KUENYEHIA
ON ENTREPRENEURSHIP

ELIKEM NUTIFAFA KUENYEHIA

Foreword by Sam Esson Jonah KBE

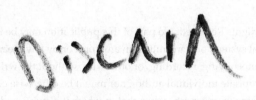

RDF business series
flipped eye publishing
accra . london . new york

RDF, accra
a business series of flipped eye publishing
www.flippedeye.net

First Published in Ghana 2012.

This book is typeset in Century Gothic and Palatino from Linotype GmbH

ISBN-13: 978-9988164713

Printed in India

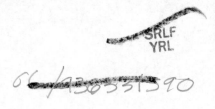

In memory of my grandmother Mrs Yaa Okyerebia Adu-
Labi formerly of Okyerebea Lodge, Abriw, Akwapim, Ghana,
the first entrepreneur I came into contact with.

To my mother, Her Excellency Judge Akua Korantema Kuenyehia
of the International Criminal Court in the Hague, who gave me
the audacity to become an entrepreneur first by allowing me to
be myself and then giving me the freedom to succeed.

Contents

FOREWORD

WITH THE LANDMARK discovery of oil and the consolidation of democracy – with its attendant respect for human rights, both personal and economic – the last decade has seen rapid growth in economic activity in Ghana. The nation's economic transformation has created fertile grounds for Ghanaians to grow enterprises that create attractive returns for investors while generating value through wages for labour and tax revenue for national development.

To be able to seize the opportunities offered by Ghana's ongoing economic transformation, the savvy entrepreneur needs to understand not just the best practices of entrepreneurship from the global stage, but also gain an insight into the Ghana-specific intricacies of turning ideas into opportunities and creating value for stakeholders. In my experience running global businesses, context is very important if an entrepreneur is to successfully navigate the business terrain of any given place.

Till now, there has not been a comprehensive resource that perfectly bridges the gap between global best practice and local knowledge. A resource that adequately equips an aspiring Ghanaian Entrepreneur with the toolkit to successfully develop an idea into an opportunity, raise capital, recruit talent, undertake legal and regulatory procedures, operate efficiently and – ultimately – to generate attractive returns on investment. In *Kuenyehia On Entrepreneurship*, Elikem Nutifafa Kuenyehia, one of Ghana's new breed of entrepreneurial stars has produced – to echo him – a 'local-content' resource that should set any entrepreneur seeking to exploit Ghana's vast economic potential on the road to success. While any book by itself will not secure the promised land of success in business; knowledge, being power, is crucial to stacking the odds in one's favour. The reader of this book, after a thorough immersion in its chapters, should have more than enough knowledge to ease the path to success.

I have always believed in the ability of Ghanaians to rise to the top; this has shaped my actions throughout my career. While the work of a few Ghanaian business pioneers have put our dear nation on the global business map, much more needs to be done to nurture a new entrepreneurial generation to succeed my generation of Ghanaian business leaders, and capitalise on Ghana's attractive prospects to deliver market-led economic development for our nation. This book has the potential to kick-start a new era of entrepreneurial growth.

Kuenyehia On Entrepreneurship is a must read for would-be entrepreneurs, start-up entrepreneurs who want to sharpen their entrepreneurial skills and anyone who wants to actively engage in the birth and growth of an enterprise. The author practices what he teaches; successfully starting and growing businesses, serving on boards of reputable companies, raising start-up and expansion capital and creating jobs. Read it, learn from it and live it; join the group of tireless champions of Ghanaian entrepreneurs, who are ardent believers that the pursuit of entrepreneurship is paramount to Ghana's economic well-being and, will deliver a true economic renaissance.

Sam Esson Jonah, KBE
Johannesburg, South Africa
16 March 2012

Introduction

WHEN I FIRST met the final year students taking the Information Technology Entrepreneurship course at the Ghana Institute of Management and Public Administration (GIMPA) in August 2007, they questioned whether the course and my approach to teaching would be 'practical' enough. Many students felt that they had taken too many courses that overemphasized academic theories of little practical application, particularly in the Ghanaian context. As *Information Technology Entrepreneurship* was an elective – rather than a compulsory – class, many of the students had come to get a sense of how practical the course (as taught by me) was going to be; they were prepared to walk out if they were not satisfied.

Over the course of that semester, the thirty or so students who stayed found out that my approach to teaching entrepreneurship is to focus less on theories and concepts, but rather to emphasise practical application, drawing on the examples of as many real-life entrepreneurs as possible.

Kuenyehia On Entrepreneurship is based on that approach. It is modelled loosely on the entrepreneurship courses I have taught at GIMPA over the last six years, and on the outstanding entrepreneurship courses I had the privilege of taking at Northwestern University's Kellogg School of Management. In my view, Entrepreneurship is a subject about doing and the proper way to teach the subject is to draw lessons from as many people as possible who have done it or are doing it.'

For each case study and for each example that made its way into this book, there are many more that did not. The lessons drawn, the questions asked and the discussions I have had with hundreds of entrepreneurs form a big part of the work presented here, adding flesh to the literature review and the primary research carried out by myself and my research team.

My fundamental premise is that entrepreneurship is a process that starts with finding an idea that removes a customer pain. An idea removes a customer pain if it meets a customer need in a novel way or in a manner that is better than existing options available to the customer.

Entrepreneurial success however requires more than just a good idea for a product or service. It also requires a solid plan of execution, adequate resources (including people and financial capital), and the ability to assemble and manage those resources according to the appropriate plan for the enterprise. These prerequisites in turn require would-be entrepreneurs to be conversant with the nuts and bolts of an amalgam of business subjects including human resource management, organizational behaviour, operations management, strategy, marketing, finance and law.

This book therefore adopts a multidisciplinary approach by considering, where relevant, aspects of other business subjects that have the most bearing on entrepreneurs. To maximise accessibility, I have not assumed any prior knowledge.

My initial objective for writing this book was to assist me in teaching my own students; in over six years of teaching, I have not found a local textbook. It is however my aspiration that this book will assist more generally in the teaching of entrepreneurship at polytechnics and universities in Ghana – and beyond.

Many of the students I teach turn up on the first day of class with a misconception that entrepreneurship is rocket science and the exclusive prerogative of a few. It is my objective in this book, as it has been in my class, to dispel this misconception by demonstrating that entrepreneurship is a simple and logical process that is open to all that aspire to it.

Apart from providing the first Ghanaian textbook on entrepreneurship – a local content resource for Ghanaian teachers and students – this book also provides a set of practical tools to give all who aspire to take the entrepreneurship route the confidence to do so. As you do so, I would love to hear from you (at **elikem@kuenyehia.com** or **@elikemkuenyehia** on Twitter) about your stories and how some of the concepts and ideas developed in this book may have helped you.

What to expect from this book

I have assumed that the reader will read this book in the order of the chapters, as in some instances earlier ideas are built upon and developed in later chapters. I have assumed no prior knowledge of entrepreneurship or of business by the reader, and have written primarily with the Ghanaian undergraduate student of entrepreneurship in mind.

While this book appears to address small or medium-sized enterprises, the concepts discussed apply to enterprises of all sizes and, wherever possible, I have drawn on examples from enterprises of different sizes and in different stages of the enterprise life cycle.

Chapter 1 provides a general introduction to the subject of entrepreneurship, entrepreneurship in the Ghanaian context and the issues that will be developed and addressed in the book. Chapter 2 focuses on the protagonist of this book – the entrepreneur – the individual who dreams the dreams for the enterprise and whose vision, energy and passion drive it. It considers the key attributes that such an individual has and considers whether anyone at all can become an entrepreneur.

Chapter 3 discusses the iterative (and sometimes illusive and confusing) process through which entrepreneurs come up with ideas for their enterprises, before going on to provide tools for evaluating ideas. Chapter 4 is devoted to the analyses that the entrepreneur should carry out to determine whether or not an opportunity is worth pursuing. Based on the insights that the entrepreneur gleans from this research, the enterprise and its offering can be positioned accordingly.

Chapter 5 helps to answer the question of whether to build a business from scratch or to buy an existing business, and, in the case of the latter, how to evaluate the value of the existing business. It also touches on operating a franchised business and managing an inherited business. Chapter 6 focuses on the legal, regulatory and policy considerations relevant to starting and leading an enterprise. Chapters 7 and 8 focus on financing: raising finance is dealt with by Chapter 7; Chapter 8 deals with managing finance.

Chapter 9 explores the most important resource of all – human capital: how to attract, manage and retain the best. Chapter 10 deals with corporate governance – the mechanism by which the key stakeholders in the enterprise make decisions and relate to each other.

It focuses in particular on establishing and working with a board of directors, and the duties and responsibilities directors have imposed on them by law.

Chapter 11 considers the process of building and developing a brand that connects meaningfully with its customers to produce maximum returns for the enterprise. Chapter 12 drills down to the operational issues that an entrepreneur will need to contend with in starting and leading an enterprise, including layout liability, insurance, risk management and technology.

Chapter 13 considers the challenges of expansion, restructuring, insolvency and bankruptcy, as well as succession planning and exit strategies that an entrepreneur may want to adopt after running the enterprise for a while.

The final chapter, Chapter 14, pulls all the prior chapters together by focusing on the process of developing and articulating an entrepreneurial strategy in a business plan.

Elikem Nutifafa Kuenyehia

May 2012

Chapter One: Introduction

"A vision without action is just a dream. Action without vision just passes time. A vision with action can change the world" - **Nelson Mandela**

Outline:

- Introduction
- History and Development of Entrepreneurship
- Entrepreneurship as a Process
- Entrepreneurship as a State of Mind or Series of Attributes
- Forms of Entrepreneurship
- Evolution of Entrepreneurship in Ghana
- The Role of Entrepreneurship in the Development of a Country's Economy
- Challenges Facing Ghanaian Entrepreneurs
- Factors Favouring Entrepreneurship
- Why Become an Entrepreneur?
- Overview of Entrepreneurial Cycle – the 4 Stages of Entrepreneurship
- Questions for Class Discussion
- Case Study: Sedina Attionu: Necessity Entrepreneur?
- Questions for Case Discussion

N THIS CHAPTER, I introduce the concept of entrepreneurship to lay the foundation for the discussions that follow in later chapters. Before suggesting my own definition, I consider some longstanding definitions of entrepreneurship and the development and usage of the word 'entrepreneur', from which entrepreneurship is derived.

The word 'entrepreneurship' is often used in everyday language to connote certain behavioural and psychological attitudes and attributes, some of which we shall explore in this chapter. The chapter also discusses the various forms of the concept of entrepreneurship.

As the primary focus of this book is on Ghanaian entrepreneurship and Ghanaian entrepreneurs, this introductory chapter sets the definition and the concept of entrepreneurship in a Ghanaian context by first tracing the evolution of entrepreneurship in Ghana, and then considering the challenges faced by Ghanaian entrepreneurs. We then consider the role entrepreneurship plays in a country's development, as well as the factors that favour entrepreneurial development.

As a book primarily targeted at tertiary students in Ghana, I explore why someone (a recent graduate, for example) might decide to become an entrepreneur rather than work for an established organisation in the private or public sector.

The chapter ends by providing an overview of the entrepreneurial cycle, the main focus of the rest of the book. The entrepreneurial cycle starts with an idea or an opportunity that the entrepreneur believes s/he can develop. Based on that conviction, s/he mobilises the requisite resources to ultimately create a profitable enterprise. In this context and throughout the book, 'enterprise' includes sole proprietorships, partnerships and companies of all sizes.[1]

History and Development of Entrepreneurship

The term entrepreneurship does not lend itself to easy definition. An understanding of the evolution and development of entrepreneurship is a necessary first step in appreciating the concept of entrepreneurship and its contextual usage over time. The word evolved from the seventeenth-century French word *entreprendre,* itself a combination of two French words: *entre* which means '*enter*' or '*between*', and *prendre* which means '*to take*'. The two words were combined to create the word *entreprendre* meaning '*to undertake*', or more literally '*between-to-take*' or '*enter-to-take*'. The word entrepreneur was thus used to generally describe individuals who 'undertook' the risk of new enterprises and bore the risks of profit or loss.

In earlier usage, entrepreneur referred to a middleman or a director of resources owned by others (for example, landowners). The entrepreneur middleman intervened by converting resources such as land, labour or capital belonging to other people but not in use economically. These resources were transformed into useful goods and services that yielded profit for the benefit of both the entrepreneur and the resource owner.

Entreprendre was also used more loosely to refer to undertaking significant projects such as the building of cathedrals or castles – taking on contracts and bearing the risks of profit or loss. The concept of entrepreneurship was further extended to tax contractors – individuals who paid money to a government for the licence to collect taxes in their region in exchange for an agreed percentage of the proceeds.

In 1734, the French economist Richard Cantillon, in his seminal work *Essai sur la Nature du Commerce en Général (The Nature of Trade in General)*[2] maintained the meaning of entrepreneur as a middleman by describing the entrepreneur as a person who pays a certain price for a product to resell it at an uncertain price, thereby making decisions about obtaining and using resources while consequently assuming the risks of enterprise. According to Cantillon, entrepreneurs were one of the three main groups of agents in every economy, the other two being the landowners (providers of primary resources) and the hirelings (those who rented the services of the entrepreneurs). Cantillon's definition is believed to be the first attempt at formalising who an entrepreneur is; his definition gave the term a distinct identity, though the meaning of entrepreneurship has since evolved greatly in practice and academia.

Jean-Baptise Say is credited with popularising the word entrepreneur. In *A Treatise on Political Economy*[3] he defined an entrepreneur as one who consciously moves economic resources from an area of lower productivity into an area of higher productivity and greater yield.

During the Industrial Revolution in the eighteenth century, inventors of new techniques who borrowed money from banks to develop their inventions, so as to earn profits from those inventions, were referred to as entrepreneurs. The period from the nineteenth century to the mid-1970s saw waves in the growth of financial institutions, technological progress and the birth of corporations and organised businesses. With these waves emerged leaders of industry who stimulated the development of industrial capitalism and became the new entrepreneurs.

In the mid-twentieth century, Joseph Schumpeter described an entrepreneur as a necessary destabilising force bringing economic growth through the disequilibrium of constant change and innovation. Schumpeter referred to the entrepreneur as an innovative generator of ideas who reformed or 'revolutionised' patterns of production and existing ways of doing things to create goods and services that are valuable to society.[4]

Hisrich, a contemporary authority, defines entrepreneurship as "the process of creating something different with value by devoting the necessary time and effort, assuming the accompanying financial, psychological and social risk, receiving the resulting rewards of money and personal satisfaction."[5]

The value entrepreneurs add is a crucial component in the modern definition of entrepreneurship. Kuratko and Hodgetts see the entrepreneurship process as being driven by "an innovator or developer who recognizes and seizes opportunities; converts those opportunities into workable/marketable ideas; adds value through time, effort, money or skills; assumes the risks of the competitive marketplace to implement these ideas; and realizes the rewards from these efforts."[6] Bolton and Thompson also describe the entrepreneur as a "person who habitually creates and innovates to build something of recognised value around perceived opportunities." [7]

Entrepreneurship as a Process

Entrepreneurship is a process of risking resources, based on an idea (or series of ideas), to develop the idea(s) into goods and/or services that people perceive as valuable, and are willing to pay for in a way that maximises returns for the enterprise. Entrepreneurship involves some element of 'adding value'; the entrepreneur must add some value to the initial primary inputs to create goods and services that people are willing to pay for, although the extent of value addition differs from entrepreneur to entrepreneur and from enterprise to enterprise, and may range from the immaterial to the material.

The process of entrepreneurship starts with an idea around which an opportunity is developed. Alternatively, it may start with an opportunity which acts as a catalyst for the development of an idea. In both scenarios, the entrepreneurial process ends with profits (or losses). The idea must be tied to an opportunity in the following sense: significant numbers of people should be willing to pay for the product or service that stems from the idea to enable the entrepreneur generate revenue from the idea.

Let us consider an example:

In 1974, while working as a computer programmer at the Volta River Authority (VRA), Mrs Elizabeth Villars, founder and former Managing Director of Camelot Ghana Ltd, came up with the idea of designing for her employer customised payslips using a computer (then a novelty). She realised there was such a demand for her product that she soon left VRA to set up Camelot to provide the customised payslip product to as many employers as possible. Today, Camelot is a leading security, business form and design printer listed on the Ghana Stock Exchange, with a subsidiary in Nigeria and the capacity to serve governments and multinational companies in ten West African countries.

The opportunity that the idea seeks to tap into, rather than the idea in itself, should be the key consideration. As in the case of Mrs Villars, there must be significant numbers of individuals and corporate entities that perceive the relevant product or service as valuable, and are willing to pay more than the cost of production for it. Whether the product or service is perceived as valuable depends on whether or not it fulfils a customer need, and to what extent it does so. For example, many would consider a shopping service for busy people in Ghana a good idea. However, due to the possible lack of Ghanaians willing to pay for this service (given the oversupply of cheap domestic labour), the entrepreneurial idea may not be profitable or worth pursuing.

For an entrepreneurial venture to be viable, the relevant product or service at the heart of the venture must remove an existing pain; it must meet an unmet need or improve an existing solution in such a manner as to attract enough potential customers to create a market for the venture. This thought will be developed in more detail in Chapter 11 but suffice to say that, for now, successful entrepreneurial practice has moved away from the sentiments captured in the notion that 'if you build it, they will come' (meaning as long as the entrepreneur makes a determination on what product or service to provide, he will find a market) to trying to figure out what customers want and/or need before deciding what to 'build' to satisfy those needs or wants.

It is generally accepted that if the opportunity is attractive enough and the idea to exploit the opportunity is realistic, resources will be found. As Johnson explains, creation (i.e. development of the idea) "is opportunity[-]driven rather than resource[-]driven."[8]

The key resources risked in creating and sustaining an entrepreneurial venture are time, human and financial capital. These resources might be risked by an individual or corporate entity acting alone or in concert with others. In many cases, the entrepreneur will establish a separate entity through which to risk the resources to provide relevant products and services that s/he hopes will generate profit. In other cases, the entrepreneur will carry on as a sole proprietor without a separate legal entity. We will discuss in Chapter 6 the different forms of business organisation open to an aspiring entrepreneur.

Entrepreneurship as a State of Mind or Series of Attributes

Entrepreneurship is also used to describe the characterisation of attributes that enable people to exploit opportunities for financial reward. These attributes (which we discuss further in Chapter 2) include passion, willingness to take risks, ability to seize opportunities and salesmanship. In this sense, entrepreneurship can be described as the state of mind that motivates an individual (alone or with others) to start a new activity and to take steps to realise a desire or dream.[9] Entrepreneurship is also viewed as a pattern of behaviour[10] that enables individuals to recognise, pursue and exploit opportunities regardless of the resources that they actually control.

In a similar vein, Timmons[11] views entrepreneurship as the ability of an individual to create and build a vision from nothing. For an individual to create and build such a vision, he must possess attributes such as opportunity obsession, tolerance of ambiguity, a sense of mission as well as commitment.

In Timmons' view, entrepreneurship is a human and a creative act of applying energy to initiative and building an enterprise or organisation, rather than just watching or analysing. The individual involved in entrepreneurship requires a willingness to take calculated risks – both personal and financial – and to do everything possible to reduce the chances of failure.

It should not be assumed from the foregoing discussion that entrepreneurship is limited exclusively to starting a new enterprise or to commercial enterprises. As we will see in Chapters 3, 5 and 6, entrepreneurship also covers the acquisition of an existing business and, in some instances, may cover the inheritance of a business.

Forms of Entrepreneurship

Entrepreneurship comes in different forms depending on a number of factors, including the reasons leading to the establishment of the venture and the socioeconomic circumstances of the entrepreneur. While it is not always possible to neatly categorise an entrepreneurial venture into one type or the other, some of the different entrepreneurship forms are discussed in the following pages.

Social Entrepreneurship

Social entrepreneurship is the process of using entrepreneurial principles to organise, create and manage a venture in order to create social change. Mission-related outcomes or social impact (rather than wealth creation) is the purpose of social enterprise. Social entrepreneurship identifies an idea relating to a social problem and then seeks the requisite resources to develop solutions to the problem.

Social entrepreneurship is as likely to be concerned with creating wide-scale social change (for example, finding a cure for HIV) as with financing narrow projects that might only benefit a small number of people (for example, South Labadi Residents Community Bank). In each case, social entrepreneurship is concerned with creating products and services that benefit society generally (or a significant subsection thereof) rather than individuals.

The spectrum of social entrepreneurship includes not-for-profit organisations that set up profit-making initiatives to support the not-for-profit aims of the organisation. Such not-for-profit organisations identify ideas and opportunities they can exploit to generate profit to support the overall not-for-profit objectives. Also included in social entrepreneurship are for-profit ventures set up with a social purpose. Examples of these types of social enterprise initiatives include the establishment of the Grameen Bank in Bangladesh in 1976 by Muhammed Yunus and the establishment in Ghana in 1994 of Sinapi Aba Trust, both of which provide microfinance to small and microenterprises that are unable to access financial assistance from the formal banking institutions due to lack of collateral, among other reasons. In doing so, Sinapi Aba Trust, for instance, aims to fulfil its mission of "providing opportunities for enterprise development and income generation to the economically disadvantaged to transform their lives."[12] Sinapi Aba Trust operates financial institutions all over Ghana through which it mobilises savings and makes loans to its target groups. Although Sinapi Aba Trust itself is set up as not-for-profit, it is important that its savings and loans arm makes a profit to help meet its objectives.

The Teachers Fund Financial Services, which focuses primarily on the provision of low-cost loans to teachers and other workers in the country, is an example of a profit-making venture set up with a social purpose. Its loans must generate enough profit to ensure that it continues to remain viable. However, the key objective of the fund is the welfare of teachers and not profit. Another example may be a religious mission hospital that charges fees for its services.

Intrapreneurship

Intrapreneurship refers to the realisation of new ideas or innovations within already existing (typically larger) enterprises. Intrapreneurship occurs when individual intrapreneurs or teams of intrapreneurs within existing organisations develop new products, services, formats or channels – sometimes outside the scope of the organisation's core business.

The intrapreneurs usually use the resources of the enterprise to develop their entrepreneurial ideas. In many instances, intrapreneurs develop within large and bureaucratic establishments. When an intrapreneur develops a new idea or opportunity which forms the basis of intrapreneurship, a smaller 'spin-off' or separate division may be developed through which resources are risked and through which the relevant newly created services or products are provided. Unlike the spin-off situation that occurs in extrapreneurship which we discuss below, in intrapreneurship, the spin-off or division would still be controlled and/or owned by the original enterprise the intrapreneur works for. In the case of extrapreneurship, this new entity is controlled by the extrapreneurs.

Intrapreneurs are motivated by a desire to overcome the shortcomings of the larger enterprise, which are inconsistent with entrepreneurship (such as bureaucracy, risk aversion, lack of innovation and enterprise inertia), and therefore often prefer to develop a separate division or entity rather than add to the existing organisational structure.

Intrapreneurship has become more relevant as technology and increased opportunities have created a more aggressive breed of entrepreneurs, posing enormous challenges for traditional corporations. Intrapreneurship should however be seen as a potential 'win-win' for the enterprises that pursue it as it enables them to retain their brightest staff who might otherwise be tempted to start their own entrepreneurial ventures. It enables companies that encourage intrapreneurship within their ranks to benefit from a wider range of ideas for new products and services and innovation than any formal approach to new product development may produce.

The intrapreneur who originates the idea however does not typically own the entrepreneurial concept; the concept will belong to the company for which the intrapreneur works as an employee. As a result, for the intrapreneur, financial and personal rewards may be limited as these go to the new enterprise or the wider organisation supporting his efforts.

However, the intrapreneur has access to resources which may have been unavailable outside the larger enterprise. Also, in an increasing number of instances, the intrapreneur is able to negotiate with his employers such that he profits directly from the success of his intrapreneurial effort – and rightly so.

Given the benefits, it is no wonder that some of the world's leading companies actively encourage intrapreneurship. At Google, for example, employees are encouraged to spend 20% of their time on independent projects, exploring ideas that interest them most. A direct result of this 20% time has been the development of products such as Gmail, Google News, Orkut, and AdSense.[13]

Similarly, 3M, a multinational manufacturing company, provides a platform that encourages the development of small teams and a plethora of employee ideas. This initiative has been at the forefront of the company's innovation and the development of innovative products such as the post-it notes, translucent dental braces, masking tape and Thinsulate.

Hewlett-Packard might have been a pioneer in the personal computer business if it had recognised and exploited the opportunity presented it by its employee at the time – Steve Wozniak – with whom it could have partnered to compete in the personal computer space. When Wozniak presented the personal computer opportunity to his employers Hewlett-Packard, they were not interested or supportive. Because of his conviction of the commercial viability of the personal computer, he left Hewlett-Packard to start Apple with Steve Jobs.

Some examples of intrapreneurship have emerged in Ghana. At Metropolitan Insurance Company, MET2U, a direct-sales format for taking personal insurance directly to the customer, and positioned largely on convenience, was developed by an employee who was figuring out ways to meet his business targets. Once he told management about the idea, he was given the requisite resources and support to develop the idea. MET2U has become a key part of Metropolitan Insurance Company's strategy of selling insurance products to individuals.

For intrapreneurship to work, top management must be committed to it. Management must be willing to encourage entrepreneurial behaviour and a culture where failure is tolerated among its ranks. The success of the intrapreneur is disproportionately dependent on his interpersonal skills because, to succeed, he needs to be able to work with and through people to obtain the requisite support and resources from management and shareholders.

Extrapreneurship

Extrapreneurship arises when individuals or groups in an enterprise break off or spin off from the parent enterprise to establish their own enterprise. The new enterprise is largely owned and/or controlled by the extrapreneurs who broke away, although they might rely on some support from their previous employers. This support may take the form of financial and social capital.

The new enterprise may be in the same line of business as the one it broke off from, or may become a customer or a supplier of a product or service for the enterprise it broke off from. The extrapreneur(s) may break off from the original enterprise to establish another venture for some of the same reasons we listed earlier as hindering intrapreneurship (bureaucracy, risk aversion, lack of innovation and enterprise inertia). Alternatively, the extrapreneur may break away because he identifies a particular opportunity he is passionate about and which he believes he can exploit, but which will not fit the overall strategy of the original enterprise. Extrapreneurship may take the form of a management buyout where managers, confident about their ability to turn a particular part of a business around (a subsidiary, for example), acquire it from its owners, breaking away from the original enterprise to run the same business that previously employed them, but as entrepreneurs and not employees.

Incubation

In ordinary English usage, incubation (in the context of rearing poultry) refers to the process of warming eggs, either by the mother hen sitting on them or by a mechanical process, until the eggs are hatched. Incubation in the entrepreneurial context is a similar notion – it involves 'nurturing' start-up businesses with an enabling environment plus material and intangible resources to grow to the stage where they can stand on their own and leave the 'mother hen'.

Typically, the investee enterprise is provided with subsidised offices, access to a network of portfolio enterprises (as potential suppliers or customers), coaching, mentoring and advice. As Hansen et al. note,[14] these services are intended to maximise the chances of success of the young enterprises, to provide sufficient resources for the enterprises to grow and also to accelerate growth and expansion within new markets.

Business incubators play an important role in creating and supporting entrepreneurs. Typically, the incubators set entry criteria for the entrepreneurs they admit. Incubators are typically set up by universities or polytechnics, high-tech parks, entrepreneurial enterprises or entrepreneurs. Incubators are critical to providing a lifeline to many enterprises through the support and resources they provide, and therefore play an important role in the development of entrepreneurs.

In Ghana there is a notable dearth of incubators. Two that deserve mention are the BusyInternet Incubation Programme and the Meltwater Entrepreneurial School of Technology. Technoserve's 'BelieveBeginBecome' Business Plan competition, although not strictly an incubator, provides critical services similar to those provided by traditional incubators.

I BusyInternet, the technology enterprise set up by Mark Davies,[15] started an Incubation programme in early 2005 with support from the World Bank's infoDev programme. The BusyInternet Incubator provided young enterprises low-cost space, access to computer equipment, electricity, and other shared services to promote new business development. These resources available at the early stage of those enterprises enabled them to survive. Between 2007 and 2008, some 35 entrepreneurs graduated from the BusyInternet Incubator, although it has since stopped running. Some of the beneficiaries who have successfully scaled up their operations include Events PmG and Topup Business Services.

I *In 2008,* Meltwater Foundation, the non-profit arm of Meltwater Group, a leading software service company, opened its non-profit incubator, Meltwater Entrepreneurial School of Technology (MEST), in Accra. MEST's objective is to foster the growth of software enterprises in Africa. The programme takes participants through three phases, the first of which is an intensive two-year course where participants, known as Entrepreneurs in Training (EITs), are taken through software development, business fundamentals and other aspects of entrepreneurship. The programme is designed to allow participants to develop software prototypes, craft business plans and have access to potential investors who will determine the commercial viability of their applications. The second stage, which also takes about two years, is the incubation stage. It allows successful MEST entrepreneurs to access start-up capital from MEST to launch their enterprises. The key focus in this phase is for the participants to develop commercially viable market strategies for their products and services. The MEST Incubator provides seed funding ranging from US$30,000 to US$300,000 for the incubated enterprises in return for minority stakes in those enterprises. In the last phase, the MEST entrepreneurs devote their time to commercialising their products and services, and scaling up their enterprises. At this stage, Meltwater provides international mentors who have relevant industry experience to work with the entrepreneurs, either as board members or advisors.

The BelieveBeginBecome business plan competition organised by TechnoServe identifies enterprising individuals who are running or intend to launch start-up enterprises, and assists them to expand or launch their enterprises. Those shortlisted for the competition undergo a structured training programme in the fundamentals of running an enterprise. They are then coached to develop a business plan which is presented before a panel of distinguished entrepreneurs and financiers. Those considered by the panel to have the best business plans are given seed capital and business development services from identified suppliers. TechnoServe has also developed a mentor network which pairs the shortlisted participants with experienced entrepreneurs. Through BelieveBeginBecome, TechnoServe has provided a springboard for a number of entrepreneurs, including Isaac Bohulu, the founder and CEO of Natural Scientific Pharmaceuticals. Isaac won US$15,000 in seed money and US$10,000 in business development services in the 2006 edition of BelieveBeginBecome; his innovation was Neemfresh, a herbal mouthwash made with extracts from the neem tree. A pharmacist by profession, Isaac now supplies Neemfresh to several dental clinics, hospitals and dental schools in Accra and beyond.[16]

The Atta Mills government signalled its intention in the 2011 Budget to develop an incubation policy to help design, develop, support and monitor private-sector business incubators in the country. While this is still no more than a mere intention of the government, it is hoped that the government will develop business incubators across the country in collaboration with universities and industry.

Opportunity vs. Necessity Entrepreneurship

The discussion so far has assumed that the starting point of an entrepreneurial venture is either an idea based on an opportunity or an opportunity which acts as a catalyst for an idea. In some cases however, the process may not be as straightforward as has been suggested in the preceding paragraphs.

The Global Entrepreneurship Monitor (GEM)[17] differentiates between two types of entrepreneurship: opportunity entrepreneurship and necessity entrepreneurship. Opportunity entrepreneurship occurs when an individual develops an idea to exploit an existing opportunity. According to the GEM, opportunity entrepreneurship is characterised by growing a business to take advantage of a unique or perceived market opportunity.

Necessity entrepreneurship, however, results from lack of options. Necessity entrepreneurs are people (typically, but not always, the poor and displaced in society) who venture into entrepreneurship out of necessity, either because it is the best option available to them or because there are no other options available. Necessity entrepreneurship may also arise as a response to changes in an individual's circumstances, including migration, mid-life crises, divorce or job loss. The effect of these changes may be such that entrepreneurship becomes the best or only option available to the individual facing the changes. After the realisation that entrepreneurship is the only real option given the changed circumstances, the individual works backwards to find an idea or opportunity that, if pursued, will yield enough to live on.

Push vs. Pull entrepreneurship

A distinction of entrepreneurs has also been made based on the behavioural motives that encourage an individual to pursue an entrepreneurial activity. This has resulted in the categorisation of entrepreneurship as either push or pull. Push entrepreneurs are individuals who are literally 'pushed' into starting an entrepreneurial venture because they are dissatisfied with their current job, while pull entrepreneurs are those people who are lured into beginning an enterprise because of the attractiveness of the business idea and its perceived benefits.[18] Many push entrepreneurs who start out as employees find that, either because of the nature of their jobs or the people involved, they do not perform as well as they would like to. This negative performance directly or indirectly pushes them to start a new venture. In the case of the pull entrepreneur, he is pulled out of his present employment because of the personal drive to initiate and successfully execute an entrepreneurial idea and reap the rewards that come with owning and controlling an enterprise.

Evolution of Entrepreneurship in Ghana

Entrepreneurship in Ghana was fairly developed before the first arrival of Europeans. Our ancestors identified opportunities for trade with other tribes and risked resources to produce or procure the relevant items for trade. They worked precious minerals into jewellery, implements and weapons. They manufactured bows, made their own mats and wove cloth, including the world-famous Kente. Although our ancestors initially produced these materials for their own immediate needs, they increasingly exchanged products with their neighbours, and later carried over the trade to larger areas.[19]

Early entrepreneurial activity in Ghana was characterised by barter in items such as trinkets, ornaments, weapons (including guns and gunpowder), alcohol and leather. Gold dust and cowries were used as the initial forms of currency, leading to the creation of gold weights, and then to nickel coins towards the close of the nineteenth century.

We can also classify the early European explorers who arrived in the Gold Coast as entrepreneurs. In the face of peril and uncertainty, they risked significant resources for the purpose of achieving profit by identifying trading opportunities with the indigenous peoples of the Gold Coast. The first Europeans to set foot in Ghana – the Portuguese, in 1471 – engaged in trade with the people of Edina (now Elmina). The Dutch and English, after forcing the Portuguese out of Ghana, issued charters to trading enterprises to strengthen their operations (including the deplorable slave trade) along the West African coast. When the slave trade was abolished, both local and European entrepreneurs participated in 'legitimate trade'. Reynolds reports that many of the early entrepreneurs were slave traders who used their experience from dealing with foreigners during the slave trade to profit from legitimate trade.[20]

After being colonised, the Gold Coast became a raw material producer for industrialised European countries, feeding the factories of European entrepreneurs as well as providing a market in which European enterprises could sell their finished goods. This spawned a further set of Ghanaian entrepreneurs – large-scale farmers and exporters of cash crops, predominant among them the Ashanti cocoa farmer.[21]

As receipts from the export of gold and cash crops led to a demand for imported textiles, beads, wines and spirits, there emerged yet another group of indigenous entrepreneurs. This group of indigenous entrepreneurs formed limited liability companies to import these products. They sought from the newly established Bank of British West Africa funding in the form of advances and overdrafts to finance their trade, although it appears that Bank of British West Africa and its successors paid more attention to foreign businesses operating in Ghana than to local entrepreneurs.[22]

The policies of the colonial government largely focused on protecting British overseas interests. As a result, Ghanaian entrepreneurship was discouraged. For example, Ghanaians whose lands contained diamonds were prevented from mining unless they were prepared to use crude 'native' methods. This undermined entrepreneurial development as this mode of operation was tedious and did not encourage large-scale mining. Consequently, instead of the Ghanaian entrepreneurs of the time channelling their energies and resources into productive ventures, they concentrated on fighting the exploitative colonial system. An example of such an entrepreneur, according to Gocking, was Nii Kwabena Bonne II, a chief who made a call to boycott European and Lebanese merchandise like cotton, textiles, canned meat, flour and spirits in 1947.[23] The boycott was meant to express displeasure at the persisting developments that were focused on protecting British overseas interests to the detriment of the Ghanaian entrepreneur.

The immediate period after independence witnessed the introduction of a mixed economic system. On one hand, the system encouraged private (mainly foreign) participation in the economy; on the other hand, it entrenched government participation in enterprises through state-owned enterprises or joint ventures established with the private sector.

Nkrumah's government initially supported private enterprise but, in 1960, Nkrumah announced that his government would place greater emphasis on Ghanaian cooperatives rather than encourage Ghanaians to start private-sector business enterprises.[24] Hug[25] argues that Nkrumah did this because he did not want to create indigenous capitalists who would be difficult to control politically. He was apparently worried that they might develop into a powerful capitalist group that could threaten his socialist regime. Thus, instead of encouraging domestic enterprises for the expansion of the economy, the government encouraged the development of foreign entrepreneurs. The 1963 Foreign Investment Act granted incentives including generous customs duties and tax relief packages to prospective foreign investors. These incentives though were not available to Ghanaian entrepreneurs.

The National Liberation Council (NLC) government, which overthrew Nkrumah's regime, showed concern for local entrepreneurs when it published a policy document titled *The Promotion of the Ghanaian Business Enterprise* in 1968. The policy sought to return the economy to one characterised by private enterprises and a decentralised system. This was to be achieved within a framework of a market-oriented economy backed by a nationalistic agenda through a policy of 'Ghanaianisation' (i.e. creating a preference for Ghanaian enterprises).

However, under the NLC, several small-scale enterprises went bankrupt due to a credit squeeze and the devaluation of the Ghanaian currency, a consequence from adhering to conditions attached to International Monetary Fund (IMF) loans the government had taken out to restore the country's economy.

It is important to note that Busia's government was the first (at least post-independence) one to extensively draw policies and establish bodies to aid in developing the Ghanaian entrepreneur. The government had an entrepreneurial development plan that sought to foster growth of private industry, and enacted the Alien's Compliance Order to get rid of foreigners in the country who were believed to have taken up most of the small and medium-sized enterprise sector which should have been in the hands of Ghanaians.[26] In the same period, the government established the Ghana Enterprises Development Commission and the Small Business Credit Scheme to help Ghanaian manufacturing enterprises access credit for their operations. Provisions were also made for Ghanaians to purchase businesses owned by foreigners.

As Appiah-Menka notes, Acheampong's National Redemption Council government (a military one that overthrew the Busia-led government) contributed enormously to the development of entrepreneurship and entrepreneurs in Ghana. Several of the contemporary giants of Ghanaian entrepreneurship emerged from the Acheampong era. These include Nana Awuah Darko, Ameen Kasardjan, Alhaji Asuma Banda, Alhadji Yusif Ibrahim, JK Siaw, Appenteng, Kowus, Appiah-Menka, Dr Bilson, BA Mensah, Dr Addison, Kwabena Darko, Kwabena Wiafe, Kwabena Pepra, Kwasi Kuffour, Mrs Georgina Kusi, Mrs Edusei Herbestein, Kofi Gyamfi Bikkai, Dr KE Appiah and Maxwell Owusu.[27]

Acheampong specified areas that were reserved for state ownership, joint state/foreign ownership, private Ghanaian/foreign ownership and purely Ghanaian ownership, which resulted in the mushrooming of many small enterprises. The policies of 'Operation Feed Yourself' and 'Operation Feed Your Industries' also benefited Ghanaian entrepreneurs because importation of certain products were banned, leading to Ghanaian production of such goods. Acheampong also apparently actively supported his political opponents in their entrepreneurial ventures.[28]

Rawlings' Provisional National Defence Council government, a socialist-leaning regime with military origins, initially opposed entrepreneurship and wealth creation, and was therefore very hostile towards successful entrepreneurs. Banks were ordered to disclose to the military all customers with a credit account of over 50,000 cedis; all customers found to possess such amounts were made to appear before the Citizen Vetting Committee on criminal charges of "illegally amassing wealth". Legitimate entrepreneurs, particularly traders, were treated as criminals and in many instances subjected to public ridicule and lashing on the basis that they were hoarding goods.[29]

Properties worth millions of cedis, including a number of private manufacturing companies, were confiscated on grounds of alleged financial and economic malpractices. A National Public Tribunal was set up where such high-profile entrepreneurs as BA Mensah (International Tobacco Company Ltd), JK Siaw (TATA Breweries Ltd) and Dr Safo Adu (Industrial Chemical Ltd) were prosecuted and lost their enterprises.[30] The justification given was that these individuals owed taxes to the state. JK Siaw, who was alleged to owe ¢10 million (old cedis) in taxes, had his multimillion-dollar brewery, gold ornaments, vehicles, furniture and cash confiscated by the state.[31]

However, due to conditions attached to aid sought from the West, the Rawlings' government was required to implement policy initiatives that sought to liberalise the economy. Under the Structural Adjustment Programme (SAP), the government embarked on a divestiture implementation policy where it sold its interests in a large number of state enterprises – including West Africa Mills, Ghana Agro-Food Company, The Coca Cola Bottling Company of Ghana Ltd and Golden

Tulip Hotel – to the private sector.[32] Typically though, given the size and the scale of the investment required, the Ghanaian entrepreneurs who were able to participate and benefit from the government's divestiture programme constituted a small number of well-connected individuals with deep pockets, or who were able to partner foreign investors. To encourage foreign direct investment (FDI) into Ghana, the Ghana Investment Promotion Centre (GIPC) was established by parliament in 1994. As a result, FDI increased from US$2.4 million in 1983 to US$5 million in 1988, US$125 million in 1993 and US$165 million in 2000. Under the Kufour regime this was to increase further to US$855 million in 2007.[33]

The Kufuor government which came into power in 2001 declared that it would make the private sector the engine of growth. As such, they embarked on a number of policies aimed at encouraging entrepreneurship in Ghana. Among others, the Kufour government took the liberalisation of the economy (started by Rawlings) one step further by deregulating the petroleum sector and seeking public-private partnerships to participate in a number of sectors including energy, information and communications technologies (ICTs) and telecommunications. The Kufour government also removed import duties and value added tax on industrial raw materials. It also established the Ghana Venture Capital Trust Fund in 2004 to provide long-term capital for small and medium-sized enterprises (SMEs), granting full tax exemption from corporate income, dividend and capital gains taxes to eligible venture capital financing companies, while making investment in eligible venture capital companies fully tax-deductible.

Through his 2006 budget, Kufour promised the introduction of an unlisted securities market on the Ghana Stock Exchange to enable SMEs secure equity. Although it never saw the light of day, this would have enabled entrepreneurs to access equity funding from the stock exchange without necessarily being listed. The Venture Capital Trust Fund is – at the time of publication – working with the Ghana Stock Exchange to develop an SME exchange.

The Atta Mills government which came to power in January 2009 also sought to support the development of microenterprises and

SMEs with its 'Better Ghana Agenda'. Among some of the initiatives, it reconstituted and strengthened the National Board for Small Scale Industry (NBSSI) to provide technical and financial support for SMEs. The NBSSI provided business development assistance and loans to over 300 SME entrepreneurs. The Rural Enterprise Skills Project also provided training and start-up kits for 4,252 rural apprentices in various professions and assisted 520 rural entrepreneurs with microcredit facilities worth GH¢1,120 (approximately US$800) each. The Business Development Services Fund helped over 140 SMEs to acquire technical assistance to enhance their productivity, increase access to markets, improve their capacity to develop new products and access finance through a grant of US$3.3 million.[34]

What is clear from the facts above is that, although entrepreneurship has been with us from pre-colonial times, Ghana has not always been the best environment for entrepreneurship. More recent governments have however made concerted – albeit fairly limited – attempts to encourage and develop entrepreneurship as they recognise the important role entrepreneurship plays in the development of a nation (see next section).

The Role of Entrepreneurship in the Development of a Country's Economy

Creates Jobs

As any economy becomes more developed, entrepreneurs play a greater role than the state in creating and providing jobs and career development opportunities for individuals. By providing jobs, entrepreneurs help create wealth for individuals. Over 80% of jobs in Ghana are in the informal sector.[35] A significant majority of these informal jobs are created by entrepreneurs.

Drives Economic Growth

SMEs make up about 94% of Ghana's industrial sector.[36] SME entrepreneurs contribute directly to the gross domestic product (i.e.

the total value of all final goods and services produced in the country) through the goods and services they provide and their aggregate demand for goods and services as inputs for their own enterprises. They also contribute to economic growth through the inflows of foreign currency they receive (by way of payment for exports), by training the labour force they employ and by paying taxes on the profits they make.

Frees Up State Resources

As entrepreneurs invest in sectors of the economy that the state may have otherwise been required to invest in, the state is able to free up some of its resources for other critical needs such as the provision of infrastructure. In Ghana, the increased participation of entrepreneurs in the economy has led to increased investment in roads, telecommunication systems, energy, ICTs, education, financial services, and real estate, among many other sectors. For example, the increase in the teledensity ratio (i.e. the number of people who own telephones as a percentage of total population) in Ghana from 1.8% in December 2002 to 14% in 2005,[37] and to 75.4% in 2010.[38] was a direct result of entrepreneurial activities by the likes of Mobitel (now tiGO, Spacefon (now MTN), Zain (now Airtel) and Kasapa (now Expresso). The increased availability of housing has also been driven largely by the efforts of members of the Ghana Real Estate Developers Association (GREDA) who risked capital resources to acquire and develop private homes for sale in several parts of the country.

Fosters Competition

An active entrepreneurial sector is one in which healthy competition exists as several firms and individuals produce similar goods and services. Customers are given greater options of services and goods and can make informed choices about which products and services best meet their peculiar needs. This in turn forces entrepreneurs to compete with each other for the patronage of the customers. It also - all things being equal – reduces the general prices of goods and services. For example, competition in the telecoms sector in Ghana has led to a reduction in the costs of owning and maintaining a mobile phone.

Mobile phone call prices dropped from an average price of 14 pesewas in 2005 to 10 pesewas in 2010.[39] The increasing number of departmental stores – such as Game, Max Mart, Koala and Melcom – all competing for the same market, has brought about competitive pricing of goods sold therein.

Fosters Innovation

Due to competition entrepreneurship can foster a culture of innovation if entrepreneurs have to compete among each other for the same limited pool of customers. To help increase their market share or margins, entrepreneurs will invest in new ways of delivering and producing goods and services in a cost-efficient manner. To do so, they rely on new technology, new processes and new efficiencies in the supply chain. An economy that fosters entrepreneurship is therefore also one in which individuals are likely to experiment to come up with new ways of doing things so as to profit from their innovation. Although there are no figures available for Ghana, anecdotal evidence suggests that innovation in most industries in Ghana has been driven by entrepreneurs and SME owners. For example, the use of DSL Internet connectivity in Ghana was pioneered by entrepreneurial outfits such as Zipnet. The increasing use of software for business solutions was driven by entrepreneurs such as Herman Chinery-Hesse of theSOFTtribe; processing juice and vegetables for export was pioneered by entrepreneurs such as Mrs Esther Ocloo.

Increases Productivity

Entrepreneurs contribute to increased productivity in the economy. As they compete for customers and seek new ways of meeting demand, they effectively reduce inefficiencies in the system, cut out waste and reduce the time needed to deliver goods and services. Also, unlike the public sector, entrepreneurs (and those working for them) can typically see direct ties between their hard work and their output, financial gain and reward. These factors motivate entrepreneurs to become far more productive than public sector employees.

Tax Revenue To The State

Entrepreneurs make a vital contribution to the public purse through a number of direct and indirect taxes they pay. They are taxed on profits of their enterprise and the incomes of their employees. Furthermore, they may pay other taxes such as capital gains tax, withholding tax on dividends and taxes on management and technology transfer agreements. Entrepreneurs also increase government revenue through value added tax and the National Health Insurance Levy paid on the goods and services that they provide.

Challenges Facing Ghanaian Entrepreneurs

The entrepreneurs surveyed by my research team highlighted the following as some of the main challenges they face:

• *Access To Finance*

Access to credit is considered to be the toughest barrier to operations and growth. It is also a major factor leading to the collapse of many Ghanaian enterprises, according to the Association of Ghana Industries.[40] Although many entrepreneurs have ideas to convert into 'bankable' enterprises, we understand that very few succeed in obtaining the requisite funding to do so. The reasons for this include:

• *Low Incomes And Low Savings Rate*

As a result of low income prevailing in Ghana and the corresponding low savings rate, banks in Ghana have had a rather limited deposit base from which to provide long-term capital for entrepreneurial development. Average gross national savings as a percentage of gross domestic investment from 1997 to 2007 was 74.3% compared, with an average of 105% for neighbouring Côte d'Ivoire and 139% for Gabon.[41] As a result of this, Ghanaian entrepreneurs have had to fund long-term financing needs with relatively expensive short-term financing.

• *Little Initiative By Banks To Be Creative*

Historically, Ghanaian banks have taken advantage of heavy government borrowing and high treasury bill rates to make profits by lending most of their deposits to the government. This has reduced the pool of funding that may have otherwise been available to fund entrepreneurial ventures.

• *Inability To Properly Evaluate and Price Entrepreneurial Credit*

Banks generally find it difficult to properly analyse and value entrepreneurial ventures presented to them. The effect is that they tend to treat entrepreneurial ventures as an amorphous set, and therefore demand the same collateral package and other requirements from all entrepreneurs instead of evaluating and pricing each entrepreneurial venture separately.

• *Human Capital*

After finance, many entrepreneurs identify 'human capital' as their biggest challenge. The most common complaint stemming from this challenge is the inability, or unwillingness, of the typical Ghanaian employee to proactively participate in developing the enterprise in which s/he finds himself. As a result, many entrepreneurs find themselves doing a lot more than they feel they ought to be doing, or would be doing, if they had motivated staff committed to developing the enterprise. As we shall see in Chapter 9, part of this problem can be avoided by entrepreneurs identifying the right people and properly rewarding, motivating and developing them.

• *Unfriendly Government Machinery*

The institutions and departments of government (such as the Ghana Revenue Authority (GRA), Companies' Registry, Trademarks Registry, Land Commission) which entrepreneurs rely on to establish and operate their enterprises are perceived by entrepreneurs as being 'entrepreneur unfriendly' and 'anti-private sector'. Many entrepreneurs we spoke to complained that the civil and public servants who populate these institutions appear (whether inadvertently or not) to discourage and hinder entrepreneurship rather than assist entrepreneurs to achieve their objectives. These public/civil servants seem more concerned with unnecessary bureaucracy and systems that add questionable value. Many are also ill-equipped to provide the level of support entrepreneurs may require. Surveys conducted by my research team revealed, for example, officers at the Companies Registry who lack basic understanding of the very Companies Code which governs how companies must be set up and registered, and officers at the Ghana Investments Promotion Centre who were unable to articulate existing investment incentives for potential foreign investors.

• *Political and Economic Instability*

This set of challenges has been a major obstacle for Ghanaian entrepreneurs over the last three decades. High inflation, instability of the cedi against major currencies and the threat of coups d'état made it difficult for entrepreneurs to properly plan for their ventures. With the fall in interest rates, the relative stability of the cedi and the peaceful democracy that has characterised the Ghanaian economy over the last decade, this set of challenges appears to be receding.

• *Access to Information*

From the initial decision to invest in an enterprise to the decision to 'harvest' the fruits of his entrepreneurial venture, the entrepreneur requires reliable market data on which to base his decisions. In Ghana, there is a marked dearth of reliable data on the economy, market size and segments. Even a reliable recent figure for unemployment in Ghana (other than the figure for the year 2000) appears to be non-existent. Even where data is not officially restricted, there is often a lack of willingness to release this data to the general public. Available data is also not updated regularly which make it difficult for entrepreneurs to make considered risk and resource allocation decisions that affect their enterprises.

In seeking reliable market data, entrepreneurs often have to conduct or commission their own research. While I suggest in Chapter 4 that research should be undertaken by entrepreneurs, sometimes the scale necessary to obtain accurate research results might be such that it may not be possible for a single entrepreneur to undertake the research. In some situations too, especially at the stage where the entrepreneur is considering a particular idea and has yet to establish the viability of the idea, it may not make sense (at least at that stage) to invest in customer research but to rely on publicly available and preferably free data.

• *Educational System*

The Ghanaian tertiary educational system does not encourage students to be entrepreneurial. Its focus is primarily on students competing and getting into corporate Ghana. The inherited colonial educational system focused on development of clerical and literacy skills deemed necessary for colonial administration and for making good employees, rather than entrepreneurs, out of locals. This legacy continues and, although most universities in Ghana have begun to offer entrepreneurship courses in recent years, entrepreneurship is taught like any of the other liberal arts subjects; students must learn concepts and sit exams that test their knowledge of the concepts, with hardly any skills being transferred. The focus should be on encouraging students to experiment within the relatively safe environment of the classroom, to test their entrepreneurial ideas and to potentially launch enterprises under the direction and supervision of lecturers. In short, it should combine classroom teaching with the acquisition of practical entrepreneurship experience.

• *Mentorship*

It is of key importance that successful entrepreneurs mentor upcoming entrepreneurs in their industries. Many of the entrepreneurs we interviewed bemoaned the difficulty of finding willing mentors who could guide and advise them, particularly at the early stages of their enterprises.

Factors Favouring Entrepreneurship

Entrepreneurship thrives in economies that have the following characteristics:

• *Political Stability*

This involves protection from political or excessive governmental influence in entrepreneurial activities. Political stability also involves having stable governments that encourage entrepreneurship through policy initiatives.

• *Macroeconomic Stability*

The risks that entrepreneurs take are largely calculated risks. Most entrepreneurs therefore like to operate in an environment of macroeconomic stability (and predictability). For most of its history, Ghana has been characterised by high rates of inflation, high lending rates and rapid depreciation of the cedi, which have made entrepreneurship very unattractive. Indeed, entrepreneurs have had to borrow at rates as high as 47% (as was prevalent in 2000). Although lending rates have fallen significantly since 2000, the average interest on loans to enterprises was still 29.87% as at the end of January 2011,[42] a figure that is still much higher than what pertains in other countries.

• *Secure Property Rights*

According to the World Bank,[43] land and buildings account for between half and three quarters of wealth in most national economies. Consequently, securing rights to land and buildings strengthens incentives to invest and facilitates trade. With formal property titles, entrepreneurs can obtain mortgages on their homes or land to start businesses. In Ghana, acquisition of land for business has been described as a major obstacle to business development and growth because of the complex land tenure system where ownership is held by a combination of traditional authorities, families, private individuals and public institutions,[44] with its attendant problem of the same land being sold to several people at a time. Property registries are so poorly organised that they provide little security of ownership. Research carried out by the Financial Times reported in 2005 that foreign investors in Ghana are deterred by high business costs and problems such as land tenure.[45] For example, a simple property transfer in Accra, Ghana takes over 382 days to register, compared to 1 day in Oslo, Norway.[46]

• *Ease of Starting Businesses*

For entrepreneurship to take root, it must be easy to start a business in terms of the number and cost of processes required to register a company, and the minimum capital required by regulation. According to the World Bank, Ghana seems a relatively easy place to start a business. It takes on average 12 days and 7 different procedures to start a business in Ghana compared to an average of 45.7 days and 9.1 procedures in the rest of Sub-Saharan Africa[47].

• *Free Flow of Information*

The free flow of information is important for entrepreneurship to thrive in any economy. Information on the market size for products and services, the laws governing the sector one wants to venture into, information on the institutions that offer capital as well as those that assist in the development of entrepreneurs must be easily accessible to prospective and established entrepreneurs to aid them in making decisions in respect of establishing, planning and developing entrepreneurial ventures.

• *The Rule of Law and Mechanisms for Contract Enforcement*

Contract enforcement is critical for entrepreneurs who enter into relationships with customers, and also for the financiers of these entrepreneurs. The more confidence an entrepreneur has in the legal system, the more likely it is that he will be willing to enter into a broader range of agreements with a wider number of people to facilitate his entrepreneurial activities. According to the World Bank's *2010 Doing Business Report*, it takes a whopping average of 487 days to enforce a simple payment dispute in Ghana, but that still compares well to 642.9 days in the Sub-Saharan region.[48]

• *Availability of Good Human Capital*

Entrepreneurs do not operate in a vacuum and therefore need to be able to tap into a talented labour pool to be able to exploit available opportunities. Many entrepreneurs complain about the calibre of the available labour pool. However,I have found that in many cases the issue about calibre is significantly exaggerated because of the unwillingness of business managers and/or owners to invest time in training.[49] There are many highly talented Ghanaians who, with the required training and coaching, can make a real contribution to enterprise growth.

• *Access to Finance*

This is a very important aspect of the entrepreneurial process. Developing ideas and opportunities, and turning them into profitable ventures, is only possible with adequate financial resources. Entrepreneurship tends to thrive in economies where banks, development finance institutions and venture capital firms are willing and able to provide finance to enterprises.

• *Demographics*

Since entrepreneurship involves turning ideas into goods and services that take away an existing pain while providing financial reward for the entrepreneur, there must exist a sizeable customer base to patronise the products and services provided. Equally important, the income levels of the target customers should be such that they can afford to pay for the perceived value added to the product or service.

• *Regulation of Enterprises*

The quality of government regulation for enterprises and the institutions that enforce those regulations are a major determinant of prosperity.[50] For example, regulations protecting trade secrets and patents, and preventing unfair competition, all determine the extent to which entrepreneurship develops in a country.

• *Culture*

Where the culture of a country encourages risk taking and boldness and celebrates honest failures, as is the case in the United States, entrepreneurship thrives. In Ghana, our culture is one where a lot of stigma and shame is attached to business failures. Mark Davies, founder of BusyInternet and an entrepreneur in Ghana for over 10 years, attributes this to the fact that because the Ghanaian society is a status-driven one, people are scared of taking any risks that might diminish whatever status they have acquired to date.[51]

• *Educational System*

Where educational institutions develop courses on entrepreneurship and, with institutional support, encourage students to initiate and develop their own ventures, it is likely that entrepreneurship will thrive.

The following institutions provide the proper framework to enable entrepreneurship to thrive:

• *An Independent Central Bank to Ensure Monetary and Economic Stability*

Monetary stability encourages the inflow of capital and prevents a flight of capital from a country. In Ghana, the Bank of Ghana Act, 2002 (Act 612) established the independence of the central bank, Bank of Ghana.[52] Through its Monetary Policy Committee, Bank of Ghana initiated policies that brought the policy or base interest rates down from 47% (when Act 612 was passed) to 15% in August 2010. The Bank has also passed other directives and policies to encourage and support entrepreneurs.

• *An Independent Judiciary to Ensure Enforcement of the Rule of Law*

An independent judiciary includes ensuring impartial enforcement of contract terms and the protection of property. Under the late Chief Justice Acquah, a Commercial Court was set up to focus exclusively on hearing commercial matters. As part of its procedural requirements, the Commercial Court requires parties to a dispute to participate in a pre-trial conference at which a judge tries to settle the matter without the parties having to continue in court. The idea is to encourage settlement rather than protracted delays in litigation (which has historically been the case in Ghana).

• *Independent Media and Easy Access to Credible Information*

An independent Media and easy access to information facilitate the exposure of corruption and other criminal acts and help to disseminate ideas that spur innovation and calculated risk taking.

• *Neutral and Professional Security Forces*

Neutral security forces help to ensure law and order as well as protect life and property from both internal and external threats and aggression.

• *Institutions of Higher Learning that Promote Entrepreneurship*

Institutions of Higher Learning can promote entrepreneurship through the development of courses and programmes that encourage individuals to learn about and then launch entrepreneurial ventures.

Why Become an Entrepreneur?

A significant majority of graduating students from universities and polytechnics in Ghana take up 'regular' executive or civil service careers. Many go on to spend the rest of their working lives climbing the ladder in big and small corporations as well as the civil service, and eventually retire on a pension paid by these corporations or the state. Increasingly, many spend their time moving from one corporate establishment to the other.

A few, after working for a number of years and gaining experience and contacts, gather the courage to go it alone in an entrepreneurial venture by starting or even buying an SME. In some rare instances, some start out in an enterprise of their own but later move to join an established company or the civil service.

In many instances, people simply dip their toes in the entrepreneurship water by starting an entrepreneurial venture on the side while they maintain their daytime jobs in Corporate Ghana, at least until their entrepreneurship venture is at a stage that gives them the confidence to plunge into full-time entrepreneurship. By doing so, they have a constant stream of income from Corporate Ghana while pursuing their more risky entrepreneurial passion. The appeal of joining Corporate Ghana or the civil service straight from university can be attributed to the following factors:

• *More Security*

Starting a business of your own requires greater initial risk. It is possible that after investment of time, energy and resources, the business might fail. Joining an existing established company or the civil service is therefore more secure.

• *Certainty of Income*

While there is great potential to make significant financial gains by going it alone, there is also a risk that at least in the initial stages the income might be pretty modest or even non-existent. Rather than face a short- or medium-term future of modest or non-existent income, many graduates gravitate towards working for an established company (banks in particular) or in the state sector, where there is certainty of income.

• *Greater Training Opportunities*

Often, graduates joining a company or a state department can expect to move on to other job functions, responsibilities or even different companies or government departments during the course of their working lives. As a result, they often consider which jobs would give them the best opportunity to train and develop their skill sets. A job in an established multinational or big local company, or in the civil service, typically offers bright graduates greater opportunities for training and personal development; this makes such jobs more attractive than entrepreneurial roles. Even where graduates definitely intend to pursue entrepreneurship as an option, they may decide to go and 'learn' in such environments before taking the plunge. It is better to learn on someone else's dime (or cedi) before making the move to private enterprise.

- *Lower Levels of Stress, Working Hour Commitment and Better Quality of Life*

Starting and managing your own enterprise as a full-time job can be extremely stressful. This makes pursuing the regular corporate or civil service path much more attractive to many. Starting and managing your own enterprise entails working many long and unpredictable hours and making personal sacrifices that many young graduates may not initially be willing to make. By contrast, taking the corporate or civil service route ensures predictable hours and less personal stress, making these routes more attractive.

- *Smaller Personal Risk*

Starting and managing an enterprise involves many personal and financial risks that may deter several people, especially those straight out of university and with relatively little capital. In a corporate or civil service job, you only need to invest your abilities.

- *Responsibility*

Starting and managing an enterprise requires a significant level of responsibility that may deter many graduates. It entails being responsible for the outcome of all decisions relating to the enterprise, and making many decisions that they might not be knowledgeable about. By contrast, joining a corporation or civil service department ensures that all responsibility given is well measured out and phased. There are several people in the organisation to bounce ideas off and it would be the exception, rather than the rule, that a fresh graduate would make major decisions on issues on which s/he is not knowledgeable.

As a result of the above factors, many graduates decide to join established companies or the civil service on graduating from universities and polytechnics in Ghana. However, a few still decide to venture out on their own and take the entrepreneurship option because of the following reasons:

• *Autonomy and Desire to Control Own Destiny*

One reason that people cite for starting their own enterprises is the desire to control their own destiny. Entrepreneurship is such that they can go as far as they want, regardless of company politics or the goodwill of employers and superiors. As the boss, they call the shots and make the fundamental decisions that concern them. They do not have to pander to the whims and caprices of superiors at work to advance.

• *Flexibility*

Entrepreneurship typically offers great flexibility as the entrepreneurs, as masters of their enterprises, are free to decide when to work and what hours to work, unlike their counterparts in 'regular' employment who have no or little flexibility. That said, in many instances, entrepreneurs find that they have little time for anything other than work, especially in the initial stages of the new enterprise's life.

• *Opportunity to Reap Unlimited Profits*

Employees typically take a limited share in the profits of the companies they work for as the bulk of profits go to shareholders. Entrepreneurs who own and manage their own enterprises can however reap unlimited profits from their venture. This makes entrepreneurship particularly attractive, although it must be borne in mind that the flip side is true as well – whereas employees typically suffer no loss in the event that their company goes out of business, the entrepreneur would most likely suffer significant personal and financial loss if this were to be the case.

• *Unemployment and Underemployment*

With high unemployment and underemployment in Ghana, some become entrepreneurs less by choice than by necessity. Rather than simply stay at home jobless for an indefinite period after graduation, affected graduates pursue entrepreneurial ventures.

• *Family*

Many people opt against the traditional route of corporate or state employment because of a family tradition steeped in entrepreneurship. Where parents or grandparents are already established entrepreneurs, it is more attractive to take a step in this direction as the requisite capital and other support is often available. However, even in such instances, it is important for the would-be entrepreneur to independently want to become an entrepreneur, rather than have entrepreneurship 'imposed' by the family.

Many of the entrepreneurs my research team spoke to admitted that entrepreneurship was challenging but hugely fulfilling and rewarding.

Overview of the Entrepreneurial Cycle - the Four Stages of Entrepreneurship

Despite the diversity of enterprises that constitute entrepreneurial ventures, it can be said broadly that entrepreneurship follows four main stages:

1. Identification of Opportunity;
2. Acquiring Resources;
3. Implementing the Plan to Take Advantage of the Opportunity;
4. Harvesting the Rewards of the Opportunity.

Identification of Opportunity

Identification of opportunities is the point at which individuals realise there are opportunities to be tapped in the marketplace. The impetus for this may come from a number of sources. An individual (for example, one who wants to leave his current employer) may actively research these opportunities. Opportunities may also come from a wide variety of sources including complaints from consumers, business associates or members of a distribution channel. In Chapters 3, 4 and 5, we discuss in more detail the identification of opportunities in the form of idea and opportunity analysis and considering whether to buy an existing business or start one from scratch.

Acquiring Resources

Once you have identified an opportunity and developed an idea to exploit the opportunity, you need to find resources to exploit the opportunity. These resources may take a number of forms but typically include time, finance and human capital. Of course, many enterprises take off without requiring any resources other than the time and human capital that the owner provides. In most enterprises though, there is a need for start-up capital, which may come from the owner's savings, loans and other parties looking to invest by way of acquiring equity. Those who offer these financial resources must be appraised by the entrepreneur, as an assessment of the needs and requirements of the providers of financial resources would put the entrepreneur in a better position to bargain for the resources at the lowest cost without losing control. In Chapters 7 and 8, we discuss the process of acquiring and managing financial resources. In Chapter 9, we discuss the process of attracting and retaining the requisite human resources.

Implementing the Plan to Take Advantage of the Opportunity

Developing a plan and implementing that plan to ensure that entrepreneur is able to achieve the maximum potential gains from his investment is an important step in the entrepreneur's journey. The odds of success in small enterprises are low so it is important that the entrepreneur develops as robust a plan as possible to take into account any contingencies that may confront him. However, it must be pointed out that several plans made for business are not actually relied on, or quickly become outdated, given the fast-paced nature of business. Nevertheless, in my opinion, the discipline of planning and thinking through the issues that might arise or not is invaluable in itself to any entrepreneur or potential entrepreneur; it is consequently highly recommended that everyone does at least some basic planning in relation to their enterprise, no matter how small the enterprise might be. Indeed, this is succinctly summed up by the old adage: 'Success is when preparation meets opportunity'. In Chapter 14, we will discuss in more detail the process of writing and implementing a business plan.

Harvesting the Rewards of the Opportunity

A farmer looks forward to the harvest season when the fruits of his hard labour, tilling the soil in the scorching Ghanaian heat, are rewarded with cash paid for his produce. Similarly, an entrepreneur who has worked hard to successfully develop his enterprise may decide to harvest that opportunity by making the decision about whether to sell a part or all of that enterprise privately, or seek an initial public offering (IPO) on the Ghana Stock Exchange. In Chapter 13, we discuss how an entrepreneur may harvest the fruits of his entrepreneurship.

Questions for Class Discussion

1. Should every entrepreneurial venture seek to remove a customer pain or satisfy a customer need in order to survive and make profit?

2. Can intrapreneurship affect the growth of entrepreneurship in Ghana?

3. Can social entrepreneurs be properly considered to be entrepreneurs?

4. Have successive Ghanaian governments stifled the growth of entrepreneurship in the country?

5. What do you think government should do to foster entrepreneurial development, considering the role entrepreneurs play in national development?

6. Considering the factors that have been identified as necessary for fostering entrepreneurship, does the Ghanaian political, social and economic environment promote entrepreneurship?

7. From your personal experience and interactions with people, how easy or difficult is it to become an entrepreneur in Ghana?

CASE STUDY: SEDINA ATTIONU: NECESSITY ENTREPRENEUR?

SEDINA ATTIONU, CHIEF EXECUTIVE OFFICER and Managing Director of The Pillbox, a chain of pharmacies in Accra, has not always been an entrepreneur. After obtaining her degree in pharmacy at the University of Science and Technology, Kumasi, she travelled to England to work with Victorian Support, a UK charity, and later for the West Middlesex University Hospital. Upon her return to Ghana she did her compulsory national service at the Pharmacy Council of Ghana. The regulatory experience she gained at the Council put her in a good position to work with SGS (Société General de Surveillance), the Swiss inspection, verification, testing and certification company. While there, she helped set up Medlab, a medical laboratory based in Accra. She subsequently worked in various capacities at Phyto-Riker, a US pharmaceutical company, and at Intravenous Infusions, a Ghanaian pharmaceutical manufacturing company based in Koforidua, where she was in charge of marketing for Francophone West Africa.

Although she did not intend using her licence to work as a pharmacist, a lack of job opportunities after relocating to Accra made her open her first pharmacy in 1999. Her strategy was to set up a chain of retail pharmacies to ensure economies of scale in bulk purchasing, which would make her products relatively cheaper. Her vision was for The Pillbox to become a household name, synonymous with world-class dispensary service, known for reliable supply and the ability to provide whatever drug a customer wants when no one else could. Within five years of her launch, she had opened five additional shops.

Sedina encountered her fair share of challenges, the major one being availability of finance for her projects. It was difficult acquiring capital from the banks for the expansion phase. Her bankers were jittery about plans for such "rapid"growth. They advised that she was new in the business and should take her time and not move at as fast a pace as she wanted to. Sedina had no alternative other than to rely on debt financing and, to date, she's still paying off loans. Working in a male-dominated industry did not make matters any easier. Most suppliers and industry gurus thought she was 'too-known' for trying to make such a big impact in their industry in so little a time; they threw as many stumbling blocks as they could in her way.

All these problems have not deterred her. She sees them as tests which have strengthened her as an entrepreneur. Although she is not working with a spelled-out business plan, her target is to own about half, if not more, of the industrial share of retail pharmacies in Ghana, and that is where she has channelled her energies. She is embarking on a social franchising model of opening at least a shop in every district in Ghana. Also, she is trying to set up as many outlets as possible. She believes that the wider spread The Pillbox chain becomes, the better its economies of scale will be, translating into cheaper products that are affordable to more Ghanaians. At the time this case was written, she had six shops and hoped to open thirty more outlets within five years.

Sedina realises that she needs to keep employees who believe in her vision and are ready to work hard to bring her plans to fruition. The 30 employees she has now were employed after a rigorous selection process and all subsequent employees will be subjected to the same procedure because the only way she can translate world-class service to her clients is through her staff.

Sedina agrees that it has not been an easy task running her business, especially when she was carrying her babies, was put on bed rest and could not go out and check on the progress in the various outlets. "It's part of the challenges that come with being a woman entrepreneur, a mother and wife" is all Sedina says about this 'inconvenience'.

Her advice to all those who want to give entrepreneurship a shot is "Just go for it!" She believes that one can do anything they set their mind to. She is however quick to caution that "you must save some money and have equity of your own before starting out because debt financing is a very strenuous and stressful situation to have to deal with in the early stages of running a business." She also recommends that chapters on management, finance, marketing and customer service be included in all books on entrepreneurship in Ghana as they would help immensely.

Asked if there was anything she wishes to have done differently, she pauses, thinks about it a bit and exclaims, "I wouldn't have expanded as quickly because of the stress, the high interest on loans and the fact that there is so much debt to be repaid!" But it is clear from the satisfied smile on her face that she has found entrepreneurship as rewarding as she has found it challenging.

QUESTIONS FOR CASE DISCUSSION:

1. Can Sedina be described as an opportunity entrepreneur or a necessity entrepreneur?
2. What is the opportunity/necessity that Sedina is seeking to exploit? What is the idea?
3. Will you say Sedina is driven by passion for her business or by need for financial stability?
4. Does the gender of a person affect his or her entrepreneurial skills and journey?
5. What are the risks faced by Sedina as a result of operating without a business plan?
6. Are Sedina's plans for expansion realistic and achievable?

Notes

1   See Chapter 6.

2   Higgs, H. *Life and Work of Richard Cantillon*. London: Macmillan, 1931.

3   Trans. C.C. Biddle, Lippincott, Grambo and Company, Philadelphia, 1855.

4   Stokes, D. *Small Business Management, An Active Learning Approach*. London; Letts Educational, 1997.

5   Hisrich, R. *Entrepreneurship, Intrapreneurship and Venture Capital*. Lexington: LexingtonBooks, 1986.

6   Kuratko, D.F. and R.M. Hodgetts. *Entrepreneurship: A Contemporary Approach*. Orlando: The Dryden Press, 1998.

7   Bolton, B. and J. Thompson. *The Entrepreneur in Focus: Achieve your potential*. Andover: Cengage Learning EMEA, 2002.

8   Johnson, D. What is innovation and entrepreneurship? Lessons for larger organisations. *Industrial and Commercial Training*, 33(4), 2001: 135-140.

9   Fortin, P.-A. *Devenez Entrepreneur*. Quebec: Publications Transcontinental, 1992.

10 *Ibid*.

11 Timmons, J. *New Venture Creation*. Homewood: Irwin, 1994.

12 Sinapi Aba Trust, www.sinapiaba.com, retrieved 23 December 2011.

13 Vise, D.A. and M. Malseed. *The Google Story*. New York: Baram Dell, 2005.

14 Hansen M.T., H. Chesbrough, N. Nohria and D. Sull. Networked Incubators: Hothouses for the New Economy. *Harvard Business Review*, 78(5), 2000: 74-84.

15 See Chapter 2.

16 Technoserve, www.technoserve.org, retrieved 18 December 2010.

17 Bosma, N., and R. Harding. Global Entrepreneurship Monitor 2009 Report (2006 and 2009 Summary Results). London: Global Entrepreneurship Monitor, 2009.

18 Amit, R. and E. Muller. Push and Pull Entrepreneurship. *Journal of Small Business and Entrepreneurship*, 12(4), 1995: 64-80.

19 Buah, F.K. *A history of Ghana*. London and Basingstoke: Macmillan, 1980.

20 Reynolds, E. Trade and Economic Change on The Gold Coast, 1807-1874. London: Longman, 1974.

21 *Ibid.*

22 Anin, T.E. *Banking in Ghana*. Accra: Woeli Publishing, 2000.

23 Gocking, R. S. *The History of Ghana*. Westport: Greenwood Publishing Group, 2005.

24 Kellick, T. *Development Economics in Action*. London: Heinemann, 1978.

25 Hug, M.M. *The Economy of Ghana*. London: Macmillan, 1989.

26 Asamoa, A. Socioeconomic Development Strategies of Independent African Countries: The Ghanaian Experience. Legon: Ghana University Press, 1996.

27 Appiah-Menka, A. *The River in the Sea*. Tema: DigiBooks, 2010.

28 *Ibid.*

29 *Ibid.*

30 Ocquaye, M. *Politics in Ghana, 1982 – 1992*. Accra: Tornado, 2004.

31 How soldiers looted J.K. Siaw, The Ghanaian Chronicle, 11 December 2002.

32 Divestiture Implementation Committee, www.dic.com.gh, retrieved on 23 December 2011.

33 Miroux, A. et al. World Investment Report 2008. Geneva: United Nations Conference on Trade and Development, 2008.

34 Government of Ghana, 2011 Budget Statement, November 2010.

35 State of the Ghanaian Economy 2009. Legon: Institute of Statistical, Social and Economic Research, 2010.

36 State of the Ghanaian Economy 2003. Legon: Institute of Statistical, Social and Economic Research, 2004.

37 State of the Ghanaian Economy 2005. Legon: Institute of Statistical, Social and Economic Research, 2006.

38 National Communications Authority, www.nca.org, retrieved

December 2010.

39 National Communications Authority, www.nca.org, retrieved December 2011.

40 Business and Financial Times, 4 February 2011.

41 Development Data Group. World Development Indicators 2008. Washington: World Bank, 2008.

42 Bank of Ghana, Monetary Policy Committee, February 2011.

43 Investment Climate Department. Doing Business in 2005 Sub-Saharan Africa: Regional Profile. Washington: World Bank, 2004.

44 Enterprise Forum, July-Dec 2004

45 Special Report: Ghana, Financial Times, 1 November 2005.

46 Investment Climate Department. Doing Business in 2010. Washington: World Bank, 2010.

47 Investment Climate Department. Doing Business in 2010. Washington: World Bank, 2010

48 Investment Climate Department. Doing Business in 2010. Washington: World Bank, 2010.

49 Kuenyehia, E. Uncommon Practice: Strategy That Works. Unpublished paper delivered at British Council Management Express Forum, Accra and Kumasi, June 2007.

50 Investment Climate Department. Doing Business in 2005 Sub-Saharan Africa: Regional Profile. Washington: World Bank, 2004.

51 Lecture delivered at Ghana Institute of Management and Public Administration, Greenhill, April 2008.

52 Banking Act, 2002 (Act 612).

Chapter Two: The Entrepreneur

"Dare to dream, but don't dream unless you are willing to live your dream" - **Bunmi Oni**

Outline

A T THE HEART of every entrepreneurial venture is the entrepreneur. Typically s/he is the person who initially 'dreams the dream' or buys into an existing dream. It is usually the entrepreneur's energy and passion that drives the process of transforming dream from mere idea into an enterprise providing products or services that people value and are willing to pay for. I use the words 'dream' and 'vision' interchangeably; like Horovitz and Ohlsson-Corboz,[1] I consider a vision merely a dream with a deadline.

This chapter explores the different ways in which someone might come to be described as an entrepreneur. Does finding yourself at the helm of an entrepreneurial venture automatically make you an entrepreneur? Who is an entrepreneur?

Outlining the traits that are considered to be necessary for a person to become a successful entrepreneur ('entrepreneurial traits'), we consider other factors that may increase the possibility of a person with entrepreneurial traits becoming a successful entrepreneur.

One of the most frequently asked questions in entrepreneurial literature is whether entrepreneurs are born or made. We examine that question in this chapter, and look at some research conducted into behaviours typical of Ghanaian entrepreneurs. The important question of why some entrepreneurs fail is covered here with thoughts on how to avoid failure. After the section on different types of entrepreneurs, a small sample of randomly selected successful Ghanaian entrepreneurs is profiled.

This chapter's objective is to demonstrate that the concept 'entrepreneur' covers a wide spectrum of people who are pursuing myriad entrepreneurial ventures in different ways. What unites all successful entrepreneurs (irrespective of industry, size of undertaking or stage in the entrepreneurial process) is a significant passion for the enterprises they are involved in. I hope that the profiled entrepreneurs, all successful locally, will inspire aspiring entrepreneurs to follow in their footsteps.

Defining the Entrepreneur

The intangible which drives or should drive every entrepreneurial venture is a vision. According to Collins and Porras,[2] a key part of a vision is the 'envisaged future' which consists of a ten- to thirty-year audacious goal and a vivid description of what it will be like to achieve this goal. I will discuss the concept of vision in more detail in Chapter 14, but it is important to point out that what becomes a vision to drive the entire organisation must start as someone's dream.

It is the dream that moves an entrepreneur to start an enterprise to achieve an envisaged future. It is the entrepreneur's passion for a dream that fires the impetus to make that dream a reality.

Once the dream is formed in the head of the entrepreneur, other people can then be persuaded to buy into it and become 'co-dreamers'. The dream might involve a completely new enterprise to be started from scratch, or it might buy into an existing enterprise through inheritance or the acquisition of an existing enterprise or a franchise. Without originating or fully embracing a dream, one can not be considered an entrepreneur.

But the dream alone, no matter how compelling, is not enough. The dream needs to be developed directly by the entrepreneur or indirectly through other people.

Entrepreneurs may be active or passive. An active entrepreneur is one who, after developing or buying into a dream, directly mobilises the resources necessary to develop an enterprise in order to achieve the vision. He is then typically involved in establishing and managing the enterprise. A passive entrepreneur, like the active one, also initially 'dreams the dream' or buys into an existing dream, but the passive entrepreneur finds other people to drive the process of turning his idea into a viable enterprise to achieve the vision. An example of a passive entrepreneur is a school teacher who sets up a fast food enterprise 'on the side' in his spare time, and hires someone else to run the enterprise while focusing fully on his teaching career. Sometimes a passive entrepreneur starts off as an active one but at some stage (perhaps when the enterprise has taken off and can run independently) may become a passive one.

In this book, I generally use the word 'entrepreneur' to mean the hands-on person who is actively involved in transforming the enterprise from an idea to profits (or, in the case of social enterprises, into a viable enterprise meeting a pressing social need). I however acknowledge in Chapter 9 that there is a stage at which the entrepreneur might have to aside for a manager to run the enterprise, unless the entrepreneur is able to become a manager as well.

The entrepreneur who initially dreams the dream and starts the entrepreneurial venture, can be regarded as a 'founding entrepreneur'.

In addition to starting an entrepreneurial venture as a founder, one may become an entrepreneur in these other instances:

• *Acquisition*

Where a person acquires an enterprise whose fundamental idea or product they buy into, with a vision to drive the existing (acquired) enterprise to become more successful than it was before the acquisition. In Chapter 5, we shall discuss the process of acquisition.

• *Franchising*

A franchise is a licence obtained by an entrepreneur (franchisee) from a (usually established) owner (franchisor), of a product, business method or service which permits the franchisee to engage in the same enterprise as the franchisor in a clearly defined location. The license is typically obtained at an initial fee and, subsequently, a percentage of revenues is paid to the franchisor as royalties. In Chapters 5 and 6 we shall discuss franchising in more detail.

• *Inheritance*

This is where one inherits a venture from another entrepreneur (in many instances, a relative or close friend). For example, the children of a successful entrepreneur who find themselves working full time on a family enterprise which they inherited on the death of a parent, and in circumstances when they would rather be pursuing other professional interests. Such persons may be better off acting in the capacity of shareholders and leaving the running of the enterprise to someone more entrepreneurial. There are however many instances where the person inheriting the enterprise continues to run the enterprise personally although they have no particular interest, passion or ability to do so. I would not consider such a person an entrepreneur but a shareholding manager.

In Chapter 1 we defined entrepreneurship as a process of risking resources to develop ideas into goods and/or services that people perceive as valuable and are willing to pay for. It is the entrepreneur, whether acting alone or jointly with others, who generates or buys into an idea and then nurtures the idea to create value for customers while capturing value for the enterprise.

Thus there are two sides to becoming an entrepreneur. The first side involves creating, developing and nurturing an idea which creates value for customers. The other side involves capturing that value for the enterprise; the fundamental basis of the entrepreneur's idea must be something that creates value for a sizeable number of customers, in a way that the enterprise through which the entrepreneur operates is able to capture value that is higher than the cost of the resources used to create the products or services delivered to customers. For commercial entrepreneurs, the captured value is typically monetary, although for social entrepreneurs, the value may take other forms.

Where an entrepreneur is acting in concert with others in an entrepreneurial venture, the other team members can only be considered entrepreneurs if they are significantly vested in the enterprise, by being, for example, a major component of the idea generation or by taking risks to such an extent that the enterprise could fairly be described as jointly theirs. Which team members can be classed as entrepreneurs will depend on the exact circumstances of the collaborative effort.

Entrepreneur vs. Businessman

The word 'entrepreneur' is a recent addition to the Ghanaian vocabulary. In Ghana, many people use the term 'businessman' to generally refer to those who undertake the risk of enterprise for financial gain. In teaching Ghanaian students of entrepreneurship, I am often asked what the difference is between the businessman and the entrepreneur.

My view is that while all commercial (as opposed to social) entrepreneurs are businessmen in so far as they run a business, not all businessmen are entrepreneurs. Beaver and Jenkins distinguish an entrepreneur from a [small] business owner who we refer to as a businessman as follows: A businessman is an individual who establishes and manages a business for the principal purpose of furthering personal goals.[3] The business is the primary source of income to meet his immediate needs and consumes majority of his time and resources. The businessman perceives the business as an extension of his personality, intricately bound with family needs and desires.

However, the entrepreneur establishes and manages a business for the principal purpose of growth and profit. The entrepreneur is therefore never really tied to a particular enterprise concept; s/he will pursue a particular enterprise so long as it remains the best use of resources. As soon as a better opportunity (higher profits, better growth opportunities, better value for the entrepreneur, etc.) arises, the entrepreneur may, in the words of Jean-Baptise Say , "shift economic resources out of an area of lower opportunities to an area of greater yield."[4] The businessman however may remain in a particular venture notwithstanding that there is an opportunity to pursue greater profits in another venture, provided their lifestyle expenses are met.

The entrepreneur, concerned with profit and growth, is likely to be more innovative than a businessman, and seeks change in a continuous and purposive way. By contrast, the businessman merely hopes for increased consumption of products and services, making the business more susceptible to competition. As a result, the businessman is usually reactive to environmental changes while the entrepreneur is usually proactive in idea generation and innovation to continuously drive improved profits and growth. The aspect of innovation also makes the entrepreneur less susceptible to competition.

Entrepreneurs are typically more focused on the long term. They pursue the vision of their enterprises to remove an existing customer pain, and often there is a sense of trying to build an enterprise that will last. The focus for an entrepreneur tends to be on the process of fulfilling the vision for the enterprise (I.e. ensuring growth of the enterprise) rather than on a mere profit motive.

The differences between an entrepreneur and a businessman may explain why some entrepreneurs still chase profit and growth opportunities long after they have reached a position when they could comfortably retire on the wealth generated through their entrepreneurial ventures. A businessman by contrast, may be more willing to sell up and retire once he is able to meet the material needs for himself and his family.

A businessman is generally more focused on the short term, largely seeking to take advantage of opportunities which present themselves to make financial gain. An example in Ghana is the stereotypical Ashanti trader in the market who does not sell any particular product but any product that is available.

Table 2.1: Differences Between an Entrepreneur and a Businessman

Entrepreneur	Businessman
Focused on developing and driving a vision which relates to removing a consumer pain	Often lacks a particular vision for the enterprise. More focused on exploiting opportunities that present themselves
Establishes business for principal purpose of growth and profit	Principal purpose of furthering personal goals (usually tied to immediate needs of self and family)
Enterprise is considered to be separate from the entrepreneur	Sees enterprise as an extension of self
Never tied to a particular enterprise	Sentimental reasons may mean s/he remains tied to a particular enterprise even if not the best use of resources
Growth motive drives innovation	Concerned with increasing consumption of particular goods and services
Usually proactive	Usually reactive
Focused on the long term	Focused on the short term
Less susceptible to competition	Highly susceptible to competition

Traits of Entrepreneurs

In determining who an entrepreneur is, existing literature on entrepreneurship gives prominence to traits that individual entrepreneurs tend to share.[5] Due to the common traits displayed by successful entrepreneurs, it is often suggested that these traits are characteristics of successful entrepreneurs. However, these traits also characterise unsuccessful entrepreneurs. This suggests that, perhaps, the traits indicate more accurately whether one is likely to become an entrepreneur, rather than how successful one might be as an entrepreneur. What determines whether an entrepreneur becomes successful is the skill set (discussed throughout this book) that, once mastered, reduces the possibility of failure.

The key traits entrepreneurial researchers identify as shared by a number of entrepreneurs include the following.

Interpersonal Skills

Entrepreneurship requires an ability to get along with people – customers, suppliers, employees, government and regulatory officials. Interpersonal skills will be called upon from registration of the enterprise at the Registrar General's Department, to wooing investors and bankers, dealing with prospective landlords, employees and customers. Interpersonal skills are so important that, in my view, it is difficult to imagine an entrepreneur succeeding without some degree of interpersonal skills.

Ability to Become 'Connected'

I differentiate 'ability to become connected' from interpersonal skills as follows: Interpersonal skills refers to an ability to get along with people in a non-specific manner, whereas 'becoming connected' refers to a more deliberate (perhaps even calculated) process of cultivating and developing relationships that will help one's enterprise succeed. In building connections, entrepreneurs generally cultivate relationships precisely because those relationships will help their enterprises. In his best-selling book *The Tipping Point*, Malcom Gladwell used the term 'connector' to describe individuals who may have many ties to different social worlds.[6]

The word 'connections' sometimes has negative connotations in the Ghanaian context because some individuals have historically abused the relationships they have built after becoming 'connected'. However, connections which concern the creation, utilisation and maintenance of economic and social relationships are extremely vital for entrepreneurial success. The groups through which connections are built include clientele, suppliers, business associates, family, friends, co-workers and schoolmates. The entrepreneur can use his connections legitimately to achieve many ends at every stage of the entrepreneurial cycle. As Byers, Kist and Sutton put it, "Successful entrepreneurs are those who can develop the right kind of relationships with others inside and outside their firm."[7] This view is shared by Sandy Osei-Agyeman, the founder of MVP, a leading brand of locally manufactured haircare products for Ghanaian women. He notes that, "in my business life, my company's longevity is only a reflection of the nurtured relationships established with my family, partners, employees, customers, friends, and of course, myself."[8]

It is highly recommended that entrepreneurs build their connections, forming as many relationships as possible and tapping into these relationships for the benefit of their ventures. Time is as scarce a resource as any of the resources that the entrepreneur requires. As a result, entrepreneurs cannot afford to build relationships with everybody. They need to strategically identify and build the relationships that are 'right' for their enterprise.

There is often a risk associated with building a network of relationships. In some cases, people in the network may try to persuade the entrepreneur to give business to or employ someone who may not be qualified to provide a particular service for the enterprise. This is something that entrepreneurs must guard against. In selecting a supplier, for example, it is important that the entrepreneur selects the best supplier for the relevant product, given the circumstances, resources and requirements of the enterprise. The network may be valuable for obtaining a shortlist of, or references for potential suppliers, but business contracts should not be awarded to someone purely because of a significant pre-existing personal or network relationship.

Ghanaian cultural norms seem to prescribe that preference be given to individuals with whom an entrepreneur has a relationship. The graveyard of Ghanaian business failures is filled with entrepreneurs who, by striving to meet this cultural expectation, employed unqualified staff or entered into contracts with people who were not qualified to execute the terms of the contracts.

A proven way of preventing such situations is for the entrepreneur to clearly write down the profile of the type of individual or company that would be ideal for their enterprise, given their objectives, resources and other circumstances, before communicating the need to the network. Depending on the particular needs of the enterprise, the profile of the ideal candidate should also be made clear to the network. The profile could, for example, include evidence of previous success in executing similar projects, financial capacity or expertise in a particular area.

Tapping into connections can save the entrepreneur time, energy and money, and help avoid mistakes and bad shortcuts in making decisions. This is particularly salient if the entrepreneur's network includes individuals who may have faced or are facing similar issues or challenges as the entrepreneur. Every entrepreneur must therefore actively reach out and connect to different types of networks in such a way as to positively assist their enterprise.

Dynamic Leadership and Vision

As I noted earlier, it is the entrepreneur's dream that provides the foundation for an enterprise to start. That dream will however remain solely in the sphere of dreams unless the entrepreneur is able to urge himself and others to make that dream a reality. Progressing from an idea or dream to a full-fledged enterprise can be a daunting task. It requires an entrepreneur who is able to effectively communicate a vision for the venture and stir excitement in a team of people who buy into the dream and are willing to turn it into reality. The members of the entrepreneur's team must therefore be encouraged to feel the same way about the enterprise by buying into the vision the same way as the founding entrepreneur. Entrepreneurs who succeed in doing so are those who exhibit leadership by living and breathing the vision. They ensure that everything they do is defined by the bigger dream for the enterprise and the values that underpin both the dream and the enterprise.[9]

Self-confidence and Optimism

Entrepreneurs sometimes pursue opportunities that most people would dismiss. Indeed, many people might discourage them from pursuing the perceived opportunities. Despite discouraging remarks and the high odds of failure, it is the self-confidence and optimism of entrepreneurs about their business ventures that urges them to continue to develop the opportunities. For example, Frederick Smith, the founder of FedEx, first set out his idea for FedEx in a term paper he wrote as an undergraduate student. His idea was to find a way of transporting computer parts and logistics to the field engineers of computer companies as quickly as possible. The term paper is said to have performed poorly at the time – he got a C for his troubles – but the poor performance of the paper did not discourage him from pursuing his dream; he went on to build FedEx into one of the world's most successful logistics companies.[10]

Salesmanship

If you don't believe in a product or service, you can't sell it. Salesmanship – the ability to sell people on an idea, product or service – is one of the most important traits of an entrepreneur, since an entrepreneur essentially sells people on an idea, a product or service. Having generated the idea, there is the important need to sell the idea (to generate funds, employ staff and target customers) so that the venture can take off. This requires good salesmanship. Underpinning the sales drive is belief in the product or service, which the entrepreneur should have in abundance.

Passion

Closely related to salesmanship is the need for the entrepreneur to have passion. Entrepreneurs should have passion in their DNA. The deep passion required for entrepreneurial success is akin to that needed for evangelism. It is this passion that enables the entrepreneur to motivate and excite employees, investors, customers and other stakeholders about the venture. Successful entrepreneurs are passionate about their underlying businesses as well as the abundant opportunities within industries they operate in. In my conversations with entrepreneurs, one thing that is always present is a passion towards their enterprises and the industries they operate in.

Risk Takers

Although entrepreneurship inevitably involves risking resources in pursuance of an enterprise's vision, successful entrepreneurs typically only take calculated risks after considering all the pros and cons of their actions. Thus, successful entrepreneurs are able to minimise the risks inherent in their ventures. McClelland found that entrepreneurs were only moderate risk takers contrary to public opinion.[11] As most entrepreneurs are driven by the need to succeed, they proactively research the environment to reduce any inherent risks confronting them. Knight,[12] in defining an entrepreneur, emphasised the calculated risk taking that an entrepreneur does.

Flexibility

Flexibility enables the entrepreneur to adapt to changes in the marketplace, the competitive environment and in consumer behaviour. Flexibility would also ensure that the entrepreneur and the enterprise do not become stale or irrelevant as a result of changes in the marketplace. It enables the entrepreneur to constantly re-position the enterprise, adapt where necessary, exploit new opportunities and abandon opportunities that are becoming less profitable or irrelevant to consumer needs and tastes. An excellent example of a flexible entrepreneur is Steve Jobs. He successfully repositioned Apple from a computer company into one of the leading consumer electronics companies in the world, while revolutionising the music industry based on a deep understanding of changing consumer tastes and desires.[13]

Unsentimental

Linked to this flexibility is a control of emotion; Bird describes entrepreneurs as unsentimental.[14] While they may be passionate about a particular business or idea, entrepreneurs are normally willing to immediately take up a better opportunity to earn higher yields as soon as that opportunity presents itself. This entrepreneurial characteristic can be contrasted with a businessman who may be sentimental, holding on to an entrepreneurial dream even when it does not make sense to do so, or go into a business which does not present new opportunities.

Discipline

Entrepreneurs must have significant personal discipline, which includes an ability to make sacrifices. They recognise that results and rewards do not materialise overnight; they are willing to practise 'delayed gratification', doing all the work now and waiting for the rewards. It is not uncommon to see entrepreneurs paying themselves very modest salaries for several months after starting their ventures so as to cut operating costs, or to pay no dividends initially so as to plough profits back into the enterprise. Unique Trust Financial Services (now UT Bank), for example, did not pay any dividends to its owners in the first eight years of its existence; it ploughed all profits back into the enterprise. It should however be noted that in the case of a privately held company controlled by no more than five persons, which does not distribute a reasonable proportion of its income to shareholders, the Commissioner of Taxes has power under Ghana's tax laws to treat what he determines a reasonable portion of the company's income as distributed to the to shareholders as dividends, therefore attracting withholding tax on dividends. This is the case irrespective of whether the distribution is ever made.

Organised

As responsibilities increase, it takes organisation and planning to stay on track. Successful entrepreneurs are able to effectively manage their time and lay out day-to-day as well as long-term schedules of activities necessary for the growth of their ventures. Planning for the venture is important as it provides overall direction for the organisation and places it in a strategic position against its competitors. Entrepreneurs who are unable to organise themselves, manage their time and/or plan for their entrepreneurial venture can easily be overtaken by time and circumstances. They are more prone to missing opportunities to expand, being overwhelmed by changing economic conditions and not recognising changes in the tastes and preferences of their target market.

Opportunity- Obsessed

Entrepreneurs generally seek out opportunities which enable them to combine personal strengths, passion and/or interest. Whether they are completely new opportunities or opportunities that complement existing ones that they are pursuing, entrepreneurs are constantly on the look out. This is exemplified by Dr Ian Kluvitse, the founder and former CEO of Medex Insurance (Ghana's first private medical insurance scheme), who says that whenever he is out of the country, he visits various shops with a notebook and pen in hand, jotting down a list of products he deems interesting but not available in Ghana and considering whether to pursue the opportunities presented by their absence in Ghana.[15] By the same token, Richard Branson also admits to constantly searching for ideas and opportunities he can exploit in the business environment.[16]

Take Initiative

Taking initiative to exploit an opportunity is the root of entrepreneurship. Entrepreneurs possess highly developed senses of personal initiative that enable them to hit the ground running irrespective of the environment they find themselves in. It is of course not enough to simply initiate; they must also be able to see through their idea and the development of the related enterprises.

Desire for Responsibility

Related to initiative is the desire for responsibility and control. Entrepreneurs typically like to take charge and be accountable for outcomes of their decisions. In this regard, taking charge does not mean they perform all activities in the enterprise by themselves. In many instances, the entrepreneur will rely on other people to perform the various activities that enable the development of the enterprise. The entrepreneur ensures accountability for non-performance and takes an interest in getting constant feedback from and providing guidance to the team members responsible for various aspects of the enterprise's activities.

Realists

Sometimes it may appear that the optimism of the entrepreneur is a blind, misplaced optimism. However, what often differentiates successful entrepreneurs from unsuccessful ones is a sound grasp of reality. Successful entrepreneurs evaluate opportunities optimistically within the context of what is realistic, given their particular skill sets and resources, or (perhaps more importantly) the skill sets and resources they can tap into. They also evaluate the size of the pie by carrying out a range of analyses (which we describe in Chapter 4), rather than merely taking a plunge into the deep end and hoping to stay afloat.

Energetic and Hardworking

High levels of energy and stamina are prerequisites for becoming a successful entrepreneur. The nature of starting up an enterprise is such that entrepreneurs spend many long hours on the venture. The entrepreneur must be able to put in the long hours and nights required to bring a venture to fruition. Many entrepreneurs routinely have to work seven days a week. Anyone thinking of becoming an entrepreneur who is already tired and cannot wait to leave the office by 5pm is probably not suited for entrepreneurship.

Sense of Mission

Although financial reward is often associated with entrepreneurial ventures, there is no guarantee of when or if these financial rewards will materialise; it could take several years to break even, for example. Consequently, there is often an underlying motive (other than financial returns) for the entrepreneur to start an enterprise. It is this underlying motive that encourages the entrepreneur to keep going even when things get tough. This underlying motive may stem from a passion for the industry or the targeted consumer segment, or may ensue from inner happiness or excitement that emanates from running an enterprise. This 'sense of mission' is best exemplified by Sergey Brin and Larry Page, the founders of Google, for whom financial success was a by-product of the passion and interest they have in making information easily accessible to customers (or, in their words, to "organise the world's information").[17] Richard Branson, who is more motivated by fun than by making money while running his business empire, states in his autobiography Losing My Virginity that "Fun... [is] one of my prime business criteria."[18]

Tolerance for Ambiguity

Even the best and most detailed business plans will not provide for every single contingency. Entrepreneurship involves significant ambiguity and anyone wanting to succeed in entrepreneurship ought to be able to tolerate and manage ambiguity. Ambiguity arises as a result of uncertainty about the level of acceptability of a product or service. Often it will never be clear who will buy the entrepreneur's product/service or how much they will buy and, indeed, how the enterprise will develop from day to day. The entrepreneur thus needs to be able to see beyond these ambiguities and make the decision to carry on.

Committed

Before taking the plunge and committing financial and other resources to a venture, it is important that the entrepreneur is completely committed to the development of the venture. This requires that the entrepreneur devotes the necessary time and energy, apart from the tangible resources, to ensuring that the venture is successful. The entrepreneur may have to commit a certain minimum number of years to see the enterprise off the ground and to develop it to such a point that their full involvement in the venture is no longer required.

Resilient

Entrepreneurs have to be tenacious. The entrepreneur must have the ability to endure the difficulties, disappointments and setbacks associated with the entrepreneurial process. On balance, these are likely to be more pronounced in the initial stages, but may also be prevalent throughout the lifespan of the enterprise. Those that succeed are the ones who are able to positively respond to all setbacks and are not derailed by obstacles. Some of the most successful entrepreneurs (including Virgin's Richard Branson, Apple's Steve Jobs and UT Bank's Prince Amoabeng) failed a few times before finally succeeding; resilience was a key driver in all instances.

Resourcefulness and Creativity

Whether it is building a multimillion-Ghana cedi enterprise from nothing, attracting outstanding talent on a shoestring budget in the initial days or coming out with a new and better mouse trap that customers want, entrepreneurs demonstrate resourcefulness and creativity in establishing and running their enterprises. Entrepreneurs must be willing (particularly in the early stages of the venture) to do whatever it takes to get the enterprise moving. They must be ready to get their hands dirty, and very often find themselves playing a jack-of-all-trades role.

Future-Oriented

True entrepreneurs tend to be forward looking and focus more on the future than the present or the past. They constantly think through how they might augment their existing cash flow, improve efficiency and grow their customer base for the growth and expansion of their enterprises. Unlike the businessman who, as we saw earlier in the chapter, is more interested in extracting short-term (short-lived) gains than long-term rewards, the successful entrepreneur is constantly looking ahead, seeking to develop the enterprise.

Unwillingness to Submit to Authority

In their study of 150 entrepreneurs, Collins and Moore concluded in part that entrepreneurs are seldom willing to submit to authority.[19] In the research conducted by my team, it was also observed that many entrepreneurs are people who like to have their own way, set their own rules and do not do well in conforming or submitting to authority. Pak-Wo Shum, founder and Managing Director of Aviation Alliance and founder of Travel King, describes himself as a "non-conformist".[20] He became an entrepreneur because he could not conform to the rules and regulations of the only employer he ever worked for.

Research conducted into personality traits of entrepreneurs shows that many entrepreneurs possess most (if not all) of the traits outlined above. It is on this basis that many give disproportionate amounts of credit to the entrepreneur at the helm of the enterprise. The classic concept of who an entrepreneur is, and the corresponding body of thought on entrepreneurship, has therefore evolved around the individual entrepreneur who drives the entrepreneurial process. This approach tends to celebrate the key individual (or in some cases, the few key individuals) behind successful entrepreneurial ventures as is the case later in this chapter, where I have profiled a few celebrated Ghanaian entrepreneurs.

Nevertheless, the tendency to celebrate key individuals does not paint an accurate picture of entrepreneurs and entrepreneurship as, in the vast majority of cases, the true story behind the entrepreneurial venture is one of collaborative teamwork (of different people with different traits), rather than one person (with classic entrepreneurial traits) driving an enterprise. Byers et al. point out that "a more accurate picture of entrepreneurship emerges when it is viewed as a social rather than an individual activity. Building an enterprise entails hiring, organizing and inspiring a collection of people who typically need to get start-up funds from others, to buy things from other people, and, ultimately, flourish or fail together as a result of the ability to sell things to yet another group of people."[21] Gartner et al., after a review of six major papers on entrepreneurship, also reiterate that entrepreneurship is a team-based process, and that entrepreneurial activity resides in a group.[22]

Other Factors Influencing Entrepreneurs

In addition to the traits we have discussed above, there are a number of other factors that may influence the decision to become an entrepreneur. These factors include:

• *Background*

Research conducted in the United States revealed that most entrepreneurs in the United States were influenced greatly by entrepreneurial parents.[23] Children of such parents, early in their lives, helped out with the family business especially during holidays. The experience gained from helping out inculcated in the children the desire to work for themselves.[24] Other entrepreneurs, in their formative years, were said to have had entrepreneurial role models who were either family members or friends of the family. Anecdotal evidence suggests that children who displayed entrepreneurial tendencies in the form of selling products such as newspapers, sweets and pencils, were more likely to become entrepreneurs later in life.

• *Age*

Cooper et al. discovered that 65% of a group of entrepreneurs interviewed in the United States launched their ventures between the ages of twenty and thirty years.[25] At forty years of age, people are usually tied down in a normal job with what Fry identified as "golden cuffs"[26] (a good salary, bonuses, and other benefit packages). People in this category are believed to become risk averse and are thus not willing to take up entrepreneurial ventures.

Bird identifies three age groups that yield the most entrepreneurs in the United States; those in their early twenties, form the first group.[27] These people are usually just out of university; some even start before they finish school, including Michael Dell, the founder of Dell Computers, who assembled personal computers in his college room. Esther Ocloo who started her food-processing venture at the age of twenty-one, falls into this category. The next group consists of those in their late twenties and early thirties. These people have worked for a while, earned some capital and experience to start their own business. Hermann Chinery-Hesse, who set up theSOFTtribe at twenty-seven, falls into this category. The last group is made up of people in their middle ages who often have no intention of starting a business but are compelled to become entrepreneurs by circumstances that occur later on in their lives. These reasons include, inter alia, retiring from work, inability to continue working for others as a result of disability, a major disagreement with an employer or being laid off. Examples include Prince Kofi Amoabeng, who turned to entrepreneurship after making the decision to quit the army, Kolawole Braimah, who set up Speedy Funds Financial Services after a distinguished career in financial services at Ecobank and United Bank for Africa (Ghana) Ltd., Ray Kroc, founder of McDonald's, and Sam Walton, founder of Wal-Mart.

• *Educational level*

The educational level of entrepreneurs vary greatly. While some entrepreneurs have little or no formal education, others are highly educated. In Ghana, uneducated entrepreneurs constituted more than 50% of the entrepreneurs surveyed. However, entrepreneurial ventures in highly specialised areas (such as knowledge-based or technology-based sectors) typically require a higher level of education for easy conceptualisation of business ideas in those areas. Madsen et al. discovered in Denmark that entrepreneurs in knowledge-based or technology-based enterprises usually had doctorate or master's degrees and, most often, a bachelor's degree (at the very least).[28]

Are Entrepreneurs Made or Born?

A large percentage of Ghanaians are involved to some degree or other in an entrepreneurial venture. A civil servant might have a store in Kaneshie where she sells beauty products. The university student may be involved in an on-campus entrepreneurial venture (for example, the sale of prepaid phone cards for mobile phones). A couple may convert part of their home into a bar and a restaurant.

Many people register sole proprietorships, limited liability companies or partnerships with the idea of setting up their own enterprises, although their dreams often never go beyond the certificates of incorporation they receive from the Registrar of Companies. On average, if you speak to a hundred Ghanaians and ask them about their dreams, 70% of them will tell you that they would like to own their own business at some point.[29]

How is it that some people make their dream a reality by launching the entrepreneurial venture(s) they dream of, while others continue to keep those dreams tucked away in a 'dream drawer', as Shefsky puts it?[30] According to him, the dream remains in a 'dream drawer' because of excuses, myths, 'better alternatives' and the fear of failure. The answer that is often suggested to this question of whether entrepreneurs are born or made is that certain individuals have certain key personality traits that make them more likely to succeed as entrepreneurs.

In his book *Entrepreneurs Are Made Not Born,* Shefsky argues that entrepreneurs are made, not born. In his opinion, although certain groups have a greater predisposition to becoming entrepreneurs (for example, migrant groups and children of entrepreneurs), most people – if adequately prepared – can become entrepreneurs.

While entrepreneurship is not for the faint-hearted, anyone can start a venture; the probability of success and growth of that venture is however dependent on certain fundamental skills, behaviours and other key factors that, once mastered, reduce the risk of failure. Subsequent chapters of this book will, among other things, focus on these skills, behaviours and success factors.

Risk Behaviours Typical of Ghanaian Entrepreneurs

Although research on Ghanaian entrepreneurs corroborates the entrepreneurial traits listed above, what I have tried to do in this section is to list risk behaviours that characterise a significant number of Ghanaian entrepreneurs encountered by my research team. The list of traits below is present among both successful and unsuccessful Ghanaian entrepreneurs, but in my opinion, they play at least a contributory role in the failure or stagnation of many Ghanaian enterprises.

Inability to Separate Oneself from the Enterprise

The mentality of owning an enterprise typically manifests itself as follows: an entrepreneur running an enterprise emotionally perceives the enterprise and self as one and, as a result, rarely makes an attempt to separate personal income and assets from that of the enterprise. Many Ghanaian entrepreneurs dip into the enterprise's coffers at will whenever they need money to sustain themselves and their families (nuclear and extended).

Personality-Driven

Too many Ghanaian businesses are built around the founding entrepreneur, and thus have no succession plan. This means that the enterprise is not managed as an entity that could potentially operate in perpetuity with the right structures in place for recruiting, decision making, operations and succession. Unsurprisingly many of these enterprises die with the entrepreneur.

Even within the supply chain, many Ghanaian entrepreneurs rely so heavily on relationships they have with particular individuals in institutions key to their enterprises that, when those individuals are no longer at the relevant institution, it can affect the entrepreneurs and their enterprises negatively. For example, a caterer may secure a contract to supply lunch to a bank based on a relationship with the bank's Human Resource Manager. When the staff of the bank complain about the food, instead of listening to and resolving the issue, the entrepreneur may rely on the relationship with the Human Resource Manager to keep the contract going and ignore the concerns of the staff. When the Human Resource Manager leaves the bank or changes function, the caterer's contract with the bank is unlikely to be secure.

Connections can be a positive thing, particularly in securing initial customers – as in the example of the caterer above. However, once the entrepreneur gets a foot in the door, the relationship should be 'institutionalised' through professionalism and hard work so that it is not solely dependent on the caterer's relationship with the Human Resource Manager. This can be achieved through quality service, responding to customer needs and building relationships widely across the bank, among others.

Lack of Planning

Many Ghanaian entrepreneurs start their ventures without seeking to determine the needs of their targeted consumers or to confirm the existence of an opportunity. Sketchy information and gut feelings very often form the bases for launching an enterprise. An example of this lack of planning, encountered in research, is that of a successful midwife who rents shop space in her neighbourhood to sell shoes for professional women, based largely on the chance availability of a shop in her neighbourhood at a rent she could afford.

After several months in business she has managed to sell a few shoes while racking up huge operational expenses. Had she carried out basic research, it would have occurred to her that her neighbourhood's profile comprised largely of low-income homes with few professional females. As majority of the professional females her enterprise was targeting rarely came to her neighbourhood, her enterprise was unlikely to take off without any modification.

Do Not Listen

Some entrepreneurs refuse to entertain ideas from anyone other than themselves. In such a set-up, the entrepreneur becomes limited to self-generated ideas, missing out on new ideas and innovations that may originate from other people. Refusing to listen to and consider the ideas of others is one of the biggest mistakes any entrepreneur can make. As no one has a patent on ideas, these good ideas can originate from several sources; many successful entrepreneurs admit that some of the ideas that have brought value to their enterprises are not their own. Kwasi Twum (founder and Chief Executive Officer of Multimedia Group Ltd, Ghana's leading broadcasting company) admits that many successful initiatives, such as the Joy Old Skuul Reunion, were conceived by his employees. Richard Branson also admits to running his business with ideas from employees, customers and suppliers. Virgin Atlantic's highly successful initiative of offering free massages in the its Upper Deck (business class) was suggested by a Japanese businessman who had flown on Virgin Atlantic from New York to Tokyo.[31]

Spread Too Thinly

Becoming an entrepreneur requires the discipline to focus on one idea at a time. Too often, people begin a promising enterprise and before it can really take off, they start investing the income generated into other enterprises, instead of re-investing in the main enterprise. This diverts financial resources and the entrepreneur's time. The likely effect (particularly at the early stages of the enterprise) is a couple of half-baked business ideas suffering from stunted growth. This amounts to killing the goose that lays – or would have laid – the golden eggs.

Some instances of business failure might have been avoided if the entrepreneur had continued to focus and devote time and other resources to one particular enterprise, instead of hopping from one idea to another.

Setting up multiple enterprises (serial entrepreneurship) does not of itself mean there is a lack of focus by the entrepreneur. However, successful serial entrepreneurs tend to ensure that any entrepreneurial activity undertaken reaches maturity before moving on to other enterprise-generating ideas.

Lack of Trust

When entrepreneurs feel unable to trust people they employ, for whatever reason, as is the case for many Ghanaian entrepreneurs, they may try to perform many of the tasks relating to the business themselves. This results entrepreneurs getting lost in the operational details of an enterprise instead of focusing on the broader picture. The focus should be on devising policies for hiring and training competent employees, and systems to monitor their progress and success.

Obsessed with Control

Entrepreneurs tend to like to take charge of outcomes, situations and resources. This trait is sometimes taken too far by some Ghanaian entrepreneurs, requiring all decisions to be approved by them. When such entrepreneurs fall ill or travel for the briefest period, their enterprises grind to a halt. There are many examples of Ghanaian businesses that go from thriving to struggling shortly after the entrepreneur dies.

The obsession with control may be related to the lack of trust outlined earlier. The entrepreneur must guard against the controlling instinct as we found this to be one of the major reasons why some of the smartest employees resigned from entrepreneurial enterprises. Any entrepreneur who wants to work with intelligent people should be prepared to relinquish some control and delegate where necessary. Although this approach entails some risk, entrepreneurs should manage the risk rather than overburdening themselves, making the enterprise inefficient.

Cut Corners

Many Ghanaian entrepreneurs retain short-term conceptions of profit and often cut corners in an attempt to maximise profits. Although the general rule in any enterprise is to keep an eye on costs, cutting costs can be dangerous to the long-term health of the enterprise. Entrepreneurs should bear in mind the popular Twi saying 'Yɛ de nam na eyi nam' (meaning to catch fish you need bait). In this context, if you want to develop a successful enterprise that makes a lot of money, you should be willing to spend some money on things that would help generate the firm's income. Beside cutting corners, many Ghanaian entrepreneurs appear unwilling to meet regulatory conditions. Filing of tax returns, paying of social security for employees and the auditing of accounts are usually left undone until there is a threat from law enforcement agencies, or the need arises to acquire additional capital to expand or grow the enterprise.

Limited Management Expertise

Entrepreneurs, particularly early stage ones, find it difficult to compete for talent with more established companies and the public sector. Indeed, many of them do not even bother to compete at all and proceed to build their enterprises without the proper level of managerial support. As put succinctly by Mrs Elisabeth Villars, "Most Ghanaians will not engage professionals to run their business. The father will be managing director, his son the accountant and his wife the administrator. All these lead to conflicts of interest and bad corporate governance."[32] It is also common to see entrepreneurs who try to wear a multitude of hats by acting as their own lawyers, accountants and other service providers. My research team came across many instances where entrepreneurs with no legal training or experience drafted or entered into contracts worth millions of cedis without engaging a lawyer. While entrepreneurship requires multi-tasking, it is important that it is not taken too far. Professionals with good track records should be sought to assist the entrepreneur in making decisions. Many professionals are happy to offer their services to aspiring entrepreneurs at a reduced fee, and even sometimes on a pro bono or deferred payment basis.

Inability to Think Big

Anecdotal evidence suggests that, compared to their counterparts in other parts of the world, notably in the United States and Europe, many Ghanaians have been schooled to limit their imagination with regards to what is achievable. As a result of our social makeup and cultural norms, many Ghanaians have not been encouraged to think big. Even at an early age, in school, students who tend to have above-average ambitions find those ambitions discouraged (consciously or unconsciously) by their teachers. Unless the parents of these students stem this trend, such lack of ambition and willingness to settle for the average will grow with the student through to adulthood. This is believed to be the reason that Ghanaian entrepreneurs generally tend to settle for small enterprises that may not be able to weather the entrepreneurial storm. I do concede, however, that the big Makola traders and fishmongers who have built thriving business empires across borders are the exception in this case.

More Ghanaian entrepreneurs need to visualise themselves owning and running bigger enterprises that can dominate markets. Thankfully, there is a small new breed of Ghanaian entrepreneurs, many of whom are referred to throughout this book, who are pursuing big dreams for themselves and their enterprises.

Unwilling to Stick it Out

There are many situations where entrepreneurs immediately want to quit entrepreneurship altogether, or to quit a particular venture, as soon as problems or crises arise. In some cases, the entrepreneur ventures into another enterprise that appears to be easier to run than the enterprise in which the problems were encountered. This unwillingness to stick with a venture through the storms associated with entrepreneurship is a particular weakness of many Ghanaian entrepreneurs. This weakness may be linked to the earlier point about lack of planning. If an entrepreneur plans adequately, undertaking the relevant research, they are better prepared for any obstacles in the life cycle of the enterprise.

Competency Dependence

Kwasi Twum, founder and Chief Executive Officer of Multimedia Group, explains that competency dependence contributes to the failure of entrepreneurs because the entrepreneurs become so good at what they do that it prevents them from adapting the enterprise where necessary to the changing world around him.[33] The competency-dependent entrepreneur prefers to stay in his comfort zone, focusing on the skill set and processes that made him successful without learning new ways of doing things. Thus, where he encounters technological changes, or changes in the attitudes, tastes and preferences of his customers, he finds that he no longer has the skills and flexibility necessary to satisfy changing customer preferences or to compete in the evolving marketplace.

Why Entrepreneurs Fail

Environmental Reasons

There are several environmental factors that may cause an entrepreneur to fail. This happens in spite of having all the traits usually associated with successful entrepreneurs, and possessing what should be a winning value proposition. In Chapter 1, I outlined periods in Ghana's history where the country's political situation was a major contributing factor to entrepreneurial failure. Consequently, no matter how great an entrepreneur a person was, and no matter how brilliant her business idea was, she was unlikely to succeed because of the political environment.

The social environment may also stifle entrepreneurship. In societies where success is not appreciated and celebrated, individuals with entrepreneurial tendencies are either unable to start their entrepreneurial ventures or may fail during the early stages of the enterprise, because the needed support and encouragement from members of the society is non-existent.

Some entrepreneurial ventures are technology-intensive. In such enterprises, inadequate technological development, or the inability to access the requisite technology may lead to failure.

Operating in a challenging economic environment of high inflation, high interest rates, wide fluctuations in exchange rates and erratic power supply could lead to – and in many instances has led to – entrepreneurial failure. For example, during the extended power crisis in Ghana in 2007, a number of cold stores in Tema, key players in the fishing industry, went out of business due to the exorbitant cost of alternative power supply.

Overoptimism

The Collins Gem English Dictionary defines optimism as the "tendency to always take the most hopeful view." Optimists can be said to believe in a positive future and possibilities that might not yet be proven. This characteristic drives entrepreneurs and encourages them to strive to meet their objectives. The problem however arises when optimism – not tempered by reality – leads to overoptimism, encouraging the entrepreneur to pursue an elusive opportunity even when it is apparent that the particular opportunity might not bear fruit.

Over-Engagement in Task-Oriented Activities

In situations where entrepreneurs are afraid to delegate – e.g. because of the fear of losing control or a lack of trust in the abilities of their employees – they tend to over-engage in task-oriented activities and get lost in details of day-to-day operations, instead of balancing an oversight of the details with greater emphasis on the wider strategic view. Such entrepreneurs, for example, can be found personally keeping the books, taking stock and making bank payments in circumstances where these tasks should be delegated. This over-engagement in the operations of the enterprise leaves the entrepreneur no time to plan strategically and provide overall direction for the venture.

Approach to Decision Making

Making decisions, under any scenario, is a systematic approach of identifying problems, finding potential solutions and choosing the best alternative in terms of the resources required to implement the chosen solution. Some entrepreneurs however prefer to take decisions based on intuition and are very individualistic in the process. Such gut-based decisions may not be the best for the enterprise, leading to its eventual failure. Often, the need to realise profits quickly makes the entrepreneur take decisions that do not properly balance the short-term and long-term needs of the enterprise.

Inability to Recognise When a Manager is Needed

The skills that may make an entrepreneur successful at the start of the enterprise may not be the same required to manage a growing and expanding enterprise. It may require someone who values systems and structures, less willing to take risks – a manager rather than an entrepreneur. In some instances, an entrepreneur is able to play both roles and can transition into the role of manager. Where this is not possible, the entrepreneur must recognise this and recruit appropriately. We will discuss this further in Chapter 9.

Lack of Discipline and Focus

The entrepreneur who is unable to defer gratification and plough profits back into the enterprise, but rather seeks to cash in immediately the enterprise starts generating income, may soon find the enterprise inadequately capitalised and unable to survive. Other entrepreneurs who fail are unable to focus on a particular idea and develop it to its maximum potential. They engage in several entrepreneurial activities at a superficial level without ever developing any properly; they become jacks of all trades and masters of none, ultimately failing in each venture.

Underestimation of Competition

Entrepreneurs can underestimate their competition due to inadequate data on the level of competition in the industry they are operating in. Further, some entrepreneurs define their market so narrowly that they fail to see certain businesses as their competitors when in fact they are. When this happens, entrepreneurs find themselves surprised by unanticipated competitors and unable to meet market projections.

Inadequate Investment in Product or Service Development

The successful take-off of new ventures may at times fog the vision of the entrepreneurs such that they fail to invest in and develop new products or services. Such entrepreneurs forget that customers are dynamic and are constantly looking out for innovations and improvements in the value of products and services. Without constantly investing in improving product or service offerings, entrepreneurs soon find customers voting with their feet, switching to other enterprises that meet their needs better.

How to Avoid Failure

Find the Right People

Human capital is crucial to the success of every entrepreneurial venture. An entrepreneur can significantly reduce the likelihood of failure by recruiting the right calibre of employees and giving them adequate training to enable them add value to the enterprise. Also, the entrepreneur must ensure that there is a right balance of people with the relevant skill sets and experience.

Give Them Freedom to Succeed

It is not enough to find bright, talented employees who are the right fit for the enterprise. The entrepreneur must also trust them and let them get on with their jobs, rather than micromanage or stifle them. While there are instances where micromanaging employees is appropriate, it is important that employees are given the freedom to succeed. To facilitate job allocation, the entrepreneur needs to spend a significant amount of time during the recruitment process and afterwards to understand the strengths and weaknesses, as well as aspirations, of each employee, then craft various jobs and projects to play to the employees' strengths. I will expand on this in Chapter 9.

Broaden the Conversation

No matter how talented entrepreneurs might be, they are limited to one head from which ideas come, one perspective and one imagination. Entrepreneurs can overcome this limitation of nature by engaging, where relevant, with a wider body of stakeholders, including employees, customers and suppliers, in respect of various aspects of the enterprise's operations. Entrepreneurs can engage potential customers very early on during idea formation by seeking their opinions on existing offerings by the competition. Sometimes, it might be in the interest of the entrepreneur to broaden the conversation to include regulators or politicians so as to be able to influence policy or legislative direction relating to the industry the entrepreneur is operating in.

Get the Right Knowledge

A deep understanding of the industry or sector an entrepreneur wishes to operate in is essential for entrepreneurial success. The necessary steps must be taken to gain insights into the operational dynamics of the industry or sector through reading, interactions with others already in that area and training one's entrepreneurial team. This is not to suggest by any means that entrepreneurs require formal training in the area of their entrepreneurial pursuit. For some entrepreneurs, formal training might be the way forward, but for the vast majority of entrepreneurs, knowledge of the industry will come informally through meeting industry players, learning by doing and through independent reading and research. Mike Nyinaku, the founder and CEO of Beige Capital, had no prior experience in microfinance prior to setting up his enterprise. He decided to bridge this gap by understudying an experienced microfinance professional for several months. He considers it a worthwhile investment he made.[34]

Prepare a Business Plan

A blueprint articulating the essential details of an enterprise is invaluable to the entrepreneur. A business plan, as we shall see in Chapter 14, provides the framework for entrepreneurs to research target markets, develop salesmanship qualities and create targets to evaluate entrepreneurial ventures. As we note in Chapter 14, one key purpose of a business plan is its ability to focus the mind of the entrepreneur on all aspects of the potential enterprise's existence, and to think through potential problems. Often, the process of putting together a thorough and well-researched business plan is in itself a valuable way to avoid failure.

Managing Financial Resources

The efficient management of financial resources will ensure that entrepreneurs always have sufficient working capital to meet liabilities. Relying entirely on revenue generated from the enterprise to pay off the operating expenses, especially at the initial stages of the venture, is not a good idea. To avoid failure, the entrepreneur must develop a realistic financial plan for the enterprise detailing the sources of financing for the enterprise and the cost of such financing, allowing for delays and challenges in revenue generation, and making adequate provision for working capital.

Adapt, Evaluate, Course-Correct

We mentioned earlier that entrepreneurs tend to have a tolerance for ambiguity and capacity for flexibility. This tendency can be used in a positive way in constantly evaluating the current entrepreneurial opportunity and the enterprise model and, if necessary, adapting it. It is also important that entrepreneurs ask themselves tough questions about how the enterprise is doing and how improvements could be made. Where appropriate, this could form the basis of broadening the conversation with employees and other stakeholders, and for the insights gleaned to be taken into account in developing the enterprise.

Don't Spread Thinly

It is essential that an entrepreneur grows an idea into a successful venture capable of standing on its own without hastening to plough profits into a different or new enterprise. An entrepreneur who fails to do this could be saidto have several half-baked cakes when time and resources could have been devoted to getting one amazing cake. For every entrepreneurial opportunity pursued there are thousands others that the entrepreneur could have pursued. Notwithstanding this, once entrepreneurs commit themselves to a particular idea and venture, they must devote all the time and resources possible to making that venture a success.

Different Types of Entrepreneurs

Lifestyle vs. High Growth Entrepreneurs

The lifestyle entrepreneur is involved in an entrepreneurial venture for the sole or predominant purpose of maintaining a particular lifestyle. This may be the case for both an individual who ventures into part-time entrepreneurship for additional income to supplement an existing income, and the full-time entrepreneur seeking a regular income. Lifestyle entrepreneurs are not motivated by the need to grow and/or expand their enterprises as long as they are able to make the amount of money that meets the demands of their lifestyles. Lifestyle entrepreneurs can also be referred to as low-growth entrepreneurs, as they often do not intend to grow their enterprises beyond a certain point and are therefore happy to remain small as long as they meet their needs from the enterprise. According to Mrs Elizabeth Villars the principal challenge limiting massive entrepreneurship growth in Ghana is that most Ghanaians want small businesses to help cater for the family, without any plans of expansion.[35]

High-growth entrepreneurs, on the other hand, are the entrepreneurs who focus significantly on expansion and growth. The primary aim of high-growth entrepreneurs is to create value and grow their venture, sometimes selling the enterprise created to begin and grow a new one.

Earlier in this chapter, we considered the differences between the Ghanaian businessman and an entrepreneur, and argued that entrepreneurs are more likely to be focused on high growth while businessmen tend to be lifestyle focused. That is not however to say that the reverse cannot be true.

Religious Entrepreneurs

We define religious entrepreneurs as mainly (but not exclusively) Christian leaders who have used entrepreneurial principles to create strong thriving churches that are financially sound and are able to finance the 'missionary' work of the church (or religion), thus making an enterprise out of preaching the gospel. Religious entrepreneurs are similar to other entrepreneurs in that they also come up with an idea (this time for a church or ministry, which typically comes from a calling). They then muster relevant resources to drive the process from idea to a full-fledged church (although in this case with a bit more spiritual input than normal).

The churches run by religious entrepreneurs in Ghana are run on strong business and entrepreneurial lines alongside the highest regards for the fundamental values of the church. These religious entrepreneurs embark on comprehensive advertising campaigns to support particular events of the church, for example, and devote time to developing the brand of the church and its leadership. In Ghana, examples of such religious entrepreneurs include Dr Heward-Mills of Lighthouse Chapel International, Pastor Mensa Otabil of the International Central Gospel Church, Apostle Sam Korankye-Ankrah of the Royalhouse Chapel International and Pastor Matthew *Ashimolowo* of Kingsway International Christian Church.

Political Entrepreneurs

According to Choi, a political entrepreneur refers to a political player who seeks to gain certain political and social benefits in return for providing the common goods that can be shared by an unorganised general public.[36] These common goods that political entrepreneurs attempt to provide to the populace generally include foreign and domestic public policy, while the benefits they hope to gain include voter support, public recognition, and personal popularity.

Politicians who brought about significant political change in their countries could be referred to as entrepreneurs. Examples of such political entrepreneurs include Kwame Nkrumah of Ghana, Nelson Mandela of South Africa, Jomo Kenyatta of Kenya and several other African leaders whose entrepreneurial capabilities in the field of politics were displayed during the struggles for independence of their respective countries. These politicians can rightly be called entrepreneurs because they 'dreamt the dream' of freedom for their countries, mobilised the requisite resources and drove the process of achieving their dream.

However, there is another type of political entrepreneur – one that is very common in Ghana, who profits from subsidies and other economic benefits received from the ruling government as a result of familiarity with the members of government, or through political influence that the entrepreneur might wield. Younkinsi however argues that these entrepreneurs should not be classified as proper entrepreneurs because they receive help from the state.[37] The main distinction of this type of political entrepreneur is that their enterprise usually does not survive beyond the term of the governments from which the special benefits are derived. While many of these entrepreneurs use their political connections to avoid fair market competition and to operate from an advantageous position, a few only use their political connections to get their foot in or to establish a footing. Once 'in', they operate their enterprises like any other commercial enterprise. In this sense they are no different from other entrepreneurs who exploit their ability to connect to seek financial gain.

Social Entrepreneurs

Social entrepreneurs are individuals or groups with innovative solutions to societal problems. Social entrepreneurs apply the entrepreneurial process in arriving at solutions to societal problems. Unlike the economic or commercial entrepreneur, the social entrepreneur is concerned with providing social change and impact rather than wealth creation. The reward to the social entrepreneur is the joy of having removed the pain and suffering that a society or group faced as a result of the non-existence of the solution provided. One of the most famous social entrepreneurs is Muhammad Yunus, the Nobel Peace Prize laureate who founded the Grameen Bank in Bangladesh to provide microfinance to the poor who, as a result of their poverty, would never have had access to conventional finance to engage in entrepreneurial activities. Although I have classified religious entrepreneurs separately, they might in fact sometimes also be classified as social entrepreneurs depending on the mission that their organisations are focused on.

Opportunity vs. Necessity Entrepreneurs

As seen in Chapter 1, opportunity entrepreneurs become entrepreneurs because they identify a consumer pain and develop an enterprise to remove that pain. Necessity entrepreneurs on the other hand are those who are pushed into entrepreneurship because of their circumstances and a lack of options. Opportunity entrepreneurs are more likely to have thought through whether or not they have the traits necessary for successful entrepreneurship. For a necessity entrepreneur though, it is usually more about survival. Necessity entrepreneurs plunge into entrepreneurship as a means of alleviating hardships that might otherwise result from their circumstances. They may be pushed into entrepreneurship because of the loss of a job, as a result of migration or other displacement, or because they must supplement their income to survive.

Intrapreneurs

The intrapreneur is an entrepreneur working within the confines of an already existing organisation. An intrapreneur conceives an idea that would remove an existing pain the same way as an entrepreneur would, and also typically goes through a similar process of transforming the idea from vision to profits. The intrapreneur however taps into the wider resources of the employer, taking on less risk and probably less reward than the independent entrepreneur.

Extrapreneurs

An extrapreneur is an individual who breaks off from an organisation to set up his own related enterprise. Extrapreneurship could result from the individual's need to remove an existing customer pain or from a lack of recognition as an intrapreneur in an organisation. The extrapreneur usually engages in the production of a value-added product or service which may be similar to or which complements that of the organisation from which he broke away. The essence of extrapreneurship is to satisfy a need that the organisation from which the extrapreneur broke away was not satisfying.

The State as an Entrepreneur?

It can be argued that the state becomes an entrepreneur when it is involved in establishing enterprises that circumvent the deficiencies usually associated with public management, enabling them to compete effectively with the private sector. Sometimes these state enterprises perform so well that they force their competitors (privately owned enterprises) out of business.

The state as an entrepreneur goes through the same processes of entrepreneurship as discussed in Chapter 1, but in this case, the capital (financial and otherwise) for the enterprise is from the state. Management positions are often held by civil or public servants, although in some instances, the state, after setting up the enterprise, will hire private-sector individuals to run the enterprise.

The Ghanaian state was an active entrepreneur during the reign of Kwame Nkrumah when many industries and other economic entities were built and operated by the state. A more recent institution that stands as an example of state entrepreneurship is the Ghana Institute of Management and Public Administration (GIMPA). GIMPA, which is owned by the state, has been very active in exploiting the demand for a wide range of undergraduate and graduate management courses in its bid to move the institution from the public service college it used to be into a full-fledged, financially-independent university offering a wide range of courses. The Graphic Corporation is another example of a state-owned institution that is run as a private company; it has succeeded in maintaining its clear market share despite a very liberal market with about 137 public and private newspapers.

Some Celebrated Ghanaian Entrepreneurs

In this section are profiles of a randomly selected group of successful Ghanaian entrepreneurs representing a number of industries spanning different time periods. The common thread that binds these entrepreneurs is that the enterprises they started were still operational at the time of publishing this book .

Alhaji Asoma Banda

Alhaji Banda is the founder and chairman of Antrak Group of Companies. The Group comprises companies such as OT Africa Line and Antrak Transport, one of the largest road transport companies in Ghana. The Antrak Group largely operates as a transport logistics business involved in trucking; stevedoring; owning, operating and broking ships; and container shipping activities around the world. It also has an off-port cargo terminal facility which is operated in Ghana's port city of Tema.

Alhaji Banda also founded Antrak Airlines, the first private airline wholly owned by a Ghanaian, to provide air service to destinations within Ghana. Despite initial challenges, Alhaji Banda has expanded the airline to serve other West African countries and it now offers both passenger and cargo services for domestic and regional routes as well as tailor-made charter services.

Since its establishment in October 2003, Antrak Airlines has established its position as a significant provider of domestic airline services, with more than 70,000 passengers using the airline in 2009,.

The most significant factor behind the company's success is the wealth of experience of its management team led by Alhaji Banda.

A member of Ghana's Council of State, Alhaji Banda is a renowned entrepreneur and has been the driving force behind a number of successful enterprises both locally and internationally including OTAL Holding Group; Cross Marine Services, Nigeria; and the Tema Container Terminal. He is a recipient of two honorary doctorate degrees from University of Cape Coast and Kwame Nkrumah University of Science and Technology, Kumasi, in recognition of his outstanding contribution to the maritime and air transport industries. In 2010, he was voted fifth in the Ghana's Most Respected CEO award scheme run by global accounting firm PricewaterhouseCoopers, and named among Ghana's 20 Most Enterprising Business Tycoons.

Barbara Baeta Bentsi-Enchill

Barbara Baeta Bentsi-Enchill is the Executive Chairman and founder of Flair Catering Services Ltd. With about 50 years of experience in the hospitality and catering industries, Barbara has successfully built a brand that stands unique in the catering services industry in Ghana. Having worked as a professional caterer in various positions in Ghana and abroad including the Gypsy Hill Training College in Surrey, UK, at the Ministry of Health and the Korle Bu Teaching Hospital in Accra., Barbara's major breakthrough was in 1964 when she was awarded a Canadian Government Technical Aid Scholarship to undertake a course in food management and interior decoration in Canada. After successfully completing the course and returning to Ghana, she was appointed an official hostess for the Ghana delegation to Expo 67 in Canada. Charged with organizing a Ghana day at the fair, she successfully cooked a Ghanaian dinner for 500 guests.

Barbara leveraged her success and catering experience to establish Flair Catering Services Ltd, one of the first privately-owned catering companies with a training school in Ghana, in 1968.

Flair is the only private catering company that has catered for every Ghanaian Head of State since 1968. The company has also served most diplomatic missions, governmental and private institutions, as well as numerous foreign dignitaries that have visited Ghana, including the late Emperor Haile Selassie of Ethiopia, His Royal Highness Prince Charles of England, The Imperial Highnesses Prince and Princess Takamado of Japan, former Secretaries-General of the United Nations U Thant and Javier Perez de Cuellar and former Presidents Jimmy Carter of the United States and Thabo Mbeki of South Africa. When President Obama visited Ghana in July 2009, Flair Catering was contracted to serve him, his family and entourage at the Castle.

Captain Prince Kofi Amoabeng

Captain P.K. Amoabeng is an ex-army officer and the Chief Executive Officer of UT Bank, a company listed on the Ghana Stock Exchange and a prestigious member of the Ghana Club 100. Although UT Bank is a bank with a universal banking licence, Captain Amoabeng previously carved a niche for himself by lending money to businessmen in need of short-term trade financing through Unique Trust Financial Services, a non-bank financial institution which filled a gap that the banks in Ghana were not servicing.

Captain Amoabeng joined the Ghana Army after graduating with a degree in Administration from the University of Ghana, intending to pursue a life-long military career. In his own words, he "loved the army and was not planning to [leave]".[38] He loved the order, the drills, the turning, the "sharp commands" and the lifestyle and discipline that the army imposed on him.[39] However, when Ghana returned to military rule in 1979, Captain Amoabeng decided to pursue entrepreneurship. Captain Amoabeng, a serial entrepreneur, set up a number of ventures including Opayesco Wood Processing Company Ltd, K K Power and Company Ltd, P.K. Amoabeng Ltd and Jam Haus, before founding Unique Trust. As an entrepreneur, Captain Amoabeng was frustrated by the lack of access to timely short-term trade finance. Traditional banks lent most of their deposits to the state at the time, and their procedures and conditions precedent to lending excluded many businessmen in need of short-term financing.

Initially, Captain Amoabeng provided a match-making service whereby he introduced his friends with money to invest, to friends who needed money quickly for business. He then obtained a banking licence from Bank of Ghana to operate a non-bank financial institution and wrote to people within his network who he felt could contribute a minimum of GH¢500, raisingGH¢25,000 cedis from 55 people to start his company. Unique Trust Financial Services began operations in a one-room office in Kantamanto, Accra (without its own washroom facilities and with one telephone line – Captain Amoabeng's mobile phone line, which was on a 'receive only' contract). In a little over 10 years, Unique Trust Financial Services merged with UT Bank after Amoabeng, through UT Holdings, successfully took over BPI Bank by listing 91 million shares to operate as a 'universal bank'. UT Bank listed on the stock exchange in an unprecedented share offering that raised GH¢25,917,000.

The company Captain Amoabeng founded now operates about 27 branches throughout the country, and has been a member of the Ghana Club 100 since 2003, rising to become second on the Ghana Club 100 list. Furthermore, the company has extended its services beyond the boundaries of Ghana to West Africa, South Africa and Germany. Captain Amoabeng has been named Ghana's Most Respected CEO for two years running in the annual PriceWaterhouseCoopers Most Respected CEO Awards.

Catherine Krobo-Edusei Benson

Catherine Benson is the founder and Chief Executive Officer of Eden Tree Ltd, an agro-processing company specializing in the packaging and supply of fresh fruits and vegetables, and Eden Tree Restaurant.

Catherine started her professional life as a banker. After obtaining a diploma in Administration from Camden College in London, she went on to work for the Saudi American Bank in the UK, before gaining further years of experience in the banking industry.

Returning to Ghana from England, Catherine found that it was difficult to find good quality fresh vegetables cultivated under hygienic conditions for her children and decided to set up a garden to produce fruits and vegetables. With start-up capital of £200 (in the form of seeds and a book on gardening sent to her by her sister-in-law), Catherine started Eden Tree Ltd in 1997. Today, Eden Tree has 12 acres of land under cultivation at Nsawam and revenue in excess of GH¢650,000. The Eden Tree logo and packaging is a familiar sight on fresh produce counters of leading supermarkets. It also has commercial agreements to supply companies such as First Catering (a company which provides catering for airlines).

To meet rapidly growing demand for fresh produce of the highest quality, Catherine spearheaded the formation of an association of outgrower farmers who supply Eden Tree. The company cultivates 40% of its total sales while outgrower farmers located in various parts of the country produce the remaining 60%.

In 2010, Eden Tree Ltd launched a GH¢50,000 Revolving Loan Fund (RLF) for the outgrower farmers. The Fund, established in collaboration with the United States Africa Development Foundation (USADF) and Development Solutions Centre (DSC), provides easily accessible loans to the farmers to boost their productivity. Rather than repay the loans in cash, beneficiaries repay their loan with the produce they cultivate from their farms. This arrangement ensures that the farmers get the needed capital to expand their farms while Eden Tree gets the produce it needs to meet market demand.

Constance Swaniker

Founder and CEO of Accents and Art, a dynamic enterprise involved in rediscovering the striking and artistic nature of wrought iron. Constance Swaniker's entrepreneurial inclination is rooted in her passion for art and a family of entrepreneurs. Her father's peregrinatory job, which led to early exposure to the range of the African continent's art, and a degree in sculpture from the Kwame Nkrumah University of Science and Technology (KNUST), provided her with the requisite foundation to establish her company. Constance also worked as an apprentice in a carpentry shop while studying at the KNUST, gaining valuable practical experience.

Constance started Accents and Art in 2001 from a backyard with only 2 artisans with a vision, inspired by an innate feeling to develop something big, and a desire to be her own boss while creating financial freedom for herself. She launched at a time when the building industry was booming and many developers were receptive to incorporating her metalwork as part of the design for their buildings. An excellent example is the African Regent Hotel, for which Accents and Art created decorative metal sculptures. Today, Accents and Art is a household name in Ghana, employing over 30 artisans. It has carved a niche in metal art and wrought iron furniture in the general furniture industry. Constance is considered to be unique; her ability to successfully move away from traditional woodwork partly accounts for her success in an industry almost entirely dominated by men.

A firm believer in hiring the right people to run a business, Constance sought and obtained a World Bank grant, the proceeds of which she used to hire consultants to help her restructure Accents and Art, developing better systems and structures.[40]

In 2007 and 2008 Constance was featured on a number of programmes and media outlets including Reuters News Agency, MNet's Studio 53, TV Africa's *Obaa Mbo* and TV3's Today's Woman and *Maasem* programmes as well as Graphic Showbiz and the Daily Graphic. The company has also received a number of awards including an award for Outstanding Industrial Metal Furniture Firm in Ghana by Women Artists in Africa (wAi Africa) in 2008. In 2010, Constance was named one of Africa's top 40 Under 40 Achievers by the New York-based The Network Journal.

Dr Esther Ocloo (deceased)

Dr Esther Ocloo began her entrepreneurial activities at the age of twenty-one with 12 jars of homemade marmalade, which she sold door-to-door in government offices. Within six months, she had managed to persuade Achimota School and the Royal West African Frontier Forces to purchase from her, becoming a major supplier of marmalade and orange juice to these institutions. She took a break from this first venture to improve her prospects by studying food processing in the UK. On her return, she set up Modern Caterers Company in 1952, which catered for banquets and private parties all over the Gold Coast, and also ran a mobile canteen.

By 1960, she started to manufacture and supply canned Ghanaian foods such as groundnut soup, jollof rice and palava sauce. Dr Ocloo was also a social entrepreneur who established enterprises such as the African Women Entrepreneurial Training Centre, and a vocational training institute in Peki to aid women who could not continue with their formal education. She was instrumental in the setting up of Aid to Artisans Ghana, a local nongovernmental organisation that offers practical assistance to artisans and designers to manufacture award-winning products for the marketplace. She also founded the Ghana Manufacturers Association (now Association of Ghana Industries) and contributed substantially to the establishment of Women's World Banking Ghana. She died in 2002, leaving a legacy matched by no other Ghanaian female entrepreneur.

Dzigbordi K. Dosoo

Dzigbordi Dosoo is the founder and Chief Executive Officer of Allure Africa Ltd, a premier day spa group with offices in Accra and Washington, D.C. She started her business after returning from the United States where she studied and worked for financial and investment companies. Although she was in full-time employment she realised that the day spa concept was a great opportunity she could capitalise on as it was non-existent in Ghana; she was determined to turn her passion for wellness and beauty into a giant spa company.

Dzigbordi opened her first salon in 2002 in the living room of her family home with one beautician. Within six months she opened another branch. After starting off as a sole proprietor, she registered Allure as a limited liability company in 2003. In 2005 she expanded to the Allure Beauty Palace East Legon, located in the A&C Shopping Mall; in 2009 the Allure Sales and Distribution Centre was established.

The bold, constantly innovative leadership of Dzigbordi led to the birth of Allure Spa in the City, West Africa's only five-star day spa, and Allure Man, a professional male grooming brand.

As an entrepreneur, Dzigbordi is constantly looking at ways of raising the standard in the wellness and beauty industry. She recently led her team in launching the first ever Spa and Beauty Expo in West Africa called Iyaba. Iyaba creates a platform for training, education and networking opportunities for enterprises in the spa and beauty industry. Allure has also introduced a new range of authentically African natural aromatherapy products under the Kanshi brand into the local and international markets, in collaboration with international partner Lydia Sarfati, the CEO of Repechage.

In recognition of her entrepreneurial excellence, Dzigbordi has been widely featured in international and spa industry magazines, including Spa Business Magazine, The Spa Hand Book, Women's Wear Daily and Pulse Magazine from the International Spa Association. She has also won several awards including the 2009 Chartered Institute of Marketing Ghana (CIMG) Marketing Woman of the Year.

Dzigbordi was educated at Accra Girls School and the Virginia State University, from which she graduated with a bachelor's degree in finance and accounting. She also went to Syracuse University for a postgraduate degree in banking and finance. She holds various spa management qualifications, including one from Harvard University.

Emmanuel Botchway

Emmanuel Botchway is the founder and chairman of the Regimanuel Gray Group, a joint venture established in 1991 between Regimanuel Ltd, a company Mr Botchway owns with his wife, and Gray Construction of Houston, Texas. A market leader in the provision of residential real estate. The group is made up of Regimanuel Gray (Ghana) Ltd, Desjoyaux Ghana, Regimanuel Estate Management Company, BessBlock Concrete Products Ltd, Regimanuel Gray (Sierra Leone) Ltd and Sierra Block Concrete Products Ltd.

Mr Botchway studied electrical engineering at St Paul's Technical School and furthered his education in the UK followed by a stint working in construction in Nigeria. However, upon his return to Ghana, he spotted an opportunity to seek out prime locations, engage in timely construction and deliver high-quality, reasonably priced housing units, ensuring that they were fused with well-developed infrastructure and social amenities for which the company has become known.

With an eclectic mix of foreign and local employees, Mr Botchway has managed to position the company as a provider of quality, peace of mind and a sense of well-being. Other business entities within the group have been built with the same qualities: Desjoyaux Ghana catering for swimming pools; BessBlock Concrete products for maintaining the quality of building blocks; Regimanuel Estate Management for estate management services. The company is still pushing boundaries and has expanded into neighbouring countries such as Sierra Leone.

The original Ghanaian arm of the group has more than 2,500 completed units with varying house types located in four different project sites to date, with ambitions to build about 200 houses a year in addition to 5,000 low cost homes over 5 years. After 20 years, the company is still delivering reasonably-priced houses and simplifying the process of home ownership.

Ernest Bediako Sampong

Ernest Sampong is the founder and CEO of Ernest Chemists Ltd, a leading pharmaceutical manufacturing and distributing company in Ghana. Mr Sampong started the company in 1986 by importing drugs from the United Kingdom, Slovenia, Belgium and Bulgaria, with support from his wife and a staff of 4 people. Today, he has over 200 employees with an ultramodern drug manufacturing plant complete with its own laboratory and storage facilities in Tema, where the company produces generic drugs including antibiotics, vitamins and analgesics. His client base consists of chemists and hospitals across the nation the company is believed to have a total market share of 25% of the pharmaceutical industry in Ghana, with intentions of expanding to market across the West African subregion[41]. Ernest Chemist is also the sole representative local pharmaceutical company for such world-leading pharmaceutical brands as GlaxoSmithKline, AstraZeneca and Pfizer.

Ernest attended the Kwame Nkrumah University of Science and Technology, spending his first three years as a medical student, before changing to pharmacy, following in the footsteps of his father and other siblings. In 2008 and 2010, he was among 10 individuals honoured at the Ghana's Most Respected Company and CEO Awards by global accounting firm Pricewaterhouse Coopers.

Herman Chinery-Hesse

Herman Chinery-Hesse founded theSOFTtribe, a market-leading software company, in 1991 with financial support from his parents. One of the first indigenous companies providing software solutions to business clients in a wide range of industries, theSOFTtribe provides a range of enterprise software solutions such as Edziban, used at restaurants to compute purchases and to provide consumers with receipts, and the bestselling Akatua, a payroll programme.

Herman began his entrepreneurial venture writing computer programmes in a bedroom in his parent's house upon returning home from the United Kingdom. His first contract was creating expense-tracking software (with his old school mate, Joe Jackson) for a travel agency. Today, he has over 65 people on his payroll, and a client base of over 300 companies including multinationals such as Nestle, Unilever and the Ford Foundation. TheSOFTtribe also has a deal with Microsoft Corporation to sell a suite of applications for which they can produce add-on programmes for the Ghanaian market.

More recently, and drawing inspiration from Amazon.com and Paypal, Herman has teamed up with some international investors to launch BSL (standing for Black Star Line), a company that will let African entrepreneurs sell products online with ease and accept payments via mobile phones. This, Herman hopes, will help push Ghana into the global economy.

Born in Ireland, Herman was educated in the United States and started his career in the United Kingdom. He has won several awards including Ghana's Millennium Excellence Award for Information Technology in 2005 and the Distinguished Alumnus Award from the Texas State University Alumni Association. He serves on several boards of companies in the country. The British Broadcasting Corporation (BBC) once described him as Africa's Bill Gates.

Joel Edmund Nettey and Daniel Ampadu Twum

Joel Nettey and the late Daniel Ampadu Twum co-founded Origin8 Saatchi & Saatchi, a top full-service advertising agency in Ghana, in 1997 to deliver effective and integrated marketing communications solutions powered by creativity. They nurtured the agency from inception to nationally-recognised company.

Daniel channelled his excellence and competitiveness into making the company one of the best advertising companies in Ghana and Joel's passion for building relationships and desire for achieving the extraordinary transformed the company. Together, they led the company in various national and pan-African campaigns that transformed Origin8 from a small Ghanaian desktop publishing company into an award-winning affiliate of global advertising giant Saatchi & Saatchi.

As Chief Operating Officer, and subsequently Chief Executive Officer, Joel oversaw the expansion of Origin8 Saatchi & Saatchi's client base to include local and international blue-chip companies such as MTN, Cadbury, Guinness Ghana Ltd, Nestlé (across West and Central Africa), Peugeot, Société General-SSB and L'Oréal West Africa. The company's motto – 'The passion to originate ideas' – underscores its commitment to producing creative, world-class marketing communications solutions for its clients.

Joel has been involved in five other companies in Ghana including

AdSpaceDDB Ghana, another advertising enterprise; Platform Ltd, a public relations, events and merchandising enterprise; Imprint, an offset and digital printing enterprise; Spectra Studios, an audiovisual production enterprise; and Engage Ltd, a media buying enterprise. In recognition of its superlative performance, Origin8 Saatchi & Saatchi has been Ghana's most lauded advertising agency in the country's Gong-Gong Awards scheme (started in 2003 and organised by the Advertisers Association of Ghana); for instance, at the 7th Gong-Gong Awards in 2010, Origin8 Saatchi & Saatchi picked up a total of 10 awards.

In May 2009, Business Initiative Directions awarded Joel the International Quality Crown in New York in recognition of "his outstanding commitment to quality and excellence in the realm of customer satisfaction, leadership, innovation and efficiency." At the end of 2011, Joel separated from Origin8 to set up his own agency, Resultz Advertising.

Joel holds a master's degree in business administration and bachelor's degree in economics and psychology from the University of Ghana.

John Maxwell Addo

The late John Maxwell Addo is the founder of JM Addo and Sons, Fanteakwa Ltd and Ellebal Ltd. Fanteakwa Ltd is a subsidiary of JM Addo and sons while Ellebal Ltd is a real estate venture engaged in the development and management of real estate in Accra. Addo also founded Leather Products Ltd, a manufacturer of handbags for ladies in the 1970s and early 1980s.

Addo established JM Addo and Sons in 1962 to deal in pharmaceutical and consumer products, incorporating it as a limited liability company in 1969. JM Addo and Sons, through its distribution hub in Okaishie, Accra, has at various stages represented different foreign companies in Ghana and distributed goods for major multinationals like Unilever, Guinness Ghana Ltd and Nestle Ghana, as well as local companies such as Achimota Brewery and Aluworks.

Chapter Two: The Entrepreneur

Addo was a versatile entrepreneur who was able to adapt his business strategy to suit the economic trends and is one of the few Ghanaian entrepreneurs who operated under all the political regimes in the country. For example, when consumer goods were in short supply in the country in the late 1970s and early 1980s, Addo focused his efforts on the importation of commodities like rice and sugar, capitalising on the high demand at the time due to limited supply. In the early 1970s, he took advantage of the Aliens Compliance Order of 1969 to acquire prime real estate to expand his business in Okaishie. Pursuant to that Order, the Busia government expelled all non-Ghanaian nationals who did not have the requisite work and resident permits from Ghana. A large proportion of those expelled were traders who were forced to dispose of their assets.

Today, the core business of JM Addo and Sons remains the wholesale and distribution of pharmaceutical and consumer goods, and the company is sole distributor for a number of companies in the UK, Spain and India. Although Addo formally retired twenty years before he died, JM Addo and Sons continues to be a key player in the pharmaceutical and consumer goods industries in Ghana, thanks to Addo's vision in ensuring proper succession. His son William Addo, a pharmacist by profession, and an Okaishie-trained businessman, is the current Managing Director of the company. Under William Addo is building on what his father started, significantly increasing the company's business and opening a branch in Lagos, Nigeria. His strategy is to expand across West Africa.

Ken Ofori-Atta and Keli Gadzekpo

Ken Ofori-Atta founded Ghana's first investment bank, Databank Financial Services Ltd, which provides services in corporate finance, stock brokerage, privatisation and portfolio management, in 1990. Ken is a good example of an opportunity entrepreneur who, after working at Morgan Stanley and Salomon Brothers in New York, moved to Ghana to take advantage of a first-mover opportunity, setting up an investment bank to provide advisory services that the newly liberalised

Ghanaian economy would require.

Ken founded Databank with Keli Gadzekpo, a former KPMG Peat Marwick and Steuart Petroleum employee and currently the Executive Vice Chairman of Databank, with seed capital of US$25,000. The company has remained the leading investment banking group in Ghana with subsidiary companies involved stock brokerage, asset management, corporate finance, advisory and private equity. Databank manages the most successful pan-African equity mutual fund, the US$60-million EPACK fund and now has offices in The Gambia and Liberia. Ken and Keli have been on the forefront of innovation in the financial services industry in Ghana over the last decade, with Databank advising numerous initial public offerings on the Ghana Stock Exchange and privatisations of state owned enterprises.

Ken, who attended Achimota School in Ghana, has a Bachelor of Arts degree in economics from Columbia University (1984) and a Master of Business Administration degree from the Yale School of Management (1988), has won several awards and was named the second Most Respected Chief Executive Officer in Ghana by the annual award scheme for the year 2009.

Keli who is responsible for the overall financial and administrative management of Databank, holds a Bachelor of Science in Accounting from the Brigham Young University in the United States and is a US-qualified Chartered Professional Account. He completed a Mason Fellowship course at Harvard University's Kennedy School of Government, and serves on the boards of Enterprise Insurance Company (EIC) and Home Finance Company of The Gambia.

Kingsley Awuah-Darko

Kingsley Awuah-Darko is the Founder and Chief Executive Officer of MoneySystems International, an open remittance management system that engages in international, regional and domestic money transfers to and within Africa. Kingsley is a second-generation entrepreneur, as his father Mr Awuah-Darko founded one of Ghana's finest insurance companies, Vanguard Assurance Company Ltd, where Kingsley worked as a Project Officer between 1992 and 1995.

After years of work in Corporate Ghana, Kingsley spotted an opportunity in the money transfer market, leading him to establish MoneySystems International in 2002. In just a year, MoneySystems successfully launched its M-SYSTEM technology platform in July 2003, enabling it to undertake large-scale processing of remittances among countries in Europe, North America and Africa. M-SYSTEM allows a network of banks and financial Institutions in Africa and Money Transfer Operators (MTOs) in the USA and Europe to transact money transfer through a standardised interconnection platform.

Kingsley has successfully expanded the operations of MoneySystems to encompass remittances from 11 states in the United States of America, 11 countries in Europe and 18 countries in Francophone and Anglophone Africa.

He holds BA in Law (Hons) from the Kwame Nkrumah University of Science and Technology and an MBA from Henley Management College, University of Reading, UK.

Kobby Asmah

Kobby Asmah is the founder and Chief Executive Officer of TYPE Company Ltd, arguably the best printing company in the country. Mr Asmah has led the company he founded in 1993 to become not only one of the fastest growing companies in Ghana but also a member of the prestigious Ghana Club 100. With its state-of-the-art facilities, Type offers a comprehensive range of printing services.

After graduating from the Kwame Nkrumah University of Science and Technology in 1988, Kobby started his career with the Ministry of Education, but retrained as a graphic designer in the United Kingdom, setting up his own company with his wife on his return.

For printing, they relied on small print shops in Accra New Town, but Kobby realised that the market was characterised by poor standards and dissatisfied clients. He decided to venture into printing and differentiate on quality. His big break came when he was able to deliver the standard of quality that Barclays Bank Ghana wanted but had been having a problem obtaining in the market. Other financial institutions followed suit and TYPE's business grew steadily.

It hasn't always been smooth for TYPE. Kobby faced various challenges building the company. He woke up one day to learn that his landlord had decided to start a printing company. With only six months' notice to leave, he decided to go for a mortgage to buy an office building, from which the company currently operates successfully. Mr Asmah changed printing in Ghana by investing in high-technology printing presses gaining a technical edge over competitors. At the moment, TYPE's machinery can produce 500,000 printed items a day.

Kwabena Adjei

Kwabena Adjei is the founder and CEO of Kasapreko Company Ghana Ltd, one of the most successful beverage manufacturers in Africa. He is an industrialist and an entrepreneur with a deep vision for entrepreneurial transformation. His entrepreneurial exploits started in the 1970s when he was introduced to the trading business by his sister. Within a short period, Kwabena had joined the growing class of small-scale traders dabbling in informal imports across the Ghana-Togo border. He also had interests in the buying and selling gold and diamonds, hardware and jewellery.

In the late 1980s, he spotted an opportunity in the alcohol business in Ghana and despite the fact that he knew little about the alcohol business at the time, he founded Kasapreko in 1989 and began making his own gin for a small market. With distinctive flavouring and competitive prices, the gin proved to be a success from the very early stages.

Working with the Centre for Scientific Research into Plant Medicine (CSRPM) at Mampong, a government-owned research institution that uses plants for scientific research into healing, Kwabena began work on his next product. After a year of dialogue and partnership, they helped him to come out with Alomo Bitters, a refined product based on herbs, the single brand that accounted for the spectacular rise of

Kasapreko.

Noting increasing consumer sophistication in the beverage market in terms of taste, quality, safety and packaging, the company identified a niche in the alcohol market that was mostly served by foreign imports. The introduction of its Kasapreko Dry Gin product, which became the ultimate consumer choice in the market, led to its rise to the leadership position of the gin market in Ghana.

Kwabena's entrepreneurial vision has been the hallmark of the company's extraordinary performance (annual turnover is currently over US$30 million). He is motivated by an inner conviction that he is destined to be the best. When asked at Empretec, where he studied, where he wanted to see himself in three years' time, he replied "I wants to be the best or the biggest alcohol manufacturing company in Ghana."[42]

Kwabena Adjei and the Kasapreko Company have won several awards. In 2000, he received the Marketing Man of the Year 2000 award from the American Biographical Institute. Two years later the Chartered Institute of Marketing Ghana awarded him the prestigious Marketing Man of the Year 2002 award. The company's performance in also saw it being admitted into the prestigious and exclusive Ghana Club 100 in 2004.

Kwaku Ofosu Bediako

Kwaku Bediako is the founder and Chief Executive Officer of Chase Petroleum Ghana Ltd, a leading oil trading and distribution company that trades actively in crude oil and bulk refined products such as gas oil, petrol, jet fuel and liquified petroleum gas (LPG). Chase also provides advisory and consultancy services in the areas of oil refinery management, value-added activities and operational efficiency to enterprises in the industry. Kwaku started out working with his father in trading commodities such as oil, sugar, fish and rice, gaining wide-ranging experience and exposure in diverse transactions.

In 1995, a unique opportunity to represent an international

oil trading company marked the beginning of his career as an entrepreneur, leading to the establishment of Chase Petroleum Ghana in 1999. The company quickly established itself as an oil trading and bulk distribution company, and was first to be issued with a bulk distributor's license in Ghana. Under the leadership of Kwaku, the business made a turnover of more than US$3 million within the first two years.

Today, Chase Petroleum is a key contributor to the oil industry and operates a far-reaching petroleum distribution network that serves both local and external markets in the subregion.

Chase Petroleum is now completing one of the most ambitious projects in the industry in Africa: the Tema Tank Farm. Its installation will increase the storage, distribution and re-distribution capacities of Chase in Ghana to enable it to better serve the West African market. The first phase of the Tema Tank Farm, already completed, has the capacity to store 70,000 cubic metres of petroleum products. The company aims to build a total capacity of about 320,000 cubic meters to create a regional hub where traders around the world can store large quantities of oil for distribution to West Africa.

Apart from Chase, Kweku is the founder and CEO of Goldkey Properties Ltd and Blackwell Ltd, both real estate developers of luxury and standard apartments, modern executive homes and commercial facilities; both companies hold land banks with a combined acreage of 17,000 square meters in prime locations across the country.

Seeing an opportunity in the persistent loss of fruit harvests to spoilage, Kwaku also set up Pinora, a fruit processing plant in Asamankese, with a group of external partners , to process tropical fruits into concentrate for export.

In his own words, he "has a passion for business and an eye for opportunity".[43] Kwaku's involvement in transformative business development partnerships is his quiet contribution to economic leadership and entrepreneurship in Ghana. In view of this, he was recognised and featured in BBC's Focus on Africa in 2006 and by Reuters in 2007. He was invited to Korea by the Korean government in 2008 as one of the successful and influential future leaders from the African continent.

Kwaku attended Achimota School, where he obtained his GCE 'O' level certificate, and Mfantsipim School where he completed his 'A' levels.

Kwasi Twum

Kwasi Twum is the founder and Chief Executive Officer of Ghana's premier independent broadcasting group, the Multimedia Group. The group is made up of Joy FM and its sister stations including Adom FM, Luv FM, Nhyira FM, Hitz FM and Asempa FM. It recently started Ghana's first free-to-air digital television service, MultiTV. Kwasi Twum has ensured the rapid growth of the stations both locally and internationally through the Internet and has entered into the Liberian broadcasting industry through acquisition.

Kwasi Twum is a good example of a focused entrepreneur. Having identified the broadcast media space as his core entrepreneurial area, he has repeatedly turned down opportunities to invest outside this core area. Rather, he continues to reinvest in his existing enterprises and to acquire other radio stations to increase his reach. Kwasi is also committed to community investment, establishing the Joy Needy Child Project, a Multimedia Group-sponsored scholarship for brilliant underprivileged students at the University of Ghana and the Kwame Nkrumah University of Science and Technology.

Kwasi Twum and the Multimedia Group have won numerous awards. In 2010, he was adjudged third while the Group was ranked sixth in the Most Respected CEO and Most Respected Company Awards schemes organised by the PricewaterhouseCoopers. The Ghana Journalist Association honoured him in 2010 for his contribution to the growth of media in the country. The Group also received the CIMG Award for Media Organisation of the Year 2008 in 2009.

Kwasi Twum attended Mfantsipim School and the University of Ghana, where he obtained a Bachelor of Arts degree in economics. He is also an alumnus of Harvard Business School.

Mark Davies

Mark Davies is the founder of BusyInternet in Accra, one of Africa's largest technological centres. Mark is Welsh and South African, but has made Ghana one of his homes. He graduated in Social Anthropology from Cambridge University in 1986, and lived in New York thereafter. Typical of some would-be entrepreneurs, Mark's diverse experiences have enriched his entrepreneurial ventures. He previously worked as a busboy and a scriptwriter for the Travel Channel in the United Kingdom, and later became a celebrity interviewer for Channel 4 (also in the United Kingdom).

Mark began his entrepreneurial activities in 1993 with Sky Electronic Publishing, a direct mail catalogue designing company through which he designed catalogues for companies such as The Body Shop and Budweiser. In 1995, he set up an online local guide called Metrobeat that later merged with CitySearch (based in California). Together, Metrobeat and CitySearch set up city guides in over seventy cities in four countries.

Mark exemplifies an opportunity entrepreneur who will go to all lengths to develop an idea. After coming across the concept of an internet café in Brazil, he carried out analysis to determine where he might obtain the highest return for such an investment and, after narrowing it down to Africa, decided to move to Ghana to pursue his entrepreneurial idea.

The BusyInternet story, which began in 2001, has evolved from a simple internet service provider into a world-class technology centre offering broadband services, data hosting services and state-of-the-art internet cafes. It has positioned itself as a technology centre focusing on transforming the Ghanaian economy to meet the growing opportunities offered by the digital world. BusyInternet's achievement has been widely featured across the world through media outlets such as the New York Times and Wall Street Journal. The company has received numerous awards over the past few years: in 2008, it received a Lifetime Achievement Award for ICT in Ghana; it was also given the West Africa International Award of Merit for 2008 and the West Africa's Best Multi-Purpose Internet Cafe Company of the Year 2008 award. In September 2010 BusyInternet was adjudged the best Internet

Service provider (ISP) of the Year 2009 at the 21st annual Chartered Institute of Marketing Ghana (CIMG) awards.

In addition to BusyInternet, Mark has been involved in a number of pioneering entrepreneurial ventures across Africa including Esoko (formerly Tradenet), a trading platform that enables farmers and traders to trade a range of commodities such as shea butter, tomatoes, onions and peppers, among others, over the mobile phone. He is also the founder of Busylabs, a bespoke software development company focused on the development of transformative, locally designed software products for the growing technological needs of African companies and economies.

Mrs Elizabeth Villars

Mrs Elizabeth Villars is the founder and immediate past Managing Director of Camelot Ghana Ltd, a company which is involved in security and commercial printing for the West African market. Mrs Villars qualified as Ghana's first female computer scientist in 1968 and started her career at the Volta River Authority (VRA).

She began her entrepreneurial career after identifying an opportunity to produce customised payslips for VRA, and decided to leave VRA in 1974 to set up on her own. Having launched Camelot, she survived coups d'état, major currency devaluations and various other barriers to successful entrepreneurship, constantly adapting her enterprise to the changing environment to enable her remain competitive. With changing global technology, Camelot has continually invested in top-of-the-range printing technology to enable the delivery of customised printing solutions in record time. Camelot has an employee base of over 50 workers and has expanded into Nigeria to take advantage of the opportunities in that market. Mrs Villars listed Camelot on the Ghana Stock Exchange in September 1999 and had market capitalisation of GH¢0.79 million at the end of December 2011.[44]

In 2004, she restructured her board, resigning from her previous combined role of Chairman/Managing Director to ensure better corporate governance. An independent chairman, Mr Sam Mensah, headed the board with Mrs Villars as Managing Director, before she handed over the Managing Director role to John Colin Villars, her son. In addition to his professional qualifications, John Villars earned the role of Managing Director by working his way up over many years.

Mrs Villars has remained committed to her goal of making Camelot a market leader in delivering high-quality business forms and document security solutions. There were many times when she found herself frustrated by what she calls "dysfunctional, inefficient public service [that] makes entrepreneurship in Ghana very difficult." According to her, "the civil service must understand the private sector and not see it as full of criminals who want to evade taxes and find quick ways of making a buck." For example, at a time when import licenses were required in Ghana, she was told by the relevant minister that "[Ghanaians] are hungry so you can't be talking about computer paper. If you needed import license to process gari, I will give you but not to import computer paper."[45]

She has faced and surmounted many challenges in manufacturing in Ghana – in the 1990s, for example, Camelot was borrowing at 52% interest – although the persistence of these challenges made it difficult to compete with foreign firms whose operational costs were much lower.

Mrs Villars has won many awards including the Chartered Institute of Marketing Ghana Marketing Woman of the Year Award in 1998, the Millennium Excellence Award in 1999 and the Most Successful Woman Entrepreneur Award in 2000. She has also served on several boards including those of the Ghana Investment Promotion Centre, the Social Investment Fund, the Ghana Trade Fair Authority and the Ghana Statistical Services. She attended Holy Child School and the IBM Training School in the United Kingdom.

RA Darko

The late RA Darko acquired Mechanical Lloyd from its parent company, a Dutch firm, in 1969. Darko, a serial entrepreneur, had experience from previous ventures such as Akuapem Trading Company, founded in 1948, and a group of companies known as Okofoh Enterprises, which included Okofoh Printing Press, Okofoh Textiles, Okofoh Arms and Ammunitions, Glyco Confectionaries, Okofoh Bookshop, Okofoh Estates, Italo-Afro, Okofoh Assembly Plant and Okofoh Timbers and Sawmill, but he is best remembered for Mechanical Lloyd Company Ltd.

After acquisition, R. A. Darko was able to, by dint of hard work, diligence, assiduity and sheer business acumen combined with personal dynamism, grow the company steadily until his death, when Terry Darko, RA's son, assumed the reins. Terry Darko, a necessity entrepreneur, successfully expanded the enterprise his father left him and transformed Mechanical Lloyd into one of the most progressive family-owned enterprises in Ghana.

In 1994, Terry Darko took the decision to list the company on the Ghana Stock Exchange, becoming the first fully Ghanaian-owned company to be listed and quoted on the Exchange, a decision that generated capital for the growth and expansion of the enterprise, and probably secured the future of the company. The extraordinary performance of the company on the Ghana Stock Exchange in 1996-97, with shares gaining 270%, led to it being awarded the Land Rover Franchise in the country. Its renounceable rights issue of shares in 1997 saw foreign fund managers taking up some 18% of the company's shares, making it the first fully Ghanaian-owned company to attract foreign equity investment. As at the end of 2011, the company had a market capitalisation of GH¢4.1 million.[46]

Sandy Osei-Agyeman

Sandy Osei-Agyeman is the founder of Slid Industries, manufacturers of MVP hair products. Sandy is a good example of someone using other people's ideas to run a successful enterprise. The MVP range of products was based on an idea generated in a term paper by a group of students from Northwestern University's Kellogg School of Management who were on a research trip to Ghana. Prior to

Slid industries, Sandy co-founded AFAM Concept, the makers of Elentee and Vitale hair products, which became a leading American manufacturer of black hair products. In 1994, he was named recipient of the Afrique Awards Entrepreneur of the Year accolade.

Sandy is a former Olympian, having represented Ghana at the 1972 and 1976 Olympic Games. He holds a Bachelor's Degree in Finance from East Illinois University, USA and a Master of Business Administration in finance and international business from Northwestern University's Kellogg School of Management. After graduating from Kellogg, Sandy worked as a banker for Continental Bank, Harris Bank and Credit Lyonnais before setting up his enterprise. He is Chairman of Ghana Athletics Commission as well as a director of Graphic Packaging Ltd.

Questions for Class Discussion

1. Can anyone become a successful entrepreneur?

2. What are the characteristics of individuals who are likely to become entrepreneurs?

3. How would you explain the expression 'Ability to become connected'? Why is this important for a prospective entrepreneur?

4. What are some of the reasons why Ghanaian entrepreneurs fail?

5. What behaviours can a prospective entrepreneur adopt to avoid failure?

6. How can political entrepreneurs survive beyond the term of political leaders they are connected to?

7. What common thread(s) do you see in the profiles of the entrepreneurs featured in this chapter?

Kuenyehia on Entrepreneurship

Case Study: The King of Travel: Pak-Wo Shum[47]

Pak-Wo Shum (or 'Shum' as he is popularly known) started his entrepreneurial activities at the age of seventeen. Prior to that, he worked for nine months at a Chinese restaurant and was fired because he could not conform to the rules and regulations that his employer required him to adhere to.

A serial entrepreneur, Shum had started, developed and managed at least seven successful enterprises by the age of thirty-five. Shum's entrepreneurial interests span a number of industries including retail, aviation, hospitality, real estate and mining. Born to Ghanaian and Chinese parents in November 1968, Shum can be said to have been a likely candidate for entrepreneurship from an early age as both his parents were entrepreneurs.

His first entrepreneurial venture was in the wholesale of cooking utensils to market women, where he served as a link between the manufacturers of cooking utensils and the women who retailed those utensils at a time when it was not easy to obtain access to the manufacturers. He subsequently went into the sale of fabrics, but decided to quit that business because he felt taking inventory of fabric was too involving. He started retailing shoes because "it was easier to count and to keep track of [them]." When his customers started asking for bags, clothing and other accessories, he expanded his range but soon decided to focus on men's clothing, opening Adeva, a shop exclusively retailing men's shirts and, later, men's accessories. Before long, Adeva became synonymous with 'shirts' in the cities of Accra and Tema.

Devaluation of the cedi and fluctuations on the foreign exchange market in the late 1980s and early 1990s made the retail of imported goods an uncertain enterprise. This situation, combined with his inner restlessness and a quest for self-development, led Shum to close down his Adeva shops in 2000 to pursue a bachelor's degree in business administration at the University of Ghana Business School as a mature student.

While in the university, Shum began to consider what business to start. He carried out research, considering a number of industries where he would not be bogged down by inventory. In his final semester (when most of his classmates were focusing on their final exams), Shum rented a small office at Aviation House near Kotoka International Airport and set up TravelKing, a travel agency.

TravelKing was initially so small that no airline would deal directly with the company. Instead, it retailed the travel services of other (bigger) travel agencies until Shum found a niche, positioning TravelKing as a leading provider of corporate travel services, with outstanding customer satisfaction ideals, winning a number of coveted industry awards. TravelKing soon became the Ghanaian strategic partner of BCD, an international corporate travel solutions provider in 95 countries with turnover in excess of US\$ 14 billion.

Shum exhibits many of the classic entrepreneurial attributes, notably, dynamic leadership and vision, self-confidence, optimism, and opportunity obsession. He has also learned by doing.

Like many Ghanaian entrepreneurs, Shum initially did not keep proper records or apply proper corporate governance practices. Neither did he separate his personal finances from those of his businesses.

However, when Delta Air Lines approached him (based on his track record with TravelKing) to act as their sole general sales agent in Ghana, Shum turned to some trusted advisers to develop a new company, a robust business plan and to identify and recruit talented staff who had experience in the Ghanaian travel industry to make up for the areas he did not consider himself an expert in. He put in place a board of directors headed by the financial consultant Sugantan Allotey (who brought a wealth of experience from his previous role at Barclays Bank Ghana, as well as knowledge of proper corporate governance). The company, Aviation Alliance had over 40,000 clients in the first six months of its operations and now operates in nine West African countries.

Shum surprised everyone by closing TravelKing down after five years to focus on Aviation Alliance. His decision is even more surprising as it appears that at least one investor was prepared to invest in TravelKing if Shum had stayed with it. But Shum concedes that he had no option but to close down TravelKing because he had failed to mentor a successor to take over from him. In his words, the Delta opportunity was one that he couldn't let go, and it was the right time for him to jump ship, particularly as he had managed to secure attractive working capital facilities from HFC Bank to pursue the opportunity offered by Aviation Alliance.

Shum's entrepreneurial interests extend beyond the travel industry. His other activities include gold exploration and real estate. He acquired a 400-square-kilometre tract of land to mine gold through two subsidiary mining companies he has founded.

Shum tries to maintain a balance in his work and social life. He values the significance of having people he can trust and talk to as an entrepreneur. He describes himself as a quiet, spiritual man who treasures quality time spent with family, friends and by himself. He attributes his success entirely to the Grace of God, having recently become a born-again Christian. When asked what his favourite pastime is, he says with a smile and with a wink: "Getting extra sleep whenever I can."

Questions for Case Discussion

1. What factors have made Shum succeed in a number of different businesses?

2. Is Shum an entrepreneur or businessman? Assuming Shum is an entrepreneur, rather than a businessman, would you say he was born an entrepreneur?

3. What traits or behaviours does Shum exhibit that assist or hamper his entrepreneurial endeavours.

4. Would you say Shum is a lifestyle or high-growth entrepreneur? A necessity or opportunity entrepreneur?

5. What traits does Shum share in common with the other celebrated Ghanaian entrepreneurs featured in this chapter?

Notes

1   Horovitz, J. and A.-V. Ohlsson-Corboz. *A Dream with a Deadline: Turning Strategy into Action.* Harlow: FT Prentice Hall, 2007.

2   Collins, J. and J. Porras 1996. Building Your Company's Vision. Harvard Business Review, *Harvard Business Review,* 74(5), 1996: 65-77.

3   Beaver, G. and P. Jenkins, Competitive advantage and entrepreneurial power. *Journal of Small Business and Enterprise Development,* Volume 12(1), 2005: 9-23.

4   Trans. C.C. Biddle, Lippincott, Grambo and Company, Philadelphia, 1855.

5   Collins, O.F. and D.G. Moore. *The Enterprising Man.* East Lansing: Michigan State University Press, 1964.

6   Gladwell, M. *The Tipping Point.* New York: Back Bay Books, 2002.

7   Byers, T., H. Kist and R. Sutton. Characteristics of the Entrepreneur: Social Creatures, Not Solo Heroes. In R.C. Dorf, ed., *The Technology Management Handbook.* Boca Raton: CRC Press, 1999.

8   Sandy Osei-Agyman, Column in *On Business Life*

9   See Chapter 14 for discussion on values.

10   Frederick W. Smith: No Overnight Success, Businessweek, 20 September 2004.

11   McClelland, D.C. Characteristics of successful entrepreneurs. In *Keys to the Future of American Business, Proceedings of the Third Creativity, Innovation, and Entrepreneurship Symposium.* Framingham: US Small Business Administration and the National Center for Research in Vocation Education, 1986.

12   Knight, F.H. *Laissez-faire: Pro and Con. Journal of Political Economy, 75, 1967: 782-795.*

13   Isaacson, W. *Steve Jobs.* New York: Simon and Schuster, 2011.

14   Bird, B.J. The Roman God Mercury: An Entrepreneurial Archetype. *Journal of Management Inquiry,* 1(3), 1992: 205-212.

15   Lecture delivered to the Business Administration class at Ghana Institute of Management and Public Administration, Greenhill, 2005.

16 Branson, R. *Losing my Virginity: The Autobiography*. London: Virgin Publishing Limited, 1998.

17 Vise, D.A. and M. Malseed. *The Google Story*. New York: Baram Dell, 2005.

18 Branson, R. *Losing my Virginity: The Autobiography*. London: Virgin Publishing Limited, 1998.

19 Collins, O.F. and Moore, D.G. *The Organization Makers*. New York: Appleton-Century-Crofts, 1970.

20 Interview for case study by Thelma Tawiah, 2007.

21 Byers, T., H. Kist and R. Sutton. Characteristics of the Entrepreneur: Social Creatures, Not Solo Heroes. In R.C. Dorf, ed., *The Technology Management Handbook*. Boca Raton: CRC Press, 1999.

22 Gartner, W.B., K.G. Shaver, E. Gatewood and J.A. Katz. Finding the entrepreneur in entrepreneurship. *Entrepreneurship Theory and Practice*, 18(3), 1994: 5-9.

23 Fry, F. L. *Entrepreneurship: A Planning Approach*. Eagan: West Publishing, 1993.

24 Hisrich, R.D. and M.P. Peters. *Entrepreneurship*. Boston: McGraw-Hill/Irwin, 2002.

25 Cooper, A.C., F.J. Gimeno-Gascon and C.Y. Woo. Initial Human and Financial Capital as Predictors of New Venture Performance. *Journal of Business Venturing*, 9(5), 1994: 371-396.

26 Fry, F. L. *Entrepreneurship: A Planning Approach*. Eagan: West Publishing, 1993.

27 Bird, B.J. The Roman God Mercury: An Entrepreneurial Archetype. *Journal of Management Inquiry*, 1(3), 1992: 205-212.

28 Madsen, H., H. Neergaard, S. Fisker and J.P. Ulhoi. Entrepreneurship in the Knowledge-intensive sector: Influential factors at the start-up and early growth phase. Paper presented at the 13th Nordic Conference on Small Business Research, Tromso, 10-12 June 2004.

29 Research carried out by the author, 2011

30 *Shefsky, L. E. Entrepreneurs Are Made Not Born*. Columbus: McGraw-Hill Companies: 1994.

31 Branson, R. *Losing my Virginity: The Autobiography*. London: Virgin

Publishing Limited, 1998.

32 Lecture delivered to the Information Technology Entrepreneurship class of Ghana Institute of Management and Public Administration, Greenhill, February 2010.

33 Keynote address delivered at the 2nd Oxford and Beaumont Retreat, Afrikiko Riverside Resort, Akosombo, December 2007.

34 As interviewed by Elikem Nutifafa Kuenyehia, October 2011.

35 Lecture delivered to the Information Technology Entrepreneurship class of Ghana Institute of Management and Public Administration, Greenhill, 28 February 2010.

36 Choi T. Promoting a Northeast Asia Economic Integration Policy. *Korea Focus*,12(2), 2004: 77-100.

37 Younkins, E. Entrepreneurship Properly Understood. *Le Quebecois Libre*, 64, 2000.

38 Keynote address delivered at the Chase Petroleum Ghana Ltd management retreat at Golden Tulip Hotel, Accra, May 2008.

39 Makura, M. *Africa's Greatest Entrepreneurs*. Johannesburg: Penguin Books Ltd, 2008.

40 Lecture delivered to the Foundations of Entrepreneurship class of Ghana Institute of Management and Public Administration, Greenhill, October 2010.

41 Summit Communications, www.summitreports.com/ghana/ernest.htm, retrieved 14 December 2011.

42 Makura, M. *Africa's Greatest Entrepreneurs*. Johannesburg: Penguin Books Ltd, 2008.

43 Lecture delivered to the Foundations of Entrepreneurship class of Ghana Institute of Management and Public Administration, Greenhill, September 2010.

44 Ghana Stock Exchange, www.gse.com.gh, retrieved 14 December 2011.

45 Lecture delivered to the Information Technology Entrepreneurship class of Ghana Institute of Management and Public Administration, Greenhill, February 2010.

46 Ghana Stock Exchange, www.gse.com.gh, retrieved 14 December 2011.

Chapter Two: The Entrepreneur

47   Based on interviews carried out by Thelma Tawiah in October 2006 and Malik Adam in December 2011.

Chapter Three: Idea Generation

"The best way to predict the future is to invent it" – **Alan Kay**

Outline

- Introduction
- The Nature of Ideas
- Sources of Ideas
- IdeaQuest Activation Tool
- Which Comes First; the Idea or the Desire to Start a Business?
- Examples of Eureka Moments
- Idea vs. Opportunity
- Concept Paper Development
- Questions for Class Discussion
- Case Study: 53 Sails: A Journey into the World of Africa's Most Successful People

THIS CHAPTER EXAMINES the nature of ideas, and concerns itself with the following fundamental questions:

1. How do entrepreneurs come up with ideas for their enterprises?
2. How does an entrepreneur determine which idea has the best chance of providing the basis for a successful venture?

I will also seek to correct the misconception that, for a successful entrepreneurial venture, an idea must be original.

Although the focus of this chapter is how people generate ideas through the brainstorming process, the principles identified in this chapter can be used when an existing business is thinking of developing new product or service lines, and can be easily built into innovation processes.

The Nature of Ideas

An idea is a conception or plan formed by mental effort.[1] I stated in Chapter 2 that the entrepreneur is the person who 'dreams the dream'; the entrepreneur's initial idea for a venture is essentially the dream.

I stated in Chapter 2 that the entrepreneur is at the heart of the entrepreneurial venture. It follows then that the entrepreneur's idea or dream is the foundation of the entrepreneurial venture, since every entrepreneurial venture rests on an idea; without an idea, the entrepreneur has nothing to develop an enterprise around. Just as it is not possible to have a tree without roots, it is not possible to create and develop an entrepreneurial venture without an idea. Every person contemplating entrepreneurship must therefore, first and foremost, have a dream or an idea that would not only form the basis on which to build a venture, but also provide the inspiration and direction for the growth of the venture.

Let us consider a few examples of the dreams that formed the bases of enterprises set up by Ghanaian entrepreneurs.

Ken Ofori-Atta dreamt of offering Ghanaian businesses investment advisory services at a time when the Ghanaian financial services sector was underdeveloped, lacking even the most basic structures. He persuaded Keli Gadzekpo and James Akpo to share in his dream and develop it together. In the process of building Databank into Ghana's most influential indigenous financial services group, they took a leadership role in helping to craft the structures and systems that have enabled the rapid evolution of Ghana's financial services space over the last two decades.

Patrick Awuah dreamt of providing a rigorous, liberal arts university education in Ghana, similar to the education he himself had benefited from while an undergraduate student at Swarthmore College in the United States. With that idea, he started Ashesi University College in March 2002 with an inaugural class of thirty students.

Dzigbordi Dosoo, the founder and Chief Executive Officer of Allure Africa Ltd, dreamt of providing stressed-out corporate executives and housewives world-class beauty and spa treatments in tranquil surroundings. With that idea as a foundation, she set up Allure Spa in the City, Allure Beauty Parlor and Allure Man to offer her target clientèle the aforementioned services.

Ladi Nylander dreamt of transforming alata samina, the traditional soap generations of Ghanaians have made from plantain leaves and other ingredients, into the fresh-smelling, attractively packaged Village Fresh toilet soap.

Kingsley Awuah-Darko dreamt of enabling millions of Africans in the diaspora to send money back home at rates significantly lower than were then available through Western Union, the dominant player in that industry. Kingsley's dream formed the basis of MoneySystems International, an electronic money transfer system operating in over 40 countries across North America, Europe and Africa.

As her colleagues at Ghana International Airlines began to pay more interest in the healthy packed fruit that she took to work for lunch, Sheila Ocansey dreamt of a business supplying health-conscious office workers fresh fruits and smoothies, a dream that evolved into a business known as Fruities.

These examples are selected at random from within the Ghanaian entrepreneurial community. There must be hundreds of thousands of other examples of entrepreneurial dreams that developed into enterprises. Of course, for each dream that actually inspired and led to the development of an enterprise, there are many more that remain in 'dream drawers,'[2] never to see the light of day.

Contrary to the view held by many, a successful business idea need not be outstanding or complicated. Indeed, as has been demonstrated in the few examples above, there are many entrepreneurs who have built extremely successful enterprises based on simple ideas. What is more important, as we see later in this chapter, is that the idea is one that is underpinned by a significant opportunity, and one that is consistent with the interest, passion, lifestyle, skill set and values of the entrepreneur. Of course, the ability to ultimately execute the dream and the will to drive the process from idea to profits, are critical.

It is also sometimes erroneously thought that for an idea to create a successful enterprise, that idea must be original. As demonstrated above as well as in many of the examples used in this book, a successful idea need not be original. Sahar and Bobby Hashemi hit the nail on the head by distinguishing inventors – "creative geniuses who come up with new things" – from entrepreneurs, who "simply make businesses out of ideas that for the most part already exist" and "for the most part, exploit the ideas capital that inventors leave behind".[3]

What entrepreneurs typically do is to 'search and spin'. Firstly they 'search' and find a pre-existing idea, and then they 'spin' (develop) that idea in the way that best suits their target market's socio-economic or personal circumstances. Alternatively, 'spinning' an idea may involve taking an idea from one part of a country, or of the world, to another location where the idea is likely to work, either in its current form or with some modification. In Chapter 2 I mentioned that both Richard Branson and Ian Kluvitse like to jot down ideas they come across in a notebook. This could form the beginning of successful searching and spinning. In fact by Kluvitse's own admission, his focus is usually on ideas that he sees overseas that have not yet been developed in Ghana, which he seeks to spin for the Ghanaian market.

Of course there are some entrepreneurs who are also inventors or become entrepreneurs because of something that they invented. Bill James Dyson, for example, is an inventor/entrepreneur; he invented and successfully commercialised the bagless vacuum cleaner. A notable Ghanaian inventor/entrepreneur is Apostle Kwadwo Safo. Through the Kristo Asafo Technology Centre (KATC) and the Great Kosa Company Ltd, he has invented and successfully commercialised products such as loud speakers, amplifiers, excavators, weed slashers, cabbage collectors and spot welding machines, both in the country and across Africa.

An entrepreneur starting an enterprise based on a 'new-to-the-world' product or service is more likely to find it difficult to launch a business around that product or service, because the potential customer base will require education about the product or service and its usage. This could take significant time and financial resources compared to a an enterprise based on an already established and understood product or service. Imagine, for example, how much money was spent educating people on how to use the personal computer when it first came out.

Rather than getting hung up on whether or not an idea is an original one, the individual looking for an idea to form the basis of an enterprise should focus on the more important question of whether or not there is an existing customer pain that the idea helps remove.

My fundamental submission is that every successful entrepreneurial venture must remove a customer pain. A customer pain may exist because a customer has a need that nobody has been able to meet. Alternatively, although there may be one or many enterprises meeting, or purporting to meet, a particular need of the customer, the customer may still have a pain because the offerings of those enterprises in fact fall short, in one way or the other, of completely removing that pain.

Let us consider an example.

Chapter Three: Idea Generation

A product that has recently captured the imagination of the Ghanaian consumer is Gari Soakings produced and distributed by Kwik Meal. This product is a pre-packaged combination of gari, sugar, powered milk, roasted groundnuts and Milo, to which a customer only needs add water to be able to enjoy a gari soakings snack.

Before the Kwik Meal Gari Soakings product was developed, there were many ways to remove a customer pain to enjoy a gari soakings snack at boarding schools, where students depend on them for survival. Generations of Ghanaian parents have sent their children away to boarding school with separate packets of gari, roasted groundnuts, sugar, and tins of Milo and milk. A student wanting a quick snack measured and mixed the relevant quantities of gari, groundnuts, sugar, milk, Milo and water.

However, as every person who spent some time in a Ghanaian boarding school will attest, the process of enjoying soakings still involved an element of 'customer pain'. At times students would find that they did not have all of the ingredients required. The entrepreneurs behind the gari soakings product recognised that pain and created a product which ensures all the ingredients come together. For the privilege of having a pre-packed product, people are willing to pay several times more than the actual cost of the individual ingredients. They are willing to pay a premium for this because it removes the inconvenience of putting the different ingredients together, as well as the possibility that, at one point, a customer may have to do without one or more ingredients. Kwik Meal even developed a cup-sized version, ideal for one serving – the customer only needs to add water and drink the soakings straight from the cup.

Where a customer's need has never been met before by anybody else, the entrepreneur's idea must provide a solution (typically a novel one) which will for the first time satisfy the customer's need. For example, the invention of mobile phones made it possible for customers to make and receive telephone calls pretty much anywhere, something that had previously not been a practical possibility.

Where the customer's need is already being met in one way or another, the entrepreneur must meet the customer's need better than the existing competitive set.

In many instances, the opportunity to remove a customer pain falls in the second category; although the customer's need is already being met to an extent, there still exists some pain that the entrepreneur can remedy by adding additional features or benefits. Kotler and Armstrong[4] examine how product strategies can be used to create additional features and benefits for the consumer. A product feature is a tangible or intangible attribute that forms part of the product. A product benefit is the outcome or effect that one derives from the usage of the product. Sugar-free chewing gum, for example, has a novel feature in the form of a substitute for sugar. The benefits of choosing this gum option include the avoidance of increased blood sugar levels and the incidence of rotten teeth.

The distinctions between the two categories of ideas that create opportunities for entrepreneurs are not as clear-cut as they appear. Take the mobile phone example used earlier. We used that example to illustrate a novel solution for a customer pain that had never been previously addressed. However, it can be argued that at the time the first mobile phones were introduced, customers could meet their needs for voice communication in a number of ways including fixed line telephones, payphones or even face-to-face contact. On that basis it can then be said that what some of the first companies to successfully commercialise the mobile phone (including ARP of Finland and NET of Japan) did, was to introduce the additional and more convenient benefit of enabling individuals to make telephone calls from anywhere.

Sources of Ideas

Ideas may come from a variety of sources, including the following:

Opportunity or environmental scanning

Entrepreneurs who develop ideas by opportunity or environmental scanning simply keep their eyes wide open and are actively alert to opportunities in the world around them. Many entrepreneurs have built successful enterprises by connecting some of the dots in the events and things they notice around them. As Dauten states, "Many inventions and innovations are a result of the inventors seeing new and different relationships among objects, processes, materials, technologies and people."[5]

To be able to develop ideas through opportunity scanning, the entrepreneur must also be sensitive to changes in the world around him. Social, economic and technological changes, as well as changing customer tastes and preferences, are sources of ideas for potentially profitable business enterprises. For example, noticing that increased prosperity in Accra within a small subset of the population has led to an increase in armed robberies and burglaries, could spark ideas around security services. Noting further that this new-found affluence has led to a mentality of health consciousness could spark an idea for developing a healthy food range. An increase in the number of busy professional women could lead to an idea around crèches located in town centres for such women to drop off and pick up their children on their way to and from work respectively.

Social, economic and technological changes offer infinite possibilities for idea generation for new and existing enterprises. Some of the changes that entrepreneurs may want to exploit for businesses in Ghana include:

- The gradual transition (at least in the urban centres) from extended family structures, leading to the rise of the nuclear family;
- Longer working hours and longer commutes to and from work and school, particularly in Accra;
- Increased health consciousness among a significant proportion of the population;
- Widespread use of mobile phones, even in the rural areas;
- An increasing proportion of the population aged below twenty-five;
- Increase in foreign direct investment into Ghana;
- Increase in global awareness and a more cosmopolitan

orientation;
- Increased urban unemployment and underemployment.

Anyone looking for an idea to develop an enterprise could list some of these changes and brainstorm potential business ideas that such changes could engender.

It is also sometimes possible that, by simply keeping your eyes open, you might notice someone providing a service or product in a way that you know you could improve on. This type of opportunity is exemplified by an enterprise which has been very successful financially, notwithstanding that it provides lousy service. In such circumstances, potential entrepreneurs simply have to figure out ways to provide better service than the incumbent(s) to attract the customers of the incumbent(s) to their venture.

Media

The media in all forms offers potential leads for ideas. Potential entrepreneurs should make time to read various newspapers and magazines, to watch television, to listen to the radio and to regularly surf the Internet. For example, reading, in the *Daily Graphic,* about the challenges of finding suitably qualified personnel in a particular area of the country could potentially lead someone to set up an employment agency to recruit and train graduates to meet the needs of businesses in that area.

To take advantage of ideas generated by the media, you must at least scan (if you are unable to read or watch in full) as many different forms of media as possible. You should also scan through particular media channels that you might not ordinarily have interacted with. For example, a man who might not otherwise read *Shika Magazine* because it is targeted at women should make time to go through it because he might otherwise miss certain idea leads. Equally, a man who might not read *CANOE Magazine* because he does not fall within *CANOE*'s upwardly mobile target market must nonetheless make time to at least scan it.

In a developing country like Ghana, where there is often a time lag between the introduction of an idea in developed countries and the introduction of the idea into Ghana, some entrepreneurs may find ideas for new business ventures by reading about new ideas or businesses in foreign newspapers, magazines and journals.

Reading

Related to the earlier point about scanning the media is the opportunity that reading generally, in as wide a variety of fields as possible, offers entrepreneurs and potential entrepreneurs in the pursuit of new business ideas. General reading may expose you to potential idea leads. Current and would-be entrepreneurs should therefore cultivate the habit of reading as much as possible, and from as wide a range of sources as possible.

Travel

Inscribed on a number of taxis and trotros in Ghana is the saying 'travel and see', which acknowledges that travel increases a person's exposure, making one knowledgeable. This is also true in the area of idea generation where people, by travelling to another city, country or region, may become exposed to new ideas for products and services. They can, in turn, develop a 'local' enterprise in their own city or country based on these 'imported' or 'foreign' ideas.

In many instances, the entrepreneur may have to tweak the idea to reflect the specific local attitudes and circumstances that might be different from the circumstances that pertain where the idea was originally imported from. Mark Davies, the founder of BusyInternet, made the decision to start Ghana's first large-scale cyber café after seeing such cyber cafés in operation in Brazil during one of his numerous trips to that country. My idea to set up a world-class corporate and commercial law firm in Ghana in the form of Oxford and Beaumont Solicitors was influenced largely by my time working in London for Linklaters LLP, one of the world's most prestigious international law firms. Oxford and Beaumont is therefore modelled along the lines of Linklaters, although there are many differences based on the different stages of each company's development, the different nature of the Ghanaian market and the resources available, among others. Many other Ghanaian entrepreneurs admit that their businesses have been influenced by ideas they have come across during periods spent outside Ghana.

Government

Governments may consciously or unconsciously create opportunities for entrepreneurs through regulatory changes, for example, the introduction of tax and other incentives to encourage individual entrepreneurs to participate in a particular sector. Governments also create opportunities when they specifically acknowledge the importance of entrepreneurship and set out to create opportunities for individual entrepreneurs to take advantage of. For example, to encourage individuals and companies to invest in the hospitality sector in a bid to increase the number of hotels available when Ghana hosted the 2008 Africa Cup of Nations, the Government introduced tax incentives for those investing in the hospitality industry.

An example of a government directly creating opportunities for entrepreneurs is the Africa Growth and Opportunity Act (AGOA), which was enacted in October 2000 by the government of the United States of America. AGOA is aimed at providing special trade preference packages for the 34 African countries that are signatories to the Act, and has helped to create several African entrepreneurs in areas such as textile and apparel production, energy-related products, agricultural products and handicrafts. An example of an AGOA beneficiary enterprise is Belin Textiles, a Ghanaian textile company that, after taking part in an AGOA-sponsored sourcing exhibition in Las Vegas, USA, secured a deal worth over US$200,000 to supply camouflage t-shirts to American retail giant Wal-Mart.[6]

In some instances, government intervention may create entrepreneurs more indirectly. This happens when the Government makes (or changes) a policy, which in turn creates opportunities that entrepreneurs can take advantage of. Examples of such instances in Ghana include deregulation of the telecommunications and petroleum markets in Ghana, which created business opportunities for telecommunications service providers, oil marketing companies and independent power producers.

Personal Experience and Frustration

While there are many examples of a deliberate effort on the part of an entrepreneur to find an idea for a business enterprise, entrepreneurs may come across opportunities inadvertently while seeking ways of meeting their own needs.

Unpleasant situations that customers experience from time to time can be a source of ideas, and it is often the case that a number of people face the same problem or irritation (customer pain), which one can then capitalise on to start an enterprise. One can start asking people (friends, family, co-workers, even strangers) about frustrations they have experienced personally as customers of other enterprises. Asking questions to understand the entire situation, and then asking oneself whether there might be an opportunity to remove the pain could lead to the generation of new business ideas. Ideas can also be generated through brainstorming with friends, focus group discussions and problem inventory assessments. A problem inventory assessment asks consumers, either through questionnaires or interviews, about the problems they have with various products and services they use. Responses to these questions could give an entrepreneur an idea of how to offer the same product or service better than the competition.

Skill Set

Based on one's professional experience and skill set, a person may become alert to a gap in the marketplace. For example, Selorm Tetteh, a veterinary surgeon employed by the Ghana Army, realised that there was a market for high-end veterinary services. This became clear after many affluent individuals approached him to assist in nursing their domestic pets back to good health. A number of these individuals had also flown their pets (with their domestic servants accompanying their pets) to countries such as Germany for treatment requiring equipment not available in Ghana. Based on that insight, he participated in Google/TechnoServe's BelieveBeginBecome competition to fine-tune his business plan to develop a high-end veterinary practice in Accra. After emerging as one of the finalists in the competition, he resigned from the army to focus fully on the veterinary practice. Vets Place is now a successful veterinary practice in Airport residential area in Accra.

In many instances, the requisite skill set would have been acquired by obtaining a professional qualification or other formal education. However, it is also the case that the skill set may have been self-taught because of a passion for a particular area. Afia Bailes' story clearly depicts this. After moving with her husband to England and subsequently to Canada, she found that she had a lot of time on her hands. She therefore taught herself how to bake novelty deserts by watching cookery shows on television and reading cookbooks. Upon her return to Ghana, when the demand from her friends to make her trademark cheese and chocolate cakes became overwhelming, Afia opened A Slice of Heaven at Ridge in Accra to provide slices of heavenly cakes and other goodies to the general public.

People who start a business based on something they have been technically trained to do or are good at, according to Gerber, often suffer the fatal assumption that "if you understand the technical work of the business, you understand a business that does that technical work."[7] Essentially, such people go into a business on the assumption that because they are skilled surgeons or hairdressers, for example, they are qualified to run a surgery or hairdressing business. This is a common failing of the many Ghanaian professionals running their own businesses as entrepreneurs.

Such professionals (or technical people as Gerber calls them) must make time to understand how to run the business through which they will provide services based on the technical skills they possess. Also, when thinking of starting a business based on technical ability, one must ensure that it is something that they love to do, and that they are doing it for the love of it rather than simply because that is what they have been trained to do. Owning an enterprise you hate is like having a job you hate. An important corollary of this is that if you are very passionate about a particular business that requires the possession of a skill you do not have, you can either acquire the skill or hire someone with that skill.

Franchising

Franchising provides a proven business format which may be attractive to prospective entrepreneurs. The advantage of the franchise option is that the franchise owners (the franchisors) would have researched the idea thoroughly and, in many cases, have several successful examples of the idea being implemented. There is therefore a ready pool of knowledge that the franchisee can rely on. I will discuss franchises in more detail in Chapters 5 and 6.

Conferences, Workshops, Exhibitions

Conferences, workshops, exhibitions and similar fora also provide a good source of business ideas as they showcase new products and service ideas, as well as provide opportunities to meet several people including inventors, manufacturer's representatives and franchisors. They provide a platform for a prospective entrepreneur to gain business ideas. Such ideas could be existing ones which can be applied in different contexts and locations. It also offers opportunities to commercialise new inventions that could remove customer pain. These professional gatherings also provide opportunities for the entrepreneur or prospective entrepreneur to meet other people, including potential business partners.

Brainstorming

Brainstorming is an effective way of generating ideas for new or existing businesses. Brainstorming is literally the process of stimulating the brain to generate as many ideas as possible. In practice, it involves one or more individuals coming up with spontaneous ideas in rapid succession.

Many of the ideas that are generated in a brainstorm will not in fact be used or may not prove suitable. However, many gems can emerge from a brainstorm which could form the basis of multimillion-Ghana cedi enterprises. The focus of any brainstorm should be to come up with as many ideas as possible. At the brainstorming stage, you should not be limited by the reality of limited or non-existent resources to develop the idea into a successful enterprise, or by the profitability of the various ideas. Those considerations, important as they are, should feature in the equation at the concept development stage when the entrepreneur must get an indication of how to generate money for and from the venture.

Drawing on his extensive experience in brainstorming sessions that have resulted in a number of revolutionary products including the Palm Pilot, Tom Kelley[8] states that sixty minutes seems to be the optimum length for a brain storming session. Kelley also advises that participants of a brainstorm exercise must build on the ideas of others and not criticise any ideas during the session. He recommends encouraging wild ideas and covering the room walls with paper to scribble down as many ideas as possible; once the various ideas are visible to participants, the written ideas will spur other ideas. Kelley also encourages 'getting physical' in a brainstorm – bringing physical objects to inspire people to generate ideas. These objects could be in the form of competitor products, magazines, books and videos.

If you are determined to start your own business but cannot come up with an idea, you can set up a brainstorming session with about four or five friends with different backgrounds and experiences. Meet in a 'cool' place or set up a room for maximum creativity – with music, colours, magazines and other visually and mentally stimulating media.

IdeaQuest Activation Tool

If you are looking to start your own enterprise but are struggling to come up with a product or service idea, or if you are already an entrepreneur but are looking for different ideas to expand or diversify your enterprise's business portfolio, you should consider using the IdeaQuest Activation tool. The tool works in the following manner.

- Make a list of your interests and passions. Write down the things that you like doing, irrespective of whether you are any good at doing them. Also, write down which industries or companies you are fascinated by.

- Keep your eyes open for inspiration; have a notebook and write down all ideas that come to you. Regularly flip through the notebook to review the ideas you have come up with in the past.

- Glance through as many magazines and newspapers as you can lay your hands on. If possible, focus on magazines that you do not typically read.

- Write a list of your major irritations – what frustrates you (or other people you know) in your day-to-day life?

- Write a list of your skills (things that you are good at, whether or not you have any interest in them).

- Write a list of things that you are not good at but have an interest in.

- Think through your personality and work style and answer questions such as: What are your values and aspirations? What times of the day and in what sort of environment do you like/ hate working? How do you like to work (as an individual or in a team)? What is your tolerance for risk?

- Also, try to figure out what products or services would make your personal life easier.

If you use this tool properly over a reasonable length of time, you will find that it spurs you on to many different ideas. Prospective entrepreneurs would need to narrow the ideas down to a single one on which they will, at least initially, focus on.

After coming up with several ideas, the entrepreneur's decision as to which idea to focus on will depend to a large extent on whether there is reasonable opportunity around the idea. I will discuss this in a bit more detail later in this chapter.

Kuenyehia on Entrepreneurship

Which Comes First, the Idea or the Desire to Start a Business?

Without the dream or idea, it is not possible to become an entrepreneur, no matter how much you might hate working for someone and want to become your own boss. A good idea is required before anyone can start a business. However, although the idea provides the foundation stone on which a prospective entrepreneur builds his enterprise, just having an idea does not guarantee that one will automatically become an entrepreneur.

Examples of Eureka Moments for Certain Entrepreneurs

▎ The idea to start the Ghana Music Awards came to Iyiola Ayoade, Chairman and Chief Executive Officer of Multiple Concepts, while on location shooting *Agoro*, the music-cum-entertainment game show produced by his company. Two top musicians, Lord Kenya and Akyeame, clashed over who should be the last to perform, as it appeared that both had quite a large following. This incident generated the idea to organise an awards programme for the public to choose the best musicians in Ghana.[9]

▎ Frustrated by her inability to obtain fresh vegetables grown under hygienic conditions for herself and her family, Catherine Krobo Edusei-Benson started a small vegetable garden with £200 which she invested in seeds and a gardening book. Eden Tree, the company that she started, now has over 12 acres under cultivation and is one of the leading suppliers of fresh fruits and vegetables to supermarkets in Accra.

▎ After his wife had to wait for over seven days for her new glasses, the founder of Vision Express, a British chain of opticians providing eyeglass services within the hour, dreamt of a world where people could get their glasses fitted or repaired within the span of a day.

I Richard Branson had flown in many airplanes but could not, in his own words, "find one positive redeeming factor in any of the airlines [he] flew." That gave him the idea to "set up an airline that treated people as human beings and was a pleasure to fly, rather than one that everyone had to grin and bear."

I Pizza Express started in 1965 in London because founder Peter Boizot was fed up that he could not get a decent pizza in London. He set up Pizza Express to provide decent pizza to the masses in London and beyond.

I Julian Metcalfe and Sinclair Beecham, who previously worked in the City of London, started Prêt-À-Manger after struggling to find sandwiches that they actually enjoyed eating for lunch.[10]

Idea vs. Opportunity

For an entrepreneur to succeed, his idea must meet the two criteria below.

It Must Have Developmental Potential

An idea has developmental potential if it can be converted into a successful enterprise by an entrepreneur given the resources to hand.

What is good for the goose is not necessarily good for the gander: one idea that has development potential for a particular entrepreneur may be seen as lacking developmental potential by another entrepreneur. As with many entrepreneurial decisions, a lot depends on the entrepreneurs, their circumstances and the type of venture that they envisage for themselves. Also, it is possible that an idea that initially lacks potential for development can acquire that potential by a change in the circumstances of the entrepreneur, or through changes in certain external factors – political regime, technology, financial market demands, etc. – that the entrepreneur might have no control over. The reverse is also true.

The Idea Must Be Underpinned by a
Potential or Actual Opportunity

An idea is only worth pursuing if it is underpinned by an opportunity. When I defined entrepreneurship in Chapter 1, I said that the process starts with an idea and ends in goods and/or services that people perceive as valuable and are willing to pay for in such a way as to maximise returns for the enterprise. This goes to the heart of whether or not there is an opportunity that underpins an idea. The existence of real opportunity will depend on a number of factors including, among others, the entrepreneur's objectives, the nature of the product and the macroeconomic environment.

An idea may be underpinned by an opportunity in one of two ways:

• *Patent Opportunity*

This is where the opportunity underpinning the idea is of an explicit nature. Typically in this situation, the idea is one which will be readily and easily understood by potential customers who will be willing to pay for it. For example, if an entrepreneur's idea is to provide laundry services, he may find that this is a patent opportunity because significant numbers of people have identified the need to have their clothes laundered, and are willing to pay the person who meets the need because of the actual value obtained by the consumer from a laundry service.

• *Tacit Discovery*

To the untrained eye this situation almost looks as though the entrepreneur is creating an opportunity to underpin his idea. This is often the case in novel idea situations where the idea (and the product or service that the idea culminates in) may not be easily or readily understood by the target customers. Creating an opportunity to underpin an idea may not only require the entrepreneur to be able to discern needs the customer herself may not know she has, but also requires an ability to anticipate the needs the customer is likely to have. Discovering these tacit opportunities (as well as learning to tease out the patent opportunities) is the focus of Chapter 4. However, it is worth dwelling a little on the nature of opportunity. In respect of the car which he popularised, Henry Ford said: "If I had asked people what they wanted, they would have said a faster horse."[11] Perhaps nobody else had previously envisaged the car, but there are currently over one billion cars in existence in the world.[12] Although the invention of the car was the capstone creation based on a novel idea, Henry Ford was able to discover an opportunity to underpin his idea, to popularise the car by educating customers in a way that expressed his vision for how people might use cars. Another way of looking at this is to say that the entrepreneur simply uses her idea to meet a customer need in a way that the customer could not have envisaged possible.

However, an opportunity only exists because the customer has a need that the entrepreneur can hang his idea on. In the case of tacit discovery, it requires a deep understanding of customer needs, wants and aspirations. It is this understanding that triggers insights into opportunities. To Henry Ford therefore, we would have said that if he had delved deeper by asking a series of 'why' questions (Why did the customer want a faster horse? Why a horse?), he would have found that what the customer wanted was not necessarily a faster horse but a faster way of getting from one place to another. Similarly, although email was a novel form of communication when it first appeared, the opportunity it presented only existed because the inventors of email (and early exploiters) could hang that invention on the need that people have to communicate as quickly, securely and cheaply as they can. Of course, to the creative entrepreneur there is room – through branding and marketing, for example – to play on people's emotions to get them to believe they have a need that might not exist.

While an idea is a mental picture, an opportunity is a function of time, place, the entrepreneur's skills and the resources available to him.

According to Timmons, "Opportunities are created through the interaction of ideas with the environment and the creativity of the entrepreneur."[13] He further describes an opportunity as having the qualities of being attractive, timely and being anchored in a product or service which creates value for, or adds value to, the lives of its buyers or users.

For an idea to be considered as an opportunity, or be capable of creating an opportunity, it should do the following.

Meet a Customer Need

Fundamentally, the idea must be able to fulfil a real (actual or perceived) need. As noted by Cagan and Vogel, "successful products fulfil a higher emotional value state, whether it is the excitement and security of driving in an SUV, the comfort and effectiveness of cooking in a kitchen, the relaxation and escapism of sipping coffee in a coffeehouse, or the independence and adventure of using a two-way communication device. The mantra that 'form follows function' is no longer relevant; we are now in a period where form and function must fulfil fantasy."[14]

Create Value for the Customers

The concept must be one that customers are willing to pay for again and again. The value of the product or service should be one that can easily be sold to customers and can stand the test of time (subject to minor tweaking from time to time). The value proposition for the customer should not be tied to a short-term fad.

Create Value for Stakeholders

These stakeholders will, in addition to the entrepreneur, include employees, investors, creditors, suppliers and the community. Value creation for stakeholders will depend on:

• *The Number of Potential Buyers*

The category of customers willing to pay for the product or service must be big enough to ensure that the venture is economically viable for the entrepreneur and his investors.

• *The Purchasing Power of Potential Buyers*

There is no point having a large number of potential buyers who are limited by their ability to purchase. The entrepreneur's target group must have sufficient purchasing power to make the venture worthwhile. A concept for a small car to carry students to lectures may seem a good idea, but the number of students who would be able to purchase such a car might be so small that, given the capital investment required, it may not be a financially viable venture.

• *Return on Investment*

Most concepts would require some kind of financial investment. A venture is only worth pursuing if the investment required to bring the concept to fruition would provide at least a reasonable level of return, given the risk involved in undertaking the venture.

Be the Right Fit:

To be the right fit, the idea must;

• *Reflect the Values, Interests and Aspirations of the Entrepreneur.*

The opportunity must also fit the personal skills and goals of the entrepreneur. The best idea in the world is completely useless in the hands of an entrepreneur who does not have a passion for, or interest in, that type of venture, or whose values are inconsistent with the idea. For example, a business concept around alcoholic beverages will be of no use to a devout Pentecostal pastor. If entrepreneurs are passionate about an industry and an idea, but do not have any technical experience in the business, they can acquire it. However, they can never acquire passion for an idea they cannot be passionate about.

• *Be Matched to the Entrepreneur's Resources and Skills*

The entrepreneur must have, or have ready access to, the requisite resources and skills required to start and develop a successful enterprise.

Realistic/Sense check

Although there is a lot of room along the entrepreneurial spectrum for big hairy audacious goals, there is an element of realism that is required for success. The question here is essentially this: Taking into account all the considerations of the entrepreneur's reality, would it be possible to develop an idea into a profitable business for the entrepreneur? Truthfully answering this question is crucial to ensuring that an entrepreneurial venture starts off on the right note.

Concept Paper Development

There is a risk of being derailed anywhere during the entrepreneurship process, but this risk is particularly acute at the idea generation stage, as the process of coming up with and refining ideas is fuzzy and undefined. One way of ensuring that the entrepreneur remains on course – imagining a logical line from idea generation to profits – is for the entrepreneur to distil the idea and the opportunity it presents into a simple one-page document.

After the eureka moment, the entrepreneur must develop the enterprise concept. This concept should address the following questions:

- What is the customer pain that the enterprise will remove?
- How is this pain being dealt with at present by those currently

offering direct or alternative solutions (the future competition)?

- How will the proposed idea/product remove customer pain (the customer value proposition)? How will this be different from current offerings on the market?
- Describe the key target customers of the proposed enterprise's products or services.
- How will the product or service be made or provided, respectively (production)?
- How will the product or service be made available to the target market (In short, mode and delivery of products or services with regard to sales points, the distribution chain, etc.)?
- An estimate of the costs of setting up the enterprise and producing products or services, and the key resources required.
- A pricing estimate for products or services.

In developing a concept paper, focus should be placed on simplicity. The entrepreneur must bear in mind the following words: "When an idea is not robust enough to stand expression in simple terms, it is a sign that it should be rejected."[15]

For entrepreneurs who do not have a eureka moment but are looking for ideas, Mark Davies, founder of BusyInternet, advises the following:

- Combine personal interests with experiences.
- Summarise strengths, weaknesses and interests.
- Write down a list of industries, jobs and products that you admire, or are interested in.
- Look for patterns in you, look for ideas in others, look for the future 'outside'.
- Develop five ideas, however bad, that are tied to your personality.
- Mature the ideas, massage the ideas, and sleep on the ideas. Dream it!

- Let your brain do the talking. Look for light bulbs. Imagine how your ideas may work.
- Pick one or two ideas you find irresistible and practical.
- Bore your friends with the idea (so they can help you develop and further refine the idea with their comments and suggestions).

The entrepreneur will need to further narrow the ideas down to a single one to focus on. Once the most appealing idea has been identified, the entrepreneur will have to determine whether the proposed idea is indeed viable, whether there is an opportunity around the idea. At this stage, entrepreneurs have to focus on carrying out research around the chosen idea to determine how they will go about developing it into a viable enterprise. The research will also enable them to determine the market potential in quantifiable terms. The research should also alert them to the inherent dangers and risks involved in developing the idea, and the return and rewards of the opportunity as viewed in the light of other possible opportunities.

The entrepreneur's research should also throw light on the competition's strengths and weaknesses, the obvious gaps in the market as well as what sort of technology and people to employ. It is after this stage that the entrepreneur should undertake a quick 'back-of-the-envelope' calculation to determine whether the venture is potentially viable. The entrepreneur must consider the worst case and best case scenarios in evaluating the potential viability of the idea.

As will be highlighted in Chapter 4, research need not be complicated or expensive to be useful. Entrepreneurs can glean a lot about a business or industry from books, news articles, the Internet and from conversations with people. Entrepreneurs can learn a lot from interviewing industry experts and people at various levels of the value chain of the industry in question. A useful framework when meeting and interviewing industry experts and participants is the Five Question Framework, summed up in the following question: What five questions do I need answered to understand the industry?

Questions for Class Discussion

1. Must a business idea be outstanding and complicated to be successful?
2. Should all successful ideas be original? Or should an idea be original to be successful?
3. Is there a difference between an inventor and an entrepreneur?
4. Explain the concept of 'removing customer pain'.
5. Should an idea remove customer pain or satisfy his need to be successful?
6. Which comes first: the idea or the desire to start a business?

53 Sails: A Journey Into the World of Africa's Most Successful People *

CANOE MAGAZINE IS A PIONEERING idea by all standards. A quarterly lifestyle magazine launched in 2007, it is fast becoming the benchmark publication for sophistication, style and luxury on the African continent. CANOE depicts success from a neo-African perspective, and guides its readers through luxury trends as well as the knowledge with which they can transform their lives and secure an exceptional lifestyle.

CANOE is an initiative started by a team of seven entrepreneurs led by Creative Director, Kwaku Nkwaye Ansah. "Each member of our team has an intimate understanding of the African continent and the ability to predict growing trends that are likely to resonate with our discerning reader," says Ansah.

CANOE uses a simple but creatively compelling layout that consists of comprehensible and highly relevant discourse and powerful imagery. It is totally world-class: from print quality, diction and style of writing to photography, design and art direction, CANOE can hold its own against any luxury magazine from anywhere in the world.

What ignited the idea for CANOE was a television show Ansah wanted to produce with the same thematic concept that now informs the creative content of the magazine. The show was designed to be a TV magazine showcasing contemporary African lifestyles and telling the story of some of the continent's most remarkable individuals. "We actually shot the first couple of episodes, but then we ran into a few hurdles that slowed the project [down]. However, at that point, we were clear in our minds about the direction we wanted to take and it was relatively easier to give life to the idea through the medium of a magazine." In a certain sense, CANOE emerged as a natural corollary of the enormous work Ansah had done (and continues to do) in advertising. Magazines all over the world survive on funding from advertisers. A graphic designer, writer and painter trained at the Kwame Nkrumah University of Science and Technology, Ansah had over two decades of experience in advertising, working in the United Kingdom, South Africa, Ghana and elsewhere in Africa. "Having worked closely with many advertisers for many years, I saw the opportunity to leverage [these] partnerships and experience to launch the CANOE platform."

One of the strongest factors that drove Ansah and his team to start CANOE is what he describes as "creative discontent". Ansah recounts an experience where he was approached by a publisher who wanted one of his (Ansah's) advertising clients to place an advertisement in a new magazine he was starting. Ansah was not convinced that the magazine's content was relevant to his client's target audience. "Looking around at the existing magazines, I did not find one with the kind of content that I felt would appeal to the emerging African elite, what we call the 'Afro-bourgeois', so we set out to offer something different, something that both readers and advertisers alike would find fascinating, relevant and rewarding."

At the same time, Ansah had this "obsession" with looking at the brighter side of Africa. In CANOE, Ansah and his team found an opportunity to create a unique platform that would serve to highlight the positive characteristics of what is often described as the 'dark continent'. "At CANOE, what we do is celebrate the evolving culture and lifestyle of the new and emerging African upper class. We are not hesitant to show success using extravagance as a merit of the prosperity of the successful African." According to Ansah, you hardly find this image of the African being portrayed in the existing media. Ansah minces no words when he says, "We are on a mission to portray positively the continent and its people."

CANOE showcases astute, high-performing, exemplary and successful people for the purpose of celebrating them as role models and, in the process, builds a database of extraordinary Africans complete with information about their paths to success.

Through exposé, CANOE encourages its readers to develop their own potential and harness their talents, skills and energies towards building a successful continent. "The people we seek to reach are high-performing individuals with remarkable personalities and distinct attributes. They are Afro-conscious, modern and have a decent standard and style of living."

The success of the early editions of CANOE is testimony to the craving within its select target market for a medium that shares their outlook and complements their lifestyle. Now in its fifth edition, CANOE is already becoming an integral part of the lifestyle of many African elites, and is expanding its distribution network to reach new audiences both on the continent and in the Diaspora.

In order to sustain the interest of its readers and advertising partners, it is crucial that the team continually charts new frontiers in creative content development. The CANOE team, keenly aware of this, are constantly brainstorming to generate new ideas and testing these ideas through research to ensure they are in tune with the tastes of their stakeholders.

After testing the concept in Ghana with four successful editions, CANOE launched internationally under the theme 53 Sails, with an exclusive and spectacular event showcasing African culture at the Vodaworld event centre in Midrand, Johannesburg, South Africa, on 6 November 2008. Ansah hopes that the international edition will showcase the finest elements in lifestyle and culture from across the continent - from fashion, jewellery and technology to real estate, luxury goods as well as investment and financial opportunities. 53 Sails is set to be the defining reference point for twenty-first-century elite African lifestyle.

However, CANOE is more than a magazine; it is a symbol of African success and sophistication. At the heart of the CANOE idea is a vision to create a network of Africa's most successful, talented and sophisticated people – entrepreneurs and business leaders, professionals, fashion designers, artists, etc: in the words of Ansah, a "network of heavy black people." The CANOE platform is based on a new optimism, a realisation that there is a group of Africans whose talents and other resources can be harnessed as forces to transform Africa's image and profile within the global community. The magazine is only the beginning of a journey to build Africa's most Creative Afro-Bourgeois Naissant Ostentatious Extraordinaire socio-economic network.

* This case was prepared by Ellis Arthur, under the supervision of Elikem Nutifafa Kuenyehia, for the purpose of class discussion rather than to document appropriate or inappropriate handling of a business situation.

Notes

1 Definition from The Concise Oxford Dictionary.

2 'Dream drawers' is an expression used by Lloyd Shefsky in *Entrepreneurs Are Made, Not Born* to describe the situation where people come out with various brilliant entrepreneurial ideas but are unable to transform such ideas into money- or profit-making ventures.

3 Hashemi, S. and B. Hashemi. *Anyone Can Do It: Building Coffee Republic from Our Kitchen Table: 57 Real-Life Laws on Entrepreneurship*. Hoboken: Wiley, 2007.

4 Kotler, P. And G. Armstrong. *Principles of Marketing*. Upper Saddle River: Pearson Education, 2007.

5 Dauten, D. *Taking Chances: Lessons in Putting Passion and Creativity into Your Work Life*. New York: Newmarket Press, 1986.

6 Africa Growth and Opportunity Act, www.agoa.gov/agoa_forum/agoa_success_storiesl.html, retrieved on 21 March 2008.

7 Michael, G. *The Entrepreneurial Myth Revisited*. New York: HarperBusiness, 1995.

8 Kelley, T. and J. Littman. *The art of innovation -lessons in creativity from Ideo, America's leading design company*. New York: Random House, 2001.

9 Interview with PaJohn Dadson for Foundations of Entrepreneurship Term Paper, April 2008.

10 Smith, S. and A. Milligan. *Uncommon Practice: People Who Deliver a Great Brand Experience*. Upper Saddle River: Pearson, 2002.

11 Sharp S, Competitive Intelligence Advantage: How to Minimize Risk, Avoid Surprises, Hoboken: Wiley, 2009

12 Wards Auto, www.wardsauto.com, retrieved 15 August 2011.

13 Timmons, J. A. *New Venture Creation, Entrepreneurship for the 21st Century*. Burr Ridge: Irwin, 1994.

14 Cagan, J. and C.M. Vogel. *Creating breakthrough products: innovation from product to program approval*. Upper Saddle River: Prentice Hall, 2002.

15 Vauvenargues, L. C. *Reflections and Maxims of Luc de Clapiers, Marquis of Vauvenargues*. Oxford: Humphrey Millford, 1940.

Chapter Four: Opportunity Analysis

"If you think education is expensive, try ignorance" - **Derek Bok**

Outline

STEVENSON ET AL.[1] argue that for an opportunity to be regarded as a good one, it must meet two key conditions. First, the opportunity must be such that it represents a future state that is attractive. Second, it must be achievable.

Although these conditions appear simple, different people will reach different conclusions about a real or perceived opportunity and the value of that opportunity, based on differing levels of information. It may be many years before all (or even a significant level) of the relevant information about an opportunity is revealed. These information asymmetries between different players in the marketplace may provide the entrepreneur armed with the most information a competitive advantage, as the information will aid evaluation and decision-making on whether or not, and how, to pursue the opportunity presented. (Information asymmetry is a term in corporate finance referring to the situation where managers know more about their companies' prospects, risks and values than outside investors.[2] In this case, we use it to refer to the situation where one or more players in the industry has more information than others, and is able to benefit from this advantage.)

On the assumption that most people will only invest in enterprises that generate returns in excess of the initial investment (or which effectively solve a pressing social need in the case of a social enterprise), the reason why an entrepreneur would carry out an opportunity analysis (an analysis of the opportunity presented by the entrepreneur's idea) is to determine whether or not the combination of skills, expertise and other resources that the entrepreneur has, or has access to, would enable the entrepreneur to effectively exploit the idea in such a manner as to generate the required returns. Sometimes, the opportunity analysis also considers whether, given the options available or potentially available to the entrepreneur, the opportunity under consideration is the best use of the entrepreneur's resources.

As Brealey and Myers[3] point out, a good investment decision requires good information. Good entrepreneurial decisions are no exception. Entrepreneurs who have better information about an opportunity they are considering are able to make better decisions relating to the resources necessary to exploit the opportunity, and relating to targeting, pricing, location and promotion.

The objective of opportunity analysis is therefore to tease out as much information as possible about the entire process from idea to profit. After identifying a customer pain, the entrepreneur must research the opportunity to determine whether or not the proposed solution for a customer pain will generate profit for the enterprise (or in the case of a social enterprise, be capable of solving the identified social need). Based on opportunity analysis, the entrepreneur may modify the original enterprise concept or abandon the initiative.

Also, when an entrepreneur determines that an opportunity

exists (for example, because of changing consumption patterns in an economy), opportunity analysis enables evaluation of the type of idea(s) that would be best suited for exploiting the opportunity, given the resources accessible.

Opportunity analysis requires a broad view to be taken of all information that may be relevant to the enterprise and the entrepreneur, and, although in the context of this chapter I discuss various aspects of the opportunity analysis under discrete headings such as Industry Analysis, PEST and Competitive Analysis, it would be wrong to assume that each of them falls into neat, tidy, distinct or sequential boxes. The reality is that information overlaps, and the entrepreneur must be prepared to analyse all information holistically.

The focus of this chapter is to examine how to obtain, analyse and make decisions about each of these factors, and how they impact the attractiveness of an entrepreneurial opportunity.

Although the context of the discussion denotes the analysis that you should carry out when contemplating an entrepreneurial venture, it is important that even when an enterprise is established, entrepreneurs maintain a culture of analysis and develop formal processes for regularly updating, collating, evaluating and disseminating the information within their enterprises.

Setting the Context

At the initial stage of the enterprise, entrepreneurs need to gain a rapid understanding of the market size, market dynamics and customer needs for the product or service they plan to offer. Tempting though as it may be for entrepreneurs to short-cut this process by relying on intuition and personal experience, I strongly advocate that the information-gathering process and the opportunity analysis should not be glossed over. As Chess advises, "even start-up teams with many years of industry experience should not rely solely on their collective experience and intuition to develop a viewpoint."[4]

By analysing information from disparate sources, the entrepreneur develops insights on which customer segments to focus on and how to differentiate against competitors. These questions are at the heart of building and developing a brand; we shall return to them in Chapter 11.

There are two main categories of information for carrying out opportunity analyses: primary data and secondary data. We shall discuss secondary data first as that is more easily available. Typically, entrepreneurs rely mainly on secondary data and limited primary data to determine whether an opportunity is broadly worth pursuing. Once satisfied that such an opportunity exists, entrepreneurs turn to primary data to develop their strategy.

Secondary Data

Secondary data refers to information that is gathered by one party and then put to use by a second person. Sources of secondary data include:

- Market reports from local market research firms, stock analysts and think tanks such as IMANI and the Institute of Economic Affairs;
- Country profiles and reports published by the international press such as the Financial Times; international organisations such as the International Monetary Fund, the United Nations Development Programme and the World Bank; and international consulting firms such as McKinsey and the Boston Consulting Group;
- Government data such as census statistics and information in the published budget;
- Newspaper, trade journal and magazine articles;
- Books and published research such as the State of The Ghanaian Economy published by the Institute of Statistical, Social and Economic Research of the University of Ghana;
- Conference reports;

- Competitor literature and websites;
- Regulator literature and websites, such as those provided by the Bank of Ghana, the National Insurance Commission, National Communications Authority and National Petroleum Authority;
- Publications from industry bodies such as Association of Ghanaian Industries and Ghana National Chamber of Commerce and Industry;
- The World Wide Web - most of the information provided by the sources above will also probably be online; in addition, the world wide web is itself a good source of secondary data.

Using secondary data can save a lot of time and can be cost-efficient as the information already exists and is generally easy to access. It can help in identifying key industry trends, gathering much of the aggregate customer and market data needed to estimate market size and appreciate growth estimates, performing initial competitive analysis and identifying where to focus primary data generation efforts. However, given that the data set was gathered by someone else for a purpose other than what you might be using it for, it is likely that it will not match your needs. It may also be out of date or biased; the quality of the data might also be questionable.

One of the biggest challenges that Ghanaian entrepreneurs face relates to obtaining relevant secondary data. Although there is a lot of secondary data available about consumers generally, it is often difficult to get Ghana-specific data. Not much research is published locally and, oftentimes, what is published can be difficult to access.

Primary Data

Primary data provides direct feedback from a sample of the population you are interested in learning about. It allows the researcher (particularly in the case of quantitative research) to reach general conclusions about a population with a certain degree of accuracy based on a small sample size and without having to survey everyone.

There are two types of primary data – exploratory primary data and conclusive primary data. Exploratory research is used to uncover the variables at work in a given situation to gain broad-based understanding and insights. Entrepreneurs would use exploratory research when the market is not understood well or the enterprise's challenges are not satisfactorily identified. As Webb put it, "exploratory research is the investigator's equivalent of dipping an elbow in the bath water in an attempt to avoid poaching the infant or wetting one's finger to find which way the wind is blowing.[5]" Exploratory research is most useful in the early stage of a research project, when the levels of uncertainty and general ignorance of the subject in question are at their highest.

Conclusive research may be descriptive or causal. Once the variables have been identified through exploratory research, descriptive research provides a valid and accurate depiction of those variables (to 'put flesh on the bones'). Causal research establishes the manner in which the variables are related to each other.

Primary data may be qualitative or quantitative. Data which are qualitative are characterised by a lack of numerical measurement and statistical analysis.[6] They typically provide in-depth, if somewhat subjective, understandings of the consumer. Primary data can be particularly helpful in obtaining background information on a market segment, enabling the entrepreneur to identify attitudes, opinions and behaviours of potential customers in the relevant target market. Qualitative data can also help in identifying variables for further study, and in providing direction for the development of questionnaires.

Qualitative Data

The most common forms of qualitative data are individual depth interviews and focus groups. In individual depth interviews the interviewer does not have a fixed set of questions; the objective is to get respondents to talk freely and in detail about a product, or their feelings on issues. The interviewer asks open-ended questions in an unstructured manner. These interviews may take the following forms.

• *Expert Interviews*

In expert interviews, people with an in-depth knowledge and understanding of the market, industry or customers are interviewed to share their opinions or views. The experts may be current or retired executives or professionals in the industry, consultants, academics researching a particular industry, suppliers, industry stock analysts, investors or industry association staff. As Chess[7] points out, this is "an excellent way to jump-start your research [programme] because experts can give you initial reality checks on market and customer assumptions, the value proposition for your product or service concept and how your product compares to competitive offerings. They also provide ideas on how to define your business concept and strategy[,] and raise additional questions that should be addressed during market research[,] as well as help locate sources of secondary data and primary interview subjects."

• *Interviews with Potential Suppliers, Distributors and Buyers*

The entrepreneur also needs to speak to potential suppliers so as to understand the supply chain as it pertains to the product or service being developed. Potential distributors and buyers can provide invaluable perspectives on the entrepreneur's proposed concept. Interviews with potential customers of the product or service give entrepreneurs an opportunity to hear opinions from the horse's own mouth. Individual depth interviews may be face-to-face interviews or telephone interviews.

• *Focus Group Interviews*

Focus groups bring together a number of people (typically 8 to 10 individuals) for an open-ended discussion led by a moderator. Although the moderator will broadly follow a script, like the individual depth interviews, he or she will seek to engage the participants in a free exchange of ideas on the subject of interest. Although the results are not strictly projectable to the larger market (because the groups are not randomly selected), interviewers can sometimes generate richer data in the relaxed, chatty format of focus groups.

• *Projective Technique*

The projective technique involves using different forms of stimuli to prompt respondents to talk in an unstructured manner about specific topics. As Cannon[8] notes, by letting respondents range freely over a subject, it is hoped that some unconscious insights or views hitherto unmentioned will emerge. The types of stimuli that lend themselves well to projective techniques include storyboard, sentence completion and concept paper. This type of research may be used to test different versions of a product on prospective customers, to gauge reaction to proposed advertising or to get a sense of how customers feel about a brand.

Quantitative Data

Quantitative research gathers valid statistical market information through surveys that numerically reinforce and highlight the extent of the issues or variables that may impact an enterprise. Unlike qualitative research, quantitative research will tell you how many people think one way or the other. Based on the results of a survey, you can generalise the results for the population as a whole. This rests on the theory that by interviewing well-chosen 'representative' respondents, it is possible to predict the attitudes of the many who were not chosen, since their opinions would be broadly mirrored by those of the respondents in the survey.

While a focus group study may highlight potential issues such as customer service, price or product variety as important for increasing sales, a survey will tell you which one of those issues is the most important to increasing sales, which one is the second most important, which the third most important, and so forth.[9]

• *Quantitative Research: Survey or the Questionnaire*

Unlike qualitative research where questions are open-ended, the objective of quantitative research is to elicit answers to very specific questions to enable generalisations to be made. The most common quantitative technique is the survey or the questionnaire, where respondents are asked targeted questions. Surveys are a flexible tool which can be used to establish motivations, lifestyle and psychographics of respondents. They are also good for learning about people's knowledge, beliefs, preferences, satisfaction and purchasing behaviour, and measuring these magnitudes in the general population. A newly opened restaurant may, for example, use a survey to find out how satisfied customers are with its service, which of its meals the customers enjoyed the most and to find out how it may improve. The survey may take any of the following forms:

- Mail Questionnaire

The questionnaire is mailed to respondents who fill them out and return them. It can be a slow way to obtain responses, and the response rate can be particularly low as respondents often do not consider the questionnaires to be urgent.

- Telephone Interview

Respondents are phoned up and asked questions on the phone. This can be a relatively cheap way of generating data over a wide segment of the population.

- Personal Interview

The respondents are visited personally and interviewed by a researcher. It can be a time-consuming and inefficient way of collecting information, although the personal contact provides a great opportunity for entrepreneurs to learn more about their target consumers.

- Online Questionnaire

The questionnaire is posted online and the link sent by email to the respondents who are asked to go to the relevant website to answer questions. It is a cheap way of generating data from a geographically dispersed group of respondents. There are a number of options online for managing such questionnaires. A favourite is SurveyMonkey (www.surveymonkey.com). Although the odd email may end up in a respondent's junk mailbox, the response rate is generally better than that of mail; it is convenient for respondents who are comfortable with and regularly use computers and the Internet. In a developing country like Ghana with low rates of computer accessibility, the online interview may eliminate a significant number of target consumers.

• *Observational Research*

This focuses on how people behave in certain situations. The premise for observational research is that watching the behaviour of respondents in controlled situations gives more insight into how respondents actually behave in practice than may have been obtained by asking respondents directly.[10] For example, an entrepreneur trying to set up a coffee shop could spend time in a number of coffee shops, observing customers when they order and consume their purchases, as well as how they interact with staff and how they generally enjoy the space. This would give the entrepreneur insights into how he might set up his own coffee shop and give him ideas about the services he may want to offer. Automobile dealers and service station managers have studied their customers' radio station preferences simply by observing the dial settings of cars brought in for service[11].

• *Behavioural Data*

The actual purchase decisions of customers provide entrepreneurs with a lot of clues as to how customers behave. For example, both Allure Spa in the City and Melting Moments (the coffee shop providing 'melting moments' in Labone, Accra) have loyalty cards that record the transactions that customers make. If the details of those transactions were to be correlated with the basic demographic and psychographic information that the customers initially provided when they signed up for the loyalty card, it would provide great insights on how certain groups of customers behave. Such data becomes invaluable in creating marketing strategies to cater to the customers from whom the information was sourced.

• *Mystery Shopping*

This is where a researcher pretends to be a customer by sampling the relevant products and services, with a view of reporting on his impression on a number of pre-agreed variables. This can be particularly helpful in already established enterprises where entrepreneurs may use mystery shopping to measure how their enterprises are doing in, for example, customer service as compared to their competitive set. In such a case, the mystery shopper will visit the premises of both entrepreneur and competitor.

• *Experimental Research*

The researcher may seek to understand the effect of variations of certain key variables. For example, an entrepreneur looking to introduce a new product into the market, but unsure of what price to offer the product at, may carry out a number of experiments where he varies price to different groups of the same market segment to see how this affects purchasing decisions. A chef looking to introduce a new range of 'waistline-friendly' lunchtime meals may decide to develop different versions of a menu, or experiment with different types of ingredients, and then observe what effects the variations have on her target market segment.

Industry Analysis and Michael Porter's Five Forces Framework

In evaluating whether or not to pursue an idea, it is important that entrepreneurs clearly understand the dynamics and drivers of the industry that they seek to compete in, and how attractive that industry is or, indeed, what its growth prospects are. The underlying structure of an industry or market sector determines how favourable it is towards small and medium-sized enterprises (SMEs).

Porter's Five Forces[12] provides a framework to catalogue and analyse the competitive situation an enterprise will face in its industry.

It can be used to determine whether the industry is attractive enough to sustain SMEs, as it provides an overview of the potential profitability of the average enterprise in the industry. The Five Forces are rivalry, barriers to entry, threat of substitutes, buyer power and supplier power.

Together, these forces determine the intensity of competition and profit potential for SMEs in a given industry or sector. In analysing each market force, the question is whether it is sufficiently strong to reduce or eliminate industry profits in a way that may significantly affect the entrepreneur's profitability. The focus at this stage is at the industry level, because industry dynamics and profits of necessity dictate profits of existing enterprises as well as new enterprises.

Also, in analysing an opportunity using the Five Forces, we want to be able to answer the following questions:

- What are the key requisites for competitive success in the particular industry?
- Does the underlying structure of the industry indicate that competitive forces in the industry will strongly or weakly affect the enterprise?

Based on these answers, entrepreneurs may determine whether, given the competitive forces in the industry, there is a strategy that they might employ to defend their enterprise, or if indeed they are able to influence the forces in their own favour.

The first step in industry analysis is to clearly and carefully define the relevant market or industry. We need to have a clear idea of what the enterprise does (or is proposing to do) and who are or will be its competition. Two common ways to define the market are in terms of products and geography. Two enterprises are considered competitors if customers are willing to use their products for the same purpose. Product similarity is the most common way that a market is defined. However, it is important to keep geography in mind as well, since firms located far away from each other may not draw from the same set of customers.

However, the entrepreneur should not get caught up in seeking a 'definitive' or 'correct' definition of the industry because, as Marciano and Mazzeo[13] point out, "In the end, industry definitions are always somewhat arbitrary. Are colas in the same product market as juices and other drinks? Are departmental stores located on opposite sides of town in direct competition?" The important thing is to have a reasonable market definition clearly stated although one must guard against defining the industry too narrowly.

Industry Rivalry[14]

Industry rivalry is the centre of the Five Forces analysis as all other forces point to it. Most forms of rivalry are unhealthy for firms, and usually result in price competition that drives away profits by pushing prices down towards costs. The following may influence rivalry.

- **Numerous Or Equally Balanced Competitors**

Where there are many competitors vying for the same cake, rivalry is more likely to be intense: some competitors might feel they can increase their market share without other enterprises noticing, competitors dissatisfied with the status quo may try to increase market share by lowering prices.

- **Slow Industry Growth**

Where there is slow industry growth, enterprises in the industry can only grow by taking market share from other enterprises, thereby leading to increased rivalry.

- **Lack Of Differentiation Or Switching Costs For Customer**

In industries where there is little or no differentiation between products or services, it is likely that there will be more rivalry. Similar or same products can only be differentiated by packaging style, after-sales service or even price. Similarly, where customers incur no cost in switching from one product to another, they are likely to move (or change) products regularly, thereby encouraging rivalry between companies in the industry. New enterprises can also enter such established markets and quickly establish a customer base. A good example would be the bottled water market in Ghana.

• High Exit Barriers

These are factors that keep an enterprise from quitting altogether, even though returns are inadequate or negative. Exit barriers for small firms can be economic (i.e. the costs of liquidation or sale and loss of income) or may relate to psychological attachment to the enterprise, loyalty to employees and the pride that comes from ownership. When those barriers are high a firm will continue for as long as possible before exiting, thus increasing the intensity of rivalry in the marketplace.

Barriers To Entry

Suppose that an industry or market is not engaged in much rivalry and operating enterprises are making healthy profits. If that is the case, we might expect more enterprises to join the market, increasing the rivalry in the industry. However, firms may be protected from this competitive threat if it is difficult for potential entrants to join the industry or if barriers to entry exist. Barriers to entry work both ways for SMEs. At first, high entry barriers act to keep entrepreneurs out but once they have entered a market, high barriers to entry can protect them from too many new competitors. In entrepreneurial ventures that require high technical knowledge and capital, such as the manufacture and distribution of drugs, only a few may be able to enter. The telecommunications industry is one of the most profitable in Ghana, yet not many entrepreneurs are venturing into telecommunications because of the limited number of telecommunication licences, the high initial costs involved and the high levels of continuous investment in technology needed to operate sustainably.

Barriers to entry may take the following forms.

• Economies of Scale

Smaller firms may find it difficult to compete in industries where profitability is dependent on economies of scale. In these industries, such as the various types of manufacturing, significant cost reductions result from high levels of output. Large firms enjoying economies of scale can use this cost advantage to establish lower market prices and lower margins which make the industry unattractive to new entrants. Where prices are kept up, bigger firms can reinvest the additional profits in marketing or research and development, again reducing the competitiveness of new entrants.

• Product Differentiation

Some industries are dominated by established firms who have built up loyalty with customers who identify with their particular product or service. Product differentiation is cultivated over a long period of time. In most instances, products put in the marketplace are as a result of extensive research on customer and consumer preferences, and are able to effectively position themselves as 'different' from the competition as they are more likely to meet the specifications, needs, preferences and requirements of their target customers. Entrepreneurs looking to compete with nationally branded products supported by huge budgets and other resources would generally find it difficult to survive such competition. They may stand a chance if they are able to effectively segment the market and identify the segment of the market that their offering appeals to the most. By doing so, even a small firm can build up significant customer loyalty which deters new competitors. Market segmentation[15] is a two-step process of naming the broad product or service markets and dividing up these broad product markets in order to select a target market. This means an entrepreneur needs to focus on producing products or services for a subset of the existing market, thus implying specialisation which can bring out the best in the enterprise. Serving a particular niche could mean that the value added would be such that prices can be higher. In the Ghanaian travel industry for instance, while it existed, TravelKing created a niche for itself in corporate travel. Krew Men's Grooming and XMen have each created a niche in providing grooming services to men in Accra.

• Capital Requirements

Some industries require such large start-up capital that only a small number of enterprises are able to accumulate. The huge levels of sunk cost are therefore a major deterrent to entry.

• *Switching Costs (For Customers)*

The idea of switching costs is as follows: Because it literally costs you more money to switch from your existing supplier to another, you will maintain the status quo and will only make the switch if the increase in value that you will obtain by making the switch is higher than the switching costs. When buyers switch from one enterprise's product or service to another, they may incur one-off 'switching costs'. These might be in the retraining of staff (for example, when a small accounting firm changes from one accounting software package to another, it will need to train staff on the new software), or purchasing other equipment (for example, in changing from one water vendor to another, a restaurant might require a different type of fountain to accommodate the new vendor's delivery systems). Switching costs represent a real, but hidden barrier. A concept that has been well researched may not pass the ultimate test of being purchased in the place of a competitive product because of the high switching costs of severing a relationship with an existing supplier.

• *Government Policy*

Some industries are controlled by government regulations which create total or partial barriers to entry. The creation of such monopolies could be because of strategic, social and/or economic goals of the state. In Ghana, for example, only State Insurance Company can insure state assets, and only Electricity Company of Ghana (ECG) can at the moment supply electricity to the ultimate consumer, although private companies can generate electricity.

Threat of Substitute Products or Services

All enterprises in an industry broadly compete with industries producing substitute products. Identifying product substitutes is a matter of searching for other products that can perform the same function for customers. When there are many substitutes closer in the 'product space' and doing better in the market, the enterprises in the given industry will be worse off. Complementary products, on the other hand, boost demand for a product, thereby enhancing the profit opportunity for the industry.

Buyer Power

Buyer power is the ability of individual customers to negotiate purchase prices that extract profit from sellers. Buyers or customers will want to get the best possible purchasing arrangement. They will try and negotiate discounts, additional services, higher quality, more after-sales support and other benefits which become added costs for the supplying enterprise.

Assume that an industry does not have much rivalry, and that the possibility of entry and substitute products do not pose substantial competitive threats. In this case, it is likely that there would be profits (surpluses) for an enterprise to earn. Nevertheless, under some conditions, buyers may be able to gain the larger share of the surplus, leaving less for the enterprise and its owners. These conditions include the following:

- The buyer purchases a large volume of the seller's output;
- The buyer's purchases represent a significant fraction of the buyer's costs or purchases, in which case the buyer is more likely to be sensitive about prices;
- The buyer purchases a standard or undifferentiated product;
- Deals in the industry are negotiated individually between buyers and sellers.

An enterprise can improve its position by finding buyers who possess the least power to adversely influence the price of its products.

Supplier Power

Powerful suppliers can squeeze profits out of an industry. If suppliers have power, they can force price increases (or quality reductions) onto enterprises in the industry. The buying enterprises may not be able to pass the price increases on to the ultimate customer. The following factors make suppliers more powerful.

- *Suppliers' Industry is More Concentrated Than the Industry it Sells To*

There are fewer suppliers of inputs to the industry than there are buyers in the relevant industry.

- *Fewer Substitutes Available Due to the Uniqueness of Inputs*

For example, theSOFTtribe's custom-made software programmes (Akatua for employers and Edziban for restaurants) would make switching relatively difficult, if not nearly impossible in the short term, for its client enterprises than if those enterprises had simply purchased off-the-shelf software.

- *The Supplier's Product is an Important Input to the Buyer's Enterprise*

Where customers have installed equipment from an original manufacturer, its parts can only be obtained from this original manufacturer. In the period when the customer is using such a machine, a switch to using another supplier may be economically inefficient, resulting in a buyer sticking with the original equipment manufacturer.

- *Buyer Has Inadequate Knowledge of the Supplier's Offerings*

This relative strength in product knowledge that the supplier has over its buyers puts the supplier in a stronger position against the buyer, enabling the supplier to extract higher prices.

It is important to note that labour must be recognised as a supplier (of human capital), and that it may exert a great deal of power in many industries, especially where labour is organised through unions.

SWOT Analysis

SWOT analysis is an assessment of an organisation's strengths (what an organisation can do) and weaknesses (what an organisation cannot do), in addition to opportunities (potential favourable conditions for an organisation's growth) and threats (potential unfavourable conditions that might impede an organisation's advancement). It is an integrated tool (including key enterprise and environmental variables) to evaluate an entrepreneur's and/or the enterprise's current position. The objective is the confrontation of the enterprise's internal strengths and weaknesses as well as enterprise-external business opportunities and risks to empower the generation of strategic options. SWOT analysis is considered one of the most important instruments for the internal analysis of a company's current situation. According to Bohm, it "in every case delivers a pretty comprehensive and resilient foundation for further entrepreneurial decisions and strategic options."[16]

On the basis of the SWOT analysis, a strategy can be developed using enterprise strengths as well as avoiding enterprise weaknesses to enable an enterprise to benefit from future opportunities while taking into account future risks. It is a well-established tool for analysing business units in larger companies as well as smaller start-ups during their launch.

The strengths and weaknesses of an enterprise are established from an internal analysis of that enterprise while its opportunities and threats emanate from an external environmental analysis.

Strengths

The objective of analysing the strengths of the enterprise and/or the entrepreneur is to identify unique strengths in relation to the competition or to an established ideal. The key questions are: What can the enterprise do that the competitors can't? What is the enterprise/entrepreneur particularly good at? Such strengths might include the following:

• *The Accumulated Knowledge and Experience of the Industry.*
This would come from having been in the industry for a long time and being able to predict market changes.

• *Proximity to Either Sources of Raw Materials or to the Consumer*
Closeness to a source of a raw material for an entrepreneur, especially if that raw material is bulky, results in a lower cost of transportation, which would reflect in a lower cost of production and hence a low cost of the product or service. Closeness to customers means that, for the rational customer, the cost of acquiring the product will be reduced.

• *Strong Financial Resources*
These will enable the entrepreneur to acquire the resources to undertake sustainable and profitable production.

Weaknesses

In assessing weaknesses, it is important that entrepreneurs have honest open conversations with themselves and their teams to identify the key impediments that could stand in the way of entrepreneurial success. The key question is: What can the competition do that the organisation can't? Weaknesses might include:

- Lack of managerial skill;
- A poor distribution network;
- Lagging competency in research and development of products or services;
- Obsolete facilities;[17]
- Limited financial resources;
- Lack of a track record in the industry.

Opportunities

In considering opportunities, the entrepreneur should answer the following questions:[18]

- What opportunities exist?
- Of what interesting trends is the entrepreneur aware?

Opportunities may arise from changes in technology, the economy, sociocultural patterns, government policy, unfulfilled customer needs, relaxation of regulations (reduction in the processes and cost associated with starting a new business in Ghana, for instance) and removal of international trade barriers.

Threats

Threats are conditions outside the organisation's direct control that stand in the way of attaining long-range goals. To identify threats, the entrepreneur should answer the following questions:

- What obstacles are there?
- Are the specifications of the enterprise's product or service changing?
- Is changing technology threatening the enterprise's position?

The same changes that may give rise to opportunities (such as changes in the economy, technology, etc.) may also pose threats for entrepreneurs, depending on the nature of their enterprises and their strengths and weaknesses.

The objective is to have a thorough assessment of all the strengths, weaknesses, opportunities and threats that apply to the entrepreneur or the enterprise. The best way of doing this is by way of a brainstorming session with the entrepreneurs and their core teams listing out on a flip chart or blackboard the various strengths, weaknesses, opportunities and threats.

Once entrepreneurs have gathered information on their (or their enterprise's) strengths and weaknesses, and the opportunities and threats that they face, they should then seek to craft strategies that can capitalise on their strengths and make greater use of them while considering how to remedy their weaknesses. Opportunities and threats are external factors. Opportunities should be sought, recognised and grasped as they arise, while threats must be acknowledged and steps taken to deal with them.[19]

PEST Analysis

Political, economic, social and technological (PEST) analysis addresses external issues that can potentially affect the performance of firms.

Political

In analysing the political environment, the entrepreneur needs to assess the governance system of the country, including political stability, the fiscal policy of the government as well as policies affecting entrepreneurial activities. A democratic government is more likely to encourage entrepreneurial activities than a dictatorship, which may put restrictions on entrepreneurial activities. The political analysis would alert the entrepreneur to opportunities and challenges. For instance, in Ghana, the transition from a military regime to a democratic one provided opportunities for many entrepreneurs (some of whom we have profiled in Chapter 2). However, it might not always be a straightforward distinction between military rule and democratic rule. As I noted in Chapter 1,[20] Appiah-Menka pointed out that the Acheampong military regime was instrumental in enabling the successes of several contemporary giants of Ghanaian entrepreneurship. Perhaps controversially, under certain circumstances, a military regime may provide greater opportunities for the few brave souls who venture into entrepreneurship.

Economic

The broader macroeconomic and microeconomic environments will have an effect on entrepreneurs operating in an economy. It is therefore important that entrepreneurs spend time to understand the key drivers of the economy to ensure that they have a view of where things are going. This will then enable them to forecast fairly accurately the prospects for their enterprises by gauging potential levels of turnover, cost of sales, etc. Researching historic and current factors in the economy that could affect the enterprise can provide the entrepreneur with a reasonable degree of certainty about how their enterprises would perform financially given certain reasonable assumptions. Such factors include economic indicators such as inflation, interest rates, growth in gross domestic product, costs of particular items that are important to the enterprise such as raw materials and the minimum wage of labour.

Social

The assessment of the social environment will aid in determining the tastes and preferences of prospective and current customers. The lifestyles, attitudes, beliefs, educational level as well as the demographic characteristics of the entrepreneur's target group provide clues on how to approach the entrepreneurial opportunity. It could, for example, help determine which products or services to focus on, and at what price points. An example of how social attitudes have informed product development is the funeral policy now sold by insurance companies in Ghana, in response to the importance many Ghanaians place on elaborate and expensive funerals.

Technological

The availability, the cost and the discovery of new technology which may have a direct or indirect impact on the (proposed) enterprise must be of particular importance to the entrepreneur. The application of appropriate technology to the production of goods or services could greatly reduce production cost and may also result in the standardisation of the product or service. Similarly, rapid technological development in the market could affect the position of an enterprise. In most instances, this requires entrepreneurs to constantly research and invest in new technologies that impact on the success of their enterprises.

Competitive Analysis

The results of the PEST and the industry analysis would give the entrepreneur a good sense of all the key potential factors that would affect the success of his enterprise, and how profitable his chosen industry is.

The competitive analysis, on the other hand, provides a framework for the entrepreneur to carry out a detailed analysis of the major players that make up the industry (those with whom he will be competing for market share). The objective is to understand how competitors respond to opportunities and threats in the industry, and what their relative strengths and weaknesses are.

It is a good idea to list a small number of the key players in the industry and carry out similar analyses on each of them to be able to compare them against each other. Such analyses will also to reveal any gaps that the competition might not be exploiting. For those chosen from the competitive set, the entrepreneur should get a good understanding of:

- How they are positioned in the market (i.e. the space they occupy in the customer's mind);[21]
- Their strengths and weaknesses;
- Their target customers and key customers;
- Their sales volumes and value, market share and growth trajectories;
- Their pricing and marketing strategies;
- Their product lines and distribution channels;

- Their business models;
- Their management styles and goals;
- Their ethos;
- Their entire value chain.

The competitive analysis can give the entrepreneur a good idea of some of the 'white spaces' or opportunity areas in the industry. It will also enable the entrepreneur anticipate potential problems, and generally help him structure his business and business strategy.

Conducting Research

The ability to elicit the right information through research is a skill and an art. Many agencies and freelance researchers specialise in various aspects of conducting research, particularly in survey design, administration, data collation and data analysis. An entrepreneur starting out may not have the budget to hire a research professional or agency. This should not be an excuse for not seeking the relevant research. Research need not be elaborate or time-consuming. A series of ten-minute conversations with even family members who fall into the potential target group would be better than simply relying on your own intuition to make certain decisions. Also, the entrepreneur could improvise by carrying out her own research. University students and their lecturers are usually a group willing to assist such entrepreneurs.

Whether the research is designed in-house by the entrepreneur or outsourced to an agency or a freelancer, a few key things must be borne in mind.

It must be clear what the objective of the research is. For example, the research carried out by a mother of three looking to start out a nursery school in her neighbourhood might first start by understanding whether there is a need for such a service and, if there is a need, what mothers would want to pay for the nursery school. She may also want to find out who currently relieves the customer pain of those mothers and for what price. Understanding generally what some of the issues may be around the delivery of services by the existing competitive set is also very useful. With these in mind, the entrepreneur may decide to arrange focus groups initially to get a sense of the different issues worth probing. Subsequently, using a questionnaire, she may ask representative mothers about important considerations for them in choosing a nursery school. She may ask them to rank, for example, price, safety, technology and experience of staff, among others, in the order of importance with regard to nursery schools.

It is important to ensure that the opportunity analysis an entrepreneur employs gets her actionable data (information that can be relied on to make decisions about the business in such a way as to meet the needs, demands and wants of a target segment), hopefully long before the competition can.

Concept Validation

Sometimes, in developing a concept or entrepreneurial idea, entrepreneurs may have an idea of what consumer segments to target, what channels of distribution to use and what pricing or promotion mechanisms to employ. They may also develop ideas about additional issues after conducting the research and analyses we have discussed previously. Concept validation is an aspect of customer research which could help hone the concept further for entrepreneurs. It can be said to be an application of the projective technique we discussed on earlier. Concept validation involves exposing individuals constituting the target segment to the concept and getting their reaction. This could take the form of identifying people entrepreneurs consider to be in their 'target group' and running the concept by them to get their reaction. The response of people to the proposal/concept would determine whether it should be developed further or not. The important thing is to ensure that as much objective data as possible is gathered, and that all responses are recorded to ensure that proper analysis can be made on customer responses to the concept.

If the product is one that lends itself to the creation (and demonstration) of a prototype, such a prototype should be commissioned and shown to members of the target consumer segments. They should be encouraged to use it and to comment on how it can be improved, how they think they will use the product, etc. In the case of a food product, it makes sense to let people taste it and express their opinions about it. Test in real life situations; if it is a product that is used at home, let them use it at home and react to it.

One of my favourite examples of how this was applied successfully is from the English brand Innocent, where the founders made a decision to quit lucrative full-time jobs and launch the brand based on feedback provided by people attending a music festival. In their book *Innocent: Our Story And Some Of The Things We've Learned*, Dan Germain and Richard Reed write:

"We needed to know what people thought of our trial smoothies at the festival. To do so, we had designed a detailed two-page questionnaire for people to fill in – age, gender, how much they liked the taste, how much they liked the label, etc., etc. But as much as we wanted to know the answers to such questions, we couldn't help but think it was a bit much to ask people to fill out a complicated form when they were at a music festival with their friends."

Rich and Andy listened to the problem and said 'Don't you just want to know if people like them or not?' to which our reply was 'Yes'. Their suggestion was keep it simple. Put up a big sign above the stall that asked 'Should we give up our jobs to make the smoothies?' and place a bin in front of the stall that had YES written on it and a bin that said NO. Then people get to vote with their empty bottles by chucking them in the appropriate bin. At the end of the weekend, we had sold out our smoothies, and the YES bin was full. There were a few bottles in the NO bin (probably from our mums). Either way, it meant that the decision was made."[22]

In the case of services and other products where prototypes are not possible, the entrepreneur should create a 'concept board' or 'concept sheet' on which the entrepreneur describes the product in as much detail as possible, together with sketches of the product (or customer receiving the service) to give readers or prospective customers as much information about the product or service to enable them provide useful suggestions and criticism to the entrepreneur. A concept board or concept sheet should be drafted such that it is readable in less than a minute.

Objectives of Concept Tests

The objective of carrying out the concept test is to validate the entrepreneur's belief that:

- The product or service meets unmet needs of customers;
- The product or service meets certain needs that customers did not know they had (for example, the benefits from certain technology-based products);
- In the case of needs that are currently being met by the competition, the product or service meets those needs in a way that exceeds, or is at least equal to, what is provided by the competition.

An entrepreneurial opportunity exists only when the scale and size of buyer need and interest in the concept is such that there is high probability that the enterprise can perform profitably by satisfying that need.

Capturing Customer Voice In Concept Validation

The stage of concept validation at which the entrepreneur captures the voice of the customer should take two forms. Firstly, concept validation should include some conversations with customers (even if only a small number) about the proposed concept. It provides good qualitative insights into the customer's needs, wants, desires and aspirations, and how the product will meet some of those needs and desires. These conversations may be done on a one-on-one basis where identified members of the target group are asked to talk generally about the features and benefits of the product and service. It can also be done in focus groups.

Secondly, a questionnaire should be designed to ask consumers to rank the product or service on a number of attributes or dimensions. This ranking has the effect of separating out the different elements in the bundle of products or services. As a further step consumers should be asked to rank which attributes or dimensions are most important to them. For example, in the case of a new telephone service, consumers may be asked to rate, in terms of importance, the following:

- Cost per call;
- Ease of use;
- Quality of telephone service;
- Quality of customer service;
- Ability to make international calls.

In the case of an entrepreneur starting out a restaurant, the relevant dimensions to measure might include:

- Waiting times for meals;
- Quality/Taste of food;
- Variety of menu offerings;
- Location;
- Drink options;
- Knowledge of waiters.

Customer responses give the entrepreneur a fair idea of the most important product or service attributes or benefits to the potential consumer. In the case of the proposed telephone service, for example, the entrepreneur may find out that for personal (as opposed to business) customers, the cost of the call may be the most important factor, and the ability to make international calls the least important factor. For the restaurant, he might find that knowledge of waiters is not as important as location and variety of menu offerings, but that the most important factor is wait times for meals and the quality/taste of the food. The entrepreneur so armed can structure his proposed venture accordingly.

Knowing what customers think about your concept and how they rank the various product or service dimensions is however not enough. Even at the concept stage, it is important to get an idea of how likely the customer will purchase the product or service, how often they will purchase and the magnitude of their purchase (likely size of purchase or level of use). These are known respectively as purchase intent, purchase frequency and purchase magnitude. The questionnaire should end with asking the customers questions about these.

• *Purchase Intent*

Customers should be asked to indicate one of the following in relation to the probability of purchase:

- Would definitely buy;
- Would probably buy;
- Neutral;
- Would probably not buy;
- Would definitely not buy.

Ideally you want 80-90% of responses to be in the top 2 boxes ('Would definitely buy' and 'Would probably buy').

• *Purchase Frequency*

Customers should be asked to estimate how often they would expect to buy a product or patronise a service. (For example, every week, once a year, twice in my lifetime, etc., depending on the type of product.)

• *Purchase Magnitude*

Apart from simply asking how often they would purchase the product, customers should also be encouraged to quantify the magnitude of their purchases (how many they expect to buy at any given time of purchase). This is intended to capture information such as a mother stating that she would purchase five ice-cream cones each time she is buying ice cream (maybe because she has five children).

Advantages and Disadvantages of Concept Testing

Concept testing, if done correctly, may prevent costly mistakes down the line. At that stage, only a minimum level of resources would have been invested and it is easily possible for the entrepreneur to modify or even abandon a concept before investing heavily in that concept.

Concept testing therefore captures directly what the potential customer is saying in relation to the product, giving the entrepreneur opportunities to feed back such information into her venture's product/ service delivery. Where a questionnaire is used, in the form described above, the information provided by potential customers gives the entrepreneur an indication of demand for the product or service. Based on the responses in relation to purchase intention, frequency and magnitude, the entrepreneur can reasonably estimate what the minimum level of demand for her product will be. For data to be meaningful though, the sample size should be large.

However, concept testing makes the entrepreneur's intentions known before she might be ready to proceed with the product or service, and therefore may make her susceptible to someone imitating her idea or beating her to market. Also, given that customers are not entirely reliable when it comes to providing information about their intended purchases and preferences, the entrepreneur may find that not all the responses given can be relied upon. Even worse is the difficulty around separating out what cannot be relied upon from what can.

It could also potentially be time-consuming for the entrepreneur, especially in the case of products where speed is of the essence. Our view is that this is not enough justification for abandoning the concept testing; rather it is better that perhaps a shorter concept test is undertaken.

Trade Area Analysis

Deciding where to locate an enterprise could make or unmake an entrepreneurial venture in certain instances. One of the reasons why entrepreneurs prefer to build their enterprises from scratch instead of buying is the advantages that come with locating their enterprise at a specific place.[23] In Ghana, for example, a number of hotels have had to close down because they were built in remote parts of Accra without good access roads or outside decent residential areas.

It is important therefore at the opportunity analysis stage for entrepreneurs to carefully research available areas to determine what locations are best suited for their enterprises. The entrepreneur must first of all determine which part of the country or which part of a particular city he intends to operate. After making this decision, he should then carry out further research to decide on the exact location within a particular city, or a particular part of the city, as the case may be. These decisions have different considerations, which are expanded on below.

Which Part of the Country to Locate In?

Among the factors that would need to be considered in making the decision of where to locate in the country are the following:

• *Proximity To Markets*

Certain parts of the country might have greater concentration of the target customers than others, and so may be more appropriate for locating a particular kind of enterprise. For example, the majority of high-end boutiques are in Accra and Kumasi because these two cities account for a disproportionately high percentage of high-income earners in Ghana. In establishing a physical fitness centre, for instance, an entrepreneur may consider locating in the urban areas where there is also a high concentration of professionals who do not have time for physical activity.

• *Proximity To Raw Materials*

Similarly (especially in the case of bulky raw materials), it may make sense to locate close to the source of raw materials so as to cut down on transportation costs, as well as to ensure a regular supply. Salt refining enterprises such as Pambros are therefore located in the coastal areas of the country.

• *Labour supply*

An enterprise may be dependent on the use of certain skills that are more commonly possessed by workers in one part of the country than others. In that case it makes sense to locate accordingly. For example, if an enterprise requires a high level of skilled labour, it makes more sense to operate in a regional capital than in a district capital, as the former tends to attract such high-calibre graduates who are often attracted by the relatively higher standards of living. However, the enterprise might be such that skills are irrelevant because all that is needed is a ready pool of unskilled labour. (Perhaps, in such a case, entrepreneurs may be attracted to parts of the country with higher unemployment).

• *Business Climate*

As a result of varied governmental policies at the regional level, some areas of the country may be more attractive for certain businesses than others, as there may be incentives available for people that set up enterprises in those parts. For example, in Ghana, the current tax legislation[24] grants tax concessions to entrepreneurs operating in industries such as agro-processing; agriculture and enterprises located in regional capitals other than Accra and rural parts of Ghana benefit from reduced corporate tax rates. In addition, businesses may be entitled to tax concessions depending on the industry in which they operate. For example, businesses engaged in agro-processing are exempt from tax during the first three years of their operations. Businesses engaged in agricultural activities such as farming of tree crops and cash crops, as well as livestock farming also enjoy various tax concessions. Further, businesses located in regional capitals other than Accra and rural parts of Ghana benefit from reduced corporate tax rates. In addition, various chiefs may also provide incentives to entrepreneurs to set up enterprises in their particular area so as to assist in the development of the area and the creation of jobs.

• Population Growth Trends, Density and Shifts

These could give an indication of opportunities available which the entrepreneur may want to take advantage of. The data collected from the national census is a good source of such information.

• Competition

The absence of competitors in parts of the country may alert entrepreneurs to potential opportunities as long as competitor absence does not mean that there would be no demand for the relevant product or service.

• Transportation Networks and Other Infrastructure

The availability or non-availability of a good transport system and other infrastructure such as good communication facilities, electricity or water may be relevant in a decision as to whether to site an enterprise in one part of the country as opposed to the other.

Where to Locate in a Particular City, Town or Village

After deciding on what part of the country to locate in, the entrepreneur has to make a decision as to exactly where to site the particular business within that part of the country. The following factors may help in making such a decision:

• Customer Traffic

A location may be better than another for an enterprise based on the customer traffic flow in that particular area. High customer traffic on Osu's Oxford Street for makes it an attractive location for fast food joints and restaurants; destination traffic in terms of customers travelling to purpose-built markets such as Makola and Mallam Atta also make them attractive locations for traders. The specific location of the physical fitness centre described above could be in residential areas to enable people exercise conveniently in the mornings and evenings before and after work.

• *Adequate Parking*

Particularly in the retail and service sectors targeting customers who own cars, the ability to provide customer parking space could determine how many customers patronise the business.

• *Room For Expansion*

Ideally, the location should be flexible enough to enable the entrepreneur to expand if the need arises.

• *Visibility*

Where an enterprise (particularly in the retail and service sector) is highly visible (for example, off a main road), it will generate a lot of walk-in business – that is, customers walking into the enterprise and transacting business with the entity simply because they notice the enterprise. Of course, this is not relevant in all cases. In some instances, it is the entrepreneur who travels to the customer to provide a service. Even in such cases, it can be argued that 'visibility' is still present in the form of phone numbers, email and website addresses through which customers can make easy contact with the service provider.

• *Competition*

This is a two-edged sword. In some instances, it may be better to locate in an area where there is little or no competition over an area preferred by competitors. However, where competitors are already established in a particular location, that area provides a well-defined market to which customers flock for the particular products offered by the competing enterprises. For instance, Abossey Okai Spare Parts Lane is widely known for its automobile spare parts shops in Accra, and Katamanto (popularly known as 'Kant' in Accra) is known for its high concentration of hand-me-down clothing sellers.

• *Cost*

Entrepreneurs would (and should) want to keep costs as low as possible. Consequently the cost of location options may be a factor in deciding where to locate. However, this must be subjected to a cost-benefit analysis. The Osu Oxford Street area in Accra commands some of the highest rental prices in Accra. However, it is also so busy with human and vehicular traffic that the returns may justify the high investment in space there.

• *Size And Layout*

The business activities to be carried out by the enterprise may impose constraints on the amount and exact types of locations that the entrepreneur can consider.

Finding Premises

Firstly, the entrepreneur needs to find out which premises are vacant before deciding which meets his needs. Having identified an appropriate one, the entrepreneur then negotiates and finalises the deal. Finding vacant premises require the use of one's social network and classified sections of newspapers (such as *Daily Graphic*) or magazines (such as *Property News*). The Internet also provides a variety of information on vacant premises. In Ghana however, reliance on personal contacts and networks is best as information on the Internet might be outdated. However, Internet sites that may be helpful are businessghana.com, ghanaweb.com and ghana.com. The use of reputable real estate agents such as Goldbrook Properties, Broll and JB Properties is another option.

Some issues that need to be considered before commitments are made regarding office premises include:

- Is the person selling or leasing the property the rightful legal owner?
- How much renovation work needs to be carried out?
- Can the premises be used for the kind of enterprise you have in mind?
- How long is the lease?
- Can you sublet part or all of the premises?
- How much rent does the landlord require in advance?

Telecommuting

With increased advances in technology, particularly information and communication technologies, the entrepreneur may, depending on the nature of his enterprise, decide that employees, instead of operating from a central location, can 'telecommute' or 'teleconference' all or part of the time. 'Telecommuting' is a situation whereby, instead of an employer commuting from home to work, he commutes via telephone and the corporate Intranet. Thus, he does not have to be physically present.

It is possible for people to work asynchronously (not at the same time) through email, voice mail, video conferencing and wikis (software that allows users to create, edit and link web pages) which enable groups to communicate with each other at any time.[25]

There is a two-stage decision an entrepreneur can make based on the availability of technology to enable telecommuting. He may decide that his enterprise can be completely virtual without the need for any offices. He can work from home, set up a website where people can place orders and then rely on a network of couriers to deliver the goods. He could also decide that although the nature of the enterprise requires a central location, the nature of work to be performed by some employees is such that they can work from home and occasionally visit the central office for training programmes and strategy meetings, among others.

Dorf and Byers[26] argue however that because social capital is based on face-to-face communication, virtual meetings work best for the discussion of focused topics such as budgets, schedules and facts. Presence, according to them, is necessary for soft functions such as negotiations. I also think it is invaluable in building a culture that creates a long-term sustainable and immutable competitive advantage.

Opportunity analysis carried out, if done well, will give the entrepreneur many insights, each with its potential for further development and further insights. It is up to the entrepreneur to connect all the dots, make meaning out of the data and turn it into actionable insights. The information can be fuzzy, messy and even contradictory. The entrepreneur's aim is to sift the data through the funnel to gain the most valuable nuggets (the needles in the haystack).

In addition to the information the entrepreneur obtains is the insights about the entrepreneur's own capacity and capability (which we discussed in Chapter 2). Together with the methods we have discussed so far, these cover broadly the eight layers of information gathering and analysis that the entrepreneur must carry out. They relate to:

- The macroeconomy;
- The entrepreneur's own capacity and capability;
- The enterprise's competencies and capacity, or potential competencies and capability;
- The target customer(s);
- The market or industry;
- The competition;
- Collaborators (key persons and enterprises the entrepreneur would need to collaborate with to empower the move from idea to profit);
- Suppliers.

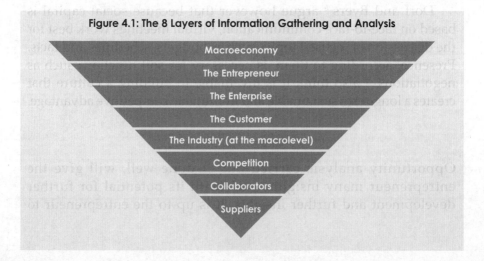

Figure 4.1: The 8 Layers of Information Gathering and Analysis

Macroeconomy

The Entrepreneur

The Enterprise

The Customer

The Industry (at the macrolevel)

Competition

Collaborators

Suppliers

If done well, the insights provided by opportunity analysis give the entrepreneur or a prospective entrepreneur the ability to design an enterprise that indeed removes an existing customer pain in a way that is hopefully better than the competitive set.

Competing and Winning with Information

Research should be employed in all aspects of building and managing the enterprise. Apart from using it to validate an idea (concept validation), it should be used to reach decisions such as which advertising medium to use, which promotional vehicle to use, what prices to charge and where to sell the product or position the service. Small enterprises benefit from getting a feel from the market about which options to pursue. However, given limited funds, research should be done in the most cost-efficient manner.

I could not agree more with Kotler when he says: "Today's marketing is becoming a battle based more on ownership of information than on ownership of other resources. Companies can copy each other's equipment, products, and procedures, but they cannot [easily] duplicate the [competitor's] information and intellectual capital. The company's information content may constitute its chief competitive advantage."[27]

I therefore recommend highly that every enterprise, no matter how small, institutionalise the process of collating and analysing customer insights on a continuous basis.

Questions for Class Discussion

1. Must research necessarily be complicated and/or expensive?
2. What are the main sources of secondary data that an entrepreneur can rely on for his research?
3. What are some of the ways that an entrepreneur can carry out research on how customers feel about a particular product or service?
4. What are projective techniques? When would you use a projective technique?
5. In what ways, if at all, is the five forces framework relevant to someone starting a small or medium size enterprise?
6. How might an entrepreneur go about validating a belief that a product or service meets an unmet customer need?
7. What are the key considerations to take into account when deciding on a suitable location for an enterprise?

Case Study: The Standard Cashless Account: Ghana's First Zero-Deposit Account [28]

N 1906 BANK OF BRITISH West Africa set up a branch in Accra, establishing the first bank in the Gold Coast, to provide banking services to the British colonial administration and British trading entities that had been established along the West African coastal corridor.[29]

In the century that followed, the banking industry in Ghana grew into a cosy gentleman's club of assured – almost guaranteed – returns with very little effort, and an absence of any real competition. A significant percentage of banking income came from treasury bill (T-bill) spreads (the 91-day T-bill rate, for example, was as high as 42.72% in 1995). Banking regulation also required banks to place 9% of their deposits in cash and 35% in secondary reserves (treasury bills, government securities and placements in discount houses and the interbank market).

Research[30] suggested that only 5% of Ghanaians had bank accounts. There was a disproportionate focus on high-net-worth and middle-income clients to the detriment of the low-income masses.

Standard Trust

Driven by its visionary founder and CEO, Tony Elumelu, Standard Trust Bank Plc, set up in August 1997, quickly became the fourth largest bank in Nigeria with over 86 branches. When it went public in 2003, it was one of Nigeria's most successful initial public offers, resulting in over 61,000 shareholders purchasing the bank's stock. Ghana was the first destination for Standard Trust outside Nigeria, and Elumelu put in place a dream team of young ambitious men and women led by seasoned banker Obeahon Ohiwerei (as Managing Director) to set up Standard Trust Bank Ghana Ltd, tasking them to replicate the success of Standard Trust Bank Plc, Nigeria.

Consumer Insights

There were many in the Ghanaian bank who felt a strategy could be developed by relying on the opinions of colleagues, many of whom had significant experience in banking in Ghana or Nigeria. Ohiwerei, for example, had brought a gamut of retail experience from Nigeria, where he had been at the epicentre of Standard Trust Nigeria's unprecedented growth. Ohiwerei therefore sought to rely on his experience in Nigeria, assuming that the Ghanaian banking consumer could not be that much different from the Nigerian consumer.

Elikem Nutifafa Kuenyehia, who was responsible for branding and strategy, however remained convinced that developing a brand strategy without consumer insight would be a fatal mistake. He would therefore not be persuaded to craft a strategy for a retail bank without such insights. Kuenyehia wanted to hire a first-class research firm to carry out thorough research into the attitudes, values and habits of banking customers in Ghana; he however faced strong resistance from Ohiwerei who felt the bank could not justify paying significant sums of money for research at a time when it was just starting out.

Without the budget he needed to hire a research company, Kuenyehia decided to carry out his own research. He hired a couple of students and took one week away from his desk to travel around the country to, as he put it, "have conversations with our profit centre". It was crucial to him to gain a deep understanding of what the Ghanaian banking customer wanted, and then communicate that knowledge internally within the bank to help drive the bank's marketing and operational strategy. Kuenyehia and his team conducted twenty focus groups over four days in Accra, Tema, Kumasi and Tamale, interviewing a total of over two hundred people drawn from various socioeconomic groups, and also across the banked and un-banked divide.

The research provided valuable insights into the opportunity that Standard Trust Bank Ghana Ltd was seeking to take advantage of. It also confirmed that the notion of the un-banked was real. Many respondents indicated that they kept their money in locked drawers at home. One person actually spoke of having a 'body bank'.

Armed with the consumer insights generated through his research, Kuenyehia hosted an idea generation and strategy session to which he invited a cross section of the bank's staff to share ideas on the bank's possible strategy. He followed this up with a number of brainstorming sessions with Joel Nettey, Dan Twum and the strategy and creative teams from the bank's advertising agency, Origin8 Saatchi and Saatchi.

Driven largely by the opportunity offered by the 95% of adult Ghanaians who did not have bank accounts, the team came up with an idea for Ghana's first zero-deposit account - The Standard Cashless Account. Launched on 28 April 2005, the product was described as one of the most revolutionary products in Ghanaian banking.[31] The research conducted to gain consumer insight had clearly shown that most adults in Ghana would like to have a bank account. It had also shown that many people, particularly in the lower socio-economic segments, were deterred from opening bank accounts because of the high deposit amounts required to open an account, and the high minimum balance one had to maintain once the account was opened. They appeared to be intimidated by banks, believing that they were not in the "class of people" that banks cater for. Some respondents actually mentioned that they felt embarrassed to go to banks to deposit "small amounts of money" in their bank accounts.

The launch of the product came at a time when both the Minister of Finance and the Governor of Bank of Ghana had criticised the bank's high opening and operating balances. The Standard Cashless Account was a product that enabled a customer to open an account with no money. The customer was then given a month to pay in at least fifty thousand cedis (GH¢5) to keep the account. This was a direct example of using consumer insights to drive business strategy.

Over 3,000 accounts were opened within months of the launch of the product. Ironically, very few people opened the account without any money. In fact a few people opened the account with as much as 50 million cedis (GH¢5,000).[32] The cashless account effectively helped to mobilise deposits at the critical period of the bank's take-off.

Notes

1 Stevenson, H. H., M.J. Roberts and H.I. Grousbeck. *New Business Ventures and the Entrepreneur*. Burr Ridge: Irwin, 1994.

2 Brealey, R. and S. Myers. *Principles of Corporate Finance*. New York: McGraw-Hill, 2000.

3 *Ibid.*

4 Chess, R. Note on Market Research. Stanford Graduate School of Business, 2003.

5 Webb, R J. *Understanding and designing research*. London: Thomson. 2002,

6 *Ibid.*

7 *Ibid.*

8 Cannon, T. *Marketing Principles and Practice*. London: Cassell, 1998.

9 Karden R.J. *Guerrilla Marketing Research*. London: Kogan Page, 2008.

10 Sanders, E. How 'applied ethnography' can improve your NPD research process. *PDMA Visions*, XXVI(2), 2002: 8-12.

11 Andreasen, A. R. Cost-Conscious Marketing Research, *Harvard Business Review*, 61(4), 1983: 74-77.

12 Porter, M.E. *Competitive Strategy: Techniques for Analysing Industries and Competitors*. New York: Free Press, 1980.

13 Draws on unpublished Kellogg School of Management Teaching Note on Michael Porter's Five Forces by S. Marciano and M. Mazzeo, 2000.

14 *Ibid.*

15 McCarthy, J.E. and W.D. Perreault. *Basic Marketing: A Global-Managerial Approach*. Burr Ridge: Irwin, 1993.

16 Bohm, A. *The SWOT Analysis*. Munich: GRIN Verlag oHG, 2009.

17 Morris, D. A new tool for strategy analysis: the opportunity model. *Journal of Business Strategy*, 26(3), 2005: 50–56.

18 Piercy, N. and W. Giles. Making SWOT Analysis Work. *Marketing Intelligence And Planning*, 7(5/6), 1989: 5-7.

19 *Ibid.*

20 See Page 35.

21 For more on positioning, see Chapter 11.

22 Germain, D. and R. Reed. *Innocent: Our story and some of the things we've learned.* London: Penguin Books, 2009.

23 Siropolis, N. *Small Business Management.* Boston: Houghton Mifflin, 1994.

24 Internal Revenue Act, 2000 (Act 592 and Regulations).

25 Richard, C. D. and H.B. Thomas. *Technology Ventures: From Idea to Enterprise.* New York: McGraw Hill, 2008.

26 *Ibid.*

27 Kotler P. *Kotler on Marketing How to create, win and dominate markets.* London: Simon & Schuster 2001

28 Distilled from a longer case, Standard Trust Bank and the democratisation of banking in Ghana, prepared by Professor Bob Hinson, Head, Marketing Department, University of Ghana Business School, with assistance from Elikem Nutifafa Kuenyehia, Thelma Tawiah and Edwin Baffour.

29 Anin, T.E. *Banking in Ghana.* Accra: Woeli Publishing, 2000.

30 Philip Buabeng, Ghana College Research,2004

31 Article by Alex Ogundadegbe, Ovation Magazine, May 2004.

32 Before redenomination of the currency, so equivalent to GH¢5,000.

Chapter Five: Build or Buy

"The beginning is the most important part of the work." - **Plato**

W HEN MANY PEOPLE think about entrepreneurship, they think of the classic case – where one or more persons come up with an idea and then marshal the requisite resources to turn that idea into an enterprise, working from scratch and often with limited initial resources. The best known examples of the start-up (many, coincidentally, starting from a garage) have inspired many entrepreneurs to also clear out their own garages or spare rooms to try their hands at entrepreneurship by starting their own enterprises.

The start-up route to entrepreneurship however is only one option. As I noted in Chapter 2, entrepreneurship is a spectrum; there are many entrepreneurs who become entrepreneurs, not by starting their own enterprises from scratch, but by inheriting an existing enterprise (typically from a relative or close friend), buying an existing enterprise or buying a franchise. Research suggests that in Ghana most entrepreneurs become entrepreneurs by starting enterprises from scratch, with only a small number buying existing enterprises although this is changing – at least to a limited extent. An increasing number of people are willing to buy existing enterprises, thereby buying into – or even buying – the dreams of other entrepreneurs, rather than starting from scratch.

In this chapter, we discuss the acquisition of an enterprise as an alternate route to entrepreneurship, and consider why an entrepreneur may buy an existing enterprise rather than start one from scratch. I use a broad meaning of the word 'acquisition': this includes the purchase of a minority or majority interest in a partnership or the share capital of a company; the acquisition of a licence for a product, service or business method through franchising; and the inheritance of an existing enterprise. We also examine the pros and cons of acquiring an existing enterprise as opposed to starting one from scratch and consider the difficulties involved in buying an enterprise, as well as the stages that one would typically go through. We then focus on the due diligence that must be undertaken to make the determination of whether or not to buy an enterprise, and at what price. That leads us to the discussion of valuation and how one might value the enterprise being acquired.

I hope to demonstrate that with the right level of due diligence, the right team in place and an enterprise that is a 'fit' for the entrepreneur and his team, buying an enterprise can be a rewarding and fulfilling route to entrepreneurship. While many large corporations acquire smaller companies that, for example, provide innovative products and technology, the focus of this chapter is on the individuals who become entrepreneurs in ways other than by starting an enterprise from scratch. The protagonist in this chapter is the buyer of the business rather than the seller, and although we consider issues from the perspectives of both buyer and seller, our focus on this chapter is more on the entrepreneur acquiring the business. In Chapter 13 – where we consider expansion options for the entrepreneur with an already existing business – we will consider the sale of the business as an option.

Buying an existing enterprise

The literature on 'build or buy' suggests that new ventures are less likely to succeed than those taken over.[1] Even with a great idea, the work and money involved in building a successful enterprise from scratch can be daunting and take many years (sometimes one or more lifetimes). At the start-up phase, there is a high degree of uncertainty with all operational aspects of the start-up venture being unknown. According to Haigh,[2] three quarters of all start-ups fail in the first year, and a quarter of those that succeed in the initial year flounder in the second year, particularly because of lack of knowledge, understanding of the market and basic working capital.

An acquired enterprise will typically have a track record based on which the buyer can make his decisions e.g. informed forecasts about the future financial prospects of the enterprise. While some of the tools we discussed in Chapter 4 can assist an entrepreneur quantify the opportunity to be exploited by a start-up, there is generally a lot less conjecture involved in the case of an existing enterprise with a location, existing customers, suppliers, branding, cash flow, infrastructure and management team. Acquiring an enterprise can however be a tricky process; it is important that would-be acquirers spend time understanding this process and doing their homework. As Adhikari puts it,[3] 'A successful acquirer needs a good balance of ACT:

- Acquisition skill (A) to understand the acquisition process, deal structure, taxes, risks and legal issues, to build credibility with the seller and to have the entrepreneurial drive to add value;
- Capital (C), his own equity and financing skills to enable the raising of additional capital;
- Technical skills (T), the management competencies in marketing, production, finance, legal, etc.

There are a number of structuring options available to entrepreneurs considering buying an existing enterprise, and these options should be considered carefully by entrepreneurs relative to their objectives and aspirations. These options are as follows.

Asset purchase

As we will see in Chapter 7, an asset may be a fixed asset or a current asset. Fixed assets include buildings, plant and machinery, fixtures and fittings, brands, intellectual property (IP) and goodwill. Current assets include accounts receivable (i.e. monies owed to the enterprise), stock, works in progress and cash reserves. For any number of reasons, an entrepreneur may want to buy assets of another company but without buying the company as a going concern.

As we will find out in Chapter 6, the company through which the entrepreneur carries out the enterprise is a different legal person from the owner(s). It is important to bear this legal principle in mind in the discussion that follows. In an asset purchase involving a company or a partnership, the seller is the company or partnership that owns the assets. The acquirer acquires some or all of the target enterprise's assets but, unless expressly agreed, will not assume the liabilities. The selling company or partnership continues to remain a company (or partnership as the case may be), albeit one which has had some or all of its assets and liabilities transferred to the buyer.

The advantage to the acquirer of pursuing an asset purchase instead of a share purchase is that the acquirer is able to buy only those assets that it desires to acquire while agreeing to assume only specified liabilities of the company or partnership. This enables the acquirer to make his money work efficiently as he only purchases the assets that he really needs, leaves behind the assets he does not need and also reduces the risk of acquiring unwanted liabilities by contractually agreeing which liabilities he agrees to assume. However, this option may be unattractive to the seller because it would mean that the seller and its shareholders (or partners) continue to retain significant known or unknown liabilities, and own assets that they may not need or want. An asset purchase by a company also results in double taxation for the sellers as follows: the gain (the difference between the value of the assets sold and the book value) on the sale of the asset attracts capital gains tax which the company pays because it owns the asset; when these gains are distributed to shareholders of the company as dividends or upon the liquidation of the company, these gains become taxable in the hands of the shareholders.

Share Purchase

In a share purchase, the acquirer buys all or a certain percentage of shares in a company. As the company would typically own the underlying enterprise together with the assets, by buying all of the shares in a company, the buyer automatically acquires the assets the company owns as well as all its liabilities. The only thing that changes in this case is that the shareholders change, as the new shareholder(s) buy out the existing shareholder(s), or become additional shareholder(s) with the original shareholder(s), depending on whether the acquirer purchases all or part of the shares of the company. However, the company continues as a going concern with all its assets, liabilities, employees and contractual relationships in place.

As Haigh puts it, "when you buy shares, you buy history. Effectively, it's a transfer of ownership and any residual issues within the company are automatically switched across, as essentially the ownership of the company has just changed hands."[4]

It means that entrepreneurs buy all the liabilities that run with the company whether they know about them or not, and whether or not they existed before they acquired the company. It is for this reason that entrepreneurs must conduct extensive due diligence on the company and its trading history to ensure that they become aware of any potential issues before making the acquisition. It should be noted, however, that in many cases, due diligence may not reveal the total extent of liabilities, many of which may come out of the woodwork only later on. To ensure that the purchaser is not left out of pocket as a result of the omission or an act of the seller, the acquirer will typically require that he is given warranties and indemnities by the seller. We will discuss due diligence later on in this chapter, together with warranties and indemnities.[5]

In a share sale, the seller is the shareholder who receives the price from the buyer. Although the seller may be subject to tax on the gains made from the disposal of shares, the only gain made is in the hands of the selling shareholder(s) and as a result, unlike the sale of an asset by the company, there is no gain attributable to the company on which the company must also pay tax. When buying shares in a company, the entrepreneur may opt for an outright purchase giving him complete ownership and control of the enterprise. Alternatively, he may opt for a stake less than 100%. Acquiring shares in a company does not automatically make the acquirer an entrepreneur, or give him a say in how the company is run. The acquirer will have the right to attend shareholders meetings of the company and other limited rights. If the acquirer is a real entrepreneur, buying into the dream of the existing enterprise and its owners, he might want more input in the running of the company. To do so, he must typically buy the majority stake in the company (so that effectively no one owns more of the company than he does). The acquirer buys an absolute majority stake if he buys anything more than 50% of the company. 50% plus one share would suffice, although generally people go for 51%.

As we will see in Chapter 10, shareholders pass resolutions to authorise officers of the company act in the name of the company. To pass a resolution, shareholders vote in one of two ways: on a show of hands or by a poll. If a vote is taken by a show of hands every shareholder has one vote. If a poll is taken, a shareholder has one vote for every share she owns.

There are two types of resolutions a company can pass – ordinary and special resolutions. For an ordinary resolution to be passed, a simple majority of shareholders (or their proxies) present and voting at the meeting must vote in favour of it. (A proxy is a person who attends a general meeting in place of a shareholder or the company. If a shareholder wants to send a proxy to a meeting rather than attending personally, he must formally appoint a person as his proxy in accordance with the terms of the company's regulations. The proxy can only exercise the vote(s) of the shareholder(s) appointing him and has no additional votes. Proxies may speak at the general meeting and may be appointed for a period of time or for a particular meeting or set of meetings.) Thus, the resolution will be passed if, on a show of hands, a majority in number of the shareholders present vote for the resolution, or if more than 50% of the votes cast in a poll are in favour.

Passing a special resolution requires 75% of shareholders present and voting at the meeting to vote in favour of the resolution. This means that on a show of hands at least three quarters of the number of shareholders (or their proxies) present and voting must vote in its favour. On a poll, 75% of the votes of the shareholders (or their proxies) present and voting at the meeting must favour the resolution.

Members act by ordinary resolution unless they are required to do otherwise by Act 196 (1963), the company's regulations or a shareholders' agreement. The Companies Code requires that certain decisions of the company (such as changing the company's regulations) can only be passed by special resolution. The shareholders' agreement may also provide that certain decisions (that would normally require only an ordinary resolution) can only be passed by a special resolution.

Clearly, then, the percentage shareholding that an acquirer obtains affects to what extent he will be able to control decisions of the company through the general or extraordinary meetings of members. Also, in the absence of any provisions to the contrary in the company's regulations or a shareholder's agreement, a shareholder (acting alone) has no right to appoint any particular director to the board, although he may exercise this right jointly with other shareholders. The acquirer buying a share that is less than 100% of the company may therefore want to use contractual provisions in the shareholders' agreement to obtain control of the company. An acquirer purchasing 25% of a company may, for example, ensure that the shareholders' agreement requires that he be consulted whenever the company has to make a decision relating to certain matters, and may want a right to appoint a minimum number of directors to ensure that his interests are properly represented at the board level. I will cover shareholders' agreements in more detail in Chapter 6.

Purchase of a Share in a Partnership

In the case of partnerships, it is possible to acquire part of a business through the acquisition of the stakes held by other partners. In rare cases, there could be an outright acquisition of a partnership, which is essentially an acquisition of the assets of that partnership rather than an acquisition of the different stakes of the partners, as the effect of a 100% sale would be to fully dilute the initial partnership set-up.

What is Included in the Acquisition?

Whether an acquirer opts for an asset purchase or acquires shares in a company or a share in a partnership, the acquirer must be clear about what it is that he is acquiring. There are a large number of permutations available to the seller and buyer to negotiate on. For example, in the US$600,000 acquisition of Kessben FC in July 2010 by Moses Armah, the owner of Medeama FC (a Ghana Division One League club) from football administrator and founder of Kessben Group of Companies, Kwabena Kesse, the acquisition was limited to such key assets such as Kessben FC's Premier League status, the players and a bus. The Anane Boateng Stadium – the home venue for Kessben FC – was excluded from the acquisition and remains the property of Kwabena Kesse.[6]

Whatever is ultimately decided, it is recommended that an annexure is developed with the seller, listing both what is included in and what is excluded from the sale. The following assets often deserve particular consideration.

Real Estate

If the intention is for real estate to be included in the purchase, it must be established in the due diligence process that the enterprise transferring the real estate has title to the real estate assets to be transferred, and also has the requisite legal authority to transfer. Where the property to be transferred is a leasehold, consent of the freeholder would normally be required.

Staff

In many instances the real value a company has lies with its employees. The acquiring entrepreneur would therefore be doomed to failure if she acquires the company, and then turns up after the champagne closing ceremony to find that the key employees have all left. It should not be taken for granted that the staff of the existing enterprise will agree to stay when there is a new owner. Some of them might have built a personal bond with the seller and may have stayed up to that point because of him. Where the acquirer is a corporate entity, some staff may refuse to stay on because they disagree with the business practices or philosophy of the acquirer. Care must be taken, at least in the case of senior employees, to engage them as soon as is practicable (subject to relevant confidentiality agreements put in place) to seek their buy-in to the purchase, and their commitment to the change of ownership. Where this is done, the due diligence process is potentially easier as the senior management can share their ideas about the opportunities and challenges facing the enterprise. Where it is intended that the acquisition will result in redundancies, the redundancy provisions of labour law (which we will discuss in Chapter 6) are applicable.

Technology

Where an enterprise relies heavily on technology, it should be ascertained whether the enterprise owns the technology or merely licences it. Where the technology is licensed as opposed to owned, consent may need to be sought from the owner of the technology, who may demand additional fees. The owner of the technology may also use it as an opportunity to negotiate a different service level agreement.

Customers and contracts

Customers and contracts of the enterprise may not necessarily remain unchanged after the change of ownership. Some agreements may have change of control provisions whereby the other party to the contract is entitled to terminate the contract in the event that there is a change in control and/or ownership of the enterprise providing the service. Where this is the case, the acquirer and the seller should engage with major customers early in the process to persuade them to stay with the enterprise as it changes hands. However, depending on the profile of the current owner(s), these contract counterparties may decide to move to a competitor. Even where there is no contractual change of control provision, it is advisable to get a sense from the biggest customers whether they are comfortable with the proposed change of ownership. For example, very early in the process by the Stellar Group to acquire Nita Travel and Tours, the buyers visited the top customers of Nita

Travel and Tours to ascertain whether they might have a problem with a change of ownership of the company. They were assured by these customers that so long as the good quality of service continued, they did not mind the change of control.[7]

Suppliers

Like customers, suppliers may not necessarily be inherited with the acquisition of the enterprise. They may also have change of control provisions or simply not want to deal with a new owner. Again, as soon as it is practicable to do so, the acquirer should engage with key suppliers.

Branding and Intellectual Property

The patents, trademarks, designs and copyrights relating to the enterprise (if any) must be properly transferred to the acquirer. In some instances, the seller would like to hold on to ownership of these rights but give the acquirer a licence to use them. Specialist advice should be sought from an intellectual property lawyer.

Whether you decide to 'build', starting a business from a mere idea and a dose of optimism, or to 'buy' an existing enterprise will depend on a number of circumstances of each entrepreneur's case. The entrepreneur must consider the pros and cons of each option before making a decision; it is to these pros and cons that we now turn our attention.

Pros of Buying vs. Starting from Scratch

There are various advantages of buying an existing enterprise as opposed to starting one from scratch. These include the following.

Easier Route to Entrepreneurship

Buying an enterprise may offer an easier and quicker route for the entrepreneur seeking to start her own enterprise, particularly where that entrepreneur does not herself have an idea that could form the basis of a successful enterprise. While these entrepreneurs may not be able to come up with ideas to start enterprises with, or may feel unable to start an enterprise from scratch, they are able to recognise opportunities to either turn around existing ventures, to expand them or to make them more profitable. Sometimes, they simply want to step into the shoes of the selling entrepreneur and to take off from the stage he is at while skipping the painstaking process of starting a venture from scratch.

The seller of the enterprise would have already spent time and effort identifying the relevant target and developing a value proposition to attract this target. The enterprise is likely to have customers, employees, suppliers, distributors and a distribution network, premises, patents and contractual relationships, among others, which the acquiring entrepreneur hopes to buy with the acquisition. All these tangible and intangible assets can then be used as a platform from which to operate (and hopefully expand) the enterprise as a 'going concern' and a market presence from day one. The venture therefore starts with a track record and a legacy of continuity. If the entrepreneur had decided to start his enterprise from scratch, he would have to go through various processes and requirements to get these resources and relationships.

A History of Success

A long history of success by an enterprise is a useful indicator by which to predict potential future success. For instance, the enterprise may have a good track record of developing products and services to meet customer preferences. It may also have other intangible assets that contribute to maximising profitability. The entrepreneur who buys such an enterprise can therefore be reasonably expected to build upon all these. It must however be noted that this is not always the case. For the entrepreneur to build upon the successes of the previous entrepreneur, he must understand the factors that have led to success in the past to ensure that he can replicate those successes when he takes over the enterprise.

Predictability of Income Stream

According to Knowles, a key advantage of buying an existing enterprise as opposed to building one from scratch is the predictability of money and an income stream.[8] If the entrepreneur conducts thorough due diligence and gets a good deal, he can start generating profit from the moment of purchase, as the enterprise already exists and is actively engaged in either production of goods or provision of services. It is hardly the case that a start-up enterprise will be able to make profit from the beginning. Some start-up enterprises take years to break even and/or to make profit.

Experience of the Previous Owner

In cases in which the enterprise has a long history of success, the new owner may be able to negotiate with the previous owner to stay on for a short time to introduce him to customers, suppliers and other strategic relationships that are crucial to the success of the enterprise. Depending on the nature of the purchase agreement, the previous owner could also be obliged to offer some managerial services and training for a period of time. Even if he does not stay on, it is often possible to at least tap into his wealth of knowledge in the form of an informal 'quasi-consultancy'. As a result, the acquirer does not have to learn the important start-up lessons the hard way. This was a key attraction for Stellar Group when they decided to acquire Nita Travel and Tours rather than start their own travel agency from scratch. They were attracted by the experience of the previous owner Nita Baptiste, and persuaded her to stay for a period of time as a non-executive director to transfer her learning and experience to Stellar, who had no experience of the travel industry in Ghana.[9]

Lower Risk

The acquirer of an existing enterprise has better information with which to evaluate its operations, its established market, existing reputation, customer base and other assets. The more information one has on any endeavour, the less risk there is. The acquiring entrepreneur who has obtained quality information from thorough due diligence on the enterprise is therefore generally considered to be taking less risk than would be the case if he was starting from scratch (where there are more uncertainties and less information on how the enterprise would turn out).

Easier to Find Finance

The relatively lower risk involved in purchasing an existing enterprise with a demonstrated track record makes it easier to find financing to fund such purchases. It is also easier to access loans for an already existing enterprise than for a start-up enterprise. Most Ghanaian banks struggle to understand and quantify the risks that are likely to follow with a start-up enterprise that has no track record and insignificant assets. Local banks want to see a track record of performance (demonstrated by financial statements) before making lending decisions. An entrepreneur who intends to raise funds for her enterprise will therefore find it easier buying an existing enterprise than starting a new one. In addition, it is generally easier to find money for other financing needs of the enterprise because (at least in the cases of successful enterprises) there is a stream of cash flow which will service the debt and the assets against which banks can lend. Apart from third-party financing, another option usually available to fund an acquisition of an existing enterprise is the seller. Many sellers help fund the acquisition of their enterprises to enable them obtain higher selling prices. They may defer part of the purchase price for a period or treat part or the entire purchase price as a loan due from the acquiring entrepreneur over a period of time.

Eliminate Competitor(s)

Sometimes, particularly in the case of larger enterprises, the decision to acquire may be influenced by a desire to consolidate the acquiring enterprise's position in the market by eliminating one or more competitors in the industry.

Eliminate Barriers to Entry

As we saw in Chapter 4, barriers to entry are potential hurdles that prevent entrepreneurs with good ideas from entering particular industries or markets. An entrepreneur, by buying an existing enterprise, rather than starting from scratch, may bypass such barriers. For example, if as a result of government policy, no more licences are being issued in a particular sector such as telecommunications or banking, an entrepreneur who buys an existing enterprise with a valid licence in place also 'buys' the licence, although in most cases the seller would have to obtain the consent of the relevant regulatory authority to transfer the licence. It is probably true to say that seeking consent for the transfer of an existing licence is normally easier to obtain than applying for a new licence.

Difficulties of Buying vs. Starting Own Enterprise

Despite the possible benefits, there are potential difficulties and disadvantages associated with buying an enterprise instead of starting from scratch. These include the following.

Legacy Issues

An acquired enterprise may have legacy problems such as disputes, debts, a bad reputation and poor management due to decisions made by the previous owner(s). An entrepreneur who acquires such an enterprise will therefore be inheriting these problems. This could have a potential impact on the future success of the enterprise, particularly if it is perceived negatively in the eyes of the consuming public. However, the new owner could turn things around by re-branding and repositioning the enterprise.

Culture/Employee Related Issues

This is another example of a legacy issue but one that deserves separate treatment. The employees that are 'inherited' with the purchase of the enterprise may not be the employees that the new owner may necessarily want to work with. They may have ways of doing things that may be inconsistent with what the new owner plans for the enterprise. The culture of the enterprise may be different from what the new owner wants. Although a change management programme can minimise the potential challenges that the cultural differences could bring, it is often difficult to implement such a change process, which can be met with serious opposition, as Vodafone found out in the retrenching exercise it undertook following its acquisition of 70% of the issued shares in Ghana Telecom. In some instances, the entrepreneur may be left with no option than to operate with the existing processes and systems.

Difficulty Finding an Enterprise That
Suits the Entrepreneur's Idea

The ideal situation for most entrepreneurs is to first come up with an idea and then to build an enterprise based on the idea to fit the aspirations of the entrepreneur. Many more compromises have to be made if the entrepreneur, after coming up with an idea, has to find an existing enterprise (conceived, developed and run by another entrepreneur) to implement his idea. Worse still, the acquiring entrepreneur may have difficulty finding the right enterprise to suit his original idea. This makes the establishment of a new venture the best option for such an entrepreneur. It is however possible for the entrepreneur to modify his original idea so as to adapt to what is available on the market.

Customer and Supplier Relationships May Not be Inherited

It should not be taken for granted that existing customers will continue to patronise the enterprise without the old owner. This is particularly true of smaller enterprises such as hairdressing salons and barbershops where the relationship with the customers is very personal. In addition, it should not be taken for granted that the new enterprise will inherit the current suppliers, or indeed the existing supply terms at that. Where there exists a special relationship with the customers and suppliers, and where that relationship is significant to the success of the enterprise, it may affect the future success of the enterprise if it cannot be easily passed on to the buyer.

Technology and/or Inventory May Be Obsolete

In acquiring an existing enterprise, particularly one that has been operating for a while, there is a risk that the technology, skill sets and/or inventory being acquired may have become obsolete. Given the rate and pace of technological change, it is important that acquirers hire the appropriate experts to value the technology, skills and/or inventory being acquired, and to advise on whether or not the value of each matches up to those recorded on the enterprise's balance sheet. In addition, they should assist in advising whether or not those assets are suitable for the acquiring entrepreneur's plans for the enterprise.

Special Talent by Owner

Berman argues that the success of some entrepreneurial ventures largely depends on the special talent and skills that the owner possesses.[10] Such special talents are particularly significant in professions like accountancy, law, medicine and art, where the entrepreneur is not just motivated by income but also by passion. In such situations, it is difficult for the new owner to succeed if she does not have that special passion-driven talent to drive the enterprise. Also related to this is the case where the owner has built a great personal relationships with customers and suppliers, who have then conducted business with the enterprise because of the owner.

Enterprise May Be Overpriced

There is always the risk that the seller may portray the enterprise as better than it is so as to get a good price for it. It is therefore possible to inherit an enterprise with many 'skeletons in the cupboard' that effectively take away from the selling price. It is important to carry out extensive due diligence before proceeding with the purchase. This problem is exacerbated because many small enterprises do not have audited accounts that reflect the true state of their enterprise. Although Ghanaian law requires companies to file audited accounts each year, the monitoring of this is so lax that many companies get away with not doing so. Those who do may file accounts that do not reflect the true state of the relevant enterprise. My researchers came across a number of auditors who also act as accountants to the company they audit and are happy to 'adapt' the company's accounts to suit the owner's purposes.

Valuation

Separate from the point about the risk that the enterprise might be over-priced is the issue of the difficulty with valuation, especially in the case of small- or medium-sized enterprises that may not have proper financial records and a strong management team. There is also the problem of asymmetric information, with the seller having most of the relevant information about the opportunities, threats and challenges of the enterprise. It is sometimes the case that most of the enterprise's value is so tied to the existing owner so that when she sells out and leaves, the enterprise loses value.

Lack of Choice

An entrepreneur may want to begin from scratch because buying an existing enterprise prevents him, for instance, from choosing employees, a banker, investors, location, suppliers, and equipment. An acquired enterprise comes with almost all of these and the entrepreneur, in the quest for continuity, may find it difficult to alter the existing relationships.

The Buying Stages

There are broadly seven stages, some of which overlap, to acquiring a company.

Decision

Although very obvious, the first step is to make the decision to proceed with the acquisition of an enterprise. For individuals not currently employed, this process first of all requires a clear understanding of the challenges and rewards of running your own enterprise, and of the traits that successful entrepreneurs possess (which we discussed in Chapter 2). The entrepreneur should be clear about his motives for going this route, and define and identify his objectives, skills, interests, abilities and passion to serve as guides in the search process.

Identification

An entrepreneur looking to buy an enterprise should develop an idea about what type of enterprise she is looking to buy and the kind of industry or industries that interest her. She should then conduct research to gather as much information as possible about the target industries and the business opportunities that are available.

The search process should take into consideration an analysis of the prospective buyer's attributes. Other criteria could be the product or service, the location of the enterprise and the available financing. Siropolis notes in particular that before buying, the prospective buyer needs to define the products that match her skills in order to determine whether she has what it takes to run the enterprise and to market its products and services.[11] Even at this stage in the buying process, the acquiring entrepreneur should have an idea of what resources she has or has access to, and a range of how much she is willing to pay for an enterprise. Being clear on this will enable her evaluate potential opportunities in the most objective light and assist in price negotiations.

The entrepreneur needs to develop a list of potential enterprises that are available for sale. There is no formal or developed market for the sale and acquisition of privately held companies or partnerships and, to my knowledge, there are no business brokers operating in Ghana. This poses both a challenge and an opportunity, the primary challenge being the difficulty of finding businesses for sale to choose from and how time-consuming the process can be because of the lack of easily accessible information – a corollary of an undeveloped market for enterprise sales. The prospective buyers will therefore typically have to keep an open eye for a period of time before they can identify an enterprise for sale that suits them. Notwithstanding this, as there are always sellers and potential sellers of businesses, the person who is able to leverage her social capital to identify the ideal target can maximise the available opportunities.

An entrepreneur may obtain information about potential acquisition targets from:

• *Professional Service Providers*

Professionals such as lawyers, accountants, investment bankers and consultants, typically learn of potential sales because they might be required by clients to advise them on these sales long in advance of the client taking the steps to sell. As close confidants of clients, clients may also share their plans with the advisors even without (or long before) instructing them.

• *Bankers*

Like the providers of professional services, bankers can also be a wealth of information on potential acquisition targets. In addition to the reason mentioned earlier for professional service providers, bankers would also have good information about companies in financial difficulty, those about to be liquidated, etc.

• *Venture Capitalists*

For every deal funded by a venture capital firm, there are several more turned down for any number of reasons although those deals might represent good opportunities. The Venture Capital Trust Fund, venture capital financing companies including Activity Venture Finance Company, Bedrock Venture Capital and venture capital providers such as Fidelity Capital Partners, Oasis Capital and Injaro Investments could provide some good leads.

• The Courts and the Registrar-General's Department

People seeking to acquire businesses are advised to develop a good relationship with court bailiffs and officers of the Registrar General's Department who can advise them of enterprises whose assets may be subject to insolvency or liquidation proceedings. Also, the courts have information about deceased individuals whose estates might include enterprises worth considering.

• Industry Executives

Where an entrepreneur is clear about the industry or industries he would like to consider, industry executives who have a good knowledge of the different enterprises operating in that industry may be able to provide good leads on potential acquisition targets.

• Newspaper Adverts

Sometimes, prospective sellers of businesses and liquidators advertise the sale of enterprises or their assets in national newspapers such as the Daily Graphic and the Business and Financial Times. However, given the wide circulation of newspapers, once the enterprise is advertised, the entrepreneur is bound to be competing with a much larger pool of interested parties. Ideally, entrepreneurs should seek to be in a situation where, because of their contacts, they hear about the information early enough to do a deal before it gets into the newspapers in the first place.

• Divestiture Implementation Committee (DIC)

DIC implements and executes all government policies relating to the divestiture of state-owned enterprises (SOEs). The DIC thus plans, monitors, coordinates and evaluate all divestitures; it develops criteria for the selection of enterprises to be divested and assumes responsibility for preparing such enterprises for divestiture, as well as ensuring consistency with regard to valuation, invitation for bids, negotiation of sales and settlement of accounts.[12] Although it is increasingly less significant, it still maintains the 'divestiture list', which holds information about enterprises that the government is trying to sell.

• Regulatory Bodies

Officials of regulatory bodies such as Ghana Investment Promotion Council, the National Insurance Commission and the National Communications Authority may also be able to provide information about enterprises that are (potentially) for sale.

• Trade Organisations

Bodies such as the Association of Ghana Industries, Ghana National Chamber of Commerce and Industry and National Board for Small Scale Industry may provide leads on enterprises that are on the market.

• Personal Contacts

An entrepreneur seeking to acquire an enterprise should inform his friends, family, professional colleagues, among others, giving them as much information about what type(s) of enterprises would be a good fit. This has proved to be a good way for people to find good acquisition leads.

• Observation and Listening

The entrepreneur should also bear in mind that it is possible to approach existing enterprise owners who may not necessarily have thought of selling their enterprises, but may be willing to sell if the price is right. Every man, after all, does have his price. So by simply observing various entrepreneurs or enterprises at work, the entrepreneur may be able to acquire an asset that was not originally for sale. For example, assume that you have been cutting your hair at the same barbershop for twenty years. Your barber is getting old and would like to retire. None of his five sons are interested in the business so the barber is thinking of closing the shop and moving to his village to enjoy retirement. You love the shop which has become part of your personal history. You have a bit of cash to invest and would like to start your own business. In such a situation, it is unlikely that your barber will not sell you the business at a fair price – especially if you offer him a non-executive board position!

Screening

After identifying and listing the entrepreneurial opportunities available, the prospective buyer needs to screen the opportunities. In order to make the process less cumbersome the entrepreneur needs detailed criteria. The criteria should revolve around the dream or idea of the entrepreneur or prospective buyer, as well as his strengths and weaknesses. He will also have to consider his preference for industry, keeping in mind his attitude to risk, the stability of the enterprise and profit projections Though it is critical for the entrepreneur to go through the screening process keeping in mind the criteria, according to Hosmer et al.,[13] it is sometimes necessary for the entrepreneur to be flexible.

Evaluation

Having screened the available opportunities, the entrepreneur will normally identify a couple of enterprises that meet his criteria. The next stage is for the entrepreneur to list all the factors that will be significant in making the purchasing decision. These include the quoted price of the enterprise, the reputation of the enterprise, the capacity of the enterprise to generate revenue, the profitability of the enterprise, the competitive environment in which the enterprise operates, the quality of its products or services, and the quality of the organisation in relation to its operational capacity and human capital. The entrepreneur will also have to evaluate the financial position of the target enterprise using audited financial statements. In doing this, the entrepreneur needs maintain a healthy scepticism about the information he is given; it is better to double-check everything from independent sources (where possible) and to seek independent advice.

In evaluating an enterprise, the entrepreneur needs to understand the seller's motives: why someone would sell an enterprise that is doing well. The seller may decide to sell an enterprise for personal reasons, such as a decision to retire, or as a result of challenges with managerial succession whereby the owner may not be happy with the likely successor, in which case she may want to sell the enterprise. However, there are instances where the seller may hide the true motive of selling the enterprise. A technological breakthrough by a competitor may result in new product development which is affecting the market share of the seller's enterprise, for example. This could adversely impact on the future financial performance of the enterprise. At the evaluation stage, the buyer may start the due diligence process although the full scale of it will depend on whether or not he has made his intention known to the seller at that stage. If he has not made his intentions known, he will not have the benefit of the seller's own information and access to management, and would thus be relying mainly on publicly available information and (possibly) the research he may commission. If and when he is ready to proceed, he will need to make his intentions known to the seller and undertake a final investigative process called due diligence. We will return to due diligence later.

Valuation

The prospective buyer needs to determine the true worth of the enterprise she is considering purchasing. At this stage, the buyer may be trying to determine on her own what the value of the enterprise is without engaging the seller because she may not necessarily have made her intention known to the seller. Different methods can be employed in the valuing process (we discuss these later in the chapter). I should point out though that valuation is more of an art than a science, incorporating many factors and assumptions that affect the final value placed on an enterprise. It is also possible that for the entrepreneur, the real value of the enterprise could depend on the future earning stream or the income that the enterprise will generate under her leadership because of the particular value that she hopes to bring. The acquiring entrepreneur should think through these issues and discuss them with her advisors.

Negotiation

After conducting an independent valuation to determine the worth of the enterprise, the buyer needs to declare an intention to buy the enterprise by offering or asking for a price. At this stage, there is a great deal of negotiation between the seller and the buyer. Formal due diligence may kick in prior to or around the initial negotiations. Typically, the buyer and the seller enter into a non-disclosure or confidentiality agreement whereby the parties agree that any information given by one party to another in connection with the potential acquisition shall not be disclosed to anyone other than advisors or others as required by law, except with the consent of all parties. The idea is to give both parties (particularly the seller) confidence to disclose information to enable a thorough evaluation of the opportunity and make the decision as to whether to proceed and at what price.

Sometimes the parties may also agree to exclusivity as follows: they agree that until they reach a firm agreement and enter into legally binding contracts, or for a certain fixed period, neither party shall deal with a third party in relation to the subject matter of the agreement (which is the enterprise to be transferred by the sale). The idea is to prevent the buyer from attempting to engage with other potential buyers at the same time as he is negotiating with the seller, and also to prevent the seller from entertaining discussions with other potential buyers while in negotiations with the current buyer.

When negotiating price, the buyer must consider both financial and non-financial factors including motivations that inform the seller's decision to sell. For example, a seller interested in finding a buyer to maintain the reputation of the enterprise, continue with his vision and treat employees well would be more interested in finding the right buyer for his enterprise than in the price alone. It is therefore important that the buyer has as much information as he can about the seller and his motivations, in addition to information about the enterprise.

The buyer must also have a sense of the realistic worth of the enterprise for the seller. This would enable the buyer to anticipate the seller's response and be able to develop effective countermeasures to the seller's demands. The buyer may make a comparison between investing the purchase price in the enterprise and investing it in alternate investments. We acknowledge though that sometimes buyers and sellers are motivated by emotional reasons that may not be backed by financial data. The buyer would almost certainly require the services of experienced corporate financiers, lawyers, auditors and tax advisors in the negotiation process; I strongly advise that these are engaged as soon as possible.

Once the parties are fairly certain that they would like to proceed in the transaction with each other, they will (with the assistance of their respective lawyers) enter into a heads of terms (also sometimes referred to as term sheet or letter of intent) which will set out the broad terms that they hope will form the basis of their agreement. This document is usually not intended to be legally binding (except in respect of specific clauses in it relating to confidentiality and dispute resolution). This is merely an agreement to agree, and will be followed by detailed negotiations on each of the areas covered in the agreement, culminating in a definitive sale and purchase agreement.

Contract

The term sheet will form the basis of the definitive sale and purchase agreement whereby the seller agrees to sell and the buyer agrees to acquire the enterprise or its assets as the case may be. Unlike the heads of terms, the sale and purchase agreement, once signed, is legally binding on the parties. However, depending on the type of asset, the sale and purchase agreement will not transfer ownership to the buyer. In the sale of shares of a private company, for example, the parties will need to enter into a separate share transfer agreement which will effect the transfer of shares. Advice must be sought from a competent solicitor to ensure that the right assets are properly transferred.

Typically, there would be a prolonged negotiation of the sale and purchase agreement, simultaneous with the due diligence being carried out by the purchaser.

The following are some of the main provisions of the sale and purchase agreement:

• *Date of the Sale and Purchase*

This is important in determining when rights and liabilities in respect of the enterprise pass on to the buyer. In some instances, the parties may sign the agreement on a particular date but provide for an 'effective date,' which is a later date that the enterprise passes over to the buyer.

• *Parties*

The buyer and the seller are the main parties. However, it is often the case in the sale of companies that the target company is also party to the contract to ensure that the company and its officers are bound by the terms of the agreement. Also, in some instances, there might be other parties such as a guarantor (of promissory notes for deferred consideration, for example) or other companies related to either buyer or seller.

• *Price and Payment Terms*

This is likely to involve long negotiations as both parties would be participating from their respective points of view and with supporting valuations and assumptions. Even after a price has been agreed, the parties must agree how and when it must be paid. The most common options are:

- Cash: The buyer uses his cash reserve or borrows using the balance sheet of the enterprise or his own balance sheet. In addition to paying the agreed price of the enterprise, the buyer and seller will have to pay the costs of closing the transaction. These costs are miscellaneous fees charged by professionals like lawyers and investment bankers who provide technical services in the negotiation and drafting of the contract.

- Deferred Cash Payments: The buyer may negotiate with the seller to defer part of the cost until a later date based on certain agreed terms. Sometimes this takes the form on an 'earn out' where the deferred payments are contingent upon achieving pre-defined financial or operating objectives after the deal is completed. For example, the total payment amount may be tied to the profit figures in the next set of audited accounts with part of the payment deferred. The parties will need to agree on the criteria on which the calculation of earn out should be based and what the period of the earn out will be. An earn out may be unattractive from the point of view of the seller who upon selling has no control of the enterprise.

- Shares: The buyer (if a company) can offer its shares as part of a share swap designed to finance the purchasing cost borne by the buyer.

- Promissory Notes: Where the seller agrees to take part payment for the sale of the enterprise, he may demand a promissory note from the buyer. A promissory note is a written, dated and signed instrument by the buyer and the seller which contains an unconditional promise by the buyer to pay a particular amount at a specified date or a date that the seller demands. The seller may require the promissory note to be guaranteed by a third party so that in case the buyer fails to pay the required amount, the guarantor will be held liable or the promissory notes may be unsecured by a third party.

• *Composition of the Board Following Completion*

Where the buyer is acquiring less than 100% of a company, he will have to ensure that he is adequately represented at the board level. Where the buyer is acquiring the entire issued shares but wants to ensure the continued involvement of the seller, the sale and purchase agreement may provide for this.

• *Transfer*

If the sale and purchase agreement is not able to legally transfer assets (.e.g. real estate and shares), the agreement will have provisions or mechanisms for the formal transfer of ownership from seller to buyer.

• *Conditions Precedent*

The conditions precedent will list the events and conditions which must occur before the sale can occur. For example, if certain authorisations and consents are required, the seller may contract to obtain them as conditions precedent. If he is unable to do so within a specific period of time, the buyer may decide not to proceed with the acquisition.

• *Warranties and Indemnities*

The principle of *caveat emptor* (buyer beware) applies to acquisitions. The law provides no protection for the buyer as to the nature of the assets and the liabilities he is acquiring. This risk is magnified in the case of a share sale because, as we explained earlier, the buyer acquires the business, with all its assets and liabilities, even if unknown or non-existent at the time of the purchase. A buyer would protect himself with warranties and indemnities in the sale and purchase agreement. Warranties are contractual statements in the acquisition agreement which take the form of assurances from the seller to the buyer as to the condition of various aspects of the target company and, in particular, in respect of any liabilities. For example, the buyer may require the seller to warrant that the company has not breached any environmental laws or regulations. In the event that this turns out to be false, the buyer (as new owner of enterprise) has a remedy against the seller for breach of warranty. However, to succeed in a breach of warranty action, the buyer would need to show not only that there was a breach of warranty on the part of the seller but that the breach resulted in quantifiable loss for the buyer.

Where there are specific risks of concern to the buyer, he may seek indemnities (instead of warranties) from the seller in respect of these risks. For example, in the example above, instead of a general warranty that the company is not in breach of any environmental laws and regulations, the buyer could seek an indemnity where he was aware of unresolved litigation involving the Environmental Protection Agency. The indemnity is a promise to reimburse the buyer in respect of a particular liability, should it arise. Unlike a warranty, an indemnity provides a guaranteed remedy (on a cedi-for-cedi basis) for the buyer. Once the litigation results in the company having to make payment to the Environmental Protection Agency, the buyer can claim back the entire amount of the payment together with incidental costs (relating to environmental clean-up or professional fees).

Warranties and indemnities work together with the due diligence process. Based on the information uncovered during the due diligence process, the buyer may decide whether to seek warranties or indemnities in respect of potential risks. However, where the risks have been disclosed, (typically through a disclosure letter by the seller), the disclosure letter operates to limit or modify the relevant warranty or indemnity. It is also typical to limit warranties and indemnities by specifying a financial maximum and a maximum time period. If that is not done, the seller might be on the hook indefinitely for a company that he is no longer involved in. My research identified a major Ghanaian company which remained on the hook for demands from a buyer making successive claims in respect of warranties and indemnities regarding the sale of one of its subsidiaries, many years after the company had been sold and the seller had no say or involvement in its operations.

• *Escrow arrangements*

In some cases an escrow arrangement will be entered into where an independent trusted third party, such as a law firm or a broker, is chosen to disburse money and transfer legal documents between the parties once certain conditions are met.

In negotiating the sale and purchase agreement, consideration will also have to be given to a number of related legal agreements or issues. These might include:

- Shareholders' agreement (which we will discuss in chapter 6), and financing agreement documents such as loan and security documentation;

- Subordination agreements, where the seller or third parties with rights against the company agree that those rights should be subordinated to the rights of the buyer;

- Non-compete agreements, in which the seller agrees not to

compete with the buyer for a certain period of time and/or in a particular location;

- Employment agreements, consultancy agreements or director service contracts, where the parties agree that the seller shall stay on, in what capacity he stays on and on what terms. Similar contracts may need to be entered into with other team members.

Post-Completion

Once the company has been acquired, the buyer should meet employees as soon as possible to motivate and encourage them to stay and help achieve the vision of the new owner. Where the buyer intends to make staff redundant, he will need to have those difficult conversations while at the same time keeping morale up. The buyer would also need to communicate the change with customers, suppliers and other stakeholders. There might also be other legal and regulatory post-completion steps (such as notifying the Registrar of Companies of the change of shareholders) that the buyer may need to take.

Due Diligence on the Acquisition of an Enterprise

Due diligence in the context of purchasing an enterprise is the process of researching and investigating an enterprise to determine the suitability or otherwise of the enterprise, given the objectives of the entrepreneur. Due diligence is, effectively, the organised 'common sense' aggregation that every entrepreneur or would-be entrepreneur ought to undertake to find out important information about the enterprise he intends to buy. This is particularly significant as it allows the prospective buyer to decide whether or not to pursue the opportunities offered by the proposed acquisition by identifying the risks inherent in the acquisition. Sometimes the nature of the risk identified by the due diligence process is not a 'deal breaker', but will require the buyer to put certain steps in place to mitigate the risk.

The objective is to use factual data to make the evaluation. However, where the plan is to keep the existing management, there is a subjective layer of assessment added to due diligence to determine whether the management team can take the enterprise to the level proposed by the prospective purchaser. The acquiring entrepreneur would normally have ideas, goals and aspirations that drive him towards the enterprise and so the due diligence process should be able to determine whether the management team will be prepared to share in the dreams of the prospective buyer.

In carrying out due diligence, one may not be able to ascertain all information. In most cases the breadth and depth of the information required will depend on the purchaser's plans for the enterprise. For example, if the purchaser intends to bring his own management team to run the company after purchase, he will focus more on investigating the industry and its prospects (using, for example, Porter's Five Forces framework discussed in Chapter 4). However, if he intends to keep the management team, the prospective purchaser will focus more on the skills, track record and competency of the existing management.

I stated earlier that an acquisition of shares is an acquisition of the company's history. However, it is also true that such an acquisition is the acquisition of the enterprise's future. It is important to bear this in mind when conducting due diligence so as not to be clouded only by the past. The entrepreneur who is mindful that he is also acquiring the company's future will put the opportunity presented by the acquisition and the revelations of the due diligence exercise in a broader context, taking into account the general prospects for the economy and market trends, as well as his own strengths, weaknesses and objectives. As a result of this, two entrepreneurs would evaluate and react differently to the same due diligence findings.

According to Blayney,[14] due diligence should focus on the three broad areas of legal, financial and commercial issues. The diagram below shows the key areas that need to be covered as part of the due diligence process. Legal due diligence involves undertaking the basic information about an enterprise and the legal status of its relationships with both internal and external parties. It also confirms ownership of all key assets, checks for past, current or potential suits, as well as examines all contractual obligations and liabilities. The significance of legal due diligence is that the buyer will be able to determine whether the operations of the enterprise are in compliance with the legal framework of the country, and also that the enterprise and seller have legal claims to all the rights that they purport to have.

Figure 5.1: Areas Of Focus For Due Diligence

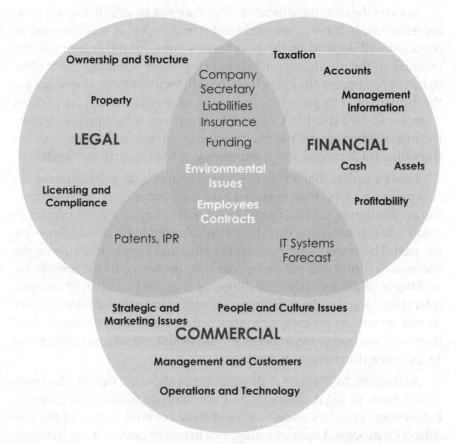

Ownership and Structure

Taxation

Accounts

Property

Company
Secretary
Liabilities
Insurance

Management
information

LEGAL

Funding

FINANCIAL

Environmental
Issues

Cash   Assets

Licensing and
Compliance

Employees
Contracts

Profitability

Patents, IPR

IT Systems
Forecast

Strategic and
Marketing Issues

People and Culture Issues

COMMERCIAL

Management and Customers

Operations and Technology

Source: Blayney 2003

Financial due diligence is used to ensure that the historical financial statements presented by the seller reflect the true position of the enterprise. It involves a rigorous process of checking management information to determine the financial standing and worth of the enterprise. It also provides the basis for the buyer to reasonably make projections of the future of the enterprise.

Commercial due diligence embodies an examination of the strategic view and the competitive position of the enterprise in the industry. Commercial due diligence allows the buyer to know how the enterprise is performing in the market – its strengths, weakness and the opportunities that exist in the sector or industry. It encompasses issues relating to the company's employees and culture as well as its suppliers and customers. Again, the tools discussed in Chapter 4 would be of invaluable help here.

Due Diligence Guidelines

Ask, Ask, Ask

Ask as many questions as you can about the enterprise, the existing owner or seller, the management and other stakeholders whose activities influence the operations of the enterprise. It is advisable to find out more about the enterprise from the outside before the prospective buyer investigates the enterprise from the inside. This allows for an objective assessment of the enterprise.

When You Hear an Answer, Make Sure You Also See the Answer

This means don't just rely on the seller or management to feed you with fanciful answers. You must double-check all answers that you are given by the seller and his management. For instance, if they tell you they have three warehouses in Kumasi, you must go and visit these warehouses to ensure they are in fact warehouses and not simply sheds in Kumasi.

Use the Colombo Method

According to Derek Collins,[15] the Colombo method (named after the persistent television detective Colombo) involves inquiring politely but persistently. It also involves asking the seller key questions multiple times in a variety of ways, all the while looking for consistency in answers.

When Co-Investing, Do Your Own Due Diligence

Don't rely only on the due diligence carried out by co-investors. It is better for each co-investor to undertake a separate due diligence to enable the group compare and contrast the facts they are presented with.

Painstakingly Review Information About
All Aspects of the Company

The point of due diligence is to help you make an informed decision about whether or not to proceed with making the purchasing decision you are contemplating. As a result, you should ensure that you find out as much as you can about the target company. Review the financial information you have, particularly the financial statements, and carry out a financial ratio analysis (see Chapter 8). A review of key documentation such as contracts and research and development information, among others, will complement the financial analysis to enable the making of informed decisions. Ask questions about products or services and find out about the key drivers of the enterprise. It will also be beneficial to speak to key customers and suppliers of the enterprise.

Valuation of an Enterprise

Valuation is the process of measuring the worth of an enterprise. It involves determining the price at which an enterprise can be sold or bought. Determining the value of an enterprise is often a complicated exercise because of the various factors that have to be taken into consideration. It is important to examine in detail, among others, the nature and type of the enterprise, its financial position, its market share, the performance of the enterprise in relation to competitors, the future earning potential of the enterprise, tangible and intangible assets as well as the seller's motives for selling the enterprise.

There are various methods that prospective buyers can use to value the worth of an enterprise. Scarborough and Zimmerer[16] outline certain guidelines that could help in the valuation process:

- The best approach to valuation is to use several methods and to choose the one that makes sense;
- The price must be satisfactory to both parties so that the seller will feel happy about the value he is receiving while the buyer should not be paying an overvalued price;
- All the records of the enterprise should be easily available to the seller and buyer;
- The value of the enterprise should be determined using facts and not imagination;
- The dealing process should be done honestly and in good faith.

In valuing an enterprise, it is worth noting that every enterprise has unique characteristics and should be treated as such. The basic techniques used in valuing an enterprise are examined below.

Balance Sheet Method

The balance sheet method of valuing an enterprise uses the book value (the value at which an asset was originally bought) of the enterprise to determine its net worth. The method determines the value of an enterprise by deducting the total liabilities from the total assets of the enterprise. The difference between the total assets and the total liabilities gives the value of the enterprise. The first part of valuing an enterprise using this method is to identify all the assets that would be sold as part of the transaction. It is important because there are cases where the seller may not want to sell some personal assets or other assets of the enterprise. Measuring the value of tangible assets such as land, buildings and equipment is often not as difficult as measuring the values of intangible assets like goodwill and patents. For the seller, these intangible assets arise out of years of commitment in developing the enterprise but, for the buyer, the importance of these intangible assets is how they can help him generate future income; if they cannot do so, those assets are worthless.

Adjusted Balance Sheet Method

The major problem with the balance sheet method of valuation is its inability to reflect the true worth of an enterprise at any given point in time because book values differ significantly from market values. Book values could either be understated or overstated; they thus do not reflect the true value of the enterprise. This limitation is corrected through the adjusted balance sheet method. This method uses the market value of the assets instead of the book values in the valuation process. For instance, if the assets of an enterprise include vehicles, land and buildings, then the market values of these assets will be used to value the enterprise and not the original amount for which these assets were bought.

In order to ensure that there is fair value, the buyer needs to check the condition of the assets before a value is placed on them. It is advisable for the buyer or his representative to see all the assets physically to determine their true state. The depreciation charge for fixed assets like vehicles should always be deducted from the original value to arrive at the true market value. The major limitation of valuing an enterprise using the balance sheet method or the adjusted balance sheet method is that the approach does not take in to consideration the future earning potential of the enterprise, unlike the other methods discussed below.

Earnings Method

When an entrepreneur decides to buy an existing enterprise instead of starting from scratch, the key consideration will be how he can increase the future earning potential of the enterprise. The earnings approach to business valuation takes into account the future earning potential of the enterprise. This can be done by preparing a budgeted income statement for the enterprise to determine its future income potential. It is prudent that the buyer prepares his own income statement, and then asks the seller to also prepare another one for comparative purposes in order to arrive at a true picture on the earnings potential of the enterprise. A five-year income statement is often preferred as it gives a good planning horizon for proper future earnings estimation. It is also essential to factor in likely future risks to the enterprise's progress against its future rate of return as part of this valuation process.

Market Multiple Method

This method of valuation uses the price/earnings (P/E) ratio to determine the value of an enterprise. The P/E ratio is the market price of a share divided by earnings per share (the dividends). If the acquiring enterprise is listed on a stock exchange, then the buyer can value the enterprise by first computing P/E and then multiplying it by the earnings. If the acquiring enterprise is not listed on the stock exchange, as the case may be with most entrepreneurial ventures in Ghana, then the prospective buyer can value the enterprise by examining the P/E ratios of similar enterprises listed on the Ghana Stock Exchange and taking their average P/E ratios. The buyer can then multiply this average ratio by the estimated net income of the target enterprise to get the value. Though this method is good in terms of determining the future earning potential of an enterprise, it does not give a true picture when one uses other enterprises as proxies in the valuation process.

Discounted Cash Flow Method

The discounted cash flow (DCF) method is considered the most theoretically sound method of valuing financial assets. It determines the value of an enterprise in relation to the future cash stream that the enterprise will be generating. It tries to work out what the total cash flows of the enterprise will be (until perpetuity), and then adjusts the future cash flow to reflect the fact that the value that might have been received over a future period of time is being received at present. The cash flows are discounted using a 'risk free' interest rate (such as the rate of return on investing in government securities).

While the earnings, market and discounted cash flow methods of valuation have a common advantage of helping the buyer to determine the future earnings potential of an enterprise, the seller or his representative should be careful which figures are being used as the bases of valuation. For instance, profit could mean any number of things including EBITDA (earnings before interest, tax, depreciation and amortisation); or EBIT (earnings before interest and tax), which is the operating income.

There are other factors that could affect a valuation of an enterprise, including the following.

• Growth
The buyer should analyse the growth trends in the enterprise and the industry in which the enterprise operates.

• Industry Attractiveness
How attractive an industry depends on the value of enterprises in that industry. This in turn is affected by such factors as the level of rivalry, threats and opportunities as we saw in Chapter 4.

• Bankability
This essentially asks how easy it is to bank (raise financing for) the enterprise. This will depend on the composition of the assets of the enterprise, their seasonality, portability, age, etc.

• Cash Flow
A proper cash flow analysis should unveil the cash flow trends of the company. A positive net cash flow gives an indication of not

just the earnings potential of the enterprise, but also the general liquidity position it is in.

• *Deal structure*

This provides the terms and conditions under which the enterprise will be bought. This generally includes the terms of payment, financing terms, and whether the transaction is going to be structured as an asset or stock sale. A seller may be prepared to sell an enterprise for a price lower than its valuation if she is being paid upfront in full.

• *Assumptions*

The parties should also agree on the basic assumptions that govern the generation of the enterprise's value so that they will be on level terms. The same valuation technique and numbers will yield different values based on the assumptions used.

• *Market Share*

The market share of the enterprise should also be considered alongside competitors in the market. The buyer should be careful when buying an enterprise with a high market share as its growth prospects might be limited. There might be more value in a company with a small market share but in a growing industry.

• *Quality of Earnings*

While examining the earning potential of the enterprise, the buyer should also look at the cost of generating income, and that the earnings are not artificial profits created by accounting anomalies or due to one-off gains.

• *Organisation and Management*

The processes and systems of operation, the culture of the organisation and the management style should be taken into account, as these could significantly affect the valuation.

• *Environmental Issues*

Particular care should be taken if the operations of the enterprise have significant impact on the environment; this is most relevant to industries capable of extensive environmental degradation, like oil and gas and mining.

Franchising

Franchising is a form of licensing by which the owner (the franchisor) of a product, service or business method obtains distribution through affiliated dealers (the franchisees). In return for the franchisor's support in starting the enterprise, the franchisee pays the franchisor an initial fee, and will usually pay an annual royalty based on gross revenues for the franchisor's continued support and the use of brands, trademarks or business formats. Examples of franchises in Ghana are KFC (Kentucky Fried Chicken), Western Union and Uniglobe Travel. Oil marketing companies have also been franchising their fuel service stations for many years. A franchise typically involves investing in a proven business model. People often go for a franchise because they do not want to take all the risks of entrepreneurship but want to benefit from the resources of the franchising organisation. This may take the form of sharing research and development, branding and other corporate support.

Advantages of Franchises for the Franchisor

• Fast Growth

Franchising can enable a business grow fairly rapidly (especially in new markets) even where there are limited resources and infrastructure. By identifying franchisees who are willing to put some of their own resources into growing and developing the business in their markets, franchisors can quickly establish a significant presence that might otherwise not have been possible.

• Economies of Scale

The rapid growth potential that franchising offers gives the franchisor an opportunity to spread costs of marketing, supply and purchasing over a wider volume base, enabling the franchisor to achieve lower cost of sales and greater profits per unit.

• *Cash Flow*

Franchising gives the franchisor a constant cash flow in terms of regular fees from the franchisees. In addition to the annual royalty based on gross revenues that the franchisees pay the franchisor, the franchisor also makes money from the franchisees by charging the franchisees to provide certain additional services including training, setup consulting, marketing and advertising. In some instances, the franchisor will acquire the relevant property and then rent it on to the franchisee, typically at a margin.

• *Motivation & Market Knowledge:*

Franchising enables the franchisor to tap into a pool of highly motivated individuals. Because they tend to have their own capital invested, franchisees are far more motivated than employees would be. Also, (especially in the case of expanding into markets not local to the franchisor), franchises provide an opportunity to tap into a wealth of local knowledge through franchisees conversant with that market.

• *Does Not Dilute Ownership*

Franchisors do not give up a stake of their equity to franchisees. Franchisees simply pay to replicate their proven business in particular markets. The ownership of the franchisor therefore remains undiluted.

Disadvantages of Franchises for the Franchisor

• *Loss of Control Over Operation*

Typically, the franchisor may try to use a legal framework to assert control over as much of the operations of the franchisee as possible so as to ensure that there is consistency in quality and appearance in its franchises. In reality though, the day-to-day operations of the franchise lie within the domain of the franchisee and not the franchisor. In the case of a large franchise, it may be difficult to completely police every franchisee to ensure that he is conforming to the franchisor's norms.

• Loss of Contact With Customers

The customers of a particular franchise are in fact the immediate customers of the franchisee rather than the franchisor. The franchisor therefore may not get as much contact with the customers as he would if the enterprise was directly owned.

• Free Riding

There is a risk of free riding. While a number of franchisees work hard to keep the quality and service standards and contribute regularly to advertising and building the brand, a few 'bad apple' franchisees regularly fail to meet the minimum quality and service levels required, and fail to contribute to advertising and brand building. However, these bad apples still benefit from the efforts of the former group who are persistent in meeting quality standards.

• Sharing Income Stream

Rather than earn all the income that comes with expansion and increased customer volumes, franchisors share this income with the franchisees; it is the pay-off for sharing the capital and manpower risks of expansion and attracting new custom with the franchisees.

Advantages of Franchises for the Franchisee

• Safety Net

Franchises provide a safety net to a would-be entrepreneur because they are based on proven business models. Consequently, the risk of failure is lower.

• Support in Terms of Training and R&D

In return for paying an annual royalty to the franchisor, the franchisee benefits from the wealth of the franchisor's experience, particularly in the area of training and research and development, as the franchisor takes on the responsibility of training both the franchisee and his staff. This has the advantage of giving a start-up franchise the same depth of expertise as an already existing company.

• *Economies of Scale*

On her own, the franchisee has limited bargaining power and therefore is unable to command lower prices for the goods and services contracted for, but the franchise concept enables her to benefit from economies of scale as the various inputs are purchased centrally through the franchisor, and then passed on to the various franchisees.

Disadvantages of Franchises for the Franchisee

• *Lack of Control*

As discussed earlier, one reason why many people decide to go into business on their own is because of the control and freedom that it gives them. In the case of franchises though, such control is limited as franchisees are always be contractually obliged to run their enterprises according to the blueprint set by the franchisor, so that, to an outsider, it is not obvious that different outlets are owned by different people. The franchisee would therefore have to choose particular types of location, hire certain types of people and market in ways consistent with the franchisor's business model.

• *Quasi-Employment*

This point is related to lack of control as explained above. Because the franchisee has to conform in many respects to the franchisor's own predetermined notions of how the enterprise is to be run, he typically has certain projections to meet in terms of revenue and income. In this way, a franchisee's position is similar to that of an employee.

• *Can Be Expensive in the Long Run*

The franchising concept enables someone to tap into an expanding business venture with far less capital than might be the case if he was starting from scratch. However, in the long run, this could become a more expensive way of doing business because the franchisor requires the franchisee to purchase most of his inputs from the franchisor at prices that may not be the most favourable for the franchisee.

• *Limit on Exit Strategy*

When the franchisee decides to exit the enterprise, he may not be free to determine who to sell it to, or indeed who he may pass the enterprise on to as an inheritance. The franchise agreement would typically limit the options of who he can pass on the enterprise to.

Working with Professionals

The vast majority of entrepreneurs who buy or sell an enterprise might only do so once in their lifetime. As a result, they will not have any prior experience of the sale or purchase process as the case may be. Notwithstanding this, I was surprised to learn from my research team that many Ghanaian entrepreneurs have acquired or sold businesses without seeking any or the full range of professional advice. In the latter case, they have usually cherry-picked from the advisors that they should have hired instead of hiring all the necessary advisors. In particular, I noticed an aversion towards hiring lawyers or lawyers with specific experience in mergers and acquisitions. In the former case, my sense is that this may be because, at least in the case of literate and educated entrepreneurs, they feel they are able to read the necessary legal documents or even create their own based on templates they find online or from elsewhere, because these documents are written in English, a language they can understand and read.

However, words, clauses and sentences used in a legal document may have a different meaning from their normal English meaning.

Without making a pitch for mergers and acquisitions lawyers, my view is that this is extremely risky.

As early as possible in the acquisition process, buyers should choose the best advisors that they can afford. Depending on the nature of the enterprise to be acquired and the complexity and value of the business, they might require different advisors at different stages. The most common advisors will be market researchers, accountants, tax advisors, financial advisors, human capital specialists, lawyers, environmental specialists, consulting engineers, architects and surveyors.

The entrepreneur should meet and agree on an engagement letter with each professional services company, covering the scope of the work to be done and other terms such as fees, timelines and staffing levels. It is important that the right lawyers with the relevant track record in advising on mergers and acquisitions, as well as other professional advisors, be engaged.

Questions for Class Discussion

1. Why might an entrepreneur decide to acquire an enterprise instead of start one from scratch?

2. 'When you buy shares you buy history' – Haigh. Discuss this statement.

3. What are some of the difficulties of acquiring an existing enterprise?

4. What are some of the key provisions you would expect to see in a contract for the sale and purchase of an existing enterprise?

5. Discuss the main valuation methods that are likely to be used by an entrepreneur selling his enterprise.

6. What type of due diligence will an entrepreneur considering the acquisition of an enterprise have to undertake?

7. What is franchising? What are the key advantages of acquiring a franchise?

Case Study: Multimedia Group's Acquisition and Rebranding of Groove FM to Adom FM

FOR KWASI TWUM, THE FOUNDER and Chief Executive Officer of Ghana's premier independent broadcasting group, Multimedia Group Ltd, the decision to acquire Groove FM in 2000 was not a mere desire to add another enterprise to his existing portfolio. Instead, it was an urgent necessity, a response to an emerging competitor that posed a threat to his market dominance of Ghana's private radio broadcasting industry.

Prior to the acquisition, he had started Joy FM in 1995 as the only private radio station in Ghana. The launch of Peace FM, a Twi-speaking private radio station, in 1999, began to affect the English-speaking Joy FM's market dominance, changing the dynamics of competition in the radio business. As Twi is widely spoken in Ghana, especially in the south, it became clear that programming in Twi had the potential of reaching a much larger audience than Joy FM's.

The launch and instant success of Peace FM was a "big bang" for the Multimedia Group, according to Mrs Jane Ohenewa Gyekye, the Chief HR Business Partner for the Group.[17] While they had previously heard that someone was going to launch a radio station in Akan, they did not expect it to succeed. Peace FM surprised them; it had adequately understood the needs of the customer of its Twi language programmes and had positioned itself to target them in mass markets.

In order to safeguard his business, Kwasi Twum had to respond and the response had to be quick. The need to rapidly diversify his service offering, triggered the decision to acquire Groove FM. With the experience of starting Joy FM from scratch, Kwasi and his team knew the difficulties they would have to go through if they were to start from scratch as opposed to acquiring an existing radio station. For instance, getting a frequency from the National Communications Authority (NCA) at the time would have taken them more than a year. Also, buying communication equipment and shipping to Ghana could have taken at least 6 months. They did not have the luxury of time as Peace FM was rapidly growing its listener base, particularly since it is difficult to steer people from radio stations once they get attached. Buying Groove FM was the best – probably the only – option.

Groove FM at the time was a music-focused radio station that was located in Accra and owned by two childhood friends, Lee Hesse and Edwin Sunkwa-Mills. After the acquisition, Joy FM rebranded it to Adom FM and changed the format from music to general entertainment, talk shows and news. In direct response to the competitor, they also changed the broadcast language to Twi to meet the mass market's needs.

Another consideration they had to take into account was where to locate Adom FM. They assessed the market and the competition, and finally chose Tema for two strategic reasons. Their experience showed that the success of radio is in how it bonds with the community. People like to feel that a radio station is 'their' radio station. They found that as Tema at the time did not have a local radio station, they could get its people to tie into it and love it. Secondly, Joy FM and Peace FM were located in Accra. Apart from Accra, the place with high earning power close to the competition was Tema. Tema, thus, was the best location for Adom FM.

There were other challenges that they had to deal with, particularly in terms of getting the right people at short notice. Given that the format of broadcasting from Groove FM to Adom FM had changed considerably, they could only keep three staff members from Groove FM. Instead, they brought in staff from Joy FM to fill in the key positions and to quickly recruit high-potential presenters.

With a new business comes a new culture; getting people used to the new culture was a hurdle they had to overcome. Adom FM was different from Joy FM in its focus and orientation. This meant that staff from Joy FM and the new ones needed to be (re-)oriented to know the difference and stick to it. They needed to be taught the Adom way of doing things, since the format and language were different and they could not use Joy FM procedures in the new business without any modifications.

Notes

1   Siropolis, N. *Small Business Management*. Boston: Houghton Mifflin, 1994.

2   Haigh, H. *Buying and Selling a Business: An Entrepeneur's Guide*. London: Piatkus Books Ltd, 2007.

3   Adhikari, M. The Art of Buying and Selling a Business. Lecture delivered to the Entrepreneurial Finance Class of Kellogg School of Management, Evanston, March 2002.

4   Haigh, H. *Buying and Selling a Business: An Entrepeneur's Guide*. London: Piatkus Books Ltd, 2007.

5   See Page 240.

6   Kessben FC Sold!, Accra Mail, 4 August 2010.

7   James, P. Build or Buy – Stellar Group's Experience Of Building Its Business Portfolio In Ghana. Presentation to GIMPA Foundations of Entrepreneurship class, Greenhill, October 2011.

8   Knowles, R. *Small Business: An Entrepreneur's Plan*. Toronto: Harcourt Brace & Company, 2003.

9   James, P. Build or Buy – Stellar Group's Experience Of Building Its Business Portfolio In Ghana. Presentation to GIMPA Foundations of Entrepreneurship class, Greenhill, October 2011.

10 Berman, P. D. *Small Business and Entrepreneurship*. Upper Saddle River: Prentice Hall, 1997.

11 Siropolis, N. *Small Business Management*. Boston: Houghton Mifflin, 1994.

12 Divestiture of State Interests (Implementation) Law, 1993 (PNDC Law 326).

13 Hosmer, L.T., A. Cooper and K.H. Vesper. *The Entrepreneurial Function: Text and Cases on Small Firms*. Upper Saddle River: Prentice Hall 1977

14 Blayney, M. 2003. *Selling Your Business For All It's Worth*. Oxford: How To Books Ltd, 2003.

15 Collins, D. Class Notes for Venture Capital Financing

(unpublished). Kellogg School of Management, 2003.

16 Scarborough, N.M. and T.W. Zimmerer. *Effective small business management: An entrepreneurial approach.* Upper Saddle River: Prentice Hall, 2003.

17 Lecture delivered to the Foundations of Entrepreneurship class at Ghana Institute of Management and Public Administration, Greenhill, November 2010.

Chapter Six: Legal and Regulatory Considerations

"No artist ever interpreted nature as freely as a lawyer interprets the truth." – **Jean Giradoux**

Outline

- Forms of Business Organisations
- Other legal forms
- Other Legal & Regulatory Considerations
- Questions for Class Discussion
- Case Study: Stolen Ownership at Yakubu and Volta International Construction Ltd

Forms of Business Organisations

AFTER MAKING THE decision to start an entrepreneurial venture, entrepreneurs must decide what form of business organisation (or legal vehicle) to use to launch the venture. There are a number of different options available so it is important that entrepreneurs think through the pros and cons of each of the possible options, in light of the nature of their particular circumstances and their objectives for the entrepreneurial venture. The exact form of business organisation that the entrepreneur ultimately chooses will be driven by a number of factors such as limited liability, tax considerations, capital and control. Essentially, there are six main options available to the entrepreneur: sole proprietorship; partnership; limited liability company; unlimited liability company; external company; and, last but not least, the cooperative.

The considerations as to the appropriate type of legal vehicle to use could apply both where an entrepreneur is starting up a venture and where he is considering the acquisition of an existing business.

Indeed, the legal implications that follow may differ depending on whether the seller is a company, a shareholder or a sole proprietor, and whether the acquirer is purchasing assets of the business or acquiring the business as a going concern. However, this chapter generally assumes that the entrepreneur is making a decision as to which form of business organisation to use in a start-up situation.

Sole Proprietorship

The most common form of business organisation in Ghana is sole proprietorship: 59.4% of all businesses registered in Ghana in the period from January 2000 to December 2011 were sole proprietorships.[1] A sole proprietorship is a business owned (and often run) by a single individual. An entrepreneur who trades as a sole proprietor or a sole trader essentially carries out business on his own behalf. He and the business are the same, as there is no distinction in law between the business he is carrying out and the individual behind the business. In fact, where the entrepreneur is carrying out business in his true personal name, surname or initials, he does not have to comply with any formal legal registration requirements.[2] However, where the entrepreneur seeks to use a name that is different from his own name, surname or initials, he must register the business with the Registrar General's Department.[3] For example, if Moses Atinga wants to set up a business to be known as Moses Atinga Enterprise, he does not need to register that business with the Registrar General. However, if he wants to call the business something else – say Kumasi Home Enterprise – he would have to register that name at the Registrar General's Department under the Registration of Business Names Act, 1962 (Act 151).

To register under the Registration of Business Names Act, the sole proprietor must purchase a copy of Form A, complete it and return the filled form to the Registrar General. Form A requires the sole proprietor to provide the following information:

- Business name;
- General nature of the business;
- Principal place of the business;

- Any other places at which the business is carried out;
- Name, nationality, residential address and business occupation of the sole proprietor.

The Registrar General, upon receipt of a duly completed application form, will issue a certificate of registration which must be renewed after a year, and annually thereafter. Failure to renew the business name may result in removal of that name from the register of business names, which will enable someone else to register and trade with that name.

Registration under the Registration of Business Names Act does not confer any distinct legal personality on any business name registered under it.[4] It only gives the entrepreneur the right to use the name, not any intellectual property rights over that name. Intellectual property rights give the entrepreneur rights over the name that can be transferred or sold.[5] This is the subject of another registration regime.[6]

A sole trader has complete responsibility for the decisions relating to his business, having no fetters on his ability to make decisions relating to the business so long as these decisions comply with the general laws of Ghana. He reports to no one and is not required to seek any formal approval for any decisions that relate to his business. This flexibility appeals to many entrepreneurs.

As there is no legal distinction between the entrepreneur-owner and the business, the assets and profits of the business, as well as its liabilities and losses – without limit – are therefore those of the entrepreneur, and his alone. He pays income tax on the profits of the business, which is treated as the entrepreneur's personal income. The law does not impose a separate tax on the profits attributable to the business run by the sole proprietor.

Although the law does not make a distinction between the sole proprietor and his business, it is highly recommended that at least from an accounting perspective, the entrepreneur takes steps to separate the finances of the business from his own finances. For example, at the very least, the sole proprietor should open a bank account separate from his personal account for the business.

There is no obligation for the sole proprietor to disclose any information about the financial performance of his business, to prepare financial statements or to have the accounts of the business audited. It is however recommended that a sole proprietor (as with any entrepreneur) keeps proper and accurate records of his business's dealings to make for easier and more responsible management. In particular, he should keep financial records that are separate from his personal financial matters.

Despite the seeming flexibility of a sole proprietorship, it would not be an appropriate form of business organisation where an entrepreneur seeks to invite others to make equity participations in his business, because equity participation in a business requires that there is a vehicle that the equity investors can buy into. In the case of a sole proprietor, there is no vehicle through which she does business other than herself; it is not possible for someone to purchase a piece of another individual. Also, for certain industries, sole proprietorship would not be an appropriate business form. Under Ghanaian law, it is not possible for a sole proprietor to set up business in industries such as banking, insurance and venture capital, where the law insists on 'body corporate' entities.

Sole proprietorship also does not lend itself easily to good corporate governance,[7] since the sole proprietor is usually the only person who makes decisions relating to the business. In practice, there is no reason why a sole proprietor cannot engage other people to share in making decisions. My view is that even the smallest of enterprises would benefit from an advisory board[8] put in place by the sole proprietor to assist in better decision making.

A sole proprietorship comes to an end on the death of the sole proprietor or a decision by the sole proprietor to discontinue the business. If the sole proprietor's business name was registered, then notice must be given to the Registrar General for the name to be removed from the register.[9]

Partnership

A partnership is "an association of two or more individuals carrying on business jointly for the purpose of making profits".[10] To carry on business jointly means that two or more persons share responsibility for the business and for the decisions that affect that business. Therefore, a partnership must necessarily consist of two or more 'proprietors'.

Under Ghanaian law, partnerships must be incorporated under the Incorporated Private Partnerships Act, 1962 (Act 152). The partners are required to submit a copy of their partnership agreement together with a duly completed Form A signed by all the partners. The partners are required to provide the following information:

- Name of partnership;
- General nature of business;
- Postal address of partnership;
- Address of principal place of business as well as details of all other places it does business;
- Personal details of each partner – name (including where applicable, former name), address and business occupation.

A partnership must consist of individuals of sound mind above the age of 18 years who have not been found guilty of any offence involving fraud or dishonesty in the preceding five years. The maximum number of persons who can form a partnership is twenty. It is not possible for a body corporate (such as a company or another partnership) to become a partner in a partnership. Where companies want to partner in this way, a more appropriate vehicle is a joint venture (discussed later in this chapter).

Upon the issue of a certificate of incorporation of the partnership by the Registrar General, a partnership becomes a separate legal entity, distinct from its partners. This means the law considers the partnership as a 'legal' person separate from the persons who own the partnership. To this extent, the law confers on the partnership all the powers of a natural person of full capacity.[11] The law treats the legal vehicle of a partnership as a separate person, even though the partnership must act through the partners and agents of the partnership.

Partners typically make joint decisions about the business, as well as share its profits and losses. A partner in a firm is jointly and severally liable with the firm and the other partners for all the debts and obligations of the firm over the duration for which he remains a partner.[12] This means that a partner can be sued individually in respect of debts and other obligations of the firm or he can be sued jointly (i.e. together with the other partners and with the partnership). This gives the person suing the partnership or its partners a choice as to whether to proceed against the partnership, a particular partner or all the partners. The decision as to whom to proceed against would probably be influenced by the claimant's perception of which target might have deeper pockets and therefore be in the best position to pay their claim.

Sometimes, a partner's involvement in running the business of the partnership may be passive. Such a partner – a 'sleeping' or 'silent' partner – relies on one or more active partners to run the business, and may only want to be consulted on the most fundamental issues relating to the partnership such as changes in ownership structure, changes in the nature of business or disposal (or acquisition) of material assets. Despite the fact that he plays only a limited (if any) role in the life of the partnership, a sleeping partner has the same liabilities and responsibilities as the other partners.

The acts of a partner bind the firm if they were authorised expressly or impliedly by the other partners, or ratified by them.[13] An act by a partner carrying on the business of the partnership in its usual way shall bind the partnership, unless the partner does not, in fact, have authority to act for the firm in the particular matter and the person with whom the partner is dealing knows that the partner does not have such authority. Where there is a restriction on the power of a partner to bind the firm, any act done in contravention of this restriction is not binding on the firm with respect to persons having notice of the agreement.[14]

Although the exact degree of the exercise of any of these rights and responsibilities among the individual partners may be varied by agreement, in the absence of this, the law will imply that they are equally shared.[15]

Individual partners are taxed on their share of partnership profits on which they pay personal income tax. The law does not impose a separate tax on the earnings of the partnership. In this sense the law treats the individual partners as if they were sole proprietors earning their proportionate share of the profits of the partnership.

Partnership firms are required by law to keep proper accounts with respect to their financial position, and to prepare financial statements (a profit and loss statement and a balance sheet) giving a true and fair view of the profitability, assets and liabilities of the firm for the relevant period.[16] There is no obligation for partnerships to have their financial statements audited. My view, however, is that it is good practice to do so because the audit process provides a good control mechanism to ensure that the firm's accounts are properly prepared. It gives another person or firm (the auditor or auditing firm) an opportunity to review and challenge, if and when necessary, the accounts prepared by the firm's accountants. It also promotes transparency and helps the partners develop confidence in the firm's financial position as reported.

It is advisable that the help of a good lawyer is sought in drafting a detailed partnership agreement to govern the relationship between the partnering parties. A typical partnership agreement would contain provisions relating to the following:

• *Commencement*
The date on which the parties regard their partnership as taking effect from.

• *Name*
The name of the partnership, under which operations will be carried out.

• *Financial Contribution*
How much money each partner is putting into the business. Generally, this tends to be a long-term investment which cannot be withdrawn until the partnership is wound up, or unless the relevant contributing partner leaves the partnership.

• *Profit (or loss) Share*

The partners will specify how profits (and losses) will be shared among them.

• *Ownership of Partnership Assets*

Although generally the ratio for sharing profits (or losses) will be the same as the ratio of the ownership of the underlying partnership assets, this need not be the case. This ratio becomes relevant, for example, where a partnership asset is disposed of, or where the partnership requires partners to contribute to acquire additional assets.

• *Drawings and/or Salaries*

A drawing is an advance that partners take in anticipation of profits. Technically, a partner only gets a share of the business profit after such profit has been computed at the end of the financial year. However, in practice, partners might need money to fund their day-to-day lives and therefore may agree to take drawings from the firm for this. This is an advance which is settled against profit when made. It is also possible for particular partners to be paid a salary (in addition to their share of profits) in recognition of (a) particular role(s) played – for example, a training partner or a managing partner of a professional services firm may be paid a salary in recognition of the additional responsibility she takes on.

• *Decision-Making and Roles*

Although each partner is entitled to make decisions relating to the partnership, roles may be split between the partners in practice. For example, there might be a partner managing the partnership, in charge of making managerial decisions. Also, based on the expertise of particular partners, certain decisions could be left to them. However, such delegation of partnership decision making would be subject to the approval of all partners.

• *Dissolution*

This typically would deal with how partnership assets and the existing business would be dealt with in the event that the partners decide to dissolve the partnership.

• Payment in the Event of Retirement or Death

The partnership agreement may have provisions relating to what should happen to the partnership's assets in the event of the retirement or death of a partner. It could, for example, provide that in such an event, the remaining partners buy the deceased partner's share of the business based on a valuation of the partnership carried out by an independent financial advisor or accountant. In the absence of any such provisions, there is no automatic right for the estate to require any such share.

• Restraint of Trade Following Departure

Partners may want to protect themselves from a situation where a partner, after obtaining all the relevant business secrets – client lists, know-how, competitive advantage, etc. – leaves the partnership and sets up exactly the same business in competition with the partnership. By so doing, he may go after the same clients, use the firm's knowledge and know-how and, in some instances, lure star employees away from the original firm. To protect partners from such situations and to align the incentives of partners to ensuring that the partnership works, the partnership agreement may have a restraint of trade provision that prevents an existing partner from competing in the same type of business, hiring employees from the partnership and/or soliciting clients for a period of time after leaving the partnership. Such a provision is extremely controversial and good legal advice must be sought in drafting one to make it enforceable. Clauses such as this provision raise tensions between two fundamental common law principles – freedom of contract and restraint of trade. On one hand, the parties seeking to enforce a clause such as this would want to rely on the principle of freedom to contract on the basis that the law must enforce contracts freely and voluntarily entered into. However, the other party (the exiting partner) may also want to rely on the other common law principle that there must be freedom to trade in a reasonable way without harming another's interest, and that a clause such as that fetters an existing freedom (to undertake whatever business the exiting partner wants to go into), restraining his ability to trade. The court may hold restraint of trade clauses void if it takes the view that they are unreasonable, unfair, contrary to the public's interest or public policy.[17] It is therefore advisable that the restraints placed (e.g. number of months the exiting partner is prohibited from competing or soliciting clients and employees or the geographical area within which he is not permitted to compete) are narrowed down as much as possible.

• *Arbitration*

Sometimes, parties may decide that in the event of a dispute, the dispute should be settled by an arbitrator appointed by the partners or on behalf of the partners, rather than through the courts. Arbitration is sometimes preferred to relying on the court because of the slow pace of court disputes, which parties may seek to avoid.

No matter how well-crafted or tightly-drafted a partnership agreement is, it is not worth the piece of paper it is written on if proper consideration has not gone into the decision of choosing who to partner with in the first place. These issues, discussed in Chapter 9, are crucially important and must be thought through to ensure that partners have complementary skills and share the same ethos, values and vision for the business. Not dissimilar from the considerations that go to choosing a spouse, people contemplating a business partnership must ensure that they take time and trouble to identify a suitable partner. Partners (like married couples and committed civil partners) must understand each other and be able to commit to the same long-term goals (again not too dissimilar from notions of 'for better for worse' and 'in health and in sickness.')[18]

Companies: Incorporating a Company

If an entrepreneur decides to incorporate a company, she must first of all conduct a search at the Companies Registry to ascertain whether or not the company name she desires is already in use by another entity. The name must also not be misleading. Assuming that the name is not already in use, the entrepreneur may apply to reserve the name or may proceed to apply to the Registrar of Companies for the company to be incorporated with the name in respect of which she carried a search. To incorporate a company, the following documents must be presented to the Registrar of Companies:

• *Regulations*

The regulations constitute the constitution of the company and bind the company, its officers, directors and shareholders.[19] They contain the objects of the company (i.e. the scope of business that the company is permitted to engage in), as well as detailed rules about decision making and the internal management of the company. The Ghanaian Companies Act, 1963 (Act 179; commonly referred to as the Companies Act) has a prescribed form of regulations for companies that an entrepreneur may adopt if he does not want to draw up his own regulations from scratch. Regulations for private limited liability companies are set out in Table A of the Companies Act. Prospective entrepreneurs must read through the regulations carefully, and if there are any provisions that entrepreneurs would like to change, they should consult with a corporate lawyer who will advise on whether the law permits amendment to that particular regulation. The initial shareholders will subscribe to the regulations by signing on the last page of the regulations. Each subscriber is required to provide his name, address, age, occupation and the number of shares he has subscribed for. The minimum number of owners, referred to as 'shareholders,' is one.

• *Form 3*

This form requires that the details of the first directors, the company secretary, the auditor and the registered office of the company be provided. Form 3 also requires that the Registrar of Companies is notified about other directorships held by the proposed directors, their residential addresses and nationalities. Every company must have a company secretary and at least two directors, one of whom must be present in Ghana at any given time. A company must also have an auditor who must be a qualified accountant qualified to practice as an auditor in Ghana. The auditor is required to audit the accounts of the company annually. The auditor must give written consent to act as an auditor. In practice, the Registrar of Companies demands evidence of such consent before incorporating the company.

• *Form 4*
This is a declaration that the requirements for setting up a company have been complied with.

• *Tax Registration Form*
This ensures that the new company acquires a tax identification number (TIN) as soon as it is set up.

In addition to the above documents, the applicant must submit the following:

- Registration and presentation fee;
- A sum equivalent to 0.5% of the stated capital of the company. The stated capital is the total capital with which the shareholders intend to start the business; the minimum acceptable capital for private limited liability companies in Ghana is GH¢500.[20]

It could take anywhere from three days to a month for the Registrar of Companies to incorporate a company by issuing it with a Certificate of Incorporation and a Certificate to Commence Business. A company is legally prohibited from starting business unless it has been issued with a Certificate to Commence Business.

Upon incorporation under the Companies Act, the law treats the company as a 'person' (as it does a partnership), albeit an artificial person (acting through its agents) but with all the powers of a natural person of full capacity.[21] The company is therefore separate and distinct from its members and can sue and be sued in its name. Property of the company belongs to the company and not to its shareholders.

Once a company has been issued with certificates ratifying its incorporation and commencement of business, it is required to display these certificates on its business premises. On its letterheads and other business stationery, it is required to show its name as well as to use the word 'Limited' (or the abbreviation 'Ltd').

Companies: shareholders' agreements

Where two or more people come together to form a company, they may want to consider whether or not, in addition to the regulations, they want to enter into a shareholders' agreement. A shareholders' agreement is a contract which can be made by either all or some of the shareholders. It may be appropriate for other people (like the company itself) who are not shareholders to be a party to the shareholders agreement. It can be entered into at any time during the lifetime of the company, but is most commonly made at initial incorporation (or acquisition), establishing areas of agreement for those involved.

Shareholders' agreements' can be important because although the regulations of the company are a binding contract in respect of membership rights, they are generally ineffective so far as non-membership rights are concerned. So if members want to agree on matters unrelated to their membership rights, they would need to use a shareholders' agreement. The regulations are also a public document open to public inspection at the Companies Registry so if there are areas of agreement which the shareholders would like to keep private, the regulations alone would be inadequate. Also, while the regulations may be altered at any time by a special resolution of members, a shareholders' agreement will need the unanimous consent of all the parties to it.

The shareholders' agreement may contain any number of issues including:

Capitalisation and funding (initial and on-going) or other contributions (for example, intellectual property rights, know-how, secondment of staff, provision of premises, etc.);

- The composition of the board and management arrangements;
- Approval of business plans;
- Dividend distribution policy;
- Transferability of shares in different circumstances;
- Deadlock and termination (including obligatory transfer events and drag along and tag along rights):
  - » Drag along rights give a majority shareholder (typically with a shareholding of 75% or above of the issued share capital) the right to 'drag along' the minority shareholders in respect of a proposed sale of the shares of the company. The majority shareholder looking to sell his shares is therefore able to require that the minority are 'dragged along'. The majority shareholder will have to give the minority shareholders the same terms as he negotiates for himself;
  - » Tag along rights give the minority shareholder a right to 'tag along' with the majority shareholder looking to sell his shares in the company on the same terms;
- Minority provisions (for example, veto rights given to minority shareholders on certain matters, also known as 'reserved matters');
- Restrictive covenants on the company and its participants;
- Confidentiality.

Companies: Types of Companies

There are two main types of companies under Ghanaian law: limited liability companies and unlimited liability companies.[22] Liability is said to be 'limited' in a limited liability company because, in general, individual shareholders of the company cannot be held liable for the debts and other obligations of the company. Liability of shareholders is limited in most cases to the amount they paid for their shares. This means that if they have paid in full for those shares, they are (in the absence of fraud or other circumstances) generally not liable for the debts of the company; if they have not paid in full for their shares, their liability is limited to the amount that remains to be paid for their shares. Another feature of limited liability is that the personal assets of the directors are not available for a company's creditors; the creditors may not proceed against such assets unless there is evidence of fraudulent trading.

In the case of a start-up or small business, the principle of limited liability may offer very little protection to shareholders and directors because entities dealing with these companies typically insist that key shareholders and/or directors are party to relevant agreements to which the company is a party. This is to prevent a situation where, for example, a bank lends money to a company which the company is subsequently unable to pay, and the shareholders and directors have assets that the bank would want to proceed against to recover the debt, but cannot. Banks therefore usually ask directors of start-up companies to provide an unlimited guarantee or indemnity to guarantee the debts and other obligations of the company. Where the company is unable to pay its debts, the bank is then able to proceed directly against the guaranteeing shareholder or director and/or his assets.

A company may be a private or a public company. A private company cannot have more than fifty persons as members (excluding employees as well as former employees who continue to be members after their employment) and is prohibited from making an invitation to the general public to acquire shares in the company. Furthermore, unlike public companies, shareholders of a private company are restricted in their ability to transfer shares to other persons,[23] as the board of directors may decline to register any transfer of shares.

Both private and public companies must file within the first eighteen months of incorporation (and thereafter annually) an annual return with the Registrar of Companies and must include a copy of their audited accounts.

Companies Limited by Shares vs. Companies Limited by Guarantee

The type of company discussed in the previous section is a company limited by shares, in which the owners or shareholders are issued shares in the company in return for the money they pay. Shares may also be issued for any consideration other than cash that is agreed on between the company and the prospective shareholder.

Another type of company that may be incorporated in Ghana is a company limited by guarantee. Members of such a company are not issued with shares and, rather than their liability being tied to shares they have purchased, the liability of the members of a company limited by guarantee is limited to such amounts as the members may respectively undertake to contribute to the assets of the company in the event of it being wound up. The amount stipulated by Ghanaian law for the settlement of such guarantee payments currently stands at GHC 700.[24] A company limited by guarantee is usually used to establish not-for-profit organisations, thus a company limited by guarantee may not lawfully be incorporated with the object of carrying on business for the purpose of making profits. The income and property of the company shall be applied solely towards the promotion of its objectives. If a company limited by guarantee carries on business for the purpose of making profits, all officers and members who were aware that the company is making a profit are liable to fines.

As with other companies, companies limited by guarantee are required by law to appoint a minimum of two directors (referred to as the Executive Council).

The regulations of the company must state that if, upon winding up of the company, there remains, after the discharge of its debts and liabilities, any property previously owned by the company, the same shall not be distributed to its members but shall be transferred to some other company limited by guarantee having similar objectives to those of the wound-up company, or applied to some charitable ends (as determined by the members prior to the dissolution of the company).

In addition to registration with the Registrar General, all not-for-profit organisations are required to be registered with the Department of Social Welfare. Registration begins at the district level where the not-for-profit organisation is to be located. The district office will, after due diligence on the proposed not-for-profit organisation, report to the head office, which will then register the not-for-profit organisation. For registration with the Department of Social Welfare, the following documents will be required:

- 4 copies of the company's certificate of incorporation issued by the Registrar General and one copy of the company's regulations;
- 4 copies of the Department of Social Welfare's investigation report;
- Copies of brochures or articles on the organisation's activities.

In addition to the filing requirements of the Companies Act, registered not-for-profit organisations are required to report annually to the Department of Social Welfare on the activities carried out within the reporting year (including details of expenditure).

Setting up a not-for-profit organisation or a company limited by guarantee does not automatically guarantee an exemption from tax for the company. To claim tax exemption (because of not-for-profit activities), the not-for-profit organisation must apply to the Commissioner General of the Ghana Revenue Authority, who administers such exemptions.

External Company

Yet another type of company is the external company. The Companies Act envisages situations in which a company already incorporated and operating in a country other than Ghana seeks to conduct business in Ghana by establishing a place of business in Ghana. Such a company is considered to have "established a place of business in Ghana" if it has "a branch, management, shares, transfer, or registration office, factory or mine, or other fixed place of business [in Ghana]."[25]

An external company does not have a separate legal personality or identity from its parent; it operates simply as a branch or offshoot of its parent. External companies are required to file within one month of establishment of a place of business in Ghana, the following documents with the Registrar of Companies:

- Certified copies of the company's constitutional documents;
- A form 3 giving the following details of the company:
  - » Name;
  - » The nature of its business or businesses or other main objects;
  - » Details of one or more persons authorised to manage the business in Ghana (referred to as the 'Local Manager'). The Local Manager should be someone who is competent to be appointed a director in Ghana. The acts of the Local Manager will bind the company unless the Local Manager has no authority to so bind the company, in which case the third party with whom the local manager is dealing should know that;
  - » Address of its registered or principal office in its country of incorporation;
  - » The address of its principal place of business in Ghana, including its postal address;
  - » The name of a process agent authorised to accept service of process and other documents on behalf of the company.

On receipt of the above by the Registrar of Companies (together with a fee of US$500), the Registrar will arrange for information about the company to be published in the Gazette, and will issue a letter to the effect that the Company has been registered on the External Register, although no certificate of incorporation will be issued.

Co-operatives

This is an association set up to provide a service or services for its members and is typically made up of members who share particular characteristics, such as same employer, trade or profession. Co-operatives are usually formed to provide benefits for members. They may be incorporated or just be a body of individuals. Where they are incorporated, they must have the word 'co-operative' in their name. They also display properties of limited liability entities where they are incorporated as such. In Ghana, a society (co-operative) that has as its object the promotion of the economic interest of its members may be registered as a body corporate with limited or unlimited liability. Co-operative societies are not permitted to grant loans to people other than their own members.[26] They may also receive deposits and loans to the extent prescribed by their regulations and by-laws. No member is allowed to hold more than 20% of the shares in a co-operative society unless it is a registered society. On the death of a member, the society shall transfer her shares and/or interest in the co-operative to an approved heir, and the liabilities of the deceased member for the debts of a registered society shall continue from the end of the financial year following the time she ceased to be a member till two years after her death. That means her estate shall bear any such liabilities for this stipulated period of time.

Table 6.1: Tabular Comparison Of The Various Types Of Incorporation In Ghana

	Sole Proprietorship	Partnership	Company	Co-operative Society
Statutory regime	Registration of Business Names, Act , 1962 (Act 151)	Incorporated Private Partnerships Act,1962 (Act 152)	Companies Act, 1963 (Act 179)	Co-operative Societies Act, 1968 (NLCD 252)
Minimum number of members	One	Two	One	Ten
Maximum number of members	One	Twenty	Fifty (for private); Unlimited for public	Unlimited
Limitation on members	Individuals only	Individuals only	Individual or corporate entities	Individuals, corporate societies and unregistered bodies of persons but with permission from the Registrar General.
Liability	Sole proprietor has unlimited liability for debts of the business	Partners liable for the debts of the partnership and the debts of other partners	Shareholders are generally not liable for company debts	Members of the society are liable for debts of the society for up to 2 years after they cease to be members
Personality	No separation between the sole proprietor and the business.	Separate legal person; can sue and be sued in its own name	Separate legal person; can sue and be sued in its own name	Separate legal person; can sue and be sued in its own name

	Sole Proprietorship	Partnership	Company	Co-operative Society
Publicity	The registered name is published in a register	The firm's name as well as the partners' names must be published in the Gazette	A notice that a certificate of incorporation has been issued to the company is published in the Gazette. A copy of the company's regulations is required to be registered with the Registrar General.	N/A
Renewal of registration	Annual renewal of registration of business name	No renewal required except in the case of businesses which are in specific sectors, such as banking or energy, where the industry regulator issues licenses which have to be renewed in accordance with the term of the relevant licence	No renewal required except in the case of businesses which are in specific sectors, such as banking or energy, where the industry regulator issues licenses which have to be renewed in accordance with the term of the relevant licence	No renewal required except in the case of businesses which are in specific sectors, such as banking or energy, where the industry regulator issues licenses which have to be renewed in accordance with the term of the relevant licence
Continuity	Ends with death of sole proprietor	Perpetual succession	Perpetual succession	Perpetual succession
Taxation	Sole proprietor is taxed as an individual; the business is not taxed separately	Individual partners are taxed on their share of partnership income; the partnership is not taxed separately	Double Taxation: Company is liable for corporate income tax on profits; once this is distributed to shareholders, shareholders also pay income tax on the dividend; if owners are also employees or directors, they pay personal income tax on their income	Society is taxed

Other Forms of Business Organisations

Joint Ventures

A joint venture occurs when two or more businesses collaborate by pooling resources to achieve a common objective of limited liability, including discrete activities or a series of transactions. A joint venture can be established with a joint venture agreement which sets out the objectives of the joint venture and the rights and responsibilities of the parties. The matters addressed in a joint venture agreement will be very similar to those we discussed in connection with partnership agreement, including decision making, roles, sharing of profits/losses and contribution to the asset base of the venture. Where a joint venture is established only by agreement, the joint venture itself is not a separate legal entity with a separate legal personality from its owners.

An alternative to establishing a joint venture solely by agreement is to establish a joint venture company. In this case a separate legal entity is set up. In Ghana, this will be in the form of a company. This joint venture company will spell out the process for decision making, for appointing board members and other activities. As the members of the joint venture are in fact 'shareholders' of the joint venture company, they may also decide to enter into a shareholders' agreement (on similar terms as we discussed earlier).

Joint ventures allow smaller companies to gain from resource and expertise which the larger joint venture partners have but which the smaller companies may not otherwise obtain. In the case of a foreign joint venture (where a company in one country enters into a joint venture with another company in another country), the joint venture may give access that the foreign company may not have otherwise had. It gives the foreign company an opportunity to tap into the local knowledge and expertise of the local partners. It may also give the foreign company an opportunity to participate in a sector of the economy where laws require local ownership of companies participating in that sector.

The choice of a joint venture partner is similar to that of choosing the right partner in forming a partnership. There must be an overall fit, with a shared vision and willingness to work together. The parties must clearly define their roles and the responsibilities with respect to all aspects necessary for the smooth running of the venture.

Franchising

We have previously discussed franchising in Chapter 5. Franchising should not be confused with other similar marketing arrangements, particularly distribution agreements and licensing agreements (discussed below), where no royalties are payable by the distributor. Franchising agreements provide more extensive restrictions than distribution and licensing agreements.

Principal/Agency

This is a legal relationship between two entities, one a principal and the other an agent, where the agent acts on behalf of the principal in managing the principal's relationship with third parties. The principal may not ratify any action an agent takes if the agent acts outside his authority. Examples of principal/agent relationships are the insurance brokerage firm which acts as an agent for the insured and a local country representative of an international company who, in certain circumstances, may be appointed as agent of the principal to act in the name and on behalf of the principal.

Distribution Agreements

Under this set-up, a manufacturer or supplier of goods appoints an independent third-party distributor to market its goods. The distributor buys the goods on his own account and trades under his own name. He may be appointed by one or any number of manufacturers or suppliers. His business name will usually have no connection with the name of the supplier of the goods. Also, the supplier will not regulate the way the distributor operates his business other than, perhaps, to oblige the distributor to reach minimum turnover levels, advertise, maintain a minimum stock of goods and spare parts as well as meet servicing criteria. No royalties are payable to the manufacturer or supplier, who makes his profit on the mark up on the goods it supplies the distributor.

Licensing Agreements

Intellectual property rights or know-how may be licensed to enable another business produce and/or sell goods. Where an entrepreneur invents a new product, for example, he may decide to licence a manufacturer to produce and distribute the product for any number of reasons, which may include the lack of manufacturing capacity of the entrepreneur or lack of resources to produce the product on the scale that makes production economically viable. He may also decide to use licensing to penetrate a country or region where he has no knowledge or contacts, instead of producing the product himself.

Mergers and Acquisitions

As discussed in Chapter 5, a merger comes about when two or more companies come together to form a new entity with a single identity. Entrepreneurs may merge as a survival strategy, to prevent unwanted or hostile takeovers, to gain technological edges or even to acquire managerial talent. Mergers are perpetual in nature. Examples of companies formed from mergers in Ghana include Guinness Ghana Breweries Limited, SG-SSB, and AngloGoldAshanti. An acquisition is the purchase of a company by another so that the acquired company loses its identity. An entrepreneur may either acquire a business or have his business acquired by another. An example of an acquisition in Ghana was the acquisition of Scancom Ghana Ltd by MTN Group of South Africa.

Other Legal Considerations

Internal Revenue Act, 2000 (Act 592 and Regulations)

All businesses are required to register with the Ghana Revenue Authority. Upon registration of the business, the company obtains a tax identification number (TIN). The TIN must be quoted on all correspondence with the Ghana Revenue Authority, and is also required to enable the company clear goods in commercial quantities from the ports, register title to or interest in land and obtain tax clearance certificates. In practice, it takes up to 14 days to complete the registration process. The company pays a stamp duty of 0.5% of the stated capital to commence business. The Companies Registry collects the money on behalf of the Ghana Revenue Authority. As an employer, the entrepreneur is required to deduct the applicable rates of income tax from the remuneration of all employees and pay the same to the Ghana Revenue Authority. There is a also a requirement for all owners/operators of factories and offices to register with the Health & Safety Directorate. A fee is payable depending on the number of employees employed at the relevant factory or office.

Subject to certain allowances, exceptions, double taxation and other reliefs granted, income brought into or received or derived from or accruing in Ghana is taxable. An individual who is present in Ghana for a total period of 183 days or more is considered to be a 'resident' person for tax purposes, and such individuals will be subject to Ghanaian income tax.

If the enterprise is set up as a company, it will be subject to corporate tax, which is currently at a rate of 25% of taxable profits. Companies are also required to file corporate tax returns four months after the end of their accounting/financial year. These returns must be accompanied by audited financial statements and detailed tax computations. Businesses may however be entitled to tax concessions depending on the industry in which they operate. For example, businesses engaged in agro-processing are exempt from tax during the first three years of their operations. Businesses engaged in agricultural activities such as farming of tree crops and cash crops as well as livestock and cattle farming also enjoy various tax concessions. Further, businesses located in regional capitals other than Accra and rural parts of Ghana benefit from reduced corporate tax rates.

National Pensions Act, 2008 (Act 766)

As an employer, the entrepreneur needs to register with the Social Security and National Insurance Trust (SSNIT), and will be required to deduct from the remuneration of all employees at the end of every month, each employee's social security contribution (an amount equal to 5.5% of the employee's monthly remuneration), which is then added to the employer's contribution of 13% of the employee's monthly remuneration, with the total amount paid to SSNIT. The latter contribution of 13% shall be paid by the employer from its own resources and cannot be deducted from the employee's remuneration. To apply for social security, the employer must attach the list of employees, their respective salaries and social security numbers, and the company's certificate of incorporation and certificate to commence business.

Value Added Tax, 1998 (Act 546)

This law stipulates the tax that is payable on all goods and services considered taxable, including all goods and services imported into Ghana. A taxable person is anyone who makes or will make a turnover in excess of what is legally stipulated. A taxable supply is a supply of goods and services that a taxable person makes in the course of or in furtherance of his business.

Ghana Investment Promotion Centre (GIPC) Act, 1994 (Act 478)

The GIPC Act applies whenever a non-Ghanaian invests and/or participates in the operation of any enterprise in Ghana, including the setting-up and operation of liaison/representative offices. The Act specifies the following minimum foreign capital investment required for non-Ghanaians:

- In the case of a joint enterprise with a Ghanaian partner, the capital required by the non-Ghanaian should not be less than US$10,000;

- In the case of an enterprise wholly owned by a non-Ghanaian, the capital required should not be less than US$50,000;

- In the case of a trading enterprise, the minimum capital (or its equivalent in goods) is US$300,000. In addition there is a requirement in this instance for at least ten Ghanaians to be employed.

All enterprises that the GIPC Act applies to are firstly required to register or incorporate under the Companies Act, after which they are required to register with the Ghana Investment Promotion Centre. Once so registered, the law guarantees unconditional transferability of dividends or net profits attributable to investment and payments in respect of servicing foreign loans, fees and charges. Expatriate personnel employed shall also be able to make remittances abroad provided that such remittances do not exceed the total wage of such personnel. The Act also gives some incentives in the form of concessionary duty when goods are imported into Ghana.

Immigration

If an entrepreneur seeks to employ a non-Ghanaian, she would have to ensure that she seeks proper authorisation from the Ministry of Interior and the Ghana Immigration Service. First of all, the non-Ghanaian national would require a visa to enter Ghana, and it is always advisable that enough time is given to obtain a business visa from the relevant Ghanaian consulate, embassy or high commission in the home country of the prospective non-Ghanaian employee. Upon arrival in Ghana, the entrepreneur has to apply to the Ministry of Interior for a residence and work permit upon submission of the following documents:

- Curriculum vitae of relevant expatriate employee (to demonstrate that he is qualified to work in the particular job);

- Photocopy of passport of the expatriate employee;

- Copies of the constitutional documents of the employer;
- Letter of application from the employer.

Typically, about one month after presentation of these documents (although this could be significantly longer), the Minister of Interior will write to the Director of Immigration (copied to the employer) granting or refusing the work permit. Upon receipt of this letter, the employee must apply to the Director of Immigration for the residence permit on a prescribed form, together with the applicant's passport, 4 passport pictures and a statutory fee (US$200 at time of press).

If successful, the expatriate employee must then present the following documents to the Ghana Immigration Service:

- Police clearance certificate from his home country;
- Medical report from any recognised hospital in Ghana;
- Appointment letter or contract of employment indicating terms of his employment.

After evaluating the application The Director of Immigration will submit a report to the Immigrant Quota Committee for consideration and approval. Both work and resident permits are typically granted for one year, and may be renewed. Work permits are tied to specific employers and become invalid once the underlying employment agreement with the named employer is terminated. Indeed, once the underlying employment agreement is terminated or the employee leaves the country for good, the resident permit must be returned to the Ghana Immigration Service for cancellation.

Labour Issues

The Labour Act, 2003 (Act 651) is the primary law that governs labour activities in Ghana. Under this Act, employment of a person for a period of six months or more must be governed by a contract of employment, which must express the rights and obligations of the parties in clear terms. Also, the employer is required to furnish the employee with a written statement of the main terms of the contract of employment. An employer under the Act is prohibited from interfering with a person's right to form and join a trade(s) union.

The Act also guarantees fifteen working days' leave with full pay; these days do not include public holidays. Hours of work must not exceed eight hours a day or forty hours a week. Extra hours worked should be considered as overtime. Contracts with temporary or casual workers need not be in writing.

The following considerations apply to all programmes of redundancy and termination.

• *Termination of Employment*

Employment may be terminated, both by the employer or the employee on the following grounds:

- by mutual agreement by the relevant parties;
- on grounds of ill-treatment or sexual harassment;
- the worker is found unfit for employment upon medical examination;
- the worker is unable to carry on work due to sickness, accident or incompetence;

Either party may terminate a contract of employment at any time by giving to the other party notice, or pay in lieu of notice, or the payment of other commitments as indicated in the employment contract binding both parties.

• *Notice of Termination*

Where a contract of employment is for three years or more, the notice period is one month or one month's salary in lieu of notice. Where the contract of employment is for less than three years, the notice period is two weeks or two weeks' salary in lieu of notice. The notice period for a contract that runs from week to week is seven days. Notice must be in writing and time begins to run on the day on which the notice is delivered.

• *Health, Safety and Environment Under the Labour Act*

According to the Act, it is the duty of the employer to ensure that every employee works under satisfactory, safe and healthy conditions. The workplace and work materials must be safe for use and safety apparel made available to employees. An employer is not liable for any injury to an employee in the work environment if the employee does not use the safety aids provided by the employer prior to injury.

• *Redundancy*

Pursuant to section 65(1) of the Labour Act, an employer may embark on a redundancy exercise where the employer contemplates that the introduction of major changes in production, programme, organisational structure and/or technology are likely to lead to the termination of employment of workers. Also, where an undertaking is closed down or undergoes an arrangement or amalgamation prior to closing down, and this arrangement or amalgamation causes a severance of the legal relationship between the employer and employee, the employee becomes redundant and is entitled to a redundancy pay.[27] Where a redundancy situation exists, the employer must adopt reasonable criteria for the selection of employees to be made redundant, and apply those criteria reasonably and fairly. In particular, if the employer adopts criteria for redundancy other than length of service, she must be able to show that those criteria were reasonably, fairly, rationally and objectively applied on a reasonably structured, comparable basis. Additionally, the employer must comply strictly with any agreed procedure or customary arrangements within the organisation while completing the redundancy selection process.[28]

An employer who intends to embark on a redundancy must do the following:

• Notification of Any Recognised Union

The employer must first of all notify the trade union to which the employees belong in writing and three months before the redundancy exercise. The notification must specify the reasons for any termination, the number and categories of employees likely to be affected and the period within which the termination is to be carried out. The employer is also required to consult the trade union concerned on measures to be taken to avert or minimise the terminations, as well as measures to mitigate the adverse effects of any terminations on the employees concerned, including their finding alternative employment.

- Notification of the Chief Labour Officer

  An employer is required under Section 65(1) of the Labour Act to provide in writing to the Chief Labour Officer, no later than three months before the redundancy, all relevant information including the reasons for any termination, the number and categories of employees likely to be affected and the period within which the termination is to be carried out.

- Interaction with Employees

  The employer is not required under the Labour Act to consult with the employees themselves. However, an employer who declares an employee redundant is required to pay the employee a sum constituting redundancy pay. The amount of any redundancy payment as well as the terms and conditions of payment are matters for negotiation between the employer or his representative and the employees or their trade union.[29] Any employee affected by the redundancy exercise may refer disputes relating to the redundancy pay and the terms and conditions of payment to the Labour Commission for settlement; the decision of the Labour Commission shall, subject to any other law, be final.

- Submission of Agreements Reached to the Chief Labour Officer

  The practice is to submit to the Chief Labour Officer copies of any redundancy agreements and/or notification of any payments made or concluded between the employer and affected employees.

- Issuance of Chief Labour Officer's fiat

  When the employer submits the redundancy agreements

(separation agreements or whatever agreements that are entered into pursuant to the redundancy), the Chief Labour Officer reviews the agreements and issues a fiat indicating the end of the redundancy process if he is satisfied that all steps have been taken as required.

Upon the termination of employment, the enterprise must pay the affected employees the following in addition to the redundancy pay:

- Any deferred pay due to the employees before the termination;
- Any compensation due to the employees in respect of sickness or accident;
- In the case of a foreign contract, in addition to the above, the necessary repatriation costs for the employee made redundant and accompanying members of his family to return to their native country;
- Any leave entitlements.

Pursuant to section 66 of the Labour Act, the provisions of the Labour Act on redundancy do not apply to the following categories of workers:

- Workers engaged under a contract of employment for specified periods to do specified work;
- Workers serving a period of probation or qualifying period of employment of reasonable duration determined in advance;
- Workers engaged on a casual basis.

Factory, Office and Shop Regulations (Act 328)

The Factories, Offices and Shops Act, 1970 (Act 328) requires that every premises to be used as a factory must be duly registered. At least one month before the occupation or use of a premises as a factory, the business must apply for the registration of the premises by sending a notice containing certain specified particulars of the premises and the business to the Chief Inspector. The registration is done within three months of submitting the notice, after which a certificate of registration is issued to the business upon the payment of the prescribed fees. Businesses in occupation of offices and shops are only required to serve a similar notice if specifically requested by the Chief Inspector.

Environmental Protection Agency

The Environmental Protection Agency may, by notice in writing, require any business engaged in an activity which, in the Agency's opinion has or is likely to have an adverse effect on the environment, to submit an environmental impact assessment. Under the Environmental Assessment Regulations, 1999 (LI 1652), it is mandatory for businesses engaged in certain industries to undertake an environmental impact assessment before commencing operations. Such businesses include those in the following sectors/categories:

Agricultural projects involving the development of more than 40 hectares of land, or that requires the resettlement of 20 families or more;

- Ports and airports;
- Drainage and irrigation;
- Land reclamation;
- Fisheries;
- Industrial activities;
- Infrastructure;
- Mining, oil and gas;
- Power generation and transmission;
- Resort and recreational development;
- Waste treatment and disposal;
- Water supply; etc.

The Environmental Assessment Regulations also require businesses engaged in manufacturing, mining, petroleum, chemicals, forestry, fishing, construction and other specified industries to obtain an environmental permit before commencing operations.

Free Zone Act, 1995 (Act 504)

An entrepreneur may establish an enterprise in an area designated as a free zone. A free zone enterprise is required to export at least 70% of the goods/services it produces/renders.

To qualify as a free zone developer or enterprise, the prospective developer or enterprise must first be registered under the Companies Act or the Incorporated Private Partnerships Act. In addition, the prospective developer/enterprise must acquire a license from the Free Zones Board. To carry on the business of banking or insurance, the enterprise must, in addition to acquiring a free zone licence, also be registered and licensed under the Banking or Insurance Acts respectively.

A free zone enterprise enjoys incentives such as exemption from direct or indirect import taxes and duties; it is also exempted from payment of income tax on profits for the first 10 years of operation. A shareholder in a free zone enterprise is exempted from paying withholding taxes on dividends accruing from investment in the enterprise.

Workmen's Compensation Regulations

The Workmen's Compensation Act, 1987 (PNDCL187) defines the terms for providing compensation (defined to include periodic payments) to employees who suffer from misfortunes arising out of or in the course of their employment. Payment is made on injuries that incapacitate an employee for a period of (at least) five conservative days. Compensation may, however, not be paid if the injury was as a result of the employee being under the influence of alcohol or drugs, or from a wilful act of misconduct. In case of death, compensation paid shall be the sum of the 42 months' worth of the employee's salary, or as decided in court.

The Constitution

Under the Constitution, every international business transaction to which the Government of Ghana is a party must be approved by Parliament in order to be valid. As a result, it is advisable that where an enterprise transacts business with the Government in conjunction with foreign partners, or if its transactions involves some other international element, the enterprise must seek appropriate legal advice on whether parliamentary approval will be required.

Public Procurement

The Public Procurement Act, 2003 (Act 663) regulates the administrative and institutional arrangements regarding procurement by public institutions to ensure transparency in the procurement process. Although it applies to public institutions and not private enterprises, entrepreneurs must ensure that public institutions to which they supply goods and services comply with the appropriate procurement procedures, or apply for the necessary exemptions.

Intellectual Property

In Ghana, trademarks are registered by the Registrar of Trademarks, and copyrights at the Copyright Office. A trademark is a sign or combination of signs capable of distinguishing the goods or services of one undertaking from the goods or services of any other undertakings, and includes words such as personal names, letters, numerals and figurative elements.[30] A copyright is the legal right and/or protection that is given to an author or originator of an artistic or literary work, which provides the author sole discretion on how to make use of his/ her creation.

• *Procedure for Registration of Trademark*

Application for the registration of a trademark in Ghana is done at the Trademark Registry at the Registrar General's Department. The application is made on a standard form that can be found in the Trademarks Regulations, 1970 (LI 667).

Due to the fact that there are numerous registered and pending trademarks, it is advisable to first conduct a search to determine whether the intended trademark is available for registration.

An application for registration of a trademark must be accompanied with the official fee as stipulated by the Trademark Registry, a representation of the proposed mark, a list of the relevant goods and/or services and an indication of the particular class(es) of goods and/or services using the international classification.[31] If available, the application may also contain a declaration claiming priority of an earlier national or regional application filed by the applicant or the predecessor in title of the applicant as provided for in article 4 of the Paris Convention.[32] The application should also contain the following details:

- The full name, description and nationality of the individual, firm or body corporate making the application;
- The names of all partners in a firm must be given in full. If the applicant is a body corporate, the country and kind of incorporation must be stated;
- Full trade or business address of the applicant;
- The trading style (if any) of the company;
- The status of the mark – that is, whether the mark is already in use or not;
- Date of the application;
- Signature of the applicant.

Upon receipt of an application to register a trademark, the Registrar will initiate a search among the registered marks and pending applications to ascertain whether there are any marks resembling the intended mark to be registered that would be a hindrance by being likely to deceive or cause confusion. If the application is approved, the Registrar shall accept the application by issuing a letter to the applicant indicating its approval of the application, subject to the publication of the trademark in the Gazette, or in an official bulletin and any print media. Any person interested in the trademark in question may file a notice of opposition within two months of the publication.

In the case of copyrights, an application for the registration and related rights in Ghana is done at the Copyright Office. The application is made on a standard form provided in the Copyright Regulations, 2010 (LI 1962).

The application is to be submitted along with a copy of the work which is to be registered and the prescribed fee, as indicated by the Copyright Office, paid. The application may either be made by the author, or on his behalf by his authorised agent, or the producer or publisher of the work to be registered.

Once the application has been filed, the Copyright Administrator shall determine whether the work submitted is subject to registration. Once confirmed, the Copyright Administrator issues a certificate of registration. However it is important to note that in Ghana, works bound by copyright do not have to be registered to be afforded protection under the law.

Questions for Class Discussion

1. What does it mean to say that a company has limited liability?
2. What does the concept of legal personality mean? Which of the different forms of business organisation available in Ghana have separate legal personality from owners?
3. What are the key provisions you would expect to see in a shareholders' agreement?
4. What are drag along and tag along rights?
5. What are the key differences between a partnership and a company?
6. When does a partnership come to an end?
7. What legal regime applies to a non-Ghanaian entrepreneur looking to invest in Ghana? What are the steps required by law?

Case Study: Stolen Ownership at Yakubu and Volta International Construction Ltd [33]

BORN AND RAISED IN **K**PANDO in the Volta Region of Ghana, Edem Kosi obtained straight A grades at A-level from Keta Secondary School, and was awarded a full scholarship to study at the University of Minnesota. He graduated with a degree in engineering and a 4.0 GPA, and joined General Electric as a Finance Analyst. Over six years, Edem worked in different divisions of the company and obtained exposure to a number of areas in the finance division.

Having set his heart on returning to Ghana 'to start his own thing', Kosi decided to pursue an MBA. He was accepted at Babson College, which had for many years been ranked by US News and World Report as the leading MBA programme in entrepreneurship in the United States. After Babson, Kosi took up an offer to join a business owned by the family of one of his Babson classmates – Johnson Family Construction Ltd. After successfully running the residential homes division of the company for several years, Kosi was approached by Haruna Yakubu, a classmate from Keta Secondary School to set up a company in Ghana to pursue real estate opportunities.

In 2005, Kosi and Yakubu formed a company called Yakubu and Volta International Construction Ltd ('Yakubu and Volta') which was registered as a limited liability company under the Ghana Companies Code of 1963 (Act 179). Kosi contributed almost US$1 million while Yakubu contributed US$2 million.

It was agreed that while Kosi remained in the United States (to allow his wife to complete her medical training), Yakubu would run the new company as Managing Director while Kosi remained a shareholder and non-executive director. However, once Kosi moved to Ghana, he would become Managing Director and Yakubu would become Executive Chairman.

Yakubu and Kosi agreed over a long-distance telephone conversation that they would own 60% and 40% of the company respectively.

As required, in the company's Regulations, the first directors of the company of Yakubu and Volta were Haruna Yakubu and Edem Kosi. However, under the same Company's Regulations, Haruna Yakubu put himself down as the sole subscriber to shares to the Regulations despite the Kosi's's contributions. As Kosi was in the United States, he had left Yakubu "to get on with the paperwork" and it had not even crossed his mind that anything like this could happen, given how long he had known Yakubu, a man he considered to be more of a brother than a friend. Yakubu had represented to the company's auditors that Kosi's contribution was in fact a director's loan, and it was recorded in the company's accounts as such.

Yakubu and Volta proved a successful company, executing many construction projects and in less than two years made more than US$10 million in profit in the process. However, before Kosi's wife could complete her medical residency, Yakubu – officially the sole shareholder of the company – suffered a heart attack and died.

Yakubu's children, inheritors of his estate, believed that Kosi's contribution was indeed a loan and refused to treat it as anything other than that.

In the ensuing arguments and disagreements regarding the ownership and control status of Yakubu and Volta, Kosi sued the estate of Yakubu and hired one of the leading litigation lawyers in Ghana. Nevertheless, the court ruled that despite his contribution, Kosi was not a shareholder of the company because the Company's Regulations did not establish him as such, and there was no evidence to show that it was intended that he be a shareholder. His US$1milion contribution was to be treated as director's loan and the court held that Kosi should be paid back his original loan together with 5% interest per annum.

Questions for Case Discussion:

1. What would you have done differently if you were Kosi?
2. Would it have made a difference if, instead of a phone conversation, Kosi and Yakubu had reached the agreement on share ownership in an email?
3. How could Kosi have realised earlier that his contribution was being treated as a loan rather than share capital?

Notes

1   Based on data from the Registrar General's Department, January 2012.

2   Registration of Business names Act, 1962 (Act 151), Section 1.

3   Registration of Business names Act, 1962 (Act 151), Section 1.

4   Barclays Bank of Ghana Ltd vs. Lartey [1978] GLR 282.

5   Baidoo vs. Sam [1987-88] 2 GLR 666. Barclays Bank vs. Lartey (supra).

6   See Page 296 on intellectual property.

7   See Chapter 11.

8   For more on advisory boards, see Chapter 11.

9   Registration of Business Names Act, 1962 (Act 151), Section 10.

10 Incorporated Private Partnerships Act, 1962 (Act 152), Section 1.

11 Incorporated Private Partnerships Act, 1962 (Act 152), Section 10(1).

12 Incorporated Private Partnerships Act, 1962 (Act 152), Section 14.

13 Incorporated Private Partnerships Act, 1962 (Act 152), Section 12(2).

14 Incorporated Private Partnerships Act, 1962 (Act 152), Section 12(4).

15 Incorporated Private Partnerships Act, 1962 (Act 152), Section 33.

16 Incorporated Private Partnerships Act, 1962 (Act 152), Section 30.

17 Accra Brewery Co Ltd vs. Guinness Ghana Ltd [[28/05/99] CS 307/99.] Unreported.

18 Of course, typically there might be provisions in the partnership agreement that may permit one party to terminate in periods of extended illnesses.

19 Companies Act, 1963 (Act 179), Section 21. See also Adehyeman Gardens Ltd vs. Assibey[2003-2004] 2 SCGLR1016, Dupaul Wood Treatment vs. Asare [2005-2006] SCGLR 667.

20 Companies Act, 1963 (Act 179), Section 28.

21 Companies Act, 1963, (Act 179), Section 24.

22 Companies Act, 1963, (Act 179), Section 9.

23 Companies Act, 1963, (Act 179), Section 9(3).

24 Companies Act, 1963 (Act 179), Section 10(3).

25 Companies Act, 1963, (Act 179), Section 302(3).

26 Co-operative Societies Act, 1968, NLCD 252, Sections 16, 19 and 20.

27 Labour Act, 2003 (Act 651), Section 65(2).

28 Kwapong vs. Ghana Cocoa Marketing Board and Others [1984-86] GLR 74, 87.

29 Labour Act, 2003 (Act 651), Section 65(4).

30 Trademarks Act, 2004 (Act 664), Section 1.

31 The International Classification referred to is the International Classification of Goods and Services for the purposes of the Registration of Marks under the Nice Agreement of 15 June, 1957, as revised at Stockholm in July, 1976, and at Geneva in May, 1977, 6th Ed. Part II.

32 Article 4 of the Paris Convention provides, inter alia, that any person who has duly filed an application for a patent, or for the registration of trademark or industrial design in any state party to the Paris Convention or his successor in title shall enjoy for the purpose of filing in the other countries a right of priority.

33 This is based on a real case but to protect the identity of the parties, the real names of the individuals and companies have been changed.

Chapter Seven: Acquiring Financial Resources

"Money isn't everything but it ranks up there with Oxygen." - **Rita Davenport**

Outline

- Introduction
- Equity Financing
- Debt Financing
- Trade Credit
- Government and Donors Sources of Funding
- Government Policy and Access to Finance
- Case Study: Smart Money for Kwasi Nyamekye and Vester Oil Mills
- Questions for Class Discussion

ENTREPRENEURS AND SMALLER enterprises often have limited access to financial resources compared with larger companies.[1] This makes financing a major challenge for most entrepreneurs, as they compete with established companies for scarce financial resources. It is argued that entrepreneurs are often at a disadvantage when competing with larger companies for capital because of the peculiar characteristics of entrepreneurial financing compared with the financing of larger and established companies.[2] Entrepreneurs often lack adequate history, including financial records, that investors require to thoroughly assess their possible risks. Prospective investors are reluctant to commit substantial resources to entrepreneurial ventures when they are not reliably informed about the operations of these enterprises, making the acquisition of adequate financial resources a crucial hindrance to achieving an entrepreneurial vision. In Sub-Saharan Africa, most entrepreneurs are likely to fail in the earlier phases of their entrepreneurial ventures because of lack of financial support.[3]

According to Abor and Biekpe, access to finance is a dominant constraint facing many Ghanaian entrepreneurs.[4] In the 1980s and

1990s, the country experienced rigid financial regulations which constrained entrepreneurs' efforts to access finance. The introduction of the Financial Sector Adjustment Programme (FINSAP) in 1989 was aimed at addressing the structural and institutional limitations of the financial sector. FINSAP was expected to bring about a strong and competitive financial sector that would significantly increase the mobilisation of domestic savings.[5] This development was seen as crucial in promoting competition in the banking and non-bank financial sectors, a necessary condition to ensuring that enterprises have access to institutional credit.

The liberalisation of the financial sector brought about significant increase in the number of banking and non-banking financial institutions, however the financial needs of entrepreneurs have not been adequately met. There are various factors contributing to this situation. Firstly, there remains a difficulty in mobilising domestic financial resources which tends to affect entrepreneurs' access to finance.[6] Ghanaians have a poor savings habit: the country's gross savings as a percentage of GDP was only 19.2% in 2005, a figure which fell rapidly in the subsequent years to just 6.6% in 2008; this occurred despite the country experiencing respectable growth in its GDP per capita from US$489 in 2005 to US$713 in 2008.[7] This poor savings culture has significant implications on the general availability of capital. The adoption of a better savings habit by Ghanaians is essential to the accumulation of capital, which would increase the availability of capital within the institutions that finance entrepreneurial ventures.

Entrepreneurs are also likely to face financing difficulties because of their lack of knowledge about potential sources of finance. For example, a survey of 200 small enterprises in Ghana found that most of the enterprises (72%) were either unaware of financing schemes outside traditional banks, or that they do not depend on sources of financing outside of banks.[8] This could be attributed to the difficulty entrepreneurs face in finding out about different sources of funding, perhaps, a result of low public education on these alternative sources.

In cases where there is available finance for Ghanaian entrepreneurs to grow their enterprises, the financing processes are often ineffective due to inadequate institutional frameworks.[9] This tends to make funding decisions very difficult: where potential investors do not have the opportunity to verify the credibility of the information that is presented for funding, and to subsequently monitor the actions and general behaviour of an entrepreneur, they may be reluctant to provide the needed capital. Under these circumstances, investors are likely to withdraw from deals or impose conditions that may be too difficult for entrepreneurs to accept. There is therefore the need for a system that ensures that investors have accessible and verifiable information about borrowers to ease the flow of credit to entrepreneurs. In Ghana, initiatives such as the proposed national identification system, under which all citizens and residents of Ghana are to be issued with uniquely numbered identification cards, as well as the recently established credit reference bureau and the collateral registry where details of all secured loans are registered, could mitigate this situation.

Thankfully the financing challenges have not prevented many entrepreneurs with viable and convincing ideas from starting-up their ventures, often with limited capital – largely personal savings – before the enterprise becomes attractive to potential investors. They employ a technique called bootstrapping. This technique involves growing a new enterprise on few resources, and using other peoples' resources when applicable.[10] By using this technique, entrepreneurs actually start their enterprises with very limited capital. They may use various tactics such as recruiting fewer people, begging, using others people's resources, leasing and in some cases bartering. These tactics allow entrepreneurs to build enterprises from the start-up phase into a growth phase where they become more attractive to external investors.

It is important that entrepreneurs reflect critically on the sources of finance to make informed decisions about the best source to fund their start-up enterprises, as this is likely to have a long lasting impact on the enterprise. Entrepreneurs must seek information on the respective advantages and disadvantages of various funding sources and consider the appropriateness of the sources for the particular stage of a venture's development. Another important factor that entrepreneurs must consider is the structure of capital. The capital structure is the proportion of an entrepreneur's financing that comes from equity and debt. This concept is discussed in detail in Chapter 8 (managing financial resources).

This chapter begins with the identification of the two major sources of finance available to the entrepreneur: equity and debt financing. It then examines government- and donor-supported schemes and governmental policies that impact on entrepreneurs' ability to access credit.

Equity Financing

Equity finance is perhaps the most important source of capital for start-up entrepreneurial ventures. It is the financial resources or capital that owners of an enterprise invest in its activities. Equity finance therefore represents the ordinary shares of an entrepreneurial venture. As shareholders, equity owners have a control over the activities of an enterprise. They exercise control by voting at meetings on important issues and major strategic decisions. A major disadvantage of equity ownership is that equity investors are often the last to receive any dividend or gains that the company makes. Also when a company is liquidated, they are the last to receive recompense, if any. Thus, should the enterprise fail, shareholders risk losing all their investments. These limitations make the cost of equity capital higher than debt capital. The cost of equity capital is the rate of return that potential investors demand for an equity stake in an enterprise.

Financing an entrepreneurial venture through equity capital as opposed to debt capital also affects how much of the enterprise an entrepreneur owns, as the financiers will automatically become part-owners (co-shareholders) of the enterprise. The entrepreneur will therefore be giving some ownership and control to the providers of equity capital in exchange for the capital needed for the growth and expansion of her enterprise. This is the essential dilemma that entrepreneurs considering equity capital face. Despite its inherent limitations, equity capital has its advantages. For example, when the enterprise grows into a profitable venture, equity owners stand a great chance of prospering from the gains after repaying debt capital.

There are different sources of equity finance that are available to the entrepreneur. The main ones are personal savings, investments by family and friends, venture capital and private equity, and the stock exchange.

Personal Savings

Personal savings is an important source of equity capital for most entrepreneurs. This is the cheapest source of capital available to the entrepreneur as he is not required to pay returns to any person for the use of the capital. A survey conducted in Ghana's ten regions found that most entrepreneurs (84%) obtained a proportion of their initial capital through personal savings.[11] In spite of the reliance on personal savings as equity capital, it is not a significant source of capital in Ghana because of the generally low income levels and the poor savings culture in the country, which in turn spring from the country's low gross domestic product per capita.

Personal savings as a source of equity finance has certain advantages over other sources of finance. An entrepreneur who depends solely on personal savings ensures that she retains complete ownership and control over the enterprise. As the next chapter shows, it is also good for cash flow since the enterprise will not be required to make the regular interest payments associated with debt capital. It also reduces the likelihood of financial distress arising from excessive borrowing. An entrepreneur who is financing her enterprise from personal savings has an added advantage – the incentive to commit to the success of the company – because she knows that should the enterprise fail she risks the personal savings she has invested.

Using personal capital also sends strong signals to potential investors and lenders that the entrepreneur is committed to the financial performance and success of the venture. This could be a possible strength should the entrepreneur decide to go for capital from external investors to expand her enterprise.

Family and Friends

Typically, once the entrepreneur has exhausted his personal savings, the first group of persons he is likely to approach for capital for his enterprise are family and friends. After personal savings, this source of finance can be the least expensive form of equity capital. As a result of family ties and close relationships with friends over the years, an entrepreneur is likely to secure financing from those friends and family. In Ghana, about 18% of small and medium-sized enterprises (SMEs) indicated that they have sought financial assistance from family and friends.[12] This source of equity capital is particularly crucial in the start-up phases of entrepreneurial ventures. The lack of history and financial records on the performance of an enterprise in its early years makes it difficult to convince impartial investors of the potential profitability of the enterprise. However, family and friends sometimes provide the capital more because of the pre-existing relationship rather than necessarily because of the merits of the business plan.

The advantage of using this source of capital is that most family members and friends will be more willing to wait for the enterprise to grow. They are not likely to ask the entrepreneur to make regular repayments, thereby reducing cash outflows. It must be noted however that should the enterprise fail, these persons risk losing their investments, which could spell the doom for the good relationship between the entrepreneur and the friends and family members involved.

Private Equity and Venture Capital

The term 'venture capital' is often used interchangeably with the term 'private equity'. The British Venture Capital Association (BVCA) uses the term 'venture capital' to refer to investments in the early (start-up to expansion) stages of unquoted companies and refers to financing at more advanced stages of a company as 'private equity'.[13] However, the US National Venture Capital Association (NVCA) refers to all the subcategories (including start-up and expansion) as private equity.[14] In this book, venture capital (VC) is used in its broadest sense to include all the various stages at which a company can receive financing.

VC firms use their own money and/or raise money from a wide variety of sources, including institutional investors (insurance companies, pension funds, mutual funds, endowments, etc.), development partners, companies and private individuals, and invest these funds in companies (called 'investee companies'). VC participation in companies usually takes the form of equity; by investing capital in the company, the venture capitalists acquire a percentage shareholding in the company. Venture capitalists will often opt for convertible preference shares, which ensure that they have a preference over other shareholders in respect of dividends and/or the assets of the company on winding up.

Venture capital investment may take the form of equity and debt, or only debt. When VC firms invest in an enterprise through debt, they often prefer convertible debt. This type of debt allows them to convert the debt capital into equity, based upon a number of factors including the performance of the enterprise.

Traditional venture capitalists typically provide capital of longer duration than banks do. Even if they wanted to, banks may not be able to provide financing of the same tenor as VC firms because they do not have access to long-term capital to match the long-term funding needs of the enterprise. VC firms, on the other hand, are set up to attract and target long-term funds from individuals and institutions and are willing to lend where banks may not because of their aversion to risk or because the enterprise does not have collateral or cash flow.

As stated earlier, venture capitalists typically have a medium-to-long-term orientation (three years and more), and so are more keen to invest in start-up ventures than traditional financiers. The venture capital market is therefore particularly significant for entrepreneurs seeking financial resources to turn their ideas into viable commercial ventures. As noted by Birch, most entrepreneurial ideas and visions are transformed into SMEs with the help of venture capital companies.[15] On average, out of every ten investee companies a venture capitalist invests in, two will fail, two will be successful and six will be marginally successful.[16] However venture capitalists expect the returns generated by the successful 20% will more than compensate for the failed investments.

Venture capitalists can be placed into two categories – institutional venture capitalists and angel investors. Institutional venture capitalists are organised professional firms that seek out and invest in new business opportunities that have high growth and profit potential. In Ghana, some of these professional venture capital companies include Activity Venture Finance Company, Bedrock Venture Capital Finance Company, Fidelity Capital Partners, Oasis Capital and Injaro Investments. Angel investors on the other hand are "wealthy business people, doctors, lawyers, and others who are willing to take an equity stake in a fledgling company in return for money to start up."[17] In many cases, angels invest in businesses for reasons other than financial motives. They may do so, for example, because of an interest in the industry or because they simply want to help develop entrepreneurs. Angel investing is characterised by relatively small sums of capital and lack of information about who the angel investors are – the real challenge with business angels, as with all angels, is finding one.

Venture capital financing is considered 'smart money' because, in addition to providing capital, the mechanism and structures of venture capital financing provides an opportunity to tap the 'brains' and other resources of the venture capitalist, including his contacts. Venture capitalists involved in an enterprise are effectively 'entrepreneurs in residence'. They act as consultants providing assistance in everything from market research, marketing, strategy development and implementation to managerial decision making as well as financial and risk management services to the entrepreneur.[18] These extras provides the entrepreneurial enterprise (particularly smaller ones) additional leverage in the form of management capacity, particularly in areas where they have no prior experience. Venture capital companies are also involved in nurturing and developing managerial competency because they will be involved (or at least have a say) in recruiting and firing key managers, determining board composition and participating as board members. They also mentor key managers and provide access to their networks to enhance the competitiveness of an enterprise.

The involvement of venture capitalists also adds credibility to an enterprise. This in turn assists in attracting additional capital, quality management as well as suppliers and customers who might not have otherwise been interested. As Green points out, "much of the value added by a venture capitalist is created through the ability to share not only direct personal experience but also the resources and lessons learned across companies that face similar issues over time."[19] It is therefore not surprising that Adjei-Boadu concludes that "perhaps, venture capital is the [most] appropriate investment vehicle for new venture creation and support for innovative ideas."[20]

In most instances, an entrepreneur considering venture capital financing will have to apply to a venture capital company presenting, among others, a comprehensive business plan or proposal. Venture capital investors will normally conduct rigorous due diligence to ascertain the veracity or otherwise of the claims in the entrepreneur's proposal. They tend to incorporate in their screening processes past experience on what worked well or did not work well for them, with their screening methodology often based on predetermined investment criteria. The main focus in the whole process is to find business opportunities that give them attractive returns. They like to examine the industry in which the entrepreneur operates, the growth potential of the enterprise, the management capacity and leadership style as well as the experience and reputation of the entrepreneur. Though their screening processes tend to be more rigorous than other investors, venture capital financiers are in reality more willing to take more risks, making it possible for risky enterprises to get funding.

Venture capital investments are usually made in stages. Rather than write out a cheque to cover the investment agreed, the venture capitalist would almost always advance it in stages or tranches, based on the occurrence of certain pre-determined events (relevant to the risk assessment of the venture capitalists) called 'milestones'. Milestones might include events such as securing a particular contract, recruiting a key manager, achieving a certain growth rate or meeting certain financial targets. The monies advanced at each milestone would be enough to get the investee company to subsequent milestones. This staged approach helps the venture capitalist to minimise the inherent risk involved in investing in such enterprises because it gives venture capitalists the opportunity to review/renew their investment decision at each milestone in the light of new information. If the milestone events do not occur, the venture capitalist may refuse to invest or re-negotiate the terms on which it is prepared to invest.

Financing an enterprise using venture capital has certain pros and cons for the entrepreneur. Typically, venture capitalists provide capital of longer duration to the entrepreneur than what other investors will offer. By their nature, venture capital firms are set up to attract and target long-term funds, making them capable of investing for long durations. Unlike other investors, venture capitalists are more willing to lend to enterprises with perceived high-risk profiles without collateral security, partly because the venture capitalist will offer technical and managerial support to help the enterprise succeed. This technical and managerial support makes them an ideal investment source for the entrepreneur. As Green points out, venture capital firms assist entrepreneurs to "launch and sustain an enterprise that can, in essence, become self-sustaining in due time".[21] Despite these, venture capital may not be attractive to entrepreneurs who wish to retain absolute control of their businesses. It is also difficult for many Ghanaian entrepreneurs to access venture capital funds due to the rigorous screening processes of VC firms.

• *What Venture Capital Firms Look For*
It has been indicated above that traditional venture capital firms invest in enterprises that meet their investment criteria and which have high potential for growth and profitability. Such enterprises often have huge market potential or other competitive advantages, such as a unique intellectual property, that can be relied upon to maximise return on investments.

Venture capitalists prefer to have some form of control over the management of an investee company. They therefore look for entrepreneurs who are willing to give away part of their ownership and control in exchange for the needed capital infusion and technical assistance.

Venture capitalists give priority to entrepreneurial ventures that commit to transparency in their dealings and management practices and, in some cases, are prepared to make changes at the top level management to ensure that a competent managerial team manages the enterprise. This means that the entrepreneur should be committed to best practices. In determining enterprises which have potential for rapid growth, Coopers and Lybrand noted that venture capital companies consider "sound management and organisation" as key performance indicators.[22] In Ghana, Mensah argues that the "lack of management skills and inappropriate management systems" accounts for the inability of most enterprises to access finance from venture capital companies.[23] The ability of an entrepreneur to assemble a competent team to drive his vision certainly attracts venture capital firms to commit their investments.

While venture capital firms may invest in different stages of the life cycle of an entrepreneurial venture, they often prefer to invest in the early and rapid growth phases. As Fry puts it, venture capitalists are mostly interested in investing in young, growing enterprises to reach their potential as quickly as possible while providing the required returns.[24] Despite this preference, they may also acquire some equity stake in ailing companies that have a realistic chance of recovery and provide an opportunity to make high returns. Such investments may involve providing direct technical and managerial support in developing new products and markets for these ailing enterprises.

In developed venture capital markets, syndicate deals are seen as an opportunity to spread risk among venture capitalists. With syndicate deals, a business opportunity from an entrepreneur is co-funded by a group of venture capital firms. This helps the co-investors to limit their exposure to investee company risk. Syndicate deals are more likely if the venture capital companies involved know each other well or have worked together in the past. In most cases, they may have the same interests, motivations and objectives.

Venture capitalists will often take a minority equity stake, although they will almost invariably want operational and management control by ensuring that certain key decisions cannot be made without their consent. Minority stake notwithstanding, these investors look for very high returns to reflect the associated high risk. To diversify their risks, venture capitalists tend to invest the proceeds of a fund in several companies with different risk profiles.

Venture capitalists are more willing to invest in enterprises that give them a competitive advantage. This could come from the area of specialisation of the entrepreneur, the uniqueness of his products and services or some intellectual capital.

• *History of Venture Capital In Ghana*

The venture capital market as a formal, organised industry is a recent development in Ghana. Despite this, venture capital as a distinct source of capital for entrepreneurs has always existed in the country in an informal manner, led by angel investors; the wealthy uncle who invests in a nephew's business, taking an equity stake and sharing all related risks and rewards, is a typical example. The first formal venture capital structure was established in the 1990s following the country's financial liberalisation under the Financial Sector Adjustment Programme (FINSAP). Under the umbrella of the financial sector reform programme, the United States Agency for International Development (USAID) and the Commonwealth Development Corporation (CDC) established the Ghana Venture Fund in 1991 with seed capital of US$5.8 million.[25] The fund, which started operations in 1992, targeted the growing long-term investment needs of Ghanaian SMEs, and was managed by the Venture Fund Management Company.

The Ghana Venture Fund invested in thirteen companies including Ghana Leasing, Achimota Brewery Ltd (subsequently acquired by Heineken), Voltic, and Pioneer Aluminium. In 1995, the European Union provided a US$4-million Enterprise Fund to the Ghana Venture Fund, which was subsequently invested in various sectors of the Ghanaian economy. The Ghana Venture Fund was subsequently subsumed by Aureos Capital Partners Ltd when it was wound up in 1997.[26]

Fidelity Capital Partners Ltd (FCPL) launched its first fund, Fidelity Equity Fund I, in 2000 with initial capital of US$4.5 million. This was subsequently increased to US$8.5 million in 2004 with additional investments from two of its main investors, the Netherlands Finance Company (FMO) and the Swiss Investment Fund for Emerging Markets (SIFEM), a Swiss government development finance institution. Fidelity Equity Fund I is a generalist fund that invests in all types of businesses with a focus on SMEs that have high growth potential. FCPL investments include investments in companies such as BusyInternet, theSOFTtribe, Aqua-In and Isopanel.[27]

Other equity investors who have provided venture capital to Ghanaian entrepreneurs include the Social Security and National Insurance Trust (SSNIT), Modern Africa Growth Fund, the Commonwealth Africa Investment Fund, the African Enterprise Fund, Databank Venture Capital and Renaissance New World Investments.

The success of some of the early entrants to the venture capital market in Ghana encouraged a number of formal venture capital financiers to enter the Ghanaian market, most of them spearheaded or financed by overseas development finance institutions. These institutions have persistently encouraged matched funding from local financial institutions for investment in locally registered venture capital companies (or funds), which are then invested in various promising enterprises.

• *Why Venture Capital is Relatively Underdeveloped in Ghana*

The vibrancy of a venture capital market depends on the existence of certain pre-conditions. Venture capital in Ghana remains largely underdeveloped for a number of reasons including:

- Small IPO Market: According to Black and Gilson, there is a direct correlation between a country's financial system and how its venture capital market performs. They argue that where there is an active stock market, the venture capital market is likely to grow faster.[28] A proper exit strategy is crucial to the development of a vibrant venture capital industry and an IPO (initial public offer) is seen as one of the most effective ways for a venture capitalist to exit. In more developed venture capital markets, even before a decision to invest is made (and as one of the considerations for the decision), the venture capitalist would consider exit options. Many venture capital funds are closed end funds, meaning by the end of the pre-determined life of the fund, all the investments must be liquidated with capital returned to the investors. After over two decades of existence, the Ghana Stock Exchange has only 36 companies listed. With this small IPO market, only a tiny percentage of venture capitalists can hope to liquidate investments in investee companies upon their floatation. While an IPO may be an exit option, this happens in very few cases. The few examples where venture capital investors have exited through an IPO include Ghana Venture Fund's exit of Pioneer Aluminum and Sam Woode Publishers through their respective IPOs.

- Relatively Few Takeovers/Mergers And Acquisitions: Another major alternative exit option for venture capital investments are takeovers, mergers and acquisitions. How vibrant the venture capital industry is in any country is significantly influenced by how buoyant takeovers and mergers and acquisitions activities are, because they remain the most common routes for providing liquidity for realising returns on venture capital investments. As Zider puts it, the idea behind venture capital is to "invest in a company's balance sheet and infrastructure until it reaches a sufficient size and credibility so that it can be sold to a corporation or so that the institutional public equity markets can step in and provide liquidity".[29] In Ghana, only few mergers and acquisitions happen and, when they do, they tend to be of mature companies getting together (e.g. Guinness Ghana Limited and Ghana Breweries to form Guinness Ghana Breweries Limited, Mobil Limited and Total Limited to form Total Limited and Ashanti Goldfields Limited and AngloGold Limited to form AngloGoldAshanti.) rather than of companies acquiring growing companies, or SMEs of similar strength combining their forces to compete effectively in the marketplace. This situation does not encourage the development of a vibrant venture capital market.

- Lack Of Alternative Sources To Exercise Put Options: A common exit strategy for venture capitalists is the use of the 'put option'. With a put option, if the venture capitalist wants to leave, it will 'put' its shares to the entrepreneur who becomes legally obliged to buy back those shares. In Ghana, put options may be difficult to enforce in practice because the entrepreneur may not have the money to acquire the shares of the venture capitalist. It is argued that in exercising put options, the entrepreneur should use capital that is separate from the company (for example, debt capital). The basis for this argument is that because the company's profits are partly as a result of the investment of the venture capitalist's capital injection, it should not be available to buy back the equity. There is also a 'call option' where the entrepreneur can compel the venture capitalist to exit by 'calling' for the venture capitalist shares. With this, the venture capitalist becomes legally obliged to sell its shares.

- Reluctance To Give Up Control: A vibrant venture capital market depends on entrepreneurs' demand for venture capital. Venture capital firms by their nature engage in medium-to-long-term investments where they have some control over the investee enterprise. As I noted in Chapter 2, entrepreneurs generally like to have as much control as possible. The average Ghanaian entrepreneur would rather own 100% of a business that is worth nothing compared to a small part of a viable business. This mindset is clearly inconsistent with venture capital funding as venture capitalists take shares in the company and also want to ensure control in other forms.

- Inflation: Historically, inflation has devalued venture capital investments and made other investment avenues such as government treasury bills more attractive forms of investment for spare cash. However, this trend has been reversed in recent years, and if the country continues to experience macroeconomic stability, this should no longer be an obstacle.

- Lack of Adequate Capital: The availability and supply of money has direct impact on venture capital activities. An active venture capital industry depends on funds from the broad masses in the form of pensions and savings. Where incomes are low, pensions and savings are correspondingly low. This is compounded by the fact that there are only a small number of venture capital providers in the country, who are unable to provide capital required by entrepreneurs seeking such financing.

- Lack of Awareness and Education: Other than the most sophisticated entrepreneurs, there is a dearth of knowledge on the operation of the venture capital industry. Therefore enterprises that could otherwise benefit from venture capital funding may not know about this source of capital. Research conducted by my team supports the view that very few entrepreneurs in Ghana are aware of venture capital as a source of financing.

- Limited Managerial Talent: There is a limited class of outstanding managers that venture capitalists can turn to to run the enterprises they invest in. Furthermore, many owner-manager enterprises lack the relevant managerial competence. As previously pointed out, the quality of management is an important criterion that venture capitalists consider before making investments. In Ghana, while venture capitalists are often willing to invest in promising smaller enterprises, the lack of managerial competence discourages them since that increases the risks and costs involved in managing their shareholding in SMEs.[30]

- Lack of Business Incubators: Venture capitalists can only be active investors if they have a pipeline of deals to choose from. A good way of ensuring a continuous pipeline of deals is the use of incubators. The idea of an incubator is to encourage as many business ideas to be 'hatched'. Incubators then provide support and mentoring to 'infant' enterprises to ensure that they grow to the stage where a venture capitalist might come in. In the West, incubators have been set up in universities, for example, to support students contemplating entrepreneurship, and the assistance given can range from seed money to subsidised rent, and will always include coaching. Incubators have also been set up to speed up and encourage the commercialisation of academic research. New high-technology enterprises being spun-out of the UK's leading universities have a failure rate of less than 10%, compared to more than 60% for similar enterprises coming out of all other institutions.[31] This is due in part to the work done by incubators that nurture such business to enable them see the light of day. As I pointed out in Chapter 1, very few incubators exist in Ghana.

- Poor Corporate Governance Practices: Many SMEs in Ghana operate without proper corporate governance structures and controls, which make them unattractive for venture capital investors.

The above factors have hindered the development of a vibrant venture capital industry in Ghana, a necessity in ensuring that the ideas of Ghanaian entrepreneurs do not remain in the graveyard of business ideas that die at birth due to lack of capital.

• *Ghana Venture Capital Trust Fund (VCTF)*

In recognition of the importance of venture capital, the Ghanaian government enacted the Venture Capital Trust Fund Act in 2004 with the stated objective to "provide financial resources for the development and promotion of venture capital financing for SMEs in priority sectors of the economy as shall be specified from time to time".[32] The Act also mandates the Fund to undertake activities and programmes as well as provide technical support that have a direct impact on promoting the health of the venture capital industry, making it capable of providing the long-term investment needs of Ghanaian SMEs. In this context, SMEs are industrial organisations, projects, undertakings or economic activities which employ not more than a hundred persons and whose total asset base, excluding land and buildings, does not exceed the cedi equivalent of US$1 million in value.[33]

The Act provided for seed capital equivalent to 25% of the proceeds of the now discontinued National Reconstruction Levy, which provided GHC22.4 million.[34] The Fund is also financed by partner institutions including banks, insurance companies and the Social Security and National Insurance Trust (SSNIT). By the end of 2010, capital under its management was GHC83 million, representing more than 300% increase over the seed capital.[35]

The Fund is managed by a Board of Trustees and a Secretariat headed by a Chief Executive Officer. It is a 'fund of funds' in that it does not invest directly in SMEs. It invests through other funds or companies known as venture capital financing companies (VCFCs). A venture capital financing company is a limited liability company "with the sole authorised business as the business of assisting in the development of SMEs by making equity and quasi-equity investments and providing business and managerial expertise to businesses in which it has made or proposes to make an investment. "[36]

There are five venture capital financing companies currently registered with the Venture Capital Trust Fund (VCTF), namely: Activity Venture Finance Company Ltd, Fidelity Equity Fund II, Bedrock Venture Capital Finance Company, Gold Venture Capital Ltd and Ebankese Fund Ltd. VCFCs who meet certain eligibility criteria may apply to the Fund for equity or debt funding that they will in turn invest in SMEs. To be eligible, the venture capital firm must:

- Be incorporated as a limited liability company under Act 179;
- Have a name that includes 'Venture Capital' or any similar abbreviation;
- Be managed by an investment adviser licensed by and in good standing with the Securities and Exchange Commission;
- Meet the minimum equity capital requirements prescribed by regulations made under Act 680 (although there are currently no such regulations in place);
- Have adequate governance and internal control and monitoring procedures for the selection of investment projects and for the monitoring and management of these projects;

- Undertake to enter into an agreement with any SME it provides funding for on broad terms and conditions approved by the board of the Trust Fund ;
- Meet other conditions prescribed by the Board.

There are various generous tax incentives provided by the Venture Capital Trust Fund Act, 2004, for venture capital investment. The VCTF is itself exempted from payments of all taxes including Value Added Tax and the National Health Insurance Levy. Provided they meet the Eligibility Criteria, VCFCs and their investors (as the case may be) are also entitled to the following tax incentives pursuant to the Internal Revenue Act, 2000 (Act 592):

- Exemption from taxes in respect of interest or dividend paid or credited to a person who has invested in a VCFC;
- Exemption from taxes for ten years in respect of dividends of the VCFC (from investments in the SMEs);
- Exemption from taxes for ten years in respect of the income of the VCFC;
- 100% of the amount invested in a VCFC by any person shall be deducted from that person's income for that year, before determining his income that may be subject to income tax;
- A loss incurred by a VCFC from the disposal of shares invested in a venture capital subsidiary during the period of tax exemption may be carried forward for up to five years;
- A loss incurred from the disposal of shares in any venture investment made with monies received from the Trust Fund may be carried forward for up to five years;
- Exemption from capital gains tax in respect of capital gains accruing to the investor in the VCFC.

Through these incentives, VCFCs have a real potential to contribute to the development of SMEs in Ghana by providing a tax-efficient mechanism for mobilising capital for SMEs. The injection of capital in participating VCFCs from the Trust Fund will also ignite their activities, making them attractive to other sources of funds like banks, insurance companies, pension funds and even foreign capital. The enactment and implementation of the Venture Capital Trust Fund Act in 2004 is thus seen as a crucial step in developing the country's underdeveloped venture capital industry.

The Venture Capital Trust Fund finances entrepreneurs through the Venture Capital Financing Companies in two ways – by debt and equity. With debt financing, VCFCs borrow from the Fund below the market rate and invest in an enterprise. The Fund requires VCFCs to have a counterpart fund to match a ratio from 1:1 up to 3:1 as a prerequisite for debt funding. The equity investments involve a partnership between the Fund and the VCFCs. The VCFC then invests in an investee company or enterprise by taking percentage of equity holding.

Entrepreneurs wishing to access these funds must provide the following:

- A completed application form;
- Tax Clearance Certificate;
- Comprehensive business plan;
- Any other information that the VCFC may require.

Since its establishment, the Fund through the VCFCs has invested in various sectors of the economy, including education, ICT, poultry farming, financial services, pharmaceuticals and waste management. By the end of 2010, the VCFCs had invested the cedi equivalent of US$17 million in entrepreneurial ventures in the country.[37]

The Venture Capital Trust Fund also operates a special purpose vehicle (SPV) financing scheme. Through this scheme, the Fund provides funds to VCFC to invest exclusively in participants with specific projects in line with the country's development needs. For instance, in 2009, the Fund provided GH¢1.04 million as part of a public private partnership (PPP) initiative involving small farmers and other stakeholders in the beverage industry to ensure a stable and sustainable high-quality sorghum supply chain as a substitute for imported grains.[38]

• *Should Venture Capital Be Left to Government?*

As mentioned in the previous section, government has played a key role in establishing venture capital as a financing option in Ghana. The Venture Capital Trust Fund was set up pursuant to the Venture Capital Trust Fund Act, 2004 (Act 680), as an initiative of the government to provide seed capital to SMEs.

Act 680 is flawed because it makes the Venture Capital Trust Fund subject to a bigger degree of governmental control than is appropriate for a venture capital firm. The Act stipulates that the chairperson and members of the Board of Trustees be appointed by the President in consultation with the Council of State.[39] The President may also remove these persons from office.[40] Also, two out of the eight members of the Board are civil servants, and the President appoints the Administrator of the Fund. The Board also formulates policies in consultation with the Minister of Finance and Economic Planning, who may give general directives in writing to the Board on matters of policy.[41] To my mind, no matter how experienced a civil servant is, s/he is unlikely to properly understand and evaluate all the dynamics venture capitalists take into account in making venture capital investments; this is because by training, the values of risk taking, venture creation and reward are inconsistent with the orientation of a civil servant. The Fund should be placed firmly in the private realm as venture capital investing has no room for governmental bureaucracy and conservatism. It is about opportunistically embracing risk and high returns which, by definition, government and its agencies are ill equipped to manage.

The policy underpinnings of the Fund are inconsistent with venture capital principles. Venture capital funding, which is generally driven by the capitalist principles of risk and reward, go naturally to the areas considered to be the 'hottest' in the economy – hottest in the sense of increasing opportunities, attractive and growing markets and massive returns on investment. The current arrangement of the Fund requires a greater percentage of the Fund to be invested in priority areas of the economy, and the rest to other viable business opportunities. While, in some cases, there might be an overlap between the 'hottest' and 'priority' areas, this is not always the case. The establishment of the Fund has been crucial in developing the venture capital industry in Ghana; however, how vibrant and sustainable the industry eventually becomes largely depends on the government allowing the forces of demand and supply to determine which areas of the economy funds must go to. Thus, the government, having identified the SME sector as the sector to support, should leave it up to the principles of risk and reward and supply and demand to determine which industries – and which companies in those industries – get venture capital funding.

The foregoing is not to suggest in any way that government should not play a role in venture capital. My view however is that this role must be limited to creating an enabling environment to develop, including a vibrant IPO market and an active mergers and acquisitions market, which will in turn spur a vibrant venture capital industry. It should also fund the establishment of incubators to help nurture and develop entrepreneurial ideas. Additionally, government can help by engaging in the development of managerial capacity in the SME sector with the creation of a technical assistance fund which can be tapped into to train entrepreneurs and venture capital managers in aspects of business management and corporate governance. This will ensure that there are enough competent managers out there to anchor the investee companies seeking and/or receiving capital from the Fund. Finally, government should invest heavily in educating Ghanaian entrepreneurs and the public on venture capital.

Stock Exchange

The stock exchange is an important market where entrepreneurs can raise long-term equity capital. It offers one of the most secure and sustainable sources of long-term financing. Raising capital for the first time from the stock exchange involves an IPO (initial public offering) where the entrepreneur offers shares in his company to the public for the first time. Subsequent offers are simply called public offerings. The decision to 'go public' is a major one that needs to be thoroughly considered. Although the stock exchange offers the potential of raising substantial capital to undertake development and expansion activities, particularly for established entrepreneurial ventures, using it involves elaborate administrative, legal and regulatory requirements.

In Ghana, the Ghana Stock Exchange (GSE) is the main market where entrepreneurs can raise long-term equity capital for their enterprises. The GSE was established in July 1989 under the Companies Code of 1963 as a private company limited by guarantee. It gained full recognition as an authorised stock exchange in October 1990 and commenced trading on 12 November 1990. It subsequently changed from a private into a public company limited by guarantee in April 1993 under the Company Code, 1963 (Act 179). Located on the fifth floor of the Cedi House in Accra, the GSE has the mandate to achieve the following objectives as an exchange[42]:

- Provide the framework and facilities for the trading in bonds, shares and other securities;
- To control all issues relating to the granting of quotations on the securities market;
- Regulate the dealings of all licensed dealing members and their clients;
- Co-ordinate stock dealing activities of members and facilitate the exchange of information;
- Co-operate with exchanges in other countries to provide useful information to members of the GSE and their clients.

Since trading commenced in November 1990, the Exchange has not been particularly vibrant, largely due to the low numbers of IPOs. There are 36 companies listed on the Exchange with a market capitalisation of GHC47.42 billion as at the end of January 2012. The failure of foreign multinationals to list on the GSE has been cited as one major reason for its low performance. This was echoed by the deputy Managing Director of the GSE, Ekow Afedzie, when he urged foreign companies in Ghana's high-yield sectors (telecoms, energy and mining) to list shares locally to help develop a buoyant and active stock exchange.[43]

Listing on the GSE requires entrepreneurs to meet a set of rules, (the Listing Rules) before and after the share offer. The key requirements as contained in the Listing Rules for an entrepreneur to offer shares to the public are as follows[44]:

- A post-floatation stated capital of at least GHC1 million for applications for listing on the First List, and GHC500,000 for the Second List (the Second List is aimed at SMEs);
- The public float of the applicant must constitute 25% of the number of issued shares[45] (this requirement may be waived if the stated capital of the applicant on floatation is at least GHC75 million and the applicant provides an undertaking to meet the percentage required within three years);
- The GSE shall refuse listings relating to partly paid shares except in exceptional circumstances;
- A prospective company shall list all the classes of shares issued or to be issued;
- The Exchange shall determine the adequacy of the spread of shareholders at the close of offer or time of listing;
- The Exchange prescribes a minimum of 100 shareholders for all listed companies.

With an average of less than 2 IPOs a year, and only 36 listed companies, the Ghana Stock Exchange has obviously not been adequately utilised by entrepreneurs to raise their long-term capital requirements.

In a bid to reverse this trend and boost capital raising and stock trading by small and medium-sized enterprises, the Ghana Stock Exchange has announced the establishment of an alternative investment market, the Ghana Alternative Investment Market (GAIM), which is will be built to cater for small and medium-sized enterprises and their typical capital profile and needs. The prospects for GAIM's launch in the near future are however slim; at the time of going to press, consultants working on the project passed the opinion that the proposed implementation timeline will most likely not be met due to technical and developmental challenges.[46]

Debt Financing

Debt financing is the most utilised source of external capital for most Ghanaian entrepreneurs. It involves borrowing money to finance entrepreneurial activities and then repaying the amount borrowed with interest. Debt finance requires an entrepreneur to pay interest, either on a fixed- or floating-rate basis, together with the principal or the initial capital. Repayment can be spread over a period of time or made in a single lump-sum payment. The need to make repayments means that debt financing tends to constrain the future cash flows of an entrepreneurial venture and, if not managed properly, could result in losses and increased financial risk.[47] Despite this inherent difficulty, debt finance remains a popular source of funding among entrepreneurs.

Debt financing appears to have wider acceptance by Ghanaian entrepreneurs compared to equity financing. As explained earlier, this is partly due to reluctance on the part of Ghanaian entrepreneurs to part with ownership and control of their business. The cost of capital for debt financing is generally less than equity financing. Interest charged by lenders on loans to entrepreneurs is generally low when compared to what equity investors demand as return on their investment. Various reasons account for this. Firstly, interest on debt is paid before dividends due equity holders. Similarly, in the event of insolvency, debt holders are paid before equity holders. Also, companies are generally allowed to deduct interest payment on loans from taxable income whereas dividends are taxed. And by using debt, an entrepreneur can maintain complete ownership of the company since debt is a liability that will be paid at a future date. Though debt is preferred, most Ghanaian entrepreneurs face challenges accessing debt capital.

Ghanaian firms rate access to credit as one of the greatest barriers to growth and the country ranks 113 out of 183 worldwide on the ease of accessing credit.[48] Some of barriers to securing debt capital include lack of assets like land and buildings to use as collateral, lack of knowledge about credit providers and lending criteria, and lengthy bureaucratic processes. All these contribute to a high cost of doing business in the country, summarily posing a direct risk to the growth of entrepreneurial ventures.

In evaluating loan applications, lenders often use a risk-return model to assess the risk profile of a company before making lending decisions, including determining the interest rate to be charged. Since Ghanaian credit providers seem to lack a satisfactory understanding of the peculiarities of entrepreneurial ventures and their operations, the onus is on the entrepreneur seeking debt capital to lessen the perceived risk associated with her enterprise by preparing adequately before applying for debt capital. This can be partly achieved by preparing financial statements which are audited by credible accounting firms; submitting historical and projected data and cash flow projections that incorporate interest and capital payments; and generally showing a solid understanding of the business and the industry.

The options open to entrepreneurs seeking debt capital to finance their short-term and long-term capital requirements include loans from banks or non-bank financial institutions, debt instruments and trade credit.

Bank Loans

Bank loans have traditionally been the most popular source of debt capital for entrepreneurs and small business owners. Although the liberalisation of the financial sector over the past decade has brought about a rapid increase in the number of banks in the country, many banks still shy away from giving credit to entrepreneurs. They typically favour less risky, larger and better established enterprises that have a borrowing history over start-up entrepreneurial ventures and smaller enterprises.[49] The difficulty that SMEs face in accessing credit from banks is partly due to the high default risk involved in doing business at that level. Despite this, research on sources of seed capital in Ghana shows that bank loans represent the second most popular financing option (32%) for entrepreneurs.[50]

Generally, banks operate with broad loan policies without specific policies targeted at SMEs. Where specific policies targeting small SMEs exist, they are more likely to be donor-funded than driven by the banks. As a result, banks' screening processes for loan applications tend to be the same for SMEs as they are for large, established companies.

Raising debt capital financing from banks for entrepreneurial ventures therefore poses various challenges to the entrepreneur. Aryeetey et al. identify high interest rates, collateral requirements and cumbersome processes as some of the main impediments that entrepreneurs face in accessing commercial loans from banks in Ghana.[51] Historically, the interest rates banks charge on loans have been high in Ghana, in some cases exceeding 40%. Banks often cite the high cost of borrowing from the central bank (Bank of Ghana) or other commercial banks as one of the reasons for this high interest rate on loans. They point to high interest rates on treasury securities as a reason for the high cost of capital as investors prefer to invest their monies in these securities, forcing the banks to compete with treasury securities to attract funds. However, even in cases where the rate at which the Bank of Ghana lends to banks have seen significant reductions – often resulting in reductions in the rate of treasury securities – average interest rates on bank loans still remain as high as 24% to 30%.

Interest rates can either be fixed or floating. With fixed rates, the entrepreneur pays the same interest over the duration of the loan. In case of the floating rate, the rate will generally be set a number of percentage points above the policy rate, which is the rate at which the Bank of Ghana lends to the banks. This means that a positive or negative change in the policy rate directly impacts on the movement of the interest rate charged under a floating-rate loan.

Audrey Selormey, the founder and Managing Director of Buka Restaurant, illustrates the frustration associated with accessing loans when she notes that "lack of access to affordable credit" is most disturbing to her as an entrepreneur. "If you don't have land or a house, banks will ask you to have a down payment of 50% of the loan value. I borrowed money at a rate of 40% in order to keep my business running, and it took three months to get the loan approved."[52]

In negotiating bank loans, there is also the possibility of asymmetric information where one party does not have adequate information essential to decision making. In most cases, banks may not have adequate and complete understanding of the entrepreneur's capacity to repay a loan. As the credit infrastructure in Ghana is not well developed, there is very little data on credit history or ratings of potential credit seekers, making it extremely difficult for banks to properly assess loan applications, which poses major risks of default to the banks. Banks tend to offset this risk through bank charges, high interest rates and demand for collateral, which entrepreneurs see as major constraints.[53] The ongoing national identification registration, as well as the recently established credit reference bureaux, are potential sources of information about all participants in the credit market. This might help drive down the cost risk of defaults and consequently the cost of loan financing.

Depending on the nature of the loan, the amount involved and the duration, banks may employ loan covenants as a way of protecting their investments. Loan covenants are legal instruments designed to put various restrictions on managerial actions that might expose a firm to a risk of default. For example, a loan covenant can stipulate that the company cannot borrow above an agreed limit.

Bank loans may be short-term or long-term. Short-term loans are loans with maturities falling within a year; this includes products like overdraft facilities and lines of credit. Overdrafts are special arrangements that allow entrepreneurs to withdraw more money than their accounts contains to finance working capital needs. A line of credit is in the form of overdraft with a predetermined limit that gives the entrepreneur short-term finance. Negotiating a line of credit with a bank allows an entrepreneur to quickly withdraw the needed capital to run an operation as and when the need for cash arises.

When entrepreneurs are granted credit in Ghana, they are mostly given short-term loans. Rarely do banks in Ghana offer long-term loans to entrepreneurs. A survey of Ghanaian entrepreneurs found that majority of loans were short-term loans with maturity periods between 3 months and a year, largely for clearing of goods at the port, or for the purpose of purchasing stock to meet seasonal demands.[54] Banks often do not provide long-term finance to entrepreneurs because they categorise them as risky. Also, even if they wanted to, banks might not be able to provide the long-term financing that other investors like venture capital firms can because banks lack access to long-term capital to match the long-term funding needs of entrepreneurs. Though banks are generally conservative in lending to start-up enterprises, they are willing to lend to entrepreneurs who are able to provide good business plans. Entrepreneurs need to demonstrate some stability in their sales and how they will generate cash flow from their products or services to enable repayment of the debt. A positive cash flow is essential for securing bank loans as it provides evidence that the company can generate funds to repay a loan.

Loans from Non-Bank Financial Institutions

Non-bank financial institutions form a significant part of the credit market in Ghana, particularly as a source of debt capital for SMEs and start-up entrepreneurs. They are often medium-sized financial companies that provide tailored products such as loans, investment and business advisory services to meet the growing needs of SMEs and other groups in a way that commercial banks are likely not to consider. In Ghana, non-bank financial institutions are regulated under the Non-Bank Financial Institutions (NBFI) Law, 1993 (PNDCL 328), and include companies like First Allied Savings and Loans, Adehyeman Savings and Loans, Beige Capital Savings and Loans, First Capital Plus Savings and Loans and Ivory Finance Company.

These financial institutions are different from banks in various ways. The regulatory requirement previously allowed them to have minimum paid-up capital of between GHC100,000 and GHC1 million. Under the newly instituted Bank of Ghana capital adequacy requirement, non-bank financial institutions are now required to have a minimum stated capital of GH7 million by the end of 2012. NBFIs are precluded from dealing in banking services such as foreign exchange transactions and direct clearing of cheques.

NBFIs tend to be highly sought after by entrepreneurs and SMEs, particularly when banks refuse loan applications because of the high-risk profile of these enterprises. Consequently, smaller enterprises have become an attractive portfolio for non-bank financial institutions. It has been found that non-bank financial institutions in Ghana are more willing to give loans to SMEs and entrepreneurs than the commercial banks.[55]

In keeping with their higher risk tolerance, these financial firms often do not require loan applicants to have a long-standing relationship with them. They are able to approve and disburse loans within very short turnaround times, but they tend to charge high interest rates relative to commercial banks. Because of their risk potential, entrepreneurs seeking loans from these institutions must charge their assets in the form of collateral. In the event of default, the charged assets can be sold to repay the debt. It is worth noting not all NBFIs require collateral, and often require minimal documentation and processes in evaluating loan applications. Further, these institutions offer further customer services including door-to-door financial service offerings and flexible loan repayment schedules that encourage customers to pay back their loans on weekly, bi-weekly and monthly bases.

The non-bank financial sector in Ghana has grown into an important segment of the economy with its services to the formal and informal sectors. The amount of loans extended by these institutions increased from GH¢70.63 million in 2003 to GH¢160.47 million in 2006.[56] The upward trend in credit provisioning demonstrates the crucial role that these institutions play in extending credit to microenterprises and SMEs in the country. With the number of non-bank financial institutions in the country increasing to 44 in 2011, their role in the credit market could become even more prominent.

In addition to being generally more willing to extend credit to entrepreneurs, non-bank financial institutions in Ghana have earned a reputation for being able to act much quicker than banks. Unique Trust Financial Services, before it became a bank, positioned itself as being able to provide a loan in less than 48 hours at a time when several banks were taking several weeks to process loan applications.

Non-bank financial institutions have developed better 'homegrown' systems for assessing and pricing risk. For example, given the country's lack of identification address system, non-bank financial institutions provide a way for their credit officers to visit homes of prospective applicants so as to map the locations of prospective applicants for easy identification in the event of default.

Debt Instruments

Debt instruments are important tools that entrepreneurs can rely on to raise loan capital either for a short or a long period of time. They are legal documents that enable one party, the issuer (in this case the entrepreneur), to raise debt capital from another party, the lender, by promising to repay the lender at a specific period of time and in accordance with the terms of the agreement. Depending on the type and the nature of the instrument, there may or may not be interest on the loan. There are various debt instruments but the commonly used ones in Ghana are bonds, commercial papers, and promissory notes.

Bonds are long-term contracts where one party, the lender, provides credit to a company in return for a promise to pay regular interest payments or coupons at predetermined intervals of time and the value of the bond on maturity. Bonds are largely long-term debt capital with maturity periods of more than a year. In Ghana, very few bonds are traded on the Ghana Stock Exchange and these are mainly issued by the government. Entrepreneurs have yet to explore the potential of raising capital through the bond market.

Ghanaian entrepreneurs are however still able to raise capital through commercial papers. Commercial papers are unsecured notes that allow entrepreneurs to raise short-term finance. The payment periods for commercial papers are usually within days or weeks. This form of debt financing is mainly used to cover working capital expenditure like inventory purchases. Entrepreneurs need to be creditworthy or be considered as posing low risk to access capital from commercial papers.

Another debt instrument available for entrepreneurs is promissory note. Promissory notes are short-term financing arrangements where an entrepreneur can raise debt capital by promising to repay the debt as and when the lender demands it. Repayment period can also be an agreed fixed date.

Trade Credit

Trade credit has always been a reliable source of capital for entrepreneurs and small business owners. Trade credit is a short-term debt financing where a customer, in this case the entrepreneur, requests a supplier, the lender, to provide a product or service, the payment of which is scheduled for a future date. Trade credit is especially crucial in financing working capital for inventory. It is useful for entrepreneurial ventures with large inventory turnover, like retail enterprises, where the inventory can be received and sold before payments are made.

It is often easier for an entrepreneur to ask a supplier to delay payment of goods and services for a period of time than seeking a loan from a bank to pay for such goods and services, particularly where an entrepreneur has developed long-standing relationships with suppliers. Also, most suppliers generally sell on credit to boost sales and retain customers. As short-term capital, trade credit is often interest free. This source of capital allows the entrepreneur to maintain a positive cash flow while continuing operations with the inventory.

Government and Donors as Sources of Funding

Government and the donor community have over the past two decades played an active role in ensuring that SMEs have access to credit. In most cases, the rationale has been to support small entrepreneurs to grow and develop their enterprises as a way of reducing poverty in the country. One such direct government intervention was the establishment of the National Board for Small Scale Industries (NBSSI). The NBSSI was established by the state with financial support from multilateral donor organisations to enhance microenterprise and SME development through access to credit and other technical assistance.

The liberalisation of the financial sector under the Financial Sector Adjustment Programme (FINSAP) provided a pivotal point in small-scale enterprise funding in the country. Under the Programme of Action to Mitigate the Social Costs of Adjustment (PAMSCAD), a special fund was created to assist microenterprises. Also, a US$30-million Fund for Small and Medium Enterprises Development (FUSMED) was initiated by the World Bank and other donors to boost credit availability to SMEs through commercial and development banks.[57] Through these funds, which were managed by the Bank of Ghana, the NBSSI assisted various start-up entrepreneurs to access credit and to grow their enterprises.

In recent years, governments have sponsored various schemes that provide credit SMEs throughout the country. These include the Social Investment Fund, the Poverty Alleviation Fund (PAF), the Presidential Special Initiatives (PSI), and the Micro Finance and Small Loan Centre (MASLOC). While these initiatives are largely geared towards poverty alleviation, they provide entrepreneurs greater access to credit.

The donor community has also been influential in promoting and providing credit to small enterprises in the form of microfinance. These donor-driven microfinance initiatives are either solely funded loan projects or co-funded by different donor groups like the World Bank and its private arm, the International Finance Corporation (IFC), the International Fund for Agricultural Development (IFAD), African Development Bank (AfDB), United Nations Development

Programme (UNDP), Danish Development Agency (DANIDA), Canadian International Development Agency (CIDA), Food and Agriculture Organisation (FAO), United States Agency for International Development (USAID), German Technical Corporation (GIZ), Netherlands Development Organisation (SNV) and CARE International.

These development partners have initiated various credit schemes that entrepreneurs can access without the usual difficulties they face in accessing funds from other sources. In some cases, these development partners assist in setting up funds to target specific industries and sectors of the economy, often working through banks and other financial institutions to administer the funds. An example of such a fund is the Export Development and Investment Fund (EDIF). EDIF was set-up to assist local businesses to export their produce to international markets. Its mission is to enhance the economic growth of Ghana by the provision of funds on concessionary terms for the development and promotion of the country's exports.

Below is a list of credit schemes and projects that have been particularly useful to Ghanaian entrepreneurs.

Rural Financial Services Project

The Rural Financial Services Project is a project sponsored by the World Bank, International Fund for Agricultural Development (IFAD) and African Development Bank (AfDB) that provides credit facilities to small enterprises. The project has established the ARB Apex Bank (which acts as a clearing house as well as a quasi-regulator) for the country's rural banks to ease the difficulties SME owners in rural areas face accessing finance to support their enterprises. It has also been proactive in building the capacity of rural and community banks by, for example, assisting them to computerise their operations to ensure greater credit provisioning accountability in rural areas.

The GRATIS Foundation

GRATIS Foundation was established to provide working capital and skills training for start-up ventures with the view to promoting small-scale industrialisation in Ghana. For over two decades, the foundation has provided basic working capital tools and the transfer of technologies to small-scale enterprises through training. With its Regional Technology Transfer Centres (RTTCs), it provides training to small entrepreneurs in areas like pottery, textile making, soap making and metal fabrication and design.

Rural Enterprise Project

The Rural Enterprise Project is a government- and donor-supported project that focuses on small-scale enterprise development in rural Ghana. The project is supported by funds from the Government of Ghana, the Agricultural Development Bank and the International Fund for Agricultural Development (IFAD). The project assists rural entrepreneurs to become profitable and enhance their growth prospects by offering them easy access to credit. In addition to providing rural financial services through the Agricultural Development Bank, the project also supports entrepreneurs in areas like business development, technology transfer and support for apprenticeship training.

Empretec Ghana Foundation

Empretec Ghana Foundation is an entrepreneurship and capacity building organisation. It started operations in Ghana in 1990 with the support of the then government, Barclays Bank and donors like the United Nations Development Programme (IUNDP), the British Department for International Development (DFID), the European Union (EU) and the International Finance Corporation. The foundation, which has become largely financially self-sufficient, provides enterprises with access to financial services, training, business advice and technology. Empretec delivers its financial assistance schemes to entrepreneurs across different sectors of the economy, including manufacturing, tourism, ICTs, agriculture, waste management, construction, wholesale and retail, education and health care, among others. It also identifies entrepreneurs and individuals with ideas that have good commercial prospects and supports them to grow their ideas into thriving enterprises. Its technical services assistance scheme supports entrepreneurs by offering them training workshops, seminars and access to networks that are valuable to their growth. Through these, the foundation has built the capacity of various entrepreneurs to grow their enterprises and to be competitive internationally.

Accessing most of these government- and donor-supported credit schemes typically does not come with the difficulties that characterise other sources of credit. Also, these initiatives often charge interest rates below the market rate, making them attractive sources of low-cost funding. The main challenge facing these schemes is that they tend to have high default rates. This may be because of the more relaxed criteria they employ in screening credit applicants.

Government Policy and Access to Finance

The interplay of demand and supply of capital to finance start-up and growing entrepreneurial ventures does not happen in a vacuum. There are several macroeconomic issues that impact on the general availability of capital for entrepreneurial financing. A country's broader macroeconomic environment informs the degree of capital flows and its direction. These, in turn, have fundamental consequences on the equity and debt markets which most entrepreneurs tap to finance their enterprises. The Ghanaian government's macroeconomic policy framework is the single most important instrument that shapes the country's macroeconomic environment and, by extension, access to finance. The Bank of Ghana as the central bank uses its monetary policy framework to determine this direction.

The interest rate is an important monetary policy tool that has a direct impact on entrepreneurs' ability to access capital, as it can be used to determine the growth of total money supply and liquidity in the country. It is the premium that lenders require for extending credit to borrowers for a period of time. For the entrepreneur, the interest rate is the cost of capital on equity and debt. There are other allied rates including policy rate, interbank rate, lending rate, deposit rate, inflation rate, treasury securities rate and exchange rate, also controlled by the Bank of Ghana, which affect capital availability and the entrepreneur's ability to access finance.

The policy rate is the reference interest rate that forms the basis for charging other interest rates like lending rates (the rate that banks and other financial institutions charge on their loans). It largely reflects the cost of capital to all lenders. A movement in the policy rate affects the interbank rates (the rate at which banks lend to each other). The entrepreneurs' cost of capital therefore depends to some extent on the upward and downward movements in the policy rate. High interest rates hinder the general accessibility of capital, which then hinder entrepreneurs' access to credit.

As a macroeconomic policy tool, the policy rate can also be used to encourage savings mobilisation in the country. As a reference interest rate, a high policy rate directly increases the rate paid by banks on deposits. This is likely to boost savings as returns increase, and subsequently the general availability of capital for the entrepreneur. However, the effect of high interest rate on savings may adversely affect the cost of capital and the rate at which capital is available to entrepreneurs.

Amonoo, Acquah and Asmah examined the relationship between interest rate and demand for credit in Ghana and found that high interest rates adversely affected access to credit due to the entrepreneurs' aversion to borrowing at high rates. They also found that high interest rates affect entrepreneurs' ability to repay back loans.[58] Indeed, high interest rates may encourage borrowers to use borrowed money to settle previous loans instead of investing them in working capital.[59] Thus, a lower policy rate could positively impact on the general availability of capital for entrepreneurs and their ability to service loans.

The policy rate can also be used to stem rising inflation rates and depreciations or falls in value of the currency. Inflation is the continual increase in the general price level in an economy over a period of time. Lower interest rates should increase the cash circulation which would increase inflation. Rising inflation affects the value of cash and discourages investment in an economy. Historically, inflation in Ghana has been very volatile, with rates as high as 30% recorded in 2000. This undervalues the currency and hinders not only entrepreneurs' access to capital but also the value of their cash. In recent times, the country has seen a downward inflation trend reducing from over 20% in 2008 to about 10% in July 2010. If this trend continues, then the negative effect of inflation on entrepreneurs should be a thing of the past.

The cedi exchange rate is the price of the cedi in relation to other currencies. Though the exchange rate largely depends on demand and supply of the relative currencies and other economic indicators like the gross domestic product and a country's international reserves, government policy in the way of buying or selling currencies may influence the movement of the rate. Depreciation of the Ghanaian currency has over the last decades affected entrepreneurs' ability to purchase the necessary goods and services to grow their enterprises.

Treasury securities rate is another important interest rate that affects entrepreneurs' access to credit. Government is the main borrower in the country. It borrows by issuing securities like treasury bills, notes and bonds. The more government borrows, the less available capital there is for lending to entrepreneurs. More importantly, the higher the rate that government is prepared to pay for debt, the higher the rate that lenders like banks and other financial institutions charge on their loans. Depositors often require banks to give them an interest rate above what government offers on its risk-free securities. With relatively high interest rates on government securities, banks typically prefer investments in securities like Treasury Bills instead of extending credit to entrepreneurs with its associated risks. Historically, government securities have been an important source of profits for banks, fetching as much as 25% of profits. The situation is now improving with lower interest rates on these securities. It is worth noting however that lending rates are not affected solely by interest rates on government securities like treasury bills.[60] The reduction in securities rate from about 25% in September 2009 to about 13% in September 2010 saw only a corresponding bank's lending rate reduction from about 30% to an average 25% for the same period. This is because banks and lenders take into consideration various factors in determining their lending rates.

Questions for Class Discussion

1. Identify the major challenges that Ghanaian entrepreneurs face in funding their enterprises.

2. What are the main types of capital available to an entrepreneur? What are the advantages and disadvantages of each source?

3. What is venture capital?

4. Is venture capital the panacea to entrepreneurial financing challenges in Ghana?

5. What role, if any, should government play in the venture capital industry?

6. What can be done to make banks more responsive to entrepreneurial financing?

7. Evaluate the role of non-governmental organisations in financing entrepreneurs in the country.

Smart Money for Kwasi Nyamekye and Vester Oil Mills

MR KWASI NYAMEKYE, THE FOUNDER and Managing Director of Vester Oil Mills Ltd (VOML) seems to have found solace in venture capital financing. Incorporated in June 2002, VOML is located at Abuontem in the Bosomtwe District of the Ashanti Region in Ghana. The company specialises in the processing of soya beans, palm nut kernels and copra into crude edible oils and their residual cakes for domestic and industrial use.

A metallurgical engineer by profession, Mr Nyamekye holds a B.Sc. in Metallurgical Engineering and an Executive MBA. Prior to his entrepreneurial exploits, he worked in the mining and mineral extraction industry for several years. Nyamekye's interest in entrepreneurial activities dates back to before 2002 when he engaged in the marketing and sale of plant oils in Kumasi with his wife, Vester Nyamekye. the Nyamekyes initially financed VOML with their personal savings of GHC500. They reinvested all profit into the company and in 2004 sought technical assistance from TechnoServe to successfully install and test the company's plants and machinery for palm nut kernel and soya processing.

VOML soon encountered challenges in funding its operating and growth expenditures. As demand for their products increased, the company urgently needed to expand its processing capacity. Apart from the need for additional mechanical expellers for processing soybeans and groundnuts into quality soy meal for livestock and crude soy oil for the paint and soap making industries, the company also needed to resolve its transportation challenges, provide electric power supply, improve its production floor and working area, enhance internal operating procedures and boost the internal management capacity of its personnel.

Fortunately, the African Development Foundation (ADF) came to its aid in 2006 by providing a soft credit facility of GHC139,350.

The amount was used to purchase two mechanical expellers and to part-fund some working capital needs. This facility allowed Mr Nyamekye to finance the company's operating activities while remaining profitable. However, growth in customer numbers and increased demand for the company's products meant the need to increase processing capacity. Long-standing problems faced in sourcing raw materials – particularly soya beans – increased. The seasonal nature of soya beans leads to high prices in the lean season, with prices often doubling compared with those in the harvest period. Securing adequate working capital to stockpile soya beans was the ideal plan for Mr Nyamekye and his management team.

Mr Nyamekye decided to seek long-term funding to mitigate the capacity and raw material challenges. For him, venture capital financing was the perfect option. According to Nyamekye, "banks were not willing to give long-term financing to VOML[,] plus the interest rates were too high for a growing business." After thorough research, Nyamekye settled on the Activity Venture Finance Company ('Activity'), and applied to Activity for equity funding. In addition to his application letter, he was required to add soft and hard copies of VOML's business plans outlining, among others, the uses of funds as well as the company's tax clearance certificate.

With its strong performance and market potential, the management of VOML expected little challenge in accessing the venture capital financing, but that was not the case. Aside the numerous requirements that Nyamekye had to fulfil, changes in the management of Activity and disagreement in the valuation of VOML delayed the approval of the funding. Yet, unlike many other local entrepreneurs, Nyamekye had an advantage. The stricter monitoring and reporting regime required by ADF for the soft credit facility in 2006 had put VOML in a solid position to meet Activity's funding requirements.

By the end of 2008, the Board of Activity approved the transfer of an amount of GH¢GHC241,800 exchange for a 25% equity stake in VOML. In addition to the equity investment, the agreement allows VOML to access a low-interest revolving credit facility of GHC106,326 per annum. This venture capital intervention allowed VOML to increase its operating capacity to 35 metric tons per day, enabling it to become one of the five leading seed oil milling companies in the country. The revolving credit facility has been particularly useful in partly resolving the raw material challenge, but the infusion of venture capital has changed the face of the company.

The involvement of the venture partner impacted significantly on the performance of the company. As Nyamekye puts it, "[the] contribution has grown the company from an annual sales of GHC881,495in 2008 to GHC1,662,049 in 2010. This is very significant in a company's growth." With its capacity and operating efficiency, VOML now has several well-known loyal customers including Agricare Ltd, Fosuka Farms Ltd, Azar Chemical Industries Ltd and the Greater Accra Poultry Farmers Association.

For Nyamekye and VOML, the financing provided by Activity really represents smart capital. He sees the monitoring, training sessions and workshops which are organised by Activity alongside financing as "incomparable. Banks and some other financial institutions do not offer [those kinds of] technical assistance." Indeed, the company's activities are constantly under the watchful eyes of Activity as VOML is required to provide monthly operating reports aside from daily interactions and regular visits to the company. Activity also has representation on the board of VOML, with board meetings held every quarter.

The technical assistance ranges from resolving regular operational problems to strategic challenges. As part of its growth strategies, VOML aims to purchase a modern 50-metric-tonne-per-day solvent extraction plant and a matching 5-metric-ton-per-day oil refinery plant. Their plan also includes procuring some farm equipment to assist soya bean farmers in northern Ghana to ensure timely and adequate supply of soya beans to the company. Activity is actively leading the process and has prepared the funding proposals to raise the required

GHC660,000 in long-term debt to partly finance the project. Such benefits scarcely come with other funding sources and that excites the management of VOML.

With this experience, Mr Nyamekye has been an advocate of venture capital financing to fellow entrepreneurs, particularly those looking for long-term investment. However, he is quick to add that venture capital financing is not for those who are "not willing to be transparent in their business dealings". While he admits that there will be pressure on you to perform, for him, at the end of the day, it is to the benefit of the entrepreneur's company.

Questions for Case Discussion

1. If Mr Nyamekye had asked you for your opinion on the valuation pursuant to which he sold 25% of his company, how would you be able to determine whether those shares were undervalued, overvalued or valued correctly?

2. Why do you think the Activity Venture Finance company agreed to fund Mr Nyamekye's business?

3. Beyond the finance, what where the expectations of Mr Nyamekye in approaching Activity Venture Finance company. Were those expectations realistic?

Notes

1   Levy, B. Obstacles to Developing Indigenous Small and Medium Enterprises: An Empirical Assessment. *The World Bank Economic Review*, 7(1), 1993: 65-83.

2   Cornwall, J.R., D.O. Vang and J.M. Hartman. *Entrepreneurial Financial Management: An Applied Approach*. Upper Saddle River: Prentice Halll: 2004.

3   Biekpe, N. Financing Small Business in Sub-Saharan Africa: Review of Some Key Credit Lending Models and Impact of Venture Capital. *Journal of African Business*, 5(1), 2004: 29-44.

4   Abor, J. and N. Biekpe. Small Business Financing Initiatives in Ghana. *Problems and Perspectives in Management*, 4(3), 2006: 69-77.

5   Antwi-Asare, T.O. and E.K.Y. Addison. Financial Sector Reforms and Bank Performance in Ghana. London: Overseas Development Institute, 2000.

6   Doni-Kwame, E. Corporate Africa: Ghana's Business Environment. *Nepad Business and Investment Guide*, 3, 2007: 4.

7   World Bank National Accounts Data and OECD National Accounts data files, 2010.

8   Abor, J. and N. Biekpe. Small Business Financing Initiatives in Ghana. *Problems and Perspectives in Management*, 4(3), 2006: 69-77.

9   Mensah, S. A Review of SME Financing Schemes in Ghana. Presented at the

    UNIDO Regional Workshop of Financing Small and Medium Scale Enterprises, Accra, Ghana, 15-16 March 2004.

10   Allen, K.R. *Launching New Ventures: An Entrepreneurial Approach*. Boston: Houghton Mifflin, 1999.

11   Ansah-Ofei, K.A. Terms and Access to Credit: Perceptions of SME /Entrepreneurs in Ghana. School of Administration, University of Ghana, Legon

12   *Ibid.*

13   British Venture Capital Association, www.bvca.co.uk/publications/

intro, retrieved January 2012.

14 *Ibid.*

15 Birch, D. L. *Job creation in America.* New York: Free Press, 1987.

16 Answers.com, www.answers.com/venture+capital, retrieved January 2012.

17 Gompers, P.A. and J. Lerner. A note on the Venture Capital Industry. Harvard Business School Note 298-083, 1994.

18 Kuratko, D.F. and R.M. Hodgetts. *Entrepreneurship: A Contemporary Approach.* Orlando: The Dryden Press, 1998.

19 Green, J. Venture Capital at a Crossroads. *Journal of Management Development,* 23(10), 2004: 972-976.

20 Adjei-Boadu, MHow venture capital investments have contributed to the development of entrepreneurship and innovation in the United Kingdom (Unpublished MSc disssertation).

21 Green, J. Venture Capital at a Crossroads. *Journal of Management Development,* 23(10), 2004: 972-976.

22 Coopers and Lybrand. *The economic impact of venture capital in the UK.* London Mimeo 1996.

23 Mensah, S. A Review of SME Financing Schemes in Ghana. Unpublished PhD Thesis, 2004.

24 Fry, F.L. *Entrepreneurship: A Planning Approach.* New York: West Publishing, 1993.

25 Mensah, S. A Review of SME Financing Schemes in Ghana. Unpublished PhD Thesis, 2004.

26 Interview with Mawuli Ababio, formerly of Ghana Venture Fund.

27 Interview with Matthew Adjei-Boadi of Fidelity Capital Partners Ltd.

28 Black, B. and R. Gilson. Venture capital and the structure of capital markets: Banks versus stock markets. *Journal of Financial Economics,* 47(3), 1998: 243-277.

29 Zider, B. How Venture Capital Works. *Harvard Business Review,* 76(6),1998: 131-139.

30 Mensah, S. A Review of SME Financing Schemes in Ghana. Unpublished PhD Thesis, 2004.

31　Gatsby Foundation funded report – January 2005

32　Venture Capital Trust Fund Act, 2004 (Act 680), Section 2(1).

33　Venture Capital Trust Fund Act, 2004 (Act 680), Section 28.

34　Venture Capital Trust Fund, www.venturecapitalghana.com.gh, retrieved January 2012.

35　Speech Delivered By Daniel Duku, CEO of Venture Capital Trust Fund, at VCTF Press Conference, 2011.

36　Venture Capital Trust Fund Act, 2004 (Act 680), Section 28.

37　Speech Delivered By Daniel Duku, CEO of Venture Capital Trust Fund, at VCTF Press Conference, 2011,

38　Annual Report on Operations of the Venture Capital Trust Fund, 2009

39　Venture Capital Trust Fund Act, 2004 (Act 680), Section 6(2).

40　Venture Capital Trust Fund Act, 2004 (Act 680), Section 8(4).

41　Venture Capital Trust Fund Act, 2004 (Act 680), Section 7(2).

42　Ghana Stock Exchange, 2010.

43　Reuters, 30 April 2010.

44　Ghana Stock Exchange, Listing Rules, 2006:

45　Rule 6(1)(b) of the Ghana Stock Exchange Listing Rules, 2006. Pursuant to Rule 49(9), in the event of a takeover, share transfers should in no way result in a reduction in volume of listed shares below 25% of market capitalisation.

46　CAL Brokers Ghana, www.calbrokersghana.com/site/newsandevents/details.php?id=210, retrieved 18 March 2012.

47　Hatten, T,S. *Small Business Management: Entrepreneurship and Beyond*. Boston :Houghton Mifflin, 2003.

48　Investment Climate Department. Doing Business in 2010. Washington: World Bank, 2004.

49　IFC/World Bank Investment Climate Team for Africa in collaboration with IFC Gender Entrepreneurship Markets (GEM) Voices of Women Entrepreneurs in Ghana, April 2007.

50　Ansah-Ofei, K. Terms and Access to Credit: Perceptions of SME /Entrepreneurs in Ghana. School of Administration, University of Ghana, Legon.

51 Aryeetey E., A. Baah-Nuakoh, T. Duggleby, H. Hettige and W.F. Steel. Supply and Demand for Finance of Small Scale Enterprises in Ghana. World Bank Discussion Paper Number 251, Washington: World Bank, 1994.

52 IFC/World Bank Investment Climate Team for Africa in collaboration with IFC Gender Entrepreneurship Markets (GEM) Voices of Women Entrepreneurs in Ghana, April 2007.

53 Deakins, D. *Entrepreneurship and Small Firms*. London: McGraw-Hill, 1996.

54 Ansah-Ofei, K. Terms and Access to Credit: Perceptions of SME /Entrepreneurs in Ghana. School of Administration, University of Ghana, Legon.

55 *Ibid.*

56 Asiama, J.P. and V. Osei. Microfinance in Ghana: An Overview. Accra: Bank of Ghana, 2007.

57 Abor, J. and N. Biekpe. Small Business Financing Initiatives in Ghana. *Problems and Perspectives in Management*, 4(3), 2006: 69-77.

58 Amonoo, E., P.K. Acquah and E.E. Asmah. The impact of interest rates on demand for credit and loan repayments by the poor and SMEs in Ghana. Geneva: International Labour Organisation, 2003.

59 Aryeetey, E., M. Nissanke and W. Steel. *Intervention and Liberalisation: Changing Policies and Performance in the Financial Sector, Economic Reforms in Ghana: The Miracle and Mirage*. Accra: Woeli Publishing, 2000.

60 Amonoo, E., P.K. Acquah and E.E. Asmah. The impact of interest rates on demand for credit and loan repayments by the poor and SMEs in Ghana. Geneva: International Labour Organisation, 2003.

Chapter Eight: Managing Financial Resources

"A lot of people make money in Africa. It is an arbitrage between perceived and actual risk." - **Tidjane Thiam**

Outline

- Introduction
- Financial Statements
- Budgeting
- Working Capital Management
- Capital Budgeting
- Ratio Analysis
- Break-Even Analysis
- Case Study: Rancard Solutions: Managing and Maximizing the Little
- Questions for Class Discussion

N THE PREVIOUS chapter we focused on the different ways in which entrepreneurs can raise the relevant financial resources to run their enterprises. But, acquiring financial resources is only one half of the essential task of financial provision for a venture; the other half is managing the financial resources after they have been acquired.

Managing an enterprise's financial resources effectively is an important aspect of growing an entrepreneurial venture into a profitable one. The entrepreneur's ability to demonstrate sound financial management goes a long way in convincing existing and potential investors that the enterprise and its managers have the managerial competence to efficiently and effectively manage its financial resources to generate a return. Yet, in most parts of Africa, financial management remains one of the biggest problems facing entrepreneurs.[1]

While most entrepreneurs are likely to delegate the finance function to accountants and other financial officers, it is important that every entrepreneur acquires at least some basic financial management skills to make meaning of the numbers, and to generally monitor and manage the health of the enterprise. The ability to do so gives entrepreneurs a crucial managerial tool that allows them to steer their way around the key pitfalls that cause many start-up businesses to fail.[2]

Sound financial planning and control also allow the entrepreneur to create value, a necessary condition for growing start-up enterprises into global giants. Ultimately, to stay in business, the enterprise must generate profits; the finance function plays a vital role in managing this process. The value of good financial management can be seen in the effect that venture capital companies have when they invest in high-potential entrepreneurial ventures. By simply providing financial management services – like initiating cost control systems, for example – venture capitalists contribute positively to the financial performance of the enterprise.[3] Taking control of the financial management of an enterprise ensures that the marginal benefit of any activity exceeds the marginal cost.

This chapter identifies and discusses the key financial tools that entrepreneurs and small business managers require to manage their enterprises more profitably. It addresses financial reporting by examining the main financial statements that entrepreneurs need to prepare and understand. I stress the importance of budgeting to ensure proper financial planning and we examine the concept of working capital in some detail. After considering how entrepreneurs can make informed investment decisions by using some basic capital budgeting techniques, we look at ratio analysis, another important financial management tool used in determining the financial health of an enterprise, and end the chapter by examining how break-even analysis can aid in making entrepreneurial investment decisions.

Financial Statements

The financial health of an enterprise is conveyed in its financial statements, which provide useful information about the financial performance of an enterprise. These statements are crucial managerial planning tools, particularly for the internal control of an entrepreneurial venture.[4] They provide important data that entrepreneurs can use to anticipate the future conditions of an enterprise.

Financial reporting also provides useful information to external parties like investors who might be considering investing their capital in the enterprise. An entrepreneur's ability to understand, generate and interpret financial statements is therefore crucial. As such, while entrepreneurs often delegate their financial statements to professional accountants, it is important that they work with these practitioners in preparing such statements to ensure that the right information is captured.[5] It is also important that the entrepreneur understands the information that goes into preparing the statements and what each different component of the financial statement says about the overall performance of the enterprise.

In Ghana, the Companies Act, 1963 (Act 179), requires that companies generate financial statements based on accepted accounting rules. This ensures consistency in financial and accounting reporting. Financial statements however do not necessarily reflect the true financial position of a firm since the book values of assets are shown instead of their current market values. They can therefore fall short of presenting the true picture of the financial status of enterprises at the time they are generated. Despite this, financial statements remain the key instrument for measuring the performance of an entrepreneurial venture. The major financial statements are the balance sheet, the income statement and the statement of cash flow.

Balance Sheet

An enterprise's balance sheet is a snapshot of its financial position at a point in time, usually at the end of the financial year. As a rule, the total assets of the enterprise must equal – i.e. balance – the total liabilities and owners' equity. In other words, for an entrepreneurial venture, the combined assets must be equal to the investments that the entrepreneur and other owners (if any) put into the enterprise plus any capital that they have borrowed, in line with the accounting rule: Assets = Liabilities + Owners' Equity. Thus movements on one

Kuenyehia on Entrepreneurship

side of the equation must be reflected by balancing movements on the other side. For instance, if the entrepreneur borrows GH¢1,000, the GH¢1,000 increase in liabilities must be balanced by an increase in assets equivalent to GH¢1,000, for example in the purchase of a computer to keep financial records.

The balance sheet can be presented in a horizontal or vertical format. If presented in a horizontal form, assets are listed in one side while liabilities and owners' equity are listed on the opposite side. With the vertical form, assets are often listed first followed by liabilities and owners' equity. Under the Generally Accepted Accounting Practices (GAAP), assets on the balance sheet must be reported at their historical cost value less depreciation (book values) and not their current market values (sale values). This is to eliminate the subjectivity that may be present in the determination of market values, thus ensuring consistency in financial reporting.

Table 8.1 shows the balance sheet of Admathar Ltd, a hypothetical fruit processing and production company in Ghana. It indicates that total assets are made up of current assets and fixed assets. Current assets are comprised of cash and assets that can be converted into cash within a short period of time. This includes cash held on hand and cash equivalents like current account balances that the enterprise holds with its bankers. Current assets also include accounts receivable, which are the are monies due from debtors. As a production company, Admathar Ltd's inventories typically include raw materials for production, work-in-progress or partly finished goods and finished goods which can be sold for cash or credit. Another notable current asset is prepaid expenses. Prepaid expenses are advance payments of expenses or bills to the company's creditors or service providers, such as paying utility bills in advance.

Fixed assets denote the long-term capital investments of Admathar Ltd and consist of items like property, plant and equipment. The net value of these assets is shown in the balance sheet instead of their original costs. This is because their accumulated depreciation over time has been deducted. Depreciation is the amount that the enterprise sets aside every year for the decline in the value of the fixed assets, and it is treated as an expense. Intangible assets like goodwill, brands, trademarks, patents, and copyrights are valuable intellectual property (IP), and must also be shown on the balance sheet. IP can either be purchased or created. Where IP is purchased, it must be recorded on the balance sheet at the purchase value less amortisation (a form of depreciation commonly attributed to intangible assets). If on the other hand IP is created, then the total cost incurred in the creation of the IP – such as research and development cost, design cost, registration cost, marketing cost, etc. – must be capitalised on the balance sheet and amortised over the expected life of the IP.

Table 8.1: Balance Sheet For Admathar Ltd For The Year Ended December 2011

	GHC	GHC
Current Assets		
Cash and cash equivalents	12,200	
Accounts receivable	10, 150	
Inventories	35, 300	
Prepaid expenses	450	
Total current assets		58, 100
Fixed Assets		
Property, plant and equipment net	42, 560	
Goodwill	6, 502	
Intangibles including brand	12, 460	
Total fixed Assets		61, 522
Total Assets		**119, 622**
Current Liabilities		
Accounts payable	11, 420	
Short-term loans	24, 000	
Income tax	4,820	
Provisions	1, 214	
Other current liabilities	1, 642	
Total current liabilities		43, 096
Non-current Liabilities		
Long-term borrowings	16, 482	
Mortgage	1, 523	
Total non-current liabilities		18, 005
Total Liabilities		**61, 101**
Owners' Equity		
Share capital	31, 879	
Reserves (retained profits)	26, 642	
		58, 521
Liabilities Plus Equity		**119, 622**

The next section of the balance sheet contains the enterprise's liabilities and equity. Liabilities are short- and long-term debts that an enterprise owes its creditors. Liabilities are divided into current and non-current liabilities. Current liabilities include such items as accounts payable (which a company owes to its trade creditors), short-term loans from banks and other lenders payable within a year, income tax that must be paid to the tax authorities as well as provisions to cover potential losses the company might incur in the course of its business operations. Non-current liabilities are debts which have a maturity period of more than a year and include long-term loans and mortgages.

The equity section provides details of the capital that the entrepreneur and other owners of the company have invested in the enterprise. The share capital represents the original value of investment that these owners actually put into the enterprise. Reserves are the retained earnings or profit that a firm reinvests in its operations. As a rule, the sum of the liabilities and equity must equal the total assets of the enterprise.

Income Statement

The entrepreneur's income statement provides a summary of the trading or operating activities for the enterprise for a specified period of time, usually a financial year. It covers all revenue and expenditure items for normal operating activities for the financial year. The first income measure on the income statement is gross profit. The two key elements that enable the calculation of gross profit are revenue and the cost of goods or services sold. Revenue represents all the income that a company receives from the sale of goods and services during the course of the financial year. The cost of goods or services rendered (also known as cost of sales) is the total cost involved in directly producing goods and services. This can be calculated by adding the inventory cost at the beginning of the year to the purchases made, and then subtracting the cost of inventory at the end of the year. Deducting the cost of goods sold from the revenue of Admathar Ltd gives the gross profit *of* GHC69,452 as indicated in Table 8.2. A positive gross profit figure means that Admathar Ltd's revenue for the period exceeded the direct cost incurred in producing the goods which were sold in the year under review.

A negative profit figure – a gross loss – would mean that the enterprise's products cost more to produce than they were sold for and would inevitably result in insolvency. Insolvency is the inability of an entity to pay its debts and obligations as and when they fall due, usually resulting in the collapse of an enterprise.

Table 8.2: Income Statement For Admathar Ltd For The Year Ended December 2011

	GHC	GHC
Revenue	105, 648	
Less: cost of goods sold	36, 196	
Gross profit		69, 452
Operating Expenses		
Advertising	2, 634	
Insurance	5, 826	
Depreciation	4, 317	
Salaries	23, 672	
Other expenses	1, 346	
Less: Total operating expenses		37, 795
Less: Operating profit		31, 657
Other expenditures		**28, 116**
Earnings Before Interest And Taxes		
Less: Finance charges	2, 986	
Less: Income tax	8, 648	
Net Profit		**18, 642**

The second income measure on the income statement is operating profit. This is arrived at by deducting all operating expenses such as advertising, insurance, depreciation and salaries from the gross profit. Depreciation is treated here as an operating expense because in the normal course of business operation, the use of plants and other fixed assets to produce goods ultimately reduces their value over time. As it would not be prudent to charge the whole value of the asset against one single year as an expense, organisations set aside a percentage of the asset's value every year until it is deemed to be worthless.

Other expenditure items which occur during the operating cycle of the enterprise but are not directly related to the production and sale of goods, such as donations, corporate social responsibility efforts and consultancy fees, are also deducted to arrive at earnings before interest and taxes. Interest, finance charges and tax are other deductible expenses that must be taken into account. Businesses are allowed to deduct finance charges incurred in the year before computing tax on the outstanding earnings. Tax is thus calculated on profits after deducting interest and other finance charges. Once tax is deducted at the applicable tax rate and remitted to the Ghana Revenue Authority (GRA), the outstanding profit represents the enterprise's net profit for the financial year, which is available for distribution to the owners or investors.

Statement of Cash Flow

The statement of cash flow is a summary of the changes in the working capital of an enterprise. It indicates the various sources of cash flows into and out of the enterprise. The health of any enterprise depends on its ability to pay its debts as they fall due. As the old adage goes, cash is king: without adequate cash, an entrepreneurial venture will struggle to survive no matter how great the idea and products of the enterprise are. The statement of cash flow can be divided into cash flow from operating activities, cash flow from investing activities and cash flow from financing activities, as depicted in Table 8.3 for Admathar Ltd.

In Table 8.3, all cash inflows are positive and cash outflows are negative. This is to ensure that cash inflows are added and cash outflows deducted to arrive at the net cash flow. Operating cash flow relates directly to the production of goods and services.

All items that result in an increase in cash are inflows and those that result in a decrease in cash are outflows. Thus, in Table 8.3, the operating profit for Admathar Ltd is treated as a cash inflow. Operating profit is used instead of net profit because, although interest and taxes are treated as payments (deducted as expenses) in the income statement, they are not incurred as part of direct operations (production of goods and services), and are thus added back to calculate operating cash flow. They are deducted under the investing and financing activities subheadings instead. Similarly, depreciation is treated as a cash inflow as all reductions in the value of fixed assets must be offset by increases in current assets, represented by cash By the same token all increases in assets and inventory imply that money has been spent and are thus treated as cash outflows. The decrease in accounts payable indicates that the enterprise settled some of its short-term liabilities (accounts payable) during the period, representing cash outflow.

Table 8.3: Statement Of Cash Flows For Admathar Ltd
For The Year Ended December 2011

	GHC	GHC
Operating Activities		
Operating profit	31, 657	
Deprecation	4, 323	
Interest paid	-2, 986	
Tax paid	-6, 488	
Change (increase) in inventory	-5, 782	
Change (increase) in accounts payable	-3, 987	
Net cash from operating activities		16, 737
Investing Activities		
Investing activities	-1, 324	
Operating investments	-2, 894	
Financing investments	950	
Net cash from investing activities		-3, 268
Financing Activities		
Financing activities	-3, 168	
Borrowings	864	
Repayments	-1, 896	
Net cash from financing activities		-4, 200
Net Cash Flows		9, 269

The investment activities consist of purchases and sale of capital assets to enhance the growth of the enterprise. It also includes investments in operating activities that will enhance the performance of the enterprise, such as buying component parts to fix plant and equipment.

Financing investments are expenditure items that improve the enterprise's ability to raise capital. The sum of all these represents net cash flow from investing activities. Lastly, the financing activities denote cash flow resulting from activities that generate debt or equity for the enterprise, and include cash borrowings and payment of interest.

A summation of the operating, investing and financing activities gives either the net increase or decrease in cash flow for the period under review. Table 8.3 shows that Admathar Ltd had a net cash flow of GHC9,269.

The statement of cash flow provides a useful source of information for the entrepreneur to critically examine the enterprise's cash flow. This helps in identifying any liquidity crisis that the enterprise might be experiencing or is likely to face in the future, providing an important indicator for the entrepreneur to determine whether she requires more cash to support her enterprise, and at what point.

Budgeting

The budget, which sets out the income and expenditure of an enterprise for future activities, is an important tool for entrepreneurs to effectively plan how they will use their financial resources.[6] . Budgeting is a planning process for the future operational activities of the entrepreneur. A budget must be specific and quantifiable in financial terms to enable an examination of its financial implications.[7] Engaging in a thorough budgeting process allows the entrepreneur to monitor and measure key cost elements crucial to an enterprise's performance management and control costs. Entrepreneurs can, for instance, categorise their costs as controllable and uncontrollable. This classification would allow them to identify the areas which they can target for cost-cutting exercises, leading ultimately to decreases in the total expenditure of their enterprises, which could in turn increase profits if they meet their revenue targets.

For a budget to achieve its objectives, it must be realistic. A budget must not necessarily be easy to achieve and must set targets that will stretch the entrepreneur and his team to get better performance. Budgets can be approached in a modular way – for example by department, by function (sales), by product or by quarter (three months) – or globally through a master budget.

Sales Budget

The sales budget provides a starting point from which other budgets like the cash budget are prepared. In most enterprises, sales represent the most important source of cash inflows; its forecasting is therefore crucial for entrepreneurs and managers. It is important that the entrepreneur undertakes the forecasting exercise with great caution. In preparing a sales budget, the entrepreneur can forecast sales by analysing the patterns and trends of past sales.

Table 8.4 is a monthly budget forecast for Admathar Ltd for the year 2012. As a major source of cash flow, an entrepreneur must be careful not to overstate the sales budget. This will not only have serious implications on other budgets but could lead to cash flow crises.

Table 8.4: Sales Budget For Admathar Ltd For The Year 2012.

Year	Jan	Feb	Mar	Apr	May	Jun	Jul	Aug	Sep	Oct	Nov	Dec
2012	GH¢	GH¢	GH¢	GH¢	GH¢	GH¢	GH¢	GH¢	GH¢	GH¢	GH¢	GH¢
	7, 623	7, 213	7, 789	8, 186	7, 936	8, 032	8, 218	8, 793	8, 645	8, 983	8, 977	9, 242

A major challenge that entrepreneurs with start-up enterprises face in preparing sales budgets is that they do not have past sales to help forecast sales figures. One way of overcoming this difficulty is to examine the general sales in the industry in which the entrepreneur intends to operate. The entrepreneur can also analyse the sales of a competitor enterprise in its first year of operations if he is able to get access to such information or generate figures through market research. As I noted in Chapter 4, an entrepreneur may be able to estimate sales based on research carried out on prospective customers. This will give the entrepreneur a rough estimate of the purchase frequency and the magnitude of the potential customer base, and thus enable him to forecast the likely sales figures. Regardless of the method, it is impossible to have an accurate sales forecast. The important thing is to ensure that the sales budget is not significantly overstated or understated. It is also important that the sales budget is updated regularly to reflect any positive or negative changes in trading conditions.

Operating Budget

Another important budget for the entrepreneur is the operating budget. This budget is similar to the income statement but it is based on estimated figures. The entrepreneur must estimate the revenue and expenses that would be incurred in the course of normal business operations so as to monitor cost and other operating activities. A comprehensive operating budget should include, forecasts for revenue, cost of goods sold and operating expenses. Table 8.5 is an operating budget for Admathar Ltd for the year 2012.

In Table 8.5, the cost of goods sold is calculated by adding the cost of opening inventory to the cost of new purchases less the cost of closing inventory. The forecasted gross profit is the difference between revenue and cost of goods sold. The operating expenses include expenses such as salaries, rents and utilities. All these expenses must be properly forecasted and deducted from the gross profit to arrive at an estimated profit.

Table 8.5: Operating Budget For Admathar Ltd For The Year 2012

Items	Jan	Feb	Mar	Apr	May	Jun	Jul	Aug	Sep	Oct	Nov	Dec
	GH¢	GH¢	GH¢	GH¢	GH¢	GH¢	GH¢	GH¢	GH¢	GH¢	GH¢	GH¢
Revenue	7, 723	7, 327	7, 968	7, 987	8, 267	8, 327	8, 421	8, 587	8, 673	9, 256	9, 489	9,862
Opening inventory	1, 217	1, 324	1, 043	1, 342	1, 398	1, 671	1, 238	1, 245	1, 324	1, 568	1, 678	1,831
Add purchases	1, 632	1, 423	1, 782	1, 878	1, 875	1, 863	1, 984	1, 986	1, 998	2, 105	2, 182	2, 001
Less closing inventory	982	971	1, 021	1, 112	1, 210	1, 231	2, 003	2, 103	1, 871	1, 934	1, 521	1, 123
Cost of goods sold	1, 867	1, 776	1, 804	2, 108	2, 063	2, 303	1, 219	3, 231	1, 451	1, 739	2, 339	2, 709
Gross Profit	**5, 856**	**5, 551**	**6, 164**	**5, 879**	**6, 204**	**6, 024**	**7, 202**	**5, 356**	**7, 222**	**7, 517**	**7, 150**	**7, 153**
Operating expenses:												
Salaries	1, 892	1, 910	1, 921	1, 927	1, 932	1, 938	1, 941	1, 948	1, 951	1, 958	1, 962	1, 981
Utilities	217	220	231	237	239	242	248	249	258	261	271	281
Advertising	221	230	235	238	244	237	289	291	286	294	298	313
Insurance	434	419	424	432	438	442	448	450	453	458	463	469
Estimated Profit	**3, 092**	**2, 772**	**3, 353**	**3, 045**	**3, 351**	**3, 165**	**2, 276**	**2, 418**	**4, 274**	**4, 546**	**4, 156**	**4, 109**

Cash Budget

As cash is central to the general liquidity of an enterprise, the cash budget is a very important managerial tool for the entrepreneur. A well-designed cash budget can help prevent cash surpluses or shortages. A cash budget will give the entrepreneur an indicator of when payments are due to be made and received, so she does not face any unexpected cash shortages. Cash outflows include payments of salaries, taxes, interest, rent, utility bills and other expenses. Cash inflows are cash receipts from sales, trade creditors and interest from investments. As certain cash outflows like salaries have fixed payment dates, the entrepreneur should use information about these fixed payment dates to improve the outflow forecast.

Cash budgets can be prepared weekly, monthly or yearly depending on the nature of business that the enterprise operates. Table 8.6 shows the monthly cash budget for Admathar Ltd for the year 2012. The cash budget indicates that the company is likely to face some liquidity crises for the months of March and April. The entrepreneur will – and should – therefore be able to make contingencies for such a situation.

Table 8.6: Cash Budget For Admathar Ltd For The Year 2012

Items	Jan	Feb	Mar	Apr	May	Jun	Jul	Aug	Sep	Oct	Nov	Dec
	GH¢	GH¢	GH¢	GH¢	GH¢	GH¢	GH¢	GH¢	GH¢	GH¢	GH¢	GH¢
Opening cash	2, 451	3, 451	2, 166	29	150	886	2, 067	2, 553	2, 346	2, 319	1, 974	2, 010
Add cash receipts	6, 321	6, 389	6, 154	7, 985	8, 167	8, 345	7, 810	7, 325	7, 621	7, 587	8, 012	7, 879
Available cash	8, 772	9, 840	8, 320	8, 014	8, 317	9, 231	9, 877	9, 878	9, 967	9, 906	9, 986	9, 889
Less cash payments	5, 321	7, 674	8, 291	7, 864	7, 431	7, 164	7, 324	7, 532	7, 648	7, 932	7, 976	7, 541
Closing cash	3, 451	2, 166	29	150	886	2, 067	2, 553	2, 346	2, 319	1, 974	2, 010	2, 348

The key element of the cash budget is time. Entrepreneurs must keep tabs on the timings of the expected inflows or outflows so as to foretell fluctuations in cash flow. An entrepreneur should, for instance, record in the cash budget only cash receipts from customers and not credit sales. Also in the cash budget, invoiced payments must be recorded at the estimated payment date and not when the entrepreneur buys the item on the invoice. The clue is in the name – the 'cash' budget. Like other budgets, cash budgets are not perfect but will reveal patterns in the cash flow that will help entrepreneurs determine when they might need to source extra cash to support their businesses.

Working Capital Management

An entrepreneur grows an enterprise by investing in assets. These assets can either be fixed or current. Working capital consists of an entrepreneur's investments in current assets. Current assets include cash and bank account balances, marketable securities, accounts receivable and inventories. In the case of a production company like Admathar Ltd, working capital is quite a high percentage of the assets because, in order to produce and process its fruits, inventory is needed in the form of raw materials, partly finished products and finished products. Purchases of raw materials are likely to be in the form of trade credit in the same way that the company will grant customers credit sales to boost sales volume. The enterprise will also need cash to meet its liquidity requirements as it grows. This is crucial to avoiding overtrading, a situation where the enterprise has insufficient working capital to sustain its trading level.[8]

Sound working capital management is a challenging task for every entrepreneur. This is because decisions on working capital need to be made at the operational level and, more often than not, such decisions need to be made quickly. For instance, where there are cash inflow problems, the entrepreneur must find the needed funds quickly and on time to prevent a liquidity crisis. In order to ensure effective working capital management, it is important to "accelerate a firm's receivables and to stretch out its payables".[9] This means ensuring that debtors (persons to whom enterprise sells to) pay their invoices on time, while simultaneously delaying payments to creditors (persons the business owes).

Cash Management

Cash plays a central role in all the activities of an enterprise. According to Arnold, enterprises need cash for transactional, precautionary and speculative motives.[10] Firstly, enterprises need cash to engage in daily transactions such as paying bills, wages and the cost of materials. Secondly, because cash flow forecasts are subject to errors, holding cash is also a precautionary measure necessary to serve as contingency for shortages in cash inflows. Lastly, a reserve of cash is required to ensure that the enterprise is in a position to take business opportunities as they emerge.

Managing cash involves setting the range within which the enterprise wants to hold cash. This requires the maintenance of a fine balance between the costs and benefits of holding cash that is not working. Effective cash management requires the entrepreneur to put cash to maximum use. She should deposit cash and process cheques quickly at the bank. Idle cash in hand should also be invested in short-term marketable securities to get some extra income. The objective of cash management for the entrepreneur is to get the highest possible returns on cash.

Entrepreneurs must ensure that they get cash into their enterprise as quickly as possible and reduce the speed of cash outflows. This can be done by managing accounts receivable, accounts payable and inventory in a manner that ensures more inflows than outflows of cash.

Accounts Receivable

Credit sales are a normal business practice for many enterprises. It is an important part of retaining customers and therefore surviving market competition. But while entrepreneurs may want to outperform competitors by granting customers more credit time, such advances could result in cash flow crises should trade debtors not pay on time. It is important therefore for enterprises granting credit to put in place effective credit policies that ensure timely collection of debt. To make this work, the enterprise should, for example, halt supplies to debtors who have exceeded their limit until they have settled their accounts.

While too strict a credit policy may drive away customers, particularly if they find market competitors are willing to offer them generous credit terms, gaining more customers through credit sales is not necessarily a good thing. Losing customers because of a strict adherence to credit polices is also not always a bad thing. Entrepreneurs must finely balance the need for an effective credit policy that will attract more customers against the need to maintain sufficient cash inflows.

A decision to grant credit to customers involves risk, particularly where the customer is not well known to the enterprise. This problem can be overcome by conducting due diligence on customers before granting them credit. One of the most common ways of establishing a customer's credit worthiness is to find out how they have dealt with other suppliers and their track record of making payments to them. Where the entrepreneur is not fully convinced about a customer, she can mitigate risk by asking for a percentage deposit payment or insisting on a guarantee provided by a bank or other third party who she can turn to should the customer default.

Accounts Payable

Accounts payable is another important component of working capital management as all payments that the entrepreneur makes to suppliers involve cash flowing out of the enterprise. Depending on the nature of the enterprise, payments to creditors could be a substantial part of cash outflows, reducing the amount of working capital. Most production, manufacturing and retail enterprises are likely to have substantial amounts going out regularly to pay accounts payable. Such large outflows of cash have an effect on the liquidity position of the enterprise. For a start-up entrepreneur, the dilemma is to ensure that he honours his accounts payable in a timely enough fashion so as not to damage his relationship with suppliers. An entrepreneur should seek to agree a payment schedule with his suppliers and other creditors to ensure that his payment obligations do not cause cash flow problems.

Inventory

Enterprises generally require some form of inventory, no matter how small it might be. Although service companies tend to utilise little inventory, inventory – comprising the essential raw materials – is the lifeblood of manufacturing and production enterprises, constituting a significant portion of working capital. Because inventories are short-term investments, the control of inventory a crucial aspect of working capital management. It is estimated that with better inventory management, an enterprise can reduce the levels of inventories by 10% to 20% without adversely affecting production and sales.[11]

Having adequate inventory prevents shortages which, for some enterprises, may lead to stoppages in production, resulting in additional costs such as paying wages for idle workers and possible losses of key customers.

However, excess inventory should be avoided due to the costs involved. The primary tangible cost associated with carrying inventory is the cost of maintaining and storing inventory. Beyond that, there is the less obvious opportunity cost – the uses to which the entrepreneur could have put the money invested in excess inventory if it were not locked in stock.

A sales forecast could be useful in estimating inventory levels so as to minimise situations where valuable cash is tied in inventory. Efficient working capital management also requires entrepreneurs to reduce the price of inventory that does not sell quickly. This will reduce inventory levels and release cash for more pressing expenses. An entrepreneur can also use the just-in-time model to manage inventories. The model requires the entrepreneur to have a supplier who can provide components and other goods as and when the entrepreneur needs them so as to prevent the situation where the entrepreneur has to acquire these goods in advance. This not only reduces excessive inventory but also eliminates storage costs.

Capital Budgeting

In the normal course of business operations, the entrepreneur will be required to make decisions that have a long-term impact on the enterprise. These could be major decisions like investment in equipment, advertising or even launching new products on the market. Capital budgeting is a technique that allows an entrepreneur to identify and justify the acquisition of capital assets and investment projects that the enterprise should undertake,[12] and then prioritise them according to the needs of the enterprise. The capital budgeting process requires an entrepreneur to identify and analyse all potential investment opportunities in order to implement those that create maximum value for the enterprise.

An entrepreneur could have different investment projects but may be unable to implement all of them due to limited financial resources and managerial capacity. By employing capital budgeting techniques, the entrepreneur is able to rank these ideas and determine which one is likely to make the most significant impact on the growth of the enterprise. As a general rule, an entrepreneur must only invest in projects and capital assets when their lifetime benefits far exceed their cost. There are various techniques that entrepreneurs can use to evaluate their capital expenditure. The most commonly used ones are the payback method, the net present value and the internal rate of return.

Payback Method

As a technique for evaluating investment projects, the payback method is the simplest of all the capital budgeting tools. An entrepreneur wishing to use this technique needs to identify a minimum period (for example, three years) in which she wants to recoup her investment. The payback period is the length of time it will take for a project's cumulative cash inflows to equal the initial capital outlay. Investment projects that are not able to pay back the capital over the target time period are rejected and the one that will pay back the initial investment in the earliest possible time will be selected.

By way of example, consider the following scenario:, Admathar Ltd has US$1,000 to invest in the expansion of its enterprise. Management has two mutually exclusive projects it would like to invest in. They are both promising but the capital available cannot fund both projects. In such a situation, the company can make a decision as to which project to invest in after using the payback method to evaluate them.

Table 8.7: Payback Method Capital Budgeting For Admathar Ltd, US$

Years	0	1	2	3	4
Project A	-1000	100	200	300	400
Project B	-1000	200	350	450	550

Based on the payback method in Table 8.7, Project B will be selected over Project A because it is able to achieve payback faster than Project A. As can be seen from Table 8.7, the cumulative cash inflows for Project A only equal the initial capital in the fourth year while Project B equals the initial capital in the third year.

The main advantage of the payback method is the ease with which the method can be used by the entrepreneur. The method also recognises the importance of the time value of money. This method is also good for cash flow as the cash inflows resulting from the quicker payback can be used for other activities. A key drawback of the payback method is that it may not give a true picture of a project that has the potential of maximising value for the entrepreneur, or yielding much higher returns over a longer period of time. For example, a project that pays back in three years may offer twice the return that a project with a two-year payback offers. Essentially, the method ignores the importance of cash inflows after the payback period.

Net Present Value

The net present value of an investment project is the "sum of the present value of all its cash flows, both inflows and outflows, discounted at a rate consistent with the project's risk."[13] It is a discounted capital budgeting method that takes into account the time value of money. The underlying assumption is that an entrepreneur will prefer to receive GH¢50 today rather than GH¢50 tomorrow because the value today is greater than the same amount in a year's time, taking into account inflation. It is the only capital budgeting technique that is consistent with maximising the entrepreneur's value-creation objective.

The net present value method satisfies the three criteria for properly analysing any investment project.[14] These are the focus on cash, the time value of money and the risk element. Focus on cash considers the cash returns that would be received from a project, from its inception to its completion, including the potential cash returns that can be derived from the disposal of the equipment that was used for the project. Time value of money analyses the exact time periods during the life of the project when cash returns would be received. For example, an amount received in the first year of the project would be more valuable than if the same amount was received in the fourth year, due to inflation. All the future cash flows from the project are thus discounted for inflation and considered in their present values. The risk element factors in the risk associated with the venture. This can be done by considering businesses already operating in the industry and benchmarking a risk rate and rate of desired return. This rate is then used to discount the cash flow.

An entrepreneur can determine the net present value of a proposed investment project by following these steps. First, the entrepreneur should estimate the net cash flows expected to be generated by the investment project. These cash flows are then discounted at an interest rate that takes into consideration the project's risk. The last step is to sum the discounted cash flows to determine the net present value of the project. A key decision rule of this method is to accept investment projects that have a net present value of more than zero.

The net present value is a good investment decision-making tool for entrepreneurs as it focuses on the actual value, discounted for inflation and risks that a given project returns to an entrepreneur. The use of the discount rate, which is equal to the returns that an investor will get from the market on similar risk profile projects, helps the entrepreneur make an informed decision on whether or not a project is worthwhile. Accepting only projects with positive net present value means that the entrepreneur sticks to the objective of maximising profits for the enterprise.

The Net Present Value can be calculated using following formula:

$$NPV = CF_0 + \frac{CF_1}{(1+r)1} + \frac{CF_2}{(1+r)2} + ... + \frac{CF_n}{(1+r)n}$$

NPV is the net present value, CF_n is the net cash flow in year n, r is the discount rate and n represents the lifespan of a project in years.

The net present value is advantageous over other capital budgeting techniques because it takes into account the time value of money allowing the entrepreneur to impose some market discipline by rejecting negative net present value projects. Investment projects are therefore subjected to market competition.

Despite this, the method is not as easy to communicate as other methods like the payback method. Also, while the NPV is technically sound and widely accepted in academia, it has caused many enterprises in the past to invest in projects with long lives that often fail to provide the cash flow forecast in the long duration, and also tends to understate cost due to factors like rises in the price of raw materials.[15]

Internal Rate of Return

The internal rate of return is another discounted cash flow method of evaluating investment projects. It takes into account the time value of money and the risk potential of projects before deriving the appropriate rate of return. The internal rate of a project measures its compound yearly rates of return, taking into account the initial capital outlay and the subsequent cash flows. Here, cash flows are discounted at a predetermined rate to ensure that the net present value of the project is equal to zero.[16] An entrepreneur with two promising projects can use this capital budgeting tool to make a decision by selecting the project with the highest internal rate of return.

In order to determine the internal rate of return of a project, the entrepreneur needs to estimate the cash flow of a project and set a rate of return that he requires on investments. The required rate of return is set based on the going market rate for investment returns on similar projects. To find out which project to select, the entrepreneur uses a discount rate which results in the present value of all the cash flow from the project being zero. Having determined the discount rate, it is then compared to the entrepreneur's preferred rate of return. The entrepreneur will only accept a project that produces an internal rate of return which exceeds the predetermined rate. Since the internal rate of return is the discount rate that makes the net present value of all cash flows equal to zero, the formula is similar to the general net present value equation.

The internal rate of return can be calculated based on the following formula:

$$NPV = 0 = CF_0 + \frac{CF_1}{(1+r)1} + \frac{CF_2}{(1+r)2} + ... + \frac{CF_n}{(1+r)n}$$

Here, NPV is the net present value and is equal to zero, CF_n is the net cash flow in year n, r is the discount rate and n also represents the lifespan of a project in years.

By using a market-based rate to determine the internal rate of return, the method incorporates a risk element. But the key drawback of the internal rate of return is that it is not as easy to use as the other methods. Using the method requires that the entrepreneur start calculating with a net present value of zero before working backwards to determine the rate. This poses various mathematical challenges.

Ratio Analysis

Financial statements have already been identified as important instruments for the internal management of an enterprise and a source of information for external parties who may have interest in the performance of an entrepreneurial venture. However, these statements by themselves do not provide enough information for the entrepreneur to determine the potential profitability and general performance of an enterprise. Ratio analysis allows entrepreneurs to calculate and interpret various figures from financial statements to determine the overall performance of an enterprise, and to monitor and control cost elements that could affect the health of a venture. According to Thomas and Evanson, expressing figures from financial statements as ratios gives insight to some salient information which might be missed when one observes the individual numbers themselves.[17]

Ratio analysis of financial statements is a useful tool that can help the entrepreneur to determine "where the business has been, where it is, and where it is going".[18] Ratio analysis gives the entrepreneur a better insight into the past performance of the enterprise and its current position. Through this, mistakes that were made in the past can be brought to light and dealt with alongside other areas that require further attention. As a tool for forecasting the future financial position of an enterprise, ratio analysis provides the entrepreneur the information to plan in advance so as to influence the future performance of his enterprise. If used properly, ratio analysis could lead to improved financial control, an essential step for a small enterprise to increase its chances of prospering through growth.[19] More importantly, entrepreneurs who are able to calculate and interpret ratios are able to gauge the health of their enterprises.

To provide the most use, financial ratios must be put in context. Ratios become more meaningful when compared to an entrepreneur's budget, past ratios, ratios of competitors, or average industrial ratios.[20] Comparing ratios with budgetary expectations allows the entrepreneur to determine whether there are variations between the budget target and actual performance. The entrepreneur can also draw more meaning from ratios by comparing the present financial ratios with previous years'. With this, the entrepreneur can identify various trends in the financial performance. Also, by benchmarking his ratios with those of similar firms in the industry or the average ratios in the industry, the entrepreneur is able to compare his performance with those of competing firms.

There are various ratios available to the entrepreneur. The choice of one ratio over the other depends largely on the nature of the industry. The entrepreneur must focus on a few ratios that, based on his industry, provide useful information for decision making. We now discuss the ratios under the headings of liquidity, activity, debt, and profitability.

Liquidity Ratios

Liquidity ratios allow the entrepreneur to measure the ability of his firm to meet its short-term obligations as they fall due. These ratios are useful cash flow indicators, allowing the entrepreneur to determine the general liquidity of the enterprise. Strong liquidity means that the entrepreneur can pay expenses like utilities and also take advantage of emerging business opportunities. The two main liquidity ratios are current ratio and quick ratio (also called the acid test ratio).

Current ratio measures the ability of an enterprise to pay its current liabilities out of its current assets. It is calculated by dividing current assets by current liabilities.

$$\text{Current Ratio} = \frac{\text{Current Assets}}{\text{Current Liabilities}}$$

A high current ratio is generally healthy since it indicates that a firm's current assets can pay for its current liabilities should they fall due. An entrepreneur must aim to attain a current ratio of at least 2:1, meaning for each GH¢1 of liability, the company has GH¢2 in assets. In interpreting ratios however, it must be noted that while a ratio will be acceptable in one industry, it may not necessarily be good for another industry. For instance, in the retail business, a lower ratio will not suggest unhealthy liquidity as in most cases the industry will have more predictable cash flows than say a manufacturing firm.

The current ratio for Admathar Ltd at the end of 2011 is calculated using the financial statement on from earlier as follows:

$$\text{Current Ratio} = \frac{58,100}{43,096} = 1.35$$

As a manufacturing company, Admathar Ltd's current ratio of 1.35 is considered low by industry averages. Manufacturing companies, unlike retail companies, may not have inflows of cash on a daily basis. This may lead to liquidity problems so the entrepreneur and his managers must take action to prevent liquidity problems.

The quick ratio or acid test ratio is similar to the current ratio except that it excludes inventory, the least liquid of the current assets. It gives the entrepreneur a more rigorous measure of his liquidity position

The quick ratio for Admathar Ltd at the end of 2011 is calculated as follows:

$$\text{Quick Ratio} = \frac{\text{Quick Assets}}{\text{Current Liabilities}}$$

Quick assets represents cash and those assets that the entrepreneur can quickly convert into cash, such as short-term securities investments and accounts receivable. A quick ratio of 1:1 is generally acceptable, but a greater ratio indicates an entrepreneur has a solid liquidity position.

$$\text{Quick Ratio} = \frac{22,800}{43,096} = 0.53$$

In the case of Admathar Ltd, the company has a larger proportion of its current assets tied in inventory at the end of the year. This explains the lower quick ratio of 0.53, which means that, should it not receive cash from sales, it is likely to encounter liquidity problems. Entrepreneurs can mitigate situations like this by employing sales promotions to convert finished goods into cash, and working to adjust purchases of raw materials to a more liquidity-friendly schedule.

Activity Ratios

Activity ratios are used to measure how fast an entrepreneur is able to convert assets into cash or sales. They provide a measure of how the entrepreneur utilises assets. The major activity ratios are inventory turnover, average collection period, fixed assets turnover and total assets turnover.

Inventory turnover measures how quickly an entrepreneur sells goods – the number of times that an entrepreneur is able to turn inventory into cash during the year. A low inventory turnover means that the inventory is not very liquid while a high ratio means that the inventory is highly liquid. Inventory turnover is calculated by dividing cost of goods sold by the inventory.

$$\text{Inventory Turnover} = \frac{\text{Cost of Goods Sold}}{\text{Inventory}}$$

This ratio is industry-dependent – for example, a retail operation will by its nature have a higher ratio than a bespoke furniture manufacturer – so it must always be used in the right context. Applied properly it can be used to establish ideal inventory levels.

The inventory turnover for Admathar Ltd at the end of 2011 is calculated as follows:

$$\text{Inventory Turnover} = \frac{36,196}{35,300} = 1.03$$

The inventory turnover ratio of 1.03 means that the Admathar Ltd is able to sell its inventory just a little over once every year. This low ratio could reflect a high proportion of long-term, high-value inventory, such as cans for the processed fruit, but it could also be as a result of poor inventory management. Comparing Admathar Ltd to other companies in the same business would give its owners a clearer picture of the situation.

Fixed asset turnover allows the entrepreneur to measure how efficiently he uses fixed assets to generate sales. Investments in fixed assets are expected to create value for an enterprise. By employing the fixed asset turnover ratio, the entrepreneur can determine in monetary terms how much value the enterprise gains from, say, GH¢10 of investment in fixed assets. This ratio is measured by dividing sales by net fixed assets (fixed assets minus depreciation and intangible assets).

$$\text{Fixed Asset Turnover} = \frac{\text{Sales}}{\text{Net Fixed Assets}}$$

A high fixed asset turnover ratio means that the enterprise generates high sales value from its fixed assets. Similarly, a low ratio means that fixed assets generate less value.

The fixed asset turnover for Admathar Ltd at the end of 2011 is calculated as follows:

$$\text{Fixed Asset Turnover} = \frac{105,648}{38,243} = 2.76$$

The ratio of 2.76 indicates that Admathar Ltd generates GH¢2.76 of sales for every GH¢1 of investment in fixed assets. This indicates that the company is efficiently managing its fixed assets and that further investment in fixed assets could yield more income.

Total asset turnover ratio measures the efficiency with which an entrepreneur uses all his assets to generate sales. Unlike fixed asset turnover it also takes into account the yield of current assets such as inventory and cash held at the bank. Total asset turnover is calculated by dividing sales by total assets.

$$\text{Total Asset Turnover} \ = \ \frac{\text{Sales}}{\text{Total Assets}}$$

Like the fixed assets turnover, a higher ratio is generally preferred to a lower ratio. Admathar Ltd's total asset turnover at the end of 2011 is calculated below.

$$\text{Total Asset Turnover} \ = \ \frac{105,648}{119,622} \ = 0.88$$

This indicates that Admathar Ltd is able to generate GH¢0.88 from every GH¢1 investment in total assets. This lower ratio could be attributed to the amount of investment tied up in inventory since inventory constitutes a significant proportion of current assets and, as indicated previously, Admathar Ltd 's inventory turnover is low.

Debt Ratios

It has been indicated earlier that entrepreneurs can finance their ventures from two main sources – equity and debt – which constitute the two main components of an enterprise's capital structure, the proportion of capital that is from lenders or shareholders. Debt ratios are used to measure the extent to which debt capital rather than equity is used to finance the operations of an enterprise. Financing an entrepreneurial venture with debt creates financial leverage that could increase the risk and influence expected returns on investment.[21] The more debt an entrepreneur uses to finance a venture, the more he increases the risk profile of the venture, particularly if the debt is serviced by regular interest and capital payments. Such regular cash outflows can negatively affect the liquidity of the enterprise. In some parts of the developing world, it has also been found that small and medium-sized enterprises with higher debt ratio are more likely to become insolvent than those with a relatively small debt ratio.[22] Two key ratios for considering the capital structure are debt ratio and debt-to-equity ratio.

Debt ratio measures the percentage of a firm's total assets that is financed by lenders. An entrepreneur who relies largely on debt finance will have a higher debt ratio. Debt ratio is equal to total liabilities divided by total assets.

$$\text{Debt Ratio} = \frac{\text{Total Liabilities}}{\text{Total Assets}}$$

The debt ratio for Admathar Ltd at the end of 2011 can be calculated as follows:

$$\text{Debt Ratio} = \frac{61,101}{119,622} = 0.51$$

This means that the enterprise finances just over half of its activities from debt capital.

Debt-to-equity ratio takes into account an entrepreneur's long-term debt relative to its shareholders equity. It is calculated by dividing long-term debt (a debt that goes beyond a financial year) by equity.

$$\text{Debt-to-Equity Ratio} = \frac{\text{Long-Term Debt}}{\text{Shareholders' Equity}}$$

Admathar Ltd's debt-to-equity ratio at the end of the year 2011 is 0.31, as calculated below.

$$\text{Debt-to-Equity Ratio} = \frac{18,005}{58,521} = 0.31$$

When interpreting debt ratios, an entrepreneur must use some discretion, bearing in mind the specific needs of her business. For example, businesses in the same industry, but located in different locations, may have peculiar differences and thus require different levels of capitalisation, including debt capitalisation.

Although high debt capital may be good, given that debt is generally cheaper than equity, it increases risk of insolvency should the enterprise be unable to generate enough income to pay the interest and the principal components of its debts.

Profitability Ratios

An important measure of an enterprise's performance is its profit. Profit is a major indicator of how an entrepreneur manages his or her enterprise. Profitability ratios measure the enterprise's ability to make profit. More importantly, profitability ratios can be used by both entrepreneurs and investors to determine the investment returns from either earnings on revenues or appreciation of assets.[23] Some important profitability ratios are gross profit margin, net profit margin, return on total assets and return on equity.

Gross profit margin measures the direct income generated from a venture after deducting the direct costs incurred in generating the income. For example, in a retail business, gross profit is the value of goods sold less the costs incurred in purchasing those goods. A high gross profit margin is widely accepted as an indication of good performance. It is calculated as follows:

$$\text{Gross Profit Margin} = \frac{\text{Gross Profit}}{\text{Sales}}$$

Admathar Ltd's gross profit margin at the end of 2011 can be calculated as follows:

$$\text{Gross Profit Margin} = \frac{69,452}{105,648} = 0.66 \text{ or } 66\%$$

A gross profit margin of 66% is very healthy, indicating that a large percentage of the enterprise's sales revenue is profit.

Net profit margin measures the profit level after all costs, including operating expenses, interest and taxes, are taken into account. It shows the returns available to the entrepreneur and his equity holders after all expenses have been deducted from income.

$$\text{Net Profit Margin} = \frac{\text{Net Profit}}{\text{Sales}}$$

The calculation below indicates that Admathar Ltd recorded a net profit margin of 0.18 or 18% at the end of 2011. This means that for every GH¢1 in sales the enterprise generates, it makes a net profit of GH¢0.18. The higher an enterprise's net profit margin, the better.

$$\text{Net Profit Margin} = \frac{18,642}{105,648} = 0.18 \text{ or } 18\%$$

Return on total assets or return on investment measures how effective the entrepreneur is in generating returns on his assets. The formula for calculating this ratio is as follows:

$$\text{Return on Total Assets} = \frac{\text{Net Income or Profit}}{\text{Total Assets}}$$

The return on total assets for Admathar Ltd at the end of 2011 is 16% as calculated below. This indicates that the enterprise earns GH¢0.16 for every GH¢1 investment in assets. As a manufacturing company, Admathar Ltd is an asset-intensive company and so this is a good return. When interpreting this ratio, it is worth noting that some companies are less asset intensive so the significance of the figure is industry-dependent.

$$\text{Return on Total Assets} = \frac{18,642}{119,622} = 0.16 \text{ or } 16\%$$

Return on equity measures the returns on shareholders' capital. It is one of the most important measures of profitability. For the entrepreneur, this ratio indicates the percentage of investment returns that comes from her equity.

$$\text{Return on Equity} = \frac{\text{Net Income or Profit}}{\text{Owner's Equity}}$$

The return on equity for Admathar Ltd at the end of the year 2011 was 0.32 or 32%. This indicates that the enterprise generated 32% of net profit based on equity investment. While a high return on equity figure is good, it can be misleading since a high figure could signal that a high percentage of the enterprise's output is financed by debt.

$$\text{Return on equity} = \frac{18,642}{58,521} = 0.32 \text{ or } 32\%$$

While ratio analysis is a useful tool for the entrepreneur, as I noted earlier, using ratios in isolation is not meaningful and may be misleading. To make sense of ratios, the entrepreneur must compare these ratios with previous years' ratios, as well as those of similar companies, or the industry averages. Comparison allows for good performance reviews. Ratios must also be compared over time to determine trends in financial performance.

Break-Even Analysis

Break-even analysis is a financial planning technique that provides accurate information for the entrepreneur's decision making. It can be considered as a back-of-the-envelope type of calculation enabling the entrepreneur to examine the potential feasibility of a project or an enterprise before investing sums of money, time and energy in the project or enterprise.[24] A firm's break-even point is the level of production or service provision at which revenues equal expenses.

Break-even analysis provides a starting point from which an entrepreneur can make profitable investment decisions. If an entrepreneur is considering entering a specific market or launching a product which cannot be sold at a break-even price point, then such an investment will not be worth pursuing. Since the technique can be used to project the level of sales required to break even, entrepreneurs are able to make quick decisions on whether to proceed with production or service delivery.

The break-even analysis can be used to prepare budgets and control various cost elements. The break-even analysis is also a useful incremental device; given that additional expenditure affects the break-even point, the technique allows entrepreneurs to determine whether it is beneficial to incur additional cost or not. By employing the break-even analysis, the entrepreneur can determine the volume of business activity it will take to support such things as additional debt service or the salary of a new recruit.[25] The technique thus helps in making pricing decisions, and also helps the entrepreneur to determine the point at which he should consider expanding his business. Break-even analysis can also be used as a cash management tool to predict and manage cash flow. The cash flow break-even point is where the cash inflows equal the cash outflows and where a shortfall is foreseen, entrepreneurs can arrange overdrafts (short-term loan finance) to maintain minimum levels of liquidity.

The major advantage of break-even analysis is that it is easy to understand. It is easy for the entrepreneur to understand that he needs to sell 20 units of a product to cover all his costs or to produce 30 units of a product to make a particular level of profit. There are two main approaches that can be used to determine a break-even point. These are the contribution margin approach and the graphic approach.

Contribution Margin Approach

The contribution margin approach uses a simple mathematical formula to calculate the break-even point. The entrepreneur can compute the break-even point using this method by identifying fixed costs, variable costs and sales revenue.

Fixed costs are costs such as rent that do not change in response to a change in activity level over a period of time. For example, an increase in production levels at a factory would not increase the rent paid for the factory space.

Variable costs, as the name suggests, vary in relation to a change in activity level. Cost of raw materials and labour are examples of variable costs. The contribution margin is the difference between the sales income from a product or service and variable costs calculated per unit. The contribution margin approach can really only be used by established enterprises as one can only calculate the variable cost-per-unit if there has already been a history of production and sales.

The break-even point is calculated by dividing total fixed cost by the contribution margin

$$\text{Break-Even Point in Units} = \frac{\text{Fixed Costs}}{\text{Contribution Margin}}$$

(Where Contribution Margin = Sale Price per unit –Variable Cost-per-unit)

For instance, if Admartha's fixed cost is 32,648, selling price of 52 and variable cost is 24, then the break even point in units can be calculated as follows:

$$\text{Break-Even PU} = \frac{\text{Fixed cost}}{\text{UCM}} = \frac{32,648}{(52-24)} = 1,166$$

(Break-Even PU - Break-Even Point In Units & UCM - Unit Contribution Margin)

For the enterprise to break even, it needs to produce 1,166 units.

The break-even point can also be calculated in sales value. For instance, if Admathar Ltd wants to make a profit of GH¢5,000, then the break-even point on sales can be computed (using the contribution margin in brackets above) as follows:

$$\text{Break-Even PSV} = \frac{\text{Fixed Cost + Desired Profit}}{\text{CMPS}}$$

$$\text{Break-Even PSV} = \frac{32,648 + 5,000}{14.56} = \text{GH¢2,585}$$

(Break-Even PSV - Break-Even Point In Sales Value & CMPS - Contribution Margin as a Percentage of Sales)

Graphic Approach

The graphic approach provides a visual presentation of a firm's break-even point. To construct the break-even graph, the entrepreneur needs the following numbers – total revenue and total cost. The point of intersection between total revenue and total cost is the break-even point as shown in Figure 8.1. Two other numbers, the variable cost and fixed cost, can be constructed on the graph to give the entrepreneur a clear picture of the relationships between the cost variables. The graph shows that Admathar Ltd's fixed cost remains constant at GH¢2,500 while variable cost increases as output increases.

Figure 8.1: Graphical Presentation of Break-Even Point

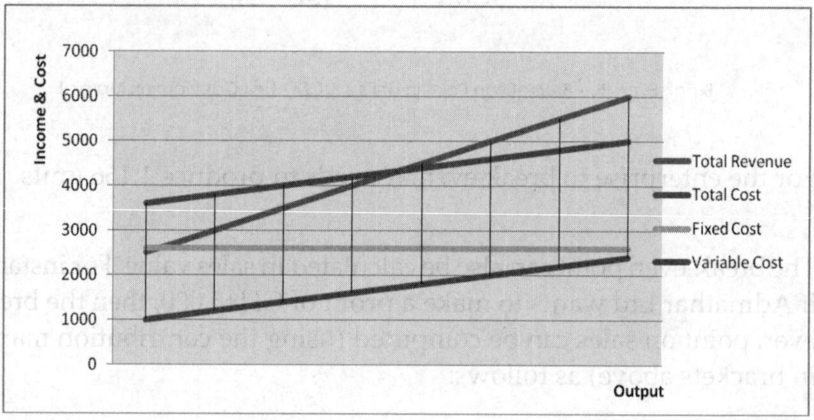

Case Study: Rancard Solutions: Managing and Maximizing the Little

KOFI DADZIE (MANAGING DIRECTOR) AND Ehizogie Binitie (Director for Product Management and Marketing) of Rancard Solutions are long-time friends, having met at Achimota School in the mid-1990s. When they co-founded Rancard in 2001, they dreamt of building a global company delivering world-class software technology. Undeterred by the modest seed capital they were able to raise, they focused on their global vision. The story of Rancard is driven by a mix of the confidence as well as the naïveté that Dadzie and Binitie had when they started the enterprise. In their own words, "[they] always thought that [they had] what it takes to grow a successful enterprise." They transitioned out of their wilderness experience (to use a Biblical analogy they closely relate to) when they figured out, with guidance from their board, the essence of marrying their technological prowess with disciplined and focused management and marketing, measured through sound financial outcomes.

Dadzie and Binitie developed Rancard's first major product in 2001 when they built a carrier-class mobile Internet (WAP) gateway to enable mobile networks deliver new data services such as push email to mobile users without additional infrastructure required of the networks. While this did not take off in 2001, its future reiteration several years down the line did eventually take off with various mobile networks signing on. Since then, they have never looked back despite encountering numerous challenges.

Prior to co-founding Rancard, Dadzie worked with a number of companies in the USA during and after completing a degree in computer engineering at Vanderbilt University. His experiences included stints at Dell Computer Corporation in Texas, where he worked as a senior analyst in the BIOS technology team and filed a patent; and at Radiant Systems Inc. in Georgia and Whirlpool Corporation in Tennessee, where he worked in various capacities related to systems technology, software automation and online commercial platforms. Binitie also had corporate experience before beginning his entrepreneurial journey. He completed an electrical engineering degree course at the Kwame Nkrumah University of Science and Technology and proceeded to work as an IT/software specialist at Intercom Data Networks (IDN). He later worked as a software architect for AQ Solutions, completing consulting projects for General Electric.

Dadzie and Binitie advocate growing your business organically. Their objective has been to grow Rancard organically up to a point by ensuring cost-effective use of and maximisation of the resources at their disposal. This sometimes involves using unconventional ways to get a product or service delivered to the customer, as was the case in one of their first enterprise software contracts to build custom payroll software. The project, which was billed at no more than US$10,000, required corresponding database software from Microsoft which cost approximately U$2,500. Dadzie and Binitie initially disagreed on whether to buy the database product, given that it would essentially deplete their margin on the contract price.

After a period of extensive search for an alternative, they found a free version of the database product with limited features but, as software engineers, they were able to ingeniously adapt and extend the limited version to get the full functionality they required for the project. As a result, they were able to save their company US$2,500, and they created a relational database interface that they could extend cheaply to future projects.

Although Dadzie and Binitie did not have the commercial or financial experience to properly manage the commercial aspect of the business, they always had an eye on cost. Aware of the value of their resources, they routinely evaluate every expense and decide whether there are other ways of getting the work done without spending more than necessary.

In 2004, for example, they restructured their business, moving from an ultra-modern and comfortable office to share office space with another company. Their objective was to get a space where they could work with all the necessary facilities without paying too much. They stayed in the building for four years before scaling up again.

In terms of managing operational expenses, they opt to cheaply rent hardware and network infrastructure in a data centre to operate their cloud-based software platform, and they extend virtual infrastructure to mobile networks over Internet-based secure VPNs (virtual private networks).

The year 2007 marked a significant milestone for Dadzie and Binitie as they successfully launched rancardmobility.com, a high-performance mobile service delivery platform (HPSDP). Using this platform, service providers and mobile network operators are able to deliver services and applications to mobile users in a cost-effective way. It has an added advantage of dynamic service configuration, speed and reliability in service delivery.

After six years of nurturing the business, their dream of building a global enterprise finally materialised as they attracted and won contracts with global brands including the BBC World Service, Google and Voice of America (VOA) with rancardmobility. com. They also provide service connectivity and an intelligent service and application management layer to major mobile network operators such as Millicom (Tigo), Vodafone, Airtel, MTN and Orange in more than 20 African, Middle Eastern and Asian countries, processing millions of mobile transactions daily.

Dadzie and Binitie advise (prospective) entrepreneurs that, in managing cash flow, it is important to look at how much you have, the expenses you have to incur and when you can – realistically! – expect your next cheque. They argue that while entrepreneurs often rejoice after a few successes, they have to be able to separate the small joys of success from realistic analyses of future prospects.

Questions for Case Discussion

1. Based on the case, are you able to identify some of the reasons why Rancard has been so successful?
2. What has been the approach of Dadzie and Binite to growing Rancard organically?
3. Do you agree with Dadzie and Binite that to maximise the little you have, the entrepreneur should always scale down on cost?

Question for Class Discussions

1. Managing financial resources is largely insignificant for entrepreneurs if their ideas/products/services are in high demand. Do you agree?
2. How significant/crucial is the financial management function to the performance of entrepreneurial ventures?
3. What are the key challenges that Ghanaian entrepreneurs face in managing their financial resources?
4. Should entrepreneurs leave the financial management function to accountants and other financial professionals?
5. Identify and discuss the essential role of financial statements for entrepreneurs in Ghana.
6. What are the key tools available for entrepreneurs to manage their working capital?
7. How can entrepreneurs best make meaning from their financial statements?
8. Advise an entrepreneur on the best way of making a capital investment decision.
9. Should entrepreneurs spend time and resources understanding break-even analysis?

Notes

1   Importance of Small Change. *The Africa Report*, 13, October – November 2008.

2   Scarborough, N. and T. Zimmerer. *Effective Small Business Management An entrepreneurial approach*. Upper Saddle River: Pearson Education, 2003.

3   Wijbenga, F.H., T.J.B.M. Postma and R. Stratling The Influence of the Venture Capitalist's Governance Activities on the Entrepreneurial Firm's Control Systems and Performance. *Entrepreneurship Theory and Practice*, 31(2), 2007: 257-277.

4   Adelman, P.J. and A.M. Marks. *Entrepreneurial Finance*. Upper Saddle River: Prentice Hall, 2007.

5   Stancill, J.M. *Managing Financial Statements: Image and Effect, Growing Concerns*. New York: Wiley, 1984.

6   Churchill, N.C. Budget Choice: Planning vs. Control. *Harvard Business Review*, 62(4), 1984: 150-164.

7   Crowther, D. *Managing Finance: A Socially Responsible Approach*. London: Elsevier, 2004.

8   Arnold, G. *Corporate Financial Management*. Upper Saddle River: Financial Times Prentice Hall, 2008.

9   Scarborough, N. and T. Zimmerer. *Effective Small Business Management An entrepreneurial approach*. Upper Saddle River: Pearson Education, 2003.

10 Arnold, G. *Corporate Financial Management*. Upper Saddle River: Financial Times Prentice Hall, 2008.

11 Singh, P. Inventory and Working Capital Management: An Empirical Analysis. *ICFAI Journal of Accounting Research*, 7(2), 2008: 53-73.

12 Megginson, W.L., S.B. Smart and B.M. Lucey. *Introduction to Corporate Finance*. Andover: Cengage Learning EMEA, 2008.

13 *Ibid.*

14 Shapiro, A.C. *Capital Budgeting and Investment Analysis*. Upper Saddle River: Prentice Hall, 2005.

15 Sagner, J.S. Capital budgeting: Problems and new approaches. *Journal of Corporate Accounting and Finance*, 19(1), 2007: 39-44.

16 Kuratko, D.F. and R.M. Hodgetts. *Entrepreneurship: A Contemporary Approach*. Orlando: The Dryden Press, 1998.

17 Thomas, J. and R.V. Evanson. An Empirical Investigation of Association between Financial Ratio Use and Small Business Success. *Journal of Business Finance and Accounting*, 14(4), 1987: 555-571.

18 Patrone, F.L. and D. DuBois. **Financial Ratio Analysis for** the **Small** Business. *Journal of Small Business Management*, 19(1), 1981: 35-40.

19 McMahon, R.G.P. and L.G. Davies. Financial Reporting and Analysis Practices in Small Enterprises: Their Association with Growth Rate And Financial Performance. *Journal of Small Business Management*, 32(1), 1994: 9-17.

20 Patrone, F.L. and D. DuBois. **Financial Ratio Analysis for** the **Small** Business. *Journal of Small Business Management*, 19(1), 1981: 35-40.

21 Megginson, W.L., S.B. Smart and B.M. Lucey. *Introduction to Corporate Finance*. Andover: Cengage Learning EMEA, 2008.

22 Kim, T., J. Kim, S. Pae and N. Pati. Accounting Ratios and Survival Rate: A Study of Korean SMEs that Received Government Loan Guarantee. *International Journal Of Business Research*, 10(1), 2010.

23 Adelman, P.J. and A.M. Marks. *Entrepreneurial Finance*. Upper Saddle River: Prentice Hall, 2007.

24 Cornwall, J.R., D.O. Vang and J.M. Hartman. *Entrepreneurial Financial Management: Applied Approach*. Upper Saddle River: Prentice Hall, 2004.

25 Thomas A. Break-even Analysis and Small Business. *Journal of Small Business Management*, 19(3), 1981: 61-62

Chapter Nine: Developing and Executing a People Strategy

"People often say that motivation doesn't last. Well, neither does bathing - that's why we recommend it daily.." - **Zig Ziglar**

Outline

- Introduction
- Developing a People Strategy
- Executing Your People Strategy – Operational Issues
- Retaining Employees
- Performance Appraisals
- Separation
- Entrepreneurial Leadership
- Building and Maintaining the Right Culture
- Building an Effective Culture
- Additional Considerations for Family-Owned Enterprises
- Case Study: Recruiting and Developing Stars at Oxford and Beaumont
- Questions for Class Discussion

Y OUR MOST IMPORTANT *assets – your reputation, your brands and your people [–] are not on the books"* – Ted Levitt

The above quotation has become a cliché. One writer has gone so far as to label it the "biggest commercial untruth since 'the cheque is in the post'"[1]. The problem is many entrepreneurs play lip service to the notion that their employees are their most important assets when seeking to attract human or financial capital. However, when it really matters – when the entrepreneurs have to approve a new employee remuneration package or invest in a training programme, rather than take out the money as dividends – they do not seem as keen to treat employees as the most important assets.

No matter how ingenious an entrepreneur is or innovative his ideas, technology, products or services, people are the most critical elements of any journey from idea to profit. The entrepreneur requires the productive energies of others to help drive his vision and enterprise.

Interestingly, the vast majority of entrepreneurs my research team spoke to complained about the difficulty of finding and retaining good and committed people, whether as employees or partners. They also complained about the attitude and motivation of their people. However, the findings from our suggest that many Ghanaian entrepreneurs fail to truly understand how central people are to creating a long-term, sustainable competitive advantage for their enterprises. Many entrepreneurs erroneously believe that the success of their enterprises comes down to their own skills, ability and contacts, and the few entrepreneurs who do not operate under this misapprehension fail to devote sufficient time to understanding the people they employ, and how those people might be better managed to contribute to the enterprise's overall objectives.

One of the more surprising responses from my research team revealed a Ghana Club 100 company that does not interview graduates, preferring to simply read their CVs and make decisions based on a host of unclear criteria.

Other trends that emerged were that it is fairly common for Ghanaian entrepreneurs to hire people they know, or who simply happen to be 'available', and not necessarily those who were the right fit[2] for the enterprise or had the required experience and/or knowledge. Although this may appear the cheaper and easier option, it consistently ended up being more expensive in the long run.

Also, a number of entrepreneurs complained about the skill set, performance and attitudes of their employees without ever having articulated to these employees their expectations of them, or given them any training. Finally, hundreds of employees and partners admitted to being frustrated because they felt undervalued, misunderstood, disrespected, underdeveloped and underemployed.

This chapter will attempt to address some of the issues that came out of the research; it also seeks to answer the question 'How do you attract, recruit, retain and motivate the right employees for your enterprise?' I have divided the chapter into two broad areas – people strategy and people operations. The few enterprises that pay attention to people issues in Ghana tend to focus more (or in some cases almost exclusively) on the operational aspects of managing people – the mechanics of filling vacancies, payroll administration, leave management, provident fund administration, etc. – without thinking about the strategy component, which is equally or perhaps even more important. It is my belief that entrepreneurs should first develop a people strategy that dovetails with the overall strategy of the enterprise. Only when that is done should the operational elements of the people equation be considered, particularly as those operational elements ought to derive from the strategy.

Ultimately, the type of people organisation that any enterprise becomes depends on its leadership and the culture that underpins and binds everything that is done in the enterprise. I therefore discuss, in some detail, the concepts of entrepreneurial leadership and culture.

Developing a People Strategy

People are so central to the success of any enterprise that the entrepreneur, if she wants to succeed, must take a strategic view of all activities relating to identifying, attracting, managing, developing and retaining the people who are the right fit for her enterprise.

My emphasis is on people who are the 'right fit' rather than the 'best' people. It is not always the case that the 'best' candidate for a given position, in terms of experience, educational background and other objective criteria, will also be the candidate who is the best fit for the role, best suited to the enterprise's culture and ethos, existing structure, values and aspirations, possessing the hard and soft skills required for the role.

According to Anthony et al., a strategic approach to human resources involves strategic planning, decision making and coordination of all human resource functions for all employees.[3] An effective people strategy starts with entrepreneurial leadership, places people at the epicentre of the strategy for the enterprise, and views the human resource function as an integral part of all the other functional areas of the enterprise (such as finance, marketing, and operations) rather than a stand-alone functional area.

The human resource function must not be left for human resource managers alone. Rather, all managers, particularly the leadership team and the entrepreneur should be actively involved in managing the human resources of the enterprise.

What I have found with Ghanaian enterprises is a general absence of a people strategy. In the vast majority of human resources functions surveyed, the focus is on the administrative or operational aspects of managing people – leave management, payroll administration, management of appraisal processes, etc.

In developing a people strategy, the following factors must first be identified and analysed to form the foundation:

• *The External Environment*

As we learnt in Chapter 4, the external environment affects the strategy, activities and profitability of an enterprise. In the context of developing a people strategy, the entrepreneur must carry out a range of analyses, particularly PEST analysis, competitive analysis and SWOT analysis, from a human resources point of view. Based on the analyses, the entrepreneurs may find their enterprises faced with threats or opportunities relating to its people strategy that it must react to. For example, as a result of increased demand in industries such as banking, insurance, technology and legal services in Ghana, qualified and motivated employees have stronger bargaining power as they have more options. Any entrepreneur targeting employees in those industries will need to ensure that he understands the typical packages and opportunities as well as the motivations and aspirations of his target employees, and adapt accordingly.

The fundamental objective in conducting analyses of the external environment is to develop a people strategy that takes into account the environment in which the enterprise does business to exploit and maximise the opportunities it presents and to minimise the threats that the enterprise faces from it.

• *The Competitive Environment*

An analysis of competitors and the evolving dynamics of the labour market will better inform the entrepreneur on how to develop a competitive people strategy. Enterprises vie to attract and retain the best talent in the market in the same way they compete to attract and retain customers. For example, the financial and telecommunications industries in Ghana compete to attract the best employees using a number of tactics including poaching staff from competitors by offering them more competitive packages and better working conditions.

There are various environmental issues that the entrepreneur needs to consider when designing his people strategy. The analysis should look at the minimum wage regulations, the rate of unemployment in the country, the skill level of potential employees, the availability of unskilled, semi-skilled and skilled labour, general working conditions, the power and influence of labour unions such as the Trade Union Congress, and the human resource strategies of their competitors. As a result of competitive analysis, the entrepreneur may, for example, decide not to compete on cash compensation given the high levels of cash offered by competitors with deeper pockets. She may instead decide to develop a strategy around training and personal development to set her enterprise apart from the competition and attract outstanding talent at lower compensation than the competition is able to.

• *Planning Horizon*

In developing a people strategy, entrepreneurs must always have a long-term focus. Since the people strategy is the bedrock of the enterprise, it must be aligned with the mission and vision of the enterprise, both of which tend to be forward looking. Attracting and retaining the right people requires significant investment which will yield dividends over a long period of time. It is important therefore that entrepreneurs develop a strategy that has a long planning horizon.

• Involve All Employees

A people strategy should take into account all the employees in an enterprise, whether they are temporary, contract or permanent staff, from the lowest ranked to the topmost executive manager, skilled and unskilled staff. It should also cover all issues that could affect the performance of their duties and responsibilities. As such their wages, salaries and benefits, should be considered together with training and development, progression and culture.

• Integrate People and Corporate Strategy

Corporate strategy should drive the people strategy. If, for example, the corporate strategy is to capture and dominate the Ghanaian non-bank financial sector, then the people strategy should focus on attracting, recruiting and retaining the people who can drive this unique corporate strategy. These people should have a common interest in financial services as well as the ambition to work with a leader or aspiring leader in the non-bank financial services sector. Some of them may come with significant experience in the non-bank or banking financial sector, while some may have diverse transferable skills from other industries, others may have just graduated. A good people strategy will aim to develop an enterprise that leverages the skills and talents of those with prior experience while fast-tracking the development of bright graduates with no prior experience. The people strategy of an enterprise that is seeking to dominate a particular industry will be vastly different from that of a lifestyle enterprise in the same industry. In the former case, the core employees are likely to be those who by nature are competitive and like to set the pace.

In developing a people strategy, the entrepreneurs may consider the following questions:

• Build or Buy?

In Chapter 5 we discussed the pros and cons of starting an

enterprise from scratch or acquiring an existing enterprise. In developing a people strategy, the entrepreneur has to make another build or buy decision: hire experienced people already trained by someone else (buy) or employ inexperienced people and spend time training and developing them (build). 'Buying' employees is more expensive than 'building' them, as experienced employees will demand a premium to reflect their experience. By virtue of their experience, they are also generally able to add value quicker, provided they are the right fit for the enterprise. My research team found that Ghanaian employers tend to prefer people with experience. Recruiting skilled staff with the necessary experience means work can start immediately, with little or no training. However, more experienced employees sometimes bring 'baggage', and may not be as adaptable or capable of fitting easily into the enterprise's culture. The major disadvantage of hiring less-experienced employees or recent graduates is that they may not be able to work immediately without extensive training. Enterprises that want standardisation of quality may find it better to hire recent graduates and train them in the required operational standards. It is easier to develop a peculiar culture by recruiting inexperienced people who have not been prejudiced by experiences of other companies or industries, and inspiring them to develop and imbibe the peculiar culture.

• *Self Recruitment or Outsourcing?*

Entrepreneurs may decide to recruit themselves or to engage the services of a recruitment agency or a headhunter. Experienced recruitment consultants can easily justify their fees because of the time they save entrepreneurs by using their databases of jobseekers. When using an external recruiter, it is important for entrepreneurs to be heavily involved in the recruitment process and to be the ones to make the final decision. They can leave it to the recruiter to pre-screen candidates and carry out relevant background checks. However, the entrepreneur should interview the candidates shortlisted by the recruiter and make the final decision. The entrepreneur should also spend time explaining to the recruiter not only the job description and specification, but also the culture and ethos of the enterprise, so as to ensure that the recruiter finds candidates who fit with the enterprise's culture.

• *Direct Employment or Outsourcing?*

In some cases there might be good reason why the entrepreneur should not hire directly but rely on an employment or placement agency to provide staff. These agencies employ the staff and place them with various enterprises, either on a temporary or short-term basis or on a much longer basis. Where employees are outsourced in this way, they remain employees of the agency, to whom the entrepreneur pays a fee, covering the salaries of the employees and other administrative costs. In Ghana, agencies such as Montran, L'ainé and Noswell provide such outsourced labour. Placement agencies can be particularly useful when targeting a special skill, groups of employees with a high turnover or employees who may be difficult to manage (such as security men, bulk cash tellers, maids and drivers). Entrepreneurs using outsourced staff should still interview the staff allocated to them to determine that they are a proper fit. Particular care must also be taken to integrate them into the firm.

• *Attitude or Aptitude?*

Sometimes the entrepreneur is faced with making the choice between two types of employee; one who has the right qualifications, technical ability and experience (aptitude) but without the right attitude on the one hand, and another who does not (as yet) have the aptitude but has a great attitude towards work. My experience supports the view that in such cases the entrepreneur should favour attitude over aptitude as, in many cases, an employee with the right attitude can, with the right coaching and development, develop the aptitude required for the job whereas the reverse is often not the case.

Employee Value Proposition

Employees contribute significantly to the consumer's total brand experience, particularly in the services sector. As a result, everyone in the organisation must understand that they are responsible for brand building; entrepreneurs should align every component of the enterprise with its brand strategy.

The brand that the enterprise communicates externally should be consistent with its internal human resource policies and vice versa. Enterprises that want to succeed in the war for talent should market themselves as good places to work based on the values of the enterprise since enterprises with great employment brands tend to recruit better. As Ama Benneh-Amponsah, Executive Director for Human Resource at MTN Ghana Ltd explains,[4] MTN's values centre around the colour yellow which signifies youth and vibrancy, thus it has an HR policy that fosters a performance-based culture, encouraging junior employees to challenge superiors if necessary.

One of the ways in which employers communicate their employee brand is through the employee value proposition, which captures the total experience which an employer offers employees in return for their labour. Based on the human resource SWOT analysis carried out, the overall strategy of the enterprise and its vision and mission, the entrepreneur should seek to create a compelling employee value proposition that distinguishes his enterprise from the competition and provides a compelling reason for employees to join. The employee value proposition must capture the compensation and benefits, the personal development opportunities, the culture, the environment and the aspiration of the enterprise. It should embody the values of the enterprise and be consistent with the brand positioning that is communicated to customers.

Executing Your People Strategy – Operational Issues

The entrepreneur will need to develop an implementation plan which translates her strategy into an operational plan. She will do this primarily through job analysis, job description and job specification, but also through operational policies relating to recruitment, retention, appraisals and separation.

Job Analysis, Job Description and Job Specification

Before hiring, entrepreneurs should be clear first of all that they need personnel. They must also be clear on the role that person is to play and where in the enterprise's organogram the role will fit. Entrepreneurs should thus begin with a job analysis, which is an analysis of the job role itself (the duties and nature of the job to be filled) and of the type of person required for the job (the skills and experience of the person who is to fill the job). It captures the entrepreneur's understanding of the requirements for the job to be filled and covers the following:[5]

- The mental and physical tasks involved (for example, judging, planning, cleaning and lifting);

- How the job will be done (the methods and the equipment to be used);

- The reason why the job exists (including an explanation of job goals and how they relate to other positions within the company);

- The qualifications needed (training, knowledge, skills and personality traits).

Lesonsky[6] advises that if you are having trouble putting a job analysis together, you should talk to employees and supervisors at other companies who have similar positions.

The objective of the job analysis is to develop a job description and a job specification. A job description is a written statement of duties, responsibilities, reporting relationships, working conditions and materials and equipment used in the job.[7] It essentially answers the question of exactly what an employee's role is in the enterprise and can be useful in giving potential applicants a sense of what the job entails.

A job specification is a profile of the kind of person who would be ideal for the role the entrepreneur has in mind. It is a written statement of the qualifications and characteristics needed for the job: educational qualifications, skills, experience and special aptitudes needed for the job (for example, mechanical, verbal, numerical skills). It may also list desirable interests and interpersonal skills, appearance, age, manner and speech. A job specification for the position of Marketing Officer may, for example, state that the ideal candidate must have at least a second class lower degree from a reputable university and three years' work experience. In addition, she must be a good listener, have empathy, be well organised, decisive, a self-starter and be able to use technology comfortably.

Ideally, at the very beginning of the enterprise, job descriptions and specifications should be developed for the team envisaged by the entrepreneur. It is important that there is consensus on the job description and job specification among all those who will interview or work with the successful candidate.

The entrepreneur should also define in what capacity he proposes to bring the person (full- or part-time employee, consultant, partner, etc.).

Recruitment

The objective of recruitment is to identify the best qualified person that an enterprise can afford to hire for a particular job. Care must be taken to avoid hiring unsuitable candidates for jobs in a bid to save money. Entrepreneurs should resist the temptation to be pesewa wise and avoid being cedi foolish; the popular adage that 'if you pay peanuts you get a monkey' is applicable in this context.

In developing the business plan, entrepreneurs must think through the number of employees required at the different stages of at least the first phase of the enterprise's life, and ensure that adequate provision is made for employing them, taking into account the costs of recruiting and retaining these people. The cost of recruitment should be included as part of the projected investment costs. Recruitment costs include advertising expenses, the cost of testing and interviews (including management time expended in testing and interviewing), training for new recruits and the equipment that the recruits will use in their roles.

Sometimes, in an attempt to save money, particularly at the beginning of the idea-to-profit journey, entrepreneurs take on roles that they are ill-equipped for. Although there is much to be said for bootstrapping and minimising costs, especially before the enterprise has begun to make profit, this should be balanced with the need to ensure that the entrepreneur has the right people to assist him in driving the enterprise towards its vision. Where necessary, entrepreneurs should hire someone with the requisite skills and expertise to take on roles beyond their capability. There are many creative ways for entrepreneurs to find people with particular skills that the enterprise may not be able to (as yet) afford; some are expanded on below.

• *Advisory Board Members*

In Chapter 10 we will discuss advisory boards. In recruiting members of an advisory board, the entrepreneur can recruit people who have skills that the entrepreneur and the enterprise may be lacking. Tapping into the knowledge and experience of advisory board members is a cost-efficient way for the entrepreneur to obtain advice and information as advisory board members would generally agree to advise the entrepreneur for free or for relatively modest sums, particularly where there is a pre-existing relationship between the advisory board members and the entrepreneur.

• *Consulting Engagements or Part-time Contracts*

Sometimes the entrepreneur can hire people on a consulting or part-time basis instead of hiring them full time. This may be especially helpful in the early days of the business when the entrepreneur might want to establish the viability of the business before committing significant resources to particular roles.

• *School Assignments*

Entrepreneurs may be able to work with professors and students of local tertiary institutions to plug the holes in their knowledge and expertise. Many tertiary institutions are open to assisting entrepreneurs with projects. This may be a very cost-efficient way for the entrepreneur to obtain the required knowledge or information. However, it may sometimes be difficult to maintain a high degree of confidentiality when there are a large number of students involved. The entrepreneur can manage this by requiring that the relevant students/lecturers sign non-disclosure agreements (sometimes called confidentiality agreements). Examples of such creativity that I have seen used include asking trainee chefs at a vocational institute to work as chefs at a start-up restaurant and asking students of the Ghana Institute of Journalism to help start a magazine. Sandy Osei-Agyemang, in developing the idea for his MVP line of haircare products, turned to students of Northwestern University's Kellogg School of Management to conduct extensive research on haircare products n Ghana.

• *National Service*

The National Service scheme is a scheme set up by the National Service Act, 1980 (Act 426), requiring all citizens of Ghana who pursue higher education to do one year of compulsory national service where they work for a rather modest monthly allowance. The use of 'national service' in this context is misleading as it is not limited to employment by the state. Private enterprises are able to apply to the National Service Secretariat (NSS) for national service personnel to be posted to their enterprises. Each year, the NSS sets the allowance to be paid to national service personnel which is always much lower than what an entrepreneur would have to pay a graduate on the market. Since National Service is compulsory, it provides entrepreneurs (and other organisations) relatively cheap labour during the national service year. My experience is that many entrepreneurs have benefited from using National Service personnel during the service year. Sometimes, after the National Service period, the entrepreneur hires the person as a full-time employee or hires another National Service person for another year. Many entrepreneurs who do this report that it is cost-effective, particularly when they are allowed to interview

National Service personnel and request that the NSS posts identified individuals to them. Although the NSS used to allow pre-screening, it appears that it has now changed its position. In my view this development is disappointing and undermines the utility of the National Service scheme for private companies and entrepreneurs.

Recruiting Methods

There are two main methods of recruiting for most enterprises. These are internal recruiting and external recruiting. In some enterprises, it is normal practice to attempt to recruit from within the enterprise before external candidates are considered.

• *Internal Recruiting*

When there is a vacant or new position in an enterprise, the first step should be to consider whether any of the existing employees would be suitable for that role. Employers communicate internal vacancies by posting the available job(s) using staff listserves, internal notice boards or the intranet. Information about internal vacancies should include as much information as possible (such as details about the position, duties and responsibilities, required skills and compensation package).

Where someone is recruited from within to fill a more senior role with more responsibility, it is a visible sign of employee progression. This is good for boosting employee morale as it inspires and motivates both the promoted person and other employees. Recruiting from within the enterprise also ensures continuity as the employee will already have knowledge and understanding of the enterprise, its operations and objectives. It is also a cheaper way of recruiting although it is not always possible to fill vacancies this way, particularly in the case of small and medium-sized enterprises with a relatively small talent pool. Employing from within can narrow the range of candidates much sooner than might have been the case if external recruiting was used, resulting in an imbalance in the types of people and the diversity of experiences and perspectives within the organisation.

• *External Recruiting*

For many entrepreneurs, one way to bring fresh ideas and skills into their enterprises is to recruit externally. There are various approaches to recruiting outside the enterprise:

- Personal Network: Entrepreneurs looking to fill a role share information about that role with those in their personal network, asking them for leads or recommendations. The advantage of recruiting through a personal network is that personal contacts are likely to be open about the strengths and weaknesses of the candidates they recommend.

- Advertising: Advertising a job opening in newspapers, magazines, radio, television and other media has the advantage of announcing the job opportunity to a wide range of potential candidates. The wide reach can however be a disadvantage as advertising generates many unsuitable candidates whose applications consume administrative time, and may divert attention away from more qualified candidates. However, advertising can also be used to target specific groups of people who might be consuming a particular media type or brand. For example, an employer seeking to recruit a chartered accountant in Ghana may advertise in the Business and Financial Times, which many accountants in Ghana read, or she may decide to advertise on the website of the Ghana Institute of Chartered Accountants. Wherever entrepreneurs decide to advertise, they should try and integrate their recruitment adverts with their other brand management initiatives. For example, job advertisements should have the same look and feel as the enterprise's other branding.

- Professional Recruiters: These go by various names including employment agencies, technical recruiters and executive search firms (or headhunters). Some are very generalised while others specialise in particular fields such as accounting, information technology or pharmaceuticals.[8] Over the past few years, there has been an increase of professional recruiters in Ghana. Companies such as Axis Human Capital, L'aine, Beekman Management Consulting, Zomelo and Associates, Jobs in Ghana, Plato Consult and KPMG are just some examples of those who scout potential talent for employers. In addition to arranging tailored searches for employers, these agencies also maintain a database of job applicants, and, for some positions, would match their database with an employer's needs. They typically screen a large number of candidates and, after interviews, present a pre-agreed number of shortlisted candidates to the employer, together with background information on skills, experience, education, and their own evaluation of the candidates. Upon hiring them, the enterprise would be required to pay a fee to the agency (up to 20% of the employee's annual compensation). Sometimes, when an employer has a high-level vacancy which requires the professional recruiter to actively headhunt for suitable candidates, the recruiter may charge a non-refundable retainer and expect to be reimbursed for expenses.

- Direct Headhunting: The entrepreneur may decide to personally identify competent individuals who may or may not be looking for new employment and approach them to interview with the enterprise, leading to a job offer if they have the right skills. For example, an entrepreneur setting up a new hotel and looking to hire front desk receptionists may loiter around the front desk of Labadi Beach Hotel and other top hotels in Ghana to get a feel for the calibre of receptionists who work there. Once he has a sense of which ones he thinks are good at their job, he may approach them to arrange interviews. Alternatively, he may find out about good candidates at a particular establishment by asking any contacts he may have who work there for leads, and then approach the recommended candidates.

- Internet: This is becoming one of the fastest ways to communicate job openings to potential candidates. More and more, job vacancies are listed on websites such as www.jobsinghana.com, www.businessghana.com and www.

ghanaweb.com. Some enterprises in the country also use their websites to advertise job vacancies and/or ask potential employees to fill their application forms and submit their resumes online. This method is becoming particularly significant as Internet penetration in the country is growing rapidly. Despite this, not everyone has access to the Internet in Ghana, and so using the Internet as a primary recruitment tool may exclude some excellent candidates.

- Employee Referrals: Existing employees are perhaps the best people to determine the skills and talents that are required to perform a particular task in an enterprise. They are therefore in a good position to recommend to the employer candidates who could perform particular roles in the enterprise. However, there is a risk that employees might recommend people who are just like them. Entrepreneurs should guard against this and pro-actively ensure that whoever they recruit adds to the diversity of the team.

- Third-Party Referrals: Third parties – business associates, suppliers and customers, etc. – are sometimes also in a good position to recommend candidates to an entrepreneur who is recruiting. Like employee referrals, these referrals, if they come from a reliable third party, can be a good source of leads, particularly where the third party has worked with the proposed candidate or knows the candidate well in other professional contexts.

- Universities And Other Tertiary Institutions: The better universities and other tertiary institutions provide a good pool of talent for entry-level positions. In some cases, through advanced degree candidates, they may also provide a pool of candidates for roles requiring experience. My experience is that entrepreneurs who take a long-term view of recruiting, and who develop relationships with tertiary institutions to build a talent pipeline, tend to have fewer retention and culture issues. Apart from recruiting students upon completion of their study to work full time, some enterprises hire university students to work as interns during vacations. A well-organised internship programme can be a good source of recruiting full-time employers after the internship period, as it provides an opportunity for both the intern and the employer to size up each other to determine whether there is a mutual fit. I highly recommend that enterprises develop a well thought-out internship programme to attract good candidates while they are still students.

- National Service: As we discussed earlier, the National Service scheme can be a good source of potential employees, particularly where employers are permitted to interview and select their own employees from the pool of eligible service personnel.

• Some Tips for Effective External Recruiting

- Do not wait until you need a new employee before you start to recruit. Always be on the lookout for prospective employees. Every time you are out and about, keep your eyes wide open. I have personal experiences of meeting some of my best employees in unlikely places such as a video library, a health farm and a bookshop.

- Make a list of all the firms you have worked at and, under each firm, list the stars you worked with that you might want to recruit and then approach them.

- List all the great people who have served with you/worked with you in different capacities, such as social committees, not-for-profit boards, parent teacher associations, church committees, etc.

- Volunteer to teach a class at a university near you or to speak at such an institution where you would be able to come into contact with potential employees. It is an excellent way for you to assess potential candidates over a long period of time where the candidates may not be aware that they are being assessed on their potential suitability for a job;

- Keep a good database in which you record details of all the good potential candidates you come across (even if it is many years before you actually need them) and keep in touch with them.

Recruiting for Fit

Beyond matching the right person to the right job, finding the 'right fit' has a cultural component. Jobs within organisations have cultural contexts. As such, entrepreneurs should make sure that all new hires strengthen those contexts, not conflict with them.

Selected employees must also fit into, enjoy and enrich both the macroculture of the enterprise and the microculture of the particular department or unit they will be working in. A macroculture is an enterprise's way of doing things, its general values, the ways in which people relate to one another, and so forth. Microculture characterises the dynamics of different departments or job functions.[9]

In addition, the entrepreneur must take time to ensure that the selected employee shares the values and ethos of the enterprise and identifies with the aspirations of the enterprise. She must be able to get along with the existing team and balance any deficiencies in the existing skill set. Her work style should also fit that of existing team members, although allowance must be made to ensure diversity. Her short- and long-term plans should be consistent with those of the enterprise.

For example, the ability to debate is an important skill for the software developers at theSOFTtribe. Herman Chinery-Hesse, the company's founder and Executive Chairman, believes that teams that succeed are the ones that encourage debate. As a result, after shortlisting the candidates, he debates with them on any number of topics and only interviews those who debated well.[10]

Application and Shortlisting

Employers can ask prospective employees to apply for vacancies by filling enterprise-specific application forms. The forms normally require candidates to fill their background information, education, work experience, and other skills. They may also have questions that allow the employer to assess certain areas of interest to him. Employers may also ask prospective candidates to submit application letters and detailed CVs. When screening candidates, it is a good idea to have the job description and job specification in front of you so as to keep the qualities and skills you are looking for clearly in mind. When you have a large number of applications, Lucke[11] advises the use of a two-part process. In the first pass eliminate applicants that have not met the basic requirements for the job. In the second pass, look out for the applications that include:

- Signs of achievement and results, stability or progressive career momentum;
- A career goal in line with the job being offered;
- Attractive overall construction and appearance.

In the second pass, also consider the subtler differences among qualified candidates before developing a list of the strongest candidates.

Many employers (sometimes in the interest of saving money) only contact shortlisted candidates and leave the other candidates wondering about their fate. The recruitment process is an opportunity to build the enterprise's brand. Writing a simple letter to the candidate to explain that there were many suitable candidates, for example, is a good way to positively project the brand of your enterprise. With the Internet, the cost of communicating with applicants is significantly reduced for those who have email access; I highly recommend that enterprises leverage this to contact and keep candidates updated on the status of their respective applications.

Testing

Testing is becoming an important technique that employers use to screen large pools of applicants. There are various testing methods that employers can use to assess potential employees. Aptitude tests help examine the various behavioural attributes and logical reasoning capabilities of candidates, while numeracy tests establish the numerical skills of candidates. Also, some employers may require that candidates carry out specific tasks similar to those they might perform in the role they are interviewing for. Testing helps employers eliminate candidates who are not well equipped for the position they intend to fill.

Ideally, entrepreneurs should carry out pre-employment tests to ensure that candidates will be able to do the job when hired. If you are recruiting for a law firm and interviewing experienced lawyers from a rival firm, you could ask them to draft an agreement of the type you might ask them to draft if employed by you. If you are hiring a chef, you could ask them to develop, cook and serve a menu.

Given the wide variances in the quality of English language instruction in primary and secondary schools in Ghana, I highly recommend that entry-level and junior staff are also tested on their command of the English language if they are expected to communicate in English on the job. I was involved in the hiring of an accounts officer who performed well on the accounting test that he was given. However it did not occur to us to test his written English. Although he could perform the relevant technical accounting work after he was hired, his command of the English language was so poor that I had to arrange private English tuition for him.

Interviews

The interview is the single most widely used device for screening job candidates; as such, the results of interviews tend to have a disproportionate amount of influence on the decision of who is hired and who is not.[12] The objective of an interview is to look at the candidate's previous experience and present capabilities, based on which the employer makes a determination of ability to perform in the role being filled.

Some thought must be put into planning the interview in advance. The entrepreneur should schedule an interview only when he has a clear idea of what he wants to get out of it. At the stage of attracting candidates, it is assumed that the entrepreneur would already have defined a clear job description and job profile, based on which he will shortlist candidates for interview.

Entrepreneurs should develop interview questions that will provide meaningful insights into an applicant's qualifications, personality and character. It is also important that there is a consistent approach taken by entrepreneurs to all interviews for a particular role to ensure that candidates can be meaningfully compared against each other. For example, all candidates should answer the same core set of questions. Admittedly, each interview will be customised depending on the responses given and the flow between the interviewer and the interviewee, but it is important that there are some core questions asked of all candidates. Where a number of people in the enterprise are responsible for interviewing candidates, efforts should be made to ensure that there is consistency across each of the interviews. It is good to have an interviewing assessment sheet which is agreed among the interviewers and applied in the evaluation process.

Where appropriate, entrepreneurs should also consider involving other stakeholders such as suppliers or customers. The no-frills American airline Southwest Airlines is famous for including customers in its interview process.

Interviewers should:

- Ask open-ended questions, rather than 'Yes' or 'No' questions. Open-ended questions are effective because they encourage the candidates to talk about their experiences, making it easier for the interviewer to determine whether the candidate exhibits the required traits or skill set;

- Leave enough time for questions specifically related to the vacant job. Too often, people spend time focusing on professional qualifications and degrees without actually finding out for sure if the interviewee can do the job. There should be some questions about scenarios the interviewee is likely to face in the job should she be recruited;

- Ask questions about the interviewee's professional work experience to determine if he or she has the required traits. If the interviewee is straight out of school, questions around participation in clubs and societies at school, taking up a leadership role, etc. could give insights into character and disposition to work.

Types of Interviews

• *One-To-One Interviews*

The candidate is interviewed by one person. The disadvantage of a one-to-one interview is that there is only one viewpoint gained on the candidate. I advise that, as much as possible, the entrepreneur should involve other people in interviewing candidates.

• *Panel Interviews*

In a panel interview, the candidate is interviewed by a selection of people. Typically, the candidate sits behind a long desk with the panel of interviewers facing him. Each member of the panel can ask any number of questions and at the end of the interview, the panel must vote on whether or not to hire the candidate or move him to the next stage of the interview process (as the case may be). Panel interviews can be a good way to get different views on the same candidate in one interview.

• *Group Interviews*

In a group interview, candidates are interviewed together with other candidates. Sometimes, they may be given topics to debate or assignments to compete in a group. The objective is usually to see how well candidates work with other people.

• *Competency Interviews*

These focus on questioning the candidate on the specific competencies required for the job. These tend to be fairly detailed interviews in which the candidate is required to answer questions based on specific examples drawn from experience.

• *Technical Interviews*

For certain jobs which require specific technical knowledge, there might be an interview focused on determining whether or not the candidate has the required technical expertise.

• *Portfolio-Based Interviews*

For some creative roles in the media and communications space, the candidate may be asked to bring a portfolio of work to the interview. Based on the portfolio, the interviewer will engage the candidate in a detailed discussion about the work making up the portfolio.

• *Case Study Interviews*

In these interviews, the candidate may be asked to solve a hypothetical or real business problem. The objective is to evaluate the candidate's thought process and his analytical ability. Case interviews are a particular favourite of consulting companies.

Face-To-Face vs. Telephone/Video Conference Interviews

The most common form of interview is the face-to-face interview. However, because it is not always possible to meet in person, employers sometimes interview candidates by telephone and video conferencing (for example, using Skype). Where there are a large number of applicants, phone interviews can be used to pre-screen candidates. My advice is that while telephone or video conference interviews may be a legitimate part of the interview process, an offer should never be made to a candidate without a face—to-face meeting. I know of too many examples of candidates appearing to be the perfect on the telephone or on a video conference, but having the wrong chemistry in person.

Type Of Interview Questions/Assessment Tools

Situational Questions

These are based on hypothetical situations (but modelled on situations that occur in the recruiting enterprise) in which the employer asks the candidate how she would react in a particular situation.

Behavioural Questions

Behavioural questions are based on how candidates have reacted to certain issues in the past, or how they have responded to challenges.

Psychometric Tests

These tests are usually used in the early stages of selection to screen out candidates who are likely to be unsuitable for the job. There are two types of psychometric tests:

- Personality Tests

  These give the employer information about aspects of a candidate's personality;

- Aptitude or Cognitive Ability Tests

  These measure intellectual abilities such as verbal comprehension and quantitative aptitude.

Assessment Days

Candidates are assessed over an extended period of time. Over the course of a few days, the candidates are interviewed by different people in a variety of situations. They may also be given a number of tasks and tests to do. Assessment days are favoured by enterprises recruiting a large number of people who have recently graduated from university (or are about to graduate). It is generally considered a fair method of selection as candidates are assessed in a situation where they have time to become comfortable, based on a number of interviews and performance on a series of tasks and tests.

The interview itself contains three phases:

• Preliminaries

This is at the beginning of the interview, where the interviewer's main role is to get the candidate to relax so as to get the best out of him or her. Also at this beginning stage, the interviewer or entrepreneur may want to take the opportunity to describe the role in a little more detail for the interviewee, and possibly provide some insights into the culture of the enterprise. It is also advised that the interviewer explain what sort of person is being sought, how many positions are involved, how the interview is to be conducted, what stages are involved in the interviewing process and how long the interview is scheduled to last.

• *Questions*

Once the interviewee is relaxed, the question stage begins. After each question, the interviewer should ensure he understands the answers and, where necessary, asks follow-up questions or questions of clarification. The 'hire' or 'no hire' decision is essentially made at this stage and, as mentioned above, it is important that the questions asked give the candidate an opportunity to demonstrate her suitability for the role.

• *Wrapping Up*

The interviewer should leave some time at the end to take questions from the interviewee as well as to sell the company and the role available. I judge interview candidates in part by the quality of questions they ask, as in my experience, the candidates that ask the most intelligent questions during the interview process tend to be more engaged employees when hired. The entrepreneur should always end the interview by thanking the interviewee and giving an indication of when a decision is likely to be made. If there are further stages in the interview process (i.e. if the candidate has to return to interview with other people or to write tests, etc.), this must be clearly communicated to the interviewee at this stage.

Robbins[13] advises that realistic job previews should be used to provide job applicants both unfavourable and favourable information before an offer is made. This is in direct contrast to the job previews that most managers give at the interview stage – carefully worded job descriptions that sell the positive aspects of the new job and the organisation. He advises that as no job or organisation is perfect, and you are more likely to keep your new hires if you are straight with them from the beginning. The evidence indicates that applicants who have been given a realistic job preview hold lower and more realistic expectations about the job they will be doing, and are better prepared for coping with the job and its frustrating elements. The result is fewer unexpected resignations.

Interviews should also be used to probe, in as much detail as possible, how much the applicant wants to work in a particular industry or for the particular enterprise. It is quite common, in countries like Ghana with high unemployment, that applicants will take whatever opportunity comes, but remain on the lookout for better opportunities. For start-ups and small enterprises, this can be a particular challenge as employees come on to 'see how it goes' while they continue their search, moving on as soon as they find something better.

Applicants must also be asked questions which seek to test their ability to do the work and to fit into the particular enterprise. Entrepreneurs must probe carefully to ensure they obtain honest answers rather than the answers they wants to hear because applicants are able to talk up their ability to do the job but, once hired, a different reality sets in.

If applicable, the entrepreneur must also try to understand why an employee has left a previous role. When recruiting experienced people, the entrepreneur should probe specific experiences that the person has to get a sense of whether or not those experiences are relevant to the enterprise and can easily be transferred.

Entrepreneurs should aim to recruit a diverse group of individuals who share the same values. How diverse a team is naturally depends on the size of the team, so diversity may be difficult to achieve in a start-up with a small team.

Preparing for the Interview

Develop Clear Objectives

Before any interview process, the entrepreneur should be clear of what her objectives are for the interview, and how they fit into her overall people strategy and her short- and long-term recruitment needs. Is the objective, for example, to find someone 'for now' until her resources allow her to find a better qualified candidate? Or is it to find a candidate with a long-term view, looking to build a career with the enterprise? The entrepreneur should answer such questions before proceeding to seek candidates.

Review Applications and CVs

Before the interview, the entrepreneur and his interviewing team should go through the applications and CVs of shortlisted candidates and note which areas will need further clarification during interviews.

Craft Standardised Questions

The interviewing team should develop a set of standardised questions so that candidates can be evaluated against common criteria.

Build Consensus on Assessment Criteria

Agree with other team members who will be monitoring the assessment criteria against which all candidates will be evaluated.

After The Interview

After the interview entrepreneurs should group candidates into three piles: acceptance, outright rejection and keep in view (KIV). Those in the acceptance pile should be called and told of the job offer before being sent a formal offer letter. Then outright rejects and KIVs should be sent letters. Outright rejects should be thanked for their time and informed they have been unsuccessful, while KIVs are also informed that their details will be kept on file for consideration should another opportunity come up.

Beyond the above, the following must also be completed.

• Offer Letters

Successful applicants should be provided with an offer letter setting out the terms and conditions of the offer and giving them enough time to evaluate and respond. I know of a prominent

Ghanaian financial institution that refuses to allow potential employees to take their offer letters away with them because, in the past, some have used offer letters to re-negotiate with their current employers. This practice should not be encouraged as there is a risk that, if employees sign without carefully understanding the terms of the offer and without being given enough time to consider its terms, they could later challenge the validity of the offer letter. Encourage employees to seek independent legal counsel to explain the terms of the offer letter to them. In practice, because many will not seek counsel, you should also go through the offer letter with them.

• *Key Performance Indicators (KPIs)*

For each position, the employer must have KPIs set for a period of time; this may be quarterly, semi-annually or annually. At the beginning of the KPI period employer and employee should agree what the KPIs are and how success will be measured. At the end of the KPI period, the employee should be appraised in respect of the KPIs as well as in respect of the culture and ethos of the firm. KPIs must be realistic targets that are achievable, although some 'stretch' must also be built in so as to challenge the employee.

• *Employee Orientation*

Employees should not start work without participating in an orientation programme. Ideally they must not even be given a desk until after orientation. No matter how small an enterprise is, an entrepreneur should ensure that he educates all new employees on the company's business, industry vision, mission, values, culture and ways of doing business. The information included in such an orientation programme might, for example, include a simplified outline of the processes used in a manufacturing enterprise so that even the receptionist can get an understanding of the employer's business. The employer needs to provide a comprehensive orientation and give new employees everything they need to start work with, including allocated mentors who will help them navigate through the transition process.

• *Probation*

Prospective employees should initially be hired for a probationary period, after which they may be confirmed as permanent staff depending on performance. The probationary period is a good way for the employer and employee to size each other up and determine whether or not both sides gel. As an alternative to probation, the entrepreneur may want to start with a short-term contract before entering into a longer-term contract upon expiry of the short-term one, with the decision based on the employee's performance in the short term. Employees may not find this option (which has the same effect as a probation period in a permanent contract) attractive as they erroneously believe it to be less secure than a conventional permanent contract with a probation period.

• *References*

After the interview, the entrepreneur should check the applicant's references. There is an increasing tendency in Ghana for employers to check references after the offer has been made and the employee has started work. In my view employers should leave enough time to check references before making an offer. References must be read cautiously. Many might be exaggerated as people feel obliged to record only positive things about previous employees. Also, as references tend to be written by people chosen by the job seeker, they will almost invariably be glowing. Try as much as possible, particularly in the case of key employees, to look beyond references. I have come across a situation where an employee who was dismissed for dishonesty in one bank managed to gain a more senior role in another bank partly because his referees (colleagues at the former work place) gave glowing references, and because his new employer carried out no additional background checks. I also remember a situation where two employees (a manager and his direct report) were fired from another company for dishonesty, yet managed to find more senior roles in two other companies.

At the very least background checks should involve the entrepreneur making independent enquiries to find out more about a candidate's work ethic, values and character.

Entrepreneurs should carry out further background checks by making discreet enquiries of other businesses or individuals that the job applicant has worked for, even if (or particularly if) they have not been listed by the applicant as referees. Care must be taken to ensure that confidentiality is maintained so that the job applicant's current position is not compromised. It is often very easy (and in my opinion, advisable) to find out significantly more about the applicant through various social channels like old school networks, church, clubs, and residential associations, or calling directly on leads where possible.

Mistakes in recruiting can be costly. In addition to the managerial time and effort involved in identifying and interviewing candidates, there are costs involved in bringing a person to an enterprise and training her in its ways only for her to leave shortly after. In a study of 54 American companies, Bradford Smith estimated that the average 'mis-hire' cost a company 24 times the individual's base compensation[14].

Entrepreneurs can avoid such costly mistakes by finding out as much as they can through the interview process, and then following up in painstaking detail when seeking references. Although, for record-keeping purposes, it is advisable that entrepreneurs ask for written references, entrepreneurs should call up or visit the referees (if possible) to have a more detailed conversation about the job applicants. There is so much more that can be found out in a face-to-face meeting or telephone conversation. This is particularly important in the case of potential key employees (no matter the size of the enterprise) and for all employees in the case of small enterprises.

References have both backward-looking and forward-looking objectives. The backward-looking objective provides the potential employer with information about how the job applicant has worked in the past and how he has dealt with certain situations. The forward-looking objective provides some indication, based on the applicant's performance in the past, about his promise for the current job under consideration. It should however be noted that the success of an employee depends in part on the environment in which he works, which suggests that he may not necessarily be successful in an enterprise just because he has been successful in a previous one. Research carried out by Groysberg et al.[15] shows that the effectiveness of top performers plummeted by as much as 20% when they moved to another firm because only 30% of a person's performance stems from individual capacities while 70% derives from resources and qualities specific to the company that developed them.

Retaining Employees

Given how much effort goes into identifying, recruiting and training the right person, the objective for any enterprise, particularly small and medium-sized ones, should be to retain as many of its employees as possible. My research shows that the factors that affect employee retention include the following:

• *Employee Engagement and Involvement*
Employee engagement refers to the heightened emotional connection that an employee feels for his organisation, which in turn influences him to exert greater discretionary effort into his work. It can be likened to the emotional connection heavy users of particular brands have towards those brands. Employees who are engaged by their employers are likely to stay. To ensure effective employee engagement, entrepreneurs must recognise that communication is a two-way process. They must broaden the conversation and listen actively to both what employees say and what they do not say. Employers must create an environment where employees feel they can speak up without fear.

• *Quality of Leadership*
Many employees told my research team that they have remained with particular enterprises because of the quality of the leadership. An enterprise with leadership that inspires and commands the

respect of employees is more likely to keep its employees than one where quality leadership is missing. It is my experience that employees (even the most confident and experienced ones) seek direction from their leaders and are motivated when leaders show an interest not only in their work, but also in their personal development.

• *Exciting and Meaningful Assignments*

Employees generally want to be challenged and given the opportunity to work on exciting, meaningful assignments that give them visibility within the enterprise, providing them with opportunities to contribute meaningfully to both their personal and the enterprise's growth. Such experiences compel employees to stay.

• *Compensation and a Progressive Reward System*

Compensation refers to the pay and benefits the enterprise gives employees in exchange for doing their job. Compensation is a tool for attracting and retaining qualified employees as well as a tool for motivating employees to contribute to the goals of the enterprise.

- Pay: For many employees, their pay is an objective measurement of their worth in an open market. They will therefore be concerned that their pay properly reflects their skills, capabilities and experience. They will also be concerned that their pay is equitable relative to what others in the same enterprise or industry are earning, and that it meets the demands of the living standard they regard as reasonable. Entrepreneurs must decide how much they will pay their employees relative to other enterprises, and how pay rates will differ among different jobs within the enterprise. What an employee gets paid should also be dependent to some extent on the effort she puts into the enterprise. It is demoralising for employees when they see that they put in as much or more effort than the next person but get paid less. Partly to prevent that, at least for more senior employees, the current trend is to tie a portion of employee pay to company profit and to employee performance. Also, some enterprises, particularly those that may not be able to afford to pay employees their true worth (such as start-ups and early-stage enterprises) develop employee share ownership plans (ESOPs) to grant shares in the company to employees based on a number of parameters (such as seniority, base compensation, and length of service). Research has shown that ESOPs are by themselves not enough to fully motivate; if they are however combined with actual employee participation in management planning, they can lead to an increase in company profits.[16]

• Other Benefits: The optional benefits provided by an enterprise should support the overall strategy, reflecting what the enterprise determines would attract the type of employees that it wants. There are a whole range of benefits – medical and dental insurance; life and disability insurance; a provident fund towards retirement; gym or club memberships; clothing allowance; transport allowance, or a car loan scheme as an alternative; etc. – that can be combined to reward employees.

• Training and Development

Constant investment in training employees is the only way an enterprise can remain competitive in the medium-to-long term. An enterprise's ability to effectively compete in the marketplace is driven by its enterprise intelligence. Enterprise intelligence is driven by the quality of staff across the enterprise. Training ensures that staff stay abreast of the industry and its trends and it is a powerful motivational tool. To employees, it is a concrete way for an employer to show interest in their personal development. I recommend that when the initial venture team is set up, or when new members join the team, they should be questioned by their immediate supervisor about their interests, strengths, weaknesses and training needs. Based on this information, the enterprise should develop a training schedule to remedy key training gaps.

The training needs analysis focuses on training that the employee requires to perform his current job. However, training should not be limited to that and should be seen in the broader context of employee personal development and as a retention tool. Training should also include what the employee considers desirable because it makes her a better person, even if it does not have a direct impact on her current job. Such training could, after all, be relevant for other jobs down the line. A more difficult decision arises when employees request training that appears to have no benefit for the enterprise, such as French language training in an enterprise that does no business in a francophone country. My view is that even such non-core training should be considered (if the enterprise can afford it) as part of its employee retention strategy.

Entrepreneurs often think of training as something run by external providers in the form of a course taken away from the office (even better if it is overseas). Due to this notion, many small business owners my research team spoke to felt that training was the preserve of larger companies with resources to match. This is a myth – every enterprise, no matter how small, must invest in training and developing its people. Start-up enterprises sometimes resist spending money to train their staff because there is a possibility that those employees may decide to leave after the investment of training. To entrepreneurs who think that way, I pose Albert Ocran's question: "To those who say that if you train them, they will leave, the perfect response is what if you do not train them and they stay?"[17] Notwithstanding this, I advise that where an enterprise spends significant sums of money on providing training for employees, it should require that those employees enter into a bond with the enterprise obliging them to stay for a minimum period after the training or pay the cost of their training back to the enterprise. Where the amounts involved are high, it is advisable to insist on a guarantor to guarantee the obligations of the employee.

There are many alternative training methods that do not involve sending employees away on a course somewhere. Indeed, I believe that the most effective training is that which is developed by the enterprise itself, focused on its particular context and challenges, and delivered by people who work in the enterprise. This enables more customisation and facilitates the capture of enterprise-wide intellectual capital to be passed on to team members in a tailored manner. It enables employees to suggest improvements to the enterprise – for example, the internal trainer can use actual examples based on her experience at the particular enterprise, which gives both trainer and trainees opportunities to challenge existing ways of doing things and to suggest improvements. In smaller enterprises, it is not uncommon for everybody to be in the training session and for decisions impacting the enterprise's operations to be made on the spot. In cases where the enterprise does not have an in-house person able to effectively facilitate training the entrepreneur should tap into her contacts to persuade someone to help train her staff (if there are no resources to pay for a training course). My experience is that subject to constraints of time, most people are willing to share their experiences, as long as it is not with a rival enterprise.

• *Empowerment*

Empowerment is the authority to take control and make decisions, and involves two elements: delegation of authority and assignment of the requisite resources for the completion of the work. Essentially, employees are given the authority to make decisions that will increase an enterprise's output and quality, and are also given the necessary resources to ensure that these goals are attained.[18] Empowerment also involves creating an environment where employees are not only encouraged to succeed but are also supported when they fail. Too many Ghanaian entrepreneurs like to take control of all aspects of their enterprises because they genuinely believe that no one can do a job better than themselves. In some cases, this is true because entrepreneurs fail to select a workforce that will add value, and also because after hiring their workforce, entrepreneurs have not invested in training their employees. If recruitment and training is done properly, there should be team members qualified to execute the enterprise's strategy excellently. For delegation to be effective, it is important that employees are given the resources needed to deliver on required objectives. According to Sam Jonah, KBE, "You should manage away your managers' excuses. You do not give [an] employee the chance to say he did not do something because he did not have some key resources necessary to be able to complete their task."[19]

• *Mentoring*

Mentoring is the process whereby a more experienced person helps to shape or guide a newcomer or an inexperienced colleague. De Long et al. advocate a hands-on, individualised feedback system rather than a formal mentoring system, which they argue helps stem talent haemorrhage. They also advise that mentoring should not be limited only to star performers but also to the solid B-team players who make up most of your workforce and on whom the enterprise's success depends.[20]

• *Stretch/Challenge*

Set challenging targets and support employees to achieve them. Many employees like to be challenged, although they do not want their employers to 'dump them in it', leaving them to sink or swim. Entrepreneurs should therefore carefully and progressively introduce stretch assignments which challenge their employees but, in doing so, they should ensure they provide an adequate support and feedback system.

• *Manage Employees As Individuals:*

Entrepreneurs should take time to learn about their employees and manage them as individuals rather than as part of a team. Entrepreneurs must understand what makes each employee tick and adapt their style as appropriate to suit the temperaments of the various team members.

• *Feedback and Recognition*

When employees do a good job, they expect to be recognised appropriately. Employees must be given both positive and negative feedback as appropriate and commensurate with performance. To encourage employees, when giving feedback, employers should start with the positives before focusing on the negatives. They should also end by giving concrete advice on how employees can improve.

• *Walking the Talk*

Actions do indeed speak louder than words. There is nothing more demotivating to employees than to see that while their superiors expect particular standards from them, those superiors do not in fact walk the talk and act by a different set of standards.

• *Benchmarking*

The employers must be conscious of the all the options available to his employees, including opportunities to move to other companies. The employer must therefore benchmark salaries, practices and trends to match – if not exceed – those of competitor companies and the industry in general. In many instances (particularly at the start-up and early stages), the entrepreneur may not be able to and should not attempt to match the competition. He must however still carry out the benchmarking exercise so as to be aware of how he compares against the competitive set, and to be able to define an employee value proposition which distinguishes him from the competition in a way that plays to the strengths of the enterprise and is meaningful to employees.

• *Career Growth and Progression*

Even in a small organisation, there should be some kind of career plan or pathway for employees. Employees are better motivated if they know there is a progression plan and that they can get from point A to point B by exhibiting certain attributes, or delivering results.

• *Personal Satisfaction*

One way that enterprises can retain their employees is to understand and attempt to satisfy their needs. Maslow,[21] in his hierarchy of needs, argued that in attempting to make the individual feel satisfied, the major needs that should be considered are physiological, safety, social, self-esteem and self-actualisation.

- Physiological Needs: To satisfy physiological needs, the employer should provide employees with appropriate working spaces and all the tools and equipment that will aid them in their work. The idea of meeting physiological needs is to make the employees feel comfortable at work. I am aware of a Ghanaian financial institution that failed to make provision for rest space for its pool drivers to relax in between assignments. The drivers, who had to stand around or wait in the cars, were highly demotivated and became easy targets for other companies.

- Safety Needs: I recommend that the employers take the employee through all operations documents and procedures relating to the enterprise, which should include employee manuals and health and safety guidelines so that the employees feel a sense of security and safety at work.

- Social Needs: People naturally want to be part of a community and want to be recognised. The social needs of employees can be met by introducing them to all staff in the enterprise, letting them know about the norms and culture of the enterprise and any social events that are organised for members of staff. In Ghana, employers try to satisfy this need by organising durbars, retreats and parties for staff, particularly at the end of the year. These events should not be limited to annual affairs. The impact of social events should not be underestimated. According to Albert Ocran, co-founder and CEO of Combert Impressions, the energy and excitement generated from the company's 'Power Wednesday' sessions (a one-hour aerobics session for employees, which started in November 2007) led to November and December 2007 contributing 40% of the total top line for 2007.[22]

- Self-Esteem: Employers can nurture employees' sense of self-worth through the performance appraisal cycle – allowing employees to challenge themselves to reach high targets and recognising their successes. Employers should also offer various promotional, training, development and assistance initiatives that employees can depend on to satisfy this need.

I have also found that creatively naming the title an employee holds can affect self esteem. A driver who had a complex around the title of Driver showed a significant improvement in self-esteem (and self-confidence) when his title was changed to Executive Chauffeur and he was given his own business card. Other creative titles I have come across include Domestic Attendant instead of Houseboy, Concierge instead of Messenger, Group Assistant instead of Secretary, Front Desk Executive instead of Receptionist and Office Environmental Assistant instead of Cleaner.

- Self-Actualisation: The highest need that employers can meet for their staff is ensuring that they achieve their highest potential in the enterprise. The employer can do this by recognising the contributions of ordinary employees to the past achievements of the enterprise and sharing the success stories with the rest of the workforce. The key goal is to make employees feel that they can achieve their fullest potential in the enterprise. Storytelling and documenting case studies of the enterprise's growth is a powerful way to help employees see the possibilities of self-actualisation through their work.

Performance Appraisals

I advised earlier that employees should be given job descriptions, job specifications and KPIs (key performance indicators). These documented guidelines make clear to employees what is expected of them and the yardsticks by which their performance will be measured. The performance appraisal is a formal system to review the performance of employees. Employees must be appraised both on technical ability and on the softer measures of contribution to life of the firm – things such as how they live the enterprise's values, contribute to teamwork and how they enhance the culture. The performance appraisal provides an opportunity for the entrepreneur not only to assess the performance of the employee, but also to highlight identified weaknesses and potential training and developmental needs.

It should be an opportunity for candid feedback to the employee with a view to improving performances. However, the employer must not wait until the formal appraisal to give feedback to his employees. Feedback must be given constantly and on the fly. If this is done, the formal appraisal process should hold no surprises for the employee but simply provide an opportunity for a more formal dialogue about, among others, training, responsibilities, potential and promotion. The most common form of appraisal is the downward appraisal where the immediate manger or supervisor carries out an appraisal of his direct reports. Less common in Ghana are the upward review system, where subordinates appraise their managers, and the 360-degree feedback system where peers, subordinates and supervisors as well as other internal and even external stakeholders appraise the employee.

Whatever form is adopted, performance appraisals must be held regularly; in my view they must be held at least twice a year. In addition to providing a written appraisal of the employee, the appraising managers should meet face to face with the employee to discuss the appraisal. Constructive criticism and an open dialogue must be established as the norms in an effective appraisal process.

Separation

As Luecke notes, "in a market-driven economy, you'll never be able to keep everyone and you shouldn't want to. A certain amount of employee turnover can actually improve the health of an organisation, infusing new energy and new ideas into the ranks."[23]

At various points in the life of an enterprise, there will be separation between enterprise and employees. This may be caused by employees resigning for any number of reasons, or it may be because the employer is terminating the employment of some employees.

Where an employee is not performing, or is failing to live up to the culture and values of the enterprise, the appraisal process should flag this for the employer, and a frank discussion should be held with the employee. The employee must be given the chance to improve but, where his non-performance is consistent, it is important that he is shown the door.

An exit interview should be arranged with the departing employee as soon as possible. Although some companies use questionnaires, I recommend a face-to-face interview where the employer seeks feedback about how the departing employee feels about the firm, its operations, strategy, management, etc. The exit interview should be seen as an important source of information for the entrepreneur to improve his enterprise. I also recommend that the parties enter into a separation agreement in which the employee acknowledges that he will not bring any causes of action against the employer.

Given that the employee would have spent some time (no matter how brief) at the enterprise, he is potentially a brand ambassador for the enterprise. It is therefore important that – perhaps other than where the departure is due to criminal conduct – the separation be as amicable as possible. Even an employee who is being fired for incompetence may harbour no grievances against the employer if the disengagement process is fair and transparent, and the employee is kept informed at all times about what is going on and the reasons for termination.

An employee today may be the supplier, customer, industry captain, regulator or politician of tomorrow. As such, it is becoming increasingly common for leading professional service firms to have regular programmes that, among others, keep track of former employees and host events that bring former employees and current employees together to network.

Entrepreneurial Leadership

Entrepreneurial Leadership is essential to attracting and managing human capital. In his capacity as leader, the entrepreneur must inspire and motivate others to join his enterprise and to work on the various tasks required to take the enterprise from idea to profit. Entrepreneurial leadership involves developing a vision for an entrepreneurial enterprise, 'selling' that vision to key stakeholders – employees, financiers, suppliers, customers, etc. – and influencing and inspiring others to work with the entrepreneur to achieve that vision. It also involves challenging employees and giving them power and freedom to achieve results.

Entrepreneurial leadership is therefore essentially about inspiring and motivating people. As Stephen Covey puts it, "Leadership deals with people; management deals with things. You manage things. You lead people. Leadership deals with vision; management deals with logistics towards that vision."[24] A leader is a team's emotional guide and must exhibit solid emotional intelligence.[25]

Leadership is critical to the success of the enterprise's efforts to create a competitive advantage based on its people. It must have a leadership that truly believes that the enterprise's success depends entirely on the people it is able to attract and retain.

There is often a tendency in start-up situations for the entrepreneur to take on a lot himself due to a desire to save costs. There is also a tendency for an entrepreneur to want to hold tightly onto the reins by making all decisions himself and micromanaging employees. While it is important that the entrepreneur proactively and closely monitors everything that goes on in his enterprise to prevent fraud, as well as to ensure that things are done the way the entrepreneur wants them to be done, it is also important that employees (especially professionals and experienced employees) feel adequately empowered to make decisions within clearly defined limits.

Effective entrepreneurial leaders exhibit the following behaviours:

Develop a Vision and Inspire People Towards the Vision

In Chapter 2, I said the entrepreneur is the person who initially dreams the dream for the enterprise. I also said that when he has dreamt the initial dream, he must persuade other people to buy into the dream to become co-dreamers with him if that dream is to become a reality. The entrepreneur must therefore both develop the enterprise's vision and inspire people to share that vision with him.

Communicate The Vision

To inspire people towards her vision, the entrepreneur must advocate the vision and give people a reason to buy into it. The entrepreneur must subsequently constantly communicate the vision and share the progress being made towards it.

Create a Set of Values and Beliefs for Employees and Passionately Pursue Them

Based on the vision and mission of the enterprise,[26] entrepreneurs must create a set of values and beliefs which are consistent with the type of enterprise that they would like to build. It is important that entrepreneurs 'walk the talk', or demonstrate their commitment and passion for the beliefs of the enterprise through action as well as words. I have come across many employees who are disillusioned because an entrepreneur's actions are inconsistent with his words.

Set the Right Example for Employees to Follow

This point is related to the point immediately above, although with a slightly different emphasis. The earlier point was about values and beliefs in the organisation. Setting the right example for employees to follow is of much wider scope. The entrepreneur, in running her business on a daily basis, should be ready to be held accountable to the same standards that she holds her employees to.

Behave With Integrity In All Situations

Integrity is a fundamental virtue of any leader. Entrepreneurs must be able to develop a reputation for themselves such that their employees and other stakeholders can trust them. They should be transparent in all their dealings. Integrity means the ability of the leader to keep his word and employees have confidence in leaders who keep their word.

Respect and Support Their Employees

While financial reward is an important motivator., it is a

universal truth that everyone wants to be accorded basic respect and courtesy. Enterprises that do best at motivating employees are those who have embedded in their culture principles of mutual respect. The entrepreneur should support employees by seeking to understand each one as a unique individual, and then correspondingly manage each according to the employee's strengths and weakness. The entrepreneur should also take interest in the personal and professional development of her employees and support them accordingly.

Constantly Communicate With Employees

The role communication plays in making or breaking an enterprise cannot be overemphasised, Effective leadership ensures that employees are constantly updated with information that affects them and relates to the enterprise in which they all have a vested interest. (Note that some information may be deemed sensitive or confidential and cannot therefore be passed on.)

Celebrate the Successes of Employees

People like to be recognised and acknowledged for a job well done. The most inspiring leaders ensure that they regularly recognise the efforts of their employees in the same way that they reprimand less-than-satisfactory performance.

Encourage Creativity

Leadership essentially involves bringing the best out of every employee. It acknowledges that everyone has significant potential and requires some room to exercise creativity. Obviously the creative output cannot be inconsistent with the enterprise's own strategy, so the entrepreneur must balance this desire for creativity with working to an agreed strategy.

Emphasise Teamwork

My experience is that the leadership of enterprises that succeed emphasise teamwork rather than individual achievement. These winning teams tend to focus on what is best for the enterprise rather than the interests of individuals.

Motivate and Reward

Entrepreneurial leaders develop relevant mechanisms to motivate employees to exhibit the behaviours the entrepreneur would like to encourage. These mechanisms (such as bonus schemes) are normally considered to be separate from salary and typically refer to programs aimed at recognising and encouraging good performance. In addition to encouraging desired behaviours, such mechanisms have the effect of retaining employees. The desired behaviours and the reward mechanisms must be clear to all employees. The rewards must be clearly tied to performance and be considered at risk when the desired objectives are not met.

Develop Succession Plans

Entrepreneurial leaders proactively manage succession, and are able to develop a talent pipeline such that they can, in effect, manage themselves out of a job because there are enough managers who are able to play the leader's role. Those managers in turn develop mid-level managers who in turn also develop more junior managers. A succession plan is a programme over a certain period of time to identify the next generation of the enterprise's leaders. It ensures that the leaders recognise other people in the enterprise who can be groomed to further grow the business. An excellent example of succession that I have encountered is at the Multimedia Group Ltd. Using the analogy of football, all key positions at Joy FM, Adom FM and other Multimedia Group broadcasting stations have a substitute who steps in when the key person is not available. That substitute also has a substitute. Substitutes are groomed to take over from the key person and undergo relevant training in this respect.

Maintain a Sense of Humour

Entrepreneurship can be a stressful route to take. There might be many different challenges on an almost daily basis. It is important that the entrepreneur maintains a sense of perspective and avoids overreacting to situations. He should maintain a sense of humour, being able to see the lighter side of even the most challenging situations. Some may wonder why this should be relevant at all. Effectively, by his conduct and actions, the entrepreneur sets the direction for the enterprise's culture. Therefore, being able to maintain a sense of humour and a sense of perspective goes a long way towards a creating a conducive environment for work, an environment where employees are not afraid to fail. I know of an entrepreneur who created employee dissatisfaction simply because he appeared too serious all the time and did not smile or laugh with his employees. At the time, the entrepreneur was dealing with personal health issues which he had not communicated to his employees.

Building and Maintaining the Right Culture

The culture of an organisation is made up of unwritten norms and practices that govern the people and style of an enterprise. Culture affects the values, attitudes, style and interactions between employees of an enterprise. As I mentioned earlier, enterprises have a macroculture and a microculture. A macroculture is an enterprise's general way of doing things, its general values and the way its people relate to each other. Microcultures characterise different departments or job functions.

Culture plays an important part of getting things done in any enterprise. In small enterprises in particular, culture can make or unmake the enterprise. It is therefore important that the right culture is fostered as it essentially determines how people work together. As Scarborough and Zimmerer rightly note, "in many small companies, culture plays as important a part in gaining a competitive edge as strategy does."[27]

Culture should reflect the deep-seated values or philosophy of the founding entrepreneurs as well as its employees, and should be able to motivate employees to give their best and to want to build careers with the enterprise. Culture will differ from enterprise to enterprise, and even within the same enterprise, from unit to unit, subsidiary to subsidiary and job function to job function. Culture is also dynamic and evolves over time.

Building an Effective Culture

My view is that, at the minimum, an effective culture should include some of the following elements.

- ### *Respect for Quality of Work*

  It is so easy to revert to the lowest common denominator when a group of people with individual standards come together. It is important therefore for the collective culture to set and enforce the minimum acceptable standard of work.

- ### *Work-Life Balance*

  I admit that work-life balance is not always easy to achieve. However, if an entrepreneur is to get the best out of his employees, he should make a conscious effort to develop a culture that tries to create some kind of balance between home life and work life, so that employees feel valued and feel that their employer has their best interests at heart. Research[28] shows that work-life balance translates to better business performance.

- ### *Respect for Diversity in All Forms*

  The importance of diversity in all forms cannot be overemphasised. Individuals from different backgrounds and with different experiences bring different perspectives to enrich the teams they join. For an enterprise to take advantage of the creative energy of a diverse group of people, the culture of the firm should celebrate diversity and deliberately recruit to reinforce it.

- ### *Integrity*

  I think integrity is fundamental to building long-lasting relationships characterised by trust and mutual respect. As a result, I believe all enterprises should have a culture that places integrity at its heart.

• *A Learning Organisation*

At the end of Chapter 4, I quoted Kotler's idea that today's marketing is becoming a battle based more on ownership of information than an ownership of other resources. This is not only true for marketing but for all functional areas of an enterprise. Given how dynamic the marketplace is becoming, it is important for the enterprise, if it is to succeed, to develop the systems and structures for developing the intellectual capacity and intelligence of its people.

• *Empowerment of Employees*

We have previously discussed the importance of empowering one's employees. This should be made a key part of the culture of any enterprise genuinely seeking to harness the potential of its people.

• *A Fair and Transparent Reward System*

An enterprise does not necessarily need to be a high-paying enterprise if it cannot afford to be. However what it pays the different categories of employees must be fair and equitable, and promotion and other reward mechanisms must be merit-based and transparent.

• *Constant Communication*

There must be constant two-way communication between the entrepreneur and his team. They should communicate on matters that affect both the output and culture of the enterprise. Effective communication is key to an effective culture, as it creates shared knowledge and responsibility among team members. Subject to things that cannot be communicated because of sensitivity or confidentiality reasons, the entrepreneur should aim to build a culture of two-way communication where he constantly shares his ideas and views with his employees, and they in turn honestly communicate with him. Because of the traditional hierarchy in Ghanaian society, it does not always feel natural for the employees to communicate their thoughts to employers. The employer should foster clear channels through which employees can get around their culture-induced hesitation. Wherever possible, employers should take time to communicate with employees on a face-to-face basis. They should encourage honest feedback from employees and provide the right environment to enable the sharing of honest opinions without fear of reprisal. During communication, employers should be as transparent as possible with employees, and vice versa.

• *Leading with the Head and Heart*

In *Pour Your Heart Into It*, Howard Schultz, says "Starbucks is living proof that a company can lead with its heart and nurture its soul and still make money. It shows that a company can provide long-term value for shareholders without sacrificing its core beliefs in treating its employees with respect and dignity."[29] I think this statement could apply to any enterprise, and I encourage entrepreneurs to lead, like Howard Schultz, with the head and the heart.

• *Walking the Talk*

For a culture to stick, people must live it throughout the enterprise. The leader must set the example and demand the same from all his employees.

As enterprises expand and take on more people, they sometimes struggle to maintain the core culture they started with. As I explained earlier, in interviewing prospective employees, the entrepreneur should be mindful of whether or not those prospective employees are the right fit for the enterprise's core culture. This consideration is even more important in a rapidly growing enterprise with a strong culture that ought to be preserved. The key question for an interview should be: Is the prospective employee the right fit for the enterprise, given the culture? During the interview and when the employee starts work, the employer should make time to explain to him the core values of the enterprise.

There should be periodic activities geared towards enhancing the culture; these could include days away or informal evening fun events. The entrepreneur (and his management team) should be the chief advocates of the culture, inspiring and motivating their employees to behave consistent with this culture. They should also live by example as enterprise leadership is, to a large extent, about creating the right examples for employees to follow.

Employers should be mindful that their actions and inactions may motivate or demotivate employees. Motivation only partly depends on financial rewards. Multifaceted motivation is especially important in the case of start-ups, as many start-ups, because they are cash constrained, cannot afford to pay their employees top-of-the-range salaries. Employee motivation should also be linked to the other factors, such as culture, and particularly to the respect that employers accord their employees. Once an employee feels as a respected and valued member of the enterprise, he is motivated to do a good job in the interest and to the benefit of the enterprise.

Gaining Competitive Advantage Through People

Entrepreneurs can gain competitive advantage through people by doing the following.

- Focusing the enterprise's strategy around its people and recognising that its distinctive competence is the skill of its employees. While this is more obvious in the case of professional service firms where professionals directly sell their skills, this point should not be underestimated in any industry. No matter what may first appear as the distinctive competence of the enterprise (for example, a new technology or brand) the only true source of competitive advantage is actually the people who have developed and manage the technology or the brand;

- Developing a culture that reflects the values and aspirations of its people, and then living, promoting and rewarding the culture.

- Identifying, attracting, developing and retaining people that fit the enterprise's culture.

- Developing relevant continuous training and development programmes – increasing technology and the pace of change in most industries means that only enterprises with the most skilled workforces will survive.

- Paying competitive total compensation (monetary and non-monetary). In a start-up, it is often hard to compete on monetary compensation so the focus of the entrepreneur should be on the environment and work culture, which are not easy to duplicate.

- Celebrating people every day and embracing mistakes.

To maintain extraordinary returns over time, any source of competitive advantage must be difficult to imitate. Although the traditional sources of competitive advantage – product and process technology, protected/regulated markets, access to financial resources and economies of scale – can still provide a source of competitive advantage, these traditional sources, as Pfeffer argues,[30] are becoming less important, with organisational culture and the capabilities derived from how people are managed being comparatively more vital sources of competitive advantage.

Entrepreneurs who focus on gaining a competitive advantage through people by implementing some of the suggestions above will be able to capture value for their enterprises because of the following.

» Reduction of employee opportunity cost as the employee has little incentive to go to another employer because the total compensation (typically the value the employee places on non-monetary compensation like culture, work environment, etc.) is so high that he is unwilling to move anywhere else;

» Customer service provided by motivated employees has consistently higher quality and is produced at a relatively lower cost. Given the quality of this customer service, the enterprise is able to capture higher prices – and higher profit – for its offerings than they were produced for.

» A number of researchers have demonstrated that there is a strong causal link between employee tenure and customer satisfaction, as employees who feel an attachment to the firm are more likely to share their positive image and feelings about the firm with customers,[31] to the accrual of greater benefits for the enterprise.

» Typically, it is more difficult to replicate things that relate to employees and culture since these tend to be very unique to the enterprise, given its history and the personalities within the enterprise.

Additional Considerations for Family Businesses

There are many advantages for involving family members in a business. According to Lagorio, "A tight-knit managerial circle, and the flexibility of related – and deeply invested – employees, has been proven to make a business resilient"[How to run a family business. Inc, March 2010]. Family enterprises may also provide peace of mind for an entrepreneur who knows that the family enterprise is able to employ his children who may be able to take over from him.

I have however been struck by the number of family enterprises that have failed, not because of an underlying business problem but because of a lack of succession planning. A typical Ghanaian scenario is follows: A successful entrepreneur employs several of his relatives who may or may not have the requisite qualifications for the roles they are employed for. As relatives of the entrepreneur, they feel a sense of entitlement and do not put in as much effort as other employees yet are given a higher compensation.

While the founding entrepreneur is alive, his ability and personality ensures that, notwithstanding some tensions as a result of hiring family members, the enterprise does well and keeps staff. However when he dies (as is also typical, without a will), all this changes. There is a fight for control of assets amongst family members who in addition to lacking the requisite skills or qualifications, do not share in the dream for the enterprise. Shortly after, the enterprise also dies. It is important that family enterprises (like non-family) develop proper succession plans. I discuss succession plans in Chapter 13.

In addition to succession, it is important that the tools discussed in this chapter are also applied to family situations. Family members should be hired based on competence and be expected to contribute fully to the business. Family members should also (at least in the context of business) not be treated differently. All employees, including family members, must have clear job descriptions and KPIs and regular appraisals should be conducted.

According to Peter Drucker 'No matter how many family members are in the enterprise and no matter how competent they are, it is always significant to have at least one top management position filled with a non-family member.'[32]

Case Study: Recruiting and Developing Stars at Oxford and Beaumont

WHEN, IN DECEMBER 2010, OXFORD and Beaumont Solicitors became the first West African law firm to be nominated in the prestigious British Legal Awards, in the category 'Middle East and Africa Law Firm of the Year,' there was no doubt in the mind of Elikem Nutifafa Kuenyehia, founder and Managing Partner of Oxford and Beaumont that it was the outstanding team that had brought him and the firm so far. Kuenyehia was not disappointed when the award went to Africa's largest law firm[33] – ENS (Edward Nathan Sonnenbergs, Inc) a South African firm established over 100 years ago with over 400 fee earners. He considered the nomination recognition enough.

Prior to setting up, Kuenyehia had been advised by a seasoned entrepreneur to keep his staff strength small and rely instead on part-timers and independent contractors. However, Kuenyehia was concerned that independent contractors and part-timers would not show the same levels of commitment as full-time employees. He was also worried about the real risk that some part-timers, because they held full-time jobs elsewhere, might be breaching the terms of their full-time employment contracts. Finally, Kuenyehia was aware of the important role that employees play in brand building and therefore ignored the advice.

Although Kuenyehia's total capital outlay of US$5,000 would not be enough to pay one month's salary for a top notch employee, let alone a whole team, it did not deter him. He refused to compromise the quality standards he set for the type of people he wanted to hire and decided to focus on hiring bright young and inexperienced stars with potential, developing them and giving them freedom to succeed within clearly defined standards, which he set out in a document named the Oxford and Beaumont Way.

To start with, Kuenyehia needed a Personal Assistant who could double as his Secretary, Office Manager, Client Service Manager and even Accounts Officer. He was unimpressed with the candidates he was sent by a recruitment firm and decided to take matters into his own hands.

Hilary Sowatey Komey

A few months earlier, he had met Hilary Komey at the Holy Trinity Spa in Sogakope where Kuenyehia had spent a weekend. Komey had dealt graciously with Kuenyehia's demands and complaints and made such an impression that Kuenyehia took his details thinking that at some point in future he might want to employ him. At the time, Kuenyehia had no idea that point would come so soon.

United Bank of Africa , where Kuenyehia worked prior to starting Oxford and Beaumont, had a policy of hiring only university degree holders. It was a policy that Kuenyehia had bought into and was hoping to apply at Oxford and Beaumont. He was therefore disappointed that Komey had a Higher National Diploma and not a degree. However, Kuenyehia was so impressed by Komey that he made him an offer as his Personal Assistant but on condition that he would enrol on the HND-to-degree upgrade programme offered at the Ghana Institute of Management and Public Administration (GIMPA). Although it meant that for an entire year, at a critical stage in the firm's development, Komey would be enrolled as a full time student and only able to work part time.

As the team expanded, Komey was promoted to Office Manager. Notwithstanding his increased responsibility, Komey was able to combine his role with his academic study, graduating with a first class degree. On the day of his graduation the team surprised him by placing a full page congratulatory advert in Ghana's biggest selling newspaper, the Daily Graphic.

After graduation, Komey was promoted to Associate Business Manager and then Business Manager, where he supported Kuenyehia in managing the firm's business. He subsequently went on to earn an Executive Masters in Business Administration from GIMPA and was promoted to Associate Director, Business Services.

Kwabena Arko Asiedu

While shopping at Kingdom Books, Kuenyehia was struck by the professionalism and curiosity of Asiedu, the sales assistant who served him. Through conversation Kuenyehia found out that Asiedu, then a first year student of the University of Ghana, had decided to work at Kingdom because he was an introvert and, because he wanted to change that, had decided to put himself in a position that forced him to deal with a lot of different people. Kuenyehia was so impressed with Asiedu that although it would be another three years before he would graduate from university, Kuenyehia gave Asiedu a number of small projects to engage him and upon graduation, Asiedu joined the firm full-time.

Nutifafa Richmond Klutse-Woanyah

The first lawyer that Kuenyehia hired was Nutifafa Richmond Klutse-Woanyah. Woanyah had been introduced to Kuenyehia when the latter requested to meet the top student of the Ghana Law School class of 2006. Indeed, Nutifafa went on to graduate top of his class at the Ghana Law School and could have joined any law firm he wanted.

When Woanyah turned up for his interview, Kuenyehia was still sharing a 323-square-foot office with Komey and had not been able to raise enough money to acquire additional space. Kuenyehia was undeterred by the possibility that a bright aspiring lawyer like Woanyah might be uninterested in joining an unknown law firm that could not even afford enough office space. After establishing during the first part of the interview that Woanyah was the right fit for the type of firm that Kuenyehia was trying to build, Kuenyehia spent the rest of the interview selling Woanyah on his vision for the firm and encouraged Woanyah to look beyond the present, but Kuenyehia was still surprised when Woanyah accepted his offer, given that his firm had only operated for two months. Woanyah joined Oxford and Beaumont as a Legal Assistant the week after he finished his final exams at the Ghana Law School. After he was called to the bar (having been awarded the prestigious Charles Mends Cann Prize for the best male graduating student), he was promoted to Associate.

In his first week as an Associate, Woanyah found himself advising a petroleum company on commodity trading contracts worth millions of dollars. He then advised the International Finance Corporation on a potential acquisition of an equity stake in a bank. After a three-month secondment in London at Berwin Leighton Paisner, where Woanyah advised on power supply agreements in Oman, Nutifafa was promoted to Senior Associate.

Thelma Tawiah

Kuenyehia conceived the idea for his book *Kuenyehia On Entrepreneurship* ('KOE') at the time he started Oxford & Beaumont. Initially he thought he could combine the role of author with his duties at the firm and therefore wanted to hire a full-time research assistant for KOE. He asked all the recent graduates he knew 'to recommend someone who was exceptionally bright'. When Kevin Dadzie recommended Thelma Tawiah, Kuenyehia was not interested. He was prejudiced because Tawiah was a recent winner of the Miss Maliaka beauty pageant. "It is a textbook I am writing, not a glossy magazine," he said to Dadzie. However, Dadzie persuaded Kuenyehia to at least interview Tawiah. Kuenyehia asked Tawiah to write a few essays and was blown away by her clarity of thought. A few weeks after leaving university, Tawiah turned down a job with a global beverage conglomerate and started working for Kuenyehia as a Research Assistant on KOE, but it became quite clear very early on that Kuenyehia had to shelve KOE to focus on running the law firm.

Given how bright Tawiah was, he did not want to lose her so Kuenyehia made up a number of projects and created a roles for Tawiah in the different organisations he was involved in . After a stint as Executive Assistant to the Managing Partner, Tawiah was promoted initially to Associate Strategy and Business Development Manager, then to Strategy and Business Development Manager, and is currently Associate Director, Strategy and Business Development.

Kuma Adusa-Amankwah

Kuenyehia had known Adusa-Amankwah, an HR specialist and a pastor, since they were both teenagers and initially sought free counsel from him.

However, Kuenyehia, under constant pressure to meet the hairy, audacious goal he had set himself and his team with rather limited resources, found that he was under pressure and often in conflict with his team members who were unable to completely understand his 'unreasonable' demands.

He therefore persuaded Adusa-Amankwah to join the firm on a part-time basis as Talent Relations Manager. As the firm expanded and a full- time manager was hired, Kuenyehia asked Adusa-Amankwa to stay on as Team Relations Manager, a role that requires him to be a counsellor, best friend, life style coach, mentor, cheerleader, barometer of the conversations around the water dispenser, a shoulder to cry on, ombudsman and the firm chaplain.

Given Adusa-Amankwah's training as an HR specialist and a pastor, he is able to build strong relationships with team members. With clearly defined authority, Adusa-Amankwah was also able to rein in any troublemakers – even if it was Kuenyehia – helping to resolve conflicts and create a more conducive place of work. Adusa-Amankwah's role supports the full time Talent Manager's role.

At the British Legal Awards dinner, hosted by *Legal Week*, and celebrating achievement, excellence and innovation in the legal industry, Kuenyehia's only regret was that the brightest lawyer he had ever worked with – Nutifafa Klutse-Woanyah – could not share in the success because he had died in a tragic car accident on 29 May 2010. But in the history of Oxford and Beaumont, Klutse-Woanyah's contribution was clearly not in doubt.

Questions for Case Discussion

1. Do you think Kuenyehia could have achieved the same results if he had hired part-time staff as advised?
2. After reading this case one student said 'Hiring people from spas and bookshops is a ridiculous idea. Kuenyehia should have turned to professional recruiters.' To what extent do you agree or disagree with this statement?
3. Should Kuenyehia have hired his childhood friend to be the firm's HR manager?
4. How important do you think the role played by Adusa-Amankwah as Team Relations Manager is?

Questions for Class Discussion

1. Why is it important that a candidate for a position not only has the required experience and skills but is also the best fit?
2. How would you go about developing your people strategy if you were starting a new enterprise?
3. What are the advantages of recruiting internally?
4. What is meant by the term 'employee value proposition'?
5. Describe the different stages in an interview.
6. What steps must you take after you have made a decision to hire a candidate based on an interview?
7. What measures must you put in place to retain your employees?
8. Must you always seek to retain all employees?

Notes

1   http://www.management-issues.com/engagement.asp, retrieved February 2012.

2   In this chapter, I use the word 'fit' to mean as follows: A candidate is said to be the right fit for an enterprise when that candidate is well suited to the enterprise and 'fits' well with the enterprise's culture, values, ethos and people.

3   Anthony, W.P., K.M. Kacmar and P.L. Perrewe. *Human Resource Management: A Strategic Approach*. Mason: South-Western Thomson Learning, 2002.

4   Seminar on Human Resources, Ghana Institute of Management and Public Administration , Greenhill, Februrary 2008.

5   Lesonsky, R. *Start your own business*. Irvine: Entrepreneur Press, 2001.

6   *Ibid.*

7   Scarborough, N. and T. Zimmerer. *Effective Small Business Management An entrepreneurial approach*. Upper Saddle River: Pearson Education, 2003.

8   Lucke, R. *Hiring and keeping the best people*. Boston: Harvard Business School Press, 2002.

9   *Ibid.*

10 Speech given to the Information Technology Entrepreneurship Class of the Ghana Institute of Management and Public Administration, Greenhill, February 2007.

11 Lucke, R. *Hiring and keeping the best people*. Boston: Harvard Business School Press, 2002.

12 Robbins, S. *The Truth About Managing People*. Upper Saddle River: Pearson Education 2008.

13 *Ibid.*

14 As quoted in Lucke, R. *Hiring and keeping the best people*. Boston: Harvard Business School Press, 2002

15 Groysberg, B., A. Nanda and N. Nohria. The risky business of

hiring stars. *Harvard Business Review*, 82(5), 2004: 92-100.

16 Kurschner, D. 5 Ways Ethical Business Creates Fatter Profits. *Business Ethics*, 10(2), 1996: 20-23.

17 Speech given to Foundations of Entrepreneurship class at Ghana Institute of Management and Public Administration, Greenhill, February 2008.

18 Kuratko, D.F. and R.M. Hodgetts. *Entrepreneurship: A Contemporary Approach*. Orlando: The Dryden Press, 1998.

19 Public lecture delivered at the Ghana Institute of Management and Public Administration, Greenhill, May2008.

20 De Long, T.J., J.J. Gabarro and R.J. Lees. Why mentoring matters in a hypercompetitive world. *Harvard Business Review*, 86(1), 2008: 115-121.

21 Maslow A.H. A Theory of Human Motivation. *Psychological Review*, 50(4), 1943: 370-396.

22 Speech given to Foundations of Entrepreneurship class at Ghana Institute of Management and Public Administration, Greenhill, February 2008.

23 Lucke, R. *Hiring and keeping the best people*. Boston: Harvard Business School Press, 2002.

24 Francis Huffman. Taking the Lead, Entrepreneur, November 1993.

25 Dorf, R. and T. Byers. *Technology Ventures: From idea to enterprise*. New York: McGraw-Hill, 2004.

26 See Chapter 14.

27 Scarborough, N. and T. Zimmerer. *Effective Small Business Management An entrepreneurial approach*. Upper Saddle River: Pearson Education, 2003.

28 Rapaport, R. and L. Bailyn. *Relinking Life and Work: Towards a better future*. New York: Ford Foundation, 1996.

29 Schultz, H. *Pour Your Heart Into It: How Starbucks Built A Company A Cup At A Time*. New York: Hyperion, 1999.

30 Pfeffer, J. Competitive Advantage Through People. *California Management Review*, 36, 1994: 9-28.

31 Ulrich, D., R. Halbrook, D. Meder, M. Stuckhlik and S. Thorpe. Employee and Customer Attachment: Synergies for competitive

Advantage. *Human Resource Planning*, 14(2), 1991: 89-103.***

32 Drucker, P. How to Save the Family Business, Wall Street Journal, 19 August 1994

33 ENS, www.ens.co.za, retrieved February 2012.

Chapter Ten: Corporate Governance

"If I have been able to see further than others, it is because I stood on the shoulders of giants." - **Isaac Newton**

Outline

- Introduction
- Agency Theory
- Principles of Corporate Governance
- Members (or Shareholders)
- Directors
- Directors' Duties and Responsibilities
- Consequences of Breach of Duty
- Board Selection
- Director Qualification
- Board of Advisors
- Pros and Cons of Boards
- Characteristics of Good Boards
- Structure and Composition of Boards
- Appointment and Termination
- Case Study: Using Board Members as a Competitive Tool at CoreNett Limited
- Questions for Class Discussion

ONKS AND MINOW define corporate governance as "the relationship among various participants in determining the direction and performance of corporations. The primary participants are (1) shareholders, (2) the management team (led by the Chief Executive Officer) and (3) the board of directors."[1]

It is generally agreed among management writers and academics that effective corporate governance can affect an enterprise's bottom line. It also plays an important role in the investment decisions of investors and potential investors. For example, studies[2] have consistently demonstrated that there is a positive relationship between the extent to which an enterprise practices good corporate governance and its performance. Corporate governance guarantees that an enterprise is directed in a responsible, professional and transparent manner towards safeguarding its long-term success. Enterprises with good corporate governance are able to command a higher valuation and generally have higher returns on capital employed. Where their shares are listed on a stock exchange, they also generally perform better. In a study commissioned by the consulting firm McKinsey, over 80% of investors agreed that they "would pay a premium for the shares of a better-governed company than for those of a poorly governed company with comparable financial performance."[3]

The primary responsibility for ensuring that good corporate governance practices prevail in an enterprise lies with the board of directors. Yet, many boards, both local and international, have failed to step up to the challenge of using their governing power to enable the companies they are involved in to achieve their economic and social objectives. Firms such as Enron and Arthur Andersen have become globally known for failures of corporate governance practices. In Ghana, there are a host of companies, including Ghana Airways, that failed because of poor corporate governance practices.

In this chapter I shall focus on how an entrepreneur can establish proper corporate governance practices which balance the interests of all key stakeholders. Firstly, we shall discuss agency theory, which provides the theoretical basis for a corporate governance structure. We will then consider the principles of good corporate governance.

Given the key role they play in ensuring proper corporate governance, we shall consider the duties and responsibilities of directors in detail, as well as what the entrepreneur should take into consideration in selecting his enterprise's board. I will also cover boards of advisors, which some enterprises set up rather than (or in addition to) boards of directors, and compare them to boards of directors.

After considering the characteristics of good boards, we discuss appointment, induction and termination. The chapter ends with the consideration of the other stakeholders in the corporate governance matrix, such as the chairman, company secretary and shareholders.

Agency Theory

Corporate governance takes as its starting point the appearance in large enterprise of a group of senior managers who are separate and distinct from the shareholders.[4] This has its theoretical underpinnings in agency theory. Agency theory teaches us that there is a potential divergence of interests between the owners of an enterprise (shareholders) and the professional managers (management) who are hired to run it. How is an investor acquiring equity in an enterprise to know that the managers appointed to run the enterprise will act in the best interests of the enterprise? How does that investor, who is generally removed from the day-to-day running of the enterprise, verify what management actually does, particularly where (as is often the case) management is better informed than the shareholders? There is potentially nothing stopping a management team from acting 'opportunistically,' pursuing their own interests to the detriment of the enterprise and its shareholders.

Dees and Lumpkin expand on the idea: "Managers may[,] for example, spend corporate funds on expensive perquisites (company jets and expensive art), devote time and resources to pet projects (initiatives in which they have a personal interest but which have limited market potential), engage in power struggles (where they may fight over resources for their own betterment, to the detriment of what is best for the firm) and negate (or sabotage) attractive merger offers because they may result in increased employment risk."[5]

There are also potential differences in attitudes and preferences towards risk. Management may prefer to take larger risks because it might increase their compensation. Shareholders, on the other hand, may be concerned that such increased risk may ultimately lead to the erosion of shareholder value.

To minimise the potential for managers to act in their own self interest or in ways that erode shareholder value, a number of 'corporate governance' mechanisms are put in place. These are:

- A committed and involved board of directors that acts in the best interests of the enterprise to create value for shareholders. Corporate governance rests largely with the board of directors;

- Shareholder activism where shareholders view themselves as owners of shares instead of mere holders of shares, and thus become actively engaged in the governance of the enterprise;

- Managerial incentives, consisting of reward and compensation agreements, which seek to align the interests of management with those of shareholders.

It is to these corporate governance mechanisms that we now turn our attention.

I should point out that although the principles of corporate governance were developed mainly in the context of large enterprises, my strongly-held view is that corporate governance principles are so valuable that they should be applied by all entrepreneurs irrespective of the size of enterprise they run, albeit with modifications where necessary to accommodate the different forms of business organisation. Putting effective corporate governance structures in place from the very beginning also supports the expansion ambitions of entrepreneurs. For example, an entrepreneur who starts out as a sole proprietor, but sets up an advisory board at the beginning, will find that by the time he sets up a company and requires external funding, he is already used to dealing with a board (albeit initially an advisory board as opposed to a statutory board).[6] Also, he will find the advice of the board invaluable in his quest to go from sole proprietor to a listed company (if that is his dream), provided he picks the right people for that board.

Principles of Corporate Governance

The key principles of corporate governance that enterprises must adhere to are as follows.

• *Compliance*

As a starting point, the enterprise must comply with the laws and regulations governing corporate governance practices, as well as accepted standard practices prescribed by professional associations, industries, and trade bodies. More specifically, the regulations (and any shareholders' agreements) governing the activities of the enterprise must be complied with in all activities.

• *Participation*

Best corporate governance practice requires the full and active involvement of all stakeholders including shareholders, management and the board of directors or advisors.

• *Accountability*

All stakeholders must be accountable in all dealings that they engage in. A reporting and information system must exist to require everyone to answer to someone. The leadership of an enterprise (management) must account to the board and the board must account to the shareholders, all on a regular basis.

• *Transparent*

All stakeholders ought to emphasise transparency in corporate governance by displaying a high degree of honesty, probity and integrity in their management and operations. Transparency enables the stakeholders of the enterprise to always be clear where the enterprise is heading, and what the opportunities as well as the challenges are.

• *Responsiveness*

Good corporate governance practice requires a timely response to the needs of stakeholders in an enterprise. There must be a properly structured system to ensure that everyone gets feedback.

The leadership of the enterprise should also always exhibit a high level of capability and representativeness, conscious of its obligations to the shareholder and the enterprise.

• *Fairness*

A well-run enterprise ensures that all stakeholders feel that they truly have a stake in it and are not excluded from the activities of the enterprise. Everyone should be treated fairly.

• *Focus on Consensus*

There are several stakeholders in corporate governance, and so good corporate governance requires mediation of the different interests in order to reach consensus that is in the best interest of the enterprise. Though the majority view must prevail, it is important that everyone is made to feel that they have won.

• *Effectiveness and Efficiency*

Good corporate governance means that the system and processes of the enterprise produce results that meet set objectives while making the best use of the resources at the enterprise's disposal.

Members (or shareholders)

As we saw in Chapters 6, the shareholders or members of a company provide equity capital for the company by acquiring shares in the company. This gives them certain rights as members (but very few liabilities as they are protected by the limited liability of the company). As we will see below, the members delegate day-to-day decision making relating to the company to the directors. However, major decisions have to be dealt with by the members passing resolutions in general meetings (meetings of members). Ghana's Companies Act, 1963 (Act 179), states that certain acts – such as removing a director from office, changing the name of the company and changing the objects of the company – can only be done by the members.

Directors

The board of directors of a company is the highest policy and decision-making body, and is a fiduciary of and accountable to the shareholders for the proper and effective administration of the company.

In Ghana, a director is a person "by whatever name called"[7] appointed to direct and administer the business of the company.[8] A director is usually appointed by shareholders or other directors under the regulations of the company. However, a person who is not duly appointed a director may be recognised as a de facto director if he holds himself or knowingly allows himself to be held out as a director. He may also be recognised as a 'shadow director' if the duly appointed directors are accustomed to acting on his instructions. In the Quality Grain trial, the late Justice Afreh found Professor John Evans Atta Mills, the then Vice President of Ghana, to be a shadow director of the company on the evidence of Professor Mills' occasional intervention in and running of the affairs of the company, and also because he had summoned the directors to him for meetings.[9]

So although one may not have been appointed as a director by the company and may therefore not consider himself to be a director, the law could find him to be a shadow director subject to the same duties and liabilities as duly appointed directors. The law does not distinguish between shadow directors and duly appointed directors when it comes to the imposition of directors' liabilities. In addition, one who holds himself out as a director or knowingly allows himself to be held out as a director commits a criminal offence, for which a fine not exceeding 250 penalty units (approximately US$1,800)[10] is payable.

The regulations of the company have provisions on the appointment of directors, and shareholders' resolutions may also make additional provisions in this regard. It is not uncommon, for example, to find shareholders' agreements providing that shareholders with a certain level of shareholding should appoint directors, that shareholders below that minimum threshold as a group should appoint a director, and that the company itself should appoint a director as an independent director. A board of five may, for example, be made up of two executive directors (two co-founders, for example), two representatives of venture capital investors who have invested in the company and one independent director.

Directors' Duties and Responsibilities

Directors owe certain duties to the companies on whose boards they sit. While there is significant overlap, these duties can be classified under four broad headings - commercial, common law, statutory and contractual duties.

Directors owe their duties to the company, which means the members of a company as a whole – members being the persons who created it or who have subsequently become members, normally by buying shares.[11] These duties are therefore owed to present and future shareholders and not merely to an individual shareholder or group of shareholders. However, these duties may also be owed to employees and other stakeholders and, where a company is insolvent, directors may owe duties to the creditors of the company.

Directors are not employees of the company but officers, and therefore have responsibilities and duties owed to the company at law. In practice, directors may enter into service agreements with the company or otherwise work for it in a full-time capacity, in which case they also become employees of the company and, in that capacity, have rights and responsibilities like other employees. Nevertheless, as officers of the company, they have certain responsibilities and owe certain duties to the company, independently of any employment contract. In addition, other duties and responsibilities may be found in the company's regulations.

Ghanaian company law makes no distinction between non-executive directors and executive directors who have the same responsibilities. In practice though, a distinction exists as follows: executive directors are those who are employed by the company on whose board they sit, such as the Managing Director or Chief

Executive Officer; non-executive directors are 'outsiders' not employed by the company, and will not be involved in day-to-day issues of the company.

Commercial Duties

The commercial duties have been developed more from the point of view of best management practice. I should point out that this categorisation is my own, and that there is some overlap between the commercial duties and the common law, statutory and contractual based duties. Where there is such an overlap, I have kept the relevant duties in the commercial category because I consider the duty to be fundamental to good management practice.

• *Provide Overall Leadership for the Enterprise*

The board of directors has a long-term responsibility for the economic vitality and viability of the enterprise, and for managing its business and financial affairs.

• *Represent Shareholders as a Whole*

Boards should serve the legitimate interests of all shareholders and act in the best interests of the enterprise and its shareholders.

• *Responsible to All Key Stakeholders*

Although their primary responsibility requires that they are accountable to shareholders, boards are also responsible to other stakeholders such as customers, employees and regulators. They should therefore seek to understand the expectations of such stakeholders and keep in reasonable contact and dialogue with them.

• *Appointment of Management*

Boards are responsible for the appointment of management (CEO and other key officers) to whom they delegate the core functions of running the enterprise. As Neuschel puts it, "[t]he selection, nurturing and retention of the CEO and other very senior members of the management are the Board's most important responsibilities."[12]

• Management Evaluation and Development

The board monitors and evaluates the performance of the CEO and his management team.

• Active Involvement in Succession Planning

The board must work closely with the CEO and senior management to ensure an effective succession process and the development of management capabilities at all levels in the corporation. After nurturing and helping the existing CEO to grow and perform, the next responsibility is to ensure that the succeeding CEO will be identified, recruited and integrated into the enterprise by an orderly process that ensures that she succeeds in the role and develops into a 'winner'. In this regard, it is suggested that the board should have a short-term or 'disaster' plan (where the CEO abruptly quits or is hit by the proverbial truck), and a longer-term, normal succession plan which assumes that the CEO will continue in place until her normal retirement date. The board should have a long-term strategic plan for identifying, nurturing and tracking CEO candidates as a prelude to ultimate selection.[13]

• Shape the Strategy of the Enterprise

The board is responsible for the active participation and strategic planning of the corporation. In addition to determining the enterprise's strategy, objectives and values, the board must have a meaningful involvement in the strategic planning and execution process. It must be focused on long-term strategic direction setting, which must be balanced by near-term needs and challenges. This does not mean that the board takes over this function which must be spearheaded by management; rather, "the board must have early involvement in the process, be part of its development with important inputs, put the ultimate 'blessing' on the strategic plan, and finally to ensure its effective implementation."[14]

• Ensure Compliance

Boards are required to ensure that there are processes in place for making the enterprise comply with laws, company's regulations and shareholders' agreements (partnership agreements in the case of partnerships), industry codes and best practices.

• *Responsible for Audits of Corporate Activities*

Boards have historically focused on ensuring that the financial statements of the enterprise reflect its true and fair position. However, the true role of boards extends beyond simply auditing the financials. Boards should play a broader corporate 'audit' role where they are responsible for 'auditing' the entire sphere of corporate activities to ensure that the management processes (including risk management) are consistent with whatever objectives the board has set for the enterprise.

• *Communication*

Communication is critical at all levels of the organisation, including at the board level. The board must ensure regular communication with shareholders and other stakeholders. Communication should be regular, honest and reliable, and be such that it enables the recipient of the communication to evaluate all the relevant facts and take action. Boards should also not knowingly or recklessly disseminate false or misleading information.

• *Technology*

Boards should ensure that the technology being used is adequate not only for running the business but also that it gives the enterprise a competitive edge.

• *Risk Management*

Boards should identify key risk areas and manage them. Financial, investment and business risks, and their attendant key performance indicators, must be benchmarked against industry norms.

• *Set Compensation*

It is the board that must set the CEO's compensation, and then shape the compensation philosophy and practices of the company.

This is an area where boards have come under a lot of criticism – for levels of executive pay which are sometimes deemed by the shareholders to be excessive. In setting compensation, boards must balance the need to motivate high-performance executives with general principles of fairness and reasonableness. The board is statutorily required to ensure that whatever remuneration is given to executive directors, which will include the CEO, is commensurate with the value of services they render to the company.

• Act As Ambassadors of the Enterprise

In the various corridors of power and other places where they find themselves, directors must articulate and represent their enterprise's interest.

• Bring Credibility to the Enterprise

This is particularly important at the very beginning of an enterprise's existence, where the board's credibility can be a key asset to business development.

Common Law Duties

These duties were initially developed by the courts, although some of them have now been codified by various statutes, particularly the Companies Act, 1963 (Act 179). The key common law duties include the following.

• Act Within Their Power

Directors must ensure that the enterprise acts within its corporate powers, that its acts are legal, and that the powers delegated to it are not exceeded and are properly exercised. The board gets its powers from the enterprise through the regulations of the company and any related shareholders' agreements and resolutions. Directors are required to administer the company's affairs within the legal framework defined by all of the above. Accordingly, each director should be aware of the provisions of the regulations, relevant shareholders' agreements and resolutions that may affect the power structure of the company. I have seen many instances where directors have assumed wrongly that the company has power to enter into particular transactions even though the company had no such power. For example, Ghanaian law[15] prohibits directors, without authority from shareholders in the form of a resolution, from borrowing money or charging any of the company's assets – where the monies to be borrowed or secured, together with the amount remaining undischarged of monies already borrowed or secured (apart from temporary loans obtained from the company's bankers in the ordinary course of business), exceeds the stated capital of the company. Yet, many Ghanaian directors have acquired loans that breach this provision of the law.

A company is generally bound by a transaction entered into by a director, just as a company is bound by a transaction authorised by the board of directors as a whole. This principle generally applies whether or not the individual director in question has authority to carry out that transaction, because a third party is usually entitled to assume that a director who usually acts for the company has the necessary authority to do so. However, if the third party had actual notice that the director did not have the power to act in the particular transaction, or that the director has acted in an irregular manner, the company will not be civilly liable to this third party. Also, where due to the relationship or position of the third party to the company, he ought to have known of the absence of power or irregularity on the part of a director, the third party will not be entitled to any action against the company.[16] A director who acts beyond the scope of his authority, however, may be personally liable to the company, as well as to third parties, for the breach of his duties as a director. However, as the director's fiduciary duties are owed to the company, the company's shareholders can, in certain circumstances, waive the fulfilment of those duties or forgive breaches.

• *Exercise Utmost Good Faith*

All directors are in a position of trust and therefore owe a number of fiduciary duties to the company. These duties are based on the simple notion that a director must show the highest loyalty and good faith to his company. Any decision a director takes must be in the best interests of the company and not for any personal motive.[17] Any transaction which is entered into by a director or by the board collectively will be deemed to have been entered into honestly and in accordance with their duties. The courts will not normally interfere unless no reasonable person could properly have taken the same view. An act of the company motivated by the personal interests of a director or undertaken for a collateral or improper purpose may be set aside at the instance of the company and, in certain circumstances, the director may be required to make good any loss suffered by the company.

Directors must therefore take account of all relevant factors when making decisions and, to safeguard their position, should ensure that full minutes are taken showing their reasons and the factors which were taken into account. In particular, a director who seriously disagrees with a decision taken by the board should insist that her disagreement is recorded in the minutes. Where the director feels that the board decision or policy is not merely commercially unwise but is unethical or illegal, he has a duty to take a lead in remedying the irregularity or illegality and, failing that, to resign.

• Have No Conflict of Duty or Interest

Directors must not allow their duty to the company to conflict with personal interest, even if such conflict is only theoretical. Each director is therefore required to disclose any interest which he or she has in a proposed contract or other arrangement to which the company may become a party. Similarly, a director must disclose any position which he or she occupies or any duty which he or she owes to a third party which might conflict with the duties owed to the company. Disclosure must be full and frank.

It is the duty of a director to disclose any interest in a contract entered into by the company,[18] or any affiliation to the other party of that contract, to avoid any conflict of interest. If such an interest is not disclosed, the director is in breach of his duties and a fine may be imposed on him, or the company may choose not to enter into the contract and demand repayment from such director.[19] A director must not be interested, directly or indirectly, apart from merely as a shareholder or debenture holder, in a public company or in any business which competes with that of the company; or be personally interested, directly or indirectly, in any contract or other transaction entered into by the company unless he has declared the extent of his interest in the proposed contract, and the contract in question has subsequently been approved by a resolution of the directors of the company.[20]

• *Must Not Misapply the Company's Property*

A director will be liable to account to the company for any loss caused by a misapplication of corporate assets in which he participated, where he knew or ought to have known that the relevant act was a misapplication. A director must not assume or pass on to another person any contract or business opportunity which arises out of the business of the company.

• *Unauthorised Profits*

A director must not make an unauthorised profit out of his position or dealings with the company. By virtue of his office, a director might be in a position to make a profit, for example, by receiving a commission on a contract or a benefit under an arrangement in which he is interested, whether or not the company itself is financially or legally able to acquire the profit in question. Directors will be required to account to the company for any profit arising out of their roles as directors. In the absence of prior disclosure to the board, such profit may only be retained legitimately by a director if the company, in a general meeting, authorises its retention.

• *Confidentiality*

A director must keep all company information confidential. Directors are under an obligation of confidence to their company. It therefore follows that any information which the director obtains by virtue of his office as director must remain confidential. This requirement extends beyond the period of office as a director.

• Duty of Skill and Care

A director owes a duty of skill and care to the company. In most circumstances, the scope of this duty is judged against the skill and care that may reasonably be expected from a person of the director's knowledge and experience, and unless the director has professed an expertise, he or she will not be expected to be an expert in relation to the company's business. A director is not liable for the acts of co-directors solely by virtue of his position. He will be liable only if he actually participates in wrongdoing. Such participation may be, for example, unquestioningly signing a cheque for an unauthorised payment or signing minutes approving the misapplication of the company's property. Subject to the regulations, the directors may delegate powers to a committee or to other officials and, in the absence of suspicious circumstances, are justified in trusting those officials to perform their duties honestly. Similarly, a director may trust experts or specialists (such as lawyers and accountants), unless he is put on notice that something is wrong. A director is liable, even if actually ignorant of another's wrong, where he or she ought to have supervised the activity or ought to have known that it was wrong. Generally, full-time directors may be expected to exhibit a higher standard of care than is expected of non-executive directors, commensurate with the amount of time they devote to the business, although this is a matter depending on prevailing circumstances.

Contractual Duties

The key contractual duties of directors derive from the following contracts.

• Regulations

This relates to the duties of directors as enshrined in the Companies Act or the regulations governing the activities of the enterprise.

• *Shareholders' Agreement*

The directors have a duty to respect and operate in accordance with any shareholders' agreement entered into by the enterprise. Although it is not usual for directors to be party to shareholder agreements in their capacity as directors, as we saw in Chapter 6, the company itself may be party to the agreement between its shareholders. Where this is the case, directors as officers of the company (and representing the company) shall be contractually bound by the shareholders' agreement the same way the shareholders are.

• *Directors' Service Contracts*

Directors are bound to perform their duties and responsibilities as contained in their service contracts.

Statutory Duties

Many other statutes impose obligations and duties, and hence potential civil or criminal liability, on directors. Such legislation now extends to almost all areas of a company's activities and can include such matters as taxation, environmental protection as well as health and safety matters and issues surrounding false accounting. In some instances the liability is strict, with the result that the consent or connivance of a director is not necessarily a precondition of civil or criminal liability. The Companies Act is littered with statutory obligations imposed on directors. The key ones include:

» It falls to the directors as officers of the company to institute (and defend) court proceedings for and on behalf of the company and in the company's name;

» Directors must deliver or make available to the company's auditors the books, accounts, vouchers and any information or explanation sought by the auditors of the company;[21]

» To prepare and circulate among members and debenture holders the financial statements of each year, namely the profit and loss accounts, balance sheet and any group accounts,[22] the directors' report on the financial statements,[23] and the auditors' report on the financial statement;[24]

» Directors must complete filing of returns as required by sections 27 and 28 (known as Forms 3 and 4) of the Companies Act, which indicate primarily the name, stated capital, particulars of the directors and secretary of the company, the number of its issued shares and the company's satisfaction of the minimum capital requirement; these returns must be filed before the company is granted the certificate to commence business;

» The company is required to maintain a number of registers which include the register of members (which indicates the list of all the shareholders of the company),[25] register of debenture holders (which list all persons who have granted loan capital, or debentures, to the company),[26] branch register (which indicates the particulars of shareholders and debenture holders held outside Ghana in a country in which some of the directors or shareholders reside),[27] and a register of charges (which indicates particulars of all charges, such as a mortgages and interest, over the company's assets).[28]

In addition to the Companies Act, there are a number of other statutes that impose certain obligations on directors. These include:

- Internal Revenue Act, 2000 (Act 592) as amended;
- Environmental Protection Agency Act, 1994 (Act 490);
- Bodies Corporate (Official Liquidation) Act, 1963 (Act 180);
- Ghana Stock Exchange Listing Rules;
- Securities and Exchange Commission Guidelines;
- Banking Act, 2004 (Act 673) as amended;
- Insurance Act, 2006 (Act 724);
- National Petroleum Authority Act, 2005 (Act 691);
- The Food and Drugs Act,1992 (PNDCL 305B) as amended.

Consequences of Breach of Duty

There are statutory penalties stipulated to be imposed on directors who breach their duty to the company.

Generally, when directors breach their fiduciary duty to the company, they are obliged to compensate the company for any loss suffered as a result of the breach, account to the company for any profit made as a result of the breach, and any contract or transaction entered into between the director and another party in breach of his duty may be rescinded by the company.[29]

Directors are in breach of their duty if they fail to register debentures.[30] Failure to register these security holdings may render the charge, in respect of the company's property, void. A director can also be criminally liable for dishonestly receiving property contrary to law.

Where a disqualified person acts as a director, that person may face a maximum of five years in prison or the payment of a fine not exceeding 1,000 penalty units (approximately US$7,200) upon conviction.[31] Measures that can prevent directors from breaching their duty are:

Insurance

Directors may find themselves in a situation where they may be held personally liable for certain acts, although there might not even be any evidence of wrongdoing. Taking out insurance for the personal liability of directors is becoming increasingly common. If the regulations of the company permit, a company should obtain such cover (referred to as Directors and Officers – or D and O – Insurance) to meet claims against its officers. Such policies will generally indemnify directors and officers against claims in respect of negligence, default, breach of duty or breach of trust committed in their respective capacities as directors or executive officers, and also against the costs of defending against such claims. Policies are generally subject to specific financial limits and specific exclusions; for example, they would not normally cover any claim arising from any criminal, dishonest or fraudulent acts. It is important to check the wording of insurance policies carefully to ensure that they cover the sort of claims likely to be faced.

Shareholder Activism

Shareholder activism can be used to prevent directors from acts that may breach the duties that they are enjoined to perform. The shareholders are entitled to bring an action in court seeking for an injunction to restrain the directors from doing anything that is illegal, including entering into any transaction that is contrary to the powers of the company as enshrined in the regulations. The shareholders can also institute proceedings to restrain the directors from a threatened breach of their duty to the company.

Compensation

Compensation packages may be used to offer incentives to directors in a way that will deter them from acts that may not be in the interest of the enterprise.

Other Stakeholders

The other stakeholders in the enterprise can also prevent directors from acting in an opportunistic manner. The stakeholders in question, and the mechanisms available to them are as follows.

- **Employees**

  The Companies Act enjoins directors to consider the interest of, among others, employees in discharging their duties to the company. This means that employees' interest must guide directors in strategising in the company's best interests.[32] Some companies have schemes where employees are made to own shares in the company, which therefore makes them instrumental in ensuring that directors seek the best interests of the company for their overall benefit.

- **Regulators**

  The industry within which a company conducts business will determine which regulatory body it is subject to. Generally, all companies are subject to the Registrar General's Department in compliance with all the provisions of their regulations and the provisions of the Companies Act. Other relevant industry-specific regulators are the Bank of Ghana, the Food and Drugs Board, the National Insurance Commission, the Securities and Exchange Commission, the National Petroleum Authority, the Environmental Protection Agency and the National Communications Authority, to mention but a few.

- **The Courts**

  The courts are also relevant in ensuring compliance by management to the relevant statutes relating to the company's business. By the applications it receives from members, directors, debenture holders, creditors and even the Registrar General's Department, the courts, through the interpretation of the law, ensure that the company's affairs are governed in accordance with the relevant legal frameworks.

Director Qualification

Other than the additional requirements imposed by certain industry regulators such as Bank of Ghana and the National Insurance Commission for directors in the banking and insurance industries respectively, the bar for becoming a director under Ghanaian law is very low.

The only persons who are disqualified from acting as directors[33] are the following:

- Infants;
- Persons found to be of unsound mind by a competent court;
- Companies;
- Undischarged bankrupts (unless the court by which the person was found bankrupt grants leave);
- Persons convicted on indictment of an offence involving dishonesty or fraud in connection with the promotion, formation or management of a company;

- Persons who have previously been ordered not to be involved in the management of any company, act as auditor, receiver or liquidator for a period specified by a court of law, must be granted leave before such persons may qualify as directors.

Board Selection

One of the most important decisions an entrepreneur will make is selecting people to form a board. Yet, as we have seen in the previous section, the bar set by law for directors to cross is rather low. Precisely because of this low bar, it is important for entrepreneurs to ensure that they set their own standards for aspiring directors to meet. Given the key role directors play and the power that they exercise, my view is that, at the very minimum, entrepreneurs choose directors who meet the criteria set out below.

• *People Who Are Accessible*

While 'star' names are important, it is more important to recruit board members who are reasonably accessible and available to contribute to the development of the enterprise. Particularly, they must be available for meetings, either in person or by telephone, and, as and when required, to counsel the CEO and other members of the senior management team.

• *Interest and Passion*

The selection of the board should take into account the candidates' interest and passion for the industry.

• *Possession of Significant Knowledge and Competencies*

The knowledge and competencies required of a director may sometimes be specific to the industry in which the enterprise operates, or may relate to another industry but should be such that the enterprise is able to benefit from the candidate's knowledge and competencies.

• *Informed Business Judgement*

Directors should have the necessary skills to make sensible decisions about the enterprise.

• *Entrepreneurial Skills*

While it should not be a prerequisite for all members, it helps if one or more board members have entrepreneurial skills that the enterprise can draw upon, especially in the more difficult start-up phase of the enterprise.

• *Wide Perspective*

Directors ought to be persons who have a wide perspective, are well-read and informed and can think beyond the box.

• *Flair for Strategic Planning*

This is particularly important so that board members can make informed decisions concerning the future direction of the enterprise.

• *Analytical and Critical Thinking Skills*

Enterprises face complicated business problems and competing priorities. It is important that the directors are able to bring their analytical and critical thinking skills to help resolve problems and to prioritise business opportunities.

• *Interpersonal Skills*

A director should be able to relate easily with all persons so that the company can benefit fully from her membership of the board and the different social networks the director belongs to.

• *Integrity*

Directors must be principled persons of the highest integrity and ethical standing. They must act as the conscience and integrity check for the company to ensure that the company and its officers act at all times in a manner consistent with the company's values.

- *Reputation*

At least one director ought to be highly regarded in the particular industry that the company operates in; all directors must necessarily have impeccable reputations.

- *Objectivity*

Directors should be able to make objective decisions, without bias, after weighing all relevant factors.

- *Communication Skills*

Directors should be able to articulate their point of view in a convincing manner. They should also be able to listen impartially.

- *Show Common Sense*

Directors should exhibit common sense, being able to display sound practical judgement in everyday matters.

- *Open-Minded and Willing To Learn About The Industry*

In many cases, only a handful of board members will come from the actual industry in which the company operates, and would have been recruited partly because it is hoped they can bring fresh perspectives (and other skill sets) from other industries. It is therefore extremely important that board members are committed to constantly learning about the company and its industry.

Board Of Advisors

At law, only companies are required to have a board of directors. Boards of companies are also referred to as statutory boards because they are the creation of statute (the Companies Act).

Although not required by law to have boards, I recommend that sole proprietors and partnerships put in place advisory boards made up of individuals who are recruited by the criteria that would have been used if the enterprise in question had been a company.

Even in the case of a company, for any number of reasons, a start-up entrepreneur may want to keep her statutory board very small and limited to the entrepreneurial team. In such a case, she would benefit by forming an advisory board to provide the enterprise with contacts and advice from time to time.

I set out the main differences between statutory boards and advisory boards in Table 10.1 as follows:

Table 10.1: Differences Between Advisory Boards and Statutory Boards

Advisory Board	Statutory Board
No obligation to do so at law	Companies are required to have a board with a minimum of two directors
No legal duties owed to the company	The law sets out the duties owed by directors to the company as a whole
Does not engage in the legal or official actions of the enterprise	Is a recognised part of the framework of companies and, as a result, forms part of its legal identity and engages in the official business of the company, often on behalf of the company
Not obliged to follow advice of the board	Management is required to follow the decisions of the board
Free from liability as long as they refrain from any legal or official role	The law imposes certain liabilities on directors

Advantages and Disadvantages of Boards

Advantages

The following are some of the advantages of having a board in place:

- *Promote Responsible, Accountable and Transparent Companies*

  Having in place an effective and engaged board promotes responsibility, accountability and transparency in all the company's dealings, provided that the structures exist to ensure that decision making is transparent.

• Recognise, Balance and Protect Stakeholder Rights

As I mentioned earlier, there are many competing interests in any enterprise. An effective board is able to identify each of the competing interests and properly balance them to protect shareholder rights.

• Assist In Attracting Investors

A well-constituted and effective board sends signals to both local and foreign investors that their investments would be secure and efficiently managed in a transparent and accountable manner, given the quality and composition of the board and the governance systems and processes in place.

• Create Competitive and Efficient Companies

A properly constituted board with the right mix of committed and experienced individuals fosters the creation of competitive and efficient companies because of the contribution board members make to shaping strategy, to debates relating to decisions the company makes and to the contact base and social network of the company.

• Enhances Accountability and Performance of the Management Team

The board is an important check on the management team and, if board members are doing their jobs properly, the board should be able to hold management accountable for their actions, which improves the performance of management because of the keen oversight that the board exercises to ensure that the right things are done for the company.

Disadvantages

Despite the obvious advantages of boards, there are a few disadvantages associated with them. The two main ones are as follows:

• *Speed*

A board may delay certain decisions because, rather than the management team simply taking the relevant decision, they would have to present it to the board and seek approval from members. Long delays in making decisions could result depending on when the board is due to meet next and how many meetings they require to reach a decision. For an entrepreneurial company, this can be frustrating. A way around this is for directors to use written resolutions to make urgent decisions without having to meet. The relevant board papers can be emailed to members who can sign an accompanying resolution to give their assent. Also, boards may meet over the telephone instead of physically to settle such urgent matters.

• *Expense*

Although fees paid to a director are typically nominal (given the stature and contribution of the director), the total amount paid to directors – sitting fees, annual or quarterly allowances, expenses relating to holding board meetings, etc. – could be significant, particularly for a small or start-up company.

Characteristics of Good Boards

While by no means exhaustive, research shows that good boards share the following characteristics.

Leadership For Continuous Prosperity

Good boards provide leadership by directing the enterprise so as to achieve continuing prosperity for all stakeholders. This requires balancing considerations of today against those of tomorrow. Good boards focus on the performance of the enterprise today, and in putting systems in place to ensure its continued performance after the involvement of the current board members. This includes the development of a succession plan to ensure that at all levels of the company, and particularly in key roles, relevant successors are in place to step into the shoes of the incumbents.

Act in the Best Interests of the Company

Good boards ensure that the overriding criterion for making any decision is that it is in the best interest of the company's commercial advancement.

Build Trust

Good boards develop a climate of trust, respect and candour in that they tend to discuss relevant issues openly and take decisions based on consensus.

Encourage Debate

Board members feel free to challenge each other and management. Members engage in constructive conflict – especially with the CEO[34] – and directors are encouraged to give their opinions and disagree each another (even the Chairman if necessary).

Teamwork

Members of good boards work together as a team and address challenges comprehensively.

Shy Away from Micromanagement

Good board members work at the appropriate level of strategic involvement and avoid micromanagement.

Diversity

High-performance boards are normally composed of a group of individuals with different experiences, strengths, profiles, backgrounds, etc. Typically, boards will include people with experience in one or more of the following: audit, finance or tax; strategy; human resources; marketing and sales; and legal. Dorf and Byers sum up the significance of this: "A premium should be placed on a wide range of expertise and backgrounds but above all, on people who will seek to expose the downsides as well as the upsides of every major decision."[35]

Commitment to Industrial Learning for Effective Strategy

Members of good boards have a superior working knowledge of the company's strategy, and try to understand the dynamics and drivers of the industry as well as the competition to help focus the firm's strategic objectives.

Commitment To Assessing Performance

Just as they are always assessing the performance of management, good boards assess their own performance, both collectively and individually.[36] Board members assess the performance of one another and discuss these assessments at board meetings. They also assess the Chairman, after which a member then discusses the Chairman's assessment with the him. The Bank of Ghana considers this so important that it now requires all boards of banks to conduct self-assessments annually.

Balanced Representation

Good boards display a balance between non-executive and executive directors, between independent directors[37] and non-independent directors and between genders, such that no individual or group of individuals can dominate the board's decision-making processes. There should also be a separation (and a balance of power) between the Chairman and the CEO. For instance, the National Insurance Commission specifically mandates that the office of the Chairman of an insurance company should be separate from that of the CEO. There is also a requirement that at least a third of the board members be independent board members (independent directors are those who are non-executives, and are free from any business with the company and its associated companies, which can materially interfere with the exercise of independent and impartial judgement; they have no close or family ties with the directors, senior management or significant shareholders of the company).[38]

A Balance Between 'Grey Hairs' and 'Wannabes'

On one level, this point can be thought of as no different from the need to balance some of the different characteristics of board members discussed above. However, I believe that the question of balance between 'grey hairs' and 'wannabes' merits special attention. It is true that board members are typically expected to contribute from their accumulated experience and wisdom. This often means that – at least, other than in the case of board members that are also part of the entrepreneurial team – board members tend to be drawn from a pool of individuals who are considered to draw on many years of experience. The enterprise then draws on this experience, not only in formulating and implementing its own strategy, but also to gain access to the pool of contacts of these board members. For example, on many of the boards that my researchers studied, the high level contacts of board members have been extremely useful in helping the company deal with anything from regulatory issues to environmental issues to averting public relations disasters. I call these people who have many years of experience 'grey hairs' and those who don't, but aspire to get there, 'wannabes'. A board that is comprised only of experienced hands is likely to be a sterile board with the risk of losing out on the perspective of the younger (and future) generations. Another advantage of ensuring a balance is that the grey hairs can groom the wannabes to take over. This is particularly important as the only way to gain boardroom experience is in the boardroom. Therefore, in setting up a board, entrepreneurs should take the time and effort to identify both experienced individuals and individuals with other relevant skill sets who may not be experienced but have potential and could be groomed in the board room to fill the shoes of older board members.

Hold Meetings with Adequate Regularity

Good boards endeavour to meet as regularly as necessary. Meetings must be held at least once a quarter to tie in with the company's quarterly management accounts. In addition, the different board committees meet as and when required. Several boards in Ghana meet on a monthly basis (and sometimes for a full day each month), but I believe that this practice (other than in exceptional circumstances) is a sign of micromanagement. It may also discourage potential board members of exceptional quality, as such people are by definition extremely busy and are typically unlikely to agree to meet every single month.

Demand Adequate Information and Preparatory Time

Board members are given adequate information and time to prepare for meetings and other discussions to enable them make informed contributions. As Nadler put it, there are two equally effective ways of keeping a board in the dark. One is to provide them with too little information. The other, ironically, is to provide too much information[39]. Receiving reams of financial information, for example, might be too much for the board to absorb or understand without considerable background information. Board members must insist that information is presented to them in advance of the meeting, and in a manner that makes sense to them. In some instances, it may be important for training to be organised for board members so that they are able to properly evaluate the information provided.

Continuous Communication

Board members engage with the company regularly at board meetings and between meetings, using both formal and informal means of communicating to keep abreast of developments. Directors regularly visit various suppliers, outlets, key sites and competitors to get a first-hand picture of what the relevant issues may be.

Members Have No Hidden Agendas

Good board members disclose conflicts of interest, abstain from voting on those issues and put the company's interest first.

Ensure That Proper Records Are Kept

Although the duty is delegated to the Company Secretary, each director should keep his own files relating to the company, double-checking and filing minutes produced by the Company Secretary to ensure they are true records of the proceedings of relevant meetings.

Strive for Consensus

The board chair steers discussions to help to arrive at consensus. Although the Companies Act gives the chair a casting vote, a good board chairman hardly uses this power. The proposed Companies Act to replace the existing Companies Act has no provision for this casting vote.

Structure and Composition of Boards

Although there are many variations to this, boards are typically structured as follows:

• Chairman

The Chairman's primary responsibility is to ensure the effective operation of the board by facilitating the effective performance of non-executive directors as well as ensuring constructive relations between executive and non-executive directors. He also ensures regular and effective communication with all shareholders. The chairman chairs all meetings of shareholders and directors. My view is that the role of chairman should be separated from that of the Chief Executive Officer, and the Chairman should as far as possible maintain a distance from the daily operations of the enterprise, which should be the responsibility of the Chief Executive Officer (sometimes called the Managing Director).

• Executive Directors

An executive directors are employed on a full- or part-time basis by the company and has a board seat because of his position in the company. Typically, one or more members of the senior executive management team are executive directors. My view is that the number of executive directors on the board should be kept to the barest minimum – ideally only the Chief Executive Officer – and certainly no more than two.

• *Non-Executive Directors*

The law does not distinguish between executive and non-executive directors but, in practice, a non-executive director is a director who is not employed by the company in any other capacity (whether on a full- or part-time basis) and devotes part of his time to the affairs of the company as an independent advisor or supervisor.[40] There are two main types of non-executive directors – nominee directors and independent directors:

» Nominee Director: A nominee director is a director representing the interest of a substantial shareholder, such as a venture capital fund, who is appointed to monitor his appointer's investment. Where the government has a significant stake in a company, it is likely to have government nominees on the board of the company, as is the case in companies such as Ghana Commercial Bank, Vodafone Ghana Ltd and Ghana Oil Company Ltd (GOIL). The fact that a director is a nominee of a substantial shareholder does nothing to modify his fiduciary duties to the company to which he is appointed, and if any conflict of interest arises, he will be fully liable to the company if he prefers the interest of his appointer.

» Independent 'Outside' Directors: A director is deemed to be independent if such director has no significant financial or personal ties to management, is free from any business or other relationship with management which could materially interfere with the exercise of his independent judgement, and receives no compensation from the company other than director's remuneration or shareholder dividends. I highly recommend that independent directors meet regularly without the insider directors present (but should inform the insider directors).

• *Company Secretary*

Strictly speaking, the Company Secretary is not a member of the board, although one can be both a board member and a Secretary. I discuss the roles and responsibilities of a secretary later.

Appointment and Termination

The Companies Act, the company's regulations and the shareholders' agreement (where relevant) govern the appointment and the termination of directors.

Appointment

A director is appointed by other directors or shareholders of the company,[41] and in the case of a private company, once appointed, a director will continue to hold office until he vacates his office or is removed by the company.

In forming boards (or appointing directors to existing boards), entrepreneurs must take action around the following considerations:

• *Candidate Due Diligence*

Entrepreneurs must complete due diligence on candidates in respect of the character, temperament, willingness to learn, ability to listen and potential to contribute to the pursuance of the company's objective. In addition, I recommend that entrepreneurs pay attention to how many boards proposed directors serve on. Some directors serve on so many boards that unless they are retired or semi-retired, they would be unable to make a significant contribution to an additional company. My experience is that there is an inverse relationship between the number of board seats a director holds and how effective that director is. I would recommend that companies limit the number of boards their directors can sit on.

• *Disclosure of Information and Expectations*

Entrepreneurs should provide prospective directors with as much information about the company as possible. This may include strategic plans, regulations, code on corporate governance, press reports, industry reviews, annual reports for the last three years (if available) and minutes of previous (board) meetings.

Also, entrepreneurs should be clear with prospective directors about their expectations. For example, does the entrepreneur expect a prospective director to use his contacts to help drive the company's sales objectives, to provide mentoring to the young leadership team or bring their wealth of experience in a particular functional area? Whichever expectations there are should be clearly communicated.

• *Developing Guidelines and Controls*

The entrepreneur should develop clear guidelines on the following:

- Matters Reserved for the Board: In practice, the board delegates the day-to-day management of the company to the executive management team. It is however important for the board to be clear about matters that the board itself must decide on. The Institute of Chartered Secretaries and Administrators (ICSA) advises that matters to be reserved for the board should include structure and capital, internal controls, board membership and other appointments, remuneration, political donations and changes to group pension schemes.

- Policy for Obtaining Independent Advice for Directorship: Directors will not always have the relevant experience and knowledge necessary to make a relevant decision. It is important that they are able to consult with experienced advisors (at the expense of the company) when such situations arise.

- Board Operation Manual/Code On Corporate Governance: Each board must have a code of corporate governance which serves as a guide (rather than a rigid code) to how the board should make decisions.

- Board Committees and Composition: It is not always possible or efficient for certain aspects of the board's work to be done by the full board. To facilitate more detailed discussion and speedy decision making, a board would typically have certain sub-committees that are charged with making recommendations to the board. It is important to note that, unless otherwise stated, a sub-committee does not make decisions on behalf of the board. It merely makes a recommendations which must be approved to be effective. The type and composition of the committee will vary from company to company and from industry to industry, and will also depend on the size and resources of the company. I believe that, at the barest minimum, every company, no matter how small the board is, should have an audit committee and a human relations committee, both chaired by non-executive directors.

» Audit Committee: This committee is primarily responsible for reviewing the integrity, reliability and accuracy of accounting and financial information. Where necessary, the committee works with external auditors to assess the adequacy and effectiveness of internal controls, risk and compliance, and to conduct forensic investigations into management practices against best practice.

» Human Relations Committee: The human relations committee is responsible for attracting, developing, managing and retaining the company's talent. It regularly reviews the compensation paid by the company to ensure that it is competitive, motivational, fair and equitable, taking into consideration the financial position of the company. It also evaluates the CEO, identifies potential board members and is responsible for board succession.

• Meetings: The entrepreneur should communicate his expectations of board meeting mechanics, including how often the board meets, quorum and voting procedures, among others.

I take the view that when a new directors join a board, inductions should be held. Executive managers must brief them on the nature of the company's business, challenges, plans, opportunities and threats. They should arrange for them to visit key locations and to meet with key stakeholders such as employees, suppliers and regulators. The Chairman of the board and the Company Secretary should also meet with the new directors to discuss board procedure, expectations of new directors and the duties and responsibilities required of all directors. I also recommend regular refresher training for continuing directors.

Termination

The appointment of directors may be terminated voluntarily or involuntarily. Directors may resign by giving notice to the company. Their appointment may also be terminated by an ordinary resolution after giving the director notice of such intention and the right to be heard.[42] To prevent the company from getting into a protracted dispute with its directors when it is trying to remove them, I recommend that upon appointment, directors be made to sign an undated letter of resignation to be effective whenever the company decides. When the company wants to remove such a director, it only needs to date the letter of resignation and file it at Companies House.

A director's appointment also comes to an end at the end of any applicable term. Although, as I noted earlier, there is no term limit for private companies, my view is that, except in exceptional circumstances, no director, however talented, should serve on any board for more than five years.

Remuneration

There is an erroneous perception that non-executive board members in Ghana are paid a lot. On the contrary, relative to the quality of the directors, their experience and value they bring to boards, our research suggests that non-executive directors of the Ghana Club 100 companies are significantly underpaid. I agree with the view taken by James Kristie: "Directors are one of the last great bargains. They are underpaid for the work they do and the responsibility they assume."[43]

This is consistent with the notion that remuneration of non-executive directors is meant to be a token, and should always be set at such a level that a director who disagrees with a position taken by the board will not refrain from resigning because of the remuneration.

The exact details vary from company to company and from industry to industry but generally non-executive directors are paid quarterly or annual fees, and then paid sitting fees for every board meeting, board committee meeting or shareholder meeting that they attend. They are also entitled to the travelling expenses and other expenses they incur in attending meetings in connection with the business of the company.[44] To arrive at a fair level of remuneration in respect of the sitting allowance, I recommend that an estimate be made first of the number of hours that a director will use to prepare for, travel to and from and attend the meeting. This should be multiplied by the going hourly charge out rate for consultants in the same industry. The quarterly or annual fee should be equal to at least twice the amount of money that would be paid directors that attend a minimum of four board meetings and two committee meetings a year, based on the formula used to compute sitting allowances. It is also generally accepted that the chairman should receive a bit more than other members of the board (probably between the range of 25% to 50% more). I think that it is also appropriate to include performance incentives and stock options for non-executive directors to align their interest with that of shareholders.

The Companies Act requires that the remuneration of directors should be determined by ordinary resolution (although the appointment letters or contracts of executive directors may stipulate the remuneration in respect of their appointment).

Company Secretary

Every company is required to have a company secretary. The appointment, duration of appointment and remuneration of the company secretary will be determined by the directors of the company. Unlike the prohibition in the case of directors, a corporate entity can be a company secretary. Secretaries play a role in summoning meetings and taking minutes of such meetings. In this regard, if a company acts for more than six months without a secretary, the company and every officer in charge will be liable to pay a fine not exceeding

25 penalty units (approximately US$180) for each day after the six months that the default continues.[45] The Companies Act also provides for clear distinction between the office of a director and a secretary by providing that, if an act is required to be done by a secretary and a director, it will not be considered as done if the act is done by one person in both capacities.[46] It is necessary that directors exercise due care in appointing a company secretary since, as an officer, the acts of a company secretary, done upon the express or implied authorisation of the board or shareholders, bind the company.

Auditors

Auditors are not officers of the company; they however stand in a fiduciary relationship to the shareholders. Their appointment is mandatory as their role is very important for the administration of the company's finances. To perfect the appointment of an auditor, the auditor must consent in writing prior to the appointment. In Ghana, auditors generally must be persons qualified as chartered accountants under the Chartered Accountants Act, 1963 (Act 170). A partnership firm may be appointed as auditors of a company. In such a situation, the appointment is deemed as an appointment of the duly qualified partners of the firm.[47] For auditors being appointed for banks and insurance companies, their appointment must receive prior approval from the Bank of Ghana and the National Insurance Commission, respectively.

A company is required to appoint its first auditors prior to the delivery of the particulars required by the Companies Act to the Registrar, or within three months of the incorporation of the company. Even though the directors appoint the first auditors and are mandated to fill in any casual vacancy in the office of the auditor, auditors are generally appointed by ordinary resolution, which means by majority votes of the members of the company. Also, the Registrar may exercise his supervisory role to appoint an auditor for a company if the company carries on business without an auditor for a continuous period of three months.

An auditor may leave office by giving notice of her resignation in writing. Also, auditors are removed by ordinary resolution just as they are appointed by the same. The company is required to give notice to the Registrar within twenty-eight days after a change of auditors.

When auditors are appointed, they must be enabled by the company to do their work. The directors are therefore supposed to give the auditors access at all times to the books, accounts and vouchers of the company. The auditors are entitled to require from the officers of the company any information and explanation that the auditors may require for their work. Auditors are also entitled to attend general meetings of the company. The company must therefore ensure that they receive all notices and other communications relating to any general meeting, and be granted hearings on any part of the meeting which concerns them as auditors.

Generally, auditors are required only to give a true and fair view of the balance sheets of the company. They are not appointed to hunt for fraud in the accounts of the company. However, an auditor may contract with a company to undertake additional obligations to detect defalcations, and to advise on accounting, costing, taxation, raising of finance and other matters.[48]

General Meetings

Shareholder meetings are called general meetings. A general meeting will be an extraordinary general meeting (EGM) except for once a year when the company has its annual general meeting (AGM). Although general meetings are meetings of members (or shareholders), it is normally the directors who call these meetings, and the directors may resolve to call a meeting of the shareholders at any time and for any reason.[49] All members are entitled to attend a general meeting and to speak at the meeting. Directors are also permitted to attend and speak, though they cannot vote unless they are also shareholders.

The AGM

The Companies Act requires that, other than for newly incorporated companies, an AGM be held once in each calendar year, with no more than fifteen months elapsing between the date of one AGM and the next. When a company is newly incorporated however, there is no need to hold an AGM in the year of incorporation, or in the following year, provided that the first AGM is held within the first 18 months of the company's existence.[50]

Notice of twenty-one clear days is required for an AGM, although members may agree unanimously that a shorter notice period is acceptable.

The AGM provides shareholders a yearly opportunity to confront the directors on their stewardship, and it is also their opportunity to see the annual accounts. It tends to be more significant in larger companies where many of the members are not also directors and are not generally informed about the day-to-day decisions that the directors make.

If the auditors of the company and all the members of the company agree in writing that an annual general meeting shall be dispensed with in any year, the company need not hold a general meeting for that year.[51]

EGMs

Although EGM stands for extraordinary general meeting, this is the name of every meeting of members other than the AGM. EGMs are convened at the discretion of the directors and can also be requisitioned by members. In both cases, they are called to discuss matters that the members consider special and urgent.

Voting

I already mentioned in Chapter 5 that voting at a general meeting of members is done in one of two ways – by a show of hands and/or by a poll. If a vote is taken by a show of hands, every member has one vote (which may be exercised by a proxy for an absent member). If a poll is taken, each member (or her proxy) has one vote for every share owned by her.

Quorum

When a general meeting is convened, it is mandatory that the requirement for quorum is satisfied. This is because no business can be transacted unless the quorum of members is present when the meeting proceeds to discuss the business of the day. Where the quorum of members is present the shareholders can proceed to discuss the business, even in situations where the quorum is only present for part of the meeting.

Quorum is said to be constituted where, in the instance that the company has only one member, that member or his proxy is present (where proxies are allowed). In any other case, quorum is said to be met by two shareholders or their proxies present, or the presence of one member who holds shares representing more than 50% of the total voting rights of the company. For most companies, quorum is determined by the regulations. Where an EGM is requisitioned by the members and quorum is not present within thirty minutes after the time appointed for the meeting, the meeting shall be dissolved. In any other case the meeting will be adjourned to the same day in the next week at the same time and place, or to any other day, time and place as the directors will determine. If on the newly appointed day the quorum is still not met within thirty minutes of the time communicated, the members present shall constitute a quorum.[52] The court also has the authority to convene a meeting if it becomes impracticable to convene and conduct meetings of the company as stipulated in the Companies Act and in the company's regulations. This power of the court is given to ensure that certain shareholders do not sabotage meetings and/or the general governance of the company.

The Chairman

The board usually has the power to elect one of its members to be the chairman. Nominally, the chairman is the head of the company, although he has no special powers other than the casting vote given him in the event of an equal vote for and against a resolution. Where there is equality of votes among the board members, the chairman is entitled to a second or casting vote.[53] Generally, the board chairman presides at meetings of the board of directors. If he is unavailable within fifteen minutes after the time appointed for the holding of the meeting, the board members are entitled to elect one of their members to chair and steer the affairs of the meeting.

The Board and the Rights of Members

The rights and liabilities attaching to the shares of a company depend on the terms of issue and of the company's regulations as far as they are consistent with the Companies Act.[54] The shareholders' agreements (if any) also operate to give rights and impose liabilities on members. The board must work at all times to safeguard these rights; some of the rights are listed below:

- *Right to Attend Meetings and to Vote*

  Every member, notwithstanding any provisions in the regulations of the company, shall have a right to attend any general meeting of the company and to speak and vote on any resolution provided before the meeting. There may be restrictions on the exercise of this right by a shareholding member who the company restricts in respect of calls or other sums payable by him with regard to the shares held.[55]

- *Right to Receive Notice of General Meetings*

  Every shareholder is entitled to receive notice of general meetings.[56] The notice may be served personally on the shareholder or through registered post or by leaving it for the shareholder with a person apparently over the age of sixteen years.[57] This portrays the importance the law attaches to every shareholder receiving notice to general meetings where they can contribute and question how the directors and management are governing the company. An accidental omission to give notice of a meeting or the non-receipt of a notice of a meeting will not invalidate proceedings.[58] This means that if the omission to give notice to a shareholder was not accidental but found to be deliberate, the shareholder can apply for invalidation of the proceedings of the meeting that was held.

• Right to a Dividend if it is Declared

The directors govern the affairs of the company to enable the shareholders reap the fruits of their investments. In this regard, they are to recommend dividends that will be distributed to members every year or within a period they determine. The company then declares dividends by ordinary resolution. The dividends declared must however not be more than the amount recommended by the directors.[59] Also, in order to ensure that the company continues as a going concern, the directors must ensure the following:

- After the dividend is paid, the company is able to pay its debts as they fall due;
- The amount declared as dividend does not exceed the income surplus of the company.

If these are not complied with, the directors will be liable to restore to the company the amount declared as dividends with 5% annual interest. If the directors are unable to restore the amount within a year of the payment of dividend, the shareholders who received the dividend will be liable to restore the amount. If the directors restore the money, they are entitled to being indemnified by the shareholders who received the dividend knowing that its payment was in contravention of the Companies Act.[60] Thus, even though shareholders have a right to dividends if they are declared, they must satisfy themselves that the requirements that attach to the declaration of dividends are complied with.

• Right to a Share Certificate

Every company is required, within two months after the issue of any of its shares or after the registration of the transfer of any issue, to deliver to registered holders a certificate which states the number and class of shares held by him, the amount paid on such shares, the amount outstanding and the name and address of the registered holder. If a share certificate is defaced, lost or destroyed, the company is required to replace the certificate.[61]

• *Right to Inspect the Register of Members*[62]

Except where the register of members is closed, every member has a right (subject to reasonable restrictions) to inspect the register of members and take a copy of the register during normal business hours.

• *Right to Call an EGM*

Any member with 10% or more of the shares of the company, or two or more members with 10% or more of the shares of the company, may require the directors to convene an EGM of the company.[63]

• *Right to Have Name Entered in the Register of Members*

Under Ghanaian law, a person who has agreed to be a member of a company must have his or her name in the register of members. Apart from subscribers, the entry into the register of members is a condition precedent to perfecting one's membership in a company.[64] Companies are mandated to keep registers of members in which they enter the names, addresses and shares held by the members, the date on which a person becomes a member and the date on which he ceases to be a member.[65] The register of members is prima facie evidence of the membership of the shareholder in the company and of all other details stated about the shareholder in the register of members.[66]

• *Right to a Copy of the Annual Accounts*

The directors of a company have a responsibility to ensure that no later than eighteen months after the company is incorporated, and subsequently at least once every year at intervals of not more than fifteen months, they circulate copies of the profit and loss account and balance sheet together with an auditors' report and directors' report on the company. These accounts will be laid before the general meeting and discussed by the shareholders, unless the general meeting is waived by the shareholders.[67]

• *The Right to an Annual General Meeting*

Shareholders are entitled to an annual general meeting (AGM).

They are entitled to attend and vote on resolutions that are passed at the meeting. The company's regulations may however restrict the right of a member to attend and vote subject to the payment of calls or other sums payable by him in respect of the shares held by him.[68] The holding of AGMs is statutorily mandatory. It can only be dispensed with if it is agreed in writing by all the shareholders and the auditor of the company.[69] AGMs give shareholders the opportunity to assess the performance of management, the board of directors and the company.

• *Right to Inspect Minutes of General Meetings*

The directors are to ensure that the minutes' book of the company's general meetings is kept at the registered office of the company. The minutes' book is to be made available during business hours, not less than two hours a day during working days, for inspection by shareholders free of charge. Shareholders are also entitled to be furnished with a copy of the minutes' book ten days after making a request for it. If an inspection is refused or a request for the minutes' book is not sent within the required time, the company and every director shall be liable, in respect of each offence, to pay a fine of 25 penalty units (approximately US$180) for each day that the offence continues, and the court is mandated to compel an immediate inspection or furnishing of a copy of the minutes' book to a shareholder.[70]

• *Right to Requisition an EGM*

Two or more shareholders of a company or a single member holding not less than 10% of the company's shares can requisition the directors to convene an extraordinary general meeting. All the members need to do is to state in their requisition the nature of the business to be transacted at the meeting, and sign and deposit the requisition at the registered office of the company. If the directors do not, within seven days after receiving the requisition at the registered office of the company, duly proceed to convene the meeting by sending notices to the other shareholders and the auditor of the company for a date not later than twenty-eight days after the receipt of the requisition, the members who requisitioned the meeting can themselves proceed to convene the meeting. However the shareholders must wait for the expiration of four months after the twenty-eight days timeline before they convene a meeting of themselves.[71] The company is required to repay to the shareholders all reasonable expenses incurred in convening the meeting and these expenses will later be deducted from the remuneration of the directors concerned.

• *Right to Restrain an Ultra Vires Act*

Acts of the company or the directors are said to be ultra vires where those acts exceed the powers conferred by the regulations of the Companies Act, or is not authorised by the regulations of the company. Shareholders have invested equity into companies and are thus entitled to ensure that their investments are being used to further the objects for which they invested. Thus if the directors and management are moving the company in a direction or into business not authorised by the company's regulations, the shareholders can bring an action in court and the court will, by an injunction, prohibit the doing of an act or the conveyance of property in pursuance of an act not authorised by the regulations of the company, or which is in excess of the powers of the company.[72]

• *Right to Have an Item Placed on the Agenda for an AGM*

Shareholders who are entitled to attend and vote at general meetings have a right to request in writing for a resolution to be put into the notices being circulated to other shareholders for general meetings. The shareholder can also attach to the request a statement of not more than 500 words with respect to the matter in the proposed resolution. The placement of the proposed resolution in the notice will be at the expense of the company.[73] Shareholders can also, at their own expense, request the company to circulate statements of not more than 1,000 words in respect of any matter to be discussed at general meetings. The member merely has to present a signed request to the registered office of the company, together with the statement and the prescribed fee necessary to enable the company circulate to all shareholders.[74] Shareholders will not be allowed to exercise this right if the company or another person applies to the court and the court is satisfied that the shareholder is abusing this right to secure needless publicity for defamatory ends.[75]

• Minority Rights and Protection

Minority protection stems from the need to counterbalance majority rule. The principle of majority rule is that the court is reluctant to interfere in the internal management of a company to cure irregularities that are otherwise curable by ordinary resolution passed by the majority, and also that for a wrong done to the company, it is only the company that can sue.

The court however makes exceptions to this rule where an act is ultra vires or constitutes a fraud against the minority and the wrongdoers are in control of the company. The court will also intervene in acts that infringe a minority member's personal rights in circumstances where a special majority was required but not sought.

For example, a shareholder can institute an action in the court in his own right for an injunction to restrain the company from doing an act or entering into a transaction which is illegal, exceeds the powers of the company or infringes the regulations of the company. A shareholder can also apply for an injunction in respect of a resolution which was passed in contravention of the regulations of the company's regulations or the Companies Act.[76]

Shareholders can also bring an action in court for an order that the affairs of the company or the powers of the board are being exercised in a manner that is oppressive to the applicant shareholders or in disregard of their proper interests. The word 'oppressive' is said not to be a term of art but must be construed in its ordinary sense, meaning an act which is burdensome, harsh and wrongful.[77] They can also bring an action where an act has been done or is threatened, or a resolution has been passed or is proposed, which unfairly discriminates or is unfairly prejudicial to them.[78]

Case Study: Using Board Members as a Competitive Tool at CoreNett Limited

MICHAEL AMANKWAH IS THE MANAGING Director of CoreNett Ltd, a transactions processing management company he started in 2005. Before CoreNett, Amankwah co-founded and was the Chief Executive Officer of Avivie, Inc. an information technology company with operations in India, and was also actively engaged in nurturing two Internet start-up companies. Prior to that, Amankwah worked with Booz Allen Hamilton in Maryland, USA, as a Senior Consultant responsible for enterprise networking management.

After a degree in accounting and accounting information systems from James Madison University, Amankwah studied for a Masters in Information and Telecommunication Systems at Johns Hopkins University and undertook several Microsoft certification courses, making the information technology sector an ideal area for his venture activities.

With his experience and an impressive range of technology solutions, Amankwah had big dreams for CoreNett. Upon setting up the company, Amankwah sent proposals to a number of financial institutions offering them innovative transaction processing solutions to facilitate their electronic transactions, including electronic purse systems, prepayment systems and bill and budget payment systems.

Although it was clear that CoreNett's offering was in many cases superior to what was being provided by the incumbents, the odds were stacked against Amankwah. He was competing against well-resourced multinationals with strong relationships built over years providing services to the very banking customers that Amankwah sought to acquire. In addition, Amankwah, who had only recently returned to Ghana from the United States and did not have a wide local network he could tap into. Apart from a few friends from Accra Academy where he had attended secondary school, most of his friends were outside Ghana. He did not know any of the decision makers of any of the financial institutions he was targeting so it was difficult for him to get in front of the key players to make a case for CoreNett. To make matters worse, Amankwah looked young for a thirty-two-year-old, so it was also difficult for the few people who consented to seeing him to meet to reconcile such rich technology experience and superior product offerings with the man in front of them. Given that the average contract he sought ran into several hundreds of thousands of dollars, the decision makers appeared uncomfortable about the fresh-faced Amankwah. Regardless, he was confident that once the right doors were opened for him, he could persuade the relevant decision makers of the superiority of CoreNett's portfolio. Amankwah was confident about the quality of his solutions and his vision for CoreNett extended beyond Ghana; he had his eyes on the entire continent of Africa.

On his drive home from work after another frustrating day in the office, it occurred to Amankwah to set up a board of directors that would help give the company the stature it required and open the doors Amankwah needed opened so that he could make his case.

Amankwah researched potential board members and settled on two in particular who, in addition to being undisputed giants in the Ghanaian banking industry, were also well known and respected throughout the African banking industry. Amankwah decided to target Dr Kobina Quansah and Dr Jean Ackah to join the board of CoreNett as Chairman and Vice-Chairman respectively. Quansah was the first Ghanaian Managing Director of Barclays Bank Ghana Ltd, and the youngest person to occupy that position when he was appointed. He had also served on the boards of United Bank for Africa, CAL Bank, Vodafone Ghana Ltd and Social Security and National Insurance Trust (SSNIT). Ackah was the Group Chief Executive Officer of Ecobank Transnational Incorporated and Managing Director for Ecobank Ghana. Prior to his appointment as Managing Director, he served as Deputy Managing Director.

When Amankwah told his lawyer about his idea, the lawyer burst out laughing, asking why on earth Quansah and Ackah would want to join the board of a company without a customer and with an uncertain future, powered mainly by Amankwah's huge dose of optimism. Undeterred, Amankwah managed to arrange meetings with Quansah and Ackah. He spent several days preparing for each of the meetings to ensure that he could clearly articulate not only the benefits to him of such banking luminaries joining CoreNett's board, but also the benefits to them of joining the board. Of course, because CoreNett had only negative cashflow, money was not a consideration. Amankwah's preparation was rewarded; Ackah accepted to join the board less than a minute after Amankwah had made his pitch, and Quansah also accepted after a brief lunchtime discussion.

Since they joined the board, the fortunes of CoreNett have changed. Besides opening several doors for Amankwah and CoreNett, they have provided Amankwah with excellent counsel on how to run the company and given the company a stamp of legitimacy. Amankwah notes that the profile of the board members alone helps when he sends proposals and business plans to bid for contracts. Amankwah wishes he had put a high-profile board in place much earlier and thinks that, perhaps, he should have involved them a bit more in his business.

Asked how he was able to persuade two distinguished bankers to join his board, Amankwah said it probably came down to how he articulated the passion behind his dream and what he wanted from them. He also believes that Quansah and Ackah, both having reached the highest heights in banking, also looked at his offer in terms of giving back to society by nurturing and supporting a new generation of business people. They joined his board because they identified with him and his vision, and wanted to help in bringing that vision to life.

Questions for Class Discussion

1. What is corporate governance? Why is it important?
2. What are the key principles of corporate governance?
3. Must a person always be formally appointed to be a director of a company?
4. Who do directors owe their duties to?
5. In selecting board members for a company, what criteria would you use?
6. What are the main differences between an advisory board and a statutory board?
7. Is there a distinction at law between a non-executive and an executive director?

Notes

1   Minow, N. and R. Monks. Corporate Governance. Chichester: John Wiley and Sons, 2011.

2   Dess G.G. and G.T. Lumpkin. *Corporate Governance Update for use with Strategic Management: Creating Competitive Advantages*. New York: McGraw-Hill, 2003.

3   McKinsey & Company, Investor Opinion Survey on Corporate Governance, June 2000.

4   Gower, L.C.B. and P. Davies. *Gower and Davies: Principles of Modern Company Law*. London: Thomson Sweet and Maxwell, 2003.

5   Dess G.G. and G.T. Lumpkin. *Corporate Governance Update for use with Strategic Management: Creating Competitive Advantages*. New York: McGraw-Hill, 2003.

6   A Table on Page 483 shows the differences between these two types of boards.

7   Companies Act, 1963 (Act 179), Section 179

8   Companies Act, 1963 (Act 179), Section 179.

9   The Republic vs. Ibrahim Adam, Dr Samuel Dapaah, Kwame Peprah, Dr George Yankey and Ato Dadzie [28/04/03], SUIT NO. FT/MISC.2/2000.

10   A penalty unit is equivalent to GH¢12, approximately US$8.

11   Gower, L.C.B. and P. Davies. *Gower and Davies: Principles of Modern Company Law*. London: Thomson Sweet and Maxwell, 2003.

12   Neuschel, R.P. Corporate Boards looking toward 2010 – 2010. Kellogg School of Management teaching note, 2001.

13   *Ibid.*

14   *Ibid.*

15   Companies Act, 1963 (Act 179), Section 202(5).

16   Companies Act, 1963(Act 179), Section 139(2)(a).

17   Companies Act, 1963 (Act 179), Section 203.

18   Companies Act, 1963 (Act 179), Section 205.

19   Companies Act, 1963 (Act 179), Section 209.

20   Companies Act, 1963 (Act 179), Section 205.

21   Companies Act, 1963 (Act 179), Section 136(1).

22   Companies Act, 1963 (Act 179), Sections 123-129.

23   Companies Act, 1963 (Act 179), Section 132.

24   Companies Act, 1963 (Act 179), Sections 124 and 133.

25   Companies Act, 1963 (Act 179), Section 32.

26   Companies Act, 1963 (Act 179), Section 96.

27   Companies Act, 1963 (Act 179), Section 103.

28   Companies Act, 1963 (Act 179), Section 111.

29   Companies Act, 1963 (Act 179), Section 209.

30   Companies Act, 1963 (Act 179), Section 107.

31   Companies Act, 1963(Act 179), Section 182(2).

32   Companies Act ,1963(Act 179), Section 203(3).

33   Companies Act, 1963 (Act 179), Section 182.

34   Finkelstein, S. and A. Mooney. Not the usual suspects. *Academy of Management Executive* (17)2, 2003: 101-112.

35   Dorf, R. and T. Byers. *Technology Ventures: From idea to enterprise.* New York: McGraw-Hill, 2004.

36   Sonnefeld, J. What makes boards great. *Harvard Business Review,* 80(9), 2002: 106-112.

37   See Pages 490 - 491 on executive, non-executive and independent directors.

38   National Insurance Commission, Composition of Boards Guidelines.

39   Nadler D, Building Better Boards, *Harvard Business Review* May 2004]

40   Practical Law, www.practicallaw.com, retrieved February 2012.

41   Companies Act, 1963 (Act 179), Section 181.

42   Companies Act, 1963 (Act 179), Section 185.

43   Shultz, S.F. *The Board Book: Making Your Corporate Board a Strategic Force in Your Company's Success.* New York: AMACOM, 2001.

44   Companies Act 1963 (Act 179), Section 194.

45   Companies Act 1963 (Act 179), Section 190.

46   Companies Act 1963 (Act 179), Section 191.

47   Companies Act 1963 (Act 179), Section 135.

48   Companies Act 1963 (Act 179), Section 136.

49   Companies Act, 1963 (Act 179), Section 150(1).

50   Companies Act, 1963 (Act 179), Section 149(1).

51   Companies Act, 1963 (Act 179), Section 149(3).

52   Companies Act 1963 (Act 179), Section 161.

53   Companies Act 1963 (Act 179), Section 200.

54   Companies Act 1963 (Act 179), Section 39 (2).

55   Companies Code, 1963 (Act 179), Section 31.

56   Companies Act, 1963 (Act 179), Section 154.

57   Companies Act, 1963 (Act 179), Section 155.

58   Companies Act, 1963 (Act 179), Section 156.

59   Companies Act,1963 (Act 179), Section 73.

60   Companies Act,1963 (Act 179), Section 71.

61   Companies Act, 1963 (Act 179), Section 53.

62   Companies Act, 1963 (Act 179), Section 33.

63   Companies Act, 1963 (Act 179), Section 271.

64   Companies Act,1963 (Act 179), Section 30.

65   Companies Act,1963 (Act 179), Section 32.

66   Companies Act,1963 (Act 179), Section 36.

67   Companies Act,1963 (Act 179), Section 124.

68   Companies Act,1963 (Act 179), Section 31.

69   Companies Act,1963 (Act 179), Section 149.

70   Companies Act,1963 (Act 179), Section 178.

71   Companies Act,1963 (Act 179), Section 124.

72   Companies Act,1963 (Act 179), Section 25.

73   Companies Act,1963 (Act 179), Section 157.

74   Companies Act,1963 (Act 179), Section 158.

75   Companies Act,1963 (Act 179), Section 15.

76   Companies Act,1963 (Act 179), Section 217.

77   Mahama v Soli [1977], GLR 215.

78   Companies Act,1963 (Act 179), Section 218.

Chapter Eleven: Building and Developing a Brand

"Your brand is formed primarily, not by what your company says about itself, but by what the company does" - **Jeff Bezos**

Outline

- Introduction
- Brand Building
- Branding and the Marketing Mix
- Choosing a Brand Name
- Segmentation, Targeting and Positioning
- E-commerce
- Media Strategy
- Creative Strategy
- Briefing and Working with an Agency
- Measurement and Evaluation
- Personal Branding
- Case study: Establishing Category Leadership Through Effective Branding at Allure
- Questions for Class Discussion

MY VIEW IS that branding is an overused and misunderstood expression in Ghana. When I speak to entrepreneurs and marketing practitioners, it is clear that many of them confuse advertising with branding. Consequently, millions of cedis are wasted every year on cluttering our lives with advertising that does not necessarily deliver on building a brand. Although advertising has an important role to play in building brands, it is one (and only one) promotional tool.

A significant percentage of those wasted millions could have been saved or better deployed if it was understood that the role of branding within an enterprise is strategic, essentially at the heart of why the enterprise exists, what it does and how it competes. An enterprise's brand strategy links directly with and is influenced by its overall business strategy and its long-term growth objectives.

It follows that branding considerations become relevant the moment the entrepreneur decides to start an enterprise. He must be clear in his mind what sort of enterprise he is looking to build and what position he would want the enterprise to occupy in the industry in which it competes, as well as in the minds of target customers. Branding considerations continue to be relevant at every stage of the enterprise, including raising finance; attracting, managing and retaining people; constituting a board of directors; expansion; etc. At each of these stages, the entrepreneur has an opportunity to enhance or hurt his brand and, whether he likes it or not, the decisions he makes and the actions he takes will affect how his brand is perceived by others.

Scott Stratten underscores this point when he says that marketing (or branding in this case) "happens every time you engage (or not) with your past, present and potential customers."[1] Kotler makes the same point as follows: "The product's styling and price, the package's shape and colour, the salesperson's manner and dress and the place's décor – all communicate something to buyers. In fact, every brand contact delivers an impression that can affect a customer's view of the company. Therefore the entire marketing mix must be integrated to deliver a consistent message and strategic positioning."[2]

Traditional branding focuses to a large extent on 'look and feel' – the associations, name, terms, signs and symbols that sellers use to distinguish their products from the competition. I think that the emphasis on this visual identity of brands accounts in part for the misunderstanding that advertising amounts to branding.

As media platforms have fragmented and as advertisers increasingly compete for space in a cluttered marketplace, the importance of branding as an integrated marketing effort becomes a bit more obvious.

In this chapter we will discuss how an entrepreneur may approach the brand building exercise holistically and from a strategic standpoint, rather than as a discrete tactical exercise considered to be the preserve of the marketing department.

Brand Building

Kotler[3] explains the brand building process with the equation:

$$R \rightarrow STP \rightarrow MM \rightarrow I \rightarrow C$$

Where:

R = Research (i.e. market research)

STP = Segmentation, Targeting and Positioning

MM = Marketing Mix (popularly known as the four Ps, i.e. product, price, place and promotion)

I = Implementaion

C = Control (getting feedback, evaluating results, and revisiting or improving STP strategy and MM tactics)

As he puts it, "Effective marketing starts with research, R. Research into a market will reveal different segments, S, consisting of buyers with different needs. The company would be wise to target T, only those segments which it could satisfy in a superior way. For each target segment, the company will have to position, P, its offering so that target customers could appreciate how the company's offering differs from the competitors' offerings. STP represents the company's strategic marketing thinking. Now the company develops its tactical marketing mix, MM, consisting of the mix of product, price, place and promotion decisions. The company then implements, I, the marketing mix. Finally, the company uses control measures, C, to monitor and evaluate results and improve its STP strategy and MM tactics."[4]

What any experienced marketer will know about the equation and the description of brand building given by Kotler in the preceding section is that the objective of research (R) is to generate customer insights: deep penetrating truths and understanding about the customer's needs, aspirations, desires and personality that hooks the brand into the consumer's needs and wants, and by so doing identifies the brand building opportunity. It is the most basic distillation of what an entrepreneur knows about the target and their needs (in the competitive environment) on which the brand is founded, and forms the basis of the entrepreneur's product or branding efforts. I made this point in Chapter 4 where I said that it is the insights provided by opportunity analysis that gives the entrepreneur or prospective entrepreneur the ability to design a product or service that indeed removes an existing customer pain, hopefully in a way that is better than competitor enterprises. In that chapter, I used the Standard Trust case study to demonstrate how a bank was able to use consumer insights to develop a revolutionary product that resonated with the broad masses, previously been excluded from banking in Ghana.

Wheeler distinguishes between research and insights as follows: "Although research is the business discipline for gathering and interpreting data, insight comes from a more personal and intuitive place. Observing the world and listening non-judgementally to ideas of others opens up possibilities."[5] Or as Dunn puts it, "analytics shouldn't be allowed to overwhelm the intuition that characterises great marketers. It's the insights that the data leads to that result in breakthrough products and compelling customer experiences."[6]

Unearthing and capturing customer insight is about delving as deeply as you can (think of peeling an onion as far back as you can) to truly understand your target's underlying motivation for purchase and usage of products. It involves continuously asking a series of 'why', 'so what' questions until the real customer pain and brand opportunity is identified. In conducting research, the objective should be to delve beneath the surface and get the true feelings that potential and current customers have about the entrepreneur's brand and the brands of his competitive set.

Customer insights help the entrepreneur gain a deep understanding of the brand or potential brand, what it means to existing and potential customers, how it performs against competitor brands and its place in the relevant category or market. Generating customer insights is at the very heart of brand building. Brands that succeed engage deeply with their target customers. The ability to engage with customers effectively requires that the entrepreneur has a vivid description and understanding of, among others, the aspirations, fears, motivations and drives of the customer. Without such a detailed understanding and description of the customer, the entrepreneur may miss out on opportunities to build relevant brand connections with the customer.

Branding and the Marketing Mix

I define a brand as the beliefs and impressions that customers form based on the sum total of their interactions, experiences and communication with an enterprise and its products, services and employees. Based on these experiences, the customer forms a particular impression and holds particular beliefs about the product or service and enterprise, and how they compare with other products and services in his frame of reference. All things being equal, the rational customer will opt for the brand that best meets his needs or most convincingly promises to meet those needs.

Brand experience is then perhaps the most important aspect of the brand building exercise. The beliefs and impressions that customers form about the brand will be most strongly shaped by their own experiences or third-party experiences reported to them. Employees thus become key in bringing a brand to life. The entrepreneur must create pride in the brand among his employees and ensure that he recruits employees who are able to live up to the brand's attributes and value proposition. Great brands are built on great products and services delivered by great people.

I think Jeff Bezos, CEO of Amazon.com, sums this up excellently when he says "The reputation of a person is such a good analogy. Somebody's reputation is largely based on what they actually do as opposed to what they actually say. That's like a brand… Your brand is formed primarily, not by what your company says about itself, but by what the company does."[7]

At the core of branding is brand essence, which is the brand's DNA or the brand's mission. All branding elements and communication channels must be consistent with the brand essence. The brand essence communicates the brand's unique values and its personality. It is the distillation of the brand into a core promise based on the deep penetrating insight(s) about the customer on which the brand is founded. It answers this question: What makes the product or service? Axe (Lynx), for example, was founded around the insight that a major obsession of teenage boys is chasing girls and being chased by girls. Axe was therefore developed as the deodorant which makes teenage guys confident and attractive to the opposite sex.

The brand essence depends largely on the brand values and brand personality. The brand values are what the brand stands for; the brand personality describes how the brand behaves ('If the brand was a person, what kind of person would it be?').

The entrepreneur must set a brand vision, the same way that, as we will see in Chapter 14, she will set a vision for the entire enterprise. The brand vision articulates the ideal position that the entrepreneur and her team would like to see the brand occupy. Based on the brand vision and her understanding of her target customers, the competition and the market, the entrepreneur's job is to ensure that she has the right product or service (product) to meet the customer's need, at the right price (price), sold through the right channel (place) and also promoted in such a way that the customer knows the product and what its value proposition is (promotion). These four elements – product, price, place and promotion – are referred to as the 4 Ps or the marketing mix, and together they constitute the major elements of brand strategy.

Lack of Awareness → Awareness → Knowledge → Evaluation → Trial → Adoption → Advocacy/Repeat Purchase

The goal of branding and operation of the marketing mix variables is to migrate the customer up the scale depicted above; to get them to try and eventually adopt the product or service. The following is a simple analysis of how this may work. Take a potential customer of a new bicycle brand. At the first stage, the customer is not aware of this bicycle. He becomes aware of it through marketing communication (promotion) and finds more about the product either through salesmen at the shop where it is sold (place) or through information contained in radio or newspaper adverts (promotion). He then makes an evaluation based on other attributes of the product and the price and decides to go for a test ride. He likes the experience and decides to purchase the bicycle. Assuming that it meets or exceeds his expectations , when he needs to replace that bicycle, he might again consider purchasing the same brand of bicycles. If the customer is happy with the bicycle, the chances are that he will recommend it to other people within his network. Given the pre-existing relationship between the customer and those in his network, they are likely to trust the recommendation. Thus the recommendation would lead to trial by those to whom he has recommended the product. If the product meets their expectations, they will also adopt it and might become advocates, creating a virtuous cycle.

We shall now consider each of the elements of the marketing mix in more detail.

Product

Product refers to both tangible products and services with no physical form. It includes the physical product itself and/or the experience of the service, the image and emotional connotations associated with the product or service as well as everything in the entire spectrum of delivering and consuming the product or service ('the magic that goes beyond the box' As intimated earlier, the product (or service) must at the minimum meet an identified customer need in a way that is equal or superior to the competition.

There are two broad approaches to new product ideation:

Proactive Approach
This approach firstly relies on research and insights to identify the unsatisfied needs of customers, and then develops products and services that provide solutions to meet the customer's unsatisfied need or removes the customer pain.

Reactive Approach

With this approach, the entrepreneur simply waits for someone else to take the lead in developing and marketing a product or service, which he then copies. In doing so, the entrepreneur may hope to have an offering that is second but better, or simply second and 'me too'.

A consideration of the product should also include a consideration of the markets the entrepreneur will serve with the product or service. The same product or service might be adapted for additional markets to reflect differing needs of people in different segments. For example, an entrepreneur selling mobile phones may have different versions of the same brand to attract different segments of customers. A basic phone with limited functions may be positioned to attract low-income customers while a sophisticated phone with several functions selling at many times the price of the basic phone may be positioned to attract the affluent user.

Price

The basis of an attainable price is the willingness of the customer to pay the price asked for the product. Although cost is an important factor in the determination of price, the cost-price ratio only becomes critical when the price asked will not cover costs within the foreseeable future. In this case, it is advisable not to get into the business in the first place or to get out of it as soon as possible. The other factors that affect pricing include price elasticity of demand, buyers' perceptions and – in particular – value for money, competitive pricing and expectations of channel members.

The price of a product should depend on perceived value in the eyes of the customer. Before making any pricing decisions regarding a product or service, the entrepreneur should understand the customer pain that the product or service seeks to remove, and how this customer pain is currently being removed by the competitive set and for how much. The entrepreneur should then quantify exactly how much his particular solution to the customer's pain is worth to the customer.

Only after doing this should the entrepreneur define a price bracket for his product or service, making sure that he verifies and refines his assumptions through discussions with potential customers and double-checking competitive pricing. The world's strongest brands develop pricing strategy based on consumers' perception of value.[8]

Pricing though is often perceived as a complex art, with many managers unaware of how price can and should relate to what customers think of a product; they therefore charge too little or too much.[9]

There are a number of pricing strategies an entrepreneur may adopt. As an entry strategy, the main options tend to be penetration pricing, where the entrepreneur penetrates the market quickly by achieving a high market share with a low price, and skimming, where the entrepreneur seeks to generate the highest possible return from the outset by pricing to reach those segments of the market for which the product has the greatest value.

Ideally, many new enterprises would like to pursue a skimming strategy rather than a penetration strategy because:

- By positioning the new product or service as 'better' than previous or existing offerings, entrepreneurs are able to justify a higher price tag;
- Higher prices generally lead to higher profit margins, thereby allowing entrepreneurs to finance their own growth; where this is the case, new investments could be financed out of profits so that outside investors may not be needed;
- Unlike the penetration strategy, the skimming strategy does not generally require high initial investment. Penetration typically requires high initial investment in order for supply to meet the high demand that will result from low prices.

A penetration strategy however may be appropriate in certain instances.

• *High Fixed costs*

Businesses with high fixed costs are forced to find a wide audience base as quickly as possible to make those costs worthwhile.

• *Competition*

If the entry barriers are low and tough competition is likely, a penetration strategy is the best way to be faster than the competition in capturing a large market share. However, it is extremely dangerous for a start-up to seek to compete primarily on price.

Another type of pricing strategy the entrepreneur might employ is value pricing, based on customer perceptions about the value of the product/service. Examples include status products and exclusive products.

For many small and medium-sized enterprises, competing on factors other than price (non-price competition) is a more effective strategy than trying to beat larger competitors in a price war. Competitive levers other than pricing, such as outstanding customer service, free trials, free delivery, lengthy warranties and money-back guarantees, tend to play down price and to stress other factors such as durability, quality, reputation or special features. It is important to note that the pricing could also set the tone for positioning the brand.

Place

Place is where the customer obtains the product. It refers to the place or method of distribution. Distribution channels aim at making available to the customer the right product at the right place at the right time.

The entrepreneur must think through the best way for his product or service to reach the customer. The choice of a distribution channel may be influenced by a number of factors including:

- The nature of the product;
- The potential customer base;
- The composition of the target market – whether individuals or enterprises;
- The shopping preferences of the target customers;

- The nature of the products or services – in particular whether or not extensive explanations and demonstrations are required;
- Whether the product is a high-end (premium) or low-end (mass-market) product;
- Whether or not after-sales service is required;
- Whether or not the customer is likely to require credit to make the purchase.

The entrepreneur may need to decide whether to handle the distribution himself or rely on a specialised third party. Some distribution channels are as follows:

• *Third-Party Retailers*

Products may be sold through third-party retailers who have easy access to potential customers (for example, consumer goods sold through supermarkets). The entrepreneur will need to offer the third-party retailer an attractive enough margin for her to accept to stock the product. Many supermarkets in Ghana have a 'sell or return policy' where they only pay the entrepreneur for products that actually sell and return those that do not sell. For a start-up, this approach could detrimentally affect cash flow.

• *Agents*

Agents take over the function of in-house salespeople. They are paid commissions only on sales made and receive nothing if they do not sell, which makes them attractive for new enterprises looking to minimise staff costs. It is important to tie commissions not only to booking the sale (recording the revenue) but also to receiving the cash (when the customer actually pays for the product), otherwise the entrepreneur may find that he is having to pay out commissions on sale transactions which the customer may never pay for or may delay significantly in paying for.

• *Franchising*

As described previously in Chapter 6, franchising is a form of licensing by which the owner (the franchisor) of a product, service or business method obtains distribution through affiliated dealers (franchisees). In return for the franchisor's support, the franchisee pays the franchisor an initial fee and would usually pay an annual royalty based on gross revenues for the franchisor's continued support and the use of brands, trademarks or business formats.

• *Wholesalers*

A wholesaler typically has many contacts across the retail trade and so a small enterprise may find it more cost-efficient to rely on the wholesaler to improve overall market penetration rather than to develop and maintain these contacts and channels itself . Wholesalers would however typically require that the products are given to them at a price low enough for them to make an attractive mark-up.

• *Stores*

Selling in the entrepreneur's own store is a good choice when the purchasing experience is central to the product decision and acquisition, and only a small number of stores are necessary to cover the market. Having own stores may require significant additional investment but also allows for the greatest control over distribution.

• *Direct Sales Representatives*

These are employees of the enterprise who call directly on its customers. Hiring a sales force can be expensive and the decision must be reached after carefully considering the pros and cons. Where the product or service requires an extensive knowledge of the product or service, as is the case in the sale of complex solutions, the entrepreneur may have to invest in his own sales force. For example, own sales staff would be a good idea in the sale of complex information technology solutions for corporate clients where the number of customers is fairly small.

• *Internet*

The Internet is a relatively cheap way of reaching a potentially global market. Since I consider the Internet to be more than a distribution channel, I discuss the Internet in more detail under e-commerce later in this chapter.

Promotions

Before potential customers can appreciate the entrepreneur's product or service, they must first hear about it and be convinced to purchase it. Promotion may involve persuading customers on a one-to-one basis, or it may involve communicating to customers through mass media such as radio, television and newspapers, with the view to attract attention to and inform, persuade and inspire confidence in the product or service.

The promotion must explain the value of the relevant product or service to potential customers as well as convince them that the particular product or service meets their needs better than competing or alternative solutions.

The key promotional tools are as follows:

• *Personal Selling*

Personal selling is probably the oldest form of marketing. It is essentially what the name suggests; directly selling a product or service to a customer either through face-to-face contact or by telephone or other electronic channels. Although it is an expensive method, it can be particularly effective in high-involvement and big-ticket categories where the customer needs guidance by sales representatives.

• *Advertising*

As Hinson notes, advertising "consists of a one-way communication about a good, service, an idea, a person or an organisation paid for by an identified sponsor or advertiser using a variety of media such as the print media (newspapers), electronic media (radio), outdoor displays (billboards), transportation, direct marketing, advertising specialties or novelties (T-shirts), catalogues, directories and films. Advertising promotes an organisation's image, reputation or idea. It also influences the sale of products and stimulates demand for specific brands."[10] The objective of advertising may be to inform (in the case of new-to-the-world products or brands, for example), persuade (highlighting particular features or benefits, compared to the competition, for example), remind (particularly with mature brands) or reinforce (assuring brand customers that they have made a good choice).

• Sales Promotion

Sales promotion refers to short-term tools and activities used to stimulate interest, trial or purchase of a product. Associated tools – coupons, discounts, competitions, sweepstakes, etc. – typically offer the customer an incentive to purchase the product.

• Public Relations/Publicity (PR)

Public relations is the means by which the enterprise relates with its 'publics'. An enterprise's publics are those who have an actual or potential interest in or impact on the enterprise's ability to achieve its objectives,[11] and may include employees, shareholders, customers (past, current and future), regulators, competitors, collaborators, business partners, industry decision makers and government officials. PR uses a wide variety of tools to promote an enterprise, its business, people and products to the enterprise's publics. PR tools include press releases, sponsorships, events, speeches, conferences, editorials, interviews and news stories. It may include articles in print media about the entrepreneur, his enterprise or product; they may be written by the entrepreneur himself or a journalist. The key difference between PR and advertising is that PR is not directly paid for by the advertiser or sponsor, and therefore tends to be cheaper than advertising. Because PR is typically positioned as being driven by a third party (the journalist, for example), it also appears to be more credible than advertising.

• Buzz Or Word-Of-Mouth Marketing

Buzz or word-of-mouth marketing involves seeking out trendsetters in each community and subtly pushing them into talking up the entrepreneur's brand to their friends and admirers.

For example, "Rather than blitzing the airwaves with 30-second television commercials for its new Focus subcompact, Ford Motor [Company] recruited just a handful of trendsetters in a few markets and gave them each a Focus to drive for six months. They were required simply to be seen with the car and to hand out Focus-themed trinkets to anyone who expressed interest in it."[12] Buzz marketing is cheap and can be particularly effective because of the credibility a recommendation by a trusted person brings. In a successful buzz campaign, each carefully cultivated recipient of the brand message becomes a powerful carrier, spreading the word to yet more carriers, arming consumers with the tools or knowledge they can take back to their peer groups so they'll be perceived as being in the know. As Scott Stratten notes, "Word of mouth is not a project or a viral marketing ploy. The mouths are already moving. You need to decide you want to be part of the conversation."[13]. However, the danger with buzz marketing is that the ultimate message is a bit more difficult to control.

• *Social Media/The New PR*
Social media relates to the way people share ideas, content, thoughts and relationships online. Social media differs from so-called mainstream media in that anyone can create, comment on, and add to social media content. Social media can take the form of text, audio, video, images and communities[14]. The most common forms are Facebook, Twitter, LinkedIn, MySpace, Google+ and blogs. Although these sites are primarily used in a domestic or social setting, they have become increasingly important and integrated into people's daily working lives. Particularly for younger people, social media is becoming the preferred method of communication. Entrepreneurs using social media should ensure that the image they present is consistent with the rest of their brand and brand identity. They must also create linkages with other customer touch points. For example, all profiles on social networking sites should include the enterprise's website address, logo and brand colours.

• Direct Marketing

Direct marketing involves communicating directly with the customer using communication tools other than face-to-face interaction, such as direct mail, telephone marketing and Internet marketing. Ghana Post has a marketing department that works with entrepreneurs to send out mailings to individuals and corporates with post boxes and private mail bags. For example, an entrepreneur wanting to advertise a salary advance product targeted at government workers could pay Ghana Post to send copies of a flier to each of the post office boxes and private mail bags at the Ministries post office in Accra, as the Ministries house a large concentration of government workers.

• Exhibitions And Fairs

Entrepreneurs may host or attend exhibitions or fairs to showcase their products and services. They may also host exhibitions that connects their customers with suppliers of other products and services in such a way as to build effective emotional connections with their customers. For example, the annual Joy FM Bridal Fair connects listeners of Joy FM who may be contemplating getting married with a wide range of professionals who cater to the wedding industry. By making this match between listeners and wedding services professionals, Joy FM creates (or reinforces) a positive affinity with its listeners.

• Visual Identity

The enterprise's visual identity is represented by a number of branding elements such as its logo, colours, stationery, business cards, brochures, website, corporate gifts, forms, uniforms and the look and feel of its offices. These become in many ways the most regular means by which the entrepreneur communicates with the public, as on any given day the enterprise will send out letters or invoices on its stationery, employees will give out business cards, people might visit the enterprise's website, etc. It is important that the visual identity that the entrepreneur settles on clearly communicates and reinforces the brand that the entrepreneur seeks to build.

• *Environments*

The environment(s) in which the customer interacts with the brand provide an opportunity for the entrepreneur to differentiate his brand from his competitive set. As Wheeler[15] puts it, "From a luxury showroom, to the inside of an airplane or a supermarket, smart businesses seize every opportunity to manage the experience and expectation of customers by branding the environment."

Table 11.1 Source: Kotler's *A Framework For Marketing Management*, 2001

Advertising	Sales Promotion	Public Relations	Personal Selling	Direct Marketing
Print, Broadcast, Online Ads, Packaging, Motion Pictures, Brochures, Booklets, Directories, Billboards, Posters, Display Signs, Point-Of-Purchase Displays, Audiovisual Material, Symbols And Logos, Videotapes, Websites and Banners	Contests, Games, Sweepstakes, Lotteries Premiums, Gifts, Sampling, Fairs, Trade Shows, Demonstrations, Coupons, Rebates, Low-Interest Financing, Trade-In Allowances, Continuity Programmes and Tie-Ins	Press Kits, Video News Releases, Speeches, Seminars, Annual Reports, Charitable Donations, Sponsorships, Publications, Community Relations, Lobbying, Identity Media and Special Events	Sales Presentations, Sales Meetings, Incentive Programmes, Fairs and Trade Shows,	Catalogues Mailings, Telemarketing, Electronic Shopping, Television Shopping Fax Mail, Email and Voicemail

• *Sponsorship*

Sponsorship of events provides an opportunity for the entrepreneur to develop and communicate his brand by associating it with an event or cause that the customer identifies with. The event or activity that the entrepreneur would like to sponsor must fit into the overall marketing goals of entrepreneur, and must ideally provide obvious 'halo effects' for the brand. For example, by sponsoring the Accra Marathon, Milo is able to reinforce its brand position as the drink of champions. Sponsorship of an event may provide the entrepreneur with an opportunity to reach his target audience in a non-intrusive manner, and to introduce his product through giveaways and sampling, for example.

• *Merchandising*

Merchandising consists of communication tools at the point of purchase (bars or shops, for example) which influence the final decision of the customer. The premise of merchandising is that in many customer markets, the consumers' final decision is made inside and not outside the point of sale. The beverage companies in Ghana, for example, use merchandising in the bars and restaurants where their products are sold; their merchandising tools, each with prominent branding, include fridges, T-shirts for bar staff, glasses, coasters, beer mats, trays, ice buckets, bottle openers, clocks and calendars.

Communication can be expensive so entrepreneurs should ensure that the chosen promotional tools are the best ones to give maximum returns, given the product or service and the target customer. In communicating with customers, the focus should be on the people who make the purchasing decisions or have the greatest influence on those purchasing decisions.

The goal of an entrepreneur's promotional efforts should be to create a brand image as well as to persuade customers to buy and to develop brand loyalty. Developing a brand for a product or service is one way to ensure that customers develop an emotional connection with a product or service. Brands try to create this emotional connection with a product or service based on name, imagery and positioning.

Choosing a Brand Name

The first step in creating a brand might be finding or developing a catchy name that is likely to appeal to potential customers, given the kind of image and personality the entrepreneur wants to build. Once the brand name has been chosen, a brand personality and image should be developed to ensure that the product or service is communicated to the customers in a manner that is consistent with the image or brand the entrepreneur is aiming for. An entrepreneur setting up a cake shop may, for example, call it 'Cakeworld' to communicate that the enterprise stocks a wide variety of cakes. He or she may then develop a brand personality and image to suggest that the brand is for discerning and upwardly mobile people wanting to treat themselves to a fine exotic cake or wanting to escape the day-to-day pressures of their lives with such a cake. If this is the case, it will be important that all the steps involved in the cake buying and eating experience at Cakeworld are consistent with this personality. Top-notch ingredients should be used and the presentation should also be consistent with this image. Alternatively, if the entrepreneur was targeting the masses, the name chosen might be 'Cheapocakes' to communicate its downmarket appeal. The cakes will probably not come in fancy boxes in a variety of colours but probably in simple polythene bags (the type the broad Ghanaian masses call 'take away'). The cakes themselves may not be of a large variety, with perhaps simply two or three key 'basic' cakes.

As we discussed in Chapter 6, depending on the name chosen, a sole proprietor may need to register under the Registration of Business Names Act, 1962 (Act 151). The elements that make up the brand identity may also require registration as a trademark at the Copyright Office.[16]

Segmentation, Targeting and Positioning

The entrepreneur must first segment the market to target the particular group of customers that he seeks to focus on for the particular product or service. It is possible (as assumed in Chapter 4 when discussing concept validation) that at the time of developing the initial concept, the entrepreneur has an idea of which customer segments to target. In such a case, the concept validation stage can help the entrepreneur to better hone these segments. However, in many cases, the entrepreneur may be unclear as to which group of customers should constitute the target market.

Customer or market segmentation consists of sub-dividing the total market into distinct and homogeneous groups of customers who have similar needs and respond similarly to the marketing mix variables. The target market consists of the core group of customers at which the enterprise aims its products and services. Customers in the target market would typically have common characteristics, aspirations, taste and features. Customer segmentation inevitably involves trade-offs based on alternative value propositions. It assumes that the entrepreneur does not have an equal chance of selling to every customer in the market, and therefore has to carve out a niche to whom his products will appeal most and focus on those customers. The entrepreneur cannot serve all possible market segments well, given the nature of the product or service, his limited resources and particular skills and competencies. Many entrepreneurs fail because they want to go after every possible segment in the market and end up pleasing no one.

Segmentation Variables

The most common variables used to segment markets include the following:

Geographic Segmentation

As the name implies it involves dividing the market into geographical zones such as cities, towns and districts, or even countries or continents. For example, it may be necessary to target on a geographic basis because customers for the same product may respond differently from Tamale to Kumasi, or because the entrepreneur can realistically only operate in certain parts of the country. An entrepreneur selling high-end coffins may decide to locate in Kumasi rather than Tamale because funerals (and high-end coffins) are a big part of life in Kumasi. In Tamale however, given the predominantly Muslim population, demand for high-end coffins and elaborate funerals is low.

Demographic Segmentation

This divides the market into groups on the basis of demographic information such as age, gender, income and social class. Through this segmentation variable, an entrepreneur may target recent graduates for his line of stylish but cheap work suits because this group generally has limited income and may be on their first proper jobs where they are required to wear suits for the first time. A provider of retirement plans would probably target middle-age couples who, after educating their children, are beginning to worry about their own future.

Psychographic Segmentation

This focuses on lifestyle, personality or values. Using this variable might reveal a group of executives who may be willing to pay for a daily summary of the key news items by email because, although they crave information, they typically do not get time to read newspapers in their entirety.

Behavioural Segmentation

This uses the behaviour of the target in relation to the particular product or service category. In Chapter 4, when we discussed quantitative research, I mentioned that both Allure and Melting Moments have consumer loyalty cards. The behavioural data provided by these loyalty cards' usage patterns could be used to segment the market and to reach and reward heavy users. Under behavioural segmentation, an entrepreneur could segment his customers based on the following:

» Occasions: The idea that people respond differently to different products based on the occasion. For example, 'last-minute' purchasers of air tickets are willing to pay more than those who book in advance.

» Usage Rate: The most frequent users of a product or service may be less price sensitive than occasional users.

Customer Profiles

To get a good understanding of the characteristics, needs, wants and desires of the various customer segments so as to determine what value propositions would work best for each of them, it is helpful to build a rich picture of the different target segments through customer profiling.

Customer profiling simply involves listing all the key segments and describing their key distinguishing characteristics, needs, wants and desires as well as attitudes, behaviour, demographics, psychographics and media consumption patterns. It is important to use as many different segmentation variables for the same target groups to build the most comprehensive picture of what those target groups really look like. After profiling, each segment is given a name based on the dominant characteristic.

The profile description should be as detailed as possible to help the entrepreneur as well as his employees and third parties he or she works with (such as advertising agencies) to get a clear understanding of the customer segments, so as to determine which to target and also how best to reach particular segments with products and service features, and benefits as well as marketing communications.

An analysis of the car market in Accra, for example, may reveal the following customer segments.

Status-Driven

This group is made up of 'posers' who want to be seen in a particular car only because of the status it confers on them. Likely to be made up of high-net -worth and high-income individuals with varying educational backgrounds. The uneducated ones will be entrepreneurs (both legitimate and non-legitimate ones) who like to 'flash' their wealth and sometimes feel that it compensates for a lack of education. The educated ones would most probably be relatively younger, ostentatious people. A disproportionate number in this group would be men. This group is likely to drive cars such as top-of-the-range models from Mercedes-Benz, BMW, Lexus, Bentley and Jaguar Land Rover.

Value-Driven

This target would cut across age ranges and would have less disposable income than the status-driven group. They typically would seek to make the most of the money they have and so in shopping for cars, they would be concerned about value for money; they would want cars that 'do the job' at an affordable cost. They would equally be open to new and second-hand cars (home-used second hand) and would favour brands like Toyota, Honda or Nissan because of their adaptability for Ghanaian roads, the price of servicing and widespread availability of spare parts.

Utility-Driven

This target is likely to see cars for the functional roles they play, and may shop accordingly. It may of consist mothers with several kids, for example, for whom estate cars hold greater appeal, or men who travel long distances, for whom 4X4 sports utility vehicles are attractive.

There are several other possible segments in the car market. The above is meant to be simply illustrative.

Given that different situations may affect who becomes a target, it is important to develop the customer profile with a view on which situations would make different groups of people target customers.

The choice of which target to serve will depend on a number of factors, which might include the size of the target group and potential growth rate, the purchasing power of the target group, the competency of the entrepreneur in meeting the needs of that target group and the gaps resulting from the lack of attention given to this target group by the competition. The opportunity analysis carried out by the entrepreneur and discussed in Chapter 4 should help in making the targeting decision and developing brand strategies and objectives which take into account the enterprise's core competencies and resource limits.

Targeting

After segmenting the market, the entrepreneur must 'position' the product or service to appeal to the target market. The marketing tactics that are used to market the product should be capable of reaching the target market, and must appeal to members of that set who in turn will be moved to purchase the product.

To position the product or service, the entrepreneur will need to define who exactly her target customer is. She will then use the marketing mix variables to target this customer with her brand-building message to get the customer to hopefully move from ignorance (of the product or service) to advocacy, in a path defined by the scale set out below. The reverse is also true – it is just as important for the entrepreneur to know which customer segments it will not serve.

Lack of Awareness → Awareness → Knowledge → Evaluation
→ Trial → Adoption → Advocacy/Repeat Purchase

The target is the person who chooses the brand. He may be the ultimate user of the product or service or a gatekeeper (like a mother or a procurement officer) who makes the decision relating to the acquisition of the product or service, although someone else (a child or an executive officer) may consume or use the product. Care must be taken to ensure that the entrepreneur understands both the ultimate consumer and the decision maker in significant detail.

The target customer is at the front, centre and end of any successful brand strategy, and all aspects of that strategy must revolve around him. In making decisions about the marketing mix, the entrepreneur must focus on the core customer he seeks to serve and ensure that whatever he is proposing would resonate with that customer.

Positioning

Positioning is an "act of designing the company's offering and image to occupy a distinctive place in the target market's mind. The end result of positioning is the successful creation of a market-focused value proposition, a cogent reason why the market should buy the product."[17] As Kotler notes, "positioning starts with the product, a piece of merchandise, a service, a company, an institution or even a person ... But positioning is not what you do to a product. Positioning is what you do to the mind of the prospect. That is, you position the product in the mind of the prospect."[18]

Through positioning the entrepreneur communicates the value he offers the target, reinforcing the product's appeal to ensure that the target purchases the product.

As the very word 'positioning' suggests, a product or service is positioned in the mind of the customer relative to other products or services – typically competitor or substitute products and services – which perform the same function for the customer.

The entrepreneur must clearly define and understand the category or market that the brand plays in. Does Club Beer, for example, compete in the beer market, the alcoholic beverage market or the beverage market?. One way that some drink brands define their market is to look at the 'share of throat' – the things that compete to go through the throat (presumably without chewing so as to exclude food). Using this approach, water can be seen as a competitor of Club Beer, as will tea and soft drinks. As a result, the category that Club Beer competes in becomes all beverages rather than simply beers or alcoholic beverages.

It is important to establish the category because the entrepreneur must have an understanding of what customers think both of the brand and the category in which the brand holds membership (i.e. the brand's market or industry). The category provides a frame of reference for the customer to evaluate the brand and compare it to other competing brands in the same category. Sometimes though, the frame of reference for the customer may not relate to any particular category, but to the goals that a particular product or service helps him achieve. The customer will consider as a frame of reference all products and services that enable him to attain a particular goal. For example, if the customer's goal is recreation and unwinding after a hard week's work, then his frame of reference may cut across a number of categories and might include sports, restaurants, cinema, gaming consoles, books, nightclubs and destination spas.

Establishing the category or frame of reference for the customer enables the entrepreneur to first position his product or service as a member of the category, and to show that the product or service provides the same basic features or benefits offered by all other products and services in the category. Such features and benefits are called points of parity. For example, Club Beer claims parity with other products in the beverages space because it refreshes and quenches thirst. Point of parity then becomes the lowest common denominator that binds all the brands in the category.

After establishing points of parity, the entrepreneur must establish the points of difference for his particular brand. This revolves around the question of exactly how his brand differs from other brands in the category. As Keller notes, "The world's most successful brands keep up with competitors by creating points of parity in those areas where competitors are trying to find an advantage while at the same time creating points of difference to achieve advantages over the competition in some other areas."[19]

Establishing category membership comes before establishing a point of difference because customers must first accept that the relevant product or service is like other products or services in the category, or that it fulfils the customer's goals. Only after establishing this can the entrepreneur proceed to establish that his product or service performs the goals better than other competing offerings, or that he has features and benefits that are superior to the other choices that the customer may have in mind.

For new-to-the-world products, the product's brand will be developed simultaneously with developing a frame of reference for the customer.

Defining the category, industry or frame of reference, establishing the generic category benefits, identifying what would be meaningful points of difference and developing a detailed and vivid description of the customer will all be informed by customer insights.

Products and services may be positioned by the following:

• *Product Attributes*

These are physical characteristics of a product such as colour, size and flavour. For some products, like computers, attributes are very important.

• *Price*

The two extremes of positioning based on price are common: where the product is positioned as a mass market product that as many people as possible can afford; and where the product is positioned as an exclusive product that is the preserve of a limited, affluent few.

• *Users and Usage Occasions*

Certain people use the product for particular occasions (e.g. cold medication when they have the flu).

• *Image*

This refers to people and occasions. Products like fragrances are positioned around image.

• *Customer Goals*

The goals that the customer is able to achieve with the product or service.

• *Benefits*

A benefit is an abstract concept such as convenience, pleasure or fun,[20] based on attributes or usage for particular occasions.

• *Origin*

Where associating with a particular geographic location connotes a particular image. For example many German cars use this positioning because of the reputation of German automobile engineering.

As products and services typically have different features and benefits, the challenge sometimes is to determine how many (or which) differences (features, benefits, solutions to the customer's goals, etc.) to promote. Given that the whole essence of segmentation, targeting and positioning is to enable the enterprise to dominate based on particular attributes or customer goals (positioning) that matter to his target, my view is that the better approach is for the entrepreneur to decide one key feature or goal on which to differentiate his offering from others. With this approach, each brand can be touted as 'number one' on a particular attribute. For example, Coca-Cola is positioned as a soft drink that refreshes, so its marketing communication aims to make you think of Coca-Cola whenever you are thirsty. Expresso (previously Kasapa) is positioned on value or price, and communicates that it is cheaper than its competitors (its original tagline 'Kasapa – good talk, great value', reflected this). Its competitor MTN however is positioned around 'reach'. MTN's initial tagline was 'communication for the nation', which evolved to 'from a local to a global network'; now it is 'everywhere you go', which captures the idea that MTN services are widely available. Key Soap is positioned around heritage and pedigree. The idea is that it is good for you because your mother and her mother before her used it.

Once a clear position has been developed for the product or service, this position must be clearly and consistently communicated. The enterprise's entire strategy must be consistent with the agreed positioning. Coca-Cola, for example, as a result of its positioning has a strategy of ensuring that there are sellers of Coca-Cola wherever you are (and are likely to be thirsty). It also encourages that the product is served cold, again to emphasise its 'refreshing' nature. MTN invests heavily in upgrading its service to ensure coverage across most parts of the country. Expresso's services, for example, could never be priced higher than MTN if it is to be true to its positioning.

For positioning to be successful, it must possess the following attributes.

• *Believable*

It must offer customers something that they believe can be

delivered by the brand. For example, the erstwhile made-in-Ghana vehicle, the Boafo, could never have positioned itself as a luxury car.

• *Competitive*

It must offer customers benefits they consider to be valuable.

• *Consistent*

It must offer customers the same message over and over again.

• *Clearly Differentiated*

It must offer customers a clearly differentiated position from the competition. Atlantis FM, for example, has positioned itself successfully as the radio station with 'less talk and more music'.

Differentiation

Positioning a product relative to the competitive set also requires that the product or service which forms the basis of targeting customers must be clearly distinguishable from the competition. This is called differentiation. Most profitable strategies are built on differentiation: offering customers something that they value that competitors don't have. Enterprises tend to focus on differentiating themselves only on the basis of their products or services. But an enterprise has the opportunity to differentiate itself at every point where it comes into contact with its customers – from the moment customers realise that they need a product or service to the time when they no longer want it and decide to dispose of it.[21]

To continually identify new points of differentiation and develop the ability to generate successful differentiation strategies, companies must do the following.

Consumption Chain Mapping

Firstly, the enterprise must map the customer consumption chain for each important customer segment. This should involve mapping the customer's entire experience with the relevant product or service. This will be done by identifying all the steps through which customers pass from the time they first become aware of the product or service to the time when they finally have to dispose of it or discontinue using it.

Analysis

After mapping, the enterprise must then analyse customers' experiences to gain insights into the their behavioural patterns by appreciating the context within which each step of the consumption chain unfolds. Then, based on the entrepreneur's strengths, his reading of the competition, etc., the entrepreneur must develop points of differentiation at all the customer touch points.[22] For a new enterprise, differentiation can start from the name (picking a name that resonates with the customer and stands out in the relevant category), recruiting staff (who will interact with customers), how the telephone is answered, the look and feel of the enterprise's website, the layout and design of the premises, the stationery, etc.

Positioning Statement

Once the entrepreneur has defined the market, segmented it, determined his target and positioned his product or service to occupy a particular place in the mind of the target, he must articulate this positioning in the form of a positioning statement. This statement will succinctly capture the value proposition for the target and form the basis of communicating with the target. The positioning statement is an internal document that may be shared with the sales team, the advertising agency and, more generally, with those for whom it is important to understand who the target is and what prompts them to choose the company's brand. It is a general summary of the key aspects of the marketing strategy and, as such, it serves as the foundation for all decisions about all elements of the marketing mix. The positioning statement addresses the following four statements:

» Who should be targeted for brand use?

» When should the brand be considered (i.e. what goal does the brand allow the target to achieve)?

» Why should the brand be chosen over other alternatives in the competitive set?
» How will choosing the brand help the target to accomplish his goal(s)?[23]

An example of a positioning statement for a new window replacement company Cocoase Windows may look like this:

> To 35-60 year old Kumasi females, Cocoase window is a window replacement specialist that you, your family and friends can trust to take the hassle out of replacing windows any day, any time.

The following is an example of how segmentation, targeting and positioning works: Kofi is a trainee chef at La Palm Royal Beach Hotel. At work one day, he mixed a number of fruits with milk to produce a delicious milk drink that he now wants to market. He has limited resources and knows that he cannot market this milk drink to everyone in the market. To determine which market segment his drink would provide the most value for, he first defines the market to be made up of all the residents of Accra, and then breaks up the market into distinct segments. Once he has done this, he picks the segments that he believes would most value the product that he is offering. There are many different ways Kofi could segment the market to determine which target to go for. His options include:

- Milk drinkers;
- People who do not drink milk;
- Mothers with babies;
- Children;
- Schools;
- Hospitals.

Each potential target group has different characteristics and needs, and would consequently respond differently to the different elements of the marketing mix. If Kofi decides to target milk drinkers he may simply position the product as a different type of milk product and in all his communication messages (i.e. his frame of reference will be milk), and he might stress the 'milk element' of the drink. He might even decide to include the word 'milk' in the name of the product. However, if he decides to target people who do not drink milk, he would stress the fruit ingredients rather than milk and position the drink closer to other fruit juices (his frame of reference being fruit juices).

If he decides to target children directly, he may have to make the product sweeter, more colourful and use vivid packaging, and perhaps stress the 'fun' aspects of drinking the milk drink. As many children do not like milk, he may achieve more success with children by not referring to the 'milk' ingredients (his frame of reference will be anything that brings fun to children). On the contrary, if he decides to target mothers with children, he might have to stress the milk ingredient, and the nutritious value of the product in particular (his frame of reference will be nutritional products for children).

As the above example demonstrates, depending on the market segment targeted, the positioning of a product can change significantly, to reflect the goals, aspirations and needs of members of the target group.

E-Commerce

The Internet is another channel which can generate additional sales of a product or service. For example, a producer of Kente artefacts at the arts centre in Accra could increase her sales if she invests in getting a presence on the web. Selling on the Web also provides a way for small businesses to expand their reach to global markets at a cost much cheaper than might be the case if they were to invest in a physical presence. The Internet is essentially a 24-hour shop that enables the entrepreneur to be always open.

If used well, the Internet can help lower the cost of doing business as it provides an efficient way of reaching a massive clientèle. For consumer products targeted at only the local masses, it could be debated if it is worth using the Internet, given the relatively low Internet penetration in Ghana. As a distribution channel, the Internet has yet to make a significant impact in Ghana because of the limited number of people with credit cards. However, emerging solutions like BSL's African Liberty card are beginning to facilitate more online transactions.

Moreover, the usefulness of the Internet to an entrepreneur goes beyond advertising; it can be a great way to connect with suppliers and customers as well as collect information about customers and the competition. The Internet, where it is appropriate to use for a business, is a good medium to educate customers. Because of the nature of the Internet and the whole process of browsing the World Wide Web, it is a good place to provide information to consumers about various products and services.

Entrepreneurs however must not underestimate the cost and time involved in setting up an effective website. It is important to seek the right technical advice to ensure that websites are set up correctly to 'entice' potential customers.

Websites can accomplish the following for enterprises:

- Promote corporate identification and be part of image building by disseminating press releases, recent articles, product and other marketing information;
- Provide information about what an enterprise makes (or sells), as well as provide links to physical places where products can be bought;
- Provide a scaled-down online version of the enterprise – particularly relevant in the case of a store – where customers can be offered some of the products sold in the main shop, and can typically be done in such a way that the customer is enticed to go to the shop for the full experience;
- Be alternative versions of the entire enterprise, where customers can shop for the product.

An entrepreneur looking to set up a website for his enterprise must have a business reason to start the website – something that he wants the site to do. He should not start a website simply because everyone seems to have a website these days.

E-commerce is however more than simply building a website. The website should form part of (and be consistent with) the entire marketing strategy. For example, the entrepreneur should conflate certain elements of his marketing mix with his website. Advertisements on television, radio or in the print media should end with a reference to the website address so that those who want further information can visit the website. The entrepreneur could also make it possible for some of the enterprise's advertisements showing on television to be viewed and/or downloaded from his website. The packaging of an item produced by an entrepreneur should also have the website address.

The Internet provides what Slywotzky calls 'choiceboards' – interactive, online systems that allow individual customers to design their own products by choosing from a menu of attributes, components, prices, and delivery options; the customer's selections send signals to the supplier's manufacturing system that set in motion the wheels of procurement, assembly and delivery, a progression that is in contrast with the guesswork carried out by suppliers to forecast what the customer might want.[24]

Because choiceboards collect precise information about the preferences and behaviours of individual buyers, they enable companies to secure customer loyalty: "With each transaction, a company becomes more knowledgeable about the customer and hence better able to anticipate and fulfil that customer's needs."[25]

Entrepreneurs relying on the World Wide Web to build brands and to drive sales must manage the consumer's online experience of the product, from first encounter through purchase to delivery and beyond. As Dayal et al. note, building a brand on the Internet requires "an approach for aligning the promises [made to] consumers, the Web design necessary to deliver those promises [online], and the economic model required to turn a profit. These three elements – the promise, the design and the economic model – together form the inseparable components of a successful Internet business or what might be called a digital brand."[26]

Media Strategy

To ensure that the entrepreneur's spend is effective and able to achieve as much bang for his buck as possible, it is important for the entrepreneur to understand both the strengths and weaknesses of the media available as well as detailed knowledge about the marketplace – in particular how customers consume media and how competitors will spend on procuring media space.

Firstly, he must select the media to transmit the relevant message. This could be broadcast media (television and radio), print media such as magazines and newspapers, as well as outdoor, transit, direct mail, the Internet and directories (such as Surf Ghana).

Once the desired media are chosen, he needs to select the appropriate vehicle. If magazines are the medium, vehicle selection may be made from among magazines such as *Business Times, Agoo, Ovation, Business World* and *Emerge*. If television is the medium, the particular programmes and the time of the day in which commercials are aired constitute the vehicles. Vehicle selection will be influenced by factors such as circulation (number of units of a newspaper sold, for example, through which the communication can be distributed), audience (the number of people who are exposed to the vehicle used to transmit the communication) and effective audience (the number of people with the target's characteristics who are exposed to the vehicle used to transmit the communication).

Finally, the vehicles selected are organised to compose a media schedule that holistically shows in which particular magazines, newspapers, television or radio programmes and Internet websites that the communication will be transmitted to target customers over a period.

Kuenyehia on Entrepreneurship

Creative Strategy[27]

Creative strategy involves developing the copy and the context in which the message content is presented. The objectives of effective creative strategy are to create brand communication that appeals and persuades the target, and to build a strong linkage between the brand name and what is said about the brand in the communication.

There are a number of options that may be used in developing creative strategy. These include:

• *Hard Sell*

This involves communication in which a simple associative bond is made between a brand and its benefit: 'buy this, get this benefit'.

• *The Big Idea*

This involves identifying a benefit that is focal to customers (usually the benefit that defines a category) and, over time, presenting a variety of attributes to imply the benefit.

• *Comparative Advertising*

This is where the benefits of a brand are compared against that of the competition.

• *Testimonials*

This is where people who have had good experiences with the brand share their experiences to convince others to adopt the relevant offering.

Briefing and Working with an Agency

Often, an entrepreneur will rely on a brand agency to execute part or all of his promotional strategy. If the entrepreneur decides to work with an agency, it is critical that the entrepreneur instructs an agency only after he himself (and his leadership team) have understood (or at least formed a view about) the key behaviours of their target customer, and the key insights around which he hopes to develop his communication strategy.

He must also take the driving position in developing and managing the brand and not simply leave it to the agency. Taking this approach prevents the problem that sometimes occurs after enterprises hire agencies – distance between managers and their key asset,, the brand, which will be the driver of future growth opportunities. Also, this approach enables the entrepreneur to challenge the agency to ensure that it focuses on a customer-led, coordinated brand-building effort that accesses alternative media rather than simply relying on the mass media channels that most agencies' talents, incentives and inclinations still lead them to suggest.[28]

The type of agency that the entrepreneur is able to hire will obviously depend on the resources the entrepreneur has. However, no matter how limited his resources are, the entrepreneur must research the different agencies available in the market who might be able to work with the resources that he has.

He should then send out a brief to each of these agencies and invite them to respond by setting out how they intend to execute the brief. He should ask for face-to-face presentations with each of the agencies to enable him to choose the agency or agencies he has the most chemistry with.

The general brand or communication brief will summarise the key elements of the brand that he wants to communicate to the public. Then, depending on the promotional tools he settles on, he will have separate briefs for each of them.

A brief will include the following.

» **Background**

   The background will set the context for the brief, and include key trends in the market and among competitors, and introduce the brand proposition or positioning.

» **Customer**

   This section will summarise who they are (gatekeepers vs.

consumers, etc.), their usage habits and the key insights that will be driving brand building.

» Objective

This states what the entrepreneur hopes to achieve by deploying the particular promotional tools (e.g. is it to generate awareness, to reinvigorate a mature brand, or to drive purchase?).

» Desired Customer Results

This considers the objective from the customer standpoint and states exactly what the entrepreneur hopes the customer will do once he has been exposed to the branding efforts.

» Functional and Emotional Benefits

This summarises the functional and emotional benefits that the product or service provides the customer.

» Reason to Believe

This sets explains why the customer should believe that the brand, product or service should be trusted to deliver the said functional and/or emotional benefits.

» Tone and Voice

This captures how the execution should sound and feel – classy, urban, upbeat, etc.

» Mandatories

These are the things that all promotional tools relating to the brand will need to incorporate, like the website address, a tagline, etc.

» Measurement and Evaluation

This lays out how the effectiveness of promotional tools will be measured and what success would look like.

» Timing

This establishes the time frame for the brand-building project.

Measurement and Evaluation

It is not enough to simply spend money building a brand without measuring the impact of the various promotional tools used and the various elements of the marketing mix. Using the marketing research concepts discussed in Chapter 4, the entrepreneur must evaluate all aspects of her brand plan. She must feed the results of this research into future brand programmes to ensure effectiveness.

Personal Branding

I agree with Tom Peter when he says that "Today, in the Age of the Individual, you have to be your own brand ... Regardless of age, regardless of position, regardless of the business we happen to be in, all of us need to understand the importance of branding. We are CEOs of our own companies: Me[,] Inc. To be in business today, our most important job is to be head marketer for the brand called You ... Everyone has a chance to stand out. Everyone has a chance to learn, improve, and build their skills. Everyone has a chance to be a brand worthy of remark."[29]

My team's research on Ghanaian business leaders who are developing personal branding shows that many of them have indeed failed to understand exactly how personal branding works. They acknowledge the importance of personal branding, but they do not go through the essential process of identifying what their brand essence is or should be, and what their target should be; they jump to choosing promotional tools, typically those that give them maximum visibility.

In my opinion, this approach dilutes the personal brand of these business leaders and indeed makes them lose the very brand differentiating factors that they aspire to promote. It is a customer truism that the more available a product is, the cheaper it is perceived to be. This is true also in personal branding: other than truly mass-target personal brands such as political leaders, it is important that individuals seeking to build personal brands ensure that they play only within identified relevant target groups.

Personal branding is not about seeing one's face in the daily newspapers regularly, or being interviewed online, or being always ready to offer an opinion on radio or television, or accepting as many speaking engagements as possible. Recall that I emphasised earlier that the whole concept of branding rests on differentiation: firstly define a market, then segment it to define a target, then define a unique position in the mind of the target so as to differentiate the brand from its competitive set.

The first step in developing an effective personal brand is to carry out a self-assessment to identity your strengths, weakness, qualities and characteristics that make you distinctive from your competitors. Competitors may be other entrepreneurs, other members of a profession, community leaders, politicians, etc.

As Peters put it, "The key to any personal branding campaign is 'word-of-mouth marketing'. Your network of friends, clients, and customers is the most important marketing vehicle you've got: what they say about you and your contributions is what the market will ultimately gauge as the value of your brand."[30]

So once you have defined what particular characteristics of your personal brand that you would want to communicate, you should focus on developing a network of people who are gatekeepers to your target group to whom you regularly communicate the core elements of your brand. If you would like to develop a brand around thought leadership in a particular sector (for example, information communication technologies (ICTs)), you might decide to put yourself up for election to the technology committee of the local chamber of commerce that you are a member of. In that capacity, you will have an opportunity to have your voice heard and to showcase your talent and expertise to a key constituent. You may also decide to first of all attend the key technology conferences where all technology decision makers gather. After attending this conference a few times, you may position yourself to be on a discussion panel, and then ultimately position yourself to give the keynote address at a future conference.

You may decide to write articles in respected technology journals or may even decide to teach at a local university. Teaching a technology elective on a MBA or an Executive MBA program, for example, will bring you into contact with many high-level decision makers and aspiring business leaders.

Just as the total customer experience is important in branding products and services, "when you are promoting brand You, everything you do – and everything you choose not to do – communicates the value and character for the brand. Everything from the way you handle phone conversations to the email messages you send to the way you conduct business in a meeting is part of the larger message that you are sending about your brand ... Partly[,] it's a matter of substance: what you have to say and how well you get it said. But it's also a matter of style."[31]

Case Study: Establishing Category Leadership Through Effective Branding at Allure

N SEPTEMBER 2010, DZIGBORDI DOSOO, the founder and chief executive officer of Allure Ghana Limited, was named the Chartered Institute of Marketing Ghana (CIMG) Marketing Woman of the Year 2009.[32] The CIMG adjudged that Allure Ghana, under Mrs Dosoo's management, had outshone its competitors in each of the thirteen selection criteria for the award,[33] including the public image criterion. The award was a deserved achievement, marking Allure Ghana's impressive growth from a two-person beauty parlour in 1998 into Ghana's premier and leading provider of day spa beauty services and wellness treatments, with two divisions: Allure Spa in the City and Allure Man.[34] Even more importantly, the award validated Allure Ghana's efforts to market its services to its target audiences by creating and managing a brand that captures and communicates the company's innovativeness and commitment to customer service.

Dzigbordi Dosoo started Allure Ghana in 1998 as a beauty parlour. Having built up companies in the financial services and consulting industries, Allure Ghana was a sideline business through which she sought to live out her passion for spa treatment and beauty service delivery. In 2005, as the beauty parlour had grown into a sustainable small-scale business, Mrs Dosoo decided to steer the young company into the spa treatment business to expand its target markets, becoming only the second provider of spa treatments in the country.[35] At the time very few Ghanaians had any idea of what spas were, or what the preventive treatments they provided were useful for.[36] This was not surprising given that the modern Ghanaian approach to healthcare has focused on disease treatment rather than prevention. Mrs Dosoo realised immediately that Allure Ghana's success depended on creating a market for her company. After careful consideration, she concluded that the best way to achieve this involved educating the Ghanaian public on the usefulness of spa treatments in reducing stress and preventing related diseases. By educating the general public, she would build up interest in a segment of the population for spa treatments, a section that could then become her potential customer base.

However, to secure the business of this potential customer base, the process of spreading the usefulness of spas needed to position Allure Ghana as the place to go to for the best possible treatment. To successfully achieve this, Mrs Dosoo had to make the Allure brand indistinguishable from spa treatments; if Ghanaians came to equate spa treatments with Allure Ghana, then her mission would have been successful.

As Mrs Dosoo recounts how she came up with the name and logo of Allure Ghana, one cannot help but admire her creativity and logical reasoning skills. "I chose to name the company Allure, because 'allure' represents 'attraction'. I wanted to appeal to people, to create attraction to my business." The butterfly logo was crafted for the same reasons, because the butterfly not only symbolises attraction; it is also emblematic of evolution, an attribute that has been important in the continuous transformation of Allure Ghana.

When it came time to create awareness about spas and to establish and grow the Allure Ghana brand, Mrs Dosoo sought professional help from Insel Communications. Mrs Dosoo and her partners at Insel brainstormed on ways to make Allure Ghana 'more unique in an already unique industry'. As Mrs Audrey Eni of Insel Communications put it, Allure Ghana needed to develop and communicate a strong and consistent identity to match its doubly unique value proposition.[37] To achieve this, Mrs Dosoo decided to position Allure Ghana as a niche provider of day spa treatments, differentiating it from its competitor.

As Allure Ghana had a limited budget for the project, both partners concluded after a lot of careful thought that the best way to reach to the market was to produce an infomercial that would simultaneously educate Ghanaians on the benefits of spa treatments while positioning Allure Ghana as the prime provider of spa treatments. The infomercial was designed for broadcast on television and on Allure Ghana's properties, and also for use on corporate road shows that aimed to educate relevant at-risk segments of the Ghanaian public on stress management, stress mitigation and stress-related disease prevention, through instruction and experience of sample treatments.

Realising that the maintenance of a positive public image of the Allure Ghana brand rests on providing excellent customer service, Allure Ghana implemented a customer relationship management (CRM) system shortly after it began operations. Consisting of, among others, customer satisfaction surveys and customer hotlines, the system is used by Mrs Dosoo and her team to manage a process of constant feedback looping, where customer praise and complaints are used as bases for continuous service improvement.

Allure Ghana's remarkable and unique service at the Kotoka International Airport (KIA) in Accra provides a prime example of the company's deployment of its strategy to drum up business in new segments of the public. In partnership with Aviance Ghana, KIA's managers, Allure Ghana launched the Akwaaba Lounge Spa. Each week, the spa provides free sampler massages and stress management education to between 800 and 1,000 business travellers in transit at the Akwaaba Lounge at the airport. With each treatment comes a discount card for use at Allure Ghana's main outlets in Accra. This sideline has quickly grown into a very successful channel of new business for Allure Ghana, with an impressive 15% of all beneficiaries using the discount cards to enjoy paid treatment at Allure Ghana's main outlets,[38] pointing to successful positioning of the Allure Ghana brand to this target audience.

With its presence established in the Ghanaian market, Allure Ghana has turned its sights to the African market. To achieve establishment and success in Africa, Allure Ghana developed the Iyaba trade fair as its dedicated vehicle. Iyaba has been positioned as "a forum that brings together [...] international expert representatives of [...] various brands to train professionals in the spa and beauty industry who will transform their clients to fulfil their desired wishes."[39] Iyaba, which is free of charge to participants, has grown from its humble beginnings into a very successful annual event, with the 2010 edition boasting over 2,000 participants from all over Africa. As the convener, Iyaba provides Allure Ghana with the opportunity to manage information flow within the industry, and to capitalise on this opportunity to market itself, along with its brand, as the leading light driving the improvement of standards on the continent. As Allure Ghana has moved into marketing related manufactured products as well, Iyaba provides a platform to market these products to leading practitioners across the continent. The newly converted practitioners then spread the message and generate further business for Allure Ghana.

In just over a decade, Allure Ghana has grown into a very successful practitioner within the spa and beauty industry. It has achieved this impressive feat by building a powerful and highly respected brand through spreading ideas and identifying and marketing remarkable treatments and services to relevant target audiences. As long as it continues to break into new territories through these means, Allure Ghana's growth, continued success, and attendant accolades to the company and its founder, should be guaranteed.

Questions for Case Discussion:

1. What factors have contributed to the success of the Allure brand?
2. What are the dangers of using brand building tools to develop the category as Allure has done? What are the advantages?
3. In what ways does Iyaba complement the Allure brand? In what ways might it hurt it?

Questions for Class Discussion

1. What steps would you take to establish a brand from scratch?
2. What are the pricing options available to an entrepreneur with a new brand? How would you go about pricing your product or service?
3. What are the key promotional tools you might consider when developing a brand?
4. Why is segmentation important in building a brand?
5. What are the key segmentation variables you must consider when developing a brand?
6. How would you go about writing a positioning statement?
7. 'Personal branding is complete nonsense' – To what extent do you agree or disagree with this statement?

Notes

1   Stratten, S. *Unmarketing: Stop marketing. Start engaging.* Hoboken: John Wiley and Sons, 2010.

2   Kotler, P. *A framework for marketing management.* Upper Saddle River: Prentice Hall, 2001.

3   Kotler, P. *Kotler on Marketing: How to create, win and dominate markets.* London: Simon and Schuster, 2001.

4   *Ibid.*

5   Wheeler, A. *Designing brand identity: a complete guide to creating, building and maintaining strong brands.* Hoboken: John Wiley and Sons, 2006.

6   As quoted in Wheeler, A. *Designing brand identity: a complete guide to creating, building and maintaining strong brands.* Hoboken: John Wiley and Sons, 2006.

7   Interbrand and Forum, *Uncommon Practice: People who deliver a great brand experience.* Harlow: Pearson Education, 2002.

8   Barwise, P. and S. Meehan, *Simply Better: Winning and keeping customers by delivering what matters most.* Boston: Harvard Business Review Press, 2004.

9   Keller, K.L. The Brand Report Card. *Harvard Busines Review,* 78(1), 2000: 147-157.

10   Hinson, R. *Marketing of Services.* Accra: Sedco, 2006.

11   Kotler, P. *A framework for marketing management.* Upper Saddle River: Prentice Hall, 2001

12   Khermouch, G. and J. Green. Buzz Marketing. *Businessweek,* ,30 July 2001: 50-51.

13   Stratten, S. *Unmarketing: Stop marketing. Start engaging.* Hoboken: John Wiley and Sons, 2010.

14   Scott, D.M. *The New Rules of Marketing and PR.* Hoboken: John Wiley and Sons, 2010.

15   Wheeler, A. *Designing brand identity: a complete guide to creating, building and maintaining strong brands.* Hoboken: John Wiley and

Sons, 2006.

16   See Page 296 on Intellectual Property.

17   Kotler, P. *A framework for marketing management*. Upper Saddle River: Prentice Hall, 2001.

18   *Ibid.*

19   Keller, K.L. The Brand Report Card. *Harvard Busines Review*, 78(1), 2000: 147-157.

20   Iacobucci, D. *Kellogg on Marketing*. New York: John Wiley and Sons, 2001.

21   MacMillan, I. and R. McGrath. Discovering new points of differentiation. *Harvard Business Review*, 75(4), 1997: 133-145.

22   *Ibid.*

23   Iacobucci, D. *Kellogg on Marketing*. New York: John Wiley and Sons, 2001.

24   Slywotzky, A.J. The Future of commerce: The age of the choiceboard. *Harvard Business Review*, 78(1), 2000: 40-41.

25   Dayal, S., H. Landesberg and M. Zeisser. Building digital brands. *McKinsey Quartely*, 2, 2000.

26   *Ibid.*

27   Draws on Professor Brian Sternthal's 2003 Kellogg School of Marketing Advertising Strategy unpublished class notes.

28   Joachimsthaler, E. and D. Aaker. Building brands without mass media. *Harvard Business Review*, 75(1), 1997: 3-10.

29   Peters, T. The Brand Called You. *Fast Company*, 10, 1997: 83.

30   *Ibid.*

31   *Ibid.*

32   Coomson, F., Graphic, Allure Ghana bosses adjudged CIMG's best marketers, http://news.myjoyonline.com/business/201009/52077.asp, retrieved 29 January 2011.

33   Chartered Institute of Marketing Ghana Annual Marketing Awards Selection Criteria, www.cimghana.org/page.php?page=79&section=10&typ=1&title=Selection%20Criteria, retrieved 29 January 2011.

34   Ghana Entrepreneurship Day 2011 Profile of Dzigbordi Dosoo,

www.ghanaeshipday.com/profile.php?id=1, retrieved 29 January 2011.

35 After the Holy Trinity Spa and Health Farm, Sogakope.

36 2005 Survey on Spas and Treatments run by Allure Ghana.

37 As interview by Eugene Adogla, May 2010

38 Ascertained from CRM analysis of customers enjoying spa treatments with the unique discount cards from the Akwaaba Lounge Spa.

39 Iyaba, *About the Event: Iyaba,* http://iyabaexpo.com/iyabaexpo/index1.php?linkid=60, retrieved 30 January 2011.

Chapter Twelve: Layout, Liability, Risk Management and Technology

"Whatever you do, don't play it safe. If you do what's expected of you, you'll never accomplish more than others expect."

– Howard Schultz

Outline

- Introduction
- Layout
- Risk Management
- Technology as a Competitive Tool
- Questions for Class Discussion
- Simulation Exercise

O NCE THE ENTREPRENEUR has settled on an idea to develop and monetise into an enterprise, and has made key decisions around opportunity analysis, whether to build or buy, the form of legal structure and corporate governance, hiring, finances and branding, among others, he must turn his attention to the operations of the enterprise.

In this chapter we focus on some of the operational issues that an entrepreneur will need to contend with in starting and building up an enterprise, and then managing the growing enterprise to keep things running smoothly within an environment of reduced risks.

While the scope of these issues is very broad, we will limit our discussion in this chapter to the following five considerations: layout, liability, insurance, risk management and technology. This is not to say that other aspects of operations are not important in growing and managing an enterprise. I have however chosen to focus on the above because they are some of the most pressing operational concerns an entrepreneur has to contend and deal with within the period of uncertainty that surrounds the start-up process (when the entrepreneur is not fully certain whether her enterprise will succeed or not).

modem (dongle; for as low as GH¢55) or a wireless modem from the telecommunications companies.

There is so much an enterprise can do to gain leverage with the Internet: every kind of information relevant to an enterprise's industry can be found via search engines – with Google, Yahoo Search and Bing being among the best-known search tools available; it is possible to create customised and branded email using solutions provided by Google; an enterprise can purchase a custom domain for as low as US$10 a year and then create a website for free with Google's GxBO programme and its Z.com initiative in partnership with Zenith Bank Ghana Ltd. These initiatives seek to place African businesses – especially small and medium-sized ones – online.

Another way to have an online presence is to register the enterprise's location on Google Maps for free, and to leverage social media platforms like Facebook, Twitter and YouTube to sell the enterprise's vision, mission and offerings to the world while engaging with customers and drumming up business. All these are free, once you discount the cost of your inexpensive Internet connection and the human resources needed to maintain such tools.

Ghana had over 17.4 million mobile phone subscriptions by the end of 2010.[8] In addition to the huge proportion of Ghana's population that this figure covers (at least theoretically), there has been a significant increase in the use of smartphones, mobile and communication devices which can connect to the Internet. A lot of enterprises are using mobile communication tools to reach out to customers and potential markets, as the huge mobile subscriber base and access to the Internet over mobile devices mean that a large percentage of any target market in (especially urban) Ghana can be reached via bulk SMS, email and mobile Internet communication.

A smartphone (RIM's Blackberry, Google Android phones from various OEMs, Apple's iPhone, Samsung's Galaxy Tab, etc.) will serve as a useful communication tool if, besides receiving calls and text messages, one can receive email, news and office updates via mobile Internet anywhere in the world. Another useful communication tool is Skype, which can be downloaded and installed on a computer and on some smartphones, and used for voice calling and video conferencing, chatting, exchange of files, collaborative teamwork and presentations from remote locations. Other messaging clients that can perform the same functions as Skype include Google Talk, Oovoo, Yahoo and MSN Messengers.

Email appears to have overtaken traditional mail such as letters and faxes as the primary mode of interpersonal communication. It is advisable that the entrepreneur invests in his own email account for his business (@name-of-the-enterprise.com), rather than rely on free email services such as Yahoo, Hotmail and Gmail. It is advisable for each email coming from the enterprise to contain a standard signature and full contact information for the person sending the email, as well as a standard confidentiality wording. Employees should be discouraged from using work email to send personal emails and it should be clear at all times that the email account belongs to the enterprise and not to the individual employees. As part of the data protection plan of the enterprise, emails should also be backed up regularly.

• *Printers, Scanners, Photocopiers*

For administrative purposes, it is advisable to purchase the items mentioned above. Some models come with printer, scanner and photocopier combined in an all-in-one console. A more cost-effective way of acquiring equipment, especially when used very frequently for high-volume tasks, is to arrange a lease agreement for your enterprise at a minimal monthly fee. That way, you do not have to worry about maintenance and replacement, and do not have to expend a lot of financial resources upfront to purchase such equipment outright.

• *Networking*

If you own a medium-sized or large-scale enterprise, you may consider networking all your computers and information technology equipment. This is a bit more costly because it requires more hardware, software and consultancy, installation and maintenance charges. However, for the purpose of storing all your data in one location and also running applications from a central location, it is necessary to have a server or a desktop computer running a server operating system, which should be purchased after a professionally completed audit of the networking enterprise's needs.

• *The Cloud*

An alternative to networking is hosting all your documents and workflows via cloud computing. Cloud computing is the delivery of computing as a service rather than as a product; shared resources, software and information are provided to computers and other devices as a utility over a network (typically the Internet). This means that you can store and share files collaboratively with your employees, over the Internet, without having to purchase any extra networking hardware and software drivers.[9] Most of these services have inexpensive recurring fees attached to them while others provide free services for limited storage space. Companies that provide such services include Google, Box.com, Dropbox, Microsoft, Salesforce.com and Amazon, with the most commonly used in Ghana being Google.

Guidelines In Using Technology

• *Proper Licensing*

Although I am aware that many entrepreneurs in Ghana do not have the appropriate licensing for the technology they use, I strongly recommend that entrepreneurs ensure that all software being used has the appropriate vendor authorisation before use. All copyrights and software licensing rules should be fully observed to avoid copyright violations and the potential legal liabilities that come with violations.

• *Security*

Employees should be discouraged from downloading or installing software on any computers without the consent of the person responsible for enterprise-wide technology. I have noticed that in many small enterprises, employees are allowed to use their personal computers to do enterprise work. I think this practice should be strongly discouraged, as it could compromise the integrity of the enterprise's technological infrastructure.

The enterprise should also invest in antivirus software, which it should regularly update to ensure that all files on the network are scanned to prevent the introduction of viruses that could destroy network integrity. Also, where the enterprise is required to send sensitive material to other parties outside the enterprise, the entrepreneur may consider investing in encryption software to ensure that her enterprise can deliver the information securely to the various authorised destinations.

• *Data Protection*

It is important that all of the enterprise's data is protected in the event of a disaster affecting the enterprise's offices. As such, it is essential that the enterprise maintains backups of all essential information, which it should store in a secure, off-site location (akin to a safety deposit box at a reputable bank). Physical backup can also be buttressed by archiving on cloud services. Backing up information must not be taken lightly and must be done frequently. The exact nature of the backup system to be put in place will vary from enterprise from enterprise, depending on the size of the enterprise and the volume and nature of the data that the enterprise deals with. Professional advice must therefore be sought from an information technology consultant to design and implement a robust solution that meets the enterprise's peculiar needs.

• *Technology is not a Magic Bullet or Substitute for Poor Processes*

While, as we have seen, technology offers tools and systems that can be used to enhance an enterprise's operations, caution must be taken by the entrepreneur and his enterprise not to regard technology in itself as the solution to all problems to the neglect of defining and establishing robust business processes. Technology should complement robust operational processes by supporting the employees of an enterprise to achieve their tasks efficiently and effectively. In a bid to develop a lean and efficient enterprise, an entrepreneur should always choose the most efficient solution rather than automatically turn to a technology-heavy solution that may cost more but generate less value.

Questions for Class Discussion

1. Why is it important for an enterprise to properly think through what type of layout to use in setting up its office/manufacturing space?

2. The set-up of an office should always prevent informal interaction among employees: do you agree with this statement? Why or why not?

3. Risk management is best left till when the enterprise is able to sustainably stand on its feet. Discuss.

4. Based on your understanding of risk management and the lessons on managing financial resources from Chapter 8, which one would you recommend: self-insurance, or buying insurance to transfer the liabilities associated with risks to an insurance company?

5. What are the technological means and related processes by which an entrepreneur can use technology to drum up business for his enterprise?

6. What measures must you put in place to ensure the security of information on an enterprise's network?

7. Must technology be the answer to every operational challenge faced by an enterprise?

Simulation Exercise

You have been put in charge of setting up ICT for your employer, a start-up enterprise providing cargo haulage services to agricultural commodity traders. You have a budget of GH¢2,500 to cover costs for eighteen months, and five members of staff – the entrepreneur/Chief Executive Officer, his Executive Assistant, the Driver and the Assistant Driver of the company's only cargo truck, and you (Business Operations Manager).

- What items of ICT does your company require? Justify your answers.

- Create an eighteen-month budget for how you would spend the GH¢2,500 available to you. Please indicate all the assumptions you have made in drawing up your budget.

Notes

1   Hansen M.T., H. Chesbrough, N. Nohria and D. Sull. Networked Incubators: Hothouses for the New Economy. *Harvard Business Review*, 78(5), 2000: 74-84.

2   Wright, W. and C. Evans. Managing the Modern Office. *British Journal of Administrative Management*, 71, 2010: 32.

3   Gensler. *These Four Walls: The Real British Office*. London: Gensler, 2005.

4   Boutellier, R., F. Ullman, J. Schreiber and R. Naef. 2008. Impact of office layout on communication in a science-driven business. *Journal of R&D Management*, 38(4), 2008: 372-391.

5   Maslow A.H. A Theory of Human Motivation. *Psychological Review*, 50(4), 1943: 370-396.

6   The development of such application markets as Google's Android and Apple's AppStore; the release of the relevant API frameworks for both stores to enable third-party development of free and low-cost technological solutions; the creation of venture capital funds like Kleiner Perkins Caufield Byers' US$200-million iFund (www.kpcb.com/initiatives/ifund), which funds innovative solutions built by third-party developers for Apple's AppStore; the growing ubiquity of smartphones and tablet computers; and the reduction is costs of purchasing traditional computing equipment and Internet connectivity: these have all led to a progressive reduction in cost and an increased myriad of products from which an enterprise can choose the technological solutions relevant to its operations.

7   World Bank, http://data.worldbank.org/country/ghana, retrieved 22 March 2012.

8   *Ibid.*

9   Infoworld.com, www.infoworld.com/d/cloud-computing/what-cloud-computing-really-means-031, retrieved 22 March 2012.

Chapter Thirteen: Expansion, Restructuring, Insolvency, Bankruptcy and Exit Strategies

"It is never too late to be what you could have been." - **George Eliot**

Outline

- Introduction
- Expansion
- Organic Growth vs. Acquisition
- Strategic Alliance and Joint Ventures
- Restructuring, Insolvency and Bankruptcy
- Exit Strategies
- Exit Options
- Succession Planning
- Case Study: The Second Generation Taking Over at Roberts & Sons
- Questions for Class Discussion

N THE PRECEDING chapters, we discussed the entrepreneurial process and looked at how entrepreneurs build enterprises from an idea. Success as an entrepreneur usually comes with an opportunity to expand in one way or the other; to take advantage of increased opportunities or to leverage expertise, skill sets, technology or economies of scales. Out of the hundreds of entrepreneurs my research team interviewed, less than 10% were happy to remain at the same size; the vast majority had plans to expand. We therefore turn our focus in this chapter to look at how entrepreneurs can grow their enterprises internally via organic growth and externally through buying an existing enterprise. We also examine how entrepreneurs can use strategic alliances and joint ventures to expand their enterprises.

It is also quite common that at some point entrepreneurs may have to rethink the direction of a business, the structure of its financial capital or the nature of its operations. This may be a result of changing market conditions, poor financial performance or a changed corporate strategy, leading entrepreneurs to restructure for more profitable and/ or efficient enterprises. We will therefore also consider restructuring.

Notwithstanding noble intentions and obvious opportunities, entrepreneurs fail for any number of reasons. In the preceding chapters we have assumed that the entrepreneur's success is a given, however, in this chapter, we consider what options a failing entrepreneur has, including insolvency and bankruptcy.

I believe that entrepreneurs are likely to improve their lot if – even at the very beginning of the enterprise – they consider what the end ought to look like and how they would reap the rewards of their entrepreneurial efforts. We therefore also consider in this chapter the exit options of a private sale or an initial public offer. Even if entrepreneurs have no plans to sell their enterprises, the reality is that they will not always be around to manage the enterprise and, as a result, it is crucial that they put in place a succession plan. We therefore end the chapter by discussing succession.

Expansion

Entrepreneurial expansion is the means by which entrepreneurs seek to realise the dreams they have for their enterprises. It involves growing an enterprise into a medium- or large-scale enterprise. Such growth can be measured using a number of indicators including growth in sales revenue, profit growth, growth in customer base, increased market share and increased assets (both tangible and intangible).

Organic Growth Versus Acquisition

Organic Growth

Organic growth is the most common expansion strategy for Ghanaian entrepreneurs. It is incremental in nature and involves the entrepreneur gradually increasing production, service levels, sales volumes and capacity to meet increased demand or new opportunities. All things being equal, this should lead to increased sales revenue and profitability. Essentially, the entrepreneur continues to do what he set out to do in the first place (make widgets, complete consulting engagements, etc.) but at an increased level.

The emphasis in organic growth is to increase output and enhance revenue growth. An enterprise can grow organically in a number of ways including the following.

• *Attracting a New Customer Base*

Selling more of the same products and services to a new group of customers.

• *Selling its Products and Services in New Areas*

The entrepreneur could, for example, open a new physical presence at another location or use distributors or franchisees to increase the volume of products sold.

• *Using More Sales Channels*

Employing additional sales channels such as increasing the network of wholesalers and retailers or even developing an Internet presence can result in increased sales volumes.

A caterer, for example, can expand a restaurant business organically by increasing the customer base and the number of plates of food served each week. This will require the caterer to either physically expand the service area or open an additional service outlet, perhaps in a different location. He may also create a delivery business by enabling additional customers to order by telephone or the Internet. Such expansion represents growth of the enterprise arising out of its core business model – the provision of cooked food.

Organic growth has implications on the performance of the entrepreneurial team. Expansion must be thought through properly. Many enterprises jump into expansion without considering whether or not the entrepreneur and her management team have the requisite capacity, skills, structures and resources to expand. Expansion should not be pursued until the entrepreneur has carried out an analysis of her strengths and weaknesses and concluded that the enterprise will be able to cope with expanded production. In order to grow organically, for example, the entrepreneur will almost inevitably have to hire additional employees and/or increase the responsibilities of existing employees.

Another key element for the entrepreneur to consider when embarking on organic growth is to ensure that the enterprise can continue to deliver quality products and services. Rapid growth can overwhelm a small enterprise, which may find that it is unable to cope with increased demand or production levels. The very customer service that first endeared the enterprise to its initial customers may put off customers of the expanding enterprise as quality drops. It is therefore important that the entrepreneur puts in place measures to ensure quality assurance and excellent customer service at the increased levels of production or service.

Organic growth has the following advantages.

- It is a much safer way to grow an enterprise because unlike an acquisition or a merger it is not rapid. Since, the business model does not change and it is tried and tested over time, it assures the entrepreneur a higher degree of safety.

- It provides the entrepreneur an opportunity to experiment and adapt at the smaller levels of output, and then to apply only those tactics and strategies that worked in the expanded enterprise.

- It does not require significant financial commitment as one can grow an enterprise organically by simply reinvesting profit, unlike most acquisitions that require massive external investment resources.

The main disadvantages of organic growth for the entrepreneur include the following.

- It takes much longer to grow an enterprise organically compared with acquisitions or mergers, making it less attractive to entrepreneurs who want to grow their enterprises rapidly.

- It is difficult to grow organically in a market full of competitors. As we learnt in Chapter 4, the growth of an enterprise depends to a large extent on the growth of the underlying industry or market. In a saturated or declining market, organic growth may not be an option.

- The incremental, gradual and somewhat piecemeal nature of organic expansion means that the entrepreneur may not have taken a holistic approach to growth to consider what the most effective approach should be for his business. It is possible, for example, that organic expansion may not be the best way to maximise returns in a rapidly growing market.

Acquisition

Acquisition as an expansion strategy involves buying an existing enterprise with its own resources and client base. Typically, with an acquisition, the entrepreneur pays a premium in order for the owner to relinquish control, but the payment of the premium ensures that (at least in theory) the entrepreneur does not face the challenges of expansion through greenfield or organic growth. [1]

The discussion in Chapter 5 on build or buy is relevant here. We considered the option of the entrepreneur starting by acquiring an existing enterprise rather than beginning from scratch. Expansion though the acquisition of an existing enterprise has the same considerations. The only difference is that instead of buying an enterprise as an entry point, the entrepreneur is already engaged in running an enterprise and acquires another enterprise to expand his existing operations to take advantage of opportunities in the market. An entrepreneur may decide to acquire a competitor enterprise to take advantage of economies of scale, for example, or he might decide to acquire a bigger share of the customer wallet by acquiring an enterprise that produces complementary products and services. He may even decide that certain functions currently outsourced to third parties are so critical to his market share that he ought to provide those services in-house by acquiring the third party enterprise to which he had previously outsourced those services.

When an entrepreneur acquires another entity as part of an expansion strategy, she may either decide to maintain the original identity or brand of the acquired enterprise or change it to reflect the new ownership.

As a growth strategy, acquiring an existing enterprise increases the entrepreneur's customer base as the buyer automatically inherits the customers of the acquired enterprise. It further increases the market share of the entrepreneur if the acquired enterprise is in the same industry. Where the acquired enterprise has a range of products, it allows the entrepreneur to develop these products in the market or use them in new markets. Acquisition can also help grow an enterprise in new territories; in fact, this expansion mechanism is often best suited for an entry into an external market, as the acquired enterprise already knows the local business environment, culture and competitive dynamics.

Nevertheless, it is important for the entrepreneur to subject every acquisition to proper investment appraisal techniques to ensure that the acquisition will add value and profitability to the existing enterprise. The appraisal should, among other things, examine the legal, accounting and tax implications of the acquisition. More importantly, the entrepreneur must take time to research the target enterprise to ensure that it will fit into the overall vision, mission and strategy of her enterprise.

When considering acquisition as a growth strategy, the crucial issue for the entrepreneur is to determine the strategic and financial values that the acquisition brings. Strategic value is the increased competitive advantage that the acquisition brings, such as improved quality or a reduced cost of doing business. Financial value is the potential for future cash flow, increased sales revenue and profit. It is important for the entrepreneur to note that acquiring an existing enterprise can only be "justified if and only if the value of the combined entity is bigger than the sum of the value of the independent entities prior to the acquisition".[2]

The entrepreneur can create value for his enterprise through acquisition in three generic ways. Firstly, it is important for the entrepreneur to buy the existing enterprise below its real value. This can be done through the application of an effective negotiation strategy for the acquisition. Secondly, there must be a strategic fit to ensure that the new business allows the existing one to achieve its strategic objectives. This is further elaborated below. Lastly, the entrepreneur and his management team ought to manage the acquisition process in an efficient and effective way. This includes ensuring that the adequate managerial capabilities are brought on board to manage the expanded enterprise.

In order to realise the growth potential inherent in an acquisition, there should be a benefit arising from synergies resulting from the acquisition. The benefit of synergy arises from cost savings and higher sales as a result of the coming together of the two entities, which could lead to the elimination of duplicated functions, increased efficiency and productivity from the use of shared assets, access to new distribution networks, and brand development, among others. These benefits can be realised if the entrepreneur considers how the acquisition will fit the strategic direction of the enterprise. Strategic fit is crucial as it is often a precondition for the realisation of the benefits of synergies. Thus, entrepreneurs should undertake an acquisition with clear strategic intent, knowing how the acquisition fits the overall strategic direction of their enterprises.

The benefits of synergies can be better enhanced through effective integration of the acquired enterprise. This starts from a clear organisational understanding on how the synergies can be realised. Some of the key issues to consider include:

- The implementation of a proper due diligence process;
- The management of the integration process;
- An examination of the cultural fit, as a cultural mismatch could lead to failure;
- How to manage people in the integration process.

As an expansion strategy, acquisition has a number of advantages over organic growth:

- Acquisition is a faster method of growing an enterprise as the entrepreneur can easily increase the sales value and market share with a good acquisition. It is therefore a faster route to increasing the enterprise's economics of scale.

- Acquisition can reduce the competitive reaction from rival enterprises that accompanies organic growth strategies.

- It allows the entrepreneur to acquire new competences and competitive advantages that his enterprise lacks.

Despite the advantages, there are various disadvantages associated with acquisition which entrepreneurs ought to take into account. These include the following:

- It can sometimes be expensive to buy an existing enterprise because of the premium that the selling entrepreneur demands, which might make acquisition a costly expansion option.

- The perceived benefits from synergies are often difficult to determine in quantitative terms. As a result, the entrepreneur cannot be assured of actually realising the gains that ought to result from the acquisition.

Strategic Alliances and Joint Ventures

Strategic alliances and joint ventures are the other options that entrepreneurs can explore to expand their enterprises. They both involve growing an existing enterprise through the collaborative efforts of entrepreneurs as they typically involve some form of relationship building with other enterprises without necessary buying those enterprises.

Strategic Alliances

Strategic alliance as a business expansion method can be used by entrepreneurs to grow their enterprises by engaging in collaborative agreements with other enterprises in order to optimise the use of resources available for their operations. An alliance involves the sharing of capabilities between two or more enterprises in order to enhance their competitive advantage, and to create new business lines or products without losing their respective strategic autonomy.[3] It is a long-term, trust-based relationship that allows two or more enterprises to pursue shared goals, which enables them to achieve a critical business need while maintaining their separate corporate identities. The focus here for the entrepreneur is to enhance the growth of his enterprise through the collaboration.

The key in creating a strategic alliance is to first and foremost define what each business entity will gain from the alliance. In doing this, it is important to bear in mind that the overall objective is to maximise quantifiable value for each enterprise. The value could be measured through revenue growth from increased sales volume, differentiated price, revenue from superior research and development, or increased cost savings from economies of scale. It is important to measure the value generated by the alliance in order to determine whether or not it has been a success.

It is for the entrepreneur to look at the overall strategic context so as to determine the value that the alliance would add to his enterprise. An alliance will be properly sustained only if it fits the strategic direction of the entrepreneur.

Strategic alliances are formed to gain competitive advantage. As such, it is important for all parties to analyse the competitive forces and industry drivers that affect their entities and how the alliance will enhance their position in the market. The analysis should point to a compelling, achievable strategic value addition which cannot be achieved without the alliance.

The enterprises also need to determine the scope and type of collaboration. According to Lasserre, there are three main types of alliance; coalition, co-specialisation and learning alliances.[4] A coalition alliance allows entrepreneurs to develop their market reach by coordinating their assets and capabilities to help them reduce costs and enhance their competitiveness. The aim of a co-specialisation alliance is for the entrepreneurs to develop new products by joining together their capabilities so that each party will focus on areas that they are best at. With learning alliances, the enterprises can transfer valuable competencies through the exchange of knowledge.

The following are some of the important questions that the entrepreneur should answer before deciding to commit to a strategic alliance:

- Is there a strategic fit in the alliance?
- Will the alliance help both parties achieve their strategic objectives?
- Do the partners have the capabilities – in terms of resources, assets and competencies – necessary to achieve the strategic intent of the alliance?
- Is there a cultural fit to ensure that the values, beliefs and norms of the partners can work together to achieve the objectives?
- Organisationally, is there a fit between the structures, systems and processes of the two enterprises such that differences will not adversely affect the partnership?

There are several benefits strategic alliances can bring to the entrepreneur. Some of these are as follows:

• Entry Into Unknown Or Foreign Markets
The entrepreneur considering entry into a new market can form an alliance with a local partner who has the knowledge and resources to help penetrate and get a share in the local market.

• Enhanced Capabilities
Alliances can be entered into to enhance the capabilities of an enterprise, increasing its competitive advantage in the market.

• *Shared Risks*

In some instances, engaging in an alliance allows the parties to share the inherent risks involved in, for instance, developing a cutting-edge new product or service. This is particularly helpful in an uncertain environment.

• *Shared Knowledge And Expertise*

As indicated earlier, strategic alliances can help entrepreneurs to learn new competencies and capabilities from each other.

Joint Ventures

In Chapter 6, we discussed joint ventures as a form of business organisation. Here, we consider the joint venture as an option for an entrepreneur to grow his enterprise.

An entrepreneur, looking to expand his existing capacity or product line but lacking the required resources, may consider entering into a joint venture with an enterprise with the requisite resources. Likewise, an entrepreneur that wishes to expand into new markets may seek a joint venture partner based in the relevant market and with local knowledge that would be able to provide the entrepreneur access he might not otherwise have. In the case of a foreign joint venture (where an enterprise in one country enters into a joint venture with another enterprise in another country), the joint venture may give access that the foreign enterprise may not have otherwise had. It gives the foreign enterprise an opportunity to tap into the knowledge and expertise of the local partners.

A joint venture may also enable enterprises that have identical products to join forces to penetrate new markets, or to work on improvements that they might be unable to pursue individually, because of the massive costs or resource requirements for such investments.

Kuenyehia on Entrepreneurship

Restructuring, Insolvency And Bankruptcy

Restructuring

Restructuring involves reorganising the legal, ownership, financial, operational and other aspects of an enterprise so as to reposition it with a view to improving its operational efficiency and profitability, and may include divesting, spinning off assets and exiting business lines.[5] The restructuring of an enterprise is usually done in response to changes in the business climate, to the competitive environment or to refocus the strategic direction of an enterprise. The changes may be to reduce excessive diversification of the enterprise, to remove unwanted assets, or to downsize the enterprise. Restructuring can also be used to redistribute limited resources to improve the efficiency of an enterprise and enhance its financial performance.

Typically, enterprises that expand through acquisition subsequently employ various restructuring mechanisms to reorganise the enterprise post-acquisition. Restructuring is thus an important post-acquisition process that entrepreneurs can use to ensure that their newly acquired enterprise fits with the existing one. In Barkema et al.'s view, the search for higher performance after an acquisition inevitably leads to large-scale organisational restructuring.[6] Restructuring is therefore an opportunity for the buyer of an enterprise to unlock and realise the potential synergies resulting from the acquisition.

Restructuring can also focus on increasing the effectiveness of a management team by making significant changes in the organisational structure.[7] In this way, key management personnel will be reassigned different positions in the enterprise; others will leave the enterprise while new top management could be brought in as part of the process.

Restructuring can also be used to change the terms of an enterprise's debt. Debt restructuring allows an enterprise facing cash flow challenges or financial distress to renegotiate existing debt agreements, reducing its repayments so as to improve its liquidity and continue operating without defaults that could lead to bankruptcy. Debt restructuring could also be used take advantage of lower interest rates, which will also improve the liquidity position of an enterprise.

The following constitute methods that an entrepreneur can use to restructure his enterprise.

Sell-Offs

This is a restructuring method in which an entrepreneur sells some assets of the enterprise to another enterprise for cash or other financial assets. This may occur where the entrepreneur is not able to maximise the potential value of all or part of the assets his enterprise owns. Thus, he sells off to a buyer who is in a better position to create value from the assets than the value that the selling entrepreneur is able to create from the same assets. An entrepreneur may also restructure his enterprise through a sell-off to reduce the debt burden that the enterprise faces. He may also sell assets so as to invest the proceeds of sale in financing a restructured strategic direction of the enterprise. Typically, sell-offs involve sale of assets outside the core business of the enterprise – assets that may have been acquired as part of an earlier expansion strategy or a discontinued strategy. A recent example of a sell-off was the sale of Barclays Bank's custody business in Africa, including the interests of its Ghanaian subsidiary, Barclays Bank Ghana Ltd, to Standard Chartered Bank in 2010.

Spin-Offs

In a spin off, an enterprise creates a separate entity into which it 'spins' the relevant assets. Unlike the sell-off situation where the assets that are sold off go to a third party for cash or other considerations, in spin-offs the original owners continue to own (directly or indirectly) the assets through a new entity. An enterprise may decide to spin-off assets into a separate entity under separate management because it might be a more efficient way to manage those assets. According to Bergh et al., where the assets to be restructured are in the core business line of the enterprise, it may be difficult for those assets to fit into another enterprise; as such, a spin-off is more preferred to sell-off.[8] In this way the spun-off entity and the restructured one can keep a long-term relationship that allows the restructured enterprise to create value more efficiently. On the other hand, they argue that where the assets are unrelated to the core business activity of the enterprise, a viable restructuring approach is to sell it off.

Insolvency and Bankruptcy: So What If You Fail?[9]

So far, we have assumed that the entrepreneur(s) at the helm of the relevant enterprise(s) will succeed. Much as this is the hope of all entrepreneurs starting out, the harsh reality is that many entrepreneurs will fail at their entrepreneurial endeavours.

How entrepreneurs manage cash flow and debts could affect the long-term survival of their enterprises. In the normal course of trading, entrepreneurs often buy goods and services from their suppliers to which they add value and sell to their own customers. Such purchases may be by way of cash, or credit sales where those suppliers become creditors of the enterprise and must be paid. Similarly, many entrepreneurs seek debt financing from individuals, banks and other financial institutions. The enterprise in its normal operations may also owe employees salaries and wages and may owe tax to the Ghana Revenue Authority. Therefore, at any given time, it is likely that an enterprise owes a number of creditors. That in itself may not be fatal; as we have seen in Chapter 8, this might be part of a deliberate strategy of managing its finances.

However, if entrepreneurs do not manage their creditors and cash flow properly, it could lead to an insolvency situation which could threaten the existence of their enterprises. An enterprise is said to be insolvent when it is unable to pay off its debts as they fall due. This occurs when the enterprise is not able to generate enough income and inflow of cash to meet its cash and debt obligations.

We should distinguish between two situations: where it is the entrepreneur himself (for example, because he is a sole proprietor) that is unable to pay his debts as they fall due; and where it is the company that is unable to pay its debts as they fall due.

In the case of the individual, a petition for a declaration of insolvency may be brought by the debtor or one or more creditors if the total debt owed by the debtor to the creditor(s) amounts to at least GH¢10,000.[10] When the petition is brought, the Official Trustee, who is the officer in charge of insolvency proceedings, makes a protection order enabling the debtor's assets to be conserved for the protection of the creditors until the affairs of the debtor have been considered by the High Court. All assets of the debtor become vested in the Official Trustee after the making of the protection order.

After the making of the protection order, the Official Trustee holds a meeting of the debtor and all the creditors, who have to prove the debts owed. After the creditors meeting, the Official Trustee makes an application to the High Court to consider the affairs of the debtor and give a decision as to the future course of the insolvency proceedings. The court may make an insolvency order, an order confirming an arrangement with creditors, or an order rescinding the protection order.

Upon the declaration of insolvency, the assets of the debtor may be liquidated to pay the debts that have been successfully proved by the creditors.

The Insolvency Act, 2006 (Act 708), makes provision for the debtor to make an arrangement with creditors for the payment of the debts owed. Any proposal for an arrangement must however be submitted at a meeting of all creditors for consideration and confirmation. The arrangement must also be confirmed by the court before it can become effective. If the court confirms the arrangement, the Official Trustee may then liquidate the assets of the debtor and pay the amount realised according to the arrangements made with the creditors.

An individual may only be declared bankrupt by a court which finds that grounds for bankruptcy exist. These grounds are as follows:

- Where for an aggregate period of 12 months within the three years preceding the making of the order, the debtor continued in trade or business in the knowledge that he was insolvent;
- Where the debtor contributed to the insolvency by rash speculations or culpable neglect of business affairs, or by gambling or extravagance;
- Where a provable debt was contracted by the debtor with the

intention that it should not be met, or without a reasonable expectation of being able to meet it;

- Where the debtor has failed to account satisfactorily for assets which have disappeared since the date of the making of the protection order or during the year previous to that date;
- If the debtor has persistently and without adequate excuse failed to carry out the duties of the debtor in the insolvency proceedings;
- If the debtor is a former bankrupt;
- If within the preceding three years the debtor has been convicted of an offence involving dishonesty in relation to property and has been sentenced to a term of imprisonment of not less than three months;
- If within the preceding three years the debtor has been convicted of an offence of making a false declaration on a statement under the Registration of Business Names Act, 1962 (Act 151).

The liquidation of companies and other insolvent bodies corporate is dealt with by the Bodies Corporate (Official Liquidations) Act, 1963 (Act 180). A petition for the declaration of insolvency may be brought by the company itself, after a special resolution has been passed to that effect, to the Registrar who doubles as the Official Liquidator. A member or creditor of the company may also bring a petition to that effect[11].

Upon the presentation of the petition, the powers of the directors of the company cease and become vested in the Official Liquidator, who manages the affairs of the company with the view to liquidating the assets and paying off the proven debts of the company.[12] The Official Liquidator publishes a notice in the Gazette or a widely read newspaper calling on all creditors of the debtor company to file a 'proof of debts', which outlines the debt owed to the creditor.

On the commencement of the insolvency proceedings, the company shall cease to carry on business, but the corporate status and the corporate powers of the company shall continue until the company is dissolved. The company shall, however, only carry on business as is necessary for the beneficial winding-up of the company[13].

When insolvency proceedings begin, all the assets of the company become vested in the Official Liquidator, who realises the assets after accountants employed by the Official Liquidator have assessed the accounts of the company. In most cases, the amounts realised after liquidation are not enough to meet all the debts of the company. Thus, the Official Liquidator may decide to pay all creditors a fixed percentage of the debt owed by the company. Usually, the percentage fixed by the Official Liquidator is non-negotiable and has to be accepted by the creditors, irrespective of the debt owed.

Unlike insolvency laws in other countries (most notably, the Chapter 11 Bankruptcy Law of the United States of America) which give insolvent companies an opportunity to reorganise their debts and continue in existence without being liquidated, under Ghanaian law, there is no alternative for the company when the petition is presented and it is proved that the company cannot pay its debts. The company will be liquidated and the amount realised used to pay off debts due to creditors. Ghanaian law does not categorise bankruptcy into liquidation and rehabilitation or reorganisation.

Alternatives to Bankruptcy or Liquidation

A declaration of bankruptcy or a liquidation should be the last possible alternative. Where possible, entrepreneurs should consider any of the following options:

Selling The Enterprise

The entrepreneur may decide to sell the shares of the company or assets of the enterprise to a willing buyer, who then assumes the debts and liabilities. It might be difficult to find a willing buyer for an enterprise facing bankruptcy, and when such a buyer is found, she is likely to exploit the situation to acquire the assets for as low a price as possible.

Reorganisation

A company that is going into liquidation may also decide to reschedule or reorganise its debts with the various creditors if they are ready and willing to do so. Since liquidation might not result in the creditors being paid the full amount due them, depending on the circumstances, these creditors might have an interest in a reorganisation that eventually results in them getting paid. The company may negotiate with its creditors for new payment terms and conditions. In some instances, the creditors may give the debtor company or individual further loans to enable the return of the enterprise to profit, resulting in the eventual payment of debts. Usually, such reorganisation or rescheduling attracts higher interest rates and more stringent conditions.

Merging

In some instances, it might also be possible for an enterprise to merge with another enterprise, and for the merged entity to absorb the debts of the bankrupt enterprise. Again, this may not be an easy option in practice.

Exit Strategies

It is important that from the onset, an entrepreneur has in place a plan to reap the rewards of her hard work. This is referred to as an exit plan or a harvest plan which means exactly that – a plan that describes how an entrepreneur will exit the enterprise or reap the rewards of her hard work. At some point, an entrepreneur will exit the venture which she started or acquired and may want to ensure that, as part of the process, she is able to extract some of the economic value of her investment and years of hard labour. Dorf and Byers take the view that "Few events in the life of the entrepreneur or the firm are more significant than the harvest. Without the opportunity to harvest, a firm's owners and investors will be denied a significant amount of value that has been created over the firm's life."[14]

The entrepreneur may exit the enterprise she founded or acquired in the following circumstances.

• *Retirement*

One of the attractions of entrepreneurship is that after working hard to build a successful enterprise, one may be able to sell the enterprise at retirement and enjoy the proceeds of the sale.

• *Desire for Diversification*

For most entrepreneurs, a vast percentage of their personal wealth may be tied to a particular enterprise. The ability to exit the enterprise by selling part or all of the enterprise may provide an opportunity to diversify their financial holdings.

• *Realising the Returns on Investment Made*

Especially where external investors such as venture capital providers have invested in the enterprise, there might be pressure on the entrepreneur to sell all or part of the enterprise so as to return the investors' money.

• *Succession*

The entrepreneur may exit the enterprise to make room for a younger generation, whom he might give an equity stake in the enterprise.

• *Death*

When an entrepreneur dies, she involuntarily exits her enterprise. It is important that an entrepreneur has a will in place dealing with how she wants her stake in the enterprise to be dealt with. It is also crucial that, during her lifetime, she develops the right succession plan to ensure that her enterprise can continue to run upon her demise.

Exit Options

An entrepreneur looking to exit his enterprise has a number of options open to him, including those expanded on below.

Private Sale to a Third Party

In Chapter 5, we discussed the option of an entrepreneur acquiring an enterprise as a route to entrepreneurship. Exiting by selling the enterprise by way of a private sale to a third party is the reverse of that process and involves allowing an entity or an individual to acquire an enterprise at an agreed price.

It may be difficult to find the right buyer for the enterprise and the entrepreneur may need to work with an investment banking or corporate finance firm to identify the right buyer. Of course, anybody can express an interest in acquiring an enterprise without having the financial muscle to do so, and so all prospective buyers should be pre-qualified to ensure that they have arranged the requisite financial resources to make the acquisition.

In many instances when an entrepreneur has been involved in building an enterprise from scratch, it is difficult for that entrepreneur to simply let the enterprise go to anybody. So beyond cash, there might be other considerations that determine whether or not the entrepreneur is willing to sell the enterprise to a particular individual, group of individuals or entity. The entrepreneur may, for example, want to ensure that the culture of the enterprise will not change significantly. He will therefore be interested in whether or not there is a cultural fit between the prospective acquirer and his enterprise.

To ensure that the entrepreneur achieves the maximum possible price, it is important that he presents the best possible face of his enterprise. It would be advisable to seek appropriate support in the form of financial and legal advisors who have gained experience in advising other entrepreneurs on the sale of their enterprises. Together with his management team and the appropriate advisors, the entrepreneur would prepare an information memorandum (IM) which sets out a detailed description of the enterprise that is being presented for sale.

The IM is typically sent to prospective buyers after they have signed and returned a non-disclosure agreement. After reviewing the IM, the prospective buyer would typically embark on a due diligence exercise; again, not dissimilar to the due diligence exercise we described in Chapter 5 in the context of an acquisition. This time though, it will be up to the entrepreneur to open up his enterprise for scrutiny by the prospective purchaser and his advisors, to justify the valuation placed on the enterprise.

Based on the results of the due diligence, the parties will negotiate the terms pursuant to which the entrepreneur will sell the enterprise; the parties will document the agreed terms in a sale and purchase agreement. Again, the discussion in Chapter 5 on the sale and purchase agreement is relevant here, as are the other considerations in that chapter on the acquisition of an enterprise.

Management Buyout

The entrepreneur may also decide to sell the enterprise to his management team. This can take the form of a management buyout where the senior managers buy the enterprise from the entrepreneur. In this case, the sale can even be properly planned so that over time a percentage of the enterprise is bought by the management team based on the achievement of certain key performance indicators. Such a plan is a good way of locking in top-performing staff, and gradually unwinds the entrepreneur from the enterprise.

A management buyout gives the entrepreneur the opportunity to sell the enterprise to a team that knows it well, already believes in it and has a track record in helping run the business. A recent example of a management buyout in Ghana is the acquisition of the shares of the construction company Taysec by the management team, led by Managing Director Geoff Fisher.

Initial Public Offering (IPO): Introduction

The ultimate dream for many entrepreneurs is to make an initial public offer. To have the general public acquire shares in a company that an entrepreneur has built from scratch is recognition of hard work and a validation of the vision for the company. It is also a key exit strategy that provides an opportunity for the entrepreneur to sell part or all of his shares to unlock some of the economic value of the enterprise. Indeed, going public is considered the ultimate exit strategy as it provides the entrepreneur with a paced and controlled exit.[15]

Not many entrepreneurs have used the IPO route in Ghana. Indeed, as I mentioned in Chapter 7, the stock market is relatively undeveloped in Ghana. However, I believe it offers tremendous potential and predict that many more Ghanaian entrepreneurs will be turning to the Ghana Stock Exchange (GSE) in the coming years to divest all or part of their companies.

An IPO may take any of the following forms.

Offer For Sale

Where there is an offer for sale, an entrepreneur (alone or together with other shareholders) offers all or part of existing shares that they own for sale to the general public.

Offer For Subscription

In the case of an offer for subscription, rather than existing shareholders selling shares that already exist, the company issues new shares which it offers to everyone, including the existing shareholders.

Offer For Sale and Subscription

This involves a combination of a sale – where existing shareholders sell existing shares – and an offer for subscription – where the company issues and offers additional shares.

Recall that in Chapter 6 we noted that listing on the Ghana Stock Exchange requires entrepreneurs to meet a set of rules (the Listing

Rules) before and after the share offer. The key requirements as contained in the Listing Rules for an entrepreneur to offer shares to the public are as follows. [16]

- A post-floatation stated capital of at least GH¢1 million for applications for listing on the First List and GH¢500,000 for the Second List. The Second List is aimed at small and medium-sized enterprises.
- The public float of the applicant must constitute 25% of the number of issued shares. (This requirement may be waived if the stated capital of the applicant on floatation is at least GH¢75 million, and the applicant provides an undertaking to meet the percentage required within three years.
- The Exchange shall refuse listing relating to partly paid shares, except in exceptional circumstances.
- A prospective company shall list all the class of shares issued or to be issued.
- The Exchange shall determine the adequacy of the spread of shareholders at the close of offer or time of listing.
- The Exchange prescribes a minimum of 100 shareholders for all listed companies.

Initial Public Offering: Key Issues to be Addressed by an Entrepreneur Seeking an IPO

• *Purpose of Offer and Nature of Shares to be Offered*

A determination must be made about whether the offer is one for sale (where the proceeds of the offer go to the shareholders), an offer for subscription (where the proceeds of the offer go to the company) or an offer for sale and subscription (where the proceeds go both to the shareholders and the company). Based on the purpose, a determination would need to be made in respect of whether additional shares need to be issued and what percentage of the shareholding will be offered to the general public, and consequently, how much the existing shareholding would be diluted due to the requirement for a minimum public float of 25% of the post-offer issued shares.

• *Application of Funds*

Tied to the purpose of the offer is the use to which the funds from the offer will be put. If a shareholder is retiring and looking to exit, he will be looking to liquidate his shareholding in full or in part. However, consideration also needs to be given to whether or not additional capital is to be invested in the company's business.

• *The Value of the Offer*

With the help of the transaction advisors, the entrepreneur will value the company and the shares to be offered.

• *The Response of the Market*

Although this can never be predicted from the onset, help should be sought from the transaction advisors who will be able to provide some idea of the capacity of the market to take up the shares on offer.

• *Preference of Existing Shareholders*

Existing shareholder(s) must consider whether or not they would like to have a controlling stake, and whether or not they would like to market the offer to identified strategic investors, foreign investors or to retail investors generally.

• *Timing of the Offer*

It is important that the offer takes into account the investment patterns of investors and other happenings in the general business environment. For example, if the offer coincides with the floatation of another company, it could impact on its success. Likewise, an offer that is close to an election is unlikely to be patronised by international investors who have a tendency of shying away from investing during an election year because of potential political uncertainty.

• *Employee Share Ownership Plan*

Just as the IPO provides an opportunity for the original entrepreneur to harvest the seeds of his hard work, it also provides an opportunity for him to reward his long-serving employees and to incentivise other employees. The entrepreneur will need to consider with his board whether or not an employee share ownership plan should be put in place to provide an opportunity for employees to own shares. If an employee share ownership plan is to be put in place, consideration will also need to be given to how employees will be required to fund the purchase of the shares subject to the plan. Typically, there will often be restrictions placed on management, shareholders and key employees to stop them selling any or all of their shares for a period after the IPO in order to help maintain confidence in the newly listed company.

Initial Public Offering: The IPO Process

Appointing Transaction Advisors

The entrepreneur will require the services of a number of professionals to ensure the success of the offer. These advisors are called transaction advisors and include the following:

» The Lead Manager: The role of the lead manager is to lead the team of transaction advisors and the IPO process, and includes obtaining all relevant approvals, leading the due diligence process, carrying out the valuation and pricing, preparing the relevant documentation and driving the flotation, allocation of shares and listing.

» The Reporting Accountant: The reporting accountant, who must be different from the auditor of the company, undertakes the financial due diligence of the company's historical and forecasted financials, and will issue an opinion on those financials for the prospectus.

» The Legal Advisor: The legal advisor will ensure that both the offer and the company comply with the relevant rules and regulations. They will conduct the legal due diligence and advise on compliance with the relevant laws and regulations, as well as issue a legal opinion for the prospectus.

» The Sponsoring Broker: To list on the GSE, the company must have a sponsoring broker who is an authorised dealing member of the GSE and who takes the responsibility of introducing the company to the GSE. In practice, the lead manager may also be the sponsoring broker. The sponsoring broker provides no guarantee as to the take up of the offer.

» Underwriter: Most of the share issues on the GSE have not been underwritten. However, where there is an underwriter, he guarantees the share issue by offering to take up any shares not taken up by the general public.

» The Marketing Consultant: The marketing consultant will develop and implement the marketing strategy for the offer.

» The Share Registrar: The share registrar will receive the application forms during the offer and liaise with the lead manager and the sponsoring broker in respect of allotment of shares.

Due Diligence

The transaction advisors will carry out due diligence of the operations of the company with the objective of identifying any issues that may be material to the transaction and the valuation. Although the exact nature of the due diligence to be conducted will vary from company to company, typically there would be financial, legal, technical and operational due diligence.

Preparation of Documents

Working with the transaction advisors, the entrepreneur will prepare the following documents: relevant resolutions passed by the board of the company and/or shareholders in respect of the IPO; and a draft prospectus which includes the historical and projected financial statements and a valuation and share pricing report.

Valuation

The company's advisors will prepare a valuation using some of the techniques we discussed in Chapter 5.

Approvals

Approvals must be sought from both GSE and the Securities and Exchange Commission (SEC). The SEC approval is in respect of the public offer of shares to the general public while the GSE approval is in connection with the listing of the shares on the GSE.

Demand Assessment (Book Building)

The company and its advisors conduct initial research and analysis to estimate the market capacity and to assess the appetite and concerns of prospective investors. Based on this assessment, they hold preliminary meetings with some potential investors to establish the likely level of demand for the company's shares and obtain, if possible, written expressions of interest.

Marketing Strategy

Using some of the promotional tools discussed in Chapter 11, the company's retained marketing consultant(s) will develop a marketing strategy to promote the offer to prospective investors.

Offer Period

The GSE does not have any time limit on the offer period; how long the offer period takes depends on the listing company, and must be featured in the prospectus. Where the company is unable to meet its minimum subscription target during its specified offer period, it can apply for an extension from the GSE.

Listing and Trading

After the offer is closed, provided that the minimum level of acceptances is met, the company will be admitted for listing on the GSE and trading will begin in its shares.

In addition to providing an exit opportunity for existing shareholders – particularly venture capitalists looking for opportunities to realise part of their investment – listing on the stock exchange provides the following advantages.[17]

• *Tax Savings*

Entrepreneurs and members of the management team who list their company on the GSE before selling their shares will not be required to pay capital gains tax on those shares. This can be a significant tax saving for entrepreneurs who would otherwise have had to pay income gains tax.

• *Access to Capital*

A listing on the stock exchange brings with it the opportunity for the company to raise equity finance both at the time of the initial listing and in the future. The broader spread of participators in the company should make it easier to raise further funds from its shareholders in the future through, for example, a rights issue.

• *Providing a Market for the Company's Shares*

A listing should make the company's shares more marketable because there is a regulated and liquid market on which the company's shares are traded.

• *Employee Commitment*

The public market in the shares may encourage employee participation in the ownership of the company through employee share ownership schemes, giving the shares a visible value and employees a liquid market on which to trade their shares. This should in turn help tie in key staff.

• *Ability to Take Advantage of Acquisition Opportunities*

Not only will the listed company have greater access to capital; it will also be able to offer listed shares rather than cash as consideration for an acquisition (unlisted shares may well be unacceptable to a seller).

• *Profile*

A listing will improve the perception of a company's financial stability and transparency. There will also be an increased public awareness of the company through greater press coverage; this may help sustain demand for and liquidity of the shares.

• *Comfort for Suppliers and Customers*

The fact that a company has undergone the rigorous due diligence and other processes required to obtain a listing may help reassure customers and suppliers as to the company's financial standing. The company's position within its industry and among its competitors is enhanced and the perceived risk of default is lower.

However, the advantages of listing a company should be weighed up against the disadvantages, which include the following.

• *Susceptibility to Market Conditions*

The fact that the value of a listed company can be adversely affected by market conditions beyond its control can be deeply frustrating for its management, who might not be used to the vagaries of the public market.

• *Potential Loss of Control*

The sale of a portion of the company's equity inevitably means a loss of control for the entrepreneur. Significant acquisitions and other such decisions may require the prior approval of shareholders. In addition, a listing can bring pressure on the management to achieve short-term targets for its shareholders at the expense of long-term strategic goals.

• *Loss of Privacy*

The greater accountability to shareholders puts every decision of the management under the spotlight. Any under-performance may attract press comment and consequently impact negatively on the share price.

• *Disclosure and Reporting Requirements*

Both during the IPO process and subsequently, the company will be subject to far greater disclosure and reporting requirements.

• *Costs and Fees*

For a small company, the costs and fees involved in floating and in maintaining its listing may be prohibitive and could outweigh the perceived benefits.

• *Management Time*

A large amount of management time will be diverted, both during the IPO process itself and afterwards, from the main job of running the business to fulfilling the continuing obligations linked to listing and, in particular, managing investor relations.

Succession Planning

Succession planning can be a rather delicate topic for many entrepreneurs, particularly in smaller enterprises where there appears to be very little, if any, distinction between the enterprise and the entrepreneur. The entrepreneur typically feels that no one else can run the enterprise as well as he can.

In Chapter 11, we introduced briefly the concept of succession planning. We stated that it is a programme over a certain period of time to identify the next generation of an enterprise's leaders. As Anderson and Dunkelberg put it, succession planning is a cognitive process of creating a plan to replace managers in any enterprise, as well as the enterprise's owner when the time comes.[18]

It is important that when the entrepreneur exits the enterprise, either voluntarily or involuntarily, there is a smooth transition to the next generation of enterprise leaders who are able to take the helm and continue in the founding entrepreneur's shoes. It tends to be a bigger challenge for someone else to run the enterprise if the founding entrepreneur is separated involuntarily from the enterprise. These circumstances could include:

- The sudden death of the entrepreneur;
- Poor health or other forms of physical or mental incapacitation that prevent him from carrying on as normal;
- Financial difficulties which result in the lenders demanding the removal of the entrepreneur as manager.

It is important that at any point in time, there is a proper succession plan across the entire enterprise delineating quite clearly who the successors are for all the key roles. One of the major challenges that most entrepreneurial ventures face, particularly in cases where the entrepreneurs are close to retiring, is lack of adequate preparation to pass on managerial control. A lack of succession planning, which often leads to incompetent or unprepared successors and unclear succession plans, has been cited as the most prevalent reason why family enterprises fail.[19] The long-term survival of many enterprises, particularly family-owned ones, therefore depends largely on a successfully crafted and executed succession plan.

In enterprises that are owned by more than one entrepreneur, the succession planning process should take into account the dual or multiple ownership, and it may be advisable to have an agreement that allows continuing owners to buy the enterprise from exiting owners in the event of death, divorce, or disability.[20]

It is important for the entrepreneur to initiate steps as early as possible to identify potential candidates as successors for all key positions at the enterprise.

There are two ways entrepreneurs can find successors: internally and externally. In most cases, when deciding who the successors will be, entrepreneurs look at internal sources, be it their sons, daughters, nephews or nieces. Entrepreneurs may also decide to train both family and non-family members in the enterprise with a view to preparing them, before selecting one as the eventual successor. The most significant thing to note when seeking internal successors is that the emphasis should be on developing the ability and credibility of successors so that they will be acceptable to the wider team.

Where entrepreneurs cannot find immediate successors within the enterprise, they may decide to select an outsider who has professional experience in the industry and has the key qualities that the entrepreneur is looking for.

Kuratko and Hodgetts advise that the following four steps should be taken when carrying out a succession plan.[21]

Identify a Successor

An entrepreneur-manager should identify a successor, or an individual who at least possesses the needed characteristics and experience to succeed the entrepreneur. In identifying the qualities, the vision and strategy of the enterprise should be considered with a view to finding a successor capable of driving the entrepreneur's dream forward.

Groom an Heir

Some entrepreneurs may pick a successor and let it be known; others may prefer that a small number of potential successors exist from which the eventual successor would be chosen, with no one knowing for sure who will actually be chosen.

Agree on a Plan

The potential candidate must be groomed by the entrepreneur. The stakeholders involved in the enterprise must crucially agree on the plan to transfer power and responsibilities from the entrepreneur to the chosen successor.

Consider Outside Help

The key question to be answered is 'How can the business be effectively run, and who has the ability to do it?' An honest answer to this question may result in reaching out to a person external to the organisation.

Case Study: The Second Generation at Roberts & Sons

AT THE AGE OF FIFTY-FIVE, after an illustrious career at NCR, the global technology company, Mr Robert Atta felt that he had reached the top of his career. After serving successfully as Managing Director of NCR's Ghana subsidiary, Atta knew that any additional responsibility would entail moving from Ghana, which he did not want to do. As a result, he decided to take early retirement.

Two years into early retirement, against the wishes of his children, Atta decided to set up an optical services company which he called Robert and Sons.

Right from the onset, one of the objectives Atta set for himself was for the company to continue long after his death. In that vein, he was significantly influenced by his experience at NCR. Set up in 1884 by John H Patterson as the National Cash Register Company, NCR was the maker of the first mechanical cash registers. It has grown into and remains – long after the death of its founder – a highly successful technology company with a number of subsidiaries around the world. The other objectives Atta set for himself were exemplary customer service, profitability and excellent relationships with all employees, especially the professional employees he relied on. Atta had no knowledge of the optical services industry and started his business with a part-time ophthalmologist providing the technical knowledge.

In 1999, at the age of sixty-eight, Atta felt that the time had come for him to pursue his plan for succession. He admits that "the idea of losing [management] control of your enterprise is an uncomfortable feeling as you have a sense that no one can manage the business like the way you do."[22] His initial motivation was to spend eighteen months participating in a Rotary International Foundation programme. However, he was also conscious that eye care was a high-fashion business that he was gradually losing touch with. He therefore thought it would be a good opportunity to hand over.

Having taken the decision to step aside, the obvious question for Atta was who would succeed him. Although, as he admits, there was no reason why he could not find a local manager to succeed him, he was keen to find someone that he knew and trusted sufficiently to take over the company.

His thoughts turned to his four children who at the time were all living in the United States. Indeed, he had suggested years ago to who is a medical doctor to pursue ophthalmology but he had not been interested. When he reached out to his first son, a doctor, to move home to succeed him, he declined. Two other sons and a daughter also showed no interest in relocating to Ghana to take over the reins at Robert and Sons.

However, when Mr Atta decided to sell the business and informed his children of his intentions, they were most unhappy; as a group, they decided that his third son Franklin should move back home to Ghana to work with his father, and take over the management of the business.

Franklin moved back home to Ghana in 2000 determined that he was "going to succeed no matter what". He found it difficult adjusting to working with his father. Where he had worked previously, he had had latitude to make decisions as long as he could justify his decisions to his boss. But, as he puts it, "working with daddy, who is strict, was different". Franklin, like his father, had no prior experience in ophthalmology and understanding the business was a steep learning curve for him. Fortunately, his father dedicated considerable time to guide him and educate him on the business before handing the reins to him.

In addition to the excellent hands-on coaching and mentoring that his father had provided, Franklin found his prior experience in finance to be helpful. Franklin had worked in the insurance industry in Houston, Texas, for five years, and studied finance at Prairie View Agricultural and Mechanical University, Texas, before pursuing his professional career.

After consolidating his hold on the business, Franklin started an expansion drive. The eyecare business was changing in Ghana and had become a lot more saturated, with competitors expanding all over the country. Franklin felt that to survive and to grow market share, Robert and Sons had no option but to expand. He focused, initially, on growing sales in the only branch the company had, and then set his sights on opening additional branches.

While his expansion drive was a success, Franklin needed to strengthen the management team to cope with the growth. After discussions with his father, they decided to hire an external person to join the management team. However, around that time, Monique, Mr Atta's youngest child and only daughter, informed him that she would also like to join the family business. She had graduated with a double major in marketing and fashion design from American Intercontinental University, and worked as the Area Manager for South Atlanta with Enterprise Rent-A Car, a Fortune 500 company founded by a father-and-son duo.

Franklin and Mr Atta felt that Monique's background in fashion and marketing would be invaluable to Robert and Sons, as would her experience in corporate relations, branch operations, marketing and employee development. It was therefore agreed that Monique would come on board as the Director for Sales and Marketing, with responsibility for branding, corporate relations, customer service, sales, branch operations, human relations and employee development. Franklin would then focus on running the finance, administration, procurement, stock management and technical departments.

Monique's arrival brought immediate changes. She oversaw the redesign of branch look and feel, a first step in developing a distinctive brand proposition for Robert and Sons around the tagline 'Seeing is Believing'.

Both Franklin and Monique, who have full management control of Robert and Sons, admit they keep going back to their father – who is their "anchor" – for advice. As Mr Atta puts it, he "sits back and provides support. Some solicited, some unsolicited".

Mr Atta now spends his time communing with his grandchildren and keeping himself involved in Rotary International activities. With five branches and counting, Franklin and Monique are not just building on the excellent foundation that their father provided; they are clearly taking Robert and Sons to the next level. While only in his early forties, Franklin admits he has already started to think about succession.

Based on a presentation by Robert Atta, Franklin Atta and Monique Atta to the Foundations of Entrepreneurship Class at Ghana Institute of Management and Public Administration' in February 2012

Questions for Case Discussion

1. What were the main factors that influenced Mr Atta's succession plan?
2. Do you think he should have put non-family members at the helm?
3. Why do you think the Attas' succession plan has been so successful?

Questions for Class Discussion

1. What options are available for entrepreneurs looking to expand their enterprises?
2. Why might an entrepreneur decide to enter into a joint venture with another company or individual?
3. In what circumstances will a court make an order for bankruptcy?
4. Who are the key players in a prospective IPO and what are their respective roles?
5. What are some of the key issues that an entrepreneur contemplating an IPO must consider?
6. What are the main advantages of listing on the Ghana Stock Exchange?
7. How would you advise the owner of a small enterprise to approach succession?

Notes

1   Megginson, W.L., S.B. Smart and B.M. Lucey. *Introduction to Corporate Finance*. London: Cengage Learning EMEA, 2008.

2   Lasserre, P. *Global Strategic Management*. Basingstoke: Palgrave Macmillan, 2007.

3   *Ibid.*

4   *Ibid.*

5   Johnson R.A. Antecedents and outcomes of corporate refocusing. *Journal of Management*, 22(3), 1996: 439–483.

6   Barkema, H.G. and M. Schijven. Toward Unlocking The Full Potential Of Acquisitions: The Role Of Organizational Restructuring. *Academy Of Management Journal*, 51(4), 2008: 696–722.

7   Bowman, E.H. and H. Singh. Corporate restructuring: Reconfiguring the firm. *Strategic Management Journal*, 14(S1), 1993: 5–14.

8   Bergh, D.D., R.A. Johnson and R. Dewitt. Restructuring through Spin-Off or Sell-Off: Transforming Information Asymmetries into Financial Gain. *Strategic Management Journal*, 29(2), 2008: 133-148.

9   This section relies heavily on Kuenyehia E.N. Insolvency and Bankruptcy: Navigating the Ghanaian System. In *Inside the Minds: Bankruptcy Law Client Strategies in the Middle East and Africa*. Boston: Aspatore Books, 2011.

10 Insolvency Act, 2006 (Act 708), Section 9.

11 Bodies Corporate (Official Liquidations) Act, 1963 (Act 180), Section 2 and Section 3.

12 Bodies Corporate (Official Liquidations) Act, 1963 (Act 180), Section 9 and Section 14.

13 Bodies Corporate (Official Liquidations) Act, 1963 (Act 180), Section 15.

14 Dorf, R. and T. Byers. *Technology ventures from idea to enterprise*. New York: McGraw-Hill, 2008.

15   Brown, G.W. 2003. Strategy Or Not, You'll Exit Sooner or Later. *Business Management,* 2003 EBSCO Publishing

16   Ghana Stock Exchange Listing Rules, 2006: 11–12.

17   A large part of this subsection (advantages and disadvantages of an IPO) relies on a practice note on the same topic at www. practicallaw.com (retrieved March 2012).

18   Anderson, R.L. and J.S. Dunkelberg. *Managing Small Business.* St. Paul: West Publishing Company, 1993.

19   Hisrich, R.D. *International Entrepreneurship: Starting, Developing and Managing a Global Venture.* Thousand Oaks: SAGE Publications, 2010.

20   Anderson, R.L. and J.S. Dunkelberg. *Managing Small Business.* St. Paul: West Publishing Company, 1993.

21   Kuratko, D.F. and R.M. Hodgetts. Succession Strategies for Family Businesses. *Management Advisor,* Spring 1989: 22-30.

22   Speech given to Foundations of Entrepreneurship class at Ghana Institute of Management and Public Administration, Greenhill, February 2012.

Chapter Fourteen: The Business Plan

"Expect the best, plan for the worst, and
prepare to be surprised." – **Denis Waitley**

Outline

- Introduction
- Developing a Business Plan
- Role of Business Plan
- Elements of a Business Plan
- Enterprise Ecosystems
- Questions for Class Discussion

H AVING SPENT THE preceding chapters of this book discussing
the journey from idea to profits (or losses), this final chapter
focuses on consolidating the learnings from that journey
into a business plan which will serve as a road map for a
new enterprise. The discussions in the preceding chapters
are an important precursor to the business plan itself, which is the
focus of this chapter.

I begin by providing an overview of business plans, focusing in
particular on the key guidelines entrepreneurs need to take note of
when developing one. We then consider the role that a business plan
plays for the entrepreneur and his enterprise. I argue that a business
plan can be used in two ways; as a planning tool for the enterprise
internally, and as a tool for seeking financial resources externally. We
then move to the business plan itself and spend the rest of the chapter
discussing its key elements. It is in developing and articulating the
different elements that make up the business plan that the entrepreneur
will pull together and consolidate the discussions and lessons from
the previous chapters.

The discussion on the opportunity, product or service will be
influenced by the concepts in Chapter 3 on idea generation and in
Chapter 4 on opportunity analysis. Likewise, ideas from Chapter 5 on
build or buy, and from Chapter 6 on legal considerations will have a

bearing on discussions on the enterprise or entity; what we read in Chapter 9 on attracting, recruiting and retaining human capital will be referenced in the discussion on the management team; the discussion on industry, market and competition will derive from explorations of opportunity analysis conducted pursuant to the contents of Chapter 4; marketing planning relates to Chapter 11 – on building and developing a successful brand; the discourse on acquiring financial resources (Chapter 7) and managing financial resources (Chapter 8) will be picked up again in the sub-section on financial requirements and financial plan; and finally, the discussion on exit strategies is drawn from lessons learned in Chapter 13.

In covering the various sections of the business plan, I will stress that the executive summary is the most important section, as it provides a snapshot of the entire business plan and is the part that determines whether the rest of the business plan will be read or not.

Developing a Business Plan

Business plans at their most basic are simply a written representation of where an enterprise is going, how it will get there, and what it will look like when it gets there. It can take many forms: from a glossy, professionally produced document to a handwritten manuscript in a three-ring binder which serves as the documentation for the goals, objectives, strategies and tactics of a company.[1]

Sahlman notes that, "judging by all the hoopla surrounding business plans, you would think that the only things standing between a would-be entrepreneur and spectacular success are glossy five-colour charts, a bundle of meticulous-looking spreadsheets, and a decade of month-by-month financial projections. Nothing could be further from the truth ... business plans rank no higher than 2 – on a scale from 1 to 10 – as a predicator of a new venture's success. And sometimes, in fact, the more elaborately crafted the document, the more likely the venture is to ... flop." Sahlman then concludes by saying that "most [business plans] waste too much ink on numbers and devote too little time to the information that really matters to investors."[2]

It is not that business plans are not important. The problem is that many people approach business plans the wrong way. All entrepreneurial ventures require a business plan that succinctly captures the entrepreneur's strategy and plans for the venture and serves as a road map for his journey from idea to profit. As the strategy and plans need to be put in context, the business plan should also contain details about the business opportunity, the market the entrepreneur wants to serve and how the entrepreneur plans to pursue the opportunity identified.[3] Beyond the opportunity and the context, the business plan should also focus on the stakeholders of the enterprise and the risk-reward assessment.

Developing a business plan can be a time-consuming and stressful exercise for the would-be entrepreneur. However, it is a valuable exercise which every entrepreneur must undertake. Although the elements of a business plan are considered to be standard, the entrepreneur should not approach writing the business plan as a template filling exercise. Rather, he should aim to use the business plan to articulate the uniqueness of his particular enterprise and the opportunity presented by it. He must develop the business plan with the target audience in mind. The goal should be to develop a business plan that gives the target audience the information they require in their decision-making processes.

A business plan should demonstrate that the entrepreneur is an expert in identifying, analysing and exploiting the opportunity he is focused on. It must show that the entrepreneur has thought through the potential venture and the key success factors. It should also demonstrate that the entrepreneur has carried out the relevant research and considered both the pros and cons of the business concept. In developing the business plan, the entrepreneur must note that timing is critical to the launch of every entrepreneurial venture, and so the entrepreneur must articulate why his chosen time is indeed the right one to launch this particular enterprise in this particular market and focused on specific opportunities.

While one business plan will vary from the other, and from one enterprise or industry to the other, there are certain key guidelines that every entrepreneur needs to note and follow when developing a business plan:

Tell a Complete Story About the Enterprise

This should cover the management team, the strategy, the opportunity, the products or services, financing needs, marketing plan, the risk involved, and the financial and non-financial goals of the enterprise.

Be Balanced and Highlight Positive and Negative Aspects of Opportunity

While the business plan should be persuasive to the target audience, such as investors, on the viability of the entrepreneurial opportunity, it should also identify the potential limitations of the business idea and explain how these limitations will be dealt with.

Be Forward-Looking with a Time Frame of About Three Years.

While the entrepreneur needs to have a long-term perspective at the back of his mind in developing the business plan, it is better to focus immediately on short-term plans and to adapt as the enterprise grows. This ensures that the business plan remains relevant in a changing business environment.

Be Clear, Concise and Organised

The key is to keep to the point, excluding information that does not add value. The business plan should be organised in a thoroughly reasoned and structured manner, and must include subheadings to make it simple to read. Any additional detailed information can be separated out and put in appendices.

Be Simple to Understand

It must contain all the information about the enterprise, but without using complex words or concepts.

Not Contain Information that Cannot be Substantiated with Facts

There must be realistic data to substantiate claims. If the objective of the business plan is to seek external financing, its persuasiveness will to a large extent depend on thorough research about the industry and supporting arguments with realistic and verifiable data, all pointing to an exciting opportunity with an attractive return on investment.

Clearly State Expected Return on Investment

The business plan should state clearly to potential investors (if the objective of the business plan is to seek investment) what the expected return on their investment will be, and also what the anticipated exit options will be. Investors make their decisions to invest partly based on the investment return they will get. They also focus on how they can profitably get out of the enterprise should they decide to exit.

Provide Projected Financial Statements

A good business opportunity should be quantifiable in financial terms. The business plan should therefore provide proforma financial statements to back the claims that the entrepreneur is making in terms of the prospects of the enterprise. In the case of an existing enterprise, the plan should also provide historical financial statements.

The exact detail of the information presented in the business plan will vary depending on whether the objective of the business plan is to solicit funding and, if it is, on the type of funding the enterprise is seeking – whether the funding is for an acquisition or to start up. In the case of a start-up, for example, the emphasis might be on providing information that substantiates the existence of market demand for the product or service. On the other hand, where the funding is for the acquisition of an existing enterprise, it should describe how the acquiring enterprise (or acquiring entrepreneur) will add value and enhance the competitive advantage of the existing enterprise.

Priority should also be placed on ensuring that investors are convinced that the management team in question has the experience and skills necessary to launch and manage the relevant enterprise. In the case of an enterprise that has undertaken significant research and development to get a product to market, or in the case of an enterprise leveraging a new technology, a research and development section should be included to highlight these efforts. However, this may not be necessary in a business plan for an import-export business or a restaurant, for example.

As much as possible, entrepreneurs should prepare the business plan themselves rather than rely on outsiders to prepare them. Even when outsiders such as consultants are used, the entrepreneur should be actively involved to make sure that the business plan represents her understanding of the opportunity and her best guess of how she will generate attractive returns by developing an enterprise that seeks to remove a particular customer pain which forms the basis of the identified opportunity. Since it is her business, idea and vision, I submit that only the entrepreneur is best placed to completely understand the business and its envisioned future. As it will be the entrepreneur (and not an external consultant) actually be running the enterprise or indeed explaining the business opportunity and the enterprise concept to potential investors, it is important that the entrepreneur is very familiar with all the details about the business, and that she is able to articulate all those details and to clearly navigate her audience through the road map to achieving her set targets. The risk of relying on someone else to prepare the business plan without complete participation is that, in the case of entrepreneurs requiring external finance, they may not appear convincing when making their case to potential investors. Other entrepreneurs may find that they have not completely grasped the business and therefore are not able to anticipate and deal with challenges that may arise.

Research shows that there is a vibrant market in business plan writing in Ghana. Many owners of small and medium-sized enterprises rely on third parties to develop business plans for them, particularly in the context of seeking external financing and often with no participation from the entrepreneurs. I think this practice is regrettable and should be discouraged.

Role of the Business Plan

Too many entrepreneurs devote time and resources to writing an elaborate business plan which they quickly forget about as they develop their enterprises. It is a complete waste of everyone's time if the business plan, after it has been developed, is left idle on the entrepreneur's shelf.

For the life of the enterprise, the business plan (and other modifications or upgrades of the plan) should be used actively by the entrepreneur in managing his enterprise. A business plan plays the following roles stated and expanded on below.

• *Acts as a Management Tool*

A business plan guides the entrepreneur by charting the future course for his enterprise, which provides a guide to devising a strategy to follow the proposed course. It helps translate a vague notion of wanting to start a business into quantifiable targets and a plan for reaching those targets. In addition to setting targets, it also provides a yardstick for measuring actual performance against those targets as well as putting those targets in the wider context of the competitive environment.

It is a tool that guides the entrepreneur over the entire life span of the business. The plan forces the entrepreneur to make an objective assessment of the performance of the enterprise. This means that at any point in time there should be a business plan in place. It is therefore important that the business plan becomes a 'living document' which is constantly evolving. The entrepreneur should constantly refer to it, and should update it at the end of each financial year in preparation for the next year of operations. Doing so affords entrepreneurs the opportunity to capture valuable lessons from that year's operation and prevent mistakes that took place during the passing/past year.

In this way, the business plan also becomes the budget for the enterprise. For instance, the financial projections can serve as a budget against which actual financial performance can be compared. In so doing, the reasons for variances between the budgeted and actual performance can be investigated and addressed on an annual basis.

Many entrepreneurs have found that just completing the steps required to develop a business plan forces them to introduce discipline and a logical thought process into all of their planning activities. They have found that a properly prepared business plan can greatly improve their company's ability to consistently establish and meet the goals and objectives in a way that best serves the company's owners' and employees' interests.[4]

• Is a Proactive Problem-Solving Document

The process of writing the business plan can reveal potential problems to the entrepreneur and give him an opportunity to think through these problems and devise potential solutions to them. It helps the entrepreneur to identify and uncover various obstacles that he might not otherwise have been prepared to handle.

Developing a business plan involves analysing all aspects of the enterprise and designing business strategies to deal with any uncertainties that may arise. Through this, it becomes a tool that allows the entrepreneur to identify the weaknesses and other significant aspects of the enterprise which he may not otherwise have given advance attention to. This becomes even more relevant when the entrepreneur asks others to review the business plan. Questions asked by those reviewing the plan may highlight omissions and gaps, and question strengths and opportunities assumed by the entrepreneur. Doing this allows the entrepreneur to take into account and address a wide range of potential factors that could negatively impact his enterprise.

Through this, the business plan becomes a tool that defines and focuses the objective of the enterprise based on the appropriate data and analysis that the entrepreneur has conducted.

• *Forces Industry Understanding*

I have stated several times that how well an enterprise does depends to a large extent on the industry in which it is competing. It is crucial therefore that the entrepreneur thoroughly understands the drivers and players in the industry, and the role her own enterprise plays or will play in the industry. Writing a business plan gives an entrepreneur an in-depth understanding of the industry in which she is competing and how her particular enterprise fits in. Also, going through the process of writing the business plan forces the entrepreneurial team to think about the business idea and opportunity from the start-up stage through to the stage of sustainable profitability.

It is also a useful exercise that helps to develop the managerial competence of the entrepreneur and his team as it forces them to constantly think about how to achieve the goals and objectives that are set in the business plan.

• *Provides Analytical Discipline*

It forces the entrepreneur to think through the question of whether his business idea can actually produce a profit or not. Sometimes, the greatest value a business plan may provide an entrepreneur is to educate him that the proposed business venture simply will not work. It is better for the entrepreneur to fail 'on paper' in the planning stages, rather than much later when he has committed time and resources to the venture.

• *Helps Attract Lenders and Investors*

By providing a framework to set out the business concept both in detail and as a summary of the key strengths and weakness and a reasonable estimate of revenue and cost projections, the business plan provides a medium for the entrepreneur to sell his business concept to potential investors. Typically, the analysis inherent in preparing a business plan provides the entrepreneur with the tools to articulate the return on investment available to investors. Investors thinking of investing in the enterprise would be primarily concerned about knowing what they would get in return for risking their capital, and also whether the entrepreneur and his team have the ability to successfully execute the plan that will deliver the anticipated returns.

As a sales tool, the business plan must be able to convince people about the viability of the entrepreneur's business idea. If a reading of the business plan cannot convince the target audience about the business idea, then the business idea is either not worth pursuing or the business plan needs to be rewritten. This means that for a business plan to be considered as a sales tool, it must be saleable and persuasive. To achieve this, the entrepreneur should avoid using fancy words and abstract theories but let his research, facts and data tell a compelling story about the entrepreneurial opportunity.

• *Communicates the Business Idea to External Parties*

The business plan is a tool that allows the entrepreneur to communicate effectively with other parties who are interested in the enterprise. In addition to potential financiers, this may include other potential partners such as suppliers, auditors, lawyers and brand consultants who may otherwise not understand the nature of the enterprise's operations.

• *Communicates the Enterprise's Story to Current and Potential Employees*

The enterprise's story must be told and retold several times internally. The business plan is often the one document that fits together all the pieces of the enterprise's story and history and is able to communicate that story to employees (both current and future), particularly senior employees. Also, as the enterprise achieves the targets set out in the business plan, it can be a great source of motivation for employees.

• *Enhances the Chances of Success*

The real value of the business plan is the analytical and research process that the entrepreneur has to go through to prepare the business plan. By providing a framework and a set of tools to subject ideas to objective critical evaluation, the business plan ensures a greater chance of success for the business. Because the process enables entrepreneurs to learn about industries, target markets, competition and key success factors, it makes them better equipped than they might otherwise have been in respect of launching the venture. It therefore reduces the risk and uncertainty of launching and managing an enterprise by teaching entrepreneurs to do it the right way.

Elements of a Business Plan

Although business plans come in many shapes, sizes and forms and no two look exactly alike, it is generally accepted that each must contain certain standard elements. It should however be noted that many people pursue business plans differently and, often, what goes into any business plan depends on a number of factors, including the end use, the target audience, the nature of the business, the stage in the businesses' life cycle and the nature of the industry. Even how the key or standard elements are presented and dealt with differs from entrepreneur to entrepreneur. The following analogy might be helpful. While all domestic dwellings must have certain key elements like a foundation, windows, doors, ventilation and sanitary facilities, different people develop homes differently depending on their objectives, resources and desires, while making provision for the key elements identified.

The key elements that constitute a business plan include the points identified and expatiated on below.

Executive Summary

The executive summary is a snapshot of the entire business plan, providing a compelling summary of the rest of the document for the targeted audience. My view is that the executive summary is the most important part of the entire business plan because it provides a window to the rest of the plan. It should be written with the view to grab the attention of readers, deepen their interest and make them want to read more about the entrepreneurial opportunity. The executive summary should provide an overview of the entire venture to enable potential investors determine whether they might be willing, at least in principle, to invest.

Venture capitalists and other investors often receive hundreds of business plans. Given the sheer volume of business plans they receive, many venture capitalists and professional investors do not go beyond the executive summary page of the business plan. If you lose such a person at the executive summary she will not see the rest of the business plan, regardless of how impressive it might be. Thus, the executive summary is often a screen or hurdle that determines whether funders will read the rest of the business plan, making it the most important yet most difficult part to develop.[5] As such, the entrepreneur and his team need to spend time crafting an excellent executive summary; it should capture the essence of the business idea and be very persuasive.

Readers of the executive summary should be able to complete it in five to ten minutes and it should be clear, after reading it, what the business concept is and what differentiates it from the competition. The executive summary should therefore capture the major highlights of the business plan and the key facts that will interest the target audience. The intention here is to make it persuasive by selling the business idea.

In one page, or two pages at most, the executive summary should explain clearly the existing customer problem or opportunity gap (customer pain) and how the enterprise will solve the problem. It should also explain the basic business model and elaborate the product or service that the enterprise is offering to consumers. This should include the business case for the product or service and an explanation of how the enterprise seeks to eliminate the customer pain with the provision of the product or service.

The executive summary should also briefly highlight the enterprise, its vision, mission and strategy. It needs to put the enterprise in historical perspective by describing how the enterprise was established, and if it is an existing enterprise, how it has been performing in the market so far. The executive summary should also briefly describe the target market that the enterprise wants to serve in the industry, going on to outline the expertise of its management in terms of their ability to turn the business idea into a profitable enterprise.

It should also discuss the existing competition and how the enterprise and its management intend to beat competitors based on certain specific competitive advantages that they have. The key marketing strategy needs to be included here, describing why the entrepreneur chose a particular market segment, the trends in that market, the risk and reward in the market, and why the market is attractive in terms of its future profitability and viability.

An important component of the executive summary is the financing requirements of the enterprise (the cedi amount requested), and how the funds will be used in the enterprise over a period of time. This part should talk about the historical financial needs of the enterprise and how it has been able to meet these financial needs so far, as well as its plans to raise additional capital if that is required. If the business plan is targeted at investors, it should state the exact financial requirement of the enterprise and the anticipated return it is offering investors. A key aspect of the executive summary is the bottom line financial performance; the executive summary should therefore should include highlights of the projected or actual sales and revenue, as well as the gross and net profit. It should further state the exit options available for investors.

The executive summary is an independent element of the business plan and should not be confused with any of the other sections. It is usually prepared after the other sections of the business plan have been completed. Indeed, its contents are contingent on the rest of the document and it cannot be written properly until the other components of the plan are essentially complete. It is therefore helpful to note one or two key sentences and some key facts and numbers from each section of the business plan proper as it is drafted, which can then be included in the executive summary.

Every executive summary must answer the following questions:

- What is the business idea? In what way is it unique?
- Who are the target customers?
- What is the value for those customers? (What is the customer pain that this business seeks to remove?)
- Who are the major customers of the enterprise?
- What test customers (if any) have been approached or could be approached?
- What distribution channels will be used?
- What partnerships (if any) will be entered into?
- What opportunities and risks are anticipated?
- What is the forecasted market volume and growth rate?
- What is the competitive environment like?
- What are the sales, costs and profit situations?
- How much investment is necessary?
- Who are the key managers and how will the entrepreneur delegate management responsibility?

Opportunity, Product or Service

The market opportunity is an essential part of the business plan as it is the platform for the entrepreneur to start an enterprise or to expand an existing enterprise. It describes the core business model and the profile of the business itself in terms of what the enterprise wants to sell and to whom, whether the business can grow fast and the likely factors that will stand in the way of success.[6] The essential premise of the business plan should be to address a current customer pain. It should recognise a customer need and then address that need. If competitors are currently attempting to address or are addressing that need, the entrepreneur will have to articulate how he will address that same need in a way that is better than the competition. It should be crystal clear to the reader of the business plan the function the product or service fulfils and the value the customer will gain from it.

The opportunity section should describe the market forces that drive the business idea, the size of the target market and its potential to grow in the future. From an investor's point of view, a growing market is more attractive than a mature market with developed competitors, because there is greater potential to gain market share. The business plan must elaborate how attractive the industry is in terms of its growth potential, and how the enterprise can make profit out of it. Where there is little evidence to support the industry's prospects, the business plan should specify how the entrepreneur intends to develop a profitable enterprise in that industry.

The opportunity should be presented in a clear and persuasive manner. It should talk about the economic factors that affect the business opportunity and how they will contribute to its success. This is also a good place to indicate the resources that the enterprise requires in order to develop the opportunity. The business plan should also state how the enterprise will develop and launch its products in the market. The emphasis should be to demonstrate that the opportunity is economically viable and one that the enterprise can undertake profitably, given the target customer base and the wider market forces at play

In describing the product or service, it is important to indicate how it differs from the competition. This section should describe the quality of the entrepreneur's product or service and its price in comparison with existing competitors. The entrepreneur should also describe the sources of inputs and the general ability of the suppliers to provide quality inputs. She needs to provide an objective assessment of the quality of her product or service by describing some strengths and weaknesses and her assessment of how marketable the product or service is.

The product or service description also needs to highlight the unique features and benefits of the product or service in comparison with the competition. If there are particular skills, experiences or technologies that are required to produce the product or provide the service, they must be listed and the entrepreneur must show that the enterprise has access to them.

The entrepreneur must convincingly substantiate the added value the customer will receive from him rather than from the existing alternatives. To do so, the entrepreneur should put himself in the place of the customer and carefully weigh the advantages and disadvantages of his offering over those of the competitive set.

Where relevant, this section should also include a short description of how far development of a product or service has progressed and what still needs to be done. The entrepreneur should also include information about the nature of the relevant innovation and the edge he has over competitors. The entrepreneur must refrain from using technical language and describe everything as simply as possible. Where possible, he must also have a finished prototype to show potential investors so as to demonstrate that he is up to meeting any technical challenges. Alternatively, a photo or sketch of the product can be included to enhance understanding of the product. Where possible, it is helpful to have pilot customers who already use the product and are able to give testimonials based on their experiences.

The following key questions should guide the entrepreneur in writing the opportunity, product or service section of the business plan:

- What are the identified customer needs that the product/service seeks to address?

- What is the value for those customers? (What is the customer pain that this business seeks to remove?)

- What are the strengths and weakness of comparable products or services and how do they compare to the entrepreneur's product or service?

- What is the nature of the business opportunity? Is there potential for growth in the coming years?

- What factors are likely to lead to the success of the business opportunity?

- What kind of service/maintenance would the entrepreneur provide to customers after they acquire the product or service?

- What is the nature of the innovation behind the business

concept?

- What is the current status of technical development?

The Enterprise or Entity

The objective of this section is to provide information on the background of the enterprise or the relevant entity behind the entrepreneurial venture. It will generally describe the concept that the enterprise is built upon, and by way of background, give the date the enterprise was set up and describe its products or service offering and the involvement of the owners of the enterprise. The section should identify the owners of the enterprise and describe the ownership structure. Where some of the owners are not actively involved in the enterprise, this section should make clear which of owners are active and which ones are passive.

The legal form or structure of the enterprise should be stated and the reasons for choosing that particular legal structure explained. If it is a sole proprietorship, it should list the name and details of the sole proprietor. If it is a partnership, the identity of the partners and their respective percentage ownership in the enterprise must be stated. In the case of a company the identity of the shareholders and their respective shareholding should be stated. If it is anticipated that the enterprise will change the ownership structure, this should also be stated here together with the rationale. For example, the owners sometimes may agree to change the ownership holding structure of an enterprise in the near future based on meeting certain targets (for example, the CEO of the enterprise could have his shareholding increased based on meeting certain financial targets under an employee share option scheme).

This section should also describe the enterprise in terms of what it does or the product and services that it provides to customers. It will describe the processes involved in providing the product or service and any decisions with respect to subcontracting any aspects of the value chain. The location of the enterprise should also be included in the description together with an explanation of why that location was chosen and the value the location provides the enterprise. If the enterprise has been in business for several years and is seeking expansion financing, this section should also contain a review of its history and sales and profit performance. If there have been any setbacks or losses in prior years, a discussion of these as well as current and future efforts to prevent a recurrence should be inserted. The description should be factual in that the entrepreneur should not present the enterprise as bigger or better than what it really is.

In this section, the entrepreneur should state clearly the goals and objectives of the enterprise, and how the entrepreneur plans to achieve these goals and objectives. The goals and objectives can be categorised under short and long terms. For instance, short-term objectives might be to reach a particular sales target, increase profit by a predetermined margin or gain a specific market share; long-term objectives can be to introduce a new product into the market, to initiate particular research and development activities or to grow the enterprise to a particular stage over a period of time.

It is expected that every enterprise owns assets. This section should also be devoted to describing all the assets, both tangible and intangible, that the enterprise has, including the state or condition in which these assets are. Some enterprises own intellectual property rights over certain products, services or even names. These should be included in the business plan. If the enterprise has a license or a franchise agreement, it should be stated.

Vision, Mission and Strategy

The business plan is an important tool to help define the philosophy of the enterprise. What does the enterprise stand for? How does it want to be perceived? What is the brand that the enterprise seeks to build? How does it intend to compete and to achieve its objectives?

As we saw in Chapter 2, dreaming has a central place in every business. You will recall that in that chapter I said the entrepreneur is the person who dreams the dream for the enterprise. The vision for the enterprise is the dream or picture of an envisaged future as seen in the eyes of the entrepreneur, provided it is quantifiable, measurable, time-bound, and articulates what the enterprise intends to achieve in the long term. Below is the original vision of Origin8 as articulated by the two founders when they set it up:

> ▌ *"One day. One day soon ... Origin8 will be acknowledged and revered around the world as a [creatively driven], efficient and results-achieving integrated marketing communications company, of truly savvy professionals. That day, we'll be listed on bourses across Africa and the rest of the world ... and in each market we choose to be listed, there'll be a 'mad rush' for Origin8 shares, not because investors the world over have nothing else to do with their funds, but because at that point and forever thereafter everybody can honestly say of us – this is truly a profitable, world-class multinational organisation."[7]*

Although it fails to clarify when the 'one day soon' is, I like this vision because it is able to paint a clear picture of the dream that the co-founders of Origin8 had for their company. My only suggestion would be for the vision to be bound by a definite time frame, with a definition of when the day of reckoning is expected to be.

Closely related to the vision is the mission of the enterprise. The mission of an enterprise is the broadest expression of its purpose and defines the direction it will take. As Collins and Porras[8] put it, this is effectively the core ideology of the enterprise. The core ideology signifies what an enterprise stands for, why it exists as an entity and embodies the key principles and tenets that guide the enterprise. The reason for the existence of the enterprise reflects the motivation that the entrepreneurial team has for initiating and implementing the business idea.

The business plan should include both the vision and the mission statement of the enterprise. Both the vision and the mission statement should be an accurate reflection of reality – where the enterprise is going and why the enterprise exists. The vision should not be too vague and unrealisable in the long term.

The entrepreneur achieves his vision by setting out a strategy. Strategy consists of a stream of decisions over time which reflects the firm's goals and the means used to achieve them.[9]

Realising the goals and objectives of an enterprise depends on how the entrepreneur executes the strategy. The business plan should therefore discuss the strategy of the enterprise in detail, including how the enterprise competes or intends to compete in the market. For example, the enterprise may decide to compete against rivals either based on price or differentiation, or a combination of both. If the enterprise is competing on price, then it must state how it is pricing its products and services in the market and how a strategy of lower prices allows it to outperform competitors.

If the enterprise seeks to differentiate itself from the market through its product or service offering, the business plan should elaborate on how different the enterprise's products and services are from the market and how that gives the enterprise a competitive advantage. The differentiation could result in the ability to provide products and services that meet a need of the customer unmet by the existing market offerings. It is important that the entrepreneur is able to articulate how the competitive advantage derived from the differentiation results in profit.

The strategy of any enterprise must be aligned with the rest of the organisation. The strategy must fit with the other aspects of the enterprise and reinforce those other aspects. In particular, the strategy must be aligned with the people, structure and governance, leadership and culture of the enterprise. For example, if the strategy of an enterprise revolves around innovation, the entrepreneur will need to put a mechanism in place to attract bright people who challenge the status quo and have a track record of innovation. The enterprise will also have to develop a governance structure that promotes innovation and develops a culture that reinforces the same.

Vision and mission do not rest with the entrepreneur or the entrepreneurial team alone. Every member of the enterprise must buy into the vision and mission, identify with, aspire to and live up to them. I noticed from the results presented by my research team that many of the enterprises that were outperforming their peers had clear visions and missions that were shared by everyone in the enterprise. When asked in 2010 about what accounted for Origin8's strong and consistent performance and rapid growth and expansion in Ghana, co-founder and ex-CEO Joel Nettey said: "A clear vision. Junior [the late Daniel Twum, his co-founder] and I knew exactly where we wanted to go from day one and we were careful to ensure that every new employee who joined [us] understood and shared this vision and had what it took to contribute towards achieving it."[10]

Albert Ocran, founder and Chief Executive Officer of Combert Impressions also explains that, in crafting the mission statement for Combert Impressions, he invited participation from all his employees, including the apprentices. As he noted, "it was therefore not difficult for them to internalise the mission statement because they had been part of developing it."[11]

Organisational Plan

An organisational plan sets out how the enterprise is or will be organised, how decisions will be made, who does what and how roles and responsibilities will be delegated to ensure that the enterprise achieves its objectives. For example, this will articulate whether the intention is to operate with a skeleton staff and to outsource all functions, or whether the enterprise will operate with the full complement of staff in departments such as research and development, production, marketing, finance and human resources. The best way to describe the organisational plan is to present it in the form of an organisational chart depicting a hierarchical order of positions, roles and responsibilities within the enterprise.

The enterprise or entity section must answer the following questions:

- What is the form of entity: sole proprietorship, partnership, company, joint venture, etc.?
- When was this entity established and by whom? What is the shareholding or partnership structure? What experience and skills do the key team members bring? What is their

involvement in the day-to-day operations of the enterprise?

- Is it a start up or a going concern?
- What is the vision, mission and strategy of the enterprise?
- What type of industry is it in: service, retail, manufacturing, etc.?
- What is the total number of employees?
- Where is the entity located or to be located?
- Are there any plans to outsource any component of the production and delivery processes?
- How is the enterprise organised in terms of roles and responsibilities?

Management Team

The people factor is perhaps the second most important element of any business plan (after the executive summary); as such the entrepreneur should devote ample space to talk about the team. Potential investors typically turn first to the management section after reading the executive summary as the success of any venture essentially drills down to the ability of the management team to execute the plan. Investors are always keen to know who is behind an enterprise, their experience and their qualifications. Bill Sahlman, a Harvard professor and seasoned investor, notes: "When I receive a business plan, I always read the resume section first. Not because the people part of the new venture is the most important, but because without the right team, none of the other parts really matter."[12]

It is therefore important for entrepreneurs to take time to select a competent team that would be able to achieve the goals set out in the business plan, and then strongly articulate the competence and experience of the team in the business plan. Even a sole entrepreneur is likely to rely on other people to perform certain tasks essential to the success of the enterprise; such people should be considered part of his team. In choosing a team, the entrepreneur should ensure that potential members have the following characteristics.

Common Vision

This is where every one of them wants to succeed in achieving the desired outcome. The team must have a common dream as to where they want to take the enterprise to, or at least buy into the dream of the entrepreneur.

Complementary Skills, Attributes and Strengths

It is important that team members complement each other in terms of skills, attributes and strengths to ensure that as balanced a team as possible is created. If the key entrepreneur is an engineer, for example, and is very strong in the operations side of the business, it is important that he takes time to recruit someone with strong complementary skills in, for example, marketing and creativity to balance his quantitative strengths.

Lean Team

It is important that the team is kept as lean as possible to ensure that the costs of running the venture are minimised. This is particularly significant in the start-up phase of the enterprise, so that additional team members can be recruited as the enterprise expands.

Resilience

The team should be one that is likely to stick together through thick and thin, one that has the ability to deal quickly with setbacks and move on.

Get Along with Each Other

It is fundamental that the people chosen to help run the enterprise respect and get along with each other. That reduces the potential for personality conflicts, which could potentially derail the attainment of the enterprise's vision and mission.

The management section should offer a brief profile of each of the management team's members, including their education, experience, skills and other credentials, as well as their responsibilities. While not all the team members are likely to have experience within the relevant market, at least one person should have some knowledge about it. When describing the management team, emphasis should be on how the opportunity fits in with the personal backgrounds and experiences of the team. This section should also include the names, background and experience of the members of the board of directors or board of advisors as the case may be.

The section should describe the experience of the team and show how familiar they are with the industry and the key players in it. It should highlight the experience, skill set and key qualifications of each team member in a way that strongly highlights their ability to perform the role assigned to them in the entrepreneurial venture. Where relevant, the entrepreneur should also present indications of commitment, such as the willingness of team members to initially accept modest salaries.

Having experienced team members and people who are known in the industry is often preferred by investors. The advantage of having experienced and prominent people in a new venture is that, while the enterprise will be new to the market, the people will not necessarily be new; subsequently, it reduces the uncertainty and risk associated with dealing with the start up. Investors actually invest in people, not ideas. The right kind of people can get a wrong idea reshaped, but bringing together the wrong people can kill a potentially excellent idea.

All the resumes of the people involved – indicating what they have done in the past that shows that they will be successful in the future – should be included as appendices.

In the management section of the business plan, the details of how responsibilities are to be delegated to the various members of management should be spelled out. It should also be clear that there is a proper balance between technical, managerial and business skills and experience.

The description of the management team must be as objective as possible, talking about both the positive and negative sides of the competencies and skill set of the people involved. Where there are gaps, the best approach is to identify the skills that the team lacks and then to describe how the entrepreneur plans to get these skills into the enterprise. If he needs to hire people with specific competencies to fill in a skill gap, the entrepreneur should state that in the business plan. If there are plans for training programmes for the team, there should be a description of how they will improve performance. Some enterprises hire certain professionals – lawyers, accountants, insurance brokers and bankers – to provide specialised advice to the enterprise. These professionals are important resources to the enterprise and, although not employees of the enterprise, who they are, the service they provide and their relationship with the enterprise must also be described in this section.

These key questions must be answered in the management section of the business plan:

- Who are the key members of management and what are their roles?
- Who are the members of the board of directors and/or the advisory board?
- What distinguishes them – education, professional experience and success, standing in the business community?
- What experience or abilities do team members possess that will be useful for implementing the business concept?
- What experience or abilities are lacking? How will these gaps be closed? By whom?
- How high is the motivation of each individual team member?
- What levels of commitment do the respective team members have to the enterprise?

Industry, Market and Competition

It is important that all entrepreneurs have a thorough understanding of the needs of their customers, as well as of the efforts that their competitors are making to meet those customer needs. An understanding of the competitive set requires a broad contextual understanding of the wider industry and the dynamics driving that industry. The entrepreneur should therefore analyse the industry or market in which she will be operating and the competitive forces that drives the industry, using the tools that we discussed in Chapter 4.

The section should provide a comprehensive analysis of the industry. In every business plan the entrepreneur must show that she is fully aware of the context in which the enterprise exists, and how that fosters or hinders the success of the enterprise. This should include, among others, the business environment, how the regulatory and policy environment will impact on the operations of the enterprise and the demographics in the country or region in which the entrepreneur is operating. This section of the business plan should also look at the level of economic activity, inflation, interest rates, exchange rates and the tax policy, and how these affect the growth and profitability of the enterprise. The business plan needs to anticipate changes in the business environment and how those changes might affect the prospects of the enterprise. It should also spell out clearly what the management team will do should the business context change in an unfavourable manner.

In addition, this section should consider market trends and patterns to determine how much opportunity there is in the market. The analysis should include current developments in the industry, such as technological breakthroughs that have a great impact on the market. There could be macro environmental factors that can affect how the product or service works, such as a shift in population, changes in customer demand and taste and sociocultural factors that are particularly significant to the industry.

An enterprise can be expected to make significant profits only if the market itself holds great potential. This section of the business plan should therefore include the entrepreneur's expectations of market growth (backed by reliable and objective data). The analysis should include the main factors affecting the development of the industry and the relevance of those factors to the enterprise. In the case of a real estate venture in Accra, for example, some linked factors may include the increase in GDP leading to increased prosperity and increased demand for housing as more and more Ghanaians build (or buy) and own their own homes. It is important to state as many of the factors as possible that the entrepreneur considers to be directly relevant (technology, legislative initiatives, socio-economic changes, etc.).

The entrepreneur should review information from sources such as the National Board for Small Scale industries, the government's annual budget statement, newspapers (particularly the Daily Graphic and Business & Financial Times), websites (like www.ghanaweb.com and www.businessghana.com) as well as statistics and census information published by the Ghana Statistical Service.

The information that the entrepreneur requires would typically not be found in one neat bundle in one place. As a result, the entrepreneur would have to be creative and combine a number of different sources to reach well-founded conclusions or estimates. He should, wherever possible, rely on verifiable figures and use logical assumptions. He should also cross-check his information by verifying facts with experts in the industry, and he must also do a 'sense-check' to make sure that any estimates he comes up with make sense.

For example, an entrepreneur estimating the market size for secondary school textbooks may find data from the Ministry of Education about the number of secondary schools, the number of students enrolled in secondary schools, the average annual increase in student numbers and the amount of money available to secondary schools for purchasing textbooks. He may also visit a few of these schools to talk to teachers (to get a feel for the number of books available compared with the number of students), to school librarians (about the wait list for certain popular books) and to parents (to gauge the willingness to purchase textbooks for their wards).

The section on industry, market and competition should also provide information about the segmentation carried out on the market and an examination of the existing competition. A comprehensive competitor analysis should identify the competitors, their strengths and weaknesses and how they are likely to respond to a new entrant into the market, as well as how the entrepreneur plans to compete with the existing competitive set. It should also analyse the market share and performance of competitors in terms of revenue and profit. This section should expand on any competitive advantage – in human capital, technology or intellectual property, for example – and also any competitive disadvantage that the competition possesses.

In sum, the key members of the competitive set must be evaluated using the same criteria, such as sales volume, revenue, pricing, growth, market share, cost positioning, product lines, target groups and distribution channels. The entrepreneur's enterprise must also be evaluated according to the same criteria. Once this is done, the entrepreneur's competitive advantage must be highlighted vis-à-vis the competitive set.

For an existing enterprise, this section will also highlight the entrepreneur's positioning in the market, explaining the differentiation in the value proposition that the entrepreneur offers/will offer customers as compared to the competitive set. Where the enterprise lags behind the competition and has plans to close the gap, this section must show how the entrepreneur intends to reposition his enterprise in the market to gain a bigger market share.

The following key questions must be answered as part of the industry, market and competition section of the business plan:

- » How is the industry developing?
- » What are the key success factors in the industry?
- » What role do innovation and technological advances play in the industry?
- » How would the entrepreneur segment the market?
- » What market volumes (value and amount) do the individual market segments have, now or in the future (rough estimates)?
- » What volumes does the entrepreneur estimate for the next five years?
- » What would influence growth in the market segments?
- » Who are the target customer groups?
- » Who are the reference customers?

» How much does the enterprise depend on large customers?

» What are the key buying factors facing customers?

» What are the barriers to market entry and how can they be overcome?

» What major competitors offer similar products/services?

» How profitable are the competitors?

» What are the competitors' marketing strategies?

» How do the strengths and weaknesses of the major competitors compare to the strengths and weaknesses of the enterprise that the business plan relates to?

» What new developments can be expected from competitors?

» How sustainable will the entrepreneur's competitive edge be?

Marketing Plan

This section of the business plan sets out the marketing and sales strategy for the enterprise. It includes a description of targeted customers, distribution, promotion, advertising strategy, pricing strategy and sales tactics and projections, based on reasonable assumptions. Increasing market share or beating the competition requires a selling strategy which states clearly how the entrepreneur intends to grow the customer base for his products and services.

This section should build upon the analysis of the market and competition by clearly stating the target customer, or the market gap that the entrepreneur intends to fill. This is the unmet need or the customer pain that the current market fails to satisfy. In stating how she plans to meet the customer pain, the entrepreneur must include the resources at her disposal and her strengths and weaknesses. It is also important that this section clearly and concisely articulates not only the core customer target but provides an indication of how large this group is. For example, an entrepreneur targeting males aged between eighteen and fifty years for a new line of men's shirts can get a feel for how large his potential market is by estimating based on census data for the region in which he conducts his business.

An important area of the marketing plan is the marketing approach the entrepreneur intends to take to satisfy target customers. Two major approaches can be used to satisfy the customer. The first approach is to develop the product or service and then look for the customer to buy. Here, the marketing approach begins with the development of a product and ends with finding a customer to buy the product. The other approach begins and ends with the customer: the customer is asked about his needs, which are then put into the design of the product or service; the final product or service is then sold on to the customer. As would have been obvious from the discussion in Chapters 4 and 11, my preferred approach is to start and end with the customer.

The characteristics of the target customer base should also be stated. This would include whether the customers are in the lower, middle or upper income group. It would also include details of their taste, preferences and lifestyles. The entrepreneur must identify the location of his target customers and articulate how he intends to reach them. He must also give an indication of whether or not he will be able to satisfy the demands of the targeted customers.

The marketing plan section of the business plan must include a brief (but rich) profile of the core customer so as to explain to the reader why that customer would react favourably to the proposed marketing and sales tactics. In some cases, the decision maker is different from the ultimate consumer. In such cases, the description of the target customer should explain that there might be a gatekeeper who makes decisions about the product. A mother, for example, may be the gatekeeper in relation to what shoes her daughter wears. As we learned in Chapter 4, the entrepreneur can obtain the relevant customer insights by talking to as many customer groups as possible, and then complement these insights with information from such secondary sources as newspapers, magazines, journals and other published and unpublished bodies of knowledge.

Once the core customer is defined, the rest of the section should seek to justify that this customer will be willing to pay the proposed asking price for the product, or shop in the way envisaged, or indeed react to the advertising medium being proposed. An expensive new product, for example, may be justified because of the technology it uses to make the life of the customer much easier; a business plan for a product targeting cocoa farmers may also argue in this section that because many cocoa farmers go to the farm with transistor radios, spending most of the advertising budget on radio advertising would be the best way to reach these farmers.

The marketing plan needs to elaborate on the marketing tools that would be used to sell the product or service, including advertising and promotion, together with the estimated marketing costs. As the first step to selling a product or service involves reaching the customer, information about how the entrepreneur plans to reach the target customer will be relevant here. Some products and services require mass advertising on television, radio or in the newspapers, while others may require tailored personal relationship building as a way to reach the target customer. It is important that the entrepreneur is able to measure the impact of the marketing tools he deploys; the anticipated impact should therefore be set out in the business plan to justify his choice of marketing tools to reach the relevant customer segments.

The business plan should also state the impact of the marketing tactics on sales and include current market share and future projections. The entrepreneur should reasonably (cautiously, but optimistically) forecast how his market share will grow relative to total market growth.

The discussion on distribution should focus on whether, for example, the enterprise will be relying on an in-house sales force, an enterprise shop or shops, third-party resellers, wholesalers, retailers or the Internet, to sell the product or service to the ultimate customer. Where relevant, this section should also include information about service and warranty policies.

Pricing Strategy

It is often a difficult exercise determining how much customers are prepared to pay for a product or service, but the business plan ought to address this question. In determining price, the production and marketing costs should be taken into account. An insightful business plan will look at the investment required and the returns expected of the enterprise and how the pricing policy will affect it.

The pricing strategy and the basis for it must be described in reasonable detail, including details of total cost, mark up, promotional policies and the general pricing structure. The pricing structure should include the price floor or the lowest price that the entrepreneur can charge and still make some profit, and the price ceiling which is determined largely by the market forces and what the customer is prepared to pay based on their perception of the enterprise's product or service offering.

More often than not, entrepreneurs make a common mistake of thinking that lowering their prices will force customers to leave competitors and buy their products or service. It is not as simple as that. When setting price, the entrepreneur must rely on the research he has carried out on the customer, and in particular on the things that customers deem important – time, quality and convenience, among others.[13] This allows the entrepreneur to set a price that customer will be happy to pay, which need not necessarily be a low price.

The trick is to establish a price that captures the value that the customer places on the product or service and, as I stated in Chapter 11, identifying what customers value and what they are willing to pay for a product or service requires detailed conversations with target consumers.

The following are the key questions that the marketing plan section must answer.

- Who are the target customers? What do they 'look' like?
- What is the potential size of the target customer base? Realistically, what percentage of this base can the entrepreneur capture?
- Who makes the ultimate decision about product purchase? Is

there a gatekeeper?

- What sales volume does the entrepreneur intend to capture?
- What is the sales price? What is the justification for that particular price?
- How will the entrepreneur draw the attention of his target market to the product or service?
- What advertising and promotional devices does the entrepreneur intend to use?
- What distribution channels does the entrepreneur intend to use? How will sales be spread over the different distribution channels?
- What market share per distribution channel does the entrepreneur intend to capture?
- What role do service and maintenance play?
- What payment policies would apply (if any)?

Financial Plan

This section of the business plan indicates the venture's financial potential, providing the benchmarks that management will aim for. The financial plan outlines the financial needs of the enterprise, how the entrepreneur plans to meet the financial needs and the actual or projected financial performance targets of the enterprise. Typically, the financial plan should be designed to show that the claims about the opportunity, the product or service and the sales and marketing strategies can work financially to create an enterprise that can survive and grow in the future.[14]

The first item to address in the financial plan is the financial needs and other capital requirements of the enterprise. The initial capital invested or to be invested in the enterprise should be outlined, with an indication of how that is broken into debt and equity capital. Evidence that the entrepreneur has invested his own money is important, as it increases his chances of raising money from external sources because it shows that he has committed his personal resources to the enterprise and will therefore be focused on attaining the greatest possible return on investment.

Where the entrepreneur seeks loan capital, he should state when the loan will be required and on what terms he is prepared to take the loan. He should list any collateral that he has and would be willing to use to secure the loan. As lenders value credit history, it will also be good for the entrepreneur to indicate his history of loan repayment, which should include any current credit facilities that he may have. The entrepreneur should also include details of how he intends to repay the loan if it is granted. Likewise, for equity capital, the entrepreneur must state the percentage of his share capital he is willing to give investors and for how much. This level of detail must be included in the financial plan to help potential investors make informed decisions about investing in the enterprise. The entrepreneur must not just give an indication of the amount he requires without showing why such an amount is needed and what plans he has for the capital. It is important to describe clearly how the entrepreneur is going to use the amount raised – to purchase assets, fund working capital or use it to expand the enterprise, for example. If the plan is to use the required capital to acquire assets, the business plan should list all the assets to be purchased and their respective costs (as an appendix).

The entrepreneur's requirement for financial capital must be justified by supporting his requirements with the market research previously conducted. For instance, his market research could have shown that if a particular product or service is improved upon, then his market share or profit margin would increase by a certain percentage. This information is important as it shows the entrepreneur's ability to repay the loan.

As part of the financial plan, the following financial statements will have to be prepared and will constitute exhibits to the business plan. It is important however to include key highlights of the financial statements in the financial plan section.

- *Actual Income Statements, Cash Flow Statements and Balance Sheets*

If the enterprise has been operating for some time, the entrepreneur must include the actual income statements, cash flow statements and balance sheets covering the current year and previous ones. These should highlight the sales revenue, the gross profit and the net profit of the enterprise over a period of time, together with its net cash flow position and its total assets and liabilities at particular points in time.

• *Proforma Income Statements for the First/Next Three Years*

These will be prepared using sales forecasts and will be based on reasonable estimates of production or operating costs. The proforma income statement shows all the sources of revenue, including sales and other income sources, as well as the total of expenditure items removed from the revenue to arrive at profit. The underlying assumptions made in preparing the proforma statements should be fully discussed. The major reason for developing proforma income statements is for the entrepreneur to demonstrate to potential lenders and investors that he has done his homework well and knows the profit potential of the market. For start-up enterprises without a track record, these projections may amount to no more than intelligent guesswork based on reasonable assumptions.

• *Proforma Balance Sheet*

This details of the anticipated assets and liabilities of the enterprise. The proforma balance sheet will show the assets and liabilities of the enterprise, as well as the sources of equity capital. It also indicates what assets the entrepreneur intends to purchase over a period of time and the sources of capital – either equity or debt – that will be secured to make such purchases. Again, the key assumptions for the projections should be included.

• *Proforma Cash Flow Analysis*

This projects the anticipated monthly cash flows for the first year of operations, and quarterly for at least the next two years. It details the amount and timing of expected cash inflows and outflows, determines the need for and timing of additional financing, indicates peak requirements for working capital and also shows how additional funding will be obtained (such as through equity financing, bank loans or short-term lines of credit from the banks). In sum, the proforma cash flow analysis should outline the present and future cash inflows and outflows, as well as the net cash flows – either surpluses or deficits. The assumptions made in respect of the timing of collection of receivables and trade discounts given must be discussed.

• Break-Even Analysis

In Chapter 8, I explained how one might go about calculating the break-even point. Recall that the break-even analysis helps the entrepreneur to indicate at which point the expenditure is equal to the sales revenue, and that it is the point at which there is no profit or loss. The entrepreneur should calculate the break-even point for the venture and indicate when it might be reached. He should also include a discussion of how the break-even point might be lowered or increased, and what conditions might necessitate such swings.

Risks Assessment and Reward

A business plan is essentially a picture of an anticipated set of events, given certain assumptions. It is therefore important to address the issue of what happens if key assumptions (such as those concerning sales and customer orders, growth rate, etc.) were to change.

Likewise, every entrepreneurial venture aims to make profit and all investors are interested in getting returns on their investments. However, they also want to know the degree to which they are risking their capital invested in the enterprise. Investors are interested in the worst- and best-case scenarios. The business plan must therefore include a thorough risk assessment unveiling all potential risks that the enterprise faces and how the entrepreneur plans to minimise these risks.

The risk assessment portion should focus on identifying all the risks that the enterprise is prone to in the course of its operations. These risks could come from the macroeconomic environment (such as interest rate and inflation risks), and even environmental or political risk.

They could also result from the degree of competition in the industry as well as from barriers to entry. The risks could be operational risks that result from the day-to-day operations of the enterprise. Such risks might include:

- Running out of cash before orders have been secured; this may be particularly relevant where the venture requires highly personalised marketing to win sales orders;

- Potential price cutting by competitors and how that will affect the competitive dynamics in the market;

- Delays caused by third parties to whom certain aspects of the business have been outsourced;

- Difficulties in obtaining bank credit;

- Breakdown of major equipment in the production line;

- Key managers leaving the enterprise.

The business plan must always anticipate obstacles that may arise and develop relevant solutions for hurdling them. This involves an assessment of everything that can go wrong and right in the enterprise, and how the entrepreneurial team is prepared to respond to the things that go wrong. Anticipating risks in this way shows that the entrepreneurial team has a complete understanding of both the positives and negatives of the business, and that team members are prepared to face uncertain situations that come their way.

In order to mitigate these potential risks, the entrepreneur should design a contingency response as part of the business plan. This will detail what he intends to do should any of the anticipated risks materialise, like, for instance, what measures the entrepreneur will take to reduce the effect of a competitor coming out with a new technology or product which results in reducing the entrepreneur's market share and profit.

The objective of this section is to highlight the key risks and to demonstrate how the entrepreneur and his team would deal with these risks were they to materialise. However, too much emphasis should not be placed on the risks. Identifying and discussing the potential risks in a venture increases the credibility of the entrepreneur and establishes confidence in his venture.

The reward portion should address the rewards that investors can expect from the enterprise's success, as well as any potential opportunities that might amplify these rewards. If the entrepreneur seeks equity investment, he needs to state in this section the potential return on equity investment and any future opportunities holders of equity may have as the enterprise grows. For debt capital, he should state the rate he is prepared to pay on the loan principal.

Another important aspect of this section is for the entrepreneur to state the exit strategies that are available to potential investors. Entrepreneurs seeking venture capital funds in particular will find that this question is of significant importance to venture capitalists. They would be interested in knowing if it is anticipated that that there will be an initial public offering or a trade sale within a particular time period, which will enable the venture capitalists to exit, hopefully profitably, from the enterprise.

The following key questions must be answered as part of the risks and reward section:

- What are the basic risks (market, regulatory, competition, technology) that the business venture faces?
- What measures would the enterprise take to counter these risks were they to materialise?
- How would investors harvest their investment? Will there be an initial public offering in future or a sale to a larger company, or is the intention that investors will only benefit in the form of successive dividend payments?

Supporting Documents

Typically, the following supporting documents will be annexed to the business plan:

» Audited and signed financial statements (balance sheet, income statement and cash flow statement) for the last three years or since the enterprise was founded, whichever is longer;

» Income statement projections for the next five years;

» Monthly cash flow statement for the next two years;

» Most recently submitted tax return and evidence of payment (or receipt of government waiver) of taxes for the enterprise since inception;

» Up-to-date monthly management accounts since the end of the previous year;

» Detailed CVs of key management team and board members;

» Copies of enterprise constitutional registration documents including (in the case of a company) regulations, certificates of incorporation and to commence business, and (in the case of a partnership) the certificate of registration of the partnership and the partnership agreement;

» Copies of relevant industry operating permits and licences, including a certificate of registration at Ghana Investment Promotion Centre (if relevant);

» Evidence of ownership, with purchase dates, of assets listed on the enterprise's balance sheet (e.g. land, buildings and equipment);

» Major project contracts including off taker agreement, supply agreements, technical assistance agreement, management agreements, loan agreements, etc.;

» Details of all bank accounts held by the enterprise and copies of the bank mandates for each account;

» Signed and dated statement of personal assets and liabilities of all shareholders;

» Copy (certified or accompanied by original document) of each shareholder's identification document (e.g. passport).

Kuenyehia on Entrepreneurship

Enterprise Ecosystem

Other than the fleeting reference in this chapter, I deliberately do not consider strategy separately in this book. That is not to say that strategy is not important. The ultimate strategy the entrepreneur settles on will be influenced by the various discussions we have had in each chapter of this book, and will come to the fore when the entrepreneur has to consolidate his thoughts and ideas into a business plan. I therefore recommend that, prior to developing each section of the business plan, the reader who is an aspiring entrepreneur should refer to each of the relevant preceding sections, in particular the discussion on opportunity analysis.

As I have demonstrated in prior chapters, in developing and executing strategy, the entrepreneur should be mindful not only of her particular enterprise but also how it relates and interacts with the 'world outside the enterprise', in particular with customers, competitors, regulators, government officials, brand consultants, recruitment consultants, accountants, lawyers, etc. Borrowing from biology, I refer to the enterprise together with the 'world outside the enterprise' as the enterprise ecosystem. As a result of my experience in setting up and assisting in the set up of entrepreneurial ventures in Ghana, as well as conversations with many other entrepreneurs in Ghana, I have come to think that it is not enough for the entrepreneur to simply focus on developing his enterprise.

We know from biology that an ecosystem is an environment consisting of all the living organisms and non-living components with which the living organisms interact, such as air, soil, water and sunlight.

Depending on the industry, the entrepreneur may find that the key players in the ecosystem that he needs to interact with to achieve his business objectives are within easy reach (and cost). However, my experience with many Ghanaian enterprises is that they find that many crucial elements of the ecosystem do not exist at all, or do not exist in the form or shape they would want, or do not exist at the price that the entrepreneur can afford to pay. In particular, I find that many Ghanaian entrepreneurs consider that there is a dearth of the right professional support (primarily at the small and medium-sized enterprise level) to help the entrepreneurs achieve their business objectives. Where there are suitable professional service providers, the entrepreneur finds that he is unable to afford those that exist. Or it may be that he is unhappy with the services currently being offered by the existing service providers.

In developing the business plan, the entrepreneur must think holistically of the ecosystem that he would consider ideal for his enterprise. Rather than relying on one of the handful of advertising agencies in the market that he can afford but is not happy with, he could, for example, build a relationship with a like-minded freelancer or full-time agency employee and encourage him to set up an agency with the understanding that he will not only support the new agency with his work but also assist in finding other clients for the agency. He may, if he has the resources, also make an investment in the agency. This template can be used for other service providers.

If an entrepreneur does this for his brand agency, IT provider and recruitment agent, for example, he will find that he has effectively 'created' his own ecosystem of people and enterprises that his enterprise relies on, rather than settling for what is available, which he may consider inadequate for his enterprise and its objectives.

Questions for Class Discussion

1. In communicating with investors, what must the entrepreneur seek to articulate in the business plan?
2. What role does the business plan play?
3. What are the key elements of a business plan?
4. Why is the executive summary of a business plan so important?
5. What is the purpose of the financial plan section of a business plan?
6. What questions would you typically expect to see answered in the entity section of the business plan?
7. What do we mean by developing an enterprise ecosystem and why is it important?

Chapter Fourteen: The Business Plan

Notes

1   Ernst and Young LLP. Outline for a business plan: A proven approach for entrepreneurs only, 1994.

2   Sahlman, W.A. How to write a great business plan, *Harvard Business Review*, 75(4),1997: 98-

3   Writing a Business Plan: The Basics. In *Entrepreneur's Toolkit: Tools and Techniques to Launch and Grow Your Business*. Boston: Harvard Business School Press, 2006.

4   Ernst and Young LLP. Outline for a business plan: A proven approach for entrepreneurs only, 1994.

5   Hisrich, R.. *International Entrepreneurship: Starting, Developing and Managing a Global Venture*. Thousand Oaks: SAGE Publications, 2010.

6   Sahlman, W.A. How to write a great business plan, *Harvard Business Review*, 75(4),1997: 98-108.

7   Plaque at Origin8 office

8   Collins, J.C. and J.I. Porras. Building Your Company's Vision. *Harvard Business Review*, 74(5),1996: 65-77.

9   Lorsch, J.W. and T.J.Tierney. *Aligning the stars: How to succeed when professionals drive results*. Boston: Harvard Business Press, 2002.

10   Interview with Ellis Arthur, August 2010

11   Presentation given to Foundations of Entrepreneurship class at Ghana Institute of Management and Public Administration, Greenhill, February 2008.

12   Sahlman, W.A. How to write a great business plan, *Harvard Business Review*, 75(4),1997: 98-108

13   Knowles, R. *Small Business: An Entrepreneur's Plan*. Toronto: Harcourt Brace and Company, 2003.

14   Allen, K.R. *Launching New Ventures: An Entrepreneurial Approach*. Boston: Houghton Mifflin, 1999.

Acknowledgements

There have been many people whose direct or indirect contribution has led to the publication of this book. The following deserve special mention.

Mr Bunmi Oni, Cecil Anetey Abbey and Funmi Afonja who inspired me to go back home. Akpe Ka ka Ka.

Dr Stephen Adei and the Ghana Institute of Management and Public Administration (GIMPA) Bachelor of Business Administration Class of 2005 who first challenged me to put in a book what I was teaching in class. Me Da si.

The people and companies who inspired me by permitting me to test my ideas in real life entrepreneurial ventures with their money at stake – Martey Akita, Tony Elumelu, Daniel Sasu, Kwaku Ofosu-Bediako, Kwame Bediako, Martin Zormelo and Sir Sam Jonah.

My Research Assistant Malik Adam and the many people who read the book at various stages and gave their comments - Mawulom Essel-Koomson, Eugene Adogla, Benjamin Abbey, Thelma Tawiah, Kwabena Asiedu , Ellis Arthur and my students who had to read successive drafts as guinea pigs. Me ne ening kpe.

The many entrepreneurs who allowed me to share their world and whose dedication and enthusiasm spurred me on to tell their stories. Ayekoo.

Teams O & B, Royal Afrideki and ENK, who by questioning everything and challenging me and my ideas, have moved me much further along my own personal journey of personal development and progress, I am most grateful.

My editor and lifelong friend Nii Ayikwei Parkes and my publisher flipped eye – Thanks for keeping the faith!

Above all, I would like to thank and acknowledge the Grace of Almighty God without whom nothing else matters.

About the Author

ELIKEM NUTIFAFA KUENYEHIA is the founder of Oxford & Beaumont, a leading law firm that, since 2006, has become internationally recognised as one of Ghana's leading law firms and has advised on over twelve billion US dollars ($12b) worth of deals for clients such as Citibank, International Finance Corporation, Coca-Cola, Goldman Sachs and Vodafone.

A graduate of Northwestern University's Kellogg School of Management, Elikem holds a bachelor's and master's degree in jurisprudence from the University of Oxford and attended Achimota School.

Prior to setting up Oxford & Beaumont, he was part of the start-up team that set up United Bank for Africa (Ghana) Limited (then Standard Trust Bank Ghana Limited), where he developed Ghana's first zero deposit account and the blueprint for the bank's market entry strategy. He also previously worked for Diageo and the leading premium international law firm Linklaters LLP.

Elikem's love affair with Entrepreneurship began in the early 1990s, when he ran a successful greeting card enterprise, co-founded the erstwhile Filla! Magazine and created, developed and co-hosted 'Second Generation', an award winning prime-time youth television show. His latest venture is Royal Afrideki, an early stage venture capital firm focused on Ghanaian small and medium sized enterprises.

Elikem serves on the boards of Metropolitan Insurance Company Limited (a member of the prestigious Ghana Club 100), Google Ghana Limited, Chase Petroleum Ghana Limited and Beige Capital Limited and was named a Young Global Leader by the World Economic Forum, and one of 'Africa's 40 under-40' achievers by The Network Journal. He also received the Millennium Excellence Awards' Young Professional of the Year Award in 2006, and, at Kellogg, the 2002 Business Leadership Award. In 1999, he was part of the team named 'Restructuring Team of 1999' by UK's Legal Business Magazine.

Elikem is a solicitor admitted in England, Wales and Ghana, and teaches entrepreneurship at the Ghana Institute of Management and Public Administration (GIMPA).